Marketing Leadership in Hospitality

Marketing
Leadership
in Hospitality

FOUNDATIONS AND PRACTICES

ROBERT C. LEWIS, PH.D.
Professor of Marketing and Research
Department of Hotel, Restaurant and Travel Administration
University of Massachusetts/Amherst

RICHARD E. CHAMBERS, MBA
President
Directional Marketing
Wellesley, MA

Van Nostrand Reinhold
_____ New York

Copyright © 1989 by Van Nostrand Reinhold
Library of Congress Catalog Card Number 88-17139
ISBN 0-442-20531-7

Printed in the United States of America

Text Design by Carla Bolte

Van Nostrand Reinhold
115 Fifth Avenue
New York, New York 10003

Van Nostrand Reinhold International Company Limited
11 New Fetter Lane
London EC4P 4EE, England

Van Nostrand Reinhold
480 La Trobe Street
Melbourne, Victoria 3000, Australia

Nelson Canada
1120 Birchmount Road
Scarborough, Ontario M1K 5G4, Canada

16 15 14 13 12 11 10 9 8 7 6 5 4 3 2

Library of Congress Cataloging-in-Publication Data

Lewis, Robert C.
   Marketing leadership in hospitality : foundations and practices /
Robert C. Lewis, Richard E. Chambers.
     p. cm.
   Bibliography: p.
   Includes index.
   ISBN 0-442-20531-7
   1. Hotels, taverns, etc.—Marketing. 2. Restaurants, lunch rooms,
etc.—Marketing. I. Chambers, Richard E. (Everett), 1956–
II. Title.
TX911.3.M3L49 1989
647'.94'0688—dc19   88-17139
                                     CIP

To
hospitality customers worldwide—
and the marketing leaders,
present and future,
who serve them

To Suze and Leslie

Contents

Preface

Market stat.

In the past ten to fifteen years, the world has witnessed a massive explosion in the hospitality industry. The industry today only vaguely resembles a second cousin of the one that existed twenty years ago. Not only has there been a proliferation of hotels, restaurants, and airlines, but the way they do business has changed drastically. Concurrently, there has been a massive change in the hospitality customer. The link between these two phenomena is marketing. This book is about that link.

The majority of the hospitality industry today is composed, for the most part, of many sophisticated organizations. While the Mom-and-Pop operations have not totally vanished, they have become increasingly scarce. The transition is not unlike what occurred during the Industrial Revolution, over a century ago. Cottage industries still exist and so does the individual entrepreneur in hospitality, but it is these same entrepreneurs who have led the way in the growth explosion.

E. M. Statler, Conrad Hilton, Howard Johnson, Kemmons Wilson, and Ray Kroc were some of these early entrepreneurs whose legends and legacies survive today. All these men were marketers par excellence. They may not have thought of themselves as such, and no doubt, terms such as *segmentation, positioning, consumer needs and wants, product life cycle, distribution,* and many others you will find in this book were not even part of their vocabulary. Nevertheless, these entrepreneurs all had one thing in common: They solved consumers' problems—and that is what marketing is all about.

It was only natural that the legacies of these individuals, and others like them, would evolve in one form or another into large organizations. Growth comes from continued solving of consumers' problems. Growth, however, also brings with it growing pains—the pains of organization, management, financing, distribution, and finally, competition.

The emphasis in these heavy growth years was on operations and costs. The person who could run a good operation and control costs was likely to be successful. In hotels, almost all general managers rose through the ranks in food and beverage departments. In restaurants, the emphasis was primarily food, beverge, and labor costs.

There were still (and always will be) the grand hotels and the grand restaurants, usually owned and run by entrepeneurs in the classic *mein host* style. By and large, however, customers took what they got for what they paid. There wasn't too much choice. Little attention was paid to selling and advertising, and marketing was a foreign word.

Marketing, in fact, did not truly begin to evolve to its present state of growth and recognition in any industry until the 1960s. It was another fifteen to twenty years before it began to evolve in the hospitality industry. When this first happened, moreover, it was not in its present form. With the growth of chain operations and regional, if not nationwide, distribution, organizations began advertising more extensively. Hotels began to fill out their sales staffs. When marketing became an accepted word in the hospitality lexicon, these two activities were largely what the word meant; merchandising and promotion were added later.

Thus, until approximately ten years ago, marketing consisted largely of what we know today as the communications mix, a subset of marketing. Today, personal selling is a major portion of the marketing mix in time and effort; it is a small portion of marketing strategy. Extensive advertising is affordable by relatively few, although merchandising and promotion are quite common in operations of all sizes.

Marketing has evolved similarly in restaurant and hotel management academic programs. The early subjects were (and in some places still are) primarily merchandising and selling. Marketing was thought by many to be something intuitive that either you were good at or you weren't, but there wasn't much point in spending an entire semester learning it. Hospitality marketing texts were largely nonexistent. What did exist concentrated primarily on merchandising, promotion, and selling.

In the early 1980s, hospitality marketing began to acquire recognition. This came about primarily as a result of two forces. The first was the recognition of marketing in other industries and its increasingly frequent mention in the business press. Individuals who had degrees from business schools and/or came from other industries entered the hospitality industry and recognized the need for marketing. Former sales departments became marketing departments. By and large, however, much of the industry was unaware of the difference.

The second force occurred in the marketplace. As competition intensified, it was no longer a case of "building another better mousetrap" and letting the people come; one had to begin to fight to obtain the business that the competition was also seeking. The customer had also changed. Demographic lines began to blur. Customers became "educated" and more demanding. After all, they now had alternatives. Properties sought to differentiate from each other.

This pattern has increased one hundredfold until it has reached its present state. The hospitality marketing trend that began in the United States is now in the heavy growth stage internationally. Businesses are now being challenged as never before to improve their marketing capabilities worldwide. Marketing is coming of age in hospitality.

Coming of age, however, does not signify expertise. The transition has been slow, if not painful, it seems, and there is still much to be learned. On the other hand, when one considers a ten-year span in the course of the long history of hospitality, the movement has been rapid—almost to the point of being mind-boggling.

It is this state that exists today and that this book addresses. Previous books on hospitality marketing have tended to be superficial, cursory, and anecdotal. These books have served the purpose of identifying "what is going on out there," but have not dealt with theoretical and conceptual foundations of why it is going on. This is a natural evolution and the time has come for the foundations.

Most academic programs, as they have evolved, have used basic marketing texts borrowed from the business school, as well as readings or a supplementary text of industry practices. The solution was less than satisfactory. Although the basic principles of marketing do not change from one discipline to another, their application does. We know now—as do the business schools, more recently—that services marketing is not a clone of goods marketing. Although services marketing (and this book) have borrowed heavily from the field of goods marketing, it has learned to round the square peg to fit the hole. It has also learned to make new holes to fit, when necessary.

This book attempts to bring all of this together. It is filled, as the title implies, with both foundations and practices. Our thesis is that the same situation rarely happens twice in the same way. Thus, knowing a practice is of minimal help when you are faced with a situation that is not quite the same and may actually be radically different. It is at these times that solid foundations lead the way in making sound marketing decisions.

On the other hand, marketing decisions can be very elusive. Marketing problems rarely provide simple solutions. Rarely do 2 and 2 add up to 4; more likely they add up to 3 or 5, and sometimes 25 or minus 10. This is because the factors in marketing are based on human behavior; there is nothing we know that is more complex than the human being. Human behavior does not offer the concrete, factual, and readily ascertainable solutions found in the areas of manufacturing goods, financial equations, or accounting manipulations.

Five different marketers can arrive at five different solutions to the same problem. All may be right; all may be wrong. In marketing we really don't know the right decision from the wrong one until after it has happened. Further, all the marketing science in the world will never eliminate the gut instinct that *sometimes* works in spite of all the evidence to the contrary.

Nevertheless, there is a logic and a system to marketing that greatly increases the probability of success. These can be learned. There are ways that we can better understand the vagaries of customer behavior. There are ways to get at the issues and to reveal the substance of marketing problems. There are underlying principles that appear time and time again.

Although marketing's elusiveness is frustrating to many on first exposure, we have no choice in the hospitality industry today but to study marketing. Marketing is the umbilical cord that connects the business to the consumer. It is the means by which the organization adjusts to the ever-changing needs of the marketplace. It is the force of change and growth and the exploration of new opportunities. It is the strongest weapon there is in fighting the competition.

We do not believe that hospitality marketing is only for hospitality marketers. Rather, it is an essential and substantial portion of all hospitality management. This is because, by contrast with manufacturing, all management decisions in hospitality affect the customer—and the customer is the soul and substance of marketing.

This book takes a leadership approach to the study of marketing in hospitality organizations. Our target audience includes those in introductory marketing courses, in marketing management courses, and in strategic marketing courses. It also includes managers and marketers now operating in the real world of the hospitality industry, at any level, who feel a need for a more foundational view of marketing with applied examples.

This book focuses on a long-range perspective rather than an operational "how-to" approach, because marketing is long-range for any organization that seeks survival and growth. This also gives it an international perspective. Although many things may change on the international scene, as we point out in Chapter 22, the basic foundations of marketing do not change.

This book also takes a realistic approach. We call it as we see it, but we don't do this lightly. Examples used come from many sources and have been checked and rechecked. Foundations presented are based on accepted principles and solid research. We editorialize and give opinions; these occasions should be clear to the reader, who should feel free to disagree. We will never claim that marketing is an exact science or that we have all the answers, but we will claim a reason and rationale for most marketing decisions. That's why marketing is also fun—we can all disagree as long as we have the foundations on which to base our decisions.

A final note: Examples used and the ads used to illustrate examples are largely drawn from well-known and international hotel companies. This should not be construed to imply that these companies do things any better or more poorly than any other company. Rather, we have used them because they are well known and most readers, worldwide, will be familar with the names and will thus be better able to identify with them.

Use of the Book

This book has six parts plus an epilogue. It is designed this way for use at different levels of expertise, background, and experience for the student, the instructor, and the practitioner. All chapters have been used, at one time or another, in the classroom at various levels and/or in industry seminars at the levels of line management, middle management, upper management, and executive.

We are acutely aware of the different class and instructor levels existing in academic institutions. For example, some programs require the introductory marketing course in the business school followed by a second course in the hospitality program; some teach the introductory course in the hospitality program. Some instructors have doctorates in marketing; others, in smaller programs where there is more diversity in subjects taught, may be simply "assigned" the marketing course for a semester. As much as possible, we have tried to accommodate all these needs.

Instructors using the book or practitioners reading it may want to revise the order of the contents. When we queried colleagues and practitioners as to the best order, we received as many different suggestions as people we asked. In some cases we adapted to those suggestions, especially when they were preponderant; in other cases we held our ground. Those situations that seemed to be especially problematic are the following.

Section II, The Marketing Environment, we believe, should come later in the book under the title of strategic marketing. Others favored it early on. We could not argue against the essentiality of this subject at any level, and capitulated. On the other hand, those who wanted it early on also wanted Chapter 20 Strategic Marketing, in the same place, concurring that the two sections should be kept together. Other marketing texts, we found, are divided in this placement, some placing strategic marketing early in the text and others placing it late.

While writing Chapter 20, Strategic Marketing, we came to believe that it requires a substantial foundation to allow readers a thorough grasp and understanding. We concur, however, with the reviewer who stated, "When the reader can understand and/or visualize the objectives and outcomes of marketing in a more tangible manner, it is then simpler to grasp the significance of individual topics in marketing as well as their relation to the outcomes."

To resolve this dilemma we have, first of all, left Chapter 20 where it is. For those who, like the above reviewer, would like to present the whole before the parts, we recommend introducing Figure 20–1 along with Chapter 1, explaining the significance of the individual topic areas.

We took the opposite approach on Chapter 19, Marketing Intelligence. Some also favored putting this section early on. We felt strongly that marketing information and research can be properly understood only after the basic concepts of marketing are understood. We left it where it is, which should not stop anyone from using it earlier.

The one other major point of difference in this book is Section V, the Marketing Mix. As we explain in Chapter 11, we do not feel that the "four Ps" adequately serve the purpose of identifying and explicating the relevant components in hospitality marketing. Some disagree with us. "They say the same thing," they argue. We agree. At the same time we have found, pedagogically, that the product/presentation/communications/distribution mix is a far more useful tool for understanding and utilizing the hospitality marketing mix. We have used both this and the "four Ps" in the classroom many times before coming to this conclusion. In the final analysis, either one is no more than a tool of understanding. When you have read Chapters 2 and 3, and then Chapters 12 through 18, and applied them to hospitality, you may find, as we have, that the hospitality mix is a more useful tool. We only ask that you try it and then let us know.

The book is intended to build one chapter upon the other. You will find common threads that run through the chapters to serve this purpose, as well as frequent referrals to previous chapters. You will also find some repetition in chapters; this is intentional and occurs in areas that we feel need especial emphasis.

In the academic classroom, this is how we have used the chapters in a fourteen-week semester.

Introductory (First) Course   We allocate Chapters 1 to 3 to the first three weeks. The first class, when the students will probably not yet have the text, is a good jumping-off point. We have avoided the usual first chapter of business marketing texts that asks "why study marketing," and so on. We think this bores students, especially if the course is required. One can start the course in the first class with a discussion of what marketing is and its role in any business enterprise. That explanation alone should make abundantly clear why anyone should study marketing. By the second class students should have read the chapter, and extensive discussion and explanation should follow.

Chapters 2 and 3, on the uniqueness of services and hospitality marketing, usually lead to extensive explanation and/or discussion. These chapters will get into the heart of hospitality marketing.

We skip Chapters 4 and 5, for reasons explained above, and spend at least a week on Chapter 6, The Hospitality Customer. There is an abundance of outside material that can be brought to this subject. Each instructor seems to have his or her own favorite topic areas. We have introduced three relatively new ones at the end of the chapter, leaving out those that are readily available in other texts for the instructor to introduce.

Chapter 7, the Organizational Customer, tied in with Chapter 6, will easily absorb the fifth week. Unlike Chapter 6, which it draws on, this chapter is relatively free of theory and is more applied than the chapters that precede it. Essentially, Chapter 7 constitutes an introduction to a hospitality sales course and the meetings markets. Some instructors may want to simply assign this chapter as outside reading.

We use Chapters 8 and 9, on segmentation, together for the sixth and seventh weeks. Segmentation is a vital topic area in marketing and can consume considerable time. Chapter 9, like Chapter 7, is again applied and theory-free, and can be assigned as outside reading to facilitate the discussion of Chapter 8. The eighth week is spent on Chapter 10, positioning. There is a lot of material in these three chapters; some instructors may want to spend an extra class or two on them.

We spend a week each on Chapters 12 (including the short Chapter 11) through 15 and a final week on Chapter 16 and 17, all of which deal with the hospitality marketing mix. Chapters 18–22 we leave for the advanced course. This leaves one week out of the fourteen that we find useful for "getting behind," additional discussion, the Epilogue, minicases, tests, or whatever.

Second Course (with First Course in Business School)   We find most business school introductory courses to be large in enrollment, quite cursory, almost totally applied to manufactured goods, and minimally memorable. Therefore, we more or less repeat the above sequence but move faster, go further, and use more outside sources.

In this course, we would cover Chapter 1 in the first class for review purposes and finish the week with Chapters 2 and 3 which will probably be new to these students. The second week we spend on Chapters 4 and 5, probably with an overlap in both weeks so we are now at the end of week three. The next five chapters (6–10) can be covered in weeks four through six. The marketing mix will cover weeks seven through ten, including Chapter 18 on distribution. Chapters 19, 20, and 21 should each fill a week. This leaves one week for "spare," or for covering Chapter 22 and/or the Epilogue.

If this second course is taught as a marketing management course with a course marketing plan project assigned, then we introduce Chapter 21 in the third or fourth week; in some cases, both Chapters 20 and 21 are introduced early on.

Second Course in Hospitality (Using Same Text)   In this case, we review Chapters 1 through 3 in the first week and carry them further into application, usually with one or two case studies utilized during class time. Chapters 4 and 5 are the second and third weeks, usually with some specific outside assignment, reading, or case. We then cover Chapters 6, 8, and 10 with a week each, including outside readings and/or case studies. In week seven, we review the marketing mix, adding Chapter 18, Distribution, which was not assigned in the introductory course. Chapter 19 consumes week eight with a minicase. We spend three or four weeks on Chapters 20 and 21, and one week on Chapter 22 and the Epilogue. This leaves one or two weeks open for cases and special assignments.

Third Course, Strategic Marketing, or Graduate Course   At these levels, we introduce numerous outside readings and case studies. Class time is spent mostly in discussion of these; students are presumed to have read and be thoroughly familiar with the readings. For example, we might assign a week each for Chapters 1, 2, 3, and 6 with two or three cases, and Chapters 4 and 5 with a case; two weeks each for Sections 4 and 5 with cases; and one week each for Chapters 19, 20, 21, 22, and the Epilogue, also with cases. This leaves three weeks for extended cases and/or other assignments and term projects.

There are numerous international references throughout the text. Because of this we have included an appendix at the end that contains maps of the various parts of the world. All cities mentioned are not on those maps, but we assume that the alert reader, both American and international, will be inquisitive enough to locate them.

Acknowledgments

Many people—friends, colleagues, and enemies—both advertently and inadvertently, have contributed to this book. Some will never realize how helpful they have been. We can only mention a few and have broken them into categories. We are grateful to these, and to many others who are unmentioned.

Early Encouragers, "Get Going, It will Only Take Four to Five Years"   Jerry Vallen, University of Nevada/Las Vegas; Margaret Shaw, University of Massachusetts/Amherst; numerous others, beyond recall, who kept saying, "When are you going to write a book?"

If You Can Do It, So Can I   Francis Buttle, University of Masschusetts/Amherst.

It's No Different from Writing a Long Thesis   Leslie Ann Chambers, wife.

Early Reviewers   John Bowen, University of Houston; Mike Leven, Days Inn; Joan Livingston, formerly of *Cornell Quarterly;* Paul Beals, formerly of IMHI/Cergy-Pontoise, France; several anonymous reviewers.

Extensive Reviewers and Classroom Testers   Venkat Chandrasekar, University of Central Florida, Orlando; Rick Warfel, Hotel Institute of The Hague; numerous students and seminar participants.

Specific Chapter Readers and Contributors   Siew Ang, Century Park Sheraton/Singapore; Steve Weisz, Marriott Corporation; Margaret Shaw, University of Massachusetts/Amherst; Chekitan Dev, Cornell University; Praveen Nair, New Delhi; Steven Fletcher, University of Massachusetts/Amherst; Linda Lowry, University of Massachusetts/Amherst, who wrote the appendix to Chapter 22 on tourism marketing; and Charles Partlow, Kansas State University and Debra Moody, Pennsylvania State University.

Anecdotal and Material Contributors   Mike Leven, Days Inn; Ingvald Fardol, Inter Nor Hotels, Oslo; Runar Warhuus, Grand Hotel, Oslo; Siew Ang, Century Park Sheraton/Singapore; Axel Kehrer, Ramada Hotels/Dusseldorf; Susan Morris, Marriott Hotel, Somerset, NJ; Laurel Walsh; Stowe Shoemaker, Restaurant Research Associates; Berit Stephansen, Royal Garden Hotel, Trondheim; Jim Nassikas, Stanford Court/San Francisco; Maurice de Rooij, The Netherlands; Saskia Radtke, Ramada International, Paris; Raja Nasri, Le Meridien, Paris; Myriam Riehl, Meridien Gestion, Paris; Uttam Dave, A.K. Dave Associates, New Delhi; Nancy Charves; Kathy Johnson; Charles Guffroy, Inter-Continental Hotels, Singapore and Cannes; Gurmit Chaudhri, Oberoi Hotels, Cairo; numerous seminar participants, industry friends and colleagues, who would probably prefer not to be mentioned.

Sub-Rosa Contributors   Executives, managers, sales and marketing people, and others, from Marriott, Hyatt, Sheraton, Omni, Hilton, Ramada, Radisson, Sara, Oberoi, Taj, Americana, Wyndham, Hilton International, Inter-Continental, Mandarin, Aircoa, Quality International, Inter Nor, Summit, Holiday Corp., Meridien, Groupe Accor, Sofitel, Peninsula, Stouffer, Four Seasons and other hotels and hotel companies; Laventhol & Horwath, and Pannell Kerr Forster; numerous restaurant chains and individual restaurants; and many, many customers.

Sources   We have used numerous printed sources as indicated by citations throughout the text. We thank all these sources for their gracious consideration in furnishing and allowing us to use these materials. Every possible effort has been made to obtain appropriate permissions and make acknowledgments under the copyright fair use laws, as well as courtesy credits. If we have missed any, please let us know and we will correct the oversight in the next edition.

In spite of all this help and support, we stand responsible for the entire contents.

About the Authors

Robert C. Lewis, Ph.D., is professor of hospitality marketing and research at the University of Massachusetts, Amherst, where he has been on the faculty since 1980. His prior career spans almost 30 years in the industry, including hotel management, airline foodservice, restaurant ownership, and consulting. He consults and does seminars in North America, Europe, and Asia, and is the author of more than 60 publications on hospitality marketing and research.

Richard E. Chambers, MBA, is President of Directional Marketing, which serves the hospitality industry in marketing research and consulting. Prior to this, he held various marketing and management positions, including Director of Sales at Hilton and Marriott franchises; Director of Marketing and General Manager of Omni properties; National Director of Sales for Omni International Hotels; and Vice President of Marketing at Tara Hotels. Mr. Chambers has authored several publications in industry trade journals and books.

PART I

Introduction to Hospitality Marketing

CHAPTER I

The Concept of Marketing

Jan Carlzon, 39, noted for his strong marketing orientation, was picked in 1981 by the Scandinavian Airways System (SAS) Board of Directors to be its president, with the challenge of turning around an ailing company. In what were tough times for the airlines, most other companies were cutting back. Carlzon went the other way; he poured it on. In a little over a year Carlzon took SAS from an $8 million loss to a gross profit of $71 million. He did it by going into the trenches, where the customer was.

Carlzon initiated the marketing concept: Make sure you're really selling what the customer wants to buy. He took SAS from a production orientation to a marketing orientation, serving the travel needs of the market. Carlzon and his top executives literally hit the road and personally visited all front-line management of the airline and many of the line employees. His intention was to change the thinking of some 20,000 employees. "He managed to get the top management of SAS to rethink the company's destiny and to come up with possibilities that enabled them to see beyond their previous conception of the business," and to ingrain this message down to the lowest level of employee.[1] Carlzon turned SAS around because he understood and practiced the concept of marketing.

Practicing the concept of marketing means recognizing the relationship between marketing and management. Marketing and management in a service business, such as the hospitality industry, are one and the same.

Practicing the concept of marketing means marketing leadership. Marketing leadership recognizes that it is marketing forces that shape the total organization.

This book is about marketing leadership in the hospitality industry. More specifically, it is about the causes and effects of marketing leadership. This book is about why people such as Jan Carlzon and companies such as SAS succeed, and why others don't

---

[1] Karl Albrecht and Ron Zemke, *Service America*, Homewood, IL: Dow Jones—Irwin, 1985, Ch. 2.

succeed or succeed less well. It is about what it is going to take to succeed in the hospitality marketplace in the years ahead. Most important, this book is about hospitality customers, because it is with the customer that marketing leadership begins.

After you have read this chapter you will understand why this is true. In short, you will understand the concept of marketing, the marketing philosophy, and the elements of marketing leadership. You will also understand why these factors are critical to the future of the hospitality industry. In the chapters that follow, you will learn how marketing leadership works.

Foundations and Practices

Marketing-oriented companies and marketing-oriented people are the ones who will be truly successful in the highly competitive hospitality marketplace in the years ahead. This has been difficult for some to realize. For a long time after World War II, a new hotel or restaurant needed only to open its doors, deliver a good product, run a good operation, control costs, and, in some cases, go out and sell in order to do the business it wanted to do and make the profit it wanted to make. Sometimes, it was the only game in town and could do well on natural demand—demand that exists without any real effort on the part of the seller. The major issue was how well you could control your costs.

In the academic world, the same has been true. Until recently, major university hospitality school programs offered only a minimum of marketing courses, most essentially sales courses with little emphasis on the customer. Tight operations and good cost controls were the mandates that graduates carried with them into the real world.

Today's world is far different: The emphasis in industry and in hospitality schools must be on the consumer and on marketing. An accountant put it this way:

> In terms of accounting procedures the difference between the cost-oriented and market-oriented approach is this: In the cost-oriented situation we are essentially concerned with the debit side of the profit and loss account, our approach is inward looking; cost manipulation and cost control are our main weapon. In the market-oriented situation we recognize that most of our costs are fixed and uncontrollable; we therefore shift our attention to the credit side of the profit and loss account.[2]

Does this mean that marketing has replaced operations and accounting? Of course not. In the academic world, only so many marketing courses can reasonably be offered. For the marketing career person these may include marketing principles, marketing management, consumer behavior, marketing strategy, and marketing research. Much of the content of these courses should be theoretical and is essential to a solid background in marketing. In the long run there is nothing as practical as good theoretical foundations, which we will discuss in this book.

But marketing is an applied discipline and these courses should also be solid in application. There is nothing as useless as a theory that can't be applied, and this book will demonstrate applications of the theories it discusses.

---

[2] Richard Kotas, "Market Orientation," HCIMA Journal, July 1973, p. 7.

The operations career individual will take fewer marketing courses per se, but must learn to apply marketing in his or her operations courses. When a menu is designed, the first question to be asked is, "How will the customer react to it?" When prices are established the first question is, "How will the consumer perceive the risk and the price/value relationship?" When engineering is taught and electric consumption is measured, the first question is, "Will the lighting be adequate for the customer?" When architectural design is evaluated, the first question to be asked is, "How does the customer use the hotel or restaurant?" When food, liquor, or labor cost controls are taught, we must ask how they impact upon the customer. The foundation is the concept of marketing; the application is its practice.

No hospitality company can continue to operate without a profit, but putting first things first, no company can begin to operate without customers. A good analogy, perhaps, is a new Broadway play. Some close down after the first night, some after the first week. The fixed costs are largely spent (accountants call them sunk costs). Ongoing variable costs are largely predetermined and are relatively minimal; there's not much that can be done to control them further. Broadway plays, like hotels, airlines, and restaurants, are in a volume-sensitive business; what is needed is customers. If the play doesn't satisfy, the customers won't come no matter how low the price, or how well the producer controls his costs.

What applies in show business also applies in the hospitality industry. For many, many years the hospitality industry has operated under the saying, "We are in the people business." Today, that axiom is useful but not quite accurate. Today we are in the "customer business." Without customers we are dead. And the way to have customers is to create them and keep them, by satisfying their needs and wants and by solving their problems.

This, then, is the marketing orientation, the foundations and practices of marketing leadership. It starts at the highest level by deed and action, not just words, and it penetrates down to the lowest level of the organization. Concern and responsibility for marketing are concerns and responsibilities of every person in a hospitality enterprise. At the highest level marketing shapes the corporate effort; at the lowest level it means the porter doesn't mop where the customer is walking. A marketing orientation says, "This is the way we do things around here."

The Concept of Marketing

For many, the term *marketing* conjures up images of selling and advertising. Because of this long standing and common belief, we call selling and advertising *traditional* marketing. Actually, however, selling and advertising are only two subsets of the broad range of marketing. While they are important, we first need to get rid of the notion that they are the only subsets. More important, we need to establish a different notion: All phases of marketing, both foundations and practices, derive from the customer. This is the concept of marketing that, as we will show, permeates both the traditional and *nontraditional* elements of marketing.

In fact, marketing differs conceptually from selling in some very important ways that will help to lead us to a definition of marketing:

- Sales-oriented management thinks in terms of volume. It aims its efforts at current sales, quotas, commissions, and bonuses. Marketing-oriented management thinks in terms of profit planning. It aims at product mixes, customer mixes, and marketing mixes to achieve profitable volume and market share from long-term customer relationships.
- Sales-oriented management thinks short run—today's products, markets, customers, and strategies. Marketing-oriented management looks at long-run trends, threats, and opportunities and how these translate into new products, markets, and marketing strategies for long-term growth.
- Sales-oriented management looks at travel-purpose segments rather than benefit-segment classes. Marketing-oriented management looks at customer types and benefit-segment differences to figure out how to offer superior value to the most profitable segments.
- Sales-oriented management thinks in terms of fieldwork and desk work, and how to sell customers. Marketing-oriented management does marketing analysis, planning, and control.
- Sales-oriented management thinks in terms of the virtues of their product and how they can persuade the customer to buy. Consciously or unconsciously, it sells the operations end of the business as dictated by other departments of the hotel or foodservice business. It thinks in terms of what they can give the customer. Marketing-oriented management thinks in terms of customer needs when it designs the product before the sale, when it delivers the product after the sale, and while the customer is consuming the product. It thinks in terms of what the customer wants.[3]

Today's marketing executives and today's hotel and foodservice managers should understand that their properties run as a system. Demand is balanced with the ability to produce. Marketing plans and strategies strike a balance between the needs of the marketing mix (sales, price, advertising, product quality, service, and distribution) and the external needs, wants, and willingness to pay of the target markets.

Defining Marketing

Every marketing textbook includes somewhere in its first or second chapter a definition of marketing. These definitions invariably include such terms as *process, exchange of goods,* and the like. In 1985, the American Marketing Association officially announced its definition of marketing: "The process of planning and executing conception, pricing, promotion, and distribution of ideas, goods, and services to create exchanges that satisfy individual and organizational objectives."[4]

---

[3] Adapted from Philip Kotler, "From Sales Obsession to Marketing Effectiveness," *Harvard Business Review,* November/December, 1977, pp. 67–75. Copyright © 1977 by the President and Fellows of Harvard College; all rights reserved.

[4] American Marketing Association, Board of Directors, 1985.

The American Marketing Association definition and others are appropriate and fitting depending upon one's particular viewpoint. Invariably, however, they focus upon a relationship that emphasizes the return inherent to the marketer by providing goods and/or services to consumers. This book will take a slightly different approach. First, we will establish some basic premises.

The Significance of Profit

It is accepted without question that any business that fails to operate at a profit will eventually cease to exist. If goods and/or services can not be offered at a price exceeding their total cost, then they should be removed from the market. Although essential to survival, however, profit is not the purpose of marketing but rather the barometer by which the validity of management decisions is measured. As well-known management guru Peter Drucker has stated: "Profitability is not the purpose of but a limiting factor on business enterprise and business activity. Profit is not the explanation, cause, or rationale of business behavior and business decisions but the *test of their validity*" (emphasis added).[5]

The Twofold Purpose of Marketing

The only valid definition of business purpose, says Drucker, is to create a customer.

> It is the customer who determines what a business is. For it is the customer, and he alone, who through being willing to pay for a good or for a service, converts economic resources into wealth, things into goods. What the business thinks it produces is not of first importance—especially not to the future of the business and to its success. What the customer thinks he is buying, what he considers "value," is decisive—it determines what a business is, what it produces and whether it will prosper.[6]

Creating a customer does not mean simply making a sale. It means creating a relationship wherein a buyer wants your product more than that of the competition. In addition to creating a customer, the purpose of both marketing and business is also to *keep* customers once they have been created. A business's purpose and marketing's purpose, in fact, are really one and the same. Any definition of marketing must emphasize that the creation and keeping of customers are primary.

The point in this difference of definition is an important one. Business revenues come from customers and nowhere else. The finest cost controls, the highest profit margins, the most highly trained management, the most innovative products, and the most efficient production lines do not produce revenue, and ultimately profit, if there are no customers.

The first consideration of any management decision should be, "Will it create and/or keep customers?" Only when that question can be answered in the affirmative is it relevant to consider the monetary implications of the decision. If the answer is negative,

---

[5] Peter F. Drucker, *Management: Tasks, Responsibilities, Practices,* New York: Harper & Row, 1974, p. 60.
[6] Peter F. Drucker, *The Practice of Management,* New York: Harper & Row, 1954, pp. 37–39.

the decision should likewise be negative even if there is no cost, or even if there is a decrease in cost. While this statement may seem self-evident and hardly worth mentioning, the number of times that it is violated are multitudinous.

Often, decisions that are made are in the best interest of the guest and may in fact create satisfaction, may not contribute to creating or keeping a customer. Although we certainly must satisfy customers to create and keep them, as we will shortly demonstrate, marketing means something more than simply satisfying. It means understanding customers' needs and wants and solving their problems. In a simplistic example, if you give me $100 I'll certainly be satisfied, but it doesn't mean I will become your customer.

For example, a hotel management might consider whether to put Godiva chocolates on each pillow during turndown service. The intent, obviously, is to increase customer satisfaction and repeat business. While customer satisfaction may well be increased (since we all appreciate getting something for nothing), it may be questionable whether it creates or keeps a customer. It is not difficult to satisfy a customer if you want to give the store away. However, satisfaction alone will not necessarily ensure that customers will return if that satisfaction does not serve their needs and wants or solve their problems.

Trying to increase satisfaction in ways that do not address needs and wants may, in fact, turn out to have a negative effect. At a cost of $4.00 per occupied room night, the Godiva chocolate decision affects profits. An alarm is sounded by the controller, whose job is not perceived as being part of marketing (although it should be). Management responds that "the customers love them; we can't stop now." A solution is found: keep the Godiva chocolates and raise the room rates, or cut out something else that might be more important to the customer. The unanswered question is: "Have we created a customer who appreciates the extra touch or have we lost one who is unwilling or unable to pay the added charge?"

Another question might be, "Does it really matter? Will this help to cause the customer to return, especially when the competition is, or soon will be, doing the same thing?" Obviously, providing Godiva chocolates would be only one of many things that the hotel must do right for the customer to want to return. There are many ways to create satisfaction, but not all of them are good marketing.

When management raises prices, in the above example, it has found a solution to its own problem, a problem that it alone created by raising customer expectations without consideration of the customer's problem. The example is an oversimplification but it demonstrates exactly what can take place when the concept of creating and/or keeping a customer is not paramount in management decisions.

The converse of this situation may also apply. A proposal is turned down because the first and only reaction to it is, "Look what it will cost," instead of, "If that's what the customer wants, how can we find a way to do it affordably?"

Occurring even more frequently are those decisions based solely on cost without any regard to customer demands. Imagine our lives today if Henry Ford had thrown in the towel when the original Ford prototype proved to be prohibitively expensive. In a lesser sense, the same is true when we understaff a front desk or a waitstaff, and let the customers wait.

We have come this far before giving our own definition of marketing because we wanted to build the case first. It should be clear now why we define marketing as we do:

Communicating to and giving the target market customers what they want, when they want it, where they want it, at a price they are willing and able to pay.

Any business that does this will fulfill its twofold purpose of creating and keeping customers and, in turn, will produce revenue. But, you might add, there are a multitude of ifs, ands, and buts with this definition. This is true. For one thing, will the company achieve a sufficient profit to satisfy its owners and to survive? That will be the test of the validity of its decisions and the extensions of marketing that we will discuss in the remainder of this book. First, let's look at what customers want and what they are willing to pay.

Solving Customers' Problems

There is a premise of marketing that is even more basic than what we have already presented. Simply put, consumers do not buy something unless they have a problem to solve and believe that a purchase will provide the solution to the problem. An example used by Levitt to make this point is that people don't buy quarter-inch drills, they buy quarter-inch holes. Here is another example, attributed to Charles Revson, founder of Revlon cosmetics: "In the factory we make cosmetics. In the store we sell hope."[7]

In this sense, customers buy solutions and nothing else. If we can think of goods and services that we want to sell in this sense only, we are a long way on the road to successful marketing. Thinking this way forces us to stand in the customer's shoes, to think as the customer thinks, and to understand what it is the customer wants, when, where, and at what price.

This point can be illustrated as follows. Perhaps you are driving down a highway and you become hungry, or you need a place to sleep. These are needs, and basic ones at that. Needs create problems—namely, how to satisfy them—so what you do next is seek a solution. You know that solution will have a cost. You have to give up something or make a sacrifice in order to get the solution. What emerges is a trade-off situation, as portrayed in Figure 1-1.

This is the trade-off thought process a consumer faces when contemplating a purchase. The decision may require long deliberation, ("Where should we spend our honeymoon?") or may be instantaneous ("Should I buy a soda?"). Nevertheless, the process takes place and the depth of deliberation depends on numerous factors that will be discussed in Chapter 6, on consumer behavior.

For the moment, let's continue the illustration and assume that a solution presents itself: A sign on the highway announces a motel ahead with rooms at $49.50. Rooms provide a solution for the need to sleep, and $49.50 is a sacrifice you are willing to make. You decide to head for the motel rather than continue driving.

Now the situation becomes complicated. You *expect* that the solution is at hand—in other words, you expect that you can get a good night's sleep at this motel. You expect, of course, that there will be a bed in the room, a bathroom, and other appointments. You also expect that the bed will be comfortable and that the room will be quiet so that you will

---

[7] Theodore Levitt, *The Marketing Imagination*, New York: The Free Press, 1986, p. 128.

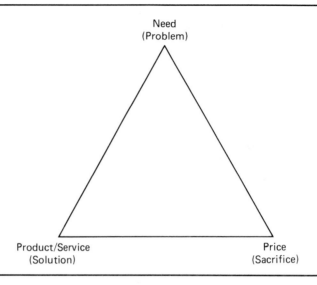

FIGURE 1-1   The trade-off of problem solutions

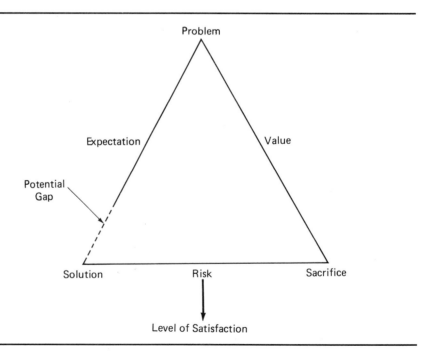

FIGURE 1-2   Expansion of the trade-off model

10

sleep well. You may not verbalize these expectations, but subconsciously they exist. You also have, consciously or unconsciously, made another decision: You have decided that spending $49.50 is worth the *risk* that your expectations will be met, the solution will solve your problem, and the value you will receive will be worth the sacrifice. The trade-off model now resembles Figure 1-2.

Obviously, consumers buy expectations at the same time that they buy solutions, both of which require a sacrifice. It then follows that the greater the sacrifice, the greater the risk, the greater the expectation, and the more demanding the customer is of the solution. To put it another way, if the solution meets the expectation and the value justifies the sacrifice, the risk becomes more justifiable, and a higher level of satisfaction becomes more likely. The result is a higher likelihood that we have created a customer. To put this in realistic terms, consider each element of Figure 1-2 in terms of going to eat at McDonald's vs. Lutèce, a French restaurant in New York City where luncheon checks average over $150 per person.

Notice now what happens when the solution does not meet the expectation. This is the potential gap on the left side of Figure 1-2, indicated by the dotted line. We have made the dotted line, let's say, "Pizza Hut length." We might make it a hair shorter for "McDonald's length," but for "Lutèce length" it might run almost to the peak of the triangle. The point is obvious: The greater the expectation, the greater the potential that it will not be fulfilled. We will explore this point in more detail in later chapters. For now, you can see very clearly why marketing and management are one and the same. If management cannot fulfill customers' expectations, it won't create and keep customers; when it does, it is marketing.

Now notice in Figure 1-2 where satisfaction occurs—at the bottom of the triangle. This places satisfaction clearly as an end product of marketing, not as part of the process, in creating and keeping the customer. If the gap is too great between expectation and fulfillment, there will be a low level of satisfaction. Now you should understand more clearly the Godiva chocolate example, and why it is expectation that marketing must serve, not just satisfaction.

In essence, Figure 1-2 represents the concept and definition of marketing—giving customers what they want, when they want it, where they want it, at a price they are willing to pay (or a sacrifice they are willing to make). Each step in Figure 1-2 can also be shown to represent the process of marketing, as we will now explain.

Marketing, of course, does not create the needs or problems associated with hunger or sleepiness.[8] However, it does identify the needs associated with what to eat and where to sleep. Marketing differentiates the available solutions through the creation of expectations. On the other side of the equation, having created expectation, marketing needs to reduce perceived risk so that the prospective customer perceives the expectation as being worth the risk.

This means not only that pricing is an important marketing tool, but also that marketing must persuade the customer that the solution is worth the price. The bottom line

---

[8] This is not totally true. A billboard or television commercial depicting a steaming pizza, or a radio commercial describing an elegant dinner can literally cause salivation. For our purposes of illustration, however, the assumption is normally true.

in the marketing model is not profit; it is the satisfaction level felt by the customer after making the sacrifice (Figure 1-2). If the satisfaction level is positive, a customer has been created. Keep in mind, of course, that the same tenets hold whether we apply them to a budget motel or a five-star hotel, to a pizza parlor or to a gourmet restaurant.

Naturally, the solution to any problem rarely exists in a vacuum. That's why marketing becomes far more complex than the example presented. If a solution to the problem of needing a night's sleep was only a room and a bed at the right price in the right place, then there would be little need for marketing. Solutions aren't that simple and include many, many other needs. The instant that one motel provides something different from another motel, competition is created and the mettle of marketing is tested. Instead of creating the thought "here's a bed" (solution to problem), marketing creates the thought "here's this bed," which represents the only solution to your specific problem.

The goal for marketers is *to present the best solution to the problem at the lowest risk*. Marketing, however, does not stop there, especially in the hospitality industry. The creation of expectations might be classified as traditional marketing. There are, however, those who believe that marketing does end there, and that it is now the job of operations management to assure that those expectations are fulfilled.

While this is surely operations management's responsibility, it also means that operations management is totally involved in the marketing effort: traditional marketing only brings the customer to the door, it is up to nontraditional marketing to create and keep the customer.

We have discussed the trade-off model at some length because it is so critical to the understanding of marketing. The concept will be developed further in later chapters, but first we need to see how marketing influences the total picture.

Management Orientations

All companies, firms, organizations, and other business entities operate under a basic philosophy or orientation. This philosophy may be spoken, written, or cast in cement; it may also be simply implied. Regardless of its articulation, it exists, and those who have been with the organization any length of time understand its force and its implications because it usually emanates from the corporate suite.

An organization's philosophy is the part of its corporate culture emphasizing that "this is the way we do business around here." It is what drives the firm, what makes it tick, and what makes it work. It is the philosophy of the organization that shapes the corporate effort and is the firm's major focus and most pervasive force from product conceptualization to market. The firm's fundamental method of managing resources is the philosophy that is exemplified in planned and goal-oriented management activities.

One example of a company philosophy is a production-line orientation: how fast, how many, and how cheaply can we produce the product to get it to the market, in bulk, at the lowest possible price? Henry Ford may have been the originator of this philosophy when he declared, "Give the customers any color they want as long as it's black." A modern-day example has been Texas Instruments, which mass-produces calculators and watches. You might say that McDonald's and Burger King also practice this philosophy, but you would be wrong. For these two companies this orientation is not a philosophy, it is one means of fulfilling their marketing philosophies.

Another example of a company philosophy is a selling orientation, as practiced by Mary Kay Cosmetics, whose legion of salespeople are driven to knock on as many doors as possible and to sell, sell, sell. We have come to know this as the "hard sell," as practiced by many automobile salespeople.

For many years Polaroid was an example of a technology-oriented company. Its founder, Edwin Land, a genius by any form of measurement, was committed to the belief that success in the marketplace was a result of the finest technological development. The Polaroid Land Camera was the original product that made Polaroid a major entity in the photographic industry. However, Land's quest to continually develop the most technologically advanced product was not always so successful. His instant movie camera proved to be too sophisticated, sold poorly, and was dropped from the product line because the market wasn't ready for it.

Polaroid's past philosophy is also similar in practice to what is called a product orientation. A firm with a product orientation puts all its emphasis on the product, assuming that the product sells itself—in other words, if the product is right, is the best, offers the best value, and so on, the customer will buy it. The emphasis is on the product rather than consumers' needs and wants.

The company philosophy that we want to emphasize here is, of course, the marketing philosophy. This orientation is best exemplified by companies like IBM and Procter and Gamble, or SAS under Jan Carlzon, as we have already pointed out. This philosophy decrees that the customer is the focal point of commitment. It further specifies that strategy and policy are executed on the basis of careful study of the market's needs consistent with the firm's skills. Markets are not assumed to exist automatically under this philosophy, as they are under the philosophy that proved to be the downfall of the instant movie camera, and effective demand is believed to be based on customers that are created, and kept.

All of these philosophies have their place and time. It is not appropriate to say that any one philosophy is the "best" a company can have. Henry Ford was right when he developed the production line to manufacture the cheapest car. Mary Kay has been enormously successful in selling cosmetics. Edwin Land was right when he invented the instant camera. And Procter and Gamble was right when it recognized customers' needs and began producing cake mix in place of unbleached flour.

Orientations in the Hospitality Industry

The hospitality industry encompasses all of these philosophies and orientations at various times and places. Many of the great European hotels, some in Asia, and some in the United States, especially some of those under individual proprietorship, are known for their emphasis on the customer's well-being, attention, and needs. When this philosophy is practiced at the highest level of management it tends to permeate the organization and is reflected in the behavior of all personnel. It was by using this philosophy that Jan Carlzon turned around SAS.

Many hospitality organizations, however, have different orientations. These orientations may be an operations, a product, or a selling orientation, or some combination of these three.

Operations Orientation   An operations orientation is categorized by its emphasis on a "smooth operation" as symbolized by the anonymous wag who once stated, "This is a great business to be in, if only the customers didn't get in the way." Another way of describing this kind of organization is the statement, "This place is run by the book." Bookshelves of operations manuals provide prescriptions for direction and behavior for almost every conceivable occurrence.

Operations-oriented hotels and restaurants have a propensity to forget the customer in the interest of a smooth operation. Although these facilities run well, customers are fickle and idiosyncratic and manuals are often inadequate to deal with all the vagaries of their behavior. This does not mean that manuals are not desirable for operations purposes. In fact, in today's large chains it would be impossible to obtain consistency in service delivery without them. Problems occur, however, when the manual becomes the "be-all and end-all" and there is no room for deviation on the customer's behalf. Or, what may be even worse, sometimes the manual is written only from an operations perspective and without consideration for the customer. In these cases the manuals or operating procedures are usually dictated from a cost perspective.

Operations philosophies, like all philosophies, come down from the executive suite. When the company or the company's executives are very bottom-line or profit-driven they tend to prescribe directives based only on cost considerations, either out-of-pocket costs or operating efficiency costs. The customer may well get caught in the squeeze.

Consider, for example, the restaurant that has a slow night. Typically, management will send wait personnel home and close part of the dining room. The section that gets closed is the exterior section, near the windows or with the view, because it is furthest away from from the kitchen and takes more effort to serve. It is also the most desirable section from the customer's perspective. The part that remains open, of course, is closest to the kitchen because it is most convenient to serve. Some company manuals actually prescribe this procedure.

Similarly, you may have had the experience of saying to a dining room hostess, "Can we have that table over there?" (instead of the one you were led to), and received the response, "I'm sorry but it's not that waiter's turn."

Another example comes from a hotel on the ocean in Jamaica. Each morning, this hotel served an extensive breakfast buffet in a beautiful poolside location by the beach. If guests desired a standard breakfast, however, they must eat inside in a coffee shop. Those who opted for just a continental breakfast must sit further inside at a counter where the sun never shines! At the same hotel, where rooms started at $160 per night, the pool closed at 6:00 P.M. although the temperature might still be 110° and many guests had been in conferences all day. To make certain there were no exceptions to this rule, the pool was chlorinated at 6:05 nightly.

In another example, consider the large flagship hotel of a major chain that claimed to be customer-oriented but rewarded all its people based on bottom-line results. This hotel was losing occupancy in the face of increasing competition, and was responding by cutting costs and raising prices. Management spent $17 million dollars on a new entryway that had little if any effect on business. The problems were inside, where staff had been cut. Normal check-in time took ten minutes, and that was when there wasn't a line. Check-out was about as bad. The indoor pool didn't open until 9:00 A.M., long after the business clientele had left for the day. The brightest light in the rooms was 67 watts, difficult to use for paperwork or reading. The widest writing space in most rooms, including suites, was 16 inches.

These types of practices are established in the name of operational or cost efficiency. Hotels and restaurants that operate by these kinds of procedures pride themselves on their operational efficiencies, rather than on their solutions to customers' problems. Obviously, such efficiencies may well cause problems instead of solving them for guests seeking a hassle-free experience.

Product Orientation   Hospitality properties that operate with a product orientation place their emphasis on the product or the service. These properties market according to the "build a better mousetrap and the world will beat a path to your door" concept. They trumpet that their property has the best food, the finest chefs, the ultimate in service, designer-decorated lobbies, or even the best location.

Consider, for example, the ads for Atlanta hotels in Figure 1-3, directed at meeting planners. At the Westin Peachtree Plaza, after Westin spent $31 million, you can have a "more than just successful" meeting because of "sumptuous new fabrics. Elegant furnishings. Italian marble. And breath-taking views." And, if you want inspiration for your meeting, there are "Twinkling arches, hidden courtyards."

At the Hotel Inter-Continental, you can have "a chauffeur-driven Rolls Royce" meet your private airplane, and you can dine "in surroundings of hand-polished wood, antique crystal and gleaming silver." At the Hyatt Regency, you get to enjoy the hotel that, 20 years later, "continues to fulfill John Portman's vision." And then, in case none of these appeal to you, as a small group you "can practically have the place to [yourself]" in "the largest best-run hotel in the Southeast, . . . with its awesome atrium, ten restaurants and lounges, indoor/outdoor pool and health club" at the Marriott Marquis.[9] At the Ritz-Carlton, on the other hand, "we concentrate on the fine points of innkeeping. Like luxurious rooms. Afternoon tea served in English bone china. Superb cuisine. Richly paneled walls graced by 18th and 19th Century oils."

Would you rather have your meeting at the Colony Square Hotel, which "assigns individuals who work behind the scenes to oversee every detail of your visit—from planning to follow-up"? and of which the manager of the Coca-Cola U.S.A. Training Center says, "They're our biggest supplier. . . . The thing I appreciate most is the flexibility. They respond quickly to our last-minute requests."

Which do you suppose meeting planners most prefer: twinkling arches, hand-polished wood, John Portman's vision, awesome atriums, English bone china, or someone who oversees every detail of their meeting?

---

[9] It should be noted that Marriott quickly changed this ad. While retaining the "awesome atrium" background, one version pictured an Executive Meeting Manager and the copy emphasized her expertise, dedication, and "attention to every last detail" of small meetings. Marriott would have preferred that we use that ad instead of the original one. Like the Colony Square ad, the emphasis is more on the problems of the meeting planner, as it should be. However, as all these ads ran together, we did not feel it would be fair to the other hotels, which may also have changed their ads, to make the switch. Instead, we applaud Marriott for its alertness in making the change and, perhaps in so doing, doubly emphasizing the point.

WE DON'T JUST ACCOMMODATE MEETINGS. WE INSPIRE THEM.

$31,000,000.

That's how much we spent to make your next meeting something more than just successful.

1074 luxurious guest rooms and suites now greet you with sumptuous new fabrics. Elegant furnishings. Italian marble. And breath-taking views of Atlanta's skyline.

We built in plenty of practicality, too. Our 41 handsome meeting rooms are now more accessible than ever. With new elevator service and spiral staircases between meeting levels. Plus new ideas in traffic flow to keep functions moving beautifully for groups to 2500.

Exhibit facilities? Loads. With our new concourse connection to the Atlanta Market Center, your guests and 176,000 square feet of first-class exhibit space are all under the same roof.

And talk about inspiration! A simple walk through our lobby will get your group's creative juices flowing. Twinkling arches, hidden courtyards—it's unique in all the world.

What's it add up to? Four Stars from Mobil *and* Four Diamonds from AAA. We're the only major hotel in Atlanta to earn both ratings.

Explore the possibilities. Call (404) 659-1400 Ext. 7060. See the difference a little inspiration—and a lot of great facilities—can make.

THE WESTIN PEACHTREE PLAZA
Atlanta

THE PEOPLE AND PLACES OF WESTIN
Caring · Comfortable · Civilized.

WESTIN
HOTELS & RESORTS

FIGURE 1-3   Hotel ads directed at the meetings market

Now your meeting will become the special event it deserves to be.

Beginning in January 1988, a new hotel in Atlanta will treat your meeting with as much importance as you do. The Hotel Inter·Continental Atlanta, with 375 luxurious guest rooms and 16,000 square feet of meeting facilities. Located in prestigious Buckhead at Lenox Square. Convenient to downtown and seconds from the finest shopping, dining, and nightlife in Atlanta.

For the meeting planner, our AdvantagePlan provides a fully staffed office, and the use of our Executive Business Center's range of telecommunications equipment. We can even provide a chauffeur-driven Rolls Royce for your special meeting needs.

We also extend the convenience of our Express Check-In, and the pleasure of conducting business in a gracious environment. With superb dining and sophisticated after-hours entertainment in surroundings of hand-polished wood, antique crystal and gleaming silver.

Hotel Inter·Continental. We have a heritage of hosting the most important meetings. Like yours. For more information, call 1-404-365-8840.

HOTEL INTER•CONTINENTAL ATLANTA
At Lenox Square.

INTER·CONTINENTAL: Atlanta (January'88), Hilton Head, S.C., Houston, Maui, Miami, Montreal, New Orleans, New York City, Philadelphia (Mid '88), Princeton, San Antonio, San Diego, San Francisco, Washington, D.C.

FIGURE 1-3   Continued

18

Small groups can practically have the place to themselves.

Most meeting planners already know that Marriott's magnificent Atlanta Marquis is the largest, best-run hotel in the Southeast, able to serve large groups superbly.

But what you may not know is that the Marquis also has a separate Executive Conference Center that's ideal for smaller groups.

It's quiet, plush and secluded. A Conference Center concierge makes sure you have everything you need, from A/V equipment to Marriott's famous food service. Even your own registration area.

There's also a separate Concierge Level of guest rooms that gives your executives the same kind of small hotel attentiveness that the Executive Conference Center gives your meetings.

And of course, the rest of the hotel, with its awesome atrium, ten restaurants and lounges, indoor/outdoor pool and health club are merely seconds away.

Book your next small meeting here. And when it's a huge success, your bosses will know who was largely responsible.

Marriott. And you.

Marriott People know how.

ATLANTA **Marriott**®
MARQUIS

Heart of Peachtree Center, (404) 521-0000 or Direct Dial (404) 586-6047

FIGURE 1-3   Continued

Hotels may have all the attributes they claim; sometimes they do not. Regardless, the claims often fail to consider whether these factors are solutions to customers' problems. In the attempt to sell the property for a group booking, as illustrated in Figure 1-3, the emphasis is on the physical attributes rather than the delivery of the service, or what these attributes will do to make the groups' meetings go smoother. More than one group has been lost forever to a hotel because of inattentive personnel, inflexible policies, bad acoustics, or stale coffee, in spite of the beautiful and very expensive chandeliers and wallpaper.

Product orientations often start before the property is built, especially in the case of hotels. For example, although atrium lobbies have become somewhat symbolic of elegance, there are many such lobbies where the noise that resounds up and across the atrium prevents many guests from obtaining a good night's sleep. Many people actually avoid atrium lobby hotels.

In the marketing sense, products should be defined only in terms of what they do for the customer. Whatever they do, they should not create even more problems, as pointed out by Meg Greenfield in an only slightly tongue-in-cheek article entitled "Who Put The Lake in the Lobby." Greenfield's column quips about needing a kayak to get to the newsstand; not being able to find the registration desk without getting a faceful of spray; elevator buttons labeled LL, MM, S, and LM that have no meaning to the guest; bedside lamps that you have to stand on the night table to turn off; and a hotel in Detroit where people trying to meet can wave at each other from different levels but can't figure out how to end up on the same level. According to Greenfield, American hotels are designed to "keep you from (a) knowing where you are or (b) getting where you want to go." We recommend the reading of Greenfield's column as an entertaining but trenchant view of hotels that are not totally planned with consumer problems in mind.[10] Greenfield clearly demonstrates the emphasis that is all too often placed on the product as opposed to the customer.

From a different perspective, it is interesting to read what Michael Leven, president of Days Inn, said when asked why he made his senior vice-president of marketing the senior vice-president of operations instead:

> The answer lies with the general managers, whose bailiwick has been soap, ashtrays, sheets, and light bills. These product-oriented people have to turn their attention to "creative revenue buildup" in today's high-supply environment and turn away from the technical approach to the hospitality business. It is the job of [the vice-president of operations] to make clear to them the customer's capability to deliver revenue if they are satisfied with the services they receive.[11]

Selling Orientation   A selling orientation in hotel and restaurant companies is one in which the effort to obtain customers emphasizes finding someone who will come through the doors, as opposed to marketing a solution to a designated market's needs. Hotel companies with this kind of orientation often have large sales forces and/or large advertising budgets. They are very conscious of their open periods and they push their salespeople to "go out and fill them" and to meet their sales quota. Or, these properties

---

[10] Meg Greenfield, "Who Put the Lake in the Lobby?" *Newsweek,* January 13, 1986, p. 76.
[11] Quoted by Connie Goldstein, *Corporate Meetings and Incentive Travel,* June, 1986, p. 6.

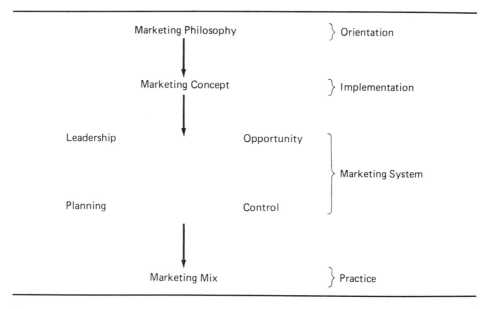

FIGURE 1-4   The marketing philosophy model

may run frequent promotions and special offers. Whichever way, everything is based on the sell, sell, sell edict rather than identifying customers' needs and wants.

There is obviously nothing wrong with running a good operation, having a fine product, or managing an effective sales force. Well-run and successful companies do all this and do it well. A truly marketing-oriented company, however, views these achievements as subsets of marketing—that is, they are accomplished with the customer as the focal point. The operations manager says "I run a tight ship," but only after making sure that the customers' needs and wants have been considered. The product manager considers first what the product will do for the customer. And the sales manager sells those benefits that will solve customers' problems and make their experiences hassle-free.

The marketing philosophy model is shown in Figure 1-4. We have discussed the initial or orientation phase of the model. This is the umbrella under which the other parts of the model exist, and these will be discussed in the remainder of this chapter.

The Marketing Concept

If a firm adopts the marketing philosophy as its orientation, then the development and implementation of that philosophy is based on what has come to be known as the marketing concept. The marketing concept is based on the premise that the customer is king, the customer has a choice, and the customer does not have to buy your product. Thus, the best way to earn a profit is to serve the customer better. According to the marketing concept, an organization should try to satisfy the needs of customers or clients through a coordinated set of activities that at the same time allows the organization to achieve its goals. Providing satisfaction to customers is the major thrust of the marketing concept. To do this [it must be found out] what will satisfy customers. With this information, the business can create satisfying products [that solve customers' problems]. But that is not enough. The business then must get these products into the hands of customers. Nor does the process end there. The business must continue to alter and adapt current products to keep pace with changes in customers' desires and preferences. Essentially the marketing concept stresses the importance of customers and emphasizes that marketing activities start and end with them.

In attempting to satisfy customers, businesses must consider not only short-run, immediate tasks, but also broad, long-run desires. Thus a business must try to satisfy current needs in a manner that will not produce adverse long-run effects which cause strong customer dissatisfaction in the future.

. . . To meet these short- and long-run needs and desires, all activities within a firm must be coordinated. Production, finance, accounting, personnel and marketing departments must work together. Lack of managerial coordination may lessen customer satisfaction or even cause severe dissatisfaction.

. . . The marketing concept stresses that a business organization can best achieve its goals by providing customer satisfaction through coordinated activities. Thus implementation of the marketing concept benefits the organization as well as its customers.[12]

. . . The marketing concept does not consist of advertising, selling and promotion. It is a willingness to recognize and understand the consumer's needs and wants, *and* a willingness to adjust any of the marketing mix elements, including product, to satisfy those needs and wants.[13]

Let us translate this definition into simpler language.

Having a marketing orientation is necessary, but not sufficient. We can believe that we are in the business of solving consumers' problems and serving their needs and wants, and we can have this philosophy permeate the entire firm, but until we do something about it—put it into practice—it will not suffice. Perhaps a more vernacular way of stating this is, "You have to put your money where your mouth is." Practicing the marketing concept does exactly that.

There is a fine but important distinction here: A company can have one without the other. A marketing orientation without practicing the marketing concept represents a good start but will not succeed in the long run. When the company dies, it will be said about it, "They were such nice people, I wonder why they didn't make it." On the other hand, practicing the marketing concept without a marketing orientation is like giving lip service to marketing; it constructs marketing as a company policy without permeating the firm as a shaper of the corporate effort. Both a marketing philosophy and the marketing concept must exist before we can define the firm as a true marketing company.

---

[12] William M. Pride and O. C. Ferrell, *Marketing: Basic Concepts and Decisions*, pp. 13–14. 2nd ed., Copyright © 1980. Used by permission of Houghton Mifflin Company.

[13] Franklin S. Houston, "The Marketing Concept: What It Is and What It Is Not," Reprinted from *The Journal of Marketing*, April, 1986, p. 85, published by the American Marketing Association.

Practicing the marketing concept means putting yourself in the customer's shoes. It means selecting market segments that can be served profitably. This translates into profitable products and services that the company can produce. Practicing the marketing concept means making the business do what suits the customer's interests. For management, it has implications of integrating and coordinating the research, planning, and systems approach of the firm. Practicing the marketing concept is a management approach to marketing that stresses problem-solving and decision-making responsibility to enhance the objectives of the entire firm. Philip Kotler, a noted marketing author and educator, says the following about the marketing concept:

> Marketing is not the art of finding clever ways to dispose of what you make. Marketing is the art of creating genuine customer value. It is the art of helping your customers become better off. The marketer's watch words are quality, service and value. Can you imagine what the world would be like if the marketing concept became a universal principle?[14]

Peters and Waterman, in their best-selling study of successful companies, found that "staying close to the customer" was one trait common to all these companies. They cite the following phrase from Lew Young, Editor-in-Chief at *Business Week* magazine:

> Probably the most important management fundamental that is being ignored today is staying close to the customer to satisfy his needs and anticipate his wants. In too many companies, the customer has become a bloody nuisance whose unpredictable behavior damages carefully made strategic plans, whose activities mess up computer operations, and who stubbornly insists that purchased products should work.[15]

Practicing the marketing concept involves a systems approach to practicing four distinct characteristics of marketing behavior, as follows and as shown in Figure 1-4.

The Marketing System

It is the marketing system in the organization that makes the marketing orientation become real and the marketing concept work. We discuss each of these briefly here, and in more detail in later chapters.

Leadership

Many researchers have studied the qualities of effective leadership by observing the characteristics of men and women generally agreed to be successful leaders. Four major characteristics seem to be

* A vision of the future
* The ability to communicate that vision

---

[14] Philip Kotler, Professor of Marketing at Northwestern University, cited in *Marketing News*, July 19, 1985, p. 1, published by the American Marketing Association, on notification that he would receive the first American Marketing Association Distinguished Educator Award.

[15] Thomas J. Peters and Robert H. Waterman, Jr., *In Search of Excellence*, New York: Harper & Row, 1982, p. 156.

- An entrepreneurial spirit
- A constant quest for excellence

These same characteristics can be applied to leadership in terms of the marketing concept. Marketing leadership accepts change as a constant. It not only recognizes needs and wants of the customer but it also recognizes that the customer changes; the customer is not in a static state, and any successful company must change with, if not before, the customer. Marketing leadership envisions these changes through constant evaluation of the market.

Business history is replete with examples of companies that failed to recognize the changes in the marketplace. Victoria Station restaurants, initially a very successful chain, entered Chapter 11 bankruptcy in 1986 after ten years of failure to understand the markeplace. Victoria Station emphasized beef and food quality and, eventually, almost every new menu item they could think of, long after the theme restaurant market had switched to new priorities of lighter, more interesting food and the total restaurant experience.

Holiday Inns came dangerously close to the edge in the mid-1970s before a new management took over and recognized the changing market. Holiday Inns originated and succeeded by creating a consistent, standard product when there were no others, and customers were happy to know what they would get when they bought a motel room. Eventually, however, customers tired of the product and its stereotype and wanted change. As dependability of the competition also occurred in the market, customers wanted variety and different features; Holiday Inns was slow to react.

Perhaps the most famous hospitality example is that of Howard Johnson's. Founded on the premise that travelers wanted assurance of consistency wherever they ate across the country, Howard Johnson's discovered a gold mine. The company was extremely successful and, based on that success, stuck to its original formula through thick and thin. When the customer changed, Howard Johnson's did not. Slowly but surely its customer base eroded.

Stopgap measures to halt the erosion brought only temporary blips in the downward trend line. In 1965, Howard Johnson's annual sales were greater than the combined sales of McDonald's, Burger King, and Kentucky Fried Chicken. By 1970, its sales were about the same as McDonald's, about a quarter of a billion dollars. For the year 1984, at the time Howard Johnson's was broken up following its sale to Marriott, its sales were less than three-fourths of a billion, compared to McDonald's sales which had grown to almost 3.5 billion.

Howard Johnson's had no marketing plan. Instead of realizing that the customer was changing, recognizing its customers' problems, and finding out what the customer wanted, Howard Johnson's concentrated on cutting costs. Said Howard B. Johnson, son of the founder and CEO until the 1979 sale to Imperial Group PLC of Britain: "We ran a very tight operation. . . . We were on top of the numbers daily." As one person quipped, "Every time I saw Howard Johnson he was always telling me how he was going to cut costs further. . . . If he'd eaten in his own restaurants more instead of lunching at '21,' he might have learned something."[16]

---

[16] John Merwin, "The Sad Case of the Dwindling Orange Roofs," *Forbes,* December 30, 1985, pp. 75–79.

Howard Johnson's made many mistakes in addition to failing to recognize that the market was changing, but they all were marketing mistakes.

Victoria Station, the earlier Holiday Inns, and Howard Johnson's were companies that fell on hard times because they lacked marketing leadership.

Besides the need for vision and an entrepreneurial spirit in marketing leadership, good leaders are never satisfied with anything less than 100 percent. Even more important, they communicate all three of these characteristics to others; they "fire everybody up" as the expression goes. This is what is meant by permeating the firm with the marketing philosophy.

Marketing leaders excel at McDonald's and the marketing philosophy permeates the firm. When Edward Carlson, a former hotel man, took over United Airlines in the late 1960s it was losing $50 million a year. Carlson traveled 200,000 miles a year practicing what he called "visible management." What's more, he made certain that his top executives did the same thing. They turned the company around, and they did this with marketing leadership. Other outstanding examples of this type of leadership are Jim Nassikas formerly of The Stanford Court Hotel in San Francisco, and Bill Marriott, president of Marriott Corporation. Both these men deserved the outstanding hotelman of the year awards they received in 1986. They are men who have a long-term vision of the customer, are entrepreneurial in nature, constantly seek excellence, and work everyday to communicate these characteristics throughout their firms.

Opportunity

Great success stories in business almost always include tales of visionary leaders who saw and grasped opportunity. Howard Johnson the founder was certainly one of those. He saw the opportunity to give traveling Americans clean, inexpensive, dependable food and service from Maine to California. Kemmons Wilson, the founder of Holiday Inns, saw the opportunity to do the same with motel rooms. Ray Kroc, the founder of McDonald's, recognized an opportunity in the families that were moving to suburbia with discretionary income, 2.3 kids in the back of a station wagon, and a mother who wanted to be able to feed them quickly and reasonably in a clean environment.

Opportunities such as these are based on needs, wants, and problems of consumers that already exist. These men were visionaries with an entrepreneurial spirit. They didn't create the needs, wants, or problems, but recognized them as opportunities. Practicing the marketing concept means constantly searching out opportunities.

Very few opportunities are as grand as those above. To find the smaller ones, marketing concept managers don't look for opportunities first; they look for problems because these are easier to identify. Some are very self-evident.

Consider, for example, the lines of people waiting to check in to a hotel. This problem is one of the most common grievances of hotel customers, but very little has been done about it at the time of this writing. One recent remedy has been to install queuing ropes at the check-in desk. This saves the customer from needing to decide which line will move the fastest, but at the same time has created another problem: making customers feel like cattle lined up for the slaughter. In some hotels, in fact, one must negotiate the maze even when the lobby is empty. This constitutes a remedy to a symptom rather than a solution to a problem.

Remedies like this come about because what is perceived as the consumer problem is really a symptom of an operations problem. A marketing mentality would perceive this as an opportunity. To gain this perception one must first recognize the real problem. The real problem is not the lines, which are a symptom and what queuing ropes attempt to resolve, but what causes the delay. In this case it is the check-in procedure. What management sees as a customer problem is caused by a management problem; in other words, this is an opportunity for management to resolve the customer problem by improving the operational efficiency.

In order to locate this opportunity, let's analyze the problem more thoroughly. What causes it? Shelley Berman, the TV and radio comedian—not a hotelier, but a customer— did it long ago. Everyone laughed but no one listened when he told a story that began something like this:

> Not long ago I checked into a fashionable and long-respected New York hotel. When the desk clerk was convinced I had a reservation, he handed me the usual registration card to fill out. The information requested was:
> The date
> My name (PLEASE PRINT)
> My home address
> My home phone number
> My city, state, and zip code
> The name of my firm
> The firm's address
> The firm's phone number
> The firm's city, state, and zip code
> My signature

If you've ever watched Shelley Berman, you can imagine the rest of the story. If you have ever checked into a hotel, you know there is even more to it than that, such as finding the reservation, asking for your credit card, finding (or making) the key, waiting for the bellman, and so forth. Shelley Berman gave this spiel before the common use of computers in hotels, but things haven't changed much. The lines are just as long today and the advent of computers has not solved the delay problem from the customer's perspective. In fact, desk clerks seem to spend more time staring into computer screens than they do talking to the customer, who stands there feeling somewhat helpless and wondering if the reservation will come up. Eventually, computers should improve the situation, much as they are helping to solve the similar problems of checking out.

In the meanwhile, here's an opportunity missed. Just suppose the desk clerk handed you the registration card to fill out while checking on your reservation. At two to five minutes per customer, think of the time it would save, apart from the aggravation, yet it happens only in a very few hotels. Or, better yet, suppose there was a desk in the lobby, like those in banks for filling out your deposit slip, where all incoming guests could have filled out their registration cards before going to the desk. Suppose the electronic lock keys had already been made. Suppose desk clerks believed, and practiced, that customers waiting in line have bigger problems than computers. A marketing opportunist could suppose a number of other things.

Opportunity continues to be the lifeblood of successful marketing. It doesn't start with fancy drapery or upholstered walls; it starts with consumers' problems. Look for a problem, the real problem, and you will find an opportunity. Ted Levitt put it most succinctly back in 1960 in his much reprinted article: "In truth, *there is no such thing* as a growth industry, I believe. There are only companies organized and operated to create and capitalize on growth opportunities."[17] No industry, no business, and no product enjoys an automatically assured growth. It is only seeking, finding, and successfully exploiting opportunities that can assure growth.

Planning

The third element of practicing the marketing concept is planning. Planning is defining what has to be done and allocating the resources to do it. It means proacting rather than reacting. It means shaping your own destiny. One writer summarizes the accomplishments attributed to good planning, as follows:

- It leads to a better position or standing for the organization.
- It helps the organization progress in the ways that its management considers most suitable.
- It helps every manager think, decide, and act more effectively for progress in the desired direction.
- It helps keep the organization flexible.
- It stimulates a cooperative, integrated, enthusiastic approach to organizational problems.
- It indicates to management how to evaluate and check up on progress toward the planned objectives.
- It leads to socially and economically useful results.[18]

Although one would expect planning to be a given in most companies, it is not difficult to find companies that do not plan, plan haphazardly, or plan only as an exercise. Good planning follows from good leadership. Visions of the future are not realized without some plan to fulfill them. Growth must be carefully planned. Opportunities, likewise, do not fall out of the sky; they must be sought and planned for in a systematic manner. Planning is essential also in choosing among opportunities when all cannot be pursued.

Planning in the marketing sense and in the sense of the marketing concept means planning with the customer in mind. It was shown that planning was neglected in the latter days of Howard Johnson's. The demise of Victoria Station restaurants was hastened by poor and haphazard planning. Marriott and McDonald's have continued to grow through, among other things, very careful planning.

Many hotels develop annual marketing plans (restaurants rarely do), but they often have very little to do with planning. After enumerating the physical assets and rack rates of the competition, these marketing plans usually turn into promotional objectives, advertising allocations, budgets, and day-by-day occupancy forecasts. Rarely do these plans address the creation of customers or the change in current operating procedures

---

[17] Theodore Levitt, "Marketing Myopia," *Harvard Business Review*, 1960. Reprinted in Theodore Levitt, *The Marketing Imagination*, New York: The Free Press, 1986, p. 147.

[18] David W. Ewing, *The Practice of Planning*, New York: Harper & Row, 1968, pp. 9–14.

needed to keep these customers coming back. Market segments are usually defined only in the broadest of terms.

While financial planning has become routine in many companies, marketing planning has yet to achieve that status. This seems strange if one accepts the premise that without customers there would be no finances to manage. Unfortunately, many hospitality companies have become only financial vehicles for their founders and owners, to whom hospitality is a foreign concern.

Many hospitality companies no longer own and operate facilities. Instead, they manage for other owners. These owners have very little experience in the industry, as they most likely made their money elsewhere. If their financial position weakens for any reason, they frequently put pressure on the property to deliver higher profits.

Compounding the problem are the management companies that provide unrealistic pro formas when bidding on management contracts.[19] Often they cannot deliver, but the owners hold them to their word. The result is severe cutbacks in operating expenses to meet the bottom line. This can result in a vicious cycle of declining business and reduced expenses. A quality level commitment must be planned for the long term. Short-term scenarios of reduced expenses only accelerate the product decline.

Much of the remainder of this book will deal with marketing planning, as it will also deal with leadership and opportunity, although those precise terms may not be used. Rather, the terms used will be those of the elements of good planning, good leadership, and the seeking of opportunity.

Control

Control is the last element of the marketing system quartet, but is also the glue that holds the other three together and makes them work. When control is lacking in hospitality firms, leadership and planning founders. Refer again, if you will, to Howard Johnson's, a classic case of a hospitality company that lost control.

Control in the sense of the marketing concept means something quite different from cost control, although certainly marketers must be aware of costs and their impact on the bottom line. Instead, control in the marketing sense means control of your destiny through leadership, planning, and opportunity by control of the customer, the market, and the product.

Control is the feedback loop of the system that tells if the system is working and provides information to management on who the market is, who the customer is, and what the customer's problems, expectations, perceptions, and experiences are. Control is knowing whether perceptions equal reality, why the customers come or don't come, how they use the product, how their complaints are handled, and whether they return. In short, control in marketing is knowing and serving the customer. Control is also knowing your employees because, as we shall see later, every employee is an integral part of the marketing effort in a hospitality firm.

---

[19]In the past, tax incentives covered up poor fiscal performance on the part of the management company. Under the 1986 tax act most of these incentives were eliminated.

There is some attempt at the customer-feedback type of control in the hospitality industry through the use of guest comment cards. Left on tables in restaurants or on dressers in hotel rooms, these cards invite customers to rate the facilities, the food, and the service. For a number of reasons, guest comment cards have been found to be unreliable and invalid indicators of performance.

One reason for the irrelevance of comment cards is that they are limited in scope and thus reveal only minimal information. Another reason is that most people do not use them, only those on opposite ends of the satisfaction spectrum. One major hotel company asked the customer to mail them directly to the president at corporate headquarters. Here they were tabulated in such a way that one negative rating out of approximately 65 possible ratings would record this customer as 98 percent satisfied. Overall, this company reported over 90 percent customer satisfaction. Management may have deceived itself, since no scientific research has ever reported this high a level of customer satisfaction in hotels.

Another major hotel company asked the customer to turn the card in at the front desk when checking out. This company reported only 47 percent customer satisfaction even though some of the front desk employees admitted a reluctance to pass on "bad cards." Discrepancies such as these make it difficult to use comment cards as a solid basis for management decisions outside of specific "this needs fixing" comments.[20]

If the definition of marketing used earlier in this chapter is to apply, it is clear that management must have access to reliable guest expectation and fulfillment information. The excerpts presented earlier from "Who Put the Lake in the Lobby" gave examples of this lack of information. If management is to seek opportunity, it needs to know customers' problems. If management is going to plan for customer change, it must know when and how the customer changes. If management intends to serve customers' needs and wants, it must know what those needs and wants are. If management plans to create customers, and keep them, it must use relevant data.

Control in marketing means a good management information system, an essential element of practicing the marketing concept. Chapter 19, on information systems and research, will discuss this in greater detail.

The Marketing Mix

The final stage of the marketing philosophy model in Figure 1-4 is what has become known as the marketing mix. The marketing mix is the product/service, the presentation, the pricing, the communication, and the distribution of the firm that directly affects the consumer. Thus far we have discussed what is essentially internal within the organization; it is not what the customer sees, but it is what the customer feels. For example, you may never hear a customer say that a hotel or restaurant company is marketing, product, or operations oriented, or that it practices the marketing concept and has visionary leadership, but you can be sure that customers are aware of those factors in one way or another.

What the customer does see is the marketing mix. To resort to the vernacular, this is where "the rubber meets the road." It is the implementation of the other parts of the philosophy model; it is what comes out at the end of the tunnel. The marketing mix is the

---

[20] Guest comment cards will be discussed further in Chapter 19.

facility, the employees, the advertising, the prices, the atmosphere, the attitude, and all the rest of the elements, both tangible and intangible, that represent to the customer the final delivery of the product and service.

The marketing mix will be discussed in detail in Chapters 11 through 18.

Summary

This chapter has introduced marketing as a philosophy and a way of life of the hospitality firm. We have defined marketing in terms of the customer and we have demonstrated how a marketing orientation, or the lack of it, affects the entire organization. We have examined the concepts of internal and relationship marketing (although without using those terms), which will be discussed in detail in Chapter 3.

We have shown that marketing is far more than selling and advertising, the traditional concepts of the field. In fact, it has been shown that advertising and selling, equated by some with the term *marketing,* are only subsets of marketing. In some cases, in fact, these activities may not even be necessary to marketing, as demonstrated by the many successful establishments that never advertise or practice direct selling.

The other side of this coin should also be apparent. You don't have to be a marketing professional to engage in marketing. Marketing is an integral part of management and the day-to-day business of running an operation. This fact has only recently approached realization for many. As Steve Powell then of Loew's Anatole Hotel in Dallas has stated,

> There's a change that's happening in the hotel industry that's developing into a trend, and that is the marketing orientation of management. . . . The industry is becoming more market or customer/client driven.
> . . . You see more [hotel executives] with customers and clients today . . . out there listening to the needs, trying to re-mold and change the industry so it's more responsive.[21]

Those readers for whom this chapter is their first real introduction to marketing may, in fact, be a little bewildered with this concept of marketing. Not to worry. In services industries, of which the hospitality industry is certainly a part, more than 80 percent of marketing may be nontraditional marketing. In Chapter 2 we will explain why.

DISCUSSION QUESTIONS

1. A very successful restaurateur says, "Who needs marketing? That's for big corporations and business students. I operate by hunch and common sense." Discuss this statement.
2. Give examples of hospitality operations you are familiar with or have read about that seem to operate by the different philosophies discussed in the chapter. Relate their philosophy to their success or lack of it.

---

[21] Quoted in *The Meeting Manager,* September, 1986, p. 22.

3. From some of your own experiences, apply the consumer trade-off model. How do you balance risk against problem solution? How does this affect your price/value perception and your expectations? Develop a scenario for how a hospitality customer might do the same thing.

4. The chapter states, "having created expectation, marketing needs to reduce perceived risk." Discuss the ways in which marketing might do this in the hospitality industry.

5. If you were the president of a hotel company with "lakes in lobbies," how would you respond to Meg Greenfield's comments?

6. Suggest ways that the front desk of a hotel might be able to speed up the check-in process, other than those given in the chapter.

CHAPTER 2

The Special Case of Hospitality Marketing

The hospitality industry is generally conceded to be a "service" industry. This notion suggests the need for special examination of the hospitality marketing activity as contrasted with that which is more indigenous to a "goods" industry. The concept of marketing will not change as it is concerned with the fulfilling of needs and wants in any industry. The orientation in the corporate suite should not change.

It was argued in Chapter 1, however, that in the hospitality industry every act of management is also an act of marketing. When this notion is contrasted with the management of a manufacturing plant and the marketing of the goods produced by that plant, it can be seen that substantive differences exist between the two types of industry. These differences and the differences between services marketing and goods marketing are worth examining before we proceed to the special case of hospitality marketing.

For more than ten years the service sector of the U.S. economy has provided over 60 percent of the nation's employment and over 50 percent of the gross national product. In 1986 these figures were approximately 71 percent and 68 percent, respectively. This expansion in the service sector has caused much to be written over the last fifteen years, by a select few individuals, about the differences between the marketing of services and the marketing of manufactured goods, and the implications of those differences.

Not surprisingly, most of those who have done the writing argue that services marketing is different from goods marketing and thus calls for different strategies and tactics. Some, however, argue that all this discussion and emphasis on services marketing as a special case constitutes much ado about nothing.

This book will take the first position. We will not dwell on the ideological controversy, which can be read about elsewhere and is recommended to the interested reader,[1] nor will we attempt a specific definition of services, as so many have tried to do. Instead, we will approach hospitality marketing as a special case of services marketing, demonstrate why this is so, and discuss the ensuing implications. First, we need to lay some groundwork.

Goods Versus Services

There is, of course, no such thing as a pure good without some elements of service attached to it. For example, there is no doubt that an automobile is a manufactured good, but few of us are strangers to the service aspects of buying and owning a car. Regardless of whether we call something a good or a service, Levitt argues for the need to make tangible the intangible service aspects.[2] Levitt notes that highly intangible products run into special problems when it comes to holding onto customers.[3]

Shostack separates goods from services by placing all products on a continuum from almost total good (table salt) to almost total service (teaching) as shown in Figure 2-1. Some others have followed Shostack's lead.

With the growth of the service sector and the advancement of viewpoints by Levitt, Shostack, and others, new emphasis has been placed on the unique characteristics of

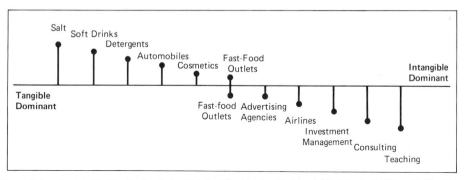

(Source: G. Lynn Shostack, "Breaking Free from Product Marketing." Reprinted from *The Journal of Marketing* (April 1977, pp. 73–80) published by the American Marketing Association.)

FIGURE 2-1   Continuum of tangible/intangible products

---

[1] For the contrary viewpoint see, e.g., Ben M. Enis and Kenneth J. Roering, "Services Marketing: Different Products, Similar Strategy," in James H. Donnelly and William R. George, eds., *Marketing of Services,* Chicago: American Marketing Association, 1981, pp. 1–4; K. Blois, "Service Marketing—Assertion or Asset?" *Service Industries Journal,* July, 1983, pp. 113–120; Victor T. C. Middleton, "Product Marketing—Goods and Services Compared," *Quarterly Review of Marketing,* July, 1983, pp. 1–10.

[2] The word *intangible* is strictly defined as "being unable to be perceived by the sense of touch." The services marketing literature tends to use the term more loosely as being unable, or difficult, to be perceived by the five senses and by conceptualization. Thus, the service of a waiter is intangible, while the steak he serves is tangible.

[3] Theodore Levitt, "Marketing Intangible Products and Product Intangibles," *Harvard Business Review,* May–June, 1981, pp. 94–102. Copyright © 1981 by the President and Fellows of Harvard College; all rights reserved.

services marketing, evidenced in a number of business and trade publications, special books on services, courses taught in some business schools, and, especially, in the American Marketing Association, which inaugurated a special services division in 1984.

As with any new scientific exploration, however, much of what comes first is clutter. One example of this is the early inference that every product that is intangible is a service, and every product that is tangible is not a service. The resulting confusion opened the floodgates for those who argue that goods and services marketing are no different. This argument is supported by the fact that there is always some good that acts like a service and some service that acts like a good.

As the state of the art of services marketing developed, researchers were led to develop taxonomies of services.[4] This, in turn, led to a new argument: Services are different from services.

Clearly, the professional services of a doctor, lawyer, or accountant are not the same as those of a hospital, a bank, a shoeshine, a drycleaning service, a barber, or a hairdresser. Thus, people like Middleton developed different measurement dimensions for classifying products. Middleton would classify all products on a continuum from convenience products (frequent purchases with minimal customer involvement or deliberation) to shopping products (less frequent purchases with high customer involvement and greater deliberation).[5]

While such classifications may be useful for academics, they bear little fruit for practitioners. What we are concerned with in this text is the product of hospitality companies. From the foregoing discussion the reader will have perceived that the hospitality product is all of the above: tangible and intangible, a service and a good, and everything in between. Perhaps it is all of these elements that make the marketing of hospitality products a special case. In this chapter we will dwell on the service, or intangible, aspects. First we need to break the product down into its various components, *as seen by the customer*. We can then examine each part.

Components of the Hospitality Product

Some writers have used the term *offering* to clarify the dichotomy between goods and services. This term, however, is somewhat awkward in use. Instead, this book will use the standard marketing terms, *product* or *product/service*, to designate the totality of what hospitality companies have to offer their customers. These terms will designate goods, services, or any combination of the two. It will also include one other element that, for lack of a better word, will be called *environment*. Research by one of the authors on hundreds of hotel customers revealed that these three elements—goods, services, and environment—are what concern customers, in relatively equal proportion, when purchasing the hospitality product.

---

[4] See, for example, Christopher Lovelock, "Classifying Services to Gain Strategic Marketing Insights," *Journal of Marketing*, Summer, 1983. pp. 9–20.
[5] Middleton, "Product Marketing."

Goods are construed to mean mostly physical factors over which management has direct, or almost direct, control and that are usually tangible. It is management decisions or practices that directly affect goods. In some cases management expertise determines the quality level of goods, as in the case of a chef. Alternatively, quality of goods may depend on management's willingness to spend or not spend money in pursuit of the target market it wishes to serve. In this category we place beds, food, room size, furnishings, location, physical amenities, porte cocheres, elevator *service,* heating and air conditioning, TVs, things that don't work, and so forth. We also define price as tangible although it is a cost of services as well as goods. To the consumer, price is very tangible in any purchase decision.

In the category of environment, we place those items over which management may also have some control, but not as directly and not as easily. While environmental items may or may not be physical and may or may not be tangible, they are something the customer feels. And what we are marketing is that feeling. For example, putting electronic locks on bedrooms doors is something very physical and tangible, but we do not sell the electronic lock to the customer. What we sell, instead, is the benefit of the feature—a feeling of security, a very important but intangible attribute for many hotel customers. Other attributes in this category are decor, atmosphere, comfort, ambience, architecture, and so forth.

The third category, service, includes nonphysical, intangible attributes that management clearly does, or *should,* control. Items in this category depend heavily on the personal elements provided by employees, such as friendliness, speed, attitude, professionalism, responsiveness, and so on. But there are other factors as well: There are those that may depend on employee aptitude, but may also depend on the system, such as the handling of reservations. Then also there are those that may strictly depend on management decisions, such as whether to offer a service. Room service is an example of this. In fact, we can use room service to demonstrate the complexity of the interrelationship among the three components of the hospitality product.

Management must first decide to offer room service. Obviously, this decision is relevant to many things including the particular property and the target market. The first question to be answered, of course, is whether offering room service will fulfill a need or want of the customers at this property. If an alert management decides that the answer is yes, it will then analyze demand, cost, resources, and facilities. If customers expect room service and it is not offered, there will be dissatisfaction.

Deciding to offer room service is not the end. There are still many opportunities to fulfill or not fulfill expectations. First, there is the service element. How many times does the phone ring before the room service department answers it? What is the attitude of the person who does answer? How long will it take to have the order delivered? Is it delivered when promised? What is the attitude of the room service waiter? Does he help to lay it out and set up chairs, or just put the tray down? Did he remember the rolls, the sugar, and enough cream for the coffee? When the meal is finished and the tray is put out in the hallway, how long does it stay there before someone takes it away?

Now, let's look at the goods element. Is the orange juice fresh, the coffee hot? Is the silverware clean? Is the china or glassware chipped? Are the eggs really soft-boiled? Is the bacon crisp or the toast soggy? Is the price fair?

What about the environment? Is there a table to put the food on without rearranging the bedroom? Are there chairs to sit on that enable one to reach the table? Is there a flower on the tray? Is the tray well presented?

If all these things are done well, consistent with the target market that determines what "well" is, does the customer say, "Boy, this is a well-managed hotel"? Probably not. But if one thing is not done well, he might well say the opposite. Why should this be? Because he EXPECTS it all to be done well. That is what he was promised when he placed the order. That is the solution to his problem. That is how he measures the price/value relationship. This is why he took the risk. All these lead to his level of satisfaction.

Proponents of the argument that all marketing is the same will respond by stating that this is no different from buying a tire. One difference, of course, and an enormous one at that, is that one cannot return room service for another room service in the same way a tire can be exchanged.

If all is done well, even if the customer will not say it, we will say, "That's good management." Yes, it is, but more important, it is good marketing! All the trivialities of running a hotel well constitute good marketing. While these trivialities may be operations-driven, they are marketing-oriented.

Does the TV work? Are the towels replaced? Is the wake-up call on time? Is there enough toilet paper? All of these are routine phases of operations, but they are also routine functions of marketing, and the way they are performed will reflect the marketing effort. Why? Because they serve the needs and wants of the customer, they keep implicit promises made to the customer, and they solve the customer's problems. Furthermore, if you don't do them well, you cause the customer problems, and that's not the way to create or keep a customer.

Now you can see why marketing the hospitality product is not exactly like marketing tires, stereo sets, a doctor's services, a hospital room, or a haircut. In the room service case, the person who answered the phone, the person who took the order, the person who fixed the breakfast, the person who delivered the meal, the person who designed the room, the person who retrieved the tray, the china, the silver, the glassware, and the room itself are all part of the product. More important, they are all part of the marketing effort.

Poor room service is one of the most common complaints of hotel customers and a good way to lose customers. Think of the cost of doing it right and keeping a customer, as opposed to the cost of selling and/or advertising to create a new customer.[6] This comparison makes it clear why marketing is such an integral part of hospitality management, and why services marketing is different from goods marketing.

Contrast the room service case, for example, to the tire manufactured in a plant hundreds of miles away from where it is sold, by someone who has no involvement with the buyer. Marketing of the tire is in the hands of the designer, corporate policy, and the advertising department of the firm. Selling at the retail location is very product-oriented. If the company is marketing-oriented, there will be no problem if something is wrong with the tire; it will be replaced without question.

---

[6] Marriott estimated the cost of getting a new customer in 1986 as approximately $120, a figure we believe is quite low.

In this chapter our concern is with the special case of marketing hospitality products, with special attention to the services element. We should bear in mind, however, that whether we call the hospitality product a good (steak), environment (decor), or service (service), in essence the entire hospitality product can be classified as an intangible service.

This is true for two reasons. First, the hospitality product is personal. The customer interacts with all phases of the product at a very personal level and judges them on the basis of personal experiences. Judgment is not based on the quality that the manufacturer puts into the product, but on the personal relationship of the customer to the product.

Second, the hospitality product is always "left behind," that is, customers do not take it with them and it can never be redone. The moment has passed forever. They go away empty-handed, with nothing to show for their money. Even the services of a doctor or a barber, which are considered by many to be more pure services than hospitality, have some elements that you can take with you. You can show your friends the scar left by the surgeon's knife, you can get a new prescription, and, generally, your hair will grow in again. The hospitality product is unique in that there is no cure or second chance. This has incredible implications for hospitality marketing and operations, as we will now explain.

Why the Marketing of Services Is Different

Writers on the services marketing scene have noted a number of important differences between services and manufactured goods. Four of these differences have found general agreement among most marketers and are those most frequently mentioned in discussions of services: intangibilty, perishability, heterogeneity, and simultaneous production and consumption. It is important to understand these differences because they are more than just pedagogical: They have important implications for marketing.

Intangibility

The notion that services are intangible as contrasted with the tangibility of goods has already been mentioned. In describing services, the term has come to mean two things: one cannot grasp a service with any of the five senses, that is, one cannot taste, feel, see, smell, or hear a service, and one cannot *grasp it conceptually*. Although services will differ in some of these respects (and it is obvious that this description is not appropriate to the hospitality product in all cases), we will continue to use the term in that common usage with license to violate it now and then.

Services are experienced, rather than possessed. There is no passing of title when a service is purchased. Buyers have nothing to be displayed, to be shown to friends or family, to put on the shelf, or ever to use again (other than the bathroom amenities which are taken home, of course). In sum, as already stated, buyers go away empty-handed. They do not, however, go away empty-headed. They have an experience to remember and to talk about.

The intangibility of services has profound implications for consumers, and thus for marketers. In the extreme, buyers are not sure what they are buying, or what they will get.

Even if they have bought it before, they cannot go back and say, "I want one of the same" and show the seller what it is that they want. Buyers cannot kick the tires, turn up the sound, choose the color, smell the aroma, measure the size, or taste the flavor. They are buying a "pig in a poke."[7]

The Consumer   It is the experience that helps create expectations for future experiences. This point demonstrates why each experience of a service rendered is a marketing effort. It is the only true way consumers have of valuing the purchase and determining if it is worth the sacrifice. Even then they are not sure if it will be repeated in an identical fashion. These factors, in turn, increase the risk for customers. Buying "blind" is indeed the riskiest of purchases.

Suppose, as may more often be the case, that prospective buyers have not previously had exactly the same experience. In this case they may have to rely on similar experiences. If there have been none, then they may choose to rely on the experiences of others, either with the same experience or with similar experiences. If this information is not available, buyers may have only the advertising, the promise, of the seller on which to rely. Without even this they are truly buying blind.

Prospective buyers of goods may well traverse the same course. With goods, however, the product can usually be tested before being purchased. In many instances one can ask for alternatives, such as when choosing between several different TVs or stereo sets, with varying attributes, in the same or different stores.[8] Or, one can personally listen to or look at the model that a friend owns, ask how it performs, and check the warranty. No such luck with services.

The Marketer   The job of marketers is to solve consumer problems and to create and keep a customer, so their task in the case of intangibles relates directly to the problems of the consumer that were just discussed.

Marketers must convince the prospective buyer that they offer the right solution to the buyer's problem. The first step, then, is to develop the expectation. Traditional methods of doing this are through advertising, personal selling, and public relations. In many cases hospitality companies use these methods but there are inherent problems: How do you advertise or sell an intangible service? You can use words, but often these are as abstract as the service itself and serve only to compound the intangibility (for example, the finest, the ultimate). You can use tangible clues (see Figure 1-3), and we will discuss these further in the chapters on positioning and advertising.

What we really do is make promises; the greater the intangibility, the greater the promise, and the greater the risk for the buyer in terms of the sacrifice that has to be made. Customers have no choice but to believe us and take our word, or not believe us and go somewhere else where they will likely get the same promise and be faced with the same dilemma. It is because of this quandary that we say that traditional marketing is only a small part of hospitality marketing.

---

[7] This term is derived from Scotch and, in turn, midwest farmers, where a poke is a bag or sack; it means that one cannot see what one is buying.

[8] One could argue, of course, that you also can look at a hotel room before buying, go to another hotel, or look at another room. In many cases, because of distance, this is impossible or extremely inconvenient. Regardless, it is not common practice in the United States or Asia. It is somewhat common in Europe outside of the chain hotels.

In fact, there are some who have raised serious questions about the value of advertising hospitality services except for purposes of creating awareness. Research has shown that, barring first-hand experience, buyers of services rely on word-of-mouth more than any other source of information. We have now come full circle. If we want to create positive word-of-mouth it is obvious that we must create positive experiences for customers.

Refer back to the example of room service and it is clear that one of the most important elements of marketing a service lies in the handling of a customer's experience. The example is compounded even further. The typical customers who experience poor room service will not complain only about room service; they will complain about the service in that hotel. The same analogy can be made for restaurants.

If services marketers must increase expectation on the one hand, they must increase value perception on the other hand. In so doing, they must also decrease risk. Both value perception and risk are, in turn, intangible abstractions to which we add two others: confidence in the seller, and image.

All of these concepts also exist in the marketing of manufactured goods. The difference lies in the intangibility of services, difficulty in marketing these intangibles, and the irretrievability of the consumer's decision once the commitment has been made.

Perishability

The second primary characteristic of services is their perishability. It has often been said, for example, that there is nothing as perishable as an airline seat or a hotel room. If not sold on a particular flight or for a particular night, that opportunity to sell it is gone forever. At first blush, the impact of this characteristic appears to be a major problem of management rather than of the consumer. That is undoubtedly true, but the repercussions are felt by the consumer as well.

Inventory management and control are important aspects in the management of a goods manufacturing company. Conversely, however, the inability to manage and control inventory is a critical factor in the ability of a service company to supply the consumer upon demand. In essence, the service company, if it wants to be able to satisfy demand, must have the capacity and capability to produce when demand occurs. If demand does not occur, that capacity and capability are lost and wasted, causing large charges to the bottom line. The result has been to push many hospitality managements into an operations mode and orientation to restrict costs in the event of unused supply.

The emphasis on operations and cost control, while necessary in many cases for survival, may have a debilitating effect on the customer relationship. Housekeeping staff, front desk staff, dining room staff, and other staff that serve the customer directly become the instruments of control. If overstaffing occurs, there is a high cost ratio and the labor cost percentage is too high. Bottom line management may resist this potential by understaffing. When unexpected demand occurs the service becomes too slow. This is a "catch 22" situation.[9]

---

[9] "Catch 22" is a vernacular expression for a situation in which something cannot happen until something else happens, but the something else cannot happen before the something happens.

One alternative has been to charge prices that are high enough so that overstaffing does not become a serious problem. Four Seasons hotels follow this strategy and are known for their high level of service regardless of the level of demand, but not without serious impact on the bottom line. Most hotels and restaurants, however, cannot afford to do this, and the result is often irate customers.

While there is no easy solution to the problem, it is one in which, once again, marketing and management are inextricably intertwined. What this means is that reduction of staff is both a marketing decision and a management decision. The impact on the customer must be the first consideration. If service is an element that is being marketed, then service is an element of customer expectation that should be provided because service is being offered as a solution to the customer's problem. It is part of the value for which a sacrifice is made and the risk is taken.

In the hospitality industry, the customer often makes an additional sacrifice beyond that of cost—that of time. Time is precious to consumers. Waiting in line at a front desk, waiting for an elevator, waiting for room service, waiting for lunch to come in a restaurant, waiting for the bottle of wine to be served, and waiting for the check to come are only a few of the annoyances that hospitality customers complain about when they have sacrificed their time to purchase the hospitality product. Recognition of this and offering an alternative has been a major factor in the success of fast-food operations.

The problem is not limited to that of speed of service. In many cases this is not desirable or expected. The problem is one of matching the service to the expectation of the buyer. It is generally recognized that it is marketing's job to forecast demand; it is less frequently recognized that concomitant with forecasting demand is forecasting supply.

If marketing is going to create expectations, make promises, offer value, and reduce risk, then surely marketing should have a say in the fulfillment of its role. This is one more example of marketing's part in keeping the customer, as well as creating the customers. If operations management is short-sighted, it may fail to see that the cost of keeping a customer is far less than the cost of creating a new one. While it is popular to talk about the perishability of the hospitality product, the oft-forgotten flip side of that characteristic is its *perpetuability,* in other words, it can be sold over and over again. Doing this, of course, depends upon demand. There is nothing better than keeping customers for maintaining constant demand.

Heterogeneity

Heterogeneity of service is concerned with the variation and lack of uniformity in the service being performed. Here we mean something different from lack of service caused by insufficient staff; instead we mean fluctuations in service caused by the human element of employees, customer perception, and the customers themselves.

In the first instance, universal performance of service is very difficult if only because of the human-intensive nature of providing service. Manuals may well prescribe exactly what every employee in a large restaurant is supposed to do in any given situation, but they can never predict what various individuals with various backgrounds, various orientations, and various personalities will actually do in a given situation. We may well hope that they never will for what a dull world it would be if we all did the same thing!

Manuals of hotel and restaurant chains, not to mention training programs and constant exhortations by supervisors, inevitably proclaim that we are in a people business, smile at the customer, call the customer by name, never argue with the customer, and the customer is always right. As necessary as these prescriptions may be, they are not sufficient. Marketing means understanding the customers' needs and wants and problems, even if you do smile at them.

Anyone who has stood behind an airline counter or the front desk of a hotel, or has waited on people in a restaurant, can tell you a great deal about customers' problems. They are infinite in number and diverse in scope but, petty or monumental, they are real to the customer and a problem to the marketer.

Marketers of services who make promises to customers have two strikes against them. The first is the question of how the employee with whom customers come face to face will handle the situation. The second is the customers themselves; what is appropriate handling to one is inappropriate to another; service to one customer may affect service to another. The consequence is that good service may equal bad service.

Consider, for example, an elderly woman at the front desk of a hotel who needs considerable help in understanding where things are in the hotel, how to work the electronic key in her door, and how to get assistance when she needs it. The service-oriented desk clerk patiently and graciously explains these things to the woman, who will depart from the hotel to tell all her friends how nice the employees are. Unfortunately, the person waiting in line behind this woman may be a business person anxious to get to a meeting. As a frequent traveler, this individual knows the ropes and only wants to register, get the key, and be on the way. This person will depart from the hotel to tell friends about the wait in line and the poor service.

For the marketer, the heterogeneity of services constitutes a lack of assurance that the product you market is what you actually sell or produce. For the consumer, it means risk and a lack of assurance that what you buy is what you get. In the hospitality industry, the consumer often perceives the personnel as the service, so that one unpleasant interaction with personnel can result in a total condemnation of the entire experience.

Another aspect of service heterogeneity is that the knowledge, experience, and proficiency of the customer affects the quality of consumption. One customer says, "Look at the full glass of wine they give you." Another says, "Don't they know that a glass of wine should never be more than half full?" One customer says, "Boy, this Veal Oscar is good." Another says, "Don't they know that Veal Oscar should be served with Béarnaise sauce, not Hollandaise?" One customer says, "Wasn't the bellman nice to show us how everything worked and to tell us about the restaurants?" Another says, "Why can't the bellman just leave the bags instead of promoting the hotel and grubbing for a bigger tip?"

Obviously, there is a wide variation in the consumers' measurement of quality, and what satisfies one may very well not satisfy another. Regardless, what consumers get they pay for; there is no opportunity to exchange their experience for another one.

For the marketer, this has many implications. A very important one is that new product innovation may require an education of the consumer, that is, the consumer must be socialized into the production process. Technological advances, such as electronic door locks and in-room movie charges, fall into this category. An outstanding example in a service sector outside the hospitality industry is the automatic teller machines. The initial introduction of these machines was less than successful because people were sure the machines would swallow their money, never to be seen again.

Many companies have attempted to overcome these difficulties through what Levitt has termed the industrialization of service.[10] Levitt sees these problems as special opportunities, and so they may well be. Certainly they should be analyzed closely with that possibility in mind. Some fast-food restaurants provide an excellent example of industrializing a service to near-uniform performance. Salad bars in restaurants provide another, and budget motels yet another.

Budget motels and salad bars are only two examples of a phenomenon to be pondered by the hospitality marketer: When is less service more service, and vice versa? Or, to put it another way, when should service be more personal and when should it be less personal? Numerous studies have shown that salad bars are very popular with a majority of the eating-out public because you can do it yourself. Yet, this is actually less service, since you have to get your own food. Whether in this case less service is more depends on the individual customer's own perception of salad bars, and clearly what satisfies one customer does not necessarily satisfy another.

Are budget motels offering service when they, sometimes literally, just throw the key at you and make sure you pay first? For some, yes, you get what you pay for; for others, no. Do computer check-ins at hotels with no personal interaction constitute less service or more service? How about ice machines on every floor? They may be seen as a convenience, but not to those who feel put out because they have to get dressed to obtain ice since room service no longer delivers it.

It is not hard to see that the marketer faces many problems when trying to cope with the heterogeneity of services, or even when trying to provide solutions to consumers' problems. The answer, at least partially, lies in knowing your market and your customers and the custom-tailoring of services. This means the emphasis should be on the customer, not on the service. We will address this subject in more detail in later chapters.

Simultaneity of Production and Consumption

The service characteristic of simultaneous production and consumption is somewhat unique among service characteristics. It is also the strongest foundation for the premise that management is marketing in the hospitality industry. This is so because in the case of simultaneous production and consumption, consumption depends on the participation of the seller, and the seller requires the participation of the buyer. The resultant effect is an interpersonal relationship between the buyer and seller that may supersede the service itself.

Consider these relationships in a hospitality situation: waiter or waitress and customer, bartender and customer, maitre d' and customer, front desk clerk or cashier and customer, housekeeper and customer, and so on. These types of personal interactions are not new, of course. We have them at the supermarket, the department store, the automobile dealership, and other places where intangible services sell very tangible products. The difference, however, is critical. Unless the situation is totally repugnant,

---

[10] Theodore Levitt, "The Industrialization of Service," in Theodore Levitt (ed.), *The Marketing Imagination*. New York: Free Press, 1986, pp. 50–71.

people are still prone to patronize the same store to buy goods even if their relationship with the salesperson is not the best. This is because they are buying something other than the service. In most cases, one can simply avoid that particular person.

In hospitality, that is not the case. The customer is buying the service. One individual can totally personify the service of a particular establishment and cause a customer not to return. We have said that we are in a people business, but that is really putting it mildly. We are totally in the marketing business. A friendly, smiling, call-you-by-your-name clerk is not enough. Each employee is literally part of the product because each employee is producing while the customer consumes.

Some people have trouble grasping this concept, so we will belabor the point a little more. Suppose you buy a car but have a bad relationship with the salesperson. You drive the car home and three months later it falls apart. By now you have long since forgotten the salesperson and you only cursorily blame the dealer; instead you blame the manufacturer. Take the hospitality situation. You check into a hotel and have a bad relationship with the front desk clerk. You go to your room and it looks out on a brick wall, the TV doesn't work, the bed sags, and the room isn't made up. You go back to the same desk clerk and explode. Three months later, guess who gets the blame—the person and the hotel because both represent the implicit promise made to you when you reserved a room.

Another facet of the simultaneous production/consumption characteristic is that you don't know what you are buying until after you have consumed it. When you think about it that seems like a pretty stupid thing to do, but that's what we do when we buy a service, even if we have bought the same service before. The heterogeneity principle of services supports this premise. Obviously, there are exceptions to this rule in services. If we have been to the same doctor twenty times, we pretty well know what to expect. In some cases this will also be true in hotels and restaurants, but to a lesser extent because of the heterogeneity principle. In the vast majority of cases, however, this will not be true and every time we purchase we assume a new risk.

The interaction of marketing and production is inescapable in the hospitality business, so let us go back to the friendly and smiling employee. The customer cannot consume what the employee cannot produce. Employees may be given smile training, but still be restricted in their ability to solve consumers' problems. Smiles in these cases are of little avail. Consider the following experience.

> A couple returned to their hotel, one of a national upscale chain, around midnight and decided to go to the revolving rooftop lounge for a nightcap. The lounge was largely empty. On each table in the lounge was a table tent promoting ice cream drinks. One of the couple decided to have some ice cream instead of a drink. When the ice cream was ordered, however, the waitress replied that she couldn't serve plain ice cream because it was served only in drinks. Sensing a desire to "build the check" the couple said they would pay for the drink but please just bring the ice cream. The waitress, very friendly and very smiling, said she couldn't do that because it was against the hotel's policy.

When you think about this incident, you see many ramifications of the simultaneous production/consumption concept and how it affects marketing. This particular couple refused ever to return to this hotel, not just because of this incident but because it was only one of a string of similar incidents that occurred in this hotel.

Management at this hotel was operations-oriented and failed to consider the customer. It could have, of course, served the ice cream and extracted the $4.00 drink price for it—probably the customers wouldn't have cared and would have soon forgotten the incident. Alternatively, the hotel could have served the ice cream, charged $1.50, and tried to keep a customer. Instead, management at this hotel gave away a free drink voucher to these guests when they checked in, called it marketing, and lost two customers plus, perhaps, a few to whom the story was told.

This story brings out another aspect of the simultaneous production and consumption of hospitality services: The buyer must follow the seller's rules for usage, and these rules become an element of the service. Some rules are necessary in hospitality premises: Many rules are operations-driven to prevent the customer from "getting in the way"; other rules are totally frivolous or archaic but management doesn't stop to question why they exist. Consider the ice cream story, or the requirement of ties and coats for men in restaurants and no slacks for women, or being unable to use the pool before nine or after six. How about only one key per room (for your security)? Or, you can only have the buffet (at $16.95 per person)? Rules like these become part of the service because they restrict the consumer's consumption.

Tying together the above four elements of service, we might come up with something like the following definition of the hospitality product:

> The hospitality product is something that prospective buyers, for the most part, cannot grasp with the senses. Consumers do not know if they will get what they buy, and they must wait until the seller produces it after they buy it but before they can consume it, sometimes after having paid for it. The seller is not totally sure that he or she can produce it. What's more, if buyers don't like what they get, they can't take it back, get an exchange, or, in most cases, get their money back.

Although this definition may appear to be a little extreme, perhaps we can better understand the inherent marketing problems of hospitality if we consider the product in this light. After all, this does describe the position in which the buyer is placed.

Other Aspects of the Service Component

There are a number of other aspects of the service component of the hospitality product that impact on the marketing effort. One of these is that the need of the buyers may be totally unrecognized by them; thus, they do not notice it until it is missing. This factor places a burden on the marketer to anticipate buyers' needs. There is really only one way to do this and that is by putting yourself in the customer's shoes and thinking like a customer. Mike Leven tells a story demonstrating this point that took place when he was Senior Vice-President of Americana Hotels.

> I was waiting in the lobby of our Jamaica property with some other of our executives about 6:00 A.M. one morning, waiting for the limo to take us to the airport. Also waiting for the same limo to catch the same flight were half a dozen guests who had just checked out. Suddenly, down the hallway came the F&B manager and a waiter wheeling a cart with fresh orange juice, coffee, and Danish. I thought to myself, "Now here's a management that knows how to take care of its customers," until I watched them wheel the cart right past the guests and in front of us.

I immediately grabbed the cart, turned it around, and wheeled it back in front of the guests. Today, this hotel has a similar cart out every morning for guests catching that early flight. I couldn't help but think, "If only we treated our customers as well as we treat ourselves."

Another marketing aspect of the intangibility of the hospitality product is the difficulty in pricing it. In contrast to tangible goods, it is difficult to base the price of a service on its "cost of goods sold," to use the common accounting term. Buyers don't understand the organization behind the product that they are paying for, and thus often come to a natural conclusion that the product is overpriced. It is also difficult for the buyer to make competitive comparisons when evaluating services.

Another critical aspect of the hospitality product are the peripheral services that affect the basic product of rooms, meals, and so on. The quality of the basic product may be affected by tangential criteria. Consider the Mike Leven story: The absence of the coffee cart might have had absolutely no effect on the guests' perception of the hotel's service quality. After all, that is not what they came to Jamaica to buy. On the other hand, the presence of the coffee cart could have considerable impact, because the customer leaves with a warm feeling about the concerns of this hotel for its customers.

Further, consider this example by John Sharpe, vice-president, operations, of Four Seasons Hotels:

> A parking valet at the Four Seasons Hotel in Seattle observed that many of our weekend guests are families with young children. After checking out of the hotel, they often face a long drive ahead and their children tend to get hungry. He suggested we pack a box of chocolate cookies and milk for each family, and leave the surprise package waiting in the guests' vehicle when they leave the hotel.[11]

Think, for a minute, of the vast multitude of similar examples. Although the customer reserves only a room, an almost endless number of peripheral services are expected to accompany that room. In the extreme, such as at a resort hotel in Jamaica, this could even include whether the sun and moon shine. Certainly it includes the beach, the pool, the entertainment, the sports facilities, and many other features that accompany the resort image. The marketer and management cannot escape the responsibility for all of these peripheral attributes, as indicated by these comments:

> You've ordered room service, but the food arrives an hour late—and it's cold. You've checked into your room, but 40 minutes later you're still waiting for the bellman to bring your luggage. The hotel laundry loses your shirts, but promises to find and return them tomorrow afternoon—five hours after you plan to check out.[12]

The term "facilitating good" was introduced by Rathmell to describe the goods component of the service product.[13] (It should be noted, as described earlier, that most goods are also accompanied by facilitating services.) A facilitating good in the case of the hospitality product could be the steak dinner, the pool, the beach, the tennis courts, the

---

[11] John Sharpe, "The Challenge of Effectively Managing," *Foodservice and Hospitality,* October, 1985, p. 68.

[12] Peter S. Greenberg, "Hotels Taking Steps to Spruce Up Flagging Service," *Los Angeles Times,* June 28, 1987, p. 7.

[13] John Rathmell, *Marketing in the Service Sector,* Cambridge, Mass.: Winthrop Publishers, 1974.

TABLE 2-1   Functional Differences Between Services and Goods

Functional Characteristics	Goods	Services
Unit definition	Precise	General
Ability to measure	Objective	Subjective
Creation	Manufactured	Delivered
Distribution	Separated from production	Same as production
Communications	Tangible	Intangible
Pricing	Cost basis	Limited cost basis
Flexibility of producer	Limited	Broad
Time interval	Months to years	Simultaneous or shortly after
Delivery	Consistent	Variable
Shelf life	Days to years	Zero
Customer perception	Standardized—what you see	Have to consume to evaluate
Marketing	Traditional, external	Nontraditional, largely internal

Source: Adapted from a talk by Thomas Fitzgerald, Vice-President, ARA Service, Ltd., American Marketing Association Services Conference, Orlando, 1981.

cocktail, or even the room itself. Although these may be essential ingredients, what the customer may really be buying is the intangibles: the service, relaxation, peace of mind, comfort, satisfaction, and so forth.

The distinction is important. In the first place, say Sasser et al., "one of the key problems in designing a service package and service delivery system is articulating the full range of elements in the purchase bundle."[14] Knowing that the consumer is buying something more than the room or the meal is understandable; articulating it is something else. In truth, hospitality marketing means getting at the something else.

In the second place, the more easily assimilated tangible components of the purchase bundle may lead management to concentrate on those elements to the detriment of the peripheral elements, or the intangible elements. As Sasser et al. point out, "A problem occurs when a service organization begins to view itself as a goods manufacturer and attempts to embody all the elements of the purchase bundle in the facilitating good."[15]

This tendency can result in neglecting the intangibles. Advertisements for both hotels and restaurants tend to emphasize the facilitating goods, the features, rather than the real reason the consumer is buying the total hospitality product, the benefits (again, see Figure 1-3). Sasser et al. sum it up as follows:

> One of the main reasons for adopting a simplistic approach is the difficulty of defining a single product for a service operation. A manufacturing organization can define its product in terms of specific cost, quality, and performance characteristics, which are

[14] W. Earl Sasser, R. Paul Olsen, and D. Daryl Wyckoff, *Management of Service Operations,* Boston: Allyn and Bacon, 1978, p. 10.
[15] Ibid.

embodied and observable in the physical goods. For a service firm the situation is almost reversed; the intangibles are an integral part of the total product bundle. In some cases the facilitating good is ancillary to the intangible benefits a consumer purchases. . . . The manufacturing process is isolated from the consumer and has an impact on the consumer only through what effect it has on the product. The elements of the manufacturing process are designed for the effective production of the physical good that is its output. . . . In contrast, the service delivery system must be designed with the presence of the consumer in mind.[16]

Table 2-1 summarizes what has been said about the differences between services and manufactured goods, and depicts some of the problems for the hospitality marketer.

Summary

The recognition of the hospitality industry as one providing services is not new. In fact, it is as old as the industry itself and many hotels and restaurants worldwide have long put this recognition into practice. Somewhere along the way, however, with the growth of chain operations and the input of developers, the emphasis is sometimes forgotten both in the corporate suite and at the unit level. The concept of customer oriented service has not always been imbedded in the management philosophy. The situation is well stated by Steve Gold of Sheraton:

In the 1950s and 1960s, hotel companies focused on technology and updating their telephone reservation systems. In the 1970s, companies like Sheraton found ourselves in the real estate business. We upgraded our properties. Now, everyone has nice properties. . . . But fewer people are bragging about their atriums. Everyone's got one. Today, we've discovered that our main focus *has* to be service. When everything is said and done, that's all the customer really wants.

Now that we've experimented with technology and upgraded our product, we've discovered that we are dealing in a nonmanufacturing society. We are in a service society, and we're catering to a much more sophisticated customer than ever before.

All of our feedback from customers is telling us that what they are now demanding is not better accommodations, but better service. . . . We're moving from high-tech to high-touch.[17]

The emphasis of this chapter has been on the differences between services and manufactured goods and the ensuing differences in marketing in these two generic and broad categories. More specifically, the attributes of services have been applied to the hospitality product and it has been shown that the marketing of that product is, indeed, a special case. That special case warrants special attention in both the foundations and the practices of hospitality marketing.

The hospitality product is different, the reasons for buying it are different, and the strategies and tactics of marketing it are different. These differences are critical to the producer of the hospitality product. More important, they are critical to the consumer of the hospitality product. The juxtaposition of these differences, by definition, causes the

---

[16] Ibid., p. 14.
[17] Greenberg, "Hotels Taking Steps to Spruce Up Flagging Services," p. 7.

necessary integration of hospitality management with hospitality marketing. The two are inseparable. This fact alone creates unique problems for the special case of the marketing of the hospitality product. The solutions to those problems lie, on the one hand, in understanding and anticipating the consumer, and on the other, in the understanding of the hospitality production process as a marketing process in both the traditional and nontraditional senses of marketing. Chapter 3 will address hospitality marketing from the nontraditional perspective.

DISCUSSION QUESTIONS

1. Discuss the argument that the marketing of goods is different from the marketing of services. Give examples both pro and con from your personal experiences.
2. Goods, environment, and service are said to be the components of the hospitality product. Which one or ones are most important to you when staying at a hotel or eating in a restaurant? Why?
3. Give an example, like the room service example in this chapter, that incorporates all three elements of the hospitality product.
4. Give examples of "facilitating goods" in hotels and restaurants other than those given in this chapter. Explain the concept. What do you think people are *really* buying? How do these and facilitating goods relate?
5. Make up a "purchase bundle" that you consciously consider when you choose a restaurant. Now, think of the things that you don't consciously consider but expect to be there. Which ones have the most impact upon your expectations and ultimate satisfaction? Discuss.

CHAPTER 3

Nontraditional Marketing in Hospitality

In the marketing of manufactured goods, the physical reality of the product is most often the basis of description—what the goods *are* to the customer. Although physical goods may well be, and often are, marketed in the abstract—that is, with statements of what they will do for the customer (e.g., Charles Revson's "in the drugstore we sell hope," p. 9)—it is the physical reality that the consumer can grasp mentally and with the five senses. In the marketing of services, on the other hand, the basis of description is most often what the services *do* for the customer

The term *service* is, in itself, one word used very frequently to describe what the service product does for the customer. There are an infinite number of other terms also used. Some of the more common in hospitality are *comfort, hassle-free, friendly, courteous, professional, relaxing,* and so forth. While these terms can certainly be used in advertising (traditional marketing), what they *do* for the customer takes place at the property. As noted in Chapter 2, this factor creates a special case for the marketing of hospitality services that is nontraditional in nature. This special marketing concept can be broken down into two major categories: internal marketing, and relationship marketing. We will discuss each in turn.

Internal Marketing

Internal marketing means "applying the philosophies and practices of marketing to people who serve the external customers so that (1) the best possible people can be employed and retained and (2) they will do the best possible work."[1] The emphasis of internal marketing is on the employee as the customer and the job as the product. Berry states: "We can think of internal marketing as viewing employees as internal customers, viewing jobs as internal products, and then endeavoring to offer internal products that satisfy the needs and wants of those internal customers while addressing the objectives of the organization."[2]

At first blush, this may appear to be a strange way to look at marketing; it is certainly not the way that we look at the marketing of goods. Careful perusal, however, makes the case obvious: If it is the employees who represent a major part of the hospitality product to the paying customer, then it is obvious that one of the first tasks of marketing and management is to have the employees believe in the product. Sasser and Arbeit, in fact, suggest that "the successful service company must first sell the job to employees before it can sell its services to customers."[3]

Looked at from this perspective, the job (or product) must satisfy the needs and wants and solve the problems of the employees (the customers). If this is not the case, we end up with dissatisfied customers (employees) who, in turn, will express, in one way or another, their dissatisfaction to the paying customers. Paying customers, in turn, find that their problems are not adequately solved, so they go elsewhere. Clearly, this is not the way to create or keep customers.[4]

What is practiced in the creation and keeping of customers of goods and services needs to also be practiced in the creation and keeping of employees. The elements of external marketing are just as appropriate and just as necessary in internal marketing. When we consider the tools of marketing such as segmentation, positioning, communication, product development, and research (tools we will elaborate on in later chapters), we can see that they are just as essential to internal marketing as they are to external marketing.

As we segment customers according to needs and wants, so too should we choose employees. As we position a product to the marketplace, so too should we position the job to each employee. As we communicate with customers, so too must we communicate with employees. As we develop new products, so too must we develop new job methods, rewards, and satisfactions. And as we research consumers, so too must we survey our employees to determine needs, wants, and attitudes. Marriott Corporation is especially noted for its employee surveys. Four Seasons Hotels uses the measurement of employee attitudes as a basis for one-third of the annual bonus given to managers.

---

[1] Reprinted by permission from BUSINESS magazine. "Services Marketing Is Different," by Leonard L. Berry, May–June 1980, p. 26.

[2] Leonard L. Berry, "The Employee as Customer," *Journal of Retail Banking,* 1981. Reprinted in C. H. Lovelock, *Services Marketing,* Englewood Cliffs: Prentice-Hall, 1984, pp. 271–278.

[3] W. E. Sasser and S. Arbeit, "Selling Jobs in the Service Sector," *Business Horizons,* June, 1976, p. 64.

[4] Although this section deals with internal marketing to employees in the interest of better customer service, it should also be noted that not fulfilling needs and wants of employees is also not the way to create and keep employees.

Demographic changes in the population have led to recent and continuing hotel and restaurant employee shortages. To counter this, both the National Restaurant Association and the American Hotel & Motel Association embarked on advertising campaigns in the mid 1980s to "sell" the industry to potential employees. This campaign touted the industry as an employment opportunity that was wonderful, exciting, fulfilling, prestigious, and so on.

Unless major personnel issues in the industry are resolved, any new enchantment of employees will be short lived. By now, the reader will be aware that this is not a selling issue, but a marketing issue, in which people buy solutions to problems. If expectations are not met, the risk will not be worth the solution.

Management Practices

The quality of services depends in large measure on the skills and attitudes of the people producing the services. An acceptable product is necessary to appeal to the external market. The same is true of the internal market. Employees, an integral part of the product in hospitality, must also be marketing oriented. Unless a firm has something to offer to its employees, it should not expect marketing-oriented behavior.

Marketing can be used to attract, keep, and motivate quality personnel. Quality personnel will improve the capability of the firm to provide quality service. Too often, acceptance of these statements is as far as they go. It is not unusual to hear such comments as "We hire the best people and give them the best training. I can't understand why they can't do the job right!" Unfortunately, in many cases, when these people are promoted they too have been indoctrinated in the system and the system perpetuates itself.

Understanding the simultaneous production and consumption nature of services is helpful in understanding how satisfied and motivated employees help to create and keep satisfied customers. Most hospitality companies are aware of this fact. Many of them conduct employee courses in customer handling, including what trainees have dubbed "smile training." Smile training, as we have previously said, is not enough. Consider the following anecdote told by a front desk clerk of a large convention hotel.

> A large convention was checking into the hotel all day and we never had a chance to get away from the desk and take a break for coffee, or even for lunch. We were smiling our damdest, dealing with all the problems, and things were going fairly smoothly considering the circumstances. After a while, however, it begins to get to you so we devised a little sing-song communication and banter among us which helped to keep our sense of humor and keep us going. While all this was going on, our supervisors were sitting in a room behind the front desk, talking and drinking coffee. Occasionally, one would step out and, seeing that all was going well, would go back to the room leaving us to carry on. When they heard our banter, however, things changed. One of us was called into the backroom and told to tell the others to cut it out. Our attitudes changed immediately. We kept on working but we couldn't have cared less about the customers and it showed.

Consider, too, the case of the waitress who couldn't sell a dish of ice cream, as described in Chapter 2. Her interest was in satisfying the customer, something she had been told in her training was as much a part of her job as serving drinks, yet company rules prohibited her from exercising her willingness to do this.

The impact of these anecdotes is that marketing principles have not been applied to these employees' jobs. Customer satisfaction has been given token attention rather than being treated as a philosophy. Employees will not "buy" the product, customer service, when it appears that management is not willing to deliver on its promise of what it is "selling." The old expression "practice what you preach" is also the essence of internal marketing.

There is an inherent conflict between company policies and the ability of the employee to satisfy customers. The very nature of the service business implies that it is impossible to anticipate all the wants of customers and the resulting interaction between customers and employees. Obviously, there must be policies to guide employee actions, and no one is suggesting that there are easy solutions to these conflicts. But it is just as obvious that there must be flexibility. If we are going to sell the concept of customer satisfaction to employees, we must also sell to those employees the "right" to use judgment to achieve it. Instead of selling the job of, for example, checking in guests, internal marketing means selling the job of solving consumers' problems. Checking in guests is only one part of that solution. This is discussed further in Chapter 6.

It is not uncommon to hear hospitality employees complain that "no one trusts you around here," or, "if you don't do it by the book, you'll get chewed out." At the same time, they are told to smile and keep the customer happy. This is not good internal marketing and often results in failure to achieve the goals that management has established.

One example of alleviating this problem is the change by some hotel companies toward allowing cashiers to deal with in-room movie charge complaints. It is not uncommon for customers to challenge a movie charge on the grounds that they did not watch the movie. In some hotels an argument ensues at the cashier desk, the hotel wins, and the customer pays and leaves, perhaps never to return. If we accept that most people are basically honest, it is hardly worth the 50 to 75 cents to lose the customer, as well as losing other customers through negative word-of-mouth.[5]

Progressive managements allow the cashier to deal with the problem on the spot and make the decision to remove the charge from the bill. Other managements insist that a supervisor be consulted first. The cashier goes looking for a supervisor, sometimes returning with an okay. Other times the supervisor appears, then argues with the customer while the cashier stands aside feeling helpless and frustrated. Of course, at the same time, whatever the outcome of the dispute, the customer (and all those in line behind) wastes another five to ten minutes and leaves the hotel fuming. It is clear that internal marketing is practiced in solving the cashier's problem by giving him or her the right to solve the customer's problem.

Customers have a wide variety of expectations, for whatever reason. These expectations can exacerbate the problems of both employees and management. The truth of the matter is that the customer is *not* always right. In the concept of marketing, the risk must be evaluated before proving the customer wrong. To a certain point, that risk must be allowed to the employee who is charged with the responsibility of fulfilling customer expectations. This constitutes marketing to both the customer and the employee.

Many years ago, motel chains began to offer "children in the same room with parents free" benefits. Signs in front of the motels proclaimed this fact, usually accompanied by wording indicating that the children must be under 16 or 18. Many arguments followed at front desks as alert clerks were instructed to be certain that the child's age did not exceed the limitation. Instead of creating customers, some properties managed to alienate them.

One Ramada property, however, must have forgotten to put the age limitation on its sign and in walked a 79-year-old mother who claimed the benefit for her 57-year-old daughter. The clerk on duty accepted them at the single rate. The result was national publicity that thousands of advertising dollars couldn't have bought.

---

[5] In most cases the movie company does not charge the hotel for the disputed charges. Hotels make about ten percent of the customer's charge on each movie watched.

The Service System

The internal marketing element has been defined as an integral part of the service system. This is because the sellers, the distributors of the service, are also part of the production process. Operations personnel thus have a high level of influence and power in the delivery of the service.

> For example, a hotel manager must simultaneously apply locally the competitive policy defined by the home office; oversee the good maintenance of the hotel and its personnel; deal with the internal problems of personnel relations, purchasing, and supply; and resolve the problems that arise from day to day with the guests. Because of this multitude of "production" problems, there is a great temptation to have a point of view that is much more "production" than "marketing." In every instance, the relationship between the internal forces at the operating level clearly favors operations rather than marketing.[6]

Eiglier and Langeard depict the service system as akin to that shown in Figure 3-1. Physical supports are the "supporting goods" necessary for the production of the service. From the physical support, both the contact personnel and the customer, and often both at the same time, will draw services. Hotel front desks and front desk computers are examples of physical supports.

The contact personnel fulfill a technical assignment that also includes some marketing facets in its adjustment to customer expectations. The customer, as shown in Figure 3-1, is both a taker and a giver in the system process. In sum, the production of services

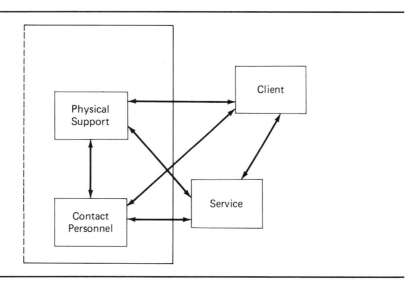

FIGURE 3-1   The fundamental elements of the service system

[6] Pierre Eiglier and Eric Langeard, "Services as Systems: Marketing Implications." In P. Eiglier, E. Langeard et al., eds. *Marketing Consumer Services: New Insights,* Cambridge, Mass.: Marketing Science Institute, 1977, pp. 85–103.

rests first and foremost on the various interactions among physical support, contact personnel, and customers. It is the internal system that ties together the physical support and contact personnel. Viewed from this perspective, the need for internal marketing is readily apparent. Eiglier and Langeard put it thus:

> The marketing implications are essentially normative: the service business must define with precision each of the elements of the system, as well as the nature, the degree, and the objective of the relationships among them. . . . In reality these tasks cannot be performed separately. It is clear, in fact, that the definition of an element is going to be a function of the relationships that one wants to see established between this element and the other elements of the system.
>
> The mechanics of the operation must also be defined, because this will have a considerable influence on the client's feelings. Here we come to the issue of the humanization of the contact, and how far the personnel are allowed to go. It can be argued that it is essential that the personnel master their own affective reactions and be capable of managing the client's. In other words, without dehumanizing the relationships, it is necessary to professionalize them with the objective of achieving a good standard of efficiency and of ambience. By his behavior and his qualification a contact person has a direct influence on the service, both on the quality and on the way in which it will be perceived by the client.[7]

Analysis of Figure 3-1 and the remarks of Eiglier and Langeard further demonstrate that smile training alone is inadequate to ensure proper service delivery from a marketing perspective.

When the system doesn't work it is often the contact employee who gets blamed. Contact personnel, often the lowest-paid employees in a hospitality company, can hardly be expected to make the system work when management doesn't understand how it should work in the first place.

Noncontact Employees

We have discussed internal marketing from the perspective of the customer-contact employee. That is certainly the most obvious way to look at it. In the hospitality industry, however, it certainly doesn't stop there and it would be unwise to think that it does. The engineers, the housekeepers, the night porters, even the accountants, and certainly the personnel department are part of the internal marketing effort in a hotel.

In a restaurant, there are the cooks, the dishwashers, the storeroom people, and others that are likewise invisible to the customer but constitute a major objective of the internal marketing effort. Management's task is to get employees to realize and feel that they are part of this effort.

Of all of the above personnel, perhaps the cooks are the most obvious case and do not need further explanation. It is the dishwasher, however, who can stop a chipped glass or a stained plate from going back into the dining room. It is the storeroom person who can make certain that the right degree of freshness is received and preserved for perishable products. In a hotel, it is the housekeeper who can be sure that all the lightbulbs are

---

[7] Ibid.

working. It is the engineer who maintains the heating and ventilating system and the TV reception. In short, ALL employees in a hospitality property are part of the marketing effort. Marketing-oriented management will make sure that this is realized—for instance, that the engineer is not just fixing the television, but helping to ensure customer satisfaction—and helping to keep a customer.

In this sense, employees must understand and realize the importance and consequences of their actions as revenue-generating marketing resources as well as production resources. This means that what influences customers must be *marketed* to employees.

Consider, for example, maids talking in a hallway. In fact, it is not uncommon for them to shout to each other the length of the hallway, annoying guests who are trying to sleep. To advise them only to not engage in this practice is not enough; they must be made aware of the impact it has on the revenue-producing customer.

The Internal Marketing Concept

It is obvious by now that internal marketing is as much a part of the marketing philosophy of an organization as is the marketing concept itself, with both strategic and tactical implications throughout. In fact, internal marketing is a separate concept in its own right. *"The internal marketing concept—as a complement to the traditional marketing concept— holds that an organization's internal market of employees can be influenced most effectively and hence motivated to customer consciousness, market orientation, and salesmindedness by a marketing-like internal approach and by using marketing-like activities internally."*[8]

Motivating employees is not a new management task in any company or industry. The problem for service companies is that it is too often perceived as an administrative task, often relegated to the personnel department. Administrative actions, however, are often inadequate to overcome problems of unfavorable attitudes among employees toward their jobs and the general internal climate. Grönroos argues, compellingly, that

> in external markets, potential customers' unfavorable attitudes and preferences are changed by marketing activities, not by administrative actions. . . . Undesired attitudes occurring internally should also be handled actively, i.e., they should be thought of in a marketing sense. . . . In regards to contact personnel, in particular, the ultimate reason for motivation is not motivation *per se*. Rather it should be customer consciousness and salesmindedness.[9]

While we agree wholeheartedly with Grönroos, it should be noted that we are not arguing, at this point, for a sales orientation. Emphasis on a sales orientation, particularly for customer-contact personnel, is not uncommon in hospitality businesses. Reservation and desk clerks are urged to "sell up," bellman are urged to sell the food and beverage facilities, and waiters and waitresses are urged to sell desserts, wine, or after-dinner drinks.

---

[8] Christian Grönroos, *Strategic Management and Marketing in the Service Sector,* Cambridge, Mass: Marketing Science Institute, 1983, p. 77.

[9] Ibid.

Such efforts are a part of marketing but a small subset that will be discussed when we get to the chapter on merchandising. What is being advocated by internal marketing, as the reader who has come this far surely realizes by now, is the enhancement of employee recognition and satisfaction of customers' needs and wants—that is, focusing the emphasis on the customer, not the product, and the ability of the employee to participate in the marketing function.

The effort that supports the concept of internal marketing starts with top management and involves management at every level of the organization. Lower-level employees, whether they are customer contact or not, cannot be expected to be customer conscious if management above them is not similarly involved. Management style and decisions must support this orientation, not counteract it. Personnel policies, likewise, must reflect this orientation and practice it in the form of job-filling, recruiting, and promotion. We can take this one step further: If internal marketing is not incorporated into management thinking, the direction of the firm may make implementation of internal marketing difficult or even impossible at lower levels.

The comments of the general manager of a large hotel are worth noting in this regard.

> The solution to this dilemma [between employee and management] lies with responsibility at all levels of management. Once the leadership role has been established, line employees will follow suit.
>
> To change the way an organization works, each manager must assume that they are 100% responsible for everything that happens in the work environment. To step this concept down, imagine the post-convention analysis of a front office manager: "The lines were too long because housekeeping didn't have the rooms ready on time, the VIP checked in one hour before she was supposed to, and check-out was screwed up because the sales office didn't tell me that it was a package plan."
>
> The result? A convention that will never come back to the hotel again. You can rest assured that the front office manager in no way feels responsible for the problem. Queries to the housekeeper and sales director will reveal similar conclusions. Line employees pick up on this attitude and begin to transfer the feelings to the next customer.
>
> Contrast this with the front office manager that checked the room status, prepared for the VIP's possible early arrival, and went to the sales office to discuss billing. This manager has taken control of the situation, satisfied the convention, and exemplified the intangible leadership necessary for internal marketing.
>
> (Unfortunately, the relatively transient nature of hotel management only intensifies the problem of responsibility: "Oh, that convention was booked before I got here, I don't know anything about it!")
>
> This scenario is typical of many managers and internal marketing will never be executed properly until the department head understands the concept of 100% responsibility.

The internal product consists of a job and work environment that depend on, among other things, management methods, personnel policy, internal training policy, procedures for planning, and implementing and following up the firm's policies. All of these areas require the right strategic decisions by management if they are not to be counterproductive. Otherwise, lower management behaviors and attitudes and personnel policies may fail to support customer consciousness on the part of employees.

Most important, personnel, especially customer-contact personnel, must realize that they are part of the total marketing effort. As Grönroos has noted, it may be more important to change employee job attitudes than to give courses on sales and communication techniques that may, in fact, turn employees away from marketing. Further, as has been pointed out, training programs must be balanced between the need to do the job technically well, and the need to understand, relate to, and resolve customers' problems.[10] In fact, the result may well be contributions from employees on how to better handle customers' problems.

Mike Leven, now president of Days Inn, tells the story of a number of years ago when he was chosen by the Washington State University Hotel and Restaurant program to be honored as "Hotel Marketer of the Year." After a long flight from New York and a long car ride from Seattle to Pullman, at the opposite end of the state, he finally came upon the motel where he was to stay. Tired as he was, Mike was gratified to see lit up in neon lights on the hotel sign the words, "Welcome, Mike Leven, Hotel Marketer of the Year." When he went to check in, however, the desk clerk, after careful perusal of the room rack, proclaimed that he had no reservation. More than a little tired, and now a little irate, Mike asked the clerk how this could possibly be when his name was in neon lights on the sign in front of the motel. "How would I know that," responded the clerk, "I came in the back door." Clearly, figuratively speaking, employees need to come in the front door to understand the customer.

A summary of the internal marketing concept is shown in Table 3-1. The following discussion also borrows from Grönroos.[11]

A management marketing orientation supports an internal marketing environment. This environment forms a basis for continuous internal marketing actions on a day-to-day basis. New services, supporting services, advertising campaigns, and other activities that affect consumers must also affect employees. Success in the targeted consumer market rests, to no small degree, on success in the internal market, the employees.

Traditional marketing activities can also play a role in influencing personnel as much as they are designed to influence customers. Employees should be kept abreast of new products, new developments, and new consumer promises even before the consumers. If a consumer wishes to claim an advertised or promoted, promised reward it is self-evident that an employee to whom the claim is made should know exactly what the customer is talking about. Personal internal marketing means not only the employee's readiness to be able to anticipate the customer; it is also a more effective means of getting people enthusiastic about a new service or campaign. Advertising can be designed for the internal customer and used to influence employees just as it is designed for the external customer and used to influence the marketplace.

Making employees aware of what is going on is not intended just to enable them to respond to customers. The flip side of the coin, unawareness, leads to embarrassment, disappointment, reduction in motivation, and lack of support for marketing efforts. Employees are, in fact, as much vital recipients of marketing campaigns as are consumers.

---

[10] "Smile buttons" are not internal marketing; the reason for wearing them is.

[11] Grönoos, *Strategic Management*, p. 77.

TABLE 3-1   The Internal Marketing Concept—A Summary

Overall Objective: To develop a motivated and customer-conscious personnel.

Strategic Level

Objective: To create an internal environment that supports customer-consciousness and sales-mindedness among the personnel through supportive

- management methods,
- personnel policy,
- internal training policy, and
- planning and control procedures.

Tactical Level

Objective: To sell services, supporting services (used as means of competition), campaigns, and single marketing efforts to the employees based on these principles:

- The personnel are the first market of the service company.
- The employees must understand why they are expected to perform in a certain manner, or in a certain situation actively support a given service or supporting service.
- The employees must accept the services and other activities of the company in order to support the service in their contact with the consumers.
- A service must be fully developed and internally accepted before it is launched.
- The internal information channels must work; personal selling is needed internally, too.

Source: Grönroos, *Strategic Management.*

John Sharpe, vice-president of operations at Four Seasons Hotels, cites a number of examples of employees' "caring" for Four Seasons' customers and then makes the following points.

> In . . . the hospitality industry, quality depends largely on the efforts of people. And service of exceptional quality can be delivered only by highly motivated people. . . . The majority of people working today are not motivated to a high pitch automatically. Yet it is possible for the majority of employees in an organization to believe and act as if their jobs really do matter.
>
>   There is no single, simple formula. . . . Motivation is not something managers do to people. Rather it is something present in everyone with its potential to drive behavior. Managers either succeed in creating a climate in which people are encouraged to release their inbuilt motivation or they create a climate which stifles it. You can't make people motivated. All you can do is create the best possible climate.
>
>   . . . creating the right climate for our employees is as important as creating the right climate for the client. The two goals go hand in hand. Success in one reinforces and enhances the other.
>
>   . . . The underlying foundation for superior service is a common philosophy and set of values that must be shared by everyone in the organization. These values serve as a guide and stimulus to behavior. They emphasize the importance not only of providing our customers with consistently excellent service and outstanding value but also the

principle of dealing with fellow employees as we would have them deal with us. . . . Understanding the sensitivity to the needs of fellow employees as well as customers.

. . . the general manager sets the tone and climate for a hotel . . . is highly visible . . . expects his division and department heads to follow his example. . . . Our GMs take their cue from the company's head office executives. . . .

. . . The employee turnover rate at Four Seasons is less than half the industry average.

. . . What our guests dwell on time and time again is the positive attitude of Four Seasons employees.[12]

In the last few years, there has been a large hue and cry about the quality of services in America. One particularly pungent comment that applies to our case follows.

The U.S. "service economy" is in big trouble. The reason: the quality of much service today, like the quality of many manufactured goods 15 years ago, stinks. When you do encounter the rare, high-quality service, the experience stands in stark and lonely contrast to the undifferentiated mass of miserable service.

This poor service has been of minor importance in the past—mostly a customer irritant. However, the service sector now faces a double-barreled competitive threat. First, the White House Office of Consumer Affairs recently released some alarming statistics: 96% of dissatisfied customers do not complain about poor quality directly to the company. Instead, they simply never buy at that company again and broadcast their dissatisfaction to friends and acquaintances.

Second, [there is] a coming onslaught of international competition in services that will challenge U.S. dominance. For example, foreign airlines are taking away market share from U.S. carriers. . . . U.S. service providers must learn the lesson that was hammered into the manufacturing sector—either shape up or face three possibilities: 1) be replaced by a competitor, probably foreign; 2) get taken over; 3) go bankrupt.

Why is the quality of service so lousy? Executives blame the poor quality of people who are willing to work in lower-paying service jobs. But this argument does not explain why higher-paying manufacturing jobs turned out poor-quality goods for many years. High pay does not equal good service, and, as McDonald's has shown, low pay need not result in poor service.

. . . There are two explanations that are more compelling. First, too many providers do not understand the nature of a service. Most are intangible: You cannot . . . take home a waiter's behavior.

. . . The second and more powerful explanation for poor service is management. Service providers treat customers similar to the way they, as employees, are treated by management. In many such organizations management treats employees as unvalued and unintelligent. The employees in turn convey the identical message to the customer. If management treats employees' concerns with indifference, then employees will not care about the customers' complaints. It is a rare employee who can rise above the effects of such poor management.

In poorly managed organizations, a pecking order exists. The boss gets the most respect and receives the widest degree of tolerance for less-than-social behavior. If the top executive treats a middle manager with rudeness and disrespect, then that manager mimics the executive by acting similarly toward his subordinate. This process

---

[12] John Sharpe, "The Challenge of Effectively Managing," *Foodservice and Hospitality,* October 1985, pp. 58, 60.

continues until the last person in the organizational chain has no one to dump on. And that person is usually the airline ticket agent, the order-taker at the fast food chain, [the waitress or the desk clerk]. Since he has no one to abuse inside the organization, he treats customers as if they were the ones on the next rung down.

If managers want to improve service quality they must treat employees the same way they want employees to treat customers. Managers are the servants of the employees, not just the bosses. They must provide services to the employees in a friendly, helpful and efficient manner that will enable those employees to better serve the customers. Customers thus become the beneficiaries of high-quality service that mirrors the organization's inner working.

. . . High-quality service depends on high-quality management. If U.S. providers fail to learn this lesson, they should not be surprised if Americans have accounts at Japanese banks, fly Singapore Airlines or eat in French-owned restaurants.[13]

Successful internal marketing considerably eases the task of implementing the second element of nontraditional marketing, relationship marketing, or the primary task of keeping customers, to which we now turn.

Relationship Marketing

Customers are assets. They are the most important assets a company can have. It is good management in business to protect your assets, but assets like buildings, or a warehouse of goods, do not produce profits; the customer that buys the goods does.

In spite of these veritably unchallenged statements, there is a tendency to concentrate efforts on obtaining new customers and, at the same time, to do a poor job of handling the present customer relationship. Sometimes, in fact, it would seem that customers are perceived as liabilities to be disposed of as quickly as possible. Consider the following situation.

A couple had gone to a certain hotel within 25 miles of their home for a long weekend following their marriage. The time was early December, when the hotel traditionally ran at about 20 percent occupancy. They continued this practice for three more years on their anniversary, each time spending about $500. They also stayed at this hotel, or ate there, four or five other times during the year. Sometimes other friends joined them.

The fifth year the couple had similar plans and made a reservation. They arrived at the hotel at about 7:00 P.M. and were welcomed by the desk clerk, whom they had come to know over the years. Upon getting to their room they changed their clothes, opened a bottle of champagne, and called the dining room to see how late they could get room service. They were informed that the dining room and kitchen were closed for the employees' annual Christmas party. Why, they asked, had they not been informed of this when they made the reservation, as they could easily have stopped and had dinner on the way; or, at the least, why had no one told them when they checked in. There was, of course, no suitable answer. Not wanting to dress again or go out at this time in a town lacking serious restaurants, they finally managed to coax two chicken sandwiches out of someone in the kitchen.

---

[13] Robert E. Kelley, "Poorly Served Employees Serve Customers Just as Poorly," *Wall Street Journal,* October 12, 1987, p. 20.

The following morning a false fire alarm forced them out of bed and down into the lobby in their nightclothes at 5:00 A.M. For this inconvenience they were given a free cup of coffee.

Checking out three days later, the husband asked for the 10 percent room discount he was entitled to as a member of an organization that had an agreement with the hotel chain. The terms of the agreement state that you must ask for the discount when making the reservation and when checking in. This he had not done, both because he forgot and because he knew the staff and realized that they knew him from many previous visits.

The clerk's response was that he was not allowed to grant the discount because it was not asked for at check-in time, even though he himself knew the customer and had personally checked him in. Furthermore, only the general manager could authorize the discount retroactively, and he was not on the premises. Although the amount was small, the customer was still upset enough when he got home to write to the general manager, explain the circumstances, and ask for the discount.

In a two-page letter explaining the policy, why employees should have Christmas parties, and why fire alarms are for the protection of guests, the general manager denied the claim in no uncertain terms.

The customer then wrote to the vice-president of marketing of the franchisor with a copy of the manager's letter. Shortly afterward, he received a very polite letter from the hotel's general manager starting, "We are always glad to know of our customers complaints because it helps us to improve our operations," and an invitation to spend a weekend at the hotel as guests of the manager. The customer never went back to the hotel and never will. Neither will some of his friends and possibly others to whom he has told the story.

Consider for a moment, the cost of granting the discount, about $25.00, against the business lost at a time when occupancy runs 20 percent, not to mention business that might be lost through word-of-mouth. Marriott estimates that it costs them $120 to get a new customer, a figure that appears, if anything, on the low side, especially for remote properties or smaller chains that are unable to spread out the cost of national advertising.

Relationship marketing is defined as marketing to protect the customer base. It sees the customer as an asset. Its function is to attract, maintain, and enhance customer relationships.

Relationship marketing should be practiced in all industries. Consider, for example, Whirlpool's hot line for customers who buy its appliances and have problems or need help. General Electric has a similar arrangement. Other companies put phone numbers or addresses on their packages for customers to use. Perhaps no one has been more cognizant of this need than the computer and software industries, many members of which provide toll-free service to help their customers become "friendly" with their user-friendly products.

Nowhere is relationship marketing more apropos than in service industries in general and the hospitality industry in particular. Relationship marketing is most applicable when

1. There is an ongoing and periodic desire for service by the customer;
2. The service customer controls the selection of the service supplier;
3. There are alternative supplier choices;

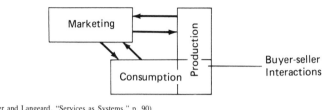

(Source: Eiglier and Langeard, "Services as Systems," p. 90)

FIGURE 3-2   The customer relation of service firms

4. Customer loyalty is weak and switching is common and easy; and
5. Word of mouth is an especially potent form of communication about a product.[14]

These conditions are obviously quite prevalent in the hospitality industry. We don't sell one-time services, and the consumer has many choices, especially today. In an era of heavy hotel building and restaurant openings, any hotel or restaurant is especially vulnerable to new competition. Most everyone likes to try a new place. The question is, will they come back? Do we offer a competitive product on dimensions that are meaningful to customers, solve customer problems, and are difficult for competitors to duplicate? This is what relationship marketing is all about, and when the above conditions pertain the opportunities to practice it are abundant.

To examine the strong need for relationship marketing in the hospitality industry, let us go back once again to the concept of simultaneous production and consumption of services. In Figure 3-2, it can be seen how this concept creates the context that makes relationship marketing so critical.

When we consider that the production of a service includes a major portion of the activities that are required to satisfy the needs of the consumer, and the consumption of the service includes a major portion of the activities that go to produce that service, the buyer-seller interaction becomes paramount. In fact, the relationship of that interaction may largely or totally supersede any other components of the sale/purchase; the relationship alone may determine the quality of the product.

Keep in mind, too, that this relationship extends from the first contact to obtain information or make a reservation, to the end of all production and consumption.

Ongoing Relationships

In relationship marketing, moreover, the process doesn't stop there. The relationship marketer works to maintain the relationship long after the formal production/consumption process has ended, seeking not only to keep customers but to bring them back as well. Levitt compares the relationship to something like a marriage.

> The relationship between a seller and a buyer seldom ends when the sale is made.
> The sale merely consummates the courtship. Then the marriage begins. How good the marriage is depends on how well the relationship is managed by the seller. That

---

[14] Adapted from L. L. Berry, "Relationship Marketing," in *Emerging Perspectives on Services Marketing*, L. L. Berry, G. D. Shostack, and G. D. Upah, eds., Chicago: American Marketing Association, 1983, p. 25.

determines whether there will be continued or expanded business or troubles and divorce, and whether costs or profits increase.

. . . It is not just that once you get a customer you want to keep him. It is more a matter of what the buyer wants. He wants a vendor who will keep his promises, who'll keep supplying and stand behind what he promised. The age of the blind date or the one-night stand is gone. Marriage is both more convenient and more necessary. . . . In these conditions success in marketing, like success in marriage, is transformed into the inescapability of a relationship.[15]

A False Case

Keeping in mind Levitt's remarks, a short detour is warranted here to discuss something that appears on the surface to be relationship marketing (and is called such by some), but in fact is not. Besides making that point, the discussion will provide an opportunity to define relationship marketing by contrast, and to explore why the point of difference is important.

In the notion of relationship marketing, American Air Lines has been applauded for its marketing coup in starting the first frequent flyer program. Other airlines quickly followed suit and, belatedly, some hotel companies, notably Holiday Inns, Marriott, Ramada, and Inter-Continental. Others, such as Sheraton and Hyatt, first affiliated with airlines and then started their own programs. Table 3-2 is Marriott's interpretation of why their "hotel guest recognition program" is better than the others. Almost all the chains make the same claim for various reasons. Table 3-3 shows Hyatt's "Gold Passport Awards" in 1987.

Frequent flyer or frequent traveler programs reward the traveler for repeat patronage with free flights, resort vacations, free car rentals, service class upgrades, free rooms, reduced rates, free newspapers, and other amenities. Some programs also give away prizes unrelated to the company's product, such as luggage, savings bonds, portable jacuzzis, grand pianos, ocean cruises, and most anything else you can think of.

Ironically, these programs also offer travelers, as members of the "club," what they thought they were buying in the first place in the room price of the upscale hotels that offer them: quick check-in/check-out, guaranteed reservations, prompt room service, telephone message delivery, bed turndown, business services (at a fee), and late check-out ("we'll do our best").

These programs have been pronounced great successes by many of the companies that sponsor them, even those companies that initiated them reluctantly, in self defense. Whether they are or not may be somewhat moot in the long term if judged in the context of whether they have actually made customers more loyal, or have taken customers from the competition. One thing is for sure, they have affected the price of hotel rooms.

---

[15] Theodore Levitt, "Marketing Intangible Products and Product Intangibles," *Harvard Business Review,* May–June, 1981, pp. 94–102. Copyright 1981 © by the President and Fellows of Harvard College; all rights reserved.

TABLE 3-2   Hotel Guest Recognition Program Comparison

	MARRIOTT Honored Guest Awards	HILTON HHonors	HOLIDAY Priority Club	HYATT Gold Passport	RADISSON Frequent Guest Awards	RAMADA Business Card	SHERATON Club International	WESTIN Premier
Membership Fee:	NONE	NONE	$10	$25	NONE	NONE	$25	NONE
Points per Room Night:	100	0	0	0	0	0	0	1
Points per Dollar Charged to Guest Room:	10	10	1 (Room Only)	5	10	1/100	4	2 (Miles)
Enrollment Bonus Points:	3,000	0	0	1,000	0	0	500	0
Activation Bonus Points:	2,000	0	0	0	5,000	1	0	3 (Nights)
Frequency Bonus:	10%	None	None	None	None	None	None	None
Do All Properties Participate?	YES*	NO	YES	YES	NO	YES	NO	NO
Travel Partner Bonuses Permitted?	YES	YES	NO	YES	YES	YES	NO	NO
AIRLINE	25%	25%	—	25%	200 (Bonus Pts.)	25%	—	—
CAR RENTAL	20%	20%	—	—	200 (Bonus Pts.)	25%	—	—
Number of Points Needed for Typical Weeklong Resort Vacation With Roundtrip Airfare for 2, Plus Additional Benefits (See Below):	130,000	200,000	45,000	250,000	100,000	300	329,000	85 (Nights)
Average Number of Hotel Nights Needed to Earn Resort Vacation:	70	126	590	333	79	217	633	82
Resort Vacation Includes:								
HOTEL NIGHTS	7	5	7	7	8	6	7	7
AIR	2	2 (U.S. only)	2	2	2 (U.S. only)	2	2	—
CAR RENTAL DAYS	7	—	7	4 (Weekends)	14 (Weekends)	7	7	—
CRUISE DAYS (50% off)	3 or 4	—	—	—	—	—	4	—
OTHER	—	—	—	Benefits	Benefits	—	—	—
Expiration Date of Program:	Indefinite	12/88	12/88	Indefinite	12/87	12/87	Indefinite	Indefinite

Source: This Hotel Guest Recognition Program Comparison was based on information supplied by each hotel chain to its program members as of May 31, 1987. Points achieved in each program were based on a composite of average room rates in a sample of major metropolitan cities.

*Courtyard By Marriott is a separate division of Marriott Corporation and does not participate in Marriott Honored Guest Awards.
Courtesy of Marriott Corp.

UNSURPASSED TRAVEL AWARDS...EXCLUSIVELY FOR HYATT GOLD PASSPORT MEMBERS

Each Gold Passport award has that unique Hyatt flair. Redeem your Hyatt Gold Passport points, and you'll enjoy a wide variety of travel experiences. You'll delight in Regency Club and Suite Upgrades, as well as deluxe weekend packages including sumptuous meals, resort vacations, and even a dream vacation at any Hyatt hotel or resort in the world.

In addition to Hyatt awards, Delta and Northwest offer you spectacular air travel awards.

And Hertz, the number one name in rent-a-car, offers great car awards, too.

These are the awards with the Hyatt difference. From a soaring atrium and lush garden lobby of a city center hotel, to the incredible landscapes of a magnificent resort, the diversity of Hyatt's world will astound you.

HYATT HOTELS & RESORTS   DELTA   NORTHWEST   Hertz

POINT LEVEL	HOTEL AWARDS		PARTNER AWARDS	
	HYATT HOTELS — OR —	HYATT RESORTS — AND —	AIRLINE AWARDS — AND —	CAR RENTAL AWARDS
5,000	A Regency Club® upgrade for up to Four Nights	A Regency Club Upgrade for up to Four Nights at All Hyatt Resorts	A Round Trip Upgrade from Coach to First Class	A One Car Class Upgrade to a Compact through a Full-size Car
7,500	Stay One Weekend Night, Get One Free	Stay One Night, Get One Free at Most Hyatt Resorts	A 25% Discount on a Companion Ticket	A Free Compact Car for One Additional Weekend Day with the Purchase of Two Weekend Days
10,000	One Free Weekend Night	One Free Night at Most Hyatt Resorts	A 25% Discount on a Companion Ticket	A Free Compact Car for One Additional Weekend Day with the Purchase of One Weekend Day
12,500	One Free Weekend Night in our Regency Club	One Free Night in our Regency Club at Most Hyatt Resorts	A 25% Discount on a Companion Ticket	A Free Full-size Car for One Additional Weekend Day with the Purchase of One Weekend Day
15,000	A Suite Upgrade for up to Four Nights	A Suite Upgrade for up to Four Nights at All Hyatt Resorts	A Round Trip Upgrade from Coach to First Class	A Two Car Class Upgrade to a Mid-size through a Full-size Car
17,500	A 50% Discount for up to Six Nights	A 50% Discount on up to Six Nights at Most Hyatt Resorts	A 50% Discount on a Companion Ticket	A 50% Discount on a Hertz Affordable Weekly™ Rental
20,000	Two Free Weekend Nights	Two Free Nights at Most Hyatt Resorts	A 50% Discount on a Companion Ticket	A Free Compact Car for One Weekend Day
25,000	Three Free Weekend Nights	Three Free Nights at Most Hyatt Resorts	A 50% Discount on a Companion Ticket	A Free Mid-size Car for One Weekend Day
30,000	Free Two Night Weekend Dreamscape	Free Two Night Dreamscape at Most Hyatt Resorts	A 50% Discount on a Companion Ticket	A Free Full-size Car for One Weekend Day
35,000	Free Two Night Weekend Regency Club Dreamscape	Free Two Night Regency Club Dreamscape at Most Hyatt Resorts	A 50% Discount on a Companion Ticket	A Free Compact Car for Two Weekend Days
40,000	Free Three Night Weekend Regency Club Dreamscape	Free Three Night Regency Club Dreamscape at Most Hyatt Resorts	A 75% Discount on a Companion Ticket	A Free Mid-size Car for Two Weekend Days
45,000	Free Three Night Weekend Suite Dreamscape	Free Three Night Suite Dreamscape at Most Hyatt Resorts	A 75% Discount on a Companion Ticket	A Free Full-size Car for Two Weekend Days
50,000	Five Free Nights	Free Two Night Dreamscape at All Hyatt Resorts	A 75% Discount on a Companion Ticket	A Free Compact Car for Three Weekend Days
60,000	Five Free Nights in our Regency Club	Free Three Night Dreamscape at All Hyatt Resorts	A 75% Discount on a Companion Ticket	A Free Mid-size Car for Three Weekend Days
70,000	Six Free Nights	Six Free Nights at Most Hyatt Resorts	One Free Round Trip Companion Ticket	A Free Full-size Car for Three Weekend Days
80,000	Seven Free Nights	Seven Free Nights at Most Hyatt Resorts	One Free Round Trip Companion Ticket	A Free Compact Car for Four Weekend Days
90,000	Seven Free Nights in our Regency Club	Seven Free Nights in our Regency Club at Most Hyatt Resorts	One Free Round Trip Companion Ticket	A Free Mid-size Car for Four Weekend Days
100,000	Seven Free Nights in a Hyatt Suite	Seven Free Nights in a Hyatt Suite at Most Hyatt Resorts	One Free Round Trip Companion Ticket	A Free Full-size Car for Four Weekend Days

TABLE 3-3 Hotel guest recognition program comparison (courtesy of Hyatt Corp.)

Question: . . . how do you feel the general increase in hotel costs . . . will affect meeting attendance . . .?

Answer by Steve Powell, Loew's Anatole Hotel, Dallas: . . . increased hotel costs . . . are a contributor to lower meeting attendance. . . . [Among other things] amenities in the rooms, costly frequent traveler plans, those of us who are partners with airlines or who have created our own plans—these factors are contributing to hotel costs.[16]

Powell's comment is not surprising. Holiday, one of the early starters, dropped their program after reportedly losing millions, then started another one (due to irate customers who were already participating). Marriott is reported to have spent $16,000,000 for their program in 1984.[17] Hilton's four-month "Instant $1 Million-a-Day 'Thank You' " program in 1987 obviously ran into the multi-millions.[18] Although no one ever asked the customer, it is likely that lower room rates would have been more appealing. At the same time, higher room rates are driving away customers.

The problem with these programs is that they do not build true, enduring loyalty. Research by the U.S. Travel Data Center showed that only 2 percent of business travelers consider a frequent traveler program important when choosing a hotel. The same study indicated that only 6 percent of all commercial travelers (two million people) belong to frequent guest programs.[19] This means that 94 percent of commercial travelers are paying the higher room rates to support a minute percentage of the market, mostly on expense account, who would stay at one of these hotels regardless. Regarding loyalty, Yesawich states:

. . . They have been particularly effective for properties (or chains) that possess no other meaningful basis of differentiating themselves from the competition. And therein lies the peril: if a guest chooses brand A over B because A offers a better premium, market share is likely to shift whenever an operator ups the ante. Hence the buy decision becomes influenced by factors other than the basic features of the brand. And any time you have to rely on the "extras" to sell the core features of the brand, you need to reevaluate the fundamental marketability of the brand. . . . The obvious question becomes, which is more important, recognition or reward? . . . for those properties or chains that truly provide a meaningful difference, there appears to be no substitute for recognition.[20]

Apparently, at least some hoteliers share these feelings (and, in fact, many appear to be in these programs against their better judgment).

William A. Vervaeke, senior vice-president sales and marketing, Trusthouse Forte: I vividly remember the car rental giveaways . . . at the height of the give-away frenzy, market shares were back where they started from. Nobody had an edge. It was just costing them more. . . . Hotel companies should look at history.

---

[16] Reported in *The Meeting Manager,* September, 1986, pp. 16–17.

[17] Steve Swartz, "How Marriott Changes Hotel Design to Lap Midpriced Market," *The Wall Street Journal,* September 18, 1985, pp. 1, 22. Marriott's costs included solicitation of members for Honored Guest Awards, a set-aside for redemption liability, and operating costs.

[18] George Taninecz, "Hilton Giveaway Hits High Gear," *Hotel & Motel Management,* January 12, 1987, pp. 2, 29.

[19] Reported by Peter Yesawich, "The Frequent Traveler Frenzy," *Lodging Hospitality,* July 1987, p. 28.

[20] Ibid.

Joe Garvey, vice-president marketing, Hyatt: . . . customers have said to us, without question, that they are confused. There are so many programs . . . that the customer has lost the ability to keep all this in mind. . . . So it comes back to where the business has always come back to and that's how best to execute the service and provide the basic product offering that we have.[21]

For many hotels and hotel companies, the net result of these programs, like the bathroom amenities programs, may be a no-gain or even a net loss when the cost is considered. This is because another unique characteristic of services is that they cannot be patented; once the competition introduces the same services, the differential advantage is lost and companies end up giving away something they should be selling.

Frequent traveler programs do not constitute relationship marketing in the true sense. The reason is that these programs are really "buying" customers and "buying" their repeated patronage; they are not creating or keeping customers in the marketing sense of creating loyalty. Most frequent traveler beneficiaries are unfaithful: They will go where the grass looks the greenest, without compunction. The reason for this is readily apparent; frequent traveler programs do not solve consumers' problems or satisfy needs and wants. Instead, they provide something for nothing; in the long run someone has to pay for it.[22]

So-called "twofer" programs (two for the price of one) and other types of restaurant promotions also have the trappings of relationship marketing but have been found lacking. Those who take advantage of these promotions often would not come to the restaurant otherwise, and don't come back when the promotion ends.

The True Case

The true sense and purpose of relationship marketing is to maintain the customer relationship and build loyalty. To offer special attractions and rewards to obtain customers, and to continue to give those rewards to keep customers are in the vein of traditional marketing. Relationship marketing means getting and keeping the customer because of his or her relationship with you. It should not be necessary to give away something that you would not give away otherwise. In fact, if the relationship is strong the customer may even be willing to pay more because of it.

Most companies devote their greatest marketing efforts to attracting new customers. Retaining existing customers, while fully agreed as desirable, seems to receive little attention. Notice sometime, for example, how when you are waiting to be seated in a restaurant, the maitre d' or hostess will go answer the phone while leaving you standing there. A major complaint of meeting planners with hotels is that there is no one present with authority to handle their problems, although they were wined and dined with the greatest attention before booking the meeting. The view of marketing as only an external activity is both short-sighted and self-defeating.

---

[21] Quoted in Steven J. Stark, "Loyalty Programs More Vital Than Ever to Hotel Chains," *Business Travel News*, February 9, 1987, p. 14.

[22] After seven years of frequent flyer plans, the airlines owe three million round-trip domestic tickets, enough to fly at least 5.4 billion miles free, and face a potential revenue loss of $1.24 billion. The probability that a frequent flier award passenger will replace a full-fare passenger in first class is 85 percent. "Ultimately, either the consumer pays or the stockholder pays." *The Wall Street Journal*, February 12, 1988, pp. 1, 7.

Relationship marketing means thinking in terms of the customers we have, rather than just in terms of the ones we hope to acquire. This is crucial in the hospitality industry. Competition is standing by, all too ready and willing to take the customers you can't keep.

Mike Leven, president of Days Inn, tells how he started his hotel career as a salesman for the Hotel Roosevelt in New York City by reading the reader boards of other hotels. He would then go back to his office and write a letter to the companies whose names he had written down and solicit their next meeting. He realized that something always went wrong at hotel meetings and the time to "steal" the business was to get them when they were still angry at the other hotel.

Attracting new customers is only the beginning of marketing in the hospitality industry. Marketing must also include building a lasting relationship, creating loyal customers, and serving customers as valued clients. Berry has noted five specific strategies for doing this.[23]

Core Service   Core services are based on central rather than peripheral market needs. It is the service around which the customer relationship is built, because it attracts new customers by meeting their needs, cements the business through its quality and enduring nature, and provides the means for offering additional services over time. A relatively recent example of offering a new core service is the suite hotel concept.

Customizing the Relationship   Because hospitality services are flexible to a large degree, they can often be customized. Here, hospitality businesses have a considerable advantage over goods manufacturers because they have the customer in-house, on premise. The customer doesn't have to be dealt with through layers of suppliers. There is tremendous opportunity to learn about particular customers and their specific requirements, and to tailor the service to meet those requirements.

Many hotels and restaurants now do this; The Stanford Court Hotel in San Francisco is a classic example. It provided customers with a reason to come back rather than starting over with another hotel by paying attention to "monumental trivialities."

The Stanford Court was individually owned and managed until bought by Stouffer Hotels in 1988, and some chain operators will argue that was is done there cannot possibly be done in a chain property. Such an attitude ignores the value of relationship marketing whether it derives from corporate policy or from an individual GM's policy. Each and every hotel and restaurant, be it a Holiday Inn or a McDonald's, is individually managed. That management individual has the same opportunity as Jim Nassikas had at The Stanford Court. In this chapter and the previous two, we have already pointed out examples of people who are in a position to customize the service to the individual.

Service Augmentation   Service augmentation means building extras into the service, especially those that it is difficult for the competition to copy. The extras must be genuine extras that have meaning and value for the customer. Bathroom amenities, although introduced in this sense, do not fill the criterion unless they are something the customer genuinely values. When the customer simply packs them to take home, they do not add value, only cost.

---

[23] Berry, "Services Marketing Is Different," p. 25.

In a hotel, it is not easy to add amenities or augmented services that the competiton cannot duplicate. This should not deter the effort when it serves a need. Recall the previous comment that one problem with services is that they are not noticed until they are missing; in these cases just the presence of a service becomes a service augmentation.

An example that demonstrates this point is the pull-out clothesline that many hotels, even older ones, have installed in bathrooms to solve a problem of women travelers. When a new 1200-room hotel of a national chain opened recently, the housekeeper was asked why these clotheslines had not been installed. The response was, "They're too much trouble."

There are many ways that today's hotels and restaurants can augment, or personal-ize, service. One way to find out what they are is to talk to customers, something the relationship marketer will do on a regular basis. Customers will always have problems that need solving.

Marriott's Club Marquis, of which a guest can become a member by spending five separate visits at Marriott hotels, entitles one to benefits over and above the normal service afforded other Marriott customers. These include higher check-cashing limits, special reservation service through a simple ID number, preregistration, and guaranteed accommodations with a $200 default penalty plus accommodations paid for elsewhere. These services all relate specifically to customers' problems. These are augmented services; in this case they are special privileges for Marriott's very best customers.

Relationship Pricing   Hotels commonly give "quantity discounts" to companies that agree to book so many room-nights a year. They also discount rooms for large groups. Frequent traveler plans were discussed earlier, but relationship pricing can go far beyond these practices, which ignore a large part of the market and should deal with rewarding loyalty.

Suppose, for example, that regular hotel customers were allowed to order wine or liquor room service, by the bottle, without paying the 300 to 500 percent markups that appear on most room service lists. Not only would customers feel privileged, they wouldn't feel taken advantage of. The hotel would also benefit, not just from the customers' loyalty but also from the service's being purchased in the hotel instead of at the package store across the street, where many hotel guests now go.

Internal Marketing   Internal marketing is the fifth strategy suggested by Berry. Because it has already been discussed in this chapter there is no need to go into further detail here. We should not, however, overlook that internal marketing may be the most critical phase of relationship marketing. As Berry states:

> In essence, internal marketing involves creating an organizational climate in general, and job-products in particular, that lead to the right service personnel performing the service in the right way. In consumption circumstances in which the performance of people is what is being sold, the marketing task is not only that of encouraging external customers to buy but also that of encouraging internal customers to perform. When internal customers perform, the likelihood of external customers *continuing* to buy is increased.[24]

---

[24] Ibid., p. 28.

Customer Complaints

If there is one place where internal marketing and relationship marketing come together it is in the handling of customer complaints. Customer complaints are a special case and deserve special treatment in this chapter because they are one of the most misunderstood and mishandled areas of customer relations in the hospitality industry. Let us look first at what customer complaints are:

- Inevitable. Nothing is perfect. The diversity of the hospitality customer and the heterogeneity of the hospitality product absolutely ensure that there will be complaints. This will be true even when everything goes according to plan. Of course, when everything doesn't go according to plan, and it almost never does, there will be additional problems and there will be complaints.

- Healthy. The old army expression is, "If the troops aren't griping look out for trouble." An absence of complaints may be the best indication management has (along with declining occupancies or covers) that something is wrong. Hospitality customers are never totally satisfied, especially over a period of time. Probably, instead, they are simply not talking to you or you are not talking to them. The communication process is not working; the relationship is deteriorating. By the time it explodes, it will be too late, à la Howard Johnson's. Some say, "If it isn't broken, don't fix it." First, you have to know if it's broken; the ones who know first are your customers. And, incidentally, the ones they tell first are your employees, which means that you had better listen to your employees as well.

- Opportunities. Customer complaints are opportunities to learn of customers' problems, whether they are idiosyncratic or caused by the operation itself. If it's broken, you have an opportunity to fix it. If it's not broken, you have an opportunity to make it better, to be creative, to develop new product, to learn new needs, and to keep old customers.

- Marketing tools. If marketing is to give customers what they want, then marketing must know what they want. All the customer surveys in the world won't tell you as much as customer complaints will tell you.

- Advertising. Yes, advertising. The advertising is negative if you don't resolve the problems, and there is nothing more devastating in the hospitality business than negative word-of-mouth. It is positive if you fix the problem. Research has shown that one of the best and most loyal customers is the one who had a complaint that was satisfactorily resolved. And this customer loves to tell others about it.

Although the importance of these five elements of customer complaints is more than obvious, many managements fear customer complaints, hide from them, avoid them, or dismiss them. The result is often a poor job by hospitality managements in handling complaints, as well as thousands of missed opportunities.

The following letter is an example of a missed opportunity in the handling of a customer complaint. This is an extreme case, to be sure, but consider the circumstances.

The letter was written by the general manager of a very famous North American resort hotel, supposedly recognized for its European concept of service. The customer who complained was the executive director of a large association; he was staying at the hotel to test it to see if he wanted to bring the association there for its annual convention. It isn't too difficult to figure out what his decision was.

Dear Mr. Smith:

Your letter of January 12 has been referred to me for reply. I am amazed to learn that you encountered so many difficulties during your brief stay with us.

Each of our guest rooms is provided with a stationery folder containing note paper and pen. The previous guest in your room must have taken the folder with them upon departing and our maid neglected to replace it, for which we apologize. We also apologize for the delay in providing a crib. We can offer no excuse for this other than our housekeeping department must have been extremely busy on your day of arrival.

We have very little call for room service before seven o'clock. The hours of operation for all food and beverage outlets are displayed prominently throughout the hotel.

We are fortunate to have an excellent Executive Housekeeper and we receive many favorable comments about the cleanliness of our rooms. I am surprised that you found it to be to the contrary.

The lamp shade in the room that you occupied has been repaired. When our hotel is running at full capacity, it is sometimes difficult to accomplish these minor repairs at once.

I reiterate my earlier statement that we are proud of our housekeeping. The carpets most certainly are vacuumed daily. Again, an oversight on the part of our maid. There should have been a room service menu in the room and the soap replaced.

I cannot understand the Express Café being out of food. We offer a limited menu in this room and it is just a matter of calling to the kitchen for additional supplies. No children's menu is offered in this room because of the nature of the restaurant.

There are always two rolls of toilet paper in the room so that our guests are not inconvenienced by running out. Again, the maid must have overlooked this as well as the Kleenex and this has been brought to her attention.

We have just had every window in the hotel cleaned. If the window in the dining room appeared dirty, it may be because of the abundance of rain. In any event, we will certainly see that they are cleaned.

We attempt at all times to relay messages received as quickly as possible. I cannot explain the delay you experienced.

I apologize also for the delay in your room service order. The service in this department is normally quite good.

In closing, I am enclosing some recent complimentary letters we have received from satisfied guests.

Because customer complaints are so critical to internal and, especially, relationship marketing, as well as word-of-mouth marketing, the results of some recent research will be presented.

Customer Complaint Research

Until 1982, no serious research had been undertaken to evaluate the impact of customer complaint behavior or management's handling of customer complaints in the hospitality industry. There were, however, a number of studies conducted to measure complaint behavior in connection with a number of other products and services. Findings from these studies indicated the tremendous impact that complainants may have on a business.

- 63 percent of complainers switch suppliers and/or warn others.
- Vocal complainers are twice as likely to believe they have been deceived as those who write complaints.
- 41 percent of complainers never verbalized their complaints; 75 percent of these stopped using the company's services.
- For every verbalized complaint there are 20 unverbalized in the expensive category, and 50 in the inexpensive category.
- Those whose complaints are not resolved tell a median of 9 to 10 others.
- 85 percent spread negative word-of-mouth to an average of 5 people.
- 53 percent were disappointed or annoyed by the company's response.
- A majority spread negative word-of-mouth without taking any action or verbalizing their complaint.
- Personal boycotts and negative word-of-mouth are prevalent because they are perceived as a low-cost way of expressing dissatisfaction.
- Customers who complain are more brand-loyal than those who remain silent.
- American Management Association studies show that a satisfied customer tells 3 people about a good experience while a dissatisfied one gripes to 11.

With such a research foundation, the time was overdue to investigate complaint behavior in the hospitality industry. Three studies in which the authors were involved were undertaken in the hotel industry. The findings carry serious import for the hospitality management.

One Hotel[25]   One hundred twenty previous guests of a specific hotel who had communicated with the hotel were surveyed by mail as to their feelings, actions, and behaviors. About 50 percent of those surveyed had written only complaints, 20 percent had written only compliments, and 30 percent had written both to complain and to compliment. Of the complainers, 60 percent had complained to management in person before leaving the hotel.

Of the guests who had complained, 71 percent said they never used guest comment cards to register their complaints. Thirty-eight percent of those who complained said they would never return, while 25 percent were unsure. For those who would choose to return, the major factor in their decision was the way the complaint was handled. Of those who complained, 63 percent were highly likely to make a point of telling others about their

---

[25] Robert C. Lewis, "When Guests Complain," *Cornell Hotel and Restaurant Administration Quarterly*, August 1983, pp. 23–32.

complaint, and 21 percent were unsure if they would; 47 percent were highly likely to tell others not to use the hotel, and 12 percent were unsure if they would.

These percentages were even higher when the complaint was not handled satisfactorily. On the other hand, the percentages decrease substantially when the complaint *was* handled satisfactorily; as few as 14 percent would tell others not to use the hotel under this condition. Extrapolation of the findings also showed that for every 10 complaints received there were 25 that were not expressed.

This research explicitly shows that once the cause of a complaint has occurred, the level of disturbance becomes a function of the handling and defusing of the situation. The disturbance level can be reduced if the complainant actively believes in management. This means that it is important for management to direct its efforts toward creating an attitude that will minimize the negative effect of the complaint.

Complainants want to feel that management is sincere and will make a sincere attempt to rectify the situation. If this belief is supported, they will probably choose the same hotel again; the tendency of complainants, however, is *not* to believe. Interestingly enough, 29 percent of the still-unsatisfied complainants in the study indicated they would have been satisfied simply with a proper response from management rather than what they felt were token gestures.

Six Unaffiliated Hotels   These findings are an unpublished part of a larger study.[26] While staying in six different hotels in a large eastern city, 1314 people were randomly surveyed. They were asked to report their complaint behavior when it related, separately, to tangible or intangible factors. The response percentages are shown in Table 3-4.

Once again, it can be seen that satisfactory complaint handling has a tremendous impact on the willingness of the complainant to return to the hotel. It can also be seen that approximately half of dissatisfied hotel customers will not take the trouble to complain at all and, of these, at least 4 out of 5 will probably not return to the hotel.

Nine Hotels of a 21-Hotel Chain[27]   Of those people who had written complaints to management over a 2-month period, 479 were surveyed by written questionnaire. Sixty-four percent had made their complaint in person at the time of the incident; 66 percent said they were extremely disturbed at the time.

Of the respondents, 50 percent said it was highly unlikely that they would ever stay at the same hotel again. Of those who had been in the area of the hotel since their complaint, 75 percent had purposely not returned to the hotel; 32 percent had purposely not returned to other hotels in the chain. An analysis of their word-of-mouth behavior is shown in Table 3-5.

Fifty-eight percent of the respondents in this study reported that they were led to complain by an entire series of problems or incidents. This indicates that the hotel

[26] Robert C. Lewis, "Getting the Most from Marketing Research," *Cornell Hotel and Restaurant Administration Quarterly*, November 1983, pp. 81–85.

[27] Susan Morris, "The Relationship Between Company Complaint Handling and Consumer Behavior," master's thesis, Hotel Restaurant & Travel Administration, University of Massachusetts/Amherst, 1985.

TABLE 3-4   Reported Complaint Behavior of 1314 Hotel Guests

	Tangible factors		Intangible factors	
	Likely	Not sure	Likely	Not sure
When you are dissatisfied how likely are you to complain to management?				
In person at the time it occurs	59%	13%	41%	18%
By using guest comment card	50%	13%	48%	13%
By mail or phone later	19%	9%	17%	8%
How likely are you to return to the same hotel when				
You do not make a complaint	5%	15%	8%	13%
Your complaint is resolved	62%	27%	57%	29%
Your complaint is not resolved	4%	3%	3%	5%

Source: Robert C. Lewis and Susan Morris, "The Positive Side of Guest Complaints." *Cornell Hotel and Restaurant Administration Quarterly* February 1987, pp. 13–15.

TABLE 3-5   Word-of-Mouth Behavior of Hotel Complainants

Likely to tell others outside family about the complaint?	
Highly likely	62%
Undecided	18%
Number of people actually told (average)	12
If the complaint was not resolved?	
Highly likely	75%
Not sure	15%
Likely to tell others not to use the hotel?	
Highly likely	43%
Not sure	13%
Number of people actually told (average)	8
If complaint was not resolved?	
Highly likely	71%
Not sure	11%

Source: Morris, "Complaint Handling and Consumer Behavior."

managements involved had a number of opportunities, if they had known of them, to resolve difficulties for the same customer. After the complaints were received, management had additional opportunities, which it failed to take advantage of in 61 percent of the cases.

This 61 percent indicated that they believed their complaint could have been better handled. How? Only 19 percent felt that they should have received a rebate or complimentary rooms or meals. Thirty-four percent thought the situation could have been better handled at the time the incident occurred. A whopping 47 percent stated they would have been satisfied with a better response from management in terms of more detailed and speedier communication or a more pleasant tone.

These three studies demonstrate the opportunities inherent in the proper handling of consumer complaints. Appropriate complaint handling just may be relationship marketing at its finest; certainly it is a tremendous marketing opportunity, which is why a marketing-oriented management should actually seek out complaints.

Complaint handling also incorporates internal marketing. Consider the case of a desk clerk who received a multitude of complaints about the same thing, which management failed to correct. Eventually, when customers came to her with this complaint, she replied with a pointing finger, "That's the complaint line over there."

On the plus side there are hotel companies addressing this issue. Marriott has a busy and well-staffed complaint-handling department at its corporate headquarters, and Bill Marriott, President, randomly answers some complaints personally. This system, however, is not entirely satisfactory and Marriott has been working on developing a new one. In new Marriott hotels a hot-line number has been installed on guest room telephones, with instructions on how to use it to get quick help when normal channels don't work.

At Days Inn every letter and phone call from a customer receives a formal response in writing within 48 hours. People who write Days Inn automatically get a 10 percent coupon to use on their next stay. Says Bob McGrail, Senior Vice President of Marketing, "The guest services department is a marketing tool, rather than a processing center for guest complaints."

Leona Helmsley, President of Helmsley Hotels, states that she personally answers all guest letters addressed to the New York City Park Lane property on Central Park South. In fact, she developed an advertising campaign out of her answers (Figure 3-3).

At the Sheraton New Orleans, staff are trained to recognize that customers with complaints offer a great "moment of truth." A priority hot line coordinates all guest requests through one 24-hour department. All calls are logged and responded to within 15 minutes, and a guest service agent returns the call to see if the guest is satisfied with the follow-through. Both the general manager and the director of guest services review the log daily for additional follow-up, if necessary.[28]

Airlines often have agents on the other side of the counter during busy periods to help customers with problems. This is a practice that could be easily emulated by hotels, with considerable benefit.

What to Do About It

Practicing relationship marketing through consumer complaint handling is not the easiest task in the world. We have already seen that many discontented customers will not take

---

[28] Letter to one of the authors from Kavin Bloomer, Director of Guest Services, Sheraton New Orleans, April 7, 1987.

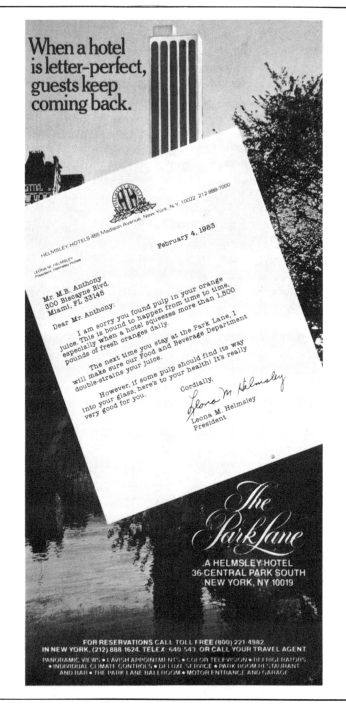

FIGURE 3-3 Capitalizing on customers' letters

the trouble to complain, yet complaints may provide some of the best opportunities. Actually encouraging complaints becomes the necessary objective.

Research has shown that people do not complain for three primary reasons:

1. It is not worth the time and effort.
2. They don't know where or how to complain.
3. They believe that nothing will be done even if they do complain.

Marketing's task is to overcome these obstacles by making it easy to complain, making it known where and how to complain, and truly doing something about the complaint (if it is reasonable—and over three-fourths of all complaints appear to fall into that category). This means setting up specific procedures.[29] Such an action will also constitute internal marketing; when employees see management taking complaints seriously they will feel more inclined to do likewise.

The benefits are clear: long-term profit from loyal customers, and more positive, and less negative, word-of-mouth advertising. There are other ancillary benefits, such as new product ideas, new product information, improved image, better-educated customers, and higher productivity and service. For line employees there are also the benefits of less customer conflict, better image and word-of-mouth about the company, and better respect for the company and the product.

Each company must devise its own system for soliciting and handling complaints. It is beyond the scope of this text to suggest procedures for doing this, but there is help available for those who want and seek it. Handling satisfied customers is easy; handling dissatisfied customers is the acid test of marketing and management.

✓ Summary

Nontraditional hospitality marketing has been explored, dissected, diagnosed, and digested in this chapter. It has been shown that both internal marketing and relationship marketing are critical areas of the marketing effort. In fact, they are essential efforts that no hospitality firm hoping to fulfill its potential can ignore.

Good customer relations are integral parts of any company's sustenance and growth. They must be developed and sustained. In a services business, this is hardly possible without similar employee relations. Employees actually are the product. Employee and guest relations march in tandem.

Once having established a good customer relation, management hopes to cherish and sustain the status quo—but customers' needs change, competition sprouts up, and the firm may be left with no customers. Understanding and anticipating the customer experience is the second key to customer loyalty, One way to do this is to talk to the customer. Complaints are healthy, customer problems are opportunities, and marketers must be opportunists.

---

[29] For more discussion of this subject, see Robert C. Lewis and Susan V. Morris, "The Positive Side of Guest Complaints," *Cornell Hotel and Restaurant Administration Quarterly*, February 1987, pp. 13–15.

DISCUSSION QUESTIONS

1. The hospitality industry has long been aware of the impact employees have on customers. Accordingly, there are many employee training programs that focus on customer relations. Why, then, are there still many problems in the employee-customer relationship? Apply the concept of marketing to this issue. How would you revise employee training?

2. What is the difference between selling a job to a prospective employee and marketing it? Explain.

3. What makes relationship marketing particularly pertinent to the hospitality industry? Discuss the cause and effect of this concept, with specific examples.

4. Write a letter to Mr. Smith (see p. 73) that you feel would have been appropriate.

5. Think of a complaint that you have had in a hotel or restaurant. What did you do about it? If you reported it, how was it handled? How many people did you tell? Would/did you return? Why? If you had been in management's place, how would you have handled it?

6. Discuss why some people complain and others don't. How does this affect relationship marketing? What would you do about it if you were guest relations director?

PART II
The Marketing Environment

CHAPTER 4
Environmental Scanning

Marketing leadership means planning for the future, but wouldn't it be nice if we knew just what the future holds in store? Of course we don't, but not for want of trying to find out. In marketing, this effort has come to be known as *environmental scanning*. Environmental scanning simply means, "What is going on out there in the environment that is going to impact on our business?"

The full treatment of environmental scanning and its full strategic implications are beyond the scope of this text. In this chapter we provide an introduction and adapt it to the marketing perspective. Fifteen years ago you would probably not have found the term *environmental scanning* in a marketing textbook, let alone a chapter on it. Today, it is impossible to write a complete marketing text without some discussion of it. What has happened in the meantime?

One of the most significant changes that has occurred is in the competitive environment. Gone are the days when one could say, "That looks like a good market; let's build a hotel (or restaurant or travel agency or airline) there." "What should it be like?" "Like the one we just built over there." In those days the risk of marketing was very often absent. There was an ever-increasing demand from an ever-increasing traveling and eating-out public. The hospitality industry responded with "me-too" products repeated over and over again, as evidenced by Howard Johnson's and Holiday Inns.

The buildings and decor were newer, but the basic product never changed. Even the atrium lobby was not a new product when first introduced by Hyatt; it was simply a new way of packaging and presenting the product. In other words, the emphasis was on the product and the operation, not the market. If you had a good product and ran a good operation, the success potential was large.

The revealing thing about the atrium lobby, in this instance, is not that Hyatt built it. It is that no one else wanted it! Why change, was the reaction of the industry, especially at added expense and maintenance costs? The same attitude prevailed in the restaurant industry; the white tablecloth, basic table setting, and the same menu that had been around for years and years prevailed. And the leaders in the industry led the way—Howard Johnson's, Holiday Inns, Statler Hotels, its successor Hilton, and many others.

In fact, it was not the clones of Conrad Hilton, Howard Johnson, or Kemmons Wilson who read the environment and changed the industry. Instead, it was the upstarts, such as Ray Kroc in the fast-food industry, Richard Melman in table dining, and Robert Hazard in hotel accommodations, who led the way. These are the people—and there are a number of others—who saw the environment changing, who had new and innovative ideas, who were willing to take the risk, and who set the stage for the competitive vigor that exists in the industry today.

Today there is no other choice. Yesterday's idea is as obsolete as yesterday itself. But rare, too, is the new brilliant concept, the great idea that no one has thought of, and the totally new innovation that may or may not catch on. Today, looking ahead means reading the environment, understanding that change is constant, and developing the product that anticipates the needs and wants of the consumer. Yesterday's success is tomorrow's failure, if there is no constant adaptation to the environment, as Howard Johnson's, Victoria Station, and Holiday Inns have proven. What was written in 1968, and proven accurate, is just as true today:

> Success in the past always becomes enshrined in the present by the over-valuation of the policies and attitudes which accompanied that success . . . with time these attitudes become imbedded in a system of beliefs, traditions, taboos, habits, customs, and inhibitions which constitute the distinctive culture of the firm. They do not adapt to change very easily.[1]

Opportunities lie in the environment and in the future. It is being alert to that environment that brings success in the future.

The Importance of Environmental Scanning

Of course, competition didn't suddenly appear. It always has been there, and there always have been innovative entrepreneurs and leaders with new ideas and the dedication to make them work. Also, the environment didn't suddenly start changing. Change has always existed as well. What has occurred, instead, is a new awareness of the need to proact, rather than react, and the need to constantly scan the environment to perceive what is happening and to anticipate what will occur. Environmental scanning as a systematic approach is a relatively new and essential leadership tool. Its leadership importance can be found in our discussion in Chapter 1: the needs and problems of the future customer, not just today's.

The critical importance of environmental planning lies in recognizing the fact that any organization is a creature of its environment. Its future depends upon the economic, political, technological, regulatory, and sociocultural changes that take place in the

---

[1] *Perspectives on Corporate Strategy,* Boston: The Boston Consulting Group, 1968, p. 93.

environment. It is here that the problems and opportunities of the future exist. Without taking into account the relevant environmental influences, it is difficult for an organization to look very far into the future. Scanning is an organization's method of improving its ability to deal with a rapidly changing environment. None of this would matter, of course, if there wasn't competition. In environmental scanning, all competition must be taken seriously.

First, we have to know who the competition is. It is too easy to identify the wrong competition or to fail to identify the right competition. Because it is so easy, it often occurs. Consider, on a broad scale, a classic example with which we are all familiar—the automobile industry.

The first real threat to this industry in America came from the Germans in the form of the Volkswagen "beetle." Industry leaders laughed at this little aberration on American highways and let it be; they wanted to show the world how tolerant they were as long as it was understood that they still called the shots. When Japanese cars appeared on the scene they laughed some more. Gradually, they laughed less and less, until they started to cry. What General Motors failed to see as a threat, the Japanese saw as an opportunity in an environmentally changing America. Another classic example is the failure of Hollywood in the early years of TV to recognize the opportunity (threat) of the massive environmental change that would occur because of a totally new form of home entertainment.

Macro Competition

How do we define competition? There are actually two forms of competition, macro, or industry generic, and micro, or product class generic. We will discuss the macro here and leave the micro for the next chapter.

In a macro sense, competition is anyone competing for the same consumer's dollar that you seek. This means that any restaurant represents competition to any other restaurant, at least in the same area, and any hotel is competition to any other hotel. We can carry it even further: We can say that any supermarket is competition to any restaurant, or that a new car is competition to a two-week cruise. In a real sense this is true and we must never forget it, as the automobile industry forgot it.

Today, fast-food operators are threatened by the competition they are getting from convenience stores, which took approximately 8 percent of the $50 billion fast-food market in 1986, and plans to take 12 percent by 1990.

Tablecloth restaurant operators are threatened by the competition they are getting from supermarkets (where TV dinners are no longer just "rubber chicken"), take-out services, and catering services. Hotel and motel operators are threatened by the competition they are getting from campers, recreational vehicles, and the hospitality of friends and relatives. One thing about services is that one can readily substitute for another, often at a much lower price. The above examples are environmental changes that are taking place, in which the competition is moving in to fulfill a need.

Why are these other businesses competition? Because they are satisfying the same needs, only with different wants. The customer wants it more cheaply, quickly, easily or conveniently, with less hassle. These are elements of current environmental change. Other industries are solving certain consumer problems that the hospitality industry is not solving.

The hospitality industry is not, of course, totally oblivious to this. McDonald's, Burger King, Wendy's, and others have gone back to drive-up windows. Many tablecloth restaurants have gone into catering. Marriott and Holiday Inns have bought or built in every tier of the hotel industry.

The above cases represent major consumer swings or decisions, the kind that Howard Johnson's totally missed. They represent recognition that the consumer changes and that good leadership foresees and responds to those changes. For those who do not respond, like the automobile industry, such consumer swings become major threats of the environment.

Notice that none of these changes started out as perceived threats, nor did the consumer wake up one morning and say, "I've changed!" The fact is that they all started out as opportunities—forerunners of environmental changes. Someone saw a need or a want that wasn't being fulfilled and thereby saw an opportunity—a niche, if you will—in the marketplace left void by the competition in a changing environment.

It is said that there are three kinds of consumer demand. *Existing demand* is demand for a good or service that is available from one or more source (restaurant food). *Latent demand* describes a need with no suitable product available to satisfy it (fast food before McDonald's). *Incipient demand* is demand for which even the customer does not yet recognize the need (cajun cooking before Paul Prudhomme). All three types of demand, but especially the latter two, affect environmental change. There are opportunities at all three levels of demand—and if you can't think of them first, watch the competition![2]

Types of Environments

Traditionally, hospitality organizations have evaluated themselves almost entirely on the basis of annual financial performance. This is still very largely true today, especially for those with profit driven owners, but there are impending signs of change in those organizations with visionary leadership. These organizations are more sensitive to technological, political, economic, regulatory, and social environments. We will discuss briefly some of the impacts of these environments upon the hospitality industry.

Technological Impacts

It was previously stated that the advent of the atrium lobby was no more than a repackaging of the same product. However, this new technology has brought about tremendous changes in the hotel environment. What it did was to open up many new opportunities for serving the customer, which are found today even in hotels with nonatrium lobbies. Lobby bars, lounges, restaurants, and other hotel services have emerged as a result of this technological advance, and these advances have encompassed the better serving of consumer needs and wants.

---

[2] Environmental changes should not be confused with fads, although there is no reason not to make an opportunity out of a fad. Fads tend to be short lived, whereas environmental changes are major shifts in the environment and society. The point at which a fad ends and a shift or trend begins can be very problematic. Marketing can take advantage of either; the risk lies in making substantial investment in what turns out to be a fad. Cajun cooking may be a fad, but this should not inhibit the opportunity to make a few menu changes that can easily be reversed.

A technological advance that has not served the customer as well is that of computerization. Computerization has been adapted largely to the needs of the operation of hotels and restaurants, rather than to the needs of the consumer. Why? The answer to that question provides an opportunity to discuss the use of environmental scanning.

Computers have certainly been one of the greatest technological advances in the world in recent times. Awareness of this fact in environmental scanning leads to analysis of its uses—that is, leads to asking how this advance can be used to competitive advantage. Until recently, few hospitality firms viewed computerization from this perspective, instead viewing it from the perspective of how it could be used to improve operations.

There is nothing wrong with this. In fact computerization soon became a necessity to many operations, but from a marketing perspective it did not deal with the needs of the consumer. In fact, for one example, initial electronic cash register or computer receipts from both restaurants and hotels, which provided a listing of all charges, were almost undecipherable by the consumer; many still are.

Let's analyze the computer revolution from a marketing standpoint. We could say something like, "Okay, here's this great new technology. How can we use it to make life better for the customer?" One answer would be at the front desk of a hotel. Here, computers improved operational control immensely, but left the customer standing in line just as long, if not longer, to check in or out. Sometimes, in fact, customers were more frustrated than before because now they were just numbers.

In fact, some of the personal touch was lost because clerks were constantly peering into a screen instead of looking at the customer. This phenomenon occurred despite the computer's ability to provide mountains of previous guest experience data upon request; with more ability to service the guest came a worse guest experience.

Things are better today, especially in the check-out area. They will get better in the check-in area, perhaps even with customers checking themselves in, but this has been a long time in coming and has created many angry customers. Thus, when we think about scanning in the technological environment from a marketing viewpoint, we need to think about the impact upon the customer.

Political Impacts

Political impacts upon the hospitality industry vary both with the stability of government and with the interest of government in developing tourism. In the United States, where the government is stable, there has been relatively little interest at the federal level in developing tourism. This places a far greater burden on the hospitality industry to develop international trade.

In other stable governments, such as those of Singapore and Bermuda, the interest in developing tourism has been a tremendous asset to the industry. In Thailand, the government decreed 1987 as the Year of Tourism and put major effort into promoting Thailand as a destination area during "Visit Thailand Year." Even in some unstable governments, such as the current Filipino government, there is a notable government effort to support the hospitality industry.

Political trends can have tremendous impact upon the hospitality industry. These should either be taken advantage of or counteracted. Both the National Restaurant Association and the American Hotel & Motel Association maintain lobbyists in Washington for this reason. State politics can be equally important. For example, political support in New York State provided the impetus for the subsequent "I Love New York" campaign. This campaign had a tremendous effect on tourism in New York and affected even the smallest motel or restaurant operator. Other states, inspired by New York's success, have followed suit. In contrast, in Massachusetts, where political support was never strong and seems to fluctuate with each election, there has never been a truly successful campaign to promote tourism.

The political environment is particularly critical for large and multinational companies in many areas of the world. The recent opening of China to trade has led to many opportunities for both hotel and fast-food companies. In India, on the other hand, there are no McDonald's because of the political and resulting regulatory environment that permits no more than 49 percent ownership by foreign entities. Political trends are also critical at the micro level, and no operator can afford to ignore them. One of the authors who once owned restaurants was heavily involved with the political environment in two very small towns because of matters concerning zoning law and liquor license restrictions.

Political impacts go far beyond this brief discussion and the scope of this chapter, but their importance should not be diminished. We will discuss them again in the chapter on international marketing.

Economic Impacts

There are many obvious economic factors that will affect any business—recessions, inflation, employment levels, gross national product (GNP), money supply, personal income, savings rates, and so forth. Foreign exchange rates, for example, affect international travel. To take a specific case, at the time this was written, it was advantageous for Europeans to travel to the United States, where their currency would buy more. Two years earlier, it was the other way around and Americans flocked to Europe. Also at the time of writing, due to economic factors, hotel rooms and restaurant meals in Mexico, Brazil, and the Philippines were so cheap that it almost cost more to stay home!

All these factors and many more must be analyzed and considered in environmental scanning, even at the local level. In 1987, because of the lowering of oil prices, Houston was suffering economically. This caused more than one restaurant and hotel, including the three-year-old Hyatt Regency West, to file for bankruptcy. At the same time the economy in most of New England was booming and prices had never been higher.

Other economic factors are affecting the hospitality customer. Price resistance is one of them, and is strong in many world areas. In the United States the expense account customer that many hoteliers had classified as "nonprice sensitive" is resisting higher prices. Corporate controllers have forced cutbacks in expense accounts, and organizational travel planner buyers are seeking reduced price contracts with both airlines and hotel companies. Even McDonald's has felt the new austerity.

It isn't just the broad economic environment that must be scanned. At the more micro level it is also the individual customer and the particular product. The automobile industry, especially General Motors, chose to ignore the trend toward price resistance, to its considerable detriment. This industry has continually raised prices, only to find itself unable to sell its product without heavy discounting and give-away programs. Among other things, this strategy has driven customers to keep their cars longer, thus reducing the total sale of automobiles. The same thing has happened with upscale hotel rooms.

Just as some companies choose to ignore these trends, others choose to capitalize on them; this is the best use of environmental scanning. Marriott, although one of those who promoted the upscale concept, found a niche in the market at the $55.00-a-night level and designed Courtyard by Marriott rooms to sell at that price. Quality Inns used the same approach to develop all-suite concepts with rack rates at $40.00 and $55.00 a night. More recently, Quality developed Sleep Inns, a downsized guestroom concept to sell at $25.00 a night.

In France, Groupe Accor, a hotel and foodservice conglomerate, beat Quality to the punch:

> In 1974 Groupe Accor developed a hotel concept called Ibis, "Economy—with style," way ahead of the rest of the industry worldwide. With less than 150 square feet per room (a standard Holiday Inn room is about 300 square feet), the Ibis room sold in France in 1987 for $32.00. With a breakeven point below the industry average, and facilities including remote control cable TV, bathrooms 50 percent larger than those in the average American economy hotel, conference rooms, bar, lounge, sidewalk cafe, swimming pool, and a restaurant to match its market, Ibis in 1988 had over 200 hotels and 20,000 rooms in nine countries outside of France, including the United States. By 1990 over half of Ibis's income is expected to come from outside France. Groupe Accor also operates four-star Sofitels[3] and three-star Novotels worldwide, but that didn't stop them from coming downscale when they scanned what was happening in the economic environment. And they didn't stop there.
>
> In 1985, Groupe Accor set out to design a hotel room to sell for 99 French francs, about U.S. $15 at the time, (for one, two, or three persons). Now called Formule 1, over 40 of these properties now exist and average 94 percent occupancy, with an average stay of three nights. Run by two people and offering only continental breakfast, these properties have a 22 percent labor cost. They also introduce two technological innovations: a self check-in procedure by credit card, eliminating any reception desk (this is not yet fully efficient, and is also being attempted by Quality in its Sleep concept); and self-cleaning toilets and showers (one for every four rooms). Plain, simple, and spartan? Yes, at 85 square feet per room, but all rooms include TV, desk, sink, and heavy insulation for soundproofing. An 80-unit Formule 1 takes two months to build on-site with a construction cost of $15,000 per room. Planned for target markets of students and low-income tourists, the market has also included trainees of local companies and visiting families of local people. An entire new market was created—those who wanted clean, modern, comfortable rooms but couldn't afford what was available, so either didn't travel or used accommodations other than hotel rooms. Yet it wasn't hard to scan the environment to find this market—it was everywhere for anyone who wanted to recognize it.

---

[3] Not always with great success. Opening a Sofitel in Toledo, Ohio, resulted from a poor analysis of the market.

Groupe Accor has been no less active in the foodservice industry, where it has fifteen different restaurant concepts serving different target markets in various contexts and times. This is a company that stays one step ahead of the environment, and it has paid off well for employees, managers, customers, and shareholders.

The economic impacts of the environment, as in the examples just given, are of course the raisons d'être behind the tier structure of the hotel industry today, started by Quality Inns in 1981. This reading of the environment by Robert Hazard at Quality Inns, and others who soon followed, gave these companies a large head start and competitive advantage. Although Marriott, Holiday Corp., Sheraton, and others of the same ilk will survive and do well in these markets, if for no other reason than sheer muscle power, they gave up a long lead through failure to scan the environment and act upon it. Marriott, in fact, having missed this early trend, is making sure that it doesn't happen again. With a large research staff, Marriott now has a good handle on customers' needs—for instance, with the middle tier Courtyard concept, the budget Fairfield Inn concept, and the future development of Residence Inns for elderly care for 1990 and beyond. Marriott has also tightly controlled its approximately 45 franchisees better than most franchisor hotel companies.

The companies mentioned above became followers where they should have been leaders. The same is true in the all-suites market, although Holiday avoided being shut out by buying out two companies that had already started development, and is now the market leader, with Embassy Suites.

Sociocultural Impacts

The hospitality industry is possibly more affected by sociocultural environmental changes than many other industries, if for no other reason than the very nature of its business. Because hospitality is a personal business and of a personal nature to everyone who buys its product, it is extremely vulnerable to social and cultural change. Jain states:

> The ultimate test of a business is its social relevance. This is particularly true in a society where survival needs are already met. It therefore behooves the strategic planner to be familiar with emerging social trends and concerns.
>
> . . . In recent years changes in [people's] values have stimulated massive regulations, deep criticisms, new demands, and challenges of the very foundation on which business rests.
>
> . . . people today seek self-gratification now rather than later. They want the good things in life immediately. They want to lead lives that are continuously improving in quality. There is a growing attitude of cynicism toward authority. . . . People seem to want a more comfortable and less risky life. . . . Profit is no longer universally accepted as the end purpose of business.[4]

All of this foretells significant impact on the hospitality industry. Two-income families, later marriages, higher divorce rates, less moral inhibition, fewer children, female careerism, physical fitness and well-being, escape from monotony and boredom, return to nature, simplification, living for today, hedonism, greater sophistication, and

---

[4] Subhash C. Jain, *Marketing Planning and Strategy.* Cincinnati: South-Western Publishing Co., 1985, pp. 267–270.

many other social changes are trends noted by researchers that have affected the hospitality industry.

The sociocultural environment also includes demographics (e.g., aging of the population), socioeconomics (e.g., increasing dual-income households), cultural values (e.g., the changing role of women), and consumerism (e.g., certain "rights" like full information and safety). Contained in the sociocultural sector is the marketplace itself and the characteristics of society.

While the industry has not been oblivious to these trends, it has been slow in catching up with them. This is hardly surprising, since so many have come so quickly, but the organization that is constantly alert and adapts to these changes will have a lead on the others.

Let's consider some examples. Hotel managements are still trying to figure out exactly what the single woman traveler wants. She says, "I just want to be treated the same way as men." But her wants also include special hangers, full-length mirrors, better lighting around mirrors (never fluorescent!), irons, softer colors, and a myriad of other things that never occurred to men. She now makes up 38 percent of the market, up from 2 percent twenty years ago, and a power with which to be reckoned. All-suite hotels are important to this traveler, but that almost developed by acccident. Electronic door lock security has become critical. And this traveler has become critical to the success of hotels.

In restaurants, sociocultural changes are affecting menus and concepts. Salad and fish are replacing meat and potatoes. "Grazing" restaurants are replacing fine dining; interesting food and presentation is replacing quantity. Local and regional specialties are replacing menus dictated by the home office in some far off place. Decaffeinated coffee, tea, substitutes for sugar and salt, truth-in-menu, and nonsmoking sections are "in." Menus in type size you can read are replacing microscopic script. Wine, Perrier water, and wine coolers are replacing hard liquor. Brighter lighting is replacing darkness. Quiet music is replacing discos. Newer concepts are replacing fern bars.

All of these sociocultural changes and many others too numerous to mention here are impacting upon the hospitality industry. Those who do not react to them will soon be left far behind.

The hospitality industry has often ignored the consumer in a heyday of growth and expansion, which is now over. Consider the baby boomers, a term applied to the product of the high birth rate immediately following World War II, who are now in their forties. They won't tolerate old product or poor service. They are taking many short vacations, they are eating out frequently, they are more sophisticated than their parents, they have more choices, and they are demanding. They want five-star standards in three-star hotels at three-star prices. They want personal service and they don't want excuses for inferior performance. They want added value—a superior product and better service at a reasonable price.

Many of the baby boomers were categorized as "yuppies," young, urban, professionals with high incomes on the fast track, who never worried about tomorrow but spent for today. Now we have the "dinks," double income, no kids, with high discretionary dollars. Other acronyms arise to categorize particular population segments as they develop.

This is the sociocultural environment facing the hospitality industry today and it continues to change. The "can you top this" policies of coupons, twofers, concierge floors, frequent traveler give-aways, pillow mints, and extended bathroom amenities are not going to satiate these social changes or take the place of better price-value relationships. The industry has worked hard at increasing customer expectations; now it has to deliver. Failing operators blame overbuilding, when the real failure may be poor marketing. Michael Diamond, then senior vice-president of marketing at the Boca Raton Hotel and Club in Florida, a five-star resort hotel, stated it this way:

> Whatever happens in the near future, there is no doubt that we're in the middle of some of the toughest competitive and most interesting times in the lodging industry. Marketing will undoubtedly play an even more important role next year, as we try to attract those returning business travelers to our hotels, regardless of type of product that you may have. But I'd like to make one very important point . . . I don't think that value can be given through added amenities . . . a good hotel provides real value through service. . . . whatever their needs, business travelers want those needs met. You can have all the amenities you want, but unless there's a friendly, knowledgeable, caring person to make those amenities work, you have nothing. . . . It's knowing what travelers need and want in a hotel and then providing it that keeps us in the travel business. If we lose sight of that, then we might as well forget the concierge floors, special menus and technologies. We're here to serve our customers' needs.[5]

Compare Diamond's remarks with the action of Hilton International France in early 1988. With occupancy down by more than 20 percentage points, and an awareness that business travelers felt they were not getting value in terms of service and product for the high room rate they were paying, Hilton made a deliberate decision to offer a "value-for-money benefits package" instead of cutting room rates. Full-rate customers were given a bottle of wine, a free drink, a morning newspaper, a telephone call credit, free pressing of one garment, a shoeshine, mineral water, and a buffet for the price of a continental breakfast. Is it surprising that occupancy showed no perceptible increase?

Relevant to this, Michael Leven, President of Days Inn, at the same Congress as Diamond, made the following comment: "After a few years in this business, I now feel that it is very difficult, or at least has been very difficult . . . for the industry to accept change."

Contrast this with the case of Holiday Inns, as reported in the *Wall Street Journal*, which in 1987 faced a system occupancy below 60 percent for the first time in its history.

> In the 1970s, Holiday Inns' effort to become a conglomerate failed, and it lost its edge in the industry it created. Now in the 1980s, this American original looks like any number of other American companies: run by the numbers and running scared from takeovers. . . . A seat-of-the-pants creation in the innocent '50s, it has turned coldly yield-driven in the sharky '80s.
>
> . . . The tale shows a company can fall victim to its own success, how a business that rode up on the demographics and developments of one time can be laid low by those of another.
>
> . . . Mr. Wilson was a throwback entrepreneur who operated . . . with a complete trust in his instincts. "I put into Holiday Inns what I like, and I think the public will like what I like."

---

[5] Presentation at World Hospitality Congress III, March 9, 1987, Boston.

. . . With their wall-to-wall carpeting and Danish furniture, Holiday Inns were on the cutting edge of '50s modern. They were cookie-cutter standard for the masses.
. . . By the mid-1960s, these standard, two-story U-shaped motels were being stamped out at a rate of one every 2½ days, or one room every 30 minutes. Holiday Inns had an 80%-plus occupancy rate.
. . . Holiday was also vulnerable because it hadn't much changed and consumers had. They were more sophisticated and widely traveled. They demanded more—and instead of getting better, many Holiday Inns had gone downhill.
. . . But now it is just another player in the overcrowded industry that Kemmons Wilson created—and it doesn't seem to have a trace of the sure instinct that guided him.
. . . The preoccupation with financial maneuverings is a far cry from the early entrepreneurial days and a source of concern for many, who fear that the good times have forever gone the way of the Great Sign. "Back in the '60s, we felt like we were part of the greatest thing ever," says Earle Jones, a Jackson, Miss. franchisee. "Now it's reached maturity, or maybe overaged."[6]

In truth, the consumer has changed in many ways and will continue to change. Scanning the sociocultural environment is *de rigueur* for any marketer, and no less the hospitality marketer, but it is also *de rigueur* to act upon what you scan, not ignore it, as some parts of the industry seem prone to do.

Even more confounding is the fact that neat, broad, homogeneous groups no longer exist, at least in the American marketplace. Target marketing, as Holiday Corp. learned as it continued to be "something-for-everyone," is the new order in the lodging industry.[7] Consider, for example, the case of the vaunted middle class.

Although many people still identify with the middle class—92% of respondents to a recent survey said they consider themselves among its members—the once tightly-knit group has broken apart.
. . . [The middle class] was marked by a broad consensus of how to live and what constitutes success. That consensus has given way to an increasingly fragmented array of life styles and values.
. . . among businesses, companies have had to learn how to cope with an eroding mass market.
. . . Some sociologists now contend that middle-class values will splinter even further.[8]

The above discussion applies to the United States. The situation is not quite the same in other countries of our experience, but it seems to be not that far behind. The need for scanning of the sociocultural environment is no less elsewhere.

The major difference, in fact, at least as regards the more developed countries, is in the education of the consumer. Consumerism has had no small part in the movement of social change affecting business in the United States. The same is true of marketing itself. Marketing, particularly as evidenced by advertising, has conditioned consumers to greater

---

[6] John Helyar, "The Holiday Inns Trip: A Breeze for Decades, Bumpy Ride in the '80s," *The Wall Street Journal*, February 19, 1987, pp. 1, 23.
[7] Ibid.
[8] John Koten, "Once Homogenous [sic], the Middle Class Now Finds Itself Divided and Uncertain." *The Wall Street Journal*, March 11, 1987, European edition, p. 3.

and greater expectation. When consumers don't get what they expect, or have been promised, they are not hesitant to make an issue out of it.

Consider airlines that changed the conditions of their frequent traveler programs in 1987 so that more mileage than previously stipulated was necessary for certain awards. "For many passengers, changing the rules in mid-game amounts to a breach of contract. A number are fighting back. . . . A class action filed in San Diego on behalf of about 2 million United, American, and TWA passengers asks that the carriers roll back their requirements."[9]

In Europe, where frequent flyer programs are not the significant factor they are in the United States, such an event would be unlikely to happen. High expectations do not exist there as they do in the United States. For example, Europeans seem to spend an inordinate amount of time in queue, in a way that Americans would never accept. They seem to accept it as a way of life. Stores and banks close for one to two hours at lunch; many stores close on Monday; any holiday (like the kind that would cause U.S. stores to have a sale) is an excuse to close. Europeans accept this presumably because it is the only expectation they know. Perhaps, at least in the hospitality industry, they accept this because when the service does come it comes in a different form. For example, you can drink coffee in a café for two hours and you are not perceived as "holding up a table."

There is evidence, however, of forthcoming change. It will be led, in this case, only partially by environmental change. Much of it will come, instead, from astute marketers who find they can beat the competition by offering better services. Others will be forced to follow suit. Eventually, this will result in consumer education and expectation and environmental change.

In Finland there is a population with high discretionary income and time (five weeks of vacation a year, mandated by law). These people have, essentially, two choices of restaurants or hotels in their own country. One is to go to the places and pay the prices designed for the foreign tourist or business traveler. The other is to eat and/or sleep in basic, inexpensive (budget category or less in the United States) restaurants and hotels. In other words, there is a mass middle area that is totally unexploited. Finnish restaurateurs and hoteliers want to change this and will create the competitive environment that will tap this essentially untouched market.

In other countries of the world, including those of a less developed nature, the hospitality industry has long catered to the foreign traveler. In these countries, there is a new awareness of their own domestic traveler. There is also a need by the industry to find other markets, and it is looking inward. In these countries, too, the environment will change.

Regulatory Impact

In April 1987, the Beverly Hills City Council banned smoking in free-standing restaurants. This had an immediate and negative impact upon business. Some restaurants suffered declines in business as high as 45 percent. Customers went to hotel restaurants, where the ban did not apply, or to competitors in neighboring cities where there were no

---

[9] "Frequent Crying: Bonus Rule Changes Rile Flyers," *Time,* European Edition, May 4, 1987, p. 39.

restrictions. According to one article on the subject, one restaurant lost a customer who regularly ordered several $500 bottles of wine for a dinner tab of $4000.[10] Restaurateurs were quick to organize. Due to their lobbying efforts, the ban was revised on July 21 to require that 50 percent of the seating be designated for nonsmokers.

Regulations tell restaurateurs who they can sell liquor to and when. They tell hoteliers what information they must obtain from a guest; in most countries, this includes a passport number, where you came from, where you are going, how and when, and a multitude of other details. Regulations tell us how much tax to add to a bill, what we can say on the menu, how much we can charge for a room, how much we have to pay employees, what to do with our waste, and whom we must accept as a customer. This is not to mention the mass of paperwork required just to comply with city, state, and national government information requirements, or the taxes we have to pay.

In fact, costs and profits can sometimes be affected as much by regulations as by management decisions or customers' preferences. This, of course, is why hospitality professional associations have lobbyists in Washington, as well as in state capitals. In many countries there is no such luxury—if the government decides it wants to do something, it simply does that thing. Wherever regulations come from, including the smallest town's local ordinance, opposing, supporting, or dealing with regulations is a science of its own. We are more concerned here with the marketing implications.

Instead of, or while, fighting proposed regulations that will affect a business, scanning the environment means preparing for the event if and when it materializes. A good example is the somewhat recent and continuing banning of "Happy Hours" in various American states and municipalities. While there has been no definitive evidence, before or after, that this would decrease drunk driving, the climate (or social environment) was ripe for such action. There was, and is, actually no concrete evidence that banning happy hours would hurt business either. Like bathroom amenities in hotels, happy hours had become universal, and they lacked competitive advantage. They also were not the reason that people drank at that time of the day. Astute operators read the writing on the wall and, before the laws were passed, turned to other promotions that did have competitive advantage.

On a national scale, a similar event occurred with the passage of the 1986 tax law allowing only 80 percent of meal expenses as a business deduction. Many restaurant operators, especially those that count heavily on the expense account customer, seemed to go into panic. After all, who else could afford to pay the exorbitant prices they were charging?

More astute operators quietly went about their business, adjusted their menus, and provided other inducements. Some, wisely, began to target other market segments that they had previously ignored.

Regulatory impacts are bound to be with us for a long time to come. There is no way that they can be successfully ignored. The marketer's task is to be aware of them, prepare for them, and develop a contingency plan before they occur. Some simply have to be lived with. We have no idea how one would get back a customer who buys $500 bottles of wine. Perhaps, however, now that nonsmokers outnumber smokers, Beverly Hills restau-

---

[10] "Hands Up and Butts Out! Beverly Hills Outlaws Smoking in Restaurants," *Time*, European edition, April 27, 1987, p. 46.

rateurs could have let the smokers go across the city lines and targeted the nonsmokers on the other side to come the other way. After all, marketing is nothing more than serving the right market in the right way.

Doing Environmental Scanning[11]

Figure 4-1 demonstrates the flow of environmental scanning information to the development of strategy and marketing planning. The steps are discussed below.

Watch for Broad Trends   Examples of this are the 1980s American change in social mores regarding drinking, later marriages, two-income families, increased travel, diet consciousness, and "grazing" eating habits. Even locally, there may be broad trends occurring. For example, as more and more New Yorkers bought second homes in Vermont, the demand for better restaurants there increased dramatically.

Determine Relevant Trends   Not everything that happens in the environment is relevant, nor can an organization adapt to everything that is relevant. The problem is determining what is relevant and what is irrelevant. Certainly, there are no hard and fast rules. Creativity, imagination, and farsightedness play an important role in this process. Some people are better at this than others and these people should be singled out. Another method is to circulate a short memo to key people (these could very well include line employees who are close to the action) and ask for reactions.

Analyze the Impact   Assuming relevance, what is the possible impact of the change, both sooner and later? Analyze it in terms of product, price, target market, competition, cost, employee attitude, and other variables that could be affected. Does it present a threat or an opportunity? If it is a threat, can it be turned into an opportunity (such as no smoking in Beverly Hills)? Again, get reactions from key people and from line employees where appropriate. At the same time, beware of those who automatically resist change and will try to minimize any impact. Two examples of very noticeable trends that were virtually ignored for years by many hoteliers were the increase of single women travelers, and the price sensitivity to increasing rack rates. Substantial competitive advantage was gained by those who acted early on these trends; such as those who moved into the middle tier market.

Forecast Direction   This is a difficult stage. One method is to use people to develop scenarios. For example, when the forthcoming increase in women travelers became apparent ten years ago, companies might have brought together groups of its women employees to do this. While that does not constitute scientific research, it is a start. The general manager or marketing director of an individual hotel could do the same, and so too could the manager of a restaurant. Another method is to use an outside consultant unconstrained by past experiences and personal biases.

---

[11] This section borrows from Jain, *Marketing Planning and Strategy,* pp. 277–280, 289, 292, and is used with permission.

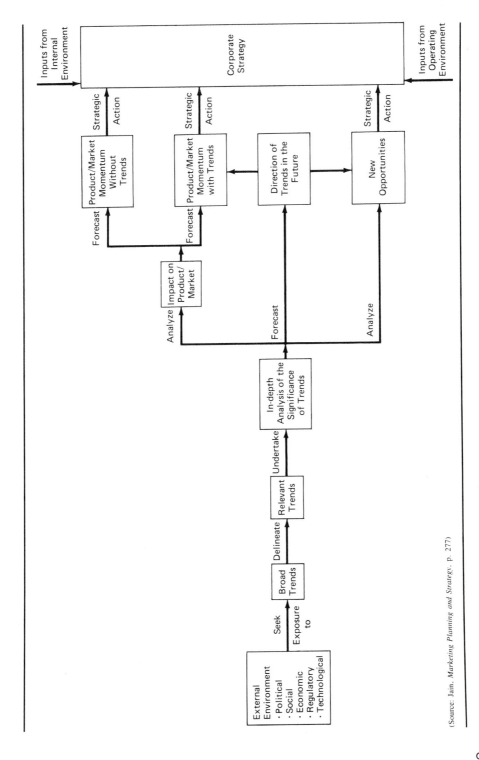

(Source: Jain. *Marketing Planning and Strategy*, p. 277)

FIGURE 4-1   Linking environmental scanning to corporate strategy

Intuitive reasoning by one person alone shoud not be used. That person's view may be too narrow—for example, one might see the marketing impact but not the financial implications, or vice versa. Alternatively, one's impact may be clouded by one's own set of values, beliefs, experiences, likes, and dislikes. Playing off opposites may not lead to consensus, but it can certainly help in getting all viewpoints. This helps particularly when management may perceive a trend but can't conceive of its relationship or impact. Serious research is another way to develop forecasting accuracy.

Assess Opportunity   As with the 1986 tax act, the banning of happy hours, the raising of drinking ages, and the banning of smoking, it is too easy to look at the bad side of things. Look too for the opportunities. Remember that "necessity is the mother of invention."

Relate the Outcome   Relate the outcome of the above five steps to the marketing strategy or marketing plan, now, next year, and five years from now. Are changes needed? If so, what are the full implications?

Environmental scanning is too important to any organization to be approached haphazardly. A systematic method is needed to fully utilize this critical marketing tool.

Environmental Scanning at Holiday Inns[12]

We conclude this chapter with an actual case situation that illustrates environmental scanning for strategic purposes at the corporate level. The assessment and forecasting were done by Holiday Inns in 1978. What is shown here is the end result and some of the conclusions that were drawn. As hindsight is always better than foresight, and we now have a number of years of hindsight to evaluate this scan, we leave it to the reader to consider the aspects and conclusions in the case, as well as the subsequent actions and fortunes of Holiday Inns (now called Holiday Corp.).

The reader should also consider the impact of this scanning process at the Holiday Inn unit level: If you were the marketing director of a Holiday Inn in 1978, what effect might this scan have had on your marketing strategies and plans?

Environmental Assessment

Holiday Inns in 1978 was composed of six major divisions, as shown in the accompanying tables. Each division was assessed in terms of "remote environment factors" (Table 4-1) and "task environment factors" (Table 4-2). In the tables and to aid in the analysis, a scale from +10 to −10 is used to identify the degree to which each environmental factor represents an opportunity or threat in the business's environment.

Comparing the remote environments in Table 4-1, Holiday Inns' most favorable opportunities appear in the three hospitality related businesses: hotels, restaurants, and casinos. Social factors in the remote environment are strongly favorable for all three

---

[12] This section is based on the work by John A. Pearce II and Richard B. Robinson, Jr., *Strategic Management: Strategy Formulation and Implementation*, Homewood, IL: Richard D. Irwin, 1982, pp. 122–126, 151–154, and is used with the authors' permission.

businesses. The remote environment is moderately opportunistic relative to the steamship operation, but inconsequential for the products group. The major remote environment threats appear in relation to the Trailway bus operation.

The most opportunistic task environments shown in Table 4-2 are found with the hotel and casino groups. The similarity of their competitive advantages (existing or potential) and favorable opportunities suggest strong synergy between the two groups from a corporate perspective. The task environment of freestanding restaurants appears favorable, with several dimensions suggesting limited but clearly exploitable opportunities. Delta Steamship encounters selectively favorable opportunities, while Trailways' task environment presents several formidable threats.

Together, the remote and task environment analyses identify factors that suggest that the greatest opportunities exist in hospitality-related businesses, and the most pressing threats face the Trailway bus operation.

Environmental Forecasting

Holiday Inns used several forecasting techniques to project changes in its remote and task environments of major importance to future strategic position. The greatest emphasis is on hospitality-related factors, which are discussed here. The primary variables on which the company places forecasting emphasis are customer, social, technological, and competition. Table 4-3 summarizes some of the forecasting techniques in terms of what they focus on relative to these key environmental factors.

Using trend analysis, surveys, and judgmental scenarios, Holiday Inns made the following forecasts about changing customer profiles and social characteristics.

1. Fewer and later marriages mean that Holiday Inn's customer base has broadened to include a great concentration of single people, couples, and business people with greater freedom to travel.
2. The demographic characteristics of a typical hotel, restaurant, and casino guest are virtually identical: age 24–49, income over $20,000, with a preference for reliable and quality service instead of the lowest price.
3. In three out of four instances, Holiday Inn guests were male, but the trend toward more women travelers is steadily growing.
4. The movement of the baby-boom generation through the prime traveling age (25–45) over the next twenty years foretells unprecedented growth opportunity in the hospitality business.
5. Futurists predict that by the end of the century, as larger numbers of people pursue business and travel, the travel industry will have become the world's largest industry.

Using similar techniques regarding competition and technology, Holiday Inns made the following forecasts.

1. Holiday Inn hotels will remain the brand preference of over one-third of the traveling public through the 1980s.
2. Hospitality facilities located in multiuser locations will dominate industry growth and development in the 1980s.

TABLE 4-1   Assessment of Remote Environment Factors

Business	Economy	Political	Social	Technology
Hotels	Reduced vacation travel during recessions/energy costs (−4)	Legal challenges to franchise agreement/political stability of international locations (−2)	Increasing leisure time/older population/single travelers and smaller families/baby boom now 25–35 years old (+8)	Electronic and computer technology in reservation and control systems/satellite communication/laborsaving technologies (+6)
Products group	Reduced demand during recession (−2)	? (0)	Changing preferences in furnishings (+3)	Laborsaving technology/obsolescence of current equipment lines (+1)
Trailways	Less travel during recession but bus is a low-priced alternative energy cost (+1)	Safety regulations/no government ownership of terminals/deregulation of airline industry (−5)	All of the factors in above hotel block applicable here, though considerably less beneficial (−2)	Laborsaving and cost-saving technology only minimal benefits, other transportation areas more (−3)

100

Delta Steamship	Recession can hurt exports and imports/ energy costs (−3)	Emergence of Third World markets/U.S. subsidies of U.S.-flag carriers and low-interest loans (+5)	Increasing concern for U.S. international trade effectiveness (+1)	Laborsaving (LASH) technologies and energy-saving technologies (+3)
Freestanding restaurants	Recession doesn't hurt family restaurant/ energy costs (+3)	Legal challenges to franchising (−1)	Increasing pattern of eating out/baby boom now 25–35/number of single-member households rising (+8)	Laborsaving and energy-saving improvements/ food preparation technology (+4)
Casino gaming	Recessionary impact on leisure travel/energy costs (−2)	Regulation of casino gambling/limited legal gaming market (−2)	All the factors mentioned in the hotel block above/increasing social acceptance of gaming (+8)	Similar to hotel block though with less impact (+3)

Source: John A. Pearce II and Richard B. Robinson, Jr., *Strategic Management: Strategy Formulation and Implementation*, Homewood, IL: Richard D. Irwin, 1982. p. 123. Reprinted by permission of the authors. All rights reserved.

TABLE 4-2 Assessment of Task Environment Factors

Business	Competition	Customers	Labor	Creditors	Suppliers
Hotel group	Substantial increase in the number of budget-chain competitors/no immediate threat to HI's leadership position, but gap is narrowing, especially with budget-conscious traveler (+5)	1 out of 6 American travelers stayed at HIs in 1978/ research shows HI to be the preference of 40 percent of traveling public—high but declining since 1975/ages 24–49 with +$20,000 incomes most frequent guest/increasing number of single travelers and women travelers (25 percent in 1979)/steady demand for HI franchises with over 60 percent of new franchise locations sought by current franchises (+6)	Adequate labor supply although HI's labor-sensitive operating margins hurt by minimum wage increases (+2)	Strong capital structure, undervalued real estate and leadership position make credit readily available (+5)	Gasoline cost for customers is rising, which begins to curtail travel (−2)

Products group	Major competition outside the HI-customer system/competitors don't operate in captive mode which can allow more freedom/some competitors more price competitive on standardized items (−2)	Large captive market via HI system/limited competitive experience outside this captive market/franchises' resistance to being required to buy through product group businesses certain standardized items (+3)	Decreasing labor intensity via mechanization (+2)	Because of low-profit margins and captive design must seek capital resources primarily within corporate structure (−1)	Available through cost-escalating raw materials (0)
Trailways	Powerful competition from Greyhound on price, facilities, size, etc./increasing competition from other transportation sectors like airlines, trains, and package delivery services/intensive price-cost squeeze (−6)	Customer profile quite different from typical HI guest, especially in income/limited gains in passenger miles since 1975/ no strong customer loyalty (−2)	Labor cost rising though some laborsaving technology improvements (−1)	Weak capital structure in highly competitive industry lessens available credit (−2)	Energy costs, especially fuel, rising significantly (−3)

(continued)

TABLE 4-2 (continued)

Business	Competition	Customers	Labor	Creditors	Suppliers
Delta Steamship	Stiff competition from foreign cargo vessels in all routes/LASH technology improving relative position/major U.S.-flag carrier (+2)	Primarily agriculture and manufacturing importers and exporters at both ends of route structure/strong in Gulf ports area (+2)	Severely dependent on independent longshore workers/decreasing labor intensity via LASH (technology) (−2)	Legislation access to U.S. government low-interest loans and cost subsidies (+5)	Energy costs, especially fuel, rising significantly (−3)
Freestanding restaurants	Stiff competition from several nationwide chains, but Perkins' position in northern U.S. rather strong/expanding primary demand which negates, to some extent, competitive impact/opportunities for additional acquisition (+1)	Customers profile quite similar to typical HI guest/family-oriented image/good brand identity in current geographic locations/trend of increased outside dining and more single households quite favorable/substantial franchise network and interest (+5)	Nonskilled labor positions/labor intensive/adequate supply though profit margins sensitive to minimum wage (+1)	Adequate capital structure and operating history for outside credit/HI corporate resources (+2)	Rising energy costs in operating units and in food products (−2)

| Casino gaming | Growing competition in each of the four legalized gambling markets in U.S./but no dominant competitor overall/rapidly growing primary demand related to increased leisure time and aging population (+5) | Customer profile very similar to typical HI guest/HI name, image, and reputation should prove quite beneficial/changing population demographics—baby boom age, single households, increasing leisure time—are strongly favorable (+8) | Temporary labor shortages but benefit by HI link in hotel, food, and lodging side/rising labor costs (−2) | Impressive profit potential but too early to tell/HI corporate resources (+1) | Fuel-sensitive business and energy-intensive facilities (−3) |

Source: John A. Pearce II and Richard B. Robinson, Jr., *Strategic Management*, p. 124–125.

TABLE 4-3   Environmental Forecasting

Main Environmental Factors	Forecasting Techniques		
	Trend Analysis	Surveys	Judgment/Scenarios
Customers	Changing demographic profile Specific HI guest characteristics Historical occupancy rate cycles	Changing consumer preferences Perceptions and brand recognition of HI	Futuristic travel patterns and destination areas
Social	Baby-boom generation Household composition Women's changing role Use of leisure time	(little use)	Worldwide status of the travel industry
Technology	Energy-saving technology, especially in automobiles and hotel operation Gas prices and impact on vacation travel	(little use)	Future travel modes Computer usage in property management Communication, especially satellite, developments
Competition	Size and growth of competitors Location emphasis of key price/value available from competition	Level of consumer name recognition Consumer image and brand preference	Which competitors represent key threats to aspects of HI operations

Source: Pearce and Robinson, *Strategic Management,* p. 152.

3. Even at $2 a gallon, highway driving habits will not change appreciably.
4. About 80 percent of U.S. adults approve of gambling and 60 percent participate in some form. Gaming is fast becoming a national pastime and is viewed by the public as a leisure activity.
5. Most countries served by Delta (Steamship) are undergoing continued development and industrial expansion. This thrust provides a market for imports of high-value goods—of which U.S. industry is a major supplier.

Holiday Inn executives summed up their various forecasts relative to the hospitality core of the company's business for the 1980s with the following statement.

The decade of the 1980s offers excellent potential for the hospitality industry. Business analysts see continued growth for travel through the end of the century.

While temporary gasoline shortages have been a short-term negative factor in our operations twice in the past six years, we remain quite optimistic about gas availability for our customers. We expect occasional brief shortages, but by and large, we believe that adequate supplies will be available.

. . . Our research tells us that our customers will continue to use their automobiles for inter-city travel and vacations. Thus, we believe we are strongly positioned for the coming decade, especially as demand for our facilities will continue to outgrow supply.

Our research tells us that the hospitality business is a good business, and will remain so for as far as we can see. We look forward to the future and see continued growth, development, and profitability.

Summary

Environmental scanning has become increasingly relevant for all businesses in the fast-moving and fast-changing world of recent years. Without it, a company is relegated to being able only to react to what happens in the environment. The basis of hospitality marketing, which was presented in the first three chapters of this book, and the application of hospitality marketing, which will be presented in the remainder of the book, lie in what is happening in the environment.

Environmental scanning looks at the big picture, the broad view, and the long range. Marketing builds on this by approaching it in an increasingly narrower perspective, resting ultimately on the individual consumer.

Environmental scanning, both in textbooks and the real world, has been largely constrained to the corporate level and to strategic planning. By definition, environmental scanning presents a macro view. We believe, however, that this macro view can be given a micro perspective. In other words, we believe that every individual or unit operator, as well as corporate and higher-level management, must be conscious of and continuously analyzing the environment, and forecasting its impact upon each unit operation. The hospitality industry today is too broad-based, too diversified, and too much operated in multiple micro environments to ignore this technique at any level.

It also follows that even if environmental scanning is done only strategically at the corporate level, it needs input from the grassroots level, where the action is that affects the individual units. In a simple example, let's say that there was a trend for business travelers to want king-size beds, or for restaurant patrons to ask for seaweed salad. These trends, and others like them, would show up at the unit level long before corporate level scanners would be able to pick them up from other sources.

More specifically, resistance to hotel room prices started ten years ago at the local level. In many cases, the corporate level chose to ignore this trend until it became a tidal wave, thus spawning a whole new layer of competition. Trends, in fact, never start at the macro level, but at the micro level. In an industry like hospitality, you can't stay too close to the customer. We continue this discussion in Chapter 5 at a more micro level.

DISCUSSION QUESTIONS

1. Consider a local restaurant or hotel. What is its competition in a macro sense? Explain. How is it affected by the three types of consumer demand?

2. Consider some current fads in eating. How long will they last? Will they turn into trends? Why/why not? If you were a restaurateur, how would you capitalize on them? What social issues have changed *your* restaurant purchase habits?

3. It was stated in the chapter that the technological advance of computers "has not served the customer as well." Do you agree or disagree? Discuss. How might computers serve customers better in the future?

4. Political impacts on the hospitality business environment can be enormous. Discuss some present potential impacts.

5. In the early 1980s it was not unusual to see headlines such as "Coming—the $300 hotel room." Although you can certainly find them, $300 rooms have not become standard. What happened? Discuss.

6. Discuss Holiday Inns environmental scanning in 1978 and where they are today. Why was Groupe Accor so successful with its Ibis and Formule1 concepts?

CHAPTER 5
Opportunities, Threats, and Competitive Analysis

In marketing, opportunity and competitive analysis go hand in hand. This is so because opportunity means being where the competition isn't, or being where the competition is weak. Someone once said that marketing opportunity is "the niche that cries out to be filled." That statement may be a little melodramatic but it does make the point. The only problem is that most opportunities don't cry out; in fact, they can be very well hidden. Perhaps it would be better to say "the niche that cries out to be found."

There are other opportunities that don't necessarily involve competitive weakness. These are the ones right under our noses, connected with improving our own product and making our customers' lives easier. These opportunities usually come under the rubric of new product development or "upselling"—selling more to the same customers. Or, they may simply involve policy or procedure changes. Obviously there is some overlap, but in this chapter we will be more concerned with market opportunities, those that exist in the marketplace. The word *market* is used here to connote customers, or groups of customers, who represent a market for the product—that is, customers who will buy and use the product. *Marketplace* means wherever the customers are who will have buying power and access to the product.

There are three broad areas that more or less fit into the category of tools that can be used to find marketplace opportunities. These are identifying existing consumer problems, conducting marketing research, and carrying out market feasibility studies. It is obvious that these areas overlap one another and that they all involve competitive analysis. We will first discuss what market opportunities are, as well as their counterparts, market threats. We will then look at competitive analysis, and then see how the three tool areas fit into the total scheme of things.

Market Opportunities and Threats

Let us begin with a basic premise that never hurts repeating: Finding marketing opportunities means finding customers, creating customers, and keeping customers. By contrast, many financial opportunities begin with the "chance to make a lot of money." Many defunct multimillion dollar projects have been based on that premise, and many supposedly great ideas have failed for lack of customers. A good example is Edwin Land's Polaroid instant movie camera, discussed in Chapter 1; another is Ford's Edsel car, a product that totally bombed and is sometimes referred to as the "marketing mistake of the century"; still another is DuPont's Corfam, a substitute for leather that the market was unwilling to accept for various reasons. Many readers will not recall these products, but they are classic cases and are discussed in many marketing textbooks.

In the restaurant area, especially in the franchise boom years of the 1960s, there were also many failures due to the introduction of products for which the marketplace wasn't ready or had no need. One of these was a concept called Sizzlebörd. Sizzlebörd franchisees sold hot open-faced sandwiches patterned after the Scandinavian smörrebörd. The market wasn't ready and didn't adapt, and the concept disappeared in less than three years. The gourmet hamburger concept, of more recent times, appears to fall into the same category although it had a strong start and launched strong chains, such as Whattaburger and Fuddruckers, both of which were forced to retrench within ten years.

Even Ray Kroc and McDonald's have introduced products that the market wouldn't buy. In fact, Kroc failed at almost every new product he personally devised, for instance, chicken pot pies. Just about every successful new product that McDonald's has introduced, from Egg McMuffin to McD.L.T., has come from the entrepreneurial franchisees who are closest to the customer and are serving customers wants.

On the flip side, Kroc's original and continued concept remains a classic case of seized market opportunity. Kroc saw families moving to the suburbs, with discretionary income and children, having a real hassle in finding a place to eat that was quick, clean, and dependable. As noted in Chapter 1, Howard Johnson (the founder) saw an opportunity in nationwide consistent restaurants; Kemmons Wilson saw the same thing with motels for Holiday Inns. More currently, founders of suite hotel and budget motel chains saw opportunities in changing needs in the lodging market. Total conference center hotels are an opportunity that grew out of companies' dissatisfaction with what they were being offered at standard hotels. All of these opportunities occurred in areas where the competition was weak or nonexistent, and where there was a consumer problem.

New markets come from only three places: They are "stolen" from the competition, they are created, or they are cannibalized, that is, we take them from ourselves. If they come from the competition, it means that we have to do something better than the competition, or we have to do something the competition isn't doing at all. If new markets are created it means that we have found a latent or incipient need that either wasn't recognized or wasn't being fulfilled. An example of creating a new market is McDonald's introduction of breakfast, which turned out to fill a real need that no one was really sure was there. In most of these cases, however, of the stolen customer or the created customer, the window of opportunity closes very quickly.

Stolen customers must be convinced to make the change—that is, they must get everything they were promised, or they will not stay stolen. Furthermore, competition will act quickly to get them back. Created customers, on the other hand, will soon be offered a myriad of similar products and/or services, sometimes at lower prices. The answer to this problem is to be continuously seeking new opportunities, since successes are usually short term. Probably nowhere is this point better exemplified today than in the computer industry, both hardware and software, but the hospitality industry is not far behind.

McDonald's has proven this point over and over. On the other hand, Hyatt Hotels stole customers when they introduced the modern hotel atrium lobby twenty years ago (a concept borrowed by architect John Portman from the Denver Brown Palace Hotel built at the turn of the century) and, as we showed in Chapter 1, are still resting on these laurels to some extent. Marriott, which is a copier in this case, emphasizes their atrium lobby hotel in Atlanta, as also shown in Chapter 1. In fact, atrium lobbies are old hat by now and that opportunity has passed, at least in major cities where there may be half a dozen or more.

In cannibalizing we steal from ourselves. We get customers to buy something instead of what they were previously buying. When Marriott developed its Courtyard by Marriott concept (an opportunity well filled), a major concern was that these hotels might draw away too many regular Marriott customers from higher-priced properties.

The other side of opportunity is threat. Competition is only one threat in the environment, but a powerful one. Competitive threats mean that the enemy did, or will, get there first, or will soon follow. Threats also come from environmental changes. We hope to be able to react quickly enough to turn the threat into an opportunity, but this may not be possible; we may just be too late.

As we saw in the case of Howard Johnson's, that company had not only new opportunities but also a head start. Others saw the opportunities when Howard Johnson's did not. Thus, the missed opportunity of Howard Johnson's turned out to be a threat when used against them, and they still failed to react until it was too late.

When another company can throw millions of dollars into an opportunity and you cannot, that is a threat of a different color. In this discussion, however, we will consider threats and opportunities as the same, recognizing that this may not always be the case. In a marketing sense, however, it probably is. The business world is full of Davids toppling Goliaths by virtue of sheer good marketing. Just look at how scared IBM became when PC clones devastated their market, forcing the company to go back to the drawing board to develop a new version of the PC.

Now that we understand what opportunities are and where markets come from, let us see how we can go about conducting competitive analysis in order to find opportunities (and diminish threats).

Competitive Analysis

In marketing, competition is the enemy. To outmaneuver the enemy we have to know its strengths and weaknesses, what it does and doesn't do well, who its customers are, why they go there, and what they do when they get there. We would also like to know something about customer loyalty, dissatisfaction, what needs and wants are not being fulfilled, and what problems customers are having. This calls for a great deal of marketing intelligence.

Competitive analysis is not limited to investigating bricks and mortar, number and size of meeting rooms, decor, what grade beef is bought, what size drink is poured, or what prices are charged. That would amount to a product orientation, and we don't want to be any more product-oriented in analyzing the competition than we do in analyzing ourselves. Of course, if the competition itself is product-oriented, we should know that as well. It may mean that we can outflank them, pull some end runs, or even throw the "long bomb."

If, on the other hand, the competition is marketing-oriented, how marketing-oriented are they? Are they creative, do they adapt quickly, will they accept short-term losses for long-term gains, do they worry about the customer, and how soon will they copy or react to what we do (or, how short-lived will any advantage we gain be)? In other words, we have to get to know the competition. Of course, we have to know something about their facilities, product (including service), and resources, but here's a basic truism that is often ignored: The competition is not simply other hotels and restaurants; it is the people who manage and operate those hotels and restaurants. Understanding these people means understanding the competition.

First, once again, we have to know who the competition is. In Chapter 4 we discussed General Motors' response to the Volkswagen Beetle and how the Japanese saw an opportunity. There is another lesson to be learned from that story. Unlike General Motors, Toyota, when it wanted to learn what Americans preferred in a small, imported car, didn't ask the people who owned Chevrolets and Pontiacs: They asked the owners of Volkswagens what they liked or disliked about the Beetle. They looked for the "niche crying out to be found"! They identified the true competition and then addressed consumers' problems.

Micro Competition

In Chapter 4 we discussed macro competition. The other form of competition is at the micro level. At this level we define competition as any business that is competing for the same customers in the same product class—in other words, a business that is a direct competitor with a similar product in a similar context. By this definition, the gourmet restaurant does not compete with fast-food restaurants, and upscale hotels do not compete with budget motels.

Caution is necessary to avoid overgeneralizing these contrasts. As mentioned above, an alternative in a different product class can become a competitor if the one product class is not fulfilling the need. In other words, we would not normally construe a three-star hotel to be a direct competitor of a five-star hotel. The situation changes, however, if the five-star hotel prices itself out of the market and consumers turn to lower-priced alternatives.

In fact, this is exactly what has happened in the hotel industry in recent years, yet it is not uncommon to hear a GM or a corporate officer say, "What? Them? They're no competition!" We once heard a GM remark about a competitor, with great disdain,

"They're not even in our class; they take airline crews!" A year later he was out soliciting airlines. Conversely, if the top end of the market overbuilds, the result may be price cutting with rates that compete in the lower end of the market. Perhaps the toughest part of competitive analysis is recognizing the realities of it.

Conversely, for marketing planning at a given time, a similar failing may be to consider as competition properties that are actually in different product classes. This failing can lead to major strategic errors. If the operator of a French restaurant says his competition is the Red Lobster across the street, he is probably basing his statement on geographic proximity rather than product class or customer needs, wants, and demand. Let us analyze this point in some detail to be certain that it is clear.

The people who eat at the French restaurant may also eat at the Red Lobster—they may even eat there more often, but this does not make the two restaurants direct competitors. The reason is that customers are fulfilling different needs and wants at the two restaurants. Except in rare cases, one of these restaurants would not be an alternative to the other.

Suppose these are the only two restaurants within 100 miles. Does the situation change? If the Red Lobster disappeared, would patronage increase at the French restaurant? Probably very little. Those times that people would have gone to the Red Lobster they will now stay home.

Suppose, however, that the Red Lobster is doing volume business and the French restaurant is doing zilch. Now does the situation change? Yes, but. . . . The *but* is not that the Red Lobster is the competition; it is that the French restaurant, assuming it is a good operation, has misjudged the market and is not catering to the needs and wants of the marketplace. If the Red Lobster now disappeared, the French restaurant would still do zilch—that is, it is not a direct competitor. The same would be true in the case of a Hyatt across the street from a Days Inn. These examples assume prices consistent with the product, but even at the same price level there would be some noncompetitive separation of needs and wants.

Choosing the Right Competition

Choosing the right competition is very critical in competitive analysis because it has tremendous bearing on the marketing strategy and tactics of any hospitality operation. Choosing the "wrong" competition is a frequently made error in hospitality marketing, which can be illustrated with three actual examples.

In the first example, management of the only French restaurant in a small city was unhappy with the volume they were doing.

> They were at a loss to explain this, since they received very favorable customer comments. In fact, cursory research showed that they were overwhelmingly rated the best restaurant in the city in terms of food, service, and atmosphere. In final desperation, after scouting all the "competition," management decided to "do as the Romans do." They put in a prime rib buffet, added steaks and chops to the menu, and did various other things that other restaurants were doing. A little less than a year later business had fallen to the point where ownership sold out.

What had happened, of course, was two things. First, the new menu had alienated the old clientele. Second, the restaurant had failed to attract a new clientele that still perceived them as an expensive French restaurant. The failing was to not recognize that their major competition was not in the same city; the competition was in adjoining cities where this restaurant lacked awareness. The appropriate strategy would have been to develop the strong niche they had and pull in customers from out of town who would have been willing to go a distance for that kind of food and service.

The second case is one of a 300-room resort hotel in a remote seasonal, oceanside location.

> In an attempt to build the off-season business, management did extensive refurbishing and remodeling so as to have extensive conference facilities. It was the only hotel in the area with the capacity and the facilities to draw groups of substantial size.
>
> In a market analysis, two large cities 75 and 175 miles away were designated as the markets. The only lodging properties within 25 miles, a Holiday Inn, a Sheraton franchise, and three or four individual properties, were designated as the competition. Marketing efforts were aimed to compete with these properties.

The effort to build off-season business failed. Once again, management failed to recognize that the customers who went to the "competition" were not the same ones or in the same market segment as the ones the property was trying to attract. The competition in this case was hundreds of miles away in similar properties that drew from diverse markets for conference and meetings business.

The third example occurs in a hotel called Rama Gardens in Bangkok.

> This hotel was located near the airport, by itself but off a very busy highway with limited exits and divided lanes going in each direction—in other words, it was a considerable nuisance for hotel guests to go elsewhere to eat. Many of the guests, in fact, had no cars because they were airline crews or people in transit from the airport. These guests were construed as a captive market with minimal, if any, competition for their foodservice patronage. The hotel had a very fine dining room with elegant service and an American-continental menu including steak, lobster, shrimp, and so forth. Prime rib was rolled out on a very expensive silver gueridon.
>
> On a good night this restaurant did about a dozen covers. Management decided to cut prices, which were quite high, and run special promotions to increase business. The effort failed.
>
> Why? In the first place, airline crews have per diem (a limited amount per day) food allowances and rarely eat in restaurants of this kind. In the second place, guests at this hotel were largely Thai or at least Asian. These people rarely include steaks, prime rib, or Continental dishes in their eating-out choices, especially when they are in transit. Thus, guests either ate in the coffee shop (cannibalization) or "found" the competition. Management completely failed to analyze the needs and wants of its market segments and, by believing it had no competition, lost an excellent opportunity to do foodservice business.

This example is not atypical of managements that, in designing their foodservice outlets, concentrate on the concept rather than the customer and the competition. We call this "conceptitis," a disease prevalent in the industry. One former food and beverage vice-president of a hotel chain was noted for his public statements that he developed hotel restaurants not just for hotel guests but for a clientele outside the hotel. This is a fine idea, as Jim Nassikas has proven at The Stanford Court Hotel in San Francisco, provided the market is there, provided you are not at the same time losing all your hotel customers, and provided the concept fits the needs of the designated market that the competition is not filling. More than one "great" concept designed by this vice-president did poorly because these rules were violated. The basis of this violation was twofold: conceptitis emphasizes the concept as opposed to either the customer or the competition.

This type of practice is so rampant that we are going to push the point one step further. Too many hotel food and beverage (F&B) outlet decisions are made when marketers are not part of the decision process, or the decision doesn't have a marketing foundation. Typically, this is a joint decision of the architect, sometimes the developer, the food and beverage executive, and other corporate officers. Successful outlets derive from the customer and the competitive analysis, and not from the concept alone, which is only the tactic that fulfills the strategy. Managing food and beverage outlets is the job of the food and beverage department; developing successful new concepts requires a marketing orientation and knowledge of the marketplace.

With all the possible alternatives, then, who is the right competition? Unfortunately, there is no simple answer to that question. The answer requires thorough analysis of any given situation. We can suggest, however, two launching points.

First, deliberately choose whom you want to, and can, compete against. Rarely do markets simply appear out of nowhere; most of the time you have to steal them. As Michael Porter has pointed out in his extensive writings on competition, choosing whom you want to compete against is one of the first decisions that has to be made in developing a product or business.[1]

Second, ask your customers where they would be if they weren't at your property. Why? Or, if you're developing a new product, research the market. Where does your target market go now? Why? The answers to these questions will tell you, at least, who the market perceives as your competition. The answers will also tell you what you have to compete against in terms of attributes and services. If the answers from the market are different from the properties you have chosen to compete against, it is clear that your perception differs from the markets. It may be necessary to rethink your competitive strategy.

We can illustrate these two points with further reference to hotel F&B outlets. Astute marketers will first determine who they want as customers and what their needs and wants are. (This includes in-house customers and the local market.) Then they will ask where these customers go now, or will go. Next, they will do a thorough analysis of this competition. Then they will go to the architect, the F&B director, and other involved parties and say, "This is what we need to do to keep/steal these customers." Then, and only then, should concept development begin because you have now chosen whom you will compete against. You have also determined the weapons you need to compete.

---

[1] See, for example, Michael E. Porter, *Competitive Strategy: Techniques for Analyzing Industries and Competitors*, New York: Free Press, 1980.

Competitive Intensity

The competitive intensity in a marketplace is the fierceness with which competing companies do battle with each other. It is an important measurement in competitive analysis because the level of intensity will often dictate the way a firm does business. This has been obvious in the computer industry, in the so-called cola wars, and in the battle of the hamburgers. In general, today, competitive intensity is very high in the hospitality industry. This can lead to less-than-wise decisions to gain competitive advantage. Jain puts it as follows:

> The degree of competition in a market depends on the moves and countermoves of the various firms that are active in the market. Usually it starts with one firm trying to achieve a favorable position by pursuing appropriate strategies [or tactics]. Since what is good for one firm may be harmful to the rival firms, however, the latter then respond with counterstrategies [or tactics] to protect their own interests. Intense competitive activity may or may not be injurious to the industry.[2]

We have already demonstrated this point with the frequent traveler program example in Chapter 3. We emphasize it again here with what took place in the so-called hotel amenities wars, because it is a marketing truism that all opportunities are not necessarily competitive advantages.

> The amenities wars probably started in the United States with one hotel chain adopting the European custom of putting a mint on the pillow and turning the bed down. Other hotel chains followed suit and the mints got better and more expensive. Then someone started with special soaps, soon followed by shampoos, body lotions, shoe horns, and so on, and then a choice of soaps, body lotions, shampoos, bubble baths, and so on. In some cases all this added well over $5.00 per occupied night to the cost of the room for the hotel. (See Figure 9-1)
>
> The makers of these products knew a good thing when they saw it and amenities manufacturers began to proliferate, their product lines proliferated, and their sales pressures intensified.
>
> Trade journals, hungry for the advertising, and without any solid research to support what they were writing, began writing feature articles and editorials, and even had "amenities contests" proclaiming the values of bathroom amenities and how they brought back customers.
>
> Among others, Procter and Gamble, the makers of Ivory and Camay soaps and other products, conducted a national survey in collaboration with the American Hotel & Motel Association. The survey revealed the earthshaking findings that soap was the most frequently used "service" of all hotel services, being used by 96 percent of the respondents. (It was not reported what the other 4 percent used.) Also, "One *surprising* finding was that personal care amenities such as shampoo and toothpaste ranked higher in use than such 'traditional' services as a restaurant or wake-up call" (emphasis added).[3]

---

[2] Subhash C. Jain, *Marketing Planning and Strategy*, Cincinnati: South-Western Publishing, 1985, pp. 155–157.

[3] *1985 Lodging Guest Survey Summary of Major Results*, New York: American Hotel & Motel Association, 1985, p. 8. This is only one of numerous similar studies with similar findings going back at least ten years.

While all this was going on (the "war" seems currently to be holding in a state of truce) no one bothered to do actual scientific research to determine what effect all these amenities really did have on the customer.[4] At the same time, hotel guests were filling their suitcases with the amenities and stocking their home medicine cabinets.

The amenities wars story demonstrates some important things about competitive intensity. First, services that can be easily duplicated offer only short-term advantage, if that, when you have aggressive competitiors. When those services are not perceived as a determinative advantage by consumers and instead end up costing them more for the core product, such services may in fact become a negative factor for the entire product class.

Second, when introducing an additional service, you need to have an idea of how your competitors will react. Third, competitive tactics should, as much as possible, be based on the customer, not on the competition unless this is essential to the firm's self-protection.

Did hotels in the same product class have to follow suit in this case in self-protection? That is difficult to answer, since no rigorous, controlled research was done and no one really knows. In San Francisco, however, The Stanford Court Hotel did not follow suit and continued to maintain one of the highest occupancies and average room rates in the city. Around 1986, Marriott began to retrench on its bathroom amenities programs and didn't appear to suffer any business falloff or negative reaction because of it.

Does this mean that a hotel or restaurant should not try to gain competitive advantage by introducing services that are easily duplicated? No, it does not or else there would never be growth or improvement. It means, instead, that the intensity of the competition is a critical factor and should be carefully weighed before making the decision. (It also means that one should not blindly believe casual, biased survey studies, or the trade press when its obvious purpose is to support its advertisers.)

It also means going back to the customer first. Does it create or keep customers? If yes, at what cost to them and at what cost to the hotel? Does it increase the price/value relationship, or just price? If it is to be done, in what meaningful way can it be done—that

---

[4] Except for a study by one of the authors of 1314 hotel guests of six hotels, in which the importance of these kinds of amenities was only a small part of the study. Amenities were found to differentiate between only two of the six hotels in the study. One of the hotels was a middle-tier property with no extra amenities; the other was a top-ranked deluxe hotel. See Robert C. Lewis, "Isolating Differences in Hotel Attributes," *Cornell Hotel and Restaurant Administration Quarterly,* November 1984, p. 73. In the same study, amenities were found to be nonsignificant in determining the choice of hotel and nonsignificant in importance when staying at a hotel, for both business and pleasure travelers. See Robert C. Lewis, "Predicting Hotel Choice: The Factors Underlying Perception," *Cornell Hotel and Restaurant Administration Quarterly,* February 1985, pp. 82–96.

In 1987, a mail panel study was conducted of 1854 frequent travelers on the importance of selected characteristics in selecting and returning to economy, midprice, and luxury hotels. This study, like previous ones, reported only frequency data on multiple response sets. Amenities failed to make the lists of important categories. The assumption that certain bathroom amenities constituted a competitive advantage was unsupported by the findings. Regardless, the sponsor, Dial Corporation, "interpreted" the results in an advertising campaign to imply that people choose hotels because they offer Dial soaps. See Bonnie J. Knutson, "Frequent Traveler Study Perceptions of Economy, Mid-Price, and Luxury Market Segments," E. Lansing: Michigan State University, 1987, pp. 7, 9, 23, 25, 40, 42. Prepared for the Dial Corporation.

is, do we know what the customer really wants? If the competition follows suit, do we retain an advantage or just an additional cost?[5]

Competitive advantages are those that are sustainable. We refer again to the frequent traveler programs, of which the most successful has probably been Marriott's. Others were hurt by the Marriott program and thus found it necessary, most probably reluctantly, to enter the fray. Hyatt, for example, clearly stated that it was more advantageous to put its money into advertising, and chose not to enter the frequent traveler arena until almost every other major chain was already in it.[6] Today all major upscale hotel chains in the United States are in the frequent traveler game, trading customers with each other and giving away rooms that previously were paid for, as well as numerous other awards. Unlike the airlines programs, the net effect has been no overall increase in the total market and little competitive advantage for most of the players. Rack rates, of course, are regularly increased to cover the cost and only a few very frequent and loyal expense account customers (not the companies which pay the bills) end up with something more than they had before.[7]

When the market is a large homogeneous unit, the intensity of competition is much greater than when the market can be segmented. This is because there are many entries into the market competing for the same customer. Small competitive advantages can become large ones if they can be sustained. On the other hand, as we have just pointed out, it becomes almost mandatory for one firm to copy another that is aggressively seeking an advantageous position, if it can do so, in order to eliminate the advantage. The best strategy in this case is, if possible, to seek segmentation advantage. We will discuss this in detail in Chapter 8.

---

[5] In *Lodging Hospitality,* February 1988, p. 24, the Gallup Organization reported that of a nationally representative sample of 1028 adults, only 29 percent expressed strong agreement with a statement that they expect a hotel or motel to provide complimentary toiletries such as shampoo. In the same issue (p. 77), it is stated that "amenity packages have essentially become marketing tools." According to Jeffrey S. Brown, a Laventhol & Horwath consultant, "the quality and reliability of the items selected influences a guest's positive or negative perception of a property."

There is no empirical foundation for this statement that is publicly known. At opposite extremes, of course, it probably pertains. When one major hotel chain, however, cut back its bathroom amenities to under $1.00 per night vs. a major competitor's $4.00 plus per night, it suffered no loss in either perception or business, based on the empirical evidence.

The article further states that, according to L&H, "special 'extras' can be used to create a competitive advantage and a lasting impression in the mind of the average traveler . . . that will help guests take home the fondest memories—and look forward to returning to the property once again." This statement also has no empirical foundation. In fact, the empirical evidence is to the contrary. The competitive advantage, if any, is gone as soon as the competition acts similarly—and it does. The best "memory" of expensive amenities probably exists at home in the guest bathroom medicine cabinet.

[6] According to Daryl Hartley-Leonard, Hyatt President, "One of us is making a terrible mistake." Quoted in Steve Swartz, "Once-complacent Hotel Industry is Forced to Learn How to Market," *Wall Street Journal,* November 29, 1985, Section 2, p. 15.

According to Warren Breaux, Hyatt North American Sales Director, "Frequent guest programs . . . are an unwanted necessity to many hotel companies. 'We were forced into it like most major hotels. We tried to stay out . . . [but Marriott] started to increase their market share.' . . . frequent guest programs [are] the biggest new cost for hotels . . . start-up costs alone for Hyatt . . . were $15 million. 'It had to be passed on to the consumer' " Quoted in *Business Travel News,* April 25, 1988, pp. 8–9.

According to Robert Collier, Sheraton senior vice president and marketing director, " . . . a proliferation of giveaways on the scale of the airline industry's triple mileage offers could 'bankrupt the hotel companies. We've really been through the worst of stealing business from each other. It's really a short-term trend in a long-term industry.' " Quoted in *Business Travel News,* June 6, 1988, pp. 80–81.

[7] For an extended opinion on listening to customers vs. competition, see Robert C. Lewis, "Are You Listening to Customers—or to Competitors?" *Hotel & Motel Management,* November 2, 1987, pp. 52, 54, 55, 76.

Competitive Intelligence

As in war, one always wants to know what the enemy is doing, their position and intentions, strengths and weaknesses, where they are most vulnerable and least vulnerable, and where the best place is to attack. There are a number of ways to get this information, and it is well worth getting. It goes beyond physical property descriptions.

First, there is public information. The media, annual reports if a publicly held company, company brochures, flyers and ads, publicity releases, and so forth are some sources. Then there is trade gossip—information from vendors and others who deal with the competition.

In some cities, hotels exchange room occupancy percentages and average rate figures nightly by mutual arrangement. (Those that drop out of the arrangement from time to time are usually considered to be doing poorly.) Many restaurant operators do likewise. (An old restaurant trick is to drive around and count cars in parking lots, but beware of employee cars!) Actually these arrangements are mutually beneficial because all they tell you is how you are doing relative to the others. The refusal of some hotel managements in some cities to share this information, or to lie to each other, is generally self-defeating. It still remains to discover why you are doing better or worse. The fact that the entire tobacco industry knows what Marlboro's market share is hasn't enabled any other company to displace Marlboro as the best-selling cigarette brand.

Comparison figures of occupancy and covers are called *market share figures* and are used to compare actual market share with fair market share. This is a national practice in many industries, where in some cases, such as the automobile industry, the figures are totally public.

In computing fair market share it is important to be certain that you are comparing apples with apples—in other words, with other properties in the same product class competing for the same customer. To do this you divide your capacity by total capacity in the product class. The resulting figure is your percentage of fair market share. To compute actual market share you divide your actual occupancy (or covers) by total product class occupancy. You then compare actual to fair market share as a measure of how well you are doing relative to the competition.

Consider the hypothetical example shown in Table 5-1 for one city area for one night. All the participants in the arrangement are not in the same product class. This does not mean that you are not interested in their occupancy—for instance, it would be worthwhile to know why middle-tier properties are running at higher occupancy than upper-tier properties. It might indicate that the upper-tier properties are pricing themselves out of the market, or it could mean something entirely different, for instance, concerning the type of business that was in town last night.

Now consider the market shares of the properties in your product class. Hotel C's actual share is considerably lower than its fair share. But look at the size of this hotel; it is still filling more rooms than any of the others in the product class. Perhaps this is primarily a convention hotel with widely fluctuating occupancies; perhaps it should not be included in the same product class. What this means is that one has to interpret these figures with discretion before making judgments.

As you can see, your hotel is barely getting its fair market share and would not be doing even that if hotel C's occupancy was up. The question is, why not? What segments

TABLE 5-1   Hypothetical Example of Market Share

	Actual Rooms	Rooms Sold	Occupancy (percent)	Fair Share (percent)	Actual Share (percent)
Upper-Tier Hotels					
A	300	220	73.3	11.5	15.5
B	500	350	70.0	19.2	24.7
C	1200	500	41.7	46.2	35.2
Yours	600	350	58.3	23.1	24.7
Total	2600	1420	54.6	100.0	100.0
Middle-Tier					
E	275	220	80.0	31.3	30.6
F	425	360	84.7	48.3	50.0
G	180	140	77.8	20.4	19.4
Total	880	720	81.8	100.0	100.0

are the others getting market share from? How are they reaching those segments and why do those segments go there? What is their track record in share and growth? Are they satisfied with their performance—that is, are they resting on their laurels or are they aggressively planning something new? What is the competency of their staff and employees?

Another technique for getting information is simply to talk to your competitors. You might do this one on one, or at industry meetings. You can also talk to your customers, who might have been their customers. You can talk to your employees, who might have been their employees, or at least might know some of their employees. Don't forget, of course, that while you are doing this, so is the competition!

In the final analysis, the management that obtains the most information will be the one that moves around, keeps its eyes and ears open, and uses good intuitive judgment. Close observation can tell you a lot about what the competition does best and why, where they are off the mark and why, what their strengths are and their weaknesses, and what they plan next. All this is good marketing intelligence and it can go a long way in helping you to develop your own marketing strategy.

We will elaborate at greater length on marketing intelligence in Chapter 19.[8]

Beating the Competition

The purpose of competitive analysis, of course, is to use it to your best advantage. If you are behind, you need to seek and increase competitive advantage. If you are ahead, you need to sustain and increase competitive advantage. In the first case, you need to

---

[8] A good analysis of gaining competitive information is given in K. Michael Haywood, "Scouting the Competition for Survival and Success," *Cornell Hotel and Restaurant Administration Quarterly,* November 1986, pp. 81–87.

overcome barriers to move ahead. In the second case you need to erect barriers to stay ahead. We will be talking more about these barriers and advantages in the chapters to come.

The essence of opportunity is beating the competition. Intense competition in an industry is neither coincidence nor bad luck.[9] It is a fact of business life. The competitive objective is to find the position where you can break down or influence the barriers, or where you can erect the best defense barriers. This means finding what makes the competition vulnerable.

Attacking vulnerability, as in the military sense, means attacking the weaknesses and avoiding the strengths in the line. The latter is as important as the former. An example of this can be seen in the fast-food hamburger industry. McDonald's set the example for this industry and it spawned many imitators. Most of these imitators tried to copy McDonald's, or attack it where it was strong. The strategy turned out to be fatal for most. Today you can count on your fingers those that survived. In the 1960s there were literally hundreds of hamburger franchise operations cropping up every place you looked.

Wendy's is one that not only has survived but has been successful. Wendy's attacked where McDonald's was weak in two areas. One was the area of "adult" hamburgers. Wendy's saw that McDonald's was not really serving this market so they set out to carve their own niche. The second area was in the product. Wendy's saw an antipathy in the market for the frozen, pre-cooked hamburger. This antipathy coincided with a portion of the adult market. Wendy's attacked and broke open the flank.

Avoid the competition's strengths, at least until you are strong enough and have the resources to challenge them with a meaningful differentiation. Look for the weaknesses. These may be in the product line, in positioning, in segmentation and target markets, in capacity, in resources, in cost disadvantages, in product differentiation, in customer loyalty, or in distribution channels.

Consider the case of distribution channels. A large, national hotel company of some longevity, such as Sheraton (used only as an example), has developed a strong reservations system. This system not only makes it easy for Sheraton's customers to make reservations, it also attracts reservations from people going to a new city because of the assumption that there will be a Sheraton there. While this is not always the case, Sheraton converts a high number of its reservations calls into actual reservations, as do other national chains such as Marriott, Days Inn, and Quality, through one central reservation number. Sheraton ran a lengthy ad campaign which advertised little more than a single 800 number. (See Figure 15-7) Contrast this with Hilton Hotel's folly of the 1970s. Hilton established over 40 individual reservation centers, each with a different 800 number, making it difficult for a customer to know what number to call.

A smaller and newer hotel company that operates in half a dozen major cities will have great difficulty competing against a reservations system like Sheraton's. In one actual case, the smaller chain found not only that its percentage of reservations made by 800 number was much smaller, but also that it was able to convert only about 12 percent of the calls into actual reservations.

---

[9] Porter, *Competitive Strategy*, p. 3.

This company must build its own channel network through a different distribution system. For example, because most of its properties are individual and unique as contrasted with the constant sameness of large competitors, its strength (and their weakness) may be in developing individual identities in a market segment that does not like chain hotel atmosphere. In fact, this company was able to do just that with incredible success in New York City, with a property that did not even identify the chain in its name. The hotel, after its initial error of trying to compete against strength, went upscale. Today it runs at high occupancy and high average rate, with only rare discounting.

The alert reader will have already noted that the above example, presented as a case in distribution, also represents a case in attacking other weaknesses of large chains. The methods used were strategies in differentiating the product line, positioning, and target marketing.

The same small chain discussed above bought a larger property in New York City a few years later. It made the same mistake by trying to attack strength. When this failed, this time, it took the opposite approach. Instead of working against the strong reservations systems of other hotels, management asked itself, "What if we did not have *any* reservations system?" The hotel went downscale with airline crews, tour groups, and lower-rated business. This and related strategies drove the occupancy, and the reservations network contribution was icing on the cake. The hotel quickly rebuilt its occupancy sufficiently to more than cover the lower rates.

Porter also cites customers as a major competitive force. For example, in a highly competitive situation, the market can force down prices, demand higher quality and more service, and play one competitor against another. This is especially true if the product is standard or undifferentiated and the customer is price sensitive.[10] This, if you look closely, is an apt description of the hotel industry today. The restaurant industry, on the other hand, has avoided much of this by being more successful in differentiating its product and segmenting the marketplace, if for no other reason than industry exigencies.

Porter suggests three strategies for beating the competition: positioning to provide the best defense, influencing the balance by taking the offense, and exploiting industry change.[11]

Defensive positioning means matching strengths and weaknesses against the competition by finding positions where it is the weakest, and strengths where the company is least vulnerable. Four Seasons Hotels have accomplished this by maintaining their level of service at all costs.

Influencing the balance by taking the offensive, or proacting, means attempting to alter the industry structure and its causes. It calls for marketing innovation, establishing brand identity, or otherwise differentiating the product. We have seen this happen with suite hotels and conference center hotels.

Exploiting industry change means anticipating shifts in the environment, forecasting the effect, constructing a composite of the future, and positioning accordingly. Robert Hazard accomplished this in his successful metamorphosis of Quality Inns in the early 1980s, when he offered three different product levels to the marketplace.

---

[10] Porter, *Competitive Strategy*, pp. 24–27.
[11] Michael E. Porter, "Note on the Structural Analysis of Industries," Harvard Business School Case Services, 1975, p. 22.

A successful company must look beyond today's competitors to those that may become competitors tomorrow (à la convenience stores in the fast-food industry). It must also watch out for new entries in the race (e.g., conference center hotels), and the threat of substitute products (e.g., supermarkets "make your own meal" bars).

The key to growth, even survival, is to obtain a position that is less vulnerable to direct attack, old or new, and less vulnerable to consumer manipulation and substitute products. This can be done by relationship marketing, actual or psychological product differentiation, and constant and foresighted competitive awareness and analysis.

Marketing and Competition

It is one thing to say "differentiate"; it is another thing to do it. There are many who say that airline seats and hotel rooms have become commodities, like a pound of salt, in that there is very little left to differentiate among them within the same product class. After all, how many changes can you make in an airline seat or a hotel room? (Although all-suite hotels certainly made a change, the first major change in many years, in the hotel room.) Restaurants have a little more flexibility.

It is at this point, however, that marketing imagination comes to the forefront.[12] It is when there is very little difference between goods or services that marketing can make the difference. Levitt points out the fallacy in the usual presumption that undifferentiated commodities are highly price sensitive, so that fractionally lower prices will sway the buyer.

Actually, he says, nothing is exempt from other considerations and it is only because price is so visible and so potentially devastating that it deflects attention from other possibilities.

The way a company manages its marketing may be the most powerful form of differentiation. It is the process, not just the product, that differentiates companies like General Foods, Procter & Gamble, IBM, and Xerox from their competitors. It is the attention to marketing details that characterizes the work of marketing managers. Levitt states, "Differentiation is possible everywhere, and one of its more powerful hidden forms is how the marketing process is managed. In this may reside for many companies, especially those selling what they think of as commodities, the opportunity to escape the commodity trap" (p. 93).

Finding Marketing Opportunities

Finding marketing opportunities is critical to the maintenance and growth of a firm. Opportunities shape an organization's efforts, determine how resources will be used, and guide the future of the firm. In many ways marketing is guided by the assumptions made regarding opportunities. Evaluating opportunities is the basis of management's decisions regarding where and how and with whom to take the firm, as well as what products and

---

[12] Theodore Levitt, *The Marketing Imagination*, New York: Free Press, 1986. See especially Chapter 4, "Differentiation—Of Anything," pp. 72–93.

services to offer. Assessing opportunities is essential to marketing strategies, tactics, and plans.

As mentioned earlier there are three broad, major, and overlapping areas for finding marketing opportunities: identifying existing consumers' problems, conducting marketing research, and carrying out market feasibility studies.

Consumers' Problems

To be sure, all marketing opportunities begin with consumers' problems. The implication here is that you have to go out and find them. That seems like an easy enough thing to do because they are all over the place and all around us, but actually, we tend to do very little to investigate these opportunities that are so vital to business health.

Drucker calls these opportunities "incongruities."[13] Incongruities here are discrepancies between what is and what ought to be. In "consumerese" this may be the difference between expectation and reality; it also may be the difference between "what I would like it to be" and "what is available." These are both true opportunities. Drucker states thus,

> Of all incongruities, that between perceived and actual reality may be the most common. Producers and suppliers almost always misconceive what it is that the customer actually buys. They must assume that what represents "value" to the producer and supplier is equally "value" to the customer. . . . And yet, no customer ever perceives himself as buying what the producer or supplier delivers. Their expectations and values are always different.[14]

If Drucker is only half right it is clear that within consumer incongruities there are tremendous opportunities. Every one is familiar with the expression "there ought to be a better way." It is in that better way that opportunities lie.

Consider, again, the case of the atrium hotel lobby, now common all over the world. John Portman was an architect who decided there ought to be a better way to design a hotel. At the time, hotel architecture had reached a degree of sameness that was so "commodity-laden" that no one thought hotels could ever be other than what they were, architecturally speaking. Portman took his design to the major hotel companies of America. They all turned him down: It wasn't practical, it was too expensive to build, it was too expensive to maintain. Finally, Portman went to Hyatt, a sleepy small hotel chain owned by the wealthy Pritzker family of Chicago but going nowhere. The Pritzkers didn't become wealthy by doing what every one else did. They saw a chance to do something different and to make a mark. The first atrium Hyatt opened in Atlanta and the industry went bananas. Every one criticized but the customers kept coming and Hyatt was on its way.

Was this a consumer problem solved? Was this a case of consumer expectations being unfulfilled? Of course it was. Hotels were dull, dreary places with long, dark corridors and dull lobbies with couches built around the antiquated concept of "a home

---

[13] Peter F. Drucker, *Innovation and Entrepreneurship*, New York: Harper & Row, 1985, p. 57.
[14] Ibid., p. 66.

away from home." Customers didn't want a home away from home; they wanted a new and exciting experience. They wanted something different, and Hyatt gave it to them. The decision by Hyatt to build an atrium lobby hotel did more than start Hyatt on its way; it started hotel architecture on its way, and today's examples are a result of that initial Portman design and Hyatt decision.

Today, we have hotel lobbies with three-story waterfalls. The New Otani in Singapore has a waterfall of seven stories that reverberates to music. There are "lakes in the lobby" as we saw in Chapter 1. Like most opportunities, this one has come full circle and may now be heading back the other way.

Consider the now ubiquitous restaurant salad bar. Who knows where or when it started? Someone saw an opportunity arising from a consumer problem. Fine wine by the glass thanks to nitrogen-filled, partially empty wine bottles solved another consumer problem. Coffee, juice, and roll carts on hotel elevators solved another consumer problem. Population shifts present other, more macro opportunities. If you want to find an opportunity, look for a consumer problem.

Opportunity solutions, to be effective, have to be simple. They have to be easily understandable by the consumer. They have to avoid increased customer risk. This was the initial problem with the automatic teller machines of banks and why they took so long to catch on. Opportunities call for innovation, leadership, and a constant awareness that there ought to be a better way. Opportunities are out there crying for solutions, but innovation to fulfull them doesn't fall in your lap. Sometimes it takes hard work, sometimes just a little common sense.

The search for opportunity begins with knowing your market, knowing your customers, and understanding your customer's problems. But never forget the first rule of marketing when you get a great opportunity idea: Will it create and/or keep a customer? When you can answer yes, then and only then ask what will it cost to do it and if you can afford it.

All opportunities to create and keep a customer are not "great" ideas. Some are just common sense, as previously mentioned. Consider a Holiday Inn in Kuala Lumpur that caters to an American market. The breakfast menu offered freshly squeezed orange juice, an obvious American favorite. The only problem was that you couldn't get it until after 10:00 A.M. Why not? "The juicer is in the bar and the bar doesn't open until 10:00 o'clock." The failing was compounded by the fact that the service personnel didn't tell you this. They simply serve canned orange juice until 10:00 o'clock! Opportunity lost.

In the Hyatt Regency in Manila, when you called room service they answered, promptly, "Good morning, Mr. Lewis." Opportunity gained. In the Sheraton Hotel in Agra, India, they served only instant coffee in spite of the many foreigners who go there to visit the Taj Mahal, not to mention the coffee-drinking Indians. In the Hyatt Regency in New Delhi, with several foodservice outlets, if you wanted fresh-brewed coffee you had to eat in the Italian dining room. Opportunities lost.

In the Sheraton Century Park in Singapore, they redesigned the bedside console that contains TV and light controls so that it projects at a 45° angle so you can see it, instead of being flat against the wall and out of vision. This means that one can wake up in the middle of the night and see the clock without raising one's head from the pillow. Opportunity gained and, incidentally, one that arose through consumer research.

Marketing Research

It is obvious that marketing research is closely aligned with consumer problems, but we use it here with a slightly different perspective. Here we are concerned with incipient needs and wants.

When you get right down to it, we know very little about the hotel or restaurant customer. This is slightly amazing when you consider that Procter and Gamble can tell you how many of us wet our toothbrush before applying the toothpaste, how many of us do it after applying the toothpaste, and how many do it both times.

The trick here is to find out how consumers use our product. What do they do when they arrive, walk in or check in, and go to their room or table? What do they do the rest of their stay? To determine incipient demand you cannot always ask customers what their problems are, because they don't always know. Management has a theory about what is important to the customer, but rarely is that theory grounded in scientific research. Here is an example:

> As the time approached for the coffee break, someone in the group asked, "What are the moments of truth involved in such a simple thing as a coffee break? What factors are important in a good break?" This led to a quick survey of the group to find out what they as individuals considered important in a coffee break.
>
> . . . the trainer conducted a little outside research.
>
> . . . The server, the food and beverage manager, and the hotel manager all agreed that the coffee should be of the highest quality, well-brewed, and served in attractive china. It should be served from a polished, elegant coffee urn on a clean, attractively arranged table.
>
> None of the people in the workshop mentioned any of these factors in their survey. They wanted to get through the line at the coffee service quickly without having to mill around in a mob scene trying to get a cup of coffee or tea. They also wanted the coffee service area to be located close to the restrooms and telephones, a factor that none of the planners had considered. It turned out that the participants thought of the coffee in the overall context of a total break that would take care of a variety of needs. None of them even mentioned the quality or flavor of the coffee.[15]

You can see that in a situation like this, if we asked the customers what problems they had, they would probably reply "none, everything is just elegant." That is because the problems are probably incipient; they are in an initial stage, just beginning to exist. Problems like this are difficult to articulate, so management concludes it is doing the best job possible; because it has satisfied customers, it fails to see the opportunities.

As an example of typical, unscientific research, like the amenities studies, assume management decided to survey what was important in a coffee break. They would make up a list of items and ask repondents to indicate the importance of each one in a coffee break. One of the items would be "quality of coffee" which 98 percent would check as very important. Voilà! The most important thing in a coffee break is the quality of the coffee. Management buys the best coffee—situation taken care of, opportunity lost.

Research as illustrated by the coffee break anecdote is used to study how people use the product. What do they do, where do they go, how do they do it? With this kind of

---

[15] Karl Albrecht and Ron Zemke, *Service America*, Homewood, Illinois: Dow Jones-Irwin, © 1985, p. 59.

information we can look for opportunities to make it all happen more easily and with less trouble.

If we succeed, does the customer go away saying, "Gee, that was sure a hassle-free experience." Of course not, because in the service offering customers often don't know what they are getting until they don't get it, or they have gotten the same thing so many times that they think this must be the norm and don't give it a second thought. But when it has all gone "better," he goes away thinking something like, "Gee, that was a great experience," and tells all his friends. This is fulfilling incipient opportunity.

Marketing research is a powerful tool in uncovering marketing opportunities. It will be discussed in greater detail in Chapter 19.

Market Feasibility Studies

Another form of marketing opportunity analysis differs somewhat from that in the previous discussion. Instead of looking for opportunities, market feasibility studies are conducted to verify whether an opportunity exists. When feasibility studies are conducted, someone already believes that there is an opportunity, such as to build a hotel or open a restaurant in a certain location. The purpose of the feasibility study is to verify that belief (and prove to the lender that it is a viable one). Measurement of market potential, or feasibility, is "to gain insights into five elements: market size, market growth, profitability, type of buying decision, and customer market structure."[16] In essence, the feasibility study should ask these questions:

- Is there a market for this property (business, concept, operation) in this location? If so, where is it, how large is it, or will be, what are its needs, and how is it currently served? What share can be captured? Will it use our property? Who are its members? Other related questions will follow naturally.
- How does the answer to the first question project into financial realities—for example, room rates or check averages, revenue, profit, return on investment, and other quantitative financial considerations?

The answers to the second question obviously depend upon the answers to the first question. Our interest here is only in the first question.

Market feasibility studies are concerned with both marketing opportunities and competitive analysis. Unfortunately, there are probably more feasibility studies done in the hospitality industry that don't truthfully address these issues than there are ones that do. While most feasibility studies in the hospitality industry go under the misnomer of market study, they often have very little to do with the study of markets. According to Ernest Acquaro, senior vice president, hotels, VMS Realty Inc., "Feasibility studies are not true research . . . They're secondary data gathering."[17]

---

[16] Subhash C. Jain, *Marketing Planning and Strategy*, p. 209.
[17] Polly M. Lattue, "Accuracy of Feasibility Studies: Cause for Concern?" *Hotel & Motel Management*, June 13, 1988, p. 74.

Feasibility studies deserve an entire chapter to themselves, but that is not within the scope of this text. Instead, we place the emphasis on the analysis of the marketing opportunity. Studying markets, as we know by now, involves studying consumers or consumer groups and how they will respond (in this case) to a given offering. In other words, having decided that we would like to do something (e.g., build a new hotel or restaurant), we seek to determine whether the opportunity is there. The opportunity, of course, lies in consumers who are ready, willing, and able to buy.

The marketing opportunity, as has been stated, depends on the consumer. If the consumer is not willing, there is no marketing opportunity. What this means is that many of the sociodemographic figures that are almost always included in so-called market feasibility studies—the number of people who pass by that location every day, the number of airport arrivals in that city, the population of the nearest large city, the growth of the area in population, and so on—mean very little (unless, of course, they have some direct relationship to the market for this property).

By the same token, as has been discussed earlier, the competive analysis of this marketing opportunity must be restricted to focus on those who are competing for the same customer under the same conditions. The six motels within a five-mile area have little to do with the competition of a proposed 300-room conference center. The alert reader will say, "Of course not," yet this is the posture that many poorly focussed market feasibility studies take.

A major portion of many feasibility study reports comes from files that have been accumulated to be inserted into any study where they might seem appropriate. For example, a developer wants to build a hotel in Chicago and hires a consulting firm to do a feasibility study to take to the lending institutions. "Get out the Chicago file," says the consultant to her secretary, "and insert it between pages 14 and 92."[18]

This is somewhat of an oversimplification but it is closer to the truth than it should be. One former consultant who performed these studies for a firm told us,

> We usually spend about a week at the site. Actually, we could do most of it in a day but it wouldn't look good to the client. We then go back to the office and pull out the file drawers, adjust the numbers, and type up the report.

Another technique used by feasibility firms to substantiate market opportunity is the "constant ratio" technique. In this technique there are, perhaps, ten properties enjoying an average 70 percent annual occupancy. With the addition of an eleventh property, the one that is the subject of the feasibility study, it is a simple calculation to show that the distribution will now be divided by 11. All properties, including the new one, will now show an average occupancy of 67 percent because the new property will obtain at least its equal share of the existing market; in fact, because it is new it will be better and therefore will do at least 70 percent occupancy while the competition will do less than 67 percent. Of course, nothing could be further from the truth unless this is a perfect competitive

[18] In one situation familiar to us, the same study was submitted to five different developers in the same area in the early 1980s. It was premised on the fact that there was presently only one major hotel in the area. For each site, the study forecast 1988 occupancy of 90 percent. Hotels were built on all five sites. In 1987 occupancies ranged from 35 percent to 62 percent.

situation, the kind that exists only in economics textbooks. Yet forecasts based on these types of calculations are not uncommon in feasibility studies.[19]

A market feasibility study should have only one purpose: to show the opportunity to attract that many customers, to pay that price, to come to that property, over a period of time. That's the hard part. Once done, the easier part is to estimate revenue, subtract cost, predict net and cash flow, and determine whether the project is "feasible"—that is, a financial opportunity.

A true market feasibility study depends, totally, on customers, whether they will come, and what they will pay. This is the competitive opportunity, or lack of it. Unfortunately, most feasibility studies crunch numbers with only a remote idea of where the customers are, whether they will come, or who the real competition is. In marketing, opportunities depend on creating paying customers—nothing else.

Consider the following excerpts from an actual feasibility study conducted for a seaside hotel at a cost of about $25,000. The report is entitled "Market Study" and is almost 100 pages in length.

> The purpose of this study was to determine the level of market support for ————. . . . to accomplish this, we . . . reviewed the markets available . . . and the major generators of demand within those markets; analyzed the group meeting market . . .; visited and evaluated various competitive hotels . . . in order to project the competitive position. . . . On the basis of our study . . . we believe there is sufficient market and operating potential to justify proceeding . . .: We have identified two distinct demand segments that should provide sufficient demand on an annual basis. These segments include transient tourists and business people and group meeting and conference attendees who are representatives of corporations and members of associations, social organizations and leisure groups.
>
> Travel to [this area is] highly seasonal; 70 percent [who come here do so within four months of the year]. This travel is also highly dependent on weather fluctuations within these months.

The next thirty or so pages present Chamber of Commerce data on the area, maps, highway routings, other things like housing statistics, employment distribution, airport arrivals for the past ten years at an airport 75 miles away, distance from metropolitan areas, location of the site, etc. This is followed by about ten pages on "competitive supply analysis," which lists properties within a 40-mile distance, their number of rooms, and a short comment on each, regardless of whether they are in the same market. Then an analysis of "potential markets":

> Based on historical geographic demand segmentation . . ., we have identified several regional areas that could generate significant demand. . . . These areas are as follows: [The two largest cities within 250 miles, the next six largest cities in the same area, and all the rest of the area in between, followed by four pages of description of the cities, their population, etc.]

---

[19] Stephen Brener, a noted hospitality financial consultant, states, "I'm convinced that the 'experts' always will be able to prove, at least on paper, the economic feasibility for a new hotel and indicate that a particular market has an unsatisfied demand for additional transient lodging, or that demand can be attracted to that market as a result of creating a unique transient lodging property" (*Lodging Hospitality*, February 1988, p. 28).

This is followed by twelve or so pages called "lodging demand analysis," basically dealing with seasonal fluctuations in the area. Then come six pages that concur with everything the developer has told them he plans to do. Finally, another ten pages that, based on all the assumptions made, project occupancy and average room rates for the next five years. And, of course, the usual disclaimer:

> . . . projections are based on estimates and assumptions. . . . However, some assumptions inevitably will not materialize, and unanticipated events and circumstances may occur; therefore, actual results achieved . . . will vary from projections, and the variations may be material.

On the basis of these statements, this study predicted a high level of success for the proposed $50+ million project. In less than two years, this hotel was in Chapter 11 bankruptcy.

Opportunities are not based on who and where people are; they are based on who and what people will buy. Notice that this report identified as "two distinct demand segments" 99 percent of the people who use hotels for any reason and the "geographic demand" segment as anywhere within 250 miles. Note, also, that it defined the competition as any property within 40 miles, including basic motels. Finally, although the report frequently mentioned seasonal fluctuations, note that the heavy four months are not the issue; the issue is the other eight months—that is, who would come to this property during these months, and why, when, historically, people didn't even come to the area?

In fact, the only feasible market for this investment was the meetings market during the 8 month off-season. The critical question was whether this market could be induced to come to this location during that time period. The competition was similar properties hundreds of miles away. The feasibility study never addressed any of these issues. If it had, the report would have been negative.

With feasibility studies like this it is no wonder that so many properties have failed in recent years. Roger Cline of Omni Hotels analyzed the first five years' results of 100 newly constructed properties. In 90 percent of the cases, the feasibility studies were 20 percent or more off the mark.[20] It is also no wonder that the firms who conduct these studies have been faced with lawsuits over the last two or three years, particularly in cities where overbuilding has occurred. Interestingly, when projected revenues fail to materialize, it is the hotel's marketing and sales staff that are questioned, not the feasibility study that was built on thin air.

In spite of these practices by some firms, we need to say a word in defense of such firms. Most important, as told to us by a member of one firm that recognizes the need for true market research in feasibility studies, is that "the client doesn't want to pay for it." In today's competitive environment, this is short-sighted folly. Saving $10 to $20 thousand dollars when launching a $50 to $150 million project doesn't make too much sense, any way you look at it. However, this is still no excuse for the superficial studies and unsubstantiated forecasts made by these firms.

At least some lenders, who have been lending for years on the basis of these studies, have come to realize that many studies are unreliable, now that the "boom" days are over.

---

[20] Lattue, "Accuracy of Feasibility Studies," p. 76.

Allen Ostroff, vice-president responsible for hospitality lending for Prudential Insurance, has told us, "After I read their study, I go out and do my own."

Fortunately, consulting firms are now tightening up their practices. Their task is to persuade developers and lenders that it is the consumer who determines true feasibility. A newcomer, San Francisco based ConStat Inc., provides new hope. Says Gary Zodrow, marketing director, "We look at specific segments to see what niches exist to properly build and meet the needs of the specific market. Studies are based on the needs of the marketplace, as opposed to what the growth rate will be."[21] Studies designed to support decisions already made are just as well not done.

Summary

Although we tend to think of marketing as a managerial activity in reaching the customer, we have shown in this chapter that there are other elements involved. Marketing, in fact, is enemy warfare and includes outwitting, outflanking, and outdoing the competition in the battle for consumer loyalty. Marketing does not live in a vacuum in solving consumers' problems and satisfying their needs and wants. A firm's marketing must perform these tasks better than the competitors do. This is the only answer to sustained advantage and growth in the hospitality industry.

Opportunities are the bedrock of marketing, the nick in the competitor's armor. They are the unsolved consumer problem or the unfulfilled consumer need and want. Seizing upon marketing opportunities means being able to analyze the competition, understand competitive strengths and weaknesses, and being able to strike when the iron is hot. To do otherwise is to court disaster.

There are, without doubt, many firms in the hospitality industry that maintain the status quo and still survive, but maintenance and survival are not the true sense of marketing. Neither objective will fulfill the potential of the firm.

This chapter has examined the competition and explored the opportunities available to alert marketers. It has shown that understanding the competition does not mean just understanding bricks and mortar. Rather, understanding the mentality of the competition—the actors that make it work—constitutes competitive analysis. Without this understanding, marketing is doomed to ignore opportunity and the property is doomed to the status of "also ran" when the final count is in.

DISCUSSION QUESTIONS

1. Consider a restaurant that you know. Analyze its competition under various market conditions discussed in the text. How should this restaurant react to these possibilities?
2. If you were the marketing director at the Rama Gardens Hotel in Bangkok, what would you do about its signature restaurant?
3. Explain *competitive intensity*. How does it impact upon marketing? Discuss.

---

[21] Ibid., p. 74.

4. How would you determine fair and actual market share for a restaurant? What would these figures tell you?
5. Discuss Porter's three strategies for beating the competition and how you would apply them for a hotel or restaurant.
6. Discuss the excerpts from the feasibility report given in the chapter. Some analysis was made; what other analysis can you make?

PART III
The Marketplace: Needs, Wants, and Problems

CHAPTER 6
The Hospitality Customer

The heavy emphasis of marketing on the consumer mandates that we know something about consumers and how and why they behave the way they do, as well as what leads them to behave in that manner. This is no small task.

There is no complete unanimity of thought to provide us with all the answers we would like to have. Instead, there are many theories, concepts, and models that have been developed to explain this complex being, the customer. These have been derived from many disciplines such as sociology, psychology, social psychology, anthropology, philosophy, and economics, and these approaches must be integrated before we can approach even a limited understanding. Our ultimate goal, of course, is to be able to influence buyer behavior. We will fall far short of that goal in its full sense but we will learn, at least, to understand some hows and whys and their causes.

It is important to begin with some basic and generally agreed upon conceptualizations of consumer behavior, because effective marketing must be based on these premises. Managerial decisions that ignore these premises will tend to lead to marketing failures.

Premise #1. Consumer behavior is purposeful and goal-oriented. What may appear to be completely illogical to the outside observer is, nevertheless, the action that an individual views as the most appropriate at the time. To assume otherwise is to underestimate the consumer.

Premise #2. The consumer has free choice. Messages and choices are processed selectively. Those that are not felt to be pertinent are either ignored, disregarded, or forgotten. Failure to realize this fundamental is a basic cause of marketing failure.

Premise #3. Consumer behavior is a process. The specific act of buying is only an intermediate stage in that process. There are many influences on consumer behavior both before and after purchase. The purchase is only a culmination of the marketing effort and its influence on the process.

Premise #4. Consumer behavior can be influenced, but only if we address perceived problems and felt or latent needs. Properly designed research can identify and assess these problems and needs.

Premise #5. There is a need for consumer education. In all their wisdom and purposeful behavior, consumers may still behave unwisely, against their own interest. Marketers have a responsibility in this effort.

Are hospitality customers any different from customers of other goods and services? Probably not. After all, they are the same people regardless of the type of purchase they are contemplating or making at any given time. It would seem, then, that basic buyer behavior theories would apply and we could confine ourselves to that domain. There is a difference, however, and it lies in the context of the purchase.

Buying a stereo is certainly not in the same context as buying a hotel room or a restaurant meal. It has been said that you can take the most gentle man in the world, put him behind the wheel of a car, in heavy traffic, at a red light, and turn him into a demon. We won't suppose that hospitality customers are demons, although if you have ever faced a really irate one you might think so, but we will suppose that they behave differently in different contexts. In this chapter we will look at the broad-based and middle-range theories of consumer behavior that have been developed in other contexts and then apply them to the hospitality context.

Needs and Wants

Abraham Maslow was a psychologist who wanted to explain how people are motivated. What he learned was that motivations are based on different needs in different contexts. Maslow labeled his theory of motivation the "hierarchy of needs."[1] This hierarchy model has stood the test of time and is the basis of much of what we know about human behavior. The model is shown in Figure 6-1.

The thrust of Maslow's hierarchy is that higher-level needs do not become primary until lower-level needs have been fulfilled. Thus, until physiological needs of hunger and thirst are satisfied, they remain primary in human motivation. Once these are satisfied, our safety needs of security and protection become primary, and so forth on up the pyramid. Of course, all of us will not act in exactly the same manner, but it has been shown, in a general sense, that the order prevails.

Maslow did not claim that the hierarchy was completely rigid or necessarily exclusive. In fact, it should be noted that we may seek to satisfy two or more diverse needs at the same time; for instance, reserving a hotel suite instead of just a room might be an attempt to satisfy needs at opposite ends of the hierarchy at the same time.

---

[1] Abraham H. Maslow, *Motivation and Personality*, New York: Harper & Row, 1954.

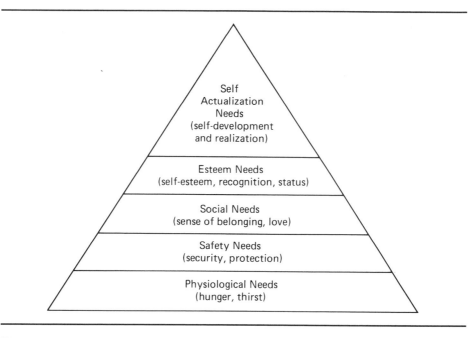

FIGURE 6-1   Maslow's hierarchy of needs

Maslow also identified two categories of cognitive needs that he did not specifically place on the hierarchy, but that he felt belonged fairly high on the scale. These additional needs are the need to know and understand, and aesthetic needs, which are designated as needs for things that are aesthetically pleasing.

It should also be noted that we may satisfy the same need in different ways, depending on the occasion, the availability, and the appropriateness at the time. This leads us into a second-level theory called *behavior primacy* theory. This theory holds that behavior is a reaction to the environment—that is, behavior changes as the environment changes, or, to use the same term used previously, as the context changes.

Application of the Theories

The application of these theories is really elementary to all of us. Do we have to know a psychological theory to know that when we say we are "starving," the first thing we want to do is eat; or that we have higher-level needs of belonging, esteem, and self-actualization? The reason the answer is yes will become clearer when we get to the chapter on segmentation and target marketing, both of which mean pinpointing particular customers. In the meantime, let us consider the need/context relationship.

The businesspeople who travel on expense accounts have been said, although it is not necessarily true, to be oblivious to the cost of their hotel rooms. They have the need to sleep, shower, change their clothes, and perhaps watch a little TV. These are basic needs, so almost any hotel will satisfy them. But they also may have, at least, the need for esteem, and the hotel they select should fulfill that need. They will expect the hotel to have "esteem," and they will expect employees there to treat them with esteem. Because cost is no object, they will select an "upscale" hotel.

At the same time, however, these businesspeople have other needs, such as a desk to write at, good lighting to read by, good telephone service, a wake-up call on time, and perhaps a stenographic service. These are not needs in the sense of Maslow's hierarchy; they are needs, or more likely wants, in the sense we mean when we say "the consumer has a problem." They seek solutions to those problems and are willing to pay for them (or have their companies pay).

Besides this, they have other wants. They want the bed to be comfortable, the room to be large, a comfortable chair to sit in, and the phone to be on the desk; they want to be able to see the TV while lying in bed, to be able to have breakfast in the room, and the front desk to have their reservation so they can check in without any hassle.

They definitely do not want to stand in line, to wait an hour for breakfast to be delivered, to have the telephone ring fifteen times before the operator answers, and to hear the housekeepers yelling at each other in the hallway.

Obviously, what we have here are complex individuals who are very strange, erratic, demanding, idiosyncratic, and unreasonable. Actually, what we have here is normal hotel customers, and we are in a business that is expected both to understand and to satisfy all their needs, wants, and problems!

The same people go home on Friday, after a very hectic week. They say to their families, "Let's get out of here. I just need to relax." For the sake of a better story, let's say they go back to the same hotel. Their basic needs haven't changed; they still need to sleep, shower, and change clothes, but the environment has changed.

Now price is a factor; it comes out of their own pocket. The phone is an unnecessary accoutrement. There is no need for a desk. They want the TV away in the corner so they won't be disturbed when the children are watching it. They still don't want housekeepers yelling in the hall, but they don't care at all when their kids run up and down the hallway screaming at each other. The hotel restaurant that was perfect for entertaining their clients is now too expensive; besides the kids won't eat that "stuff" and the service is too slow for them. Where's the nearest McDonald's? In short, the needs are the same: What has changed is the wants and problems.

The upshot of all this is that we have to understand the need hierarchy, the wants that go with each level of the hierarchy, the "problems" of given individuals, and we have to understand the context or environment in which they will consume the hospitality product. This calls for a lot of understanding! On the other hand, it is so elementary that it is, in fact, the substance of the hospitality marketer's job. "Marketer's job? That's management's job; all I do is get them here!" Ah, ha! Now you're beginning to get the picture.

Let us not forget Maslow's hierarchy of needs; it is a critical foundation of human behavior. At the same time, let us not forget that it is only a foundation upon which we must build.

In short, understanding consumer behavior means understanding the needs, wants, and problems of the consumer, within the context where they take place. These are extremely fertile areas for consumer research which will be discussed at greater length in Chapter 19. As has been stated, needs and wants cannot be generalized across the entire population. Consider, then, what hoteliers and restaurateurs might like to know of the needs and wants of women vs. men, meeting planners vs. corporate planners, incentive planners, tour planners, and self-employed business travelers, just to mention a few of the broader possibilities.

Perceptions

For the consumer, perception is reality. This point is so critical that it is worth repeating: *Perception is reality*. Perhaps one of the greatest mistakes we make as marketers is thinking that what we perceive is also what the customer perceives. If the customer doesn't perceive it, it doesn't exist. Marketers make a critical error when they assume that what they see is what the customer sees, and a greater error when they try to force that view upon the customer. You cannot make something what it is not by simply saying so; you have to *change* perception. Or, to paraphrase T. H. Huxley "perceptions do not cease to exist just because they are ignored."

Self-touting hotels and restaurants follow practices that are self-defeating *unless* they can live up to their boasts. When they promise the moon to someone who hasn't been at the property before, and then fail to deliver the moon (in fact, are bewildered when the customer asks for the moon), they have defeated their own purpose: they have alienated a customer.

We have returned, of course, to the expectation gap in Figure 1-2 in Chapter 1, but have gone one step further. Peruse again the claims made in the hotel ads in Figure 1-3, both express and implied. Would you really expect all those claims to be fulfilled—for example, "A simple walk through our lobby will get your group's creative juices flowing"? Probably not. We are usually willing to allow a little braggadocio and hyperbole in advertising. Do you even care about lobbies that stimulate creative juices? Probably not, but your perception goes beyond this, doesn't it? In this example, you would expect everything to go right for your meeting at this hotel; at least, that is the perception that the ad is intended to create. Now you see how expectations derive from perceptions.

To emphasize this point we need to go back to our discussion of traditional vs. nontraditional marketing.

Initial perception depends on *stimulus* factors. This is the area of traditional marketing. A resort hotel brochure illustrates an indefinitely long (as far as the eye can see) stretch of white sandy beach, a quiet remote setting, elegant dining on your own private patio overlooking the ocean, and a romantic full moon. These are stimulus factors and your perception is, "What a perfect place for a honeymoon!" You book your honeymoon with great expectations.

Actual perception depends on *personal* factors: needs, moods, experiences, values and, most of all, expectations. We have reversed the order: Perceptions now derive from expectations. This is the area of nontraditional marketing.

You find the beach all right. It's on the other side of the island; the one at the hotel is the size of a postage stamp. When you check in, you find that a 300-room convention is checking in ahead of you. The remote setting is in the flight path of the airport. The private patio overlooking the ocean is in the $800 suite, which you didn't reserve. You can eat in your room or in the enclosed dining room without view, or even windows. It rains the entire week. Now, reality is perception; expectations were not fulfilled and your perceptions are negative. You go back home and say, "What a bummer."

Then you meet the couple who stayed in the suite the following week, when the convention was gone and the moon shone. They couldn't have cared less about the beach; they spent all their time in their room, and had room service for every meal. They tell you what a fantastic place it was. *Reality is perception.*

Perception Is Selective   We cannot possibly perceive all the stimulus objects that are presented to us, so we select what we want to perceive. If you are looking for a honeymoon spot, you select to perceive the beach, the patio, the quiet, and the moon from the brochures, ads, or materials presented you. If you are looking for a spot for your company's next sales meeting, you select to perceive the meeting rooms, the banquet facilities, and the sports facilities from the very same brochures, ads, and materials. When you are at a hotel you may select to perceive the decor, the elevator service, the bar, the golf course, or anything that you felt was promised you. Perceptions are images, and images influence purchase behavior. We will illustrate this point further when we discuss information processing, which we will come to shortly.

Consider the hotel brochure cover shown in Figure 6-2. Do you selectively choose to perceive the picture of the hotel reflected in the mirror being held by the woman? If you do, you would not be disappointed. The hotel looks just as it does in the picture, on the main street of a small town. Or do you selectively choose to perceive the woman in the bikini, the water, and the people swimming? You might be disappointed, because they are some distance from the hotel.

Marketers must deal very acutely with perceptions. Marketers must create images with the stimuli pertinent to the specific target market they are trying to attract. They must use stimuli that are relevant to that market, and they must be certain that reality equals, or almost equals, expectation, so that reality doesn't negatively influence perception. Failure to do this will create a dissatisfied customer and negative word-of-mouth. Recall, in the hospitality business, that it is not enough just to create a customer; it is necessary, as well, to keep the customer.

Perception Research   Consumer perception is another fertile research area. In fact, it is almost the only way of really knowing what customers really think about your property. Figure 6-3 illustrates a "gap" model that indicates nine potential gaps in the delivery of service quality that should clearly be management concerns. To illustrate two of them, a research study was conducted at a hotel. Both guests and management were asked to rate their perception of how the hotel delivered on 44 different attributes.

There were 19 significant ($p < .05$)[2] gaps between customer-expected service and customer-perceived service (Gap 4). In 13 of these cases, customer perception exceeded

---

[2] $p < .05$ is a statistical expression meaning that there is less than a 5 percent possibility that the finding could have occurred by chance.

FIGURE 6-2　Two choices of perception

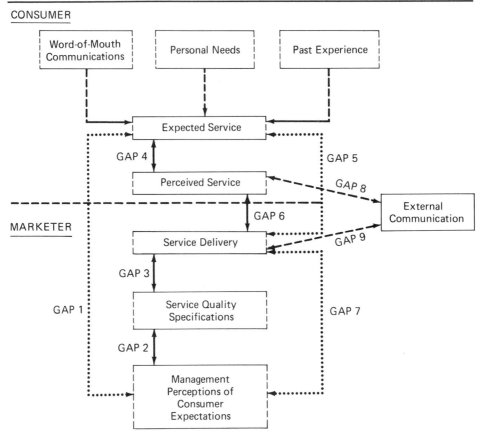

CONSUMER

(Adapted from A. Parasuraman, V. A. Zeithaml, and L. L. Berry, "A Conceptual Model of Service Quality and its Implications for Future Research," *Journal of Marketing*, Fall 1985, pp. 41–50, published by the American Marketing Association.)

FIGURE 6-3   Potential gaps in service quality

expectation; either management was doing a good job or expectations were not high. In 6 cases, and these were critical areas for management, perception was lower than expectation; either management was doing poorly or expectation was too high.

Confirming what was happening, it was found in 25 of 44 attributes that guests' perception of service delivery was significantly lower ($p < .05$) than what management believed its delivery to be (Gap 6). This finding provided a clear mandate to management to readjust its thinking and improve its service delivery.[3]

Important perception research also takes place using noncustomers, and such research may be more important because these are the people whom we want as customers. In proprietary research for a French restaurant, it was found that noncustomers who had heard of the restaurant but had not been there judged that the restaurant's check

[3] For further discussion of the model and findings of the study, see Robert C. Lewis, "The Measurement of Gaps in the Quality of Hotel Services," *International Journal of Hospitality Management*, Vol. 6, No. 2, 1987, pp. 83–88.

average was between $50 and $75. In fact, it was between $25 and $30. This finding provided a mandate to management to change perceptions.

Unrealistic Perceptions There is another side to the perception issue that needs to be mentioned because, like it or not, the marketer must deal with it. This side is the totally unrealistic perceptions of consumers that have been created in their own minds through no fault of the marketer.

When customers' perceptions are unrealistic or wrong, it will be almost impossible to fulfill their expectations. As an example, a person who travels infrequently might perceive that a $75 hotel room in New York City would be a "great" hotel room; in fact, the room may be closet-sized. There are no great hotel rooms in New York City for $75. The customer has created an unrealistic perception of a $75 room. This type of scenario is important to understand when we are faced with an irate customer.

Beliefs, Attitudes, and Intentions

Figure 6-4 is a comprehensive model of consumer behavior, perhaps too comprehensive. Although applicable, the model is also complex. Because so many things affect behavior, it is difficult to apply the model in a given situation. Instead, we will break it down piece by piece, and add some variations on the theme.

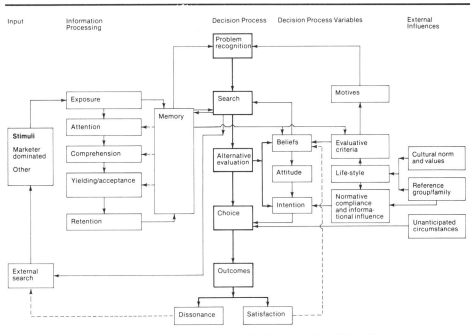

(Source: J. F. Engel and R. D. Blackwell, *Consumer Behavior*, 4th ed., New York: Dryden Press, 1982, p. 687)

FIGURE 6-4   A comprehensive model of consumer behavior

Perceptions lead to beliefs. Beliefs, in turn, affect attitudes. Attitude is a complex phenomenon that has been subjected to a great deal of research, controversy, change of definition, and misunderstanding over time. On the other hand, so much of marketing deals with attitudes and the changing of attitudes that it is essential to try to understand this complexity. It is beyond the scope of this book to attempt to deal with the wide-ranging literature on the subject, but serious marketers are recommended to further reading. Here we will address the subject with a summarized approach.

In a general sense, attitudes are considered by many to be one part of the belief-attitude-intention trilogy that leads to behavior. Others say that attitude is the combination of belief, attitude (affect), and intention. Used this way, some would argue (and this is the longest-term argument) that attitude precedes behavior. For example, if your attitude toward a certain restaurant is favorable, you will patronize that restaurant.

More recently, others argue that attitude follows behavior. In this case, if you patronize a certain restaurant, then you will have a favorable attitude toward that restaurant. Whichever view you take, and it is probable that both are true in different situations, it is clear that attitude and behavior are closely related. That relationship is important to marketers. First we will examine attitude as a component of the trilogy, as shown below, along with the other components.

BELIEFS———→ATTITUDES———→INTENTIONS

Beliefs

Belief can be defined as something we actually think is fact; it derives from perceptions. We attach a belief to an object. An object could be a restaurant, and a belief could be that it is expensive. Whether or not the restaurant is expensive is incidental to the belief. Beliefs are cognitive; they exist in the mind regardless of where or whom they come from. If beliefs are accurate—if the restaurant is expensive—and we want consumers to have that belief, then we can be satisfied with the status quo in that respect.

Sometimes, however, marketers want to change or create beliefs. The restaurant is really not expensive, we say. But how can we say that? For some people it may be very expensive, and for others it may be quite inexpensive. The solution lies in the definition of the target market. These are the people we want as customers; what are their beliefs? We have to learn this before we decide whether we want to change them.

The same is true if we want to create beliefs, as for a new restaurant. Creating beliefs, however, is much easier than changing them, because essentially what exists already is a vacuum and all we have to do is fill it. When we want to change a belief we have to both get rid of the old one and replace it with a new one. This is why it is important that we try to "do things right" in the first place.

People change beliefs frequently without any effort on the part of marketers, or maybe because of lack of effort. Consider the case of Howard Johnson's, described in Chapter 1. Customers changed their beliefs over time to include unclean facilities, poor service, and mediocre food. This belief became so ingrained that a massive effort was necessary to change it. Howard Johnson's tried to clean up their act and then tried to persuade the public that it had done so. The persuasion effort failed, and not only because they failed to clean up their act sufficiently. They also failed to understand that their orange roofs epitomized negative beliefs. People were not going to be persuaded simply because they were told that things were different.

Research by Howard Johnson's failed to uncover this problem. Howard Johnson's research analyzed attitude. They responded to this analysis with the notion that if they could change attitude they would change behavior. But the problem wasn't attitudes. People's attitudes were and continued to be negative toward unclean restaurants with poor service. The problem was the belief that these elements were inherent in Howard Johnson's.

Howard Johnson's then committed a major blunder. Their research showed that people's *attitude* toward family restaurants was that they liked them to be "homelike." Based on this revelation, Howard Johnson's commenced an advertising campaign to convince the public that its restaurants were homelike. The headline of the campaign was, "If it's not your mother, it must be Howard Johnson's." Consider the subliminal impact: First, I still *believe* that Howard Johnson's is unclean and has poor service; and second, I'm insulted by your telling me that my mother has an unclean house and poor service. Of course, beliefs did not change, they only became more negative. With a better understanding of consumer behavior, the story might have had a different ending.

Attitudes

Attitudes, as used in this case, are considered the affective component of the trilogy. *Affective* means the subjective and emotional feelings toward the belief. *Attitudes* are tendencies to respond toward beliefs, as in the Howard Johnson's case above. If you believe that a restaurant is expensive, how do you actually feel about going there? In a sense, this is the application of our beliefs; this is how we judge our beliefs and how we react to them.

Let's assume that our restaurant is expensive and our target market believes this. There is no point here in trying to change belief, because it is true. Yet people are not coming to the restaurant because of their affective response to their belief that it's too expensive. Unless, of course, we want to change the restaurant to lower prices (and research may show that to be the only viable course of action, given this market), what we have to change is attitude and affect. One way to do this might be to try and persuade people that the restaurant is expensive but worth the price. If we could succeed in this effort, we will have changed attitude while maintaining the same belief.

Research contrary to that of Howard Johnson's makes this point. Coca-Cola found that a significant majority of 40,000 people who taste-tested "new" Coke against "old" Coke preferred the new variety. When they switched their formula to the new Coke, the market revolted. What Coca-Cola's research did was to measure beliefs and ignore attitudes. People believed that new Coke was better, but their attitude toward changing was negative.

Intentions

The final stage of the trilogy is called the *conative* stage, covering what people intend to do. This is not behavior, but it may be as close to behavior as we can get, as will be discussed shortly. There is no way we can positively be assured of behavior until after it happens. Even Pavlov's animals weren't 100 percent predictable. Failing this, we want to know what people intend to do.

Let us assume that we have a restaurant that we believe is expensive, but worth it. We have a positive disposition to this restaurant. Do we intend to go there? No! We can't afford it. Our positive attitude thus turns out to mean nothing for the marketer who wants our patronage. Of course, the specific context may change: Would you intend to go there on your tenth wedding anniversary next week? Perhaps now the answer is, Yes. It can be seen now how context can change behavior, or at least intended behavior. It can also be seen that simply asking people what they intend to do can be very misleading without also measuring belief, attitude, time, and context.

The Ajzen/Fishbein Model

Icek Ajzen and Martin Fishbein have brought the understanding of attitudes and behavior to its present state of knowledge in what they call "a theory of reasoned action."[4] According to this theory people do not normally act capriciously, but are usually quite rational and make systematic use of the information available to them. To predict whether someone will do something, the simplest and most efficient approach is to ask the person whether he or she intends to do this, but the answer will depend on attitudes and beliefs.

People's intentions are a function of two basic determinants. The first is a personal factor, the *attitude toward the behavior*. This refers to the judgment that performing the behavior is good or bad, that they are in favor of or against performing the behavior. This attitude rests on beliefs about the outcome of performing the behavior.

The second determinant of intention reflects social influence. This is people's perceptions of the social pressures put on them to perform or not perform the behavior. This factor is called the *subjective norm* because it is based on perceived impressions. The balance between the two determinants of intention lies in the weight given each by each individual. These weights will vary from one person to another.

Consider, for example, two businesspeople who hold positive attitudes toward staying at a particular middle-tier hotel, but perceive negative social pressures against not staying at an upper-scale hotel. If one person's intention was weighted heavily by attitudinal considerations, that person would stay at the middle-tier hotel. If the other person's intentions were more heavily weighted by the social norms, that person would not stay there.

Both attitude toward the behavior and subjective norms are affected by beliefs. The model that depicts the theory of reasoned action is shown in Figure 6-5.

If you examine the Ajzen/Fishbein model in Figure 6-5 more closely, you will notice in the second column of the model that what the individual is concerned with is the outcome of the behavior. Because a number of different behaviors can lead to the same outcome (e.g., either eating at Club 21 or at McDonald's will satisfy my hunger), we have to be concerned with the desired outcome, and the belief that the behavior will lead to that outcome.

---

[4] Icek Ajzen and Martin Fishbein, *Understanding Attitudes and Predicting Social Behavior*, Englewood Cliffs, New Jersey: Prentice-Hall, 1980. This section draws heavily from this work.

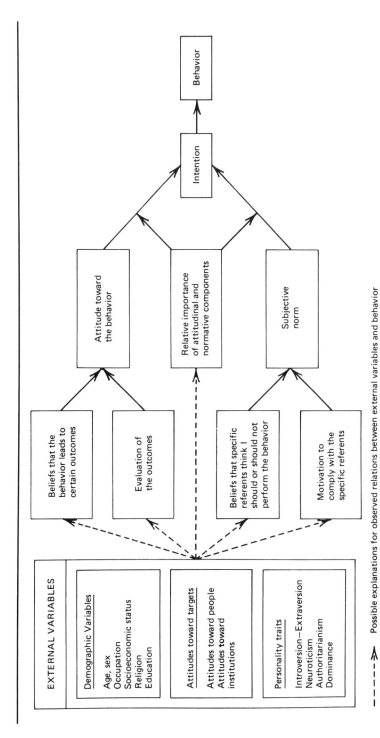

- - - - → Possible explanations for observed relations between external variables and behavior

———→ Stable theoretical relations linking beliefs to behavior

(Source: Icek Ajzen/Martin Fishbein, UNDERSTANDING ATTITUDES AND PREDICTING SOCIAL BEHAVIOR. © 1980, p. 84. Reprinted by permission of Prentice-Hall, Inc., Englewood Cliffs, New Jersey.)

FIGURE 6-5 Effects of external variables on behavior

Three other elements impinge upon behavior and intention to perform that behavior: the target, the context, and the time. The target is what the behavior is directed toward. The target might be a generic category such as fast-food restaurants: Do I intend to eat my lunch at a fast-food restaurant? Or the target may be a single instance of the generic category: Do I intend to eat my lunch at McDonald's?

The target intention is influenced by context and time. I might intend to go to McDonald's alone, but would I go there with the vice-president? I might intend to go there for lunch, but I will never go there for dinner. Variations in any of these elements defining the behavior—target, context, and time—may influence the relative importance of the attitudinal and normative components.

Notice also in the second column of the model the use of the word *beliefs*. Beliefs are what underlie a person's attitudes and subjective norms, as well as the contemplated outcome. Thus, beliefs ultimately determine intentions and behavior. Attitudes toward the behavior, as we saw in the Howard Johnson's and Coca-Cola cases, can be independent of the object of the attitude and also independent of the attitude toward that object.

To try and predict behavior, then, without knowing intention, we would need to know the attitude toward performing the behavior and the beliefs about the object and outcome—to wit: My attitude toward eating in an unclean place is that it makes me uncomfortable; I believe that a certain restaurant is unclean; I believe that the outcome of eating at that restaurant would be discomfort; therefore, I do not intend to eat there. On the other hand, if I am in my car on an interstate highway with only that restaurant on it, I am in a hurry, and it will take me time to go off the highway, I just might eat there. My attitude toward the behavior (eating there) is independent of my attitude toward the object (the restaurant).

We have now come full circle. If we refer back to the needs, wants, and problems of the consumer; if we evaluate how perceptions create beliefs of reality; and if we follow through the Ajzen/Fishbein model, we should now have a good conceptualization of why consumers do what they do.

It should also be apparent that two people who associate the same set of consequences with performing a specific behavior may hold different attitudes toward the behavior if they evaluate the consequences differently, or if the strength of their beliefs differs. By the same token, if two people associate different consequences with performing a behavior, they may nevertheless have the same attitudes.

Where do marketers come in? The following list should answer that.

1. First, as has been emphasized so much, they must understand needs, wants, and problems.
2. Second, they must understand the target, the context, and the time elements.
3. Third, they must be aware of perceptions and the beliefs those perceptions have created, which marketers may seek to change or reinforce.
4. Fourth, they should know the attitude toward the target and the attitude toward the behavior, which they also may or may not seek to change.
5. Fifth, they should understand the subjective norms under which people operate. Subjective norms can sometimes be changed as well, but with greater difficulty.
6. Finally, if marketers have all this information, they may be able to predict intention and, one hopes, behavior.

In practice, of course, marketers don't really want just to predict intention or behavior. What they want is to know *what* predicts intention and behavior. Intention and behavior are not directly manipulable, but what causes them is.

Subjective Norm Influences

When Ajzen and Fishbein talk about subjective norms in their model, they describe those norms as a function of beliefs, but beliefs of a different kind than beliefs about an object. These are beliefs that certain individuals or groups think we should or should not perform the behavior. They are called *normative* beliefs. These beliefs might also be called *social pressures*. The social forces they come from are called *referents,* or *reference groups.* These people or groups influence attitudes about particular topics.

Referents or reference groups have many sources that influence normative compliance. These sources include cultures and subcultures, nationalities, religious groups, labor groups, professional groups, educational groups, and so forth. These societal groups help to shape values, ideas, attitudes, and other aspects of human behavior.

The marketer has two concerns with these groups. One arises when a market segment includes a total culture, religion, nationality, or social group such as Hispanics, Jews, union members, or doctors. In hospitality marketing this is rarely the case so we will pass it over, with only a caution to watch out for, identify, and recognize the particular needs of these groups when they are in your market segment.

We are more concerned with the second type of group. These are referents or reference groups which form small pockets of influence that affect consumers. In some cases they are direct intermediaries with special needs of their own, such as travel agents. By influencing these groups, we hope to affect the consumers whom they influence.

Primary reference groups are small, usually intimate groups that may have direct influence on individuals who belong to the group. These include families, neighborhood groups, country clubs, business colleagues, travel clubs, and other social clubs. These groups develop norms for what is and is not appropriate behavior in many situations. They can influence the hotels one stays at, the restaurants one eats at, the airlines one flies on, the destinations one goes to, and the activities in which one participates. People who purchase certain items or eat in certain restaurants to "keep up with the Joneses" are affected by one or more of these groups. Primary referents may even be singular, as with a husband, a wife, or a secretary. The question of who makes purchase decisions such as "Where do we eat tonight?" is one that marketers can answer through research.

In Chapter 2, on services, it was mentioned that one cannot possess, take home, and display a service. Instead, one can only "possess" the pride of having been the recipient of a service. When people go back to their groups they like to talk about the countries they have visited, the hotels they have stayed at, and the restaurants they have eaten in. They then receive admiration, or even adulation, from their groups. If the experience was good or bad, they pass on the appropriate information and details so the next group member will know whether to do the same.

Influencing these groups is not easy in hospitality marketing. The groups are small, and relatively few hospitality firms have the power of large-scale advertising that will reach them. Instead, in hospitality, influence probably works best in reverse direction, through individual members; in other words we influence individuals and send them back to the group with the appropriate information. This is no less than word-of-mouth advertising, of course, except it is directed at special groups, or special target markets.

Secondary groups are larger organizations in which there is less direct personal contact among members, at least on the large-scale level, but in which it is often easier to reach the members as a body. For example, take the case of the Golden Agers, a national organization of older people who are prime targets for bus tours, package tours, and other diversions. Locally, where members have direct face-to-face contact, it would be difficult for anyone other than a local restaurant or bus company to reach the group. Through publications that reach all members, however, the entire membership can be approached.

Another group that may have considerable influence on your customers is called a *comparative* group. Individuals use it to assess themselves or as a goal to emulate. A group that fits this description in the hospitality field is the so-called jet-set group or, more recently, the yuppie or dink groups.

Today, hotel companies consider single women travelers as a large secondary group with its own norms of behavior. Influencing this group has become critical, since it now represents more than one-third of hotel and restaurant customers.

The important thing to remember about reference groups is that they may represent opportunities and specialized target markets that need reaching. Many may not be obvious and you may learn of them only through customer research. The alert marketer is constantly on the lookout for special groups whose needs can be satisfied by the firm. Ramada Inns has made a special effort to attract the single woman traveler and has appointed one corporate person just to look after the needs of that market segment. Days Inn has done the same with the senior citizen market. An inn in northwestern Connecticut has built several special, otherwise dead, weekends around New England antique car collectors.

Information Processing

It was stated at the beginning of this chapter that consumer behavior is a process and many influences affect this process both before and after the act of purchase. We will now examine that process in some detail. Only by understanding the processes can the marketer hope to do more than tangentially influence it. The model we will follow is shown in Figure 6-6.

Needs, Wants and Problems   The process normally begins with needs, wants, and problem recognition or identification. In Figure 6-6 we also show stimuli in parentheses at the beginning of the model. This is because sometimes the need, want, or problem recognition will come as a response to stimuli, for example, TV commercial, an ad, or a billboard.

In the case of problem recognition coming first, consumers know, or think, they have a problem and begin a search for a solution. We should understand that this may be a very subtle stage. Consumers do not suddenly jump up and shout, "I have a problem." In fact, consumers may not even think of it as a problem; they might simply say, "I'm hungry [problem]; let's eat [solution]." On the other hand, they might think, "I'd really like to go to a quiet [want] place for a good [want] dinner [need] tonight. Where should we go [problem]?"

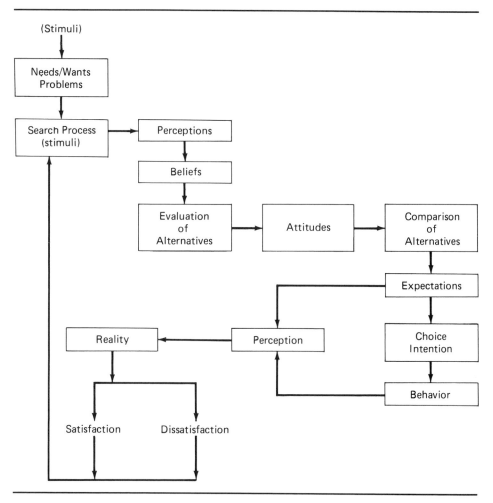

FIGURE 6-6   Consumer information processing model

They then begin the search process for a solution. They may simply search their memories, they may ask others, they may look to the newspaper or the telephone directory, or they may do any number of other things to obtain either new information or additional information. They may do this in split seconds if there is a suitable restaurant right around the corner, or they may take a year to do it, as in planning an annual vacation. They may give the task to someone else, such as a subordinate, a secretary, a spouse, an airline, or a travel agency.

Keep in mind that many things will affect this process until it is completed. These things include all that has been discussed in this chapter so far, such as culture, reference groups, attitudes, and beliefs; many things we have yet to discuss; and many things that will not be discussed because they are beyond the framework of this book.

In the example given above the consumer has recognized the problem unaided. Marketing has had little, if any, impact upon that recognition. Once the problem has been recognized, however, marketing can begin to take an active role. Where consumers go for information, what they read or hear there, whether the information was already in their memory, for whatever reason—marketing has had an influence on this part of the process.

At other times the problem may arise not through recognition, but through identification. In this case, consumers are unaware that they have a problem until it is presented to them and identified for them. Now marketing has a role right from the beginning. Let us say that these same consumers plan, as usual, to eat at home tonight. They are reading the newspaper or watching television when suddenly they see an ad for what appears to be a nice quiet restaurant. They think, "Boy, wouldn't that be nice for a change?" Their wants and problem have been identified for them. Marketing has not created a need—that was already there. Marketing has created a want and caused a problem that needs a solution.

These simplistic examples can be applied to the begining of any purchase decision process, whether it be for a glass of milk or a year-long trip around the world. For simple purchases the process may be totally subconscious and/or parts of it may be skipped. For similar decisions that have been made many times before, the process may be instantaneous because of what has become a learned reaction. Of course, the process could also end in a nonpurchase decision. This might be the case when marketing has not done its job adequately. Regardless, the role of marketing is apparent even at this early stage. It is also apparent that if marketers want to affect the process at this stage, they must be aware of the complexities of the decision and the influences that will modify it.

Stimuli Selection   In the first case above, consumers determined their own problem; in the second case it was caused by a stimulus. In either case, stimuli may affect the process at some stage. The degree of impact, as well as the intensity of the entire search process, is determined by the level of involvement the consumer has with the purchase decision.

The impact and intensity is greater in cases of *high involvement*. These are cases when the decision has high personal importance or relevance to the consumer, such as high cost, high risk, high effect on self-image, or high reference group influence. When *low involvement* exists the process is similar except that it proceeds far more quickly and some stages may be skipped, especially when information is readily at hand. Regardless, consumers are affected by stimuli that they can choose to select or not to select.

The selection process applies especially, but not only, to advertising at four stages. The first stage is selective attention. We attend only to that which is of interest to us, as discussed above. When we know specifically what we are looking for, then we search for it. Marketers, however, cannot depend on that, so they try to direct advertising at us that will get our attention, or they use special media such as special interest magazines. If the subject, or even just the headline, is of interest to us we pay attention. Hyatt, for example, is a hotel company that tries to get attention by using sometimes startling graphics in its ads. Holiday Corp. at times has done the same. Examples of each can be seen in Figures 6-7 and 6-8.[5]

---

[5] Hyatt's ad was accompanied by bowls of pears with light bulbs in them, on front desks and other places, much to the perplexity of customers. How many hotel rooms this campaign sold is moot.

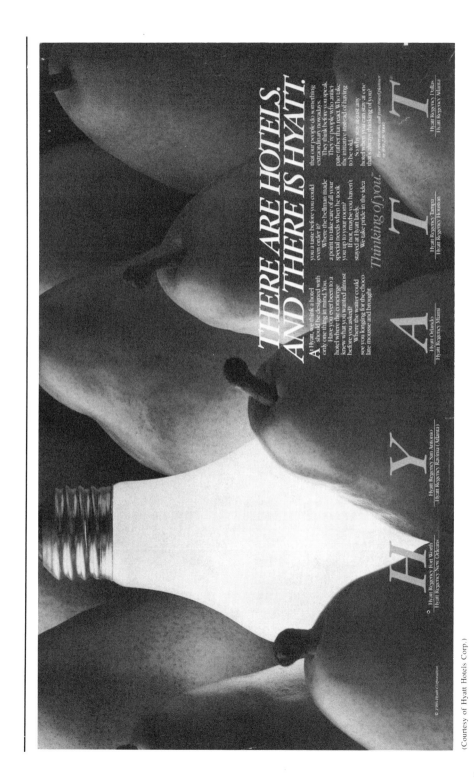

(Courtesy of Hyatt Hotels Corp.)

FIGURE 6-7 Using graphics to get attention

153

Waiting in line after line can bring your business to a halt.

Crowne Plaza® hotels make your time our business. Guaranteed reservations through an advanced hotel reservation system and an efficient front desk staff make your check-in and check-out fast and easy. And, if you stay on the Concierge Floor, you'll enjoy private check-in/check-out service.

More service without more cost. At Crowne Plaza hotels the service you deserve doesn't carry a high cost. You'll enjoy spacious rooms, special Concierge Floors, cafe and

fine dining, recreation/health facilities, tele-conferencing and car rental offices.

So, the next time you need a hotel that really understands the way you do business, call 1-800-HOLIDAY or your travel agent.

HOLIDAY INN
CROWNE PLAZA

AT SOME HOTELS, THERE'S JUST NO END TO THE CHECK-OUT LINES.

Atlanta, GA International Airport	**Houston, TX** Park 10	**New Orleans, LA** French Quarter Area	**Sao Paulo, Brazil**	*OPENING SOON*
Boston-Natick, MA MetroWest Area	**Lisle-Naperville, IL** Chicago Area	**Orlando, FL** Florida Mall — Spring 1986	**Seattle, WA** Downtown	Amsterdam, The Netherlands Cologne, West Germany
Dallas, TX North Dallas	Fall 1986	**San Francisco, CA** International Airport	**Stamford, CT** Downtown	Manchester, England Monterrey, Mexico
Frankfurt, West Germany Fall 1986	**Los Angeles, CA** International Airport	**Santiago, Chile**	**Washington, D.C.** Rockville, MD	St. Johns Newfoundland, Canada Washington, D.C.
Houston, TX Galleria Area	**Memphis, TN** Convention Center **Mexico City, Mexico**		**White Plains, NY** Downtown	© 1986 Holiday Inns, Inc.

(Courtesy of Holiday Inns, Inc.)

FIGURE 6-8   Using graphics to get attention

154

FIGURE 6-9   Using sex to get attention

Sex has long been used in all kinds of advertising to gain attention. In hospitality this is especially true for resort hotels. In fact, the picture of a bikini-clad female on a beach, in the water, or in front of a hotel has become so common that it may well have lost its impact, yet is still widely used. The French tend to put a different twist on it, as shown in Figure 6-9.

The second stage of the selection process is selective comprehension. Attention goes only so far. If we are still interested after reading or watching what got our attention, we will try to comprehend, digest, and evaluate it. Leona Helmsley, president of Helmsley Hotels, in her ads for the Helmsley Palace hotel in New York City, stands in an evening gown with the headline "The only palace in the world where the queen stands guard" (Figure 15-1). The headline gets attention; the next step is to try and comprehend the connection between that and a hotel, so we may read further if we select to interpret this headline as reflecting a customer concern.

The third stage of the selection process is selective acceptance. If we have comprehended why the Helmsley Palace is the only hotel in the world where the queen stands guard, and if we are still interested, we go further. Do we accept this contention? Does it have some importance to us in choosing a hotel? Is the claim valid? We selectively decide whether we want to accept this into our beliefs. If so, we may add it to memory, at least for a short time.

Finally, we select whether to retain the message for future reference. If we selectively retain the message, we add it to long-term memory, where it will be available when we want to use it again.

Because consumers only selectively attend, comprehend, accept, and retain messages, we should be aware that much of what we direct at them does not sink in. Unless we can bombard them, à la McDonald's, we need to be certain that what we want them to select is directed in a manner that appeals to their needs, wants, and problems. This truism applies not only in advertising but also in selling, in-house merchandising, public relations, and any other way in which consumers gather information. As we have already discussed, this selective process is weighted by the perception and belief stages shown in Figure 6-6.

Alternative Evaluation   Rarely is there only one possible solution, and the consumer now has to compare the alternatives. Reference groups and other evaluative criteria have strong impact at this stage. More important, how well have the marketers done their job? Has the case been well presented? Does the solution look viable? Is the risk worth it? Is the price/value relationship appropriate? Does it cover the necessary needs and wants? What is the word-of-mouth medium report? Is it different or better than the other alternatives, and if so, why? This approximates the mental process of the consumer. Again, the higher the involvement, the lengthier and more deliberate the process and the greater the search for more information.

The marketer's most critical impact is probably at this stage, at least for medium- to high-involvement purchases. The level of involvement will vary with the individual. Eating at McDonald's is low involvement but that does not stop McDonald's from having one of the largest advertising budgets in the country. McDonald's truly wants you to have high involvement with them.

As the price gets higher and, in the hospitality industry, as the service element becomes more important, the level of involvement increases. But the involvement level in choosing a hotel is always relatively high, because the product is consumed as purchased, unlike a good, which can be returned if it doesn't work. It is also because the entire hotel experience is personal; if it's a bad experience, it affects the user personally.

Alternative evaluation is the point at which the total marketing effort, including especially internal and relationships marketing, will pay off.

Alternative Comparison   Consumers make many assumptions, with or without their search findings, in the comparison of alternatives, but they will first have gathered what they perceive as facts. Now attitude and affective response will play their roles.

Hospitality purchase choices often include many elements. There are the obvious elements such as price, location, accessibility, reputation, and quality. There are also the less obvious or anticipated elements such as service, ambience, attitude, newness, and other clientele. Researchers have developed what are called multiattribute models in attempts to explain these choice processes.

Some of these models are called *compensatory* models under the assumption that people make trade-offs of one attribute for another in order to make a decision—that is, a weakness in one attribute is compensated for by a strength in another. The most widely accepted of the compensatory models is the *expectancy-value* model. This model assumes that people have a measurement of belief about the existence of an attribute (say, service), and that each attribute has an importance weight relative to the other attributes (service is very important). The model is depicted mathematically in Figure 6-10.

According to this model, a consumer's attitude (A) is obtained by multiplying his beliefs (B) about attributes by the respective importance weights (W), and summing to derive a total attitude score for the brand. Applying this model, marketers would try to increase the measure of belief about key attributes, by saying, for example, "Our service is of the highest level." Alternatively, they might even try to increase importance of attributes in which there tends to be high belief—for instance, by asking, "When you feel like being pampered, what's more important than good service?" Using this model a consumer might, for example, trade-off a poor location for good service.

Another compensatory model contends that consumers measure alternative choices against ideals. In this case, the marketer would have to know something about the ideals. This can be learned through research using techniques such as multidimensional scaling and conjoint analysis.

Using *noncompensatory* models (no trade-off of attributes), consumers might establish a minimum acceptable level for each important product attribute and make a choice only if each attribute equals or exceeds the minimum level. This is called the *conjunctive* model. Another model, called the *disjunctive* model, would have the consumer establish a minimum level on only one or a few attributes—for example, price.

$$A_{jk} = \sum_{i}^{n} W_{ik}B_{ijk}$$

where: A_{jk} = consumer k's attitude score for brand j

W_{ik} = the importance weight assigned by consumer k to attribute i

B_{ijk} = consumer k's belief as to the amount of attribute i offered by brand j

n = the number of important attributes in the selection of a given brand

---

FIGURE 6-10   Mathematical depiction of the expectancy value model

These choice models and others require consumer research to determine the target market's choice process. Unit customers will vary, and it may be very difficult to find any one model that will fit. On the other hand, the research effort is eased and the models fit better when applied to larger groups such as meeting planners or incentive planners. The important point for us right now is to understand the use consumers make of beliefs and importance weights in developing attitudes.

Expectations   The expectation here, of course, is whether the solution will solve the problem and satisfy the needs and wants. In a hotel or restaurant many things accompany this expectation: the reservation, food, decor, ambience, attitude, service, accoutrements, and all the vast multitude of minutiae called "monumentally magnificent trivialities."

Choice and Outcomes   The choice is made and the performance takes place. What is the outcome? Does performance match expectation? Is perception changed? We have managed to create a customer, but have we managed to keep one? Will he or she come back? Tell others? Is the new customer satisfied, dissatisfied, or just so-so? Notice the feedback loop in Figure 6-6; notice how it will affect the process the next time the same problem arises for this consumer.

We could never hope to know if every customer left satisfied or dissatisfied but we certainly should have a good idea of many of them. With individuals, we will have to randomly sample to find this out; with groups and large parties, we should have some contact with each one.

Marketing hasn't stopped yet. Remember, we want to keep these new customers. As much as we can, let's follow up with them. If they are satisfied, let's find out why. Maybe it will teach us something. When will they be back?

If they are not satisfied, why not? What can we do about it? Can we still get them to come back? Can we correct the problem? Perhaps they are suffering from a malady called *cognitive dissonance*, a state of mind in which attitude and behavior don't mesh—in other words, when what we do is not the same as our attitude toward it. This state causes us to have second thoughts or doubts about the choice that we made. This is especially true when the choice was an important one psychologically and/or financially and when there were alternative choices with a number of favorable features.

Most people try to reduce their own cognitive dissonance. We can't change the behavior, so we try to change our attitude to feel better about having done it. Marketers can help customers reduce cognitive dissonance by convincing them that they did in fact make the right choice.

Research has shown that people try to reduce dissonance by seeking or choosing to perceive information that supports the wisdom of the decision, by finding fault with the alternatives so that they look less favorable, and by downplaying the negative aspects of the choice and enhancing the positive elements. Advertising that supports the choice or personal communication that commends the wisdom of the choice have been found to be helpful in reducing dissonance and increasing loyalty.

The Consumer Mental Process

Let us break consumer information processing down another level at the first stage of needs, wants, and problem recognition to the second stage of alternative evaluation. This

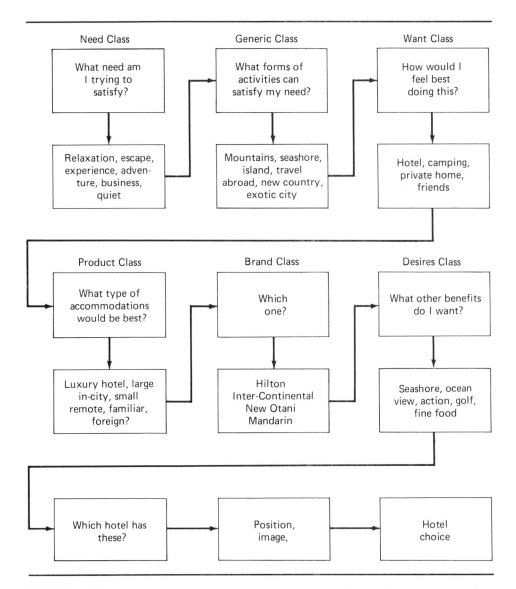

FIGURE 6-11   Consumer mental evaluation process (conscious and/or unconscious)

will enable us to see how marketing can affect the needs and wants process at this stage. The process is shown in Figure 6-11. It is self-explanatory so further discussion here is unnecessary, but the reader should trace through the steps to see how they fit the elements of consumer behavior we have discussed thus far. This analysis will make the theory more practical. You might even attempt fitting to the model your own particular mental process on a recent or proposed purchase to see how it fits.

Figure 6-11 is an oversimplication of a very complex process. In fact, this process is so complex that only one's own mind can process it for oneself, as it is laden with a multitude of variables, many idiosyncratic in nature. The process in an overall consumer behavior sense, however, is important and marketers should understand it. The labels given to the boxes in Figure 6-11 are class categories that will be discussed in more detail later in the book. Here, we tie them together so as to understand their synergism.

Other Aspects of Hospitality Customer Behavior

Because of the unique nature of purchasing services in general, and the hospitality product in particular, there are some aspects of consumer behavior that pertain more particularly to the hospitality customer. In this section we will address some of those aspects.

Evaluation Processes[6]

We have seen in the preceding discussion of information processing that consumers go through a search process in order to limit alternative solutions and to gain information about those alternatives. Prior to purchase, this is the most common method of evaluation available. In the case of manufactured goods, consumers, as a final step and having obtained all the information they can otherwise, may go to a store to examine and evaluate the good before making a final decision.

Particularly when purchasing high-involvement items, however, we like to try out things whenever possible. We test drive a car, we watch a television screen, we listen to a stereo set, and we try on a suit of clothes before making a final decision. In some cases we are even allowed to take an item home or purchase by mail for a trial period.

The reason we are allowed to do this, of course, is because the seller wants to reduce perceived risk. We are all afraid to buy a pig in a poke, so we feel the risk is much lower when we are allowed to try the item first. With most goods we have the advantage of being able to examine most of the attributes before purchasing. We call these attributes "search qualities." They include such things as color, fit, feel, and so on—that is, they are largely tangible qualities. Even the feel of a car is largely tangible and "searchable."

Attributes that can only be evaluated after purchase or during consumption are called "experience qualities." These attributes include such things as taste and wearability, but even many of these can be sampled. When we come to hospitality services, however, there is no opportunity for sampling and we are almost totally dependent on experience qualities. (An exception would be, for example, meeting planners who stay at a hotel before booking their group.)

Although we can gather information, read ads and brochures, and listen to others, we cannot truly evaluate the hospitality products until we have consumed them; these include plane rides, vacations, restaurant meals, and other aspects of the hospitality product.

---

[6] This section is largely based on work by Valerie Zeithaml. See Valerie Zeithaml, "How Consumer Evaluation Processes Differ Between Goods and Services," reprinted from J. H. Donnelly and W. R. George, eds., *Marketing of Services*, published by the American Marketing Association, 1981, pp. 186–190.

The characteristics of services—heterogeneity, intangibility, perishability, and simultaneous production and consumption—and even the facilitating and supporting goods of the hospitality product, cause them to possess a far greater proportion of experience qualities than search qualities. While this may not be significant in ordering a hamburger at McDonald's, it can be very significant in the purchase of other hospitality products. Even the jaded business traveler will be upset when things do not go right. This is because the consumption of the hospitality product is so personal and leaves the customer vulnerable to a myriad of private feelings. When things go wrong, the customer feels personally "violated."

This situation often causes purchasers of the hospitality product to employ different evaluation processes from those they use with goods dominated by search qualities. Some of these differences follow.

Information Search   Hospitality consumers seek and rely on personal sources to a greater extent, so as to obtain experience qualities vicariously. Media advertising is highly inadequate for conveying the intangible and experience qualities of services. Pictures of hotel buildings, couples in hotel rooms, or people eating in dining rooms do little to permit realistic evaluation. In attempts to differentiate from the competition—a difficult task at best—hospitality advertising is rampant with puffery (e.g., in Figure 1-3), which in itself constitutes as much uniformity as pictures of buildings.

Although there are notable exceptions to the rule, hospitality advertising is largely most effective as awareness advertising. It may be time for the industry to reevaluate the use of media and find new ways to reach the consumer.

Hospitality consumers engage in greater postpurchase evaluation and information-seeking. This may be true if for no other reason than that this cannot be done beforehand. The customer develops beliefs and attitudes through a greater use of both personal and vicarious experiences. The dissonance response model becomes more pertinent for the hospitality product, with which most evaluation follows purchase.

Evaluating Quality   In the case of goods, consumers have many tangible cues for evaluating quality before purchase. In the case of hospitality services, consumers have few if any real cues before purchase although, as in Figure 1-3, advertising attempts to provide them. Consumers may, in some cases, have a name-brand identity as a cue, which in fact is a very strong cue. They still, however, have no real cue as to the delivery. Unlike, say, computers, the service in a chain hotel or restaurant in Acapulco may not be the same as that in London. However, the consumer does have a large number of both tangible and intangible cues after purchase.

Goods are often packaged to evoke quality and it may be the package that sells the good. A Hyatt hotel is also packaged to evoke quality, but the best restaurant in town may reside behind a dowdy old storefront in a back alley. The package, in fact, may be totally negative. Restaurant-goers have come to know this, but must rely on either their own experience or the experience of others to evaluate the package. For example, an un-knowledgeable couple looking at the front of Lasserre in Paris could not know that it would probably cost them $250 apiece to have one of the finest dinners in the city there.

If intangibles are so important in the hospitality product, as we have suggested, it is apparent that the customer must evaluate quality based to a large degree on intangibles. In this sense, quality is perceived as the outcome of experiences, that is, the result desired by the customer.

And what is that? Obviously it will depend to some extent on the particular customer. We can generalize, however, that quality is defined as *perceived* service matching *expected* service. This definition clearly places the criteria of quality on the consumer, not management, as we have already shown in the previous discussion of so-called gaps.

Research has shown that expectations of service quality are quite different from expectations of the quality of goods. Table 6-1 shows some reasons for this. Although the list in Table 6-1 is not unique to services, it can be seen that customers obtain many of their quality cues from the delivery or performance of the service. Most of the cues are absent prior to purchase.

Perceived Risk   Hospitality consumers assume greater risk when buying hospitality products than when buying goods. Services are nonstandardized and are usually sold without guarantees or warranties. A room service order that takes two hours is nonredeemable. An overcooked steak may be replaced but only at the sacrifice of time to oneself and others in the party. A room not prepared for a meeting has no possible replacement in time lost. A surly desk clerk or waiter can ruin one's day without redemption. The consumer seeks greater assurance.

As with quality, the consumer evaluates risk. We call this *value,* which is closely akin to quality. Value incorporates other perspectives such as quality, need, expectation, and price. Value perception is used by consumers to choose, or rechoose, to buy specific products and services.

Unlike quality perception, however, for something to have value it must satisfy a need—that is, high quality does not necessarily have high value. Consider again, as just one example, the high-quality bathroom amenities package. If lemon, herbal, or leather soap does not satisfy a need any better than a basic soap, it will have little value to the customer.

Value is the relationship of the benefits derived from a purchase to the sacrifice made on account of that purchase. Pricing authority Kent Monroe defines value as the ratio of quality (as perceived by the customer) to price.[7] Either way, it is clear that perceived risk is based on various relationships. The subjects of value and risk are discussed further in Chapter 14.

Brand Loyalty   Brand loyalty has small reward in the purchase of hospitality services. Although frequent traveler programs have tried to overcome this resistance, they do not really build brand loyalty, as we have shown, and many properties cannot afford them, especially restaurants.

A few years ago brand loyalty was an insignificant factor in the hospitality industry. Most brands amounted to only one property, or very few properties. With the current advent of larger and larger chains, this situation has changed but brand loyalty is still relatively rare. Such words as *undependable, unreliable,* and *inconsistent* crop up. Travelers in the same product class prefer one chain's hotel in one city and another chain's hotel in another city.

---

[7] Kent Monroe, *Pricing—Making Profitable Decisions,* New York: McGraw-Hill, 1979, p. 38.

TABLE 6-1   Determinants of Service Quality

RELIABILITY involves consistency of performance and dependability.

It means that the firm performs the service right the first time.

It also means that the firm honors its promises.

RESPONSIVENESS concerns the willingness or readiness of employees to provide service.

It involves timeliness of service.

COMPETENCE means possession of the required skills and knowledge to perform the service.

It involves knowledge and skill of the contact personnel.

ACCESS involves approachability and ease of contact.

It means the service is easily accessible by telephone (lines are not busy and they don't put you on hold).

Waiting time to receive service is not extensive.

The hours of operation are convenient.

COURTESY involves politeness, respect, consideration, and friendliness of contact personnel (including receptionists, telephone operators, etc.).

COMMUNICATION means keeping customers informed in language they can understand and listening to customers. It may mean that the company has to adjust its language for different consumers—increasing the level of sophistication with a well-educated customer and speaking simply and plainly with a novice.

It involves
- explaining the service itself
- explaining how much the service will cost
- explaining the trade-offs between service and cost
- assuring the consumer that a problem will be handled

CREDIBILITY involves trustworthiness, believability, and honesty. It involves having the customer's best interests at heart.

Contributing to credibility are company, company reputation, personal characteristics of the contact personnel, and the degree of hard sell involved in interactions with the customer.

SECURITY is the freedom from danger, risk, or doubt.

It involves physical safety, financial security, and confidentiality.

UNDERSTANDING/KNOWING THE CUSTOMER involves making the effort to understand the customer's needs.

It involves learning the customer's specific requirements, providing individualized attention, and recognizing the regular customer.

TANGIBLES include the physical evidence of the service:
- physical facilities
- appearance of personnel
- equipment used to provide the service
- physical representation of the service
- other customers in the service facility

Source: Adapted from A. Parasuraman et al., "Service Quality and Its Implications."

Franchise companies such as Hilton and Sheraton, for example, have a wide range of product inconsistencies. In general, corporate-managed hotels are of a quality equal to the name. Franchisees run the gamut from superior to unacceptable. The customer becomes uncertain when purchasing the product. Marriott has done an excellent job in controlling franchisees. Customers can hardly tell the difference between the 100-plus Marriott corporate-managed hotels and the 45-plus or -minus franchised hotels.

Consider the first-time buyer. She's heard a brand name so she tries it in Salt Lake City. The experience is good so she tries it again in Boise, Idaho. The experience is bad; next time in Boise she'll try another brand. Research has shown that it is the individual property and the individual management that make the difference in many cases.

These elements of consumer evaluation of hospitality services have implications for marketers. For the effect on information search, it may be wise to reduce advertising cost and rely more on public relations, publicity, or other means to stimulate and simulate word-of-mouth communication, and to concentrate more on reducing after-purchase dissonance. This is not to mention, of course, relationship marketing. The same suggestions apply to projecting a quality image.

The marketer of hospitality services must seek to reduce perceived risk. Guarantees of satisfaction may be necessary, as Holiday Inns provides. Standardization may become more necessary so that consumers learn to expect a given level of quality and satisfaction. Restaurant chains have certainly tried this, but then there is always the problem of consumer boredom with which to contend. If you look closely, you will see that McDonald's works hard to overcome this problem.

The lack of brand loyalty has its good and its bad aspects. The bad side is that it is harder to keep a customer; the good side is that it is easier to steal one from the competition. Marketers who can gain an edge in loyalty over their competitors will have a crucial advantage.[8]

Personal Control[9]

Personal control means being in control of personal situations in your life. The demand for personal control over events is common in everyday life. Psychologists suggest that people will react differently to stressful situations if they can personally control those situations than if they cannot. Whether control is perceived or actual, it can significantly affect people's responses in a service encounter or situation.

In fact, at least the perception of control can avoid aggravation, defuse antagonistic situations, and eliminate feelings of stress and dissatisfaction. Because service encounters can be stressful for both customer and employee, the concept of personal control has serious implications for both internal and relationship marketing in the hospitality industry.

There are three kinds of personal control. The first is *behavioral control*, which is the ability to directly influence or modify behavior. *Cognitive control* refers to interpreta-

---

[8] "Loyalty" comes in a number of different colors. For a good discussion of this, see "Winning the Market Share Game," *Cornell Hotel and Restaurant Administration Quarterly*, November 1986, pp. 73–79.

[9] This section is based on work done by John Bateson and others. See John E. G. Bateson, "Perceived Control and the Service Encounter," in J. A. Czepiel, M. R. Solomon, and C. F. Surprenant, eds., *The Service Encounter: Managing Employee/Customer Interaction in Service Businesses,* Lexington, MA: Lexington Books, 1985, pp. 67–82.

tion of an event and constitutes information that leads to predictability and anticipation of an event. *Decisional control* represents a choice in the selection or outcome of goals.

The three types of control may interact. Regardless of the type of control, what is significant is that control, or perceived control, can exert considerable benefit in stressful situations.

A number of elements have been found to affect the sense of control in service encounters:

- the amount of time involved
- personal control of the situation
- the efficiency of the process
- the need to depend on others
- the amount of human contact involved
- the risk involved
- the amount of effort involved

All these elements are critical in the control process in the hospitality industry. Envision, if you will, waiting in line at the front desk of a hotel, waiting for room service, waiting to be seated in a restaurant, waiting for someone to take your order or give you the check, or waiting for some one to take your telephone reservation after you have been placed on hold.

Better yet, envision these scenarios: "we don't seem to have your reservation"; you have finally decided to take a shower when room service knocks on the door; the hostess tells you for the fourth time, "just 20 minutes more"; the waiter never looks at your frantic waving as he repeatedly passes your table; you're on hold on the telephone listening to a recorded commercial to book your next meeting at Hyatt, and you get disconnected. You are out of control!

In a study of how meeting planners (who have an especially large amount of risk and effort involved) make the meeting purchase decision, Renaghan and Kaye found that, "For the planner, the key to a successful meeting lies in his or her ability to control as many of the meeting variables as possible."[10] This is no surprise; it is hard to find a meeting planner who doesn't have some horror story about things going wrong. The prominence of personal control as a critical element in the hospitality customer's attitude is readily apparent.

Other studies have also supported the idea that perceived control is an important variable in the behavior of the customer in the service encounter. More important, they suggest that control can significantly influence customer satisfaction with a service.

On the other side of the coin, the same thing has been found to be true of employees in the service encounter. That is, the contact person working for a service firm also desires to have control. Consider the constraints on the employees in the situations mentioned above: It is rare that they actually do *not* want to provide better service.

Based on these findings, Bateson suggests that the service encounter is "a compromise between partially conflicting parties: the customer, the server, and the service firm as embodied in the environment and rules and procedures it creates for the service encounter."

---

[10] Leo M. Renaghan and Michael Kaye, "What Meeting Planners Want: The Conjoint Analysis Approach," *Cornell Hotel and Restaurant Administration Quarterly*, May 1987, pp. 67–76.

The service firm seeks to achieve efficiency through standardization. The price paid for such efficiency may be high in terms of the perceived behavioral control of both customer and server, both of whom desire control. From the employee's point of view there is no autonomy and everything must be done by the book. This may even lead to a situation that the employee knows will upset the customer.

When the customer dominates the encounter the situation changes and the customer essentially takes control. The firm is organized to serve the customer who is "always right." From the employees' point of view, they are there only to serve the customer and satisfy the customer's orders.

In some cases, employees will have control. In this case, they are placed in autonomous positions and will perceive themselves as having high control over the situation. The customer will have little control, will be ordered about by the employees, and will be quite unhappy. (This seems to be the model in many government agencies, as when one is attempting to obtain a driver's license.)

It is not difficult to visualize any one of these situations occurring in a hospitality establishment. In many cases it can depend upon the individuals. As one example, consider a waitress: Some do it by the book (no ice cream served here); some take control, and you had better be nice to her if you want your dinner; still others are dominated by customers with a strong personality.

These are extremes but they make the point. There is an inherent triadic conflict among the three forces, as shown in Figure 6-12.

Because our goal is satisfied customers, and we now know that that necessitates satisfied employees, the best service encounter balances the need for control of both the customer and the contact personnel against the efficiency demands of the operation. While this may seem impossible on the face of it, it will be impossible only if we accept as inviolate the boundaries of the behavioral control model in Figure 6-12.

If, however, we adopt the concept of perceived control included with the notion of cognitive control, then we can envision a situation in which all parties can be satisfied.

In a hospitality encounter, the customer must give up some control and obey the procedures and the service personnel. While this may incur a negative reaction from the customer, it goes without saying that the employee must treat customers as if they were in control. For this to occur, management will obviously have to give up something as well, if the employee is to have the autonomy to give the customer a sense of control. This is tricky but critical, because on it rests the foundation of internal and relationship marketing. In this light, Bateson raises the following questions:

- Can we increase perceived control of the customer and thus increase his or her perceived value?
- How does the customer view the encounter in terms of perceived control relative to competitors' encounters?
- Through using information to increase cognitive control, can the customer be educated so that the encounter is predictable?
- Can we sort out the components of the encounter to see how each one influences the perceived control of the customer?
- Can we build perceived control into our encounters?

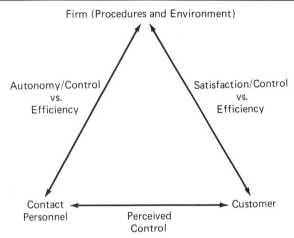

Firm (Procedures and Environment)

Autonomy/Control
vs.
Efficiency

Satisfaction/Control
vs.
Efficiency

Contact
Personnel

Perceived
Control

Customer

(Source: Bateson, 1985. Reprinted by permission of the publisher, from *The Service Encounter*, edited by Jon A. Czepiel, Michael R. Solomon, and Carol F. Surprenant, Lexington, Mass.: Lexington Books, D.C. Heath and Company, © 1985, D.C. Heath and Company).

FIGURE 6-12   Perceived behavioral control conflicts in the service encounter

- Can we give more control to the contact personnel to allow them to serve the customer better?
- Can we give more real or perceived control to the contact personnel to satisfy their need for control?
- How do the contact personnel currently see their perceived control? What factors and procedures do they see limiting their control?
- How can we balance giving control to the contact personnel against operational efficiency?
- Is personnel and marketing effectiveness worth more than operational efficiency?

Work on balancing the control among the customer, the contact employee, and the requirements of the organization has not received much attention in the hospitality industry. If anything, emphasis has been on organizational requirements first, the customer second, and the employee last.

Balancing these three elements can provide substantial benefits, as shown by work in twenty-three branches of an east coast bank. The resultant changed environment was described as an "enthusiasts' climate," where the focus is more on the customer, and procedures and attitudes encourage flexibility to meet customers' needs. Employees were also found to have higher levels of satisfaction.[11]

Control conflict situations are exceedingly common in hospitality establishments. This is becoming even truer as larger and larger companies dominate the scene, with properties owned more and more by strictly bottom line-oriented individuals and organizations. This is an area of consumer behavior—both employee and customer—that needs to be fitted to the marketing philosophy.

[11] Benjamin Schneider, "The Service Organization: The Climate Is Crucial," *Organizational Dynamics,* Autumn, 1980, pp. 52–65.

Personal Constructs[12]

We have already discussed a number of times the notion that services are intangible. This notion presents particular problems for the consumer and, in turn, for the hospitality marketer. Accordingly, it has been suggested by a number of authorities that the need is to provide intangible services with tangible evidence in market positioning.

Levitt, for one, has declared that the implications derive from asking consumers to buy intangible promises. The greater the degree of intangibility in the product and the lesser the ability of the consumer to test or experience the product in advance, the bigger the promise. "Promises, being intangible, have to be 'tangibilized' in their presentation. . . . Metaphors and similes become surrogates for the tangibility that cannot be provided or experienced in advance."[13]

Personal constructs are devices that individuals use to interpret or make sense out of what they confront. Personal constructs determine what are termed perceived realities. They are also used to *validate* perceived reality. What this means is that we develop an image of what something means, when we encounter it, on a bipolar scale. For example, we have a bipolar scale that runs from good to bad. "Good to bad" is a construct. When we see someone behave in a certain way, we place that person somewhere on our construct scale by saying that's "bad," that's "good," or that's somewhere in between.

What we perceive is a function of our personal constructs. For example, we might place shrimp on a tough-to-tender construct scale, with large shrimp being tough and small shrimp being tender. Now we perceive reality based on that construct—that is, if we see a large shrimp we perceive that the shrimp will be tough, and vice versa. When we say we validate perceived reality with our constructs, we mean this: If the large shrimp is actually tough, we have validated the construct. If, however, the large shrimp turns out to be tender we have an invalidation and we revise our construct: Large shrimp are not tough, at least not all the time.

Developing personal constructs is something that we all do although we may never have thought of it in that way; it describes the way we go through life making judgments. Constructs for tangibles are relatively easy to determine. We can take a very tangible item such as a hotel building and place it on any number of constructs: large-small, modern-historic, attractive-ugly, new-old, and so forth.

The problem occurs when we try to do the same thing with intangibles such as service, atmosphere, friendliness, and so on. This relates to what Levitt means when he says we need to "tangibilize" the intangible, or that metaphors and similes become surrogates for the tangibility that doesn't exist. In other words, we have to provide consumers with tangible surrogates so they can "get a handle on" the intangible that we are promising. Otherwise it becomes very difficult to communicate to the hospitality customers what it is that we are trying to sell them.

The best examples of this come from other industries. Merrill Lynch's bull tangibilizes investment services as strong and unique, "a breed apart." Prudential tangibilizes

---

[12] This section draws heavily on work by Lewis and Klein. See Robert C. Lewis and David M. Klein, "Personal Constructs: Their Use in the Marketing of Intangible Services," *Psychology and Marketing*, Fall 1985, Vol. 2, No. 3, pp. 201–216.

[13] Theodore M. Levitt, "Marketing Intangible Products and Product Intangibles," *Harvard Business Review*, May–June, 1981, pp. 94–102. Copyright © 1981 by the President and Fellows of Harvard College; all rights reserved.

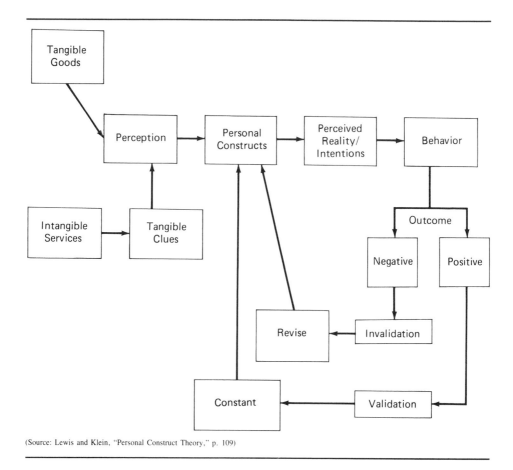

(Source: Lewis and Klein, "Personal Construct Theory," p. 109)

FIGURE 6-13   Personal constructs as filters leading to behavior

solidarity and endurance in insurance with the Rock of Gibralter, "a piece of the rock." Allstate Insurance tangibilizes care in insurance with a pair of open hands, saying, "You're in good hands with Allstate."

In the hotel industry, the Stanford Court Hotel in San Francisco tangibilized class with a Napoleonic clock in its lobby for "people who understand the subtle differences" (Figure 10–4). The president of Marriott tangibilizes quick service by standing in the doorway of a bedroom looking at this watch as the breakfast cart rolls in, saying, "If you don't get it in 15 minutes it's on us" (Figure 15-8). McDonald's tangibilizes "good times" with Ronald McDonald.

Refer back to the ads in Figure 1-3 and in Figures 6-7 to 6-9. What intangibles do they tangibilize? What is their intent? What does it do for the customer?

The trick to marketing intangibles, then, is to find the reality perceived by the consumers, which is determined by the construct that is fashioned from their needs and wants and interpreted through the perceptions of tangible surrogates. Figure 6-13 shows the model depicting this viewpoint. Notice that intangible services have to move through tangible clues in order to reach perception, then be interpreted through personal constructs, then be construed as perceived realities, and finally be consummated in behavior.

For the marketer, these are the questions: What are the important intangible attributes that I want to represent? What are the constructs that determine perception of those attributes? What are the tangible clues that a consumer uses in the determination of construct validation?

Suppose you wanted to promote your restaurant as romantic—an intangible attribute: How would you answer the three questions?

Summary

This chapter has looked at the behavior of consumers from a number of different viewpoints. We have moved from the broad-based theories of human behavior to theories on the specific behaviors of hospitality customers. We have also omitted a good deal. Because consumer behavior theory derives from the theory of many other disciplines, its depth and width is enormous and total coverage is beyond our scope. Instead, the emphasis has been on the service customer in general and on the hospitality customer in particular.

Some of the concepts introduced in this chapter, such as personal control and construct theory, are relatively new, at least in marketing and certainly in hospitality. Others are much older and more accepted, such as Maslow's hierarchy and information processing, yet they have received surprisingly little application in hospitality marketing.

All of the theories and concepts introduced in this chapter are directly applicable to the hospitality industry. Those that seem not to apply as well have not been included but can be found in any good text on consumer behavior. New research may prove that they do apply. Their exclusion is not intended to derogate them; it only means that space was limited.

Dealing with theory takes hard thought and good powers of conceptualization. In the long run, however, no theory is worthwhile if it can not be applied. Everything in this chapter is highly applicable to the hospitality industry. We have tried to show how this is true, but the best test can come only in application.

The key to marketing today is to understand the customer. Good theory provides the basis for that understanding. It works, and applying it will put you light-years ahead of those who are still selling when they should be marketing.

DISCUSSION QUESTIONS

1. Consider Maslow's hierarchy in terms of a hotel and of a restaurant. In each case, name as many attributes as you can that fit each level of the hierarchy. Be prepared to discuss.
2. From a recent paper or magazine, collect a half-dozen hotel or restaurant ads. Discuss them in terms of perception, expectation, beliefs, and tangibility.

3. Explain the relationship among beliefs, attitudes, and intentions. What are the four elements of the Ajzen/Fishbein model? Discuss how all these interrelate in hospitality consumer behavior.

4. The chapter did not delve much into subjective norms. Elaborate on the discussion from your own experiences and background. How would they affect your choice of a hotel or restaurant?

5. Consider Figure 6-11. Take an example of something you have done or might want to do in terms of a hospitality purchase. Apply the model.

6. Elaborate on Figures 6-12 and 6-13. Discuss them in terms of experience and application.

CHAPTER 7

The Organizational Customer

The organizational customer is defined as the purchaser of hospitality products for a group of people with a common purpose. This customer's needs are somewhat different needs from those of the individual customers described in Chapter 6. Although all of the basic principles are the same—perceptions, beliefs, attitudes, subjective norms, control, and personal constructs—organizational customers are essentially buying for someone else. They seek to satisfy all the needs and wants of the others, as a group. Like the travel agent, then, organizational customers are intermediaries. Unlike the travel agent, they don't "sell" the customer; rather, they organize and plan on demand of the customer.

Business travelers may book a room or an airline seat by themselves or through a secretary. Neither they nor the secretary can be considered an organizational customer, since they are not purchasing for a group of people. The tour operator we do not consider an organizational customer. While a group of people is involved, individuals can each singly purchase the tour, thereby nullifying the common purpose.

What, then, is the organizational market? Although there are a sizable number of target market categories, we can define them in four major segments: the corporate travel market, the corporate meetings market, the incentive market, and the association, convention, and trade show market. Each of these categories of customers purchases hotel, restaurant, and airline facilities and services for a group of people with a common purpose.

For marketing purposes, as we have said, there is a difference between organizational customers' needs and the needs of individual customers. The organizational customer is not, in the true sense, the end-user of the product. When a couple books a hotel room on a weekend package, it knows what its expectations will be: The expectations are their own. Similarly, business travelers may choose to be close to their business location for the next day, sometimes at the expense of comfort. The needs and purpose of these customers are individualized; the similarity, of course, is that in either case if expectations are not met, the customer may go somewhere else the next time.

The Generic Organizational Market

The organizational customer plans to satisfy, perhaps, 25 to 5000 individual needs. Although the group may have a common purpose, such as a business meeting of a corporation, a convention for the computer industry, or an incentive trip for pen salespeople, each member of the group has different individual needs. This makes the overall task for planning somewhat more formidable for the organizational customer.

Specifically, the organizational customer must try to anticipate the needs of the group, as well as to select the proper facilities to accomplish the common purpose. For example, the meeting planner of a corporation may be given the task of planning a sales conference for the international division. The planner must understand the needs of that particular department within the company, with which he or she normally has very little contact, as well as the needs of the individual members.

At times, organizational customers may not even visit the hotels or restaurants to which they send their organizational group. Thus, to make the right decision, the organizational customer needs to rely on a different set of stimuli from those used by other customers. While advertising may be construed as the appropriate method for affecting these decision-makers, word-of-mouth from fellow organizational customers ranks first as probably the predominant factor in choosing facilities.

It has been found that recommendations from others within the group rank second in the decision-making process, with direct sales efforts by suppliers ranking third. Advertising has been found to rank tenth out of fourteen possible influences for the organizational customer.[1]

Organizational customers do, however, rely on salespeople of a hotel far more than do individual customers. Also, conference coordinators of the hotel, who handle the details, become extremely important in the decision to book, and to rebook after the event is over. Even the chef, who is going to be serving perhaps 300 attendees three meals a day, becomes critical. The organizational customer is at far more risk from a bad meal than the weekend package customer who is not pleased with an individual meal.

There is evidence, however, that as organizational customers gain more experience on the job, they are less influenced by the salespeople. In the case of the incentive buyer, it has been found that only about 25 percent of those planners with more than five years' experience are greatly influenced by salespeople.[2] These people and many other organizational buyers want to see for themselves, and will visit the property before booking it. There is an increased professionalism among planners, evident in the way they go about inspecting properties and setting up meetings.[3]

---

[1] Heidi Bloom, "Marketing to Meeting Planners: What Works?" *Cornell Hotel and Restaurant Administration Quarterly*, August 1981, pp. 45–50.

[2] Robert C. Lewis, "The Incentive Travel Market: How to Reap Your Share," *Cornell Hotel and Restaurant Administration Quarterly*, May 1983, pp. 19–27.

[3] Margaret Shaw, *The Group Market: What It Is and How to Sell It*, Washington D.C.: The Hotel Sales and Marketing Association International Foundation, p. 8.

The smart salesperson moves the selling session away from price and toward service. All planners, no matter what their depth of competence, are most concerned that the hotel and its staff perform so that their meetings are successful. Quite often a planner's promotion—or even his job—is on the line.

Even if the hotel was entirely at fault, it is ultimately the responsibility of the planner who chose the wrong site for the meeting.[4]

Other surveys strongly support the meeting planners' concerns. For example, an informal survey by H&MM brought the following comments from meeting planners.

You can have the most gorgeous facility in the world. . . . I still need professional staff to augment what I do. . . . I often follow the same people as they move from hotel to hotel.

The people I do meetings for like to be pampered a little bit. A property may be less than desirable, but if they can provide service and if the food is good we can overlook the other things.

What's important to me is . . . that everything I've ordered is there.

Problems occur when hotels don't deliver what they say they can deliver.[5]

To begin to understand the needs of the organizational customer, it is important to see how the planning process should go for a meeting or function. With this tool, the sales and operations departments of a hotel can anticipate the problems before they happen, perhaps preserving the success of the entire meeting.

The Organizational Customer Buying Process

The example of marketing to the meeting planner is used to demonstrate the organizational customer buying process.

Assess the Needs   Each body of people with a common purpose has different needs as an organization. The Elks Club convention certainly has a different reason for meeting than does the new product development team for IBM, yet both of these organizations may meet in the same meeting room, in the same hotel, at the same time of the year. Both the organizational customer and the hotel employees must understand the purpose of the meeting. If, in fact, the meeting is purely a social one, theme parties, golf outings, fashion shows, and so on are expected and welcomed. If, in fact, the purpose of the meeting is to devise strategies that will bring a corporation out of bankruptcy, the entire agenda will be altered accordingly. These are obvious differences; there are many far more subtle ones.

The most common complaint planners have about hotel salespeople does not relate either to high-pressure selling or to cold calls—though they don't particularly like either one. It is that the salesperson has not taken the time to find out about their business. Often they are pitched by a property wholly unsuited to their needs and resent the fact that their time is being wasted by someone who didn't even make the effort to find out what they were like.[6]

---

[4] Ibid., p. 9.

[5] Kathy Seal, "Staff, Service, Top Priorities for Planners," *Hotel & Motel Management*, July 20, 1987, pp. 40, 42, 43.

[6] Shaw, *Group Market*, p. 15.

Set Measurable Goals   For the organizational customer, nothing can be managed if it cannot be measured. It is critical that the needs of the meeting be translated into measurable results. Corporate planners can measure results from their agenda. If the meeting purpose was to brainstorm for a new product, the success of the meeting can be judged on whether the product was ever developed. For the incentive planner, post-trip evaluations are helpful. The goal may be that 90 percent of the winners of the incentive would return next year if given the opportunity. From the hotel side, if the planner does not have measurable goals set, success for the meeting becomes subjective rather than objective and minor discrepancies are susceptible to magnified scrutiny.

Develop a Plan   The plan needs to be concise and to lead directly from the goals and needs of the organization. The plan should include hotel and nonhotel related activities. Airline tickets, ground transportation to and from the airport, and transportation of materials are all items that must be incorporated into the plan. An organizational planner without a plan is one who must be helped through the process.

It is the responsibility of the hotel that wants satisfied customers to assist in-experienced planners with all phases of the meeting. Sometimes the planner is placed in that position with no experience. For example, the bylaws of the organization may stipulate that the secretary of the group is responsible for the annual convention. If the newly elected secretary has no prior planning experience, the hotel staff needs to give assurance that all phases of the meeting will be accommodated. It will do the hotel no good to have a disorganized function come to fruition. Once the salesperson senses an absence of knowledge, a different selling scenario should be employed.

During the planning process, it may be found that the planner did not allow the proper timing between sessions for the group to move from the meeting rooms to the ballroom for lunch. The conference coordinator must be knowledgeable enough to steer the planner toward the correct time frame.

On the other hand, planners are also becoming more educated as to what is best for their meetings. For example, a hotel salesperson might book another group into the meeting room next to the general session of the conference. The planner might, in this instance, insist that the space be utilized for his or her luncheon, thereby preventing any unanticipated interruptions from the group next door.

Resolve Conflicts   Organizational customers have to work in tandem with both the hotel and their own organizations to anticipate and resolve potential problems. While planning may alleviate possible conflicts, the hotel may be only half of the problem. The organization itself presents problems that must be addressed before the function occurs. There may be a hierarchy within the organization that needs suites, first-class travel, and seats at the head table. Failing to accommodate these needs can cause conflicts that ruin the meeting through no fault of the hotel. A hotel staff can anticipate these needs by asking to review the V.I.P. list.

There are numerous other potential issues. Nonsmoking guest rooms and sections of meeting rooms are entering into the spectrum of worries. Individual special meals during a banquet are no longer limited to just kosher meals. Many banquet meals now require low salt or vegetarian plates to satisfy the needs of attendees.

A good way to resolve possible conflicts for both sides is to have a preconference meeting. The term *preconference* is generic, and can be applied to incentive trips as well as to corporate meetings. At this meeting, the organizational customer reviews the details of the meeting with each department to ensure that communications were not distorted through the conference coordinator. The front office and banquet managers, and general manager if the situation warrants, should be in attendance with the salesperson and conference coordinator to ensure that all potential conflicts are discussed and remedied before the function occurs.

Execute the Meeting   This may be the simplest phase of the organizational customer's job, if all the previous steps were followed. If they were not, this is certainly the hardest portion of the process. The execution of the meeting could occur without the planner's being in attendance. The needs of the planner are now being transposed onto the group.

Sometimes, even if the organizational planner is on the site, the end-users' needs are not met. For example, the association planner may want the general session set up theater-style, with the room having chairs that face the podium for a guest speaker. The guest speaker might demand that the room be set up classroom-style, with each chair having a desk in front of it so that participants can write in conjunction with the presentation.

This is a classic example of how the planner is not the end-user, and the needs of the group change right up to the last minute. The hotel that adjusts accordingly will be the one that receives the future business. There are no right and wrong sides to this scenario. The task must be completed to satisfy the needs of both the end-user and the organizational planner.

Evaluate the Results   Based upon the goals of the organization, was the meeting a success? The hotel should be interested in the results as much as the organizational customer is. The evaluation process can take place in a postconference meeting held shortly after the conclusion of the function. Department heads and the planner can review face-to-face all the things that went right, as well as those that went wrong. The marketing-oriented organization will take immediate steps to correct the malfunctions and to reinforce the positive aspects.

The evaluation process is also critical for the organizational customer. When these customers are the buyers, but may not be present at the actual event, it may be difficult for them to understand exactly what took place. Even when the hotel delivered as promised, the organization may not have accomplished its goals. The planner will need to assess the results before starting to plan the next similar function, and should be made aware of the problem areas and where they lie.

The Corporate Travel Market

The organizational customer for the corporate market plans the travel and entertainment for a corporate entity. The term *group* needs to be interpreted loosely here. The corporate travel planner is different from the corporate meeting planner in that he or she plans for a group of people with a common purpose, albeit with individual travel schedules. A common purpose still exists, since the corporate entity is relatively homogeneous. In some organizations, the travel planner and the meeting planner are the same person. Corporate meeting planning will be discussed in the next section.

The size of the corporate travel market is very large, running into tens of millions of business travelers. About half of these end-users are directed or influenced by the corporate organizational customer who plans, controls, mediates, negotiates, evaluates and/or approves their travel expenditures. This market is very desirable for hotels because it tends to pay good rates, is large in size, and travels consistently throughout most of the year.

The corporate planner in this case needs to find the correct products for the entire corporate entity. Once the product is identified, the best rates are negotiated. The supplier needs to understand the culture of the organization to fulfill its needs. For example, some companies go to the top of the line for their hospitality and service needs. From first-class airplane seats, to limousines for ground transport, to the best hotel in the area, some companies spare no expense when entertaining themselves or their customers.

Some corporate cultures are just the opposite. They use hotel rooms sparingly, have meetings in their own offices, and use cabs or airport shuttles to reach hotels. Most companies are somewhere in between in spite of the hotel ads that seem to assume that corporate customers all expect Rolls Royces to whisk them to the hotel. Typically, corporate executives get the best treatment and company trainees the least. It mostly comes down to examining the purpose of travel, who is traveling, and where they are going.

Only recently have many companies come to realize the extent of their travel and entertainment budgets. In some cases, this can be as much as 25 percent of an organization's costs. Today, the situation had drastically changed from what it was just five years ago. A majority of corporations are tightening the screws on travel costs. As one corporate travel planner told us, "You can't believe what $5 a night means over a year's time." Hyatt Hotels apparently realizes this, as can be seen from its ad in Figure 7-1.

The emergence of corporate travel buyers is a result of this cost control effort. Essentially, such people's task is to control the cost without losing the quality of the product. Corporate travel buyers first ascertain the level and service of product that the organization is willing to accept; they then negotiate the prices and proceed more or less as follows.

Know the Volume It is difficult to negotiate anything without knowing the parameters with which both parties are dealing. A hotel might give a discount based upon expected volume, only to find that the volume never materializes. A corporation, on the other hand, might be unaware of its true rooms volume at a destination and be paying more than it could negotiate at that volume. The same is true with airline travel, where companies can often negotiate volume discounts.

With hotel rack rates at their present heights, the organizational customer has come to expect a discount no matter what the volume. One of the authors once received a call from a corporate travel department asking for a discounted rate. The company, which happened to sell shoes, claimed its volume would be about 100 room nights annually. The hotel happened to enjoy high occupancies and rarely discounted rooms, even for 1500 room nights a year. The shoe company planner was not convinced that his perception of

(Courtesy of Hyatt Hotels Corp.)

FIGURE 7-1   Marketing to the corporate travel planner

volume did not apply in this case. Finally, the author asked if he could get a discount on shoes if he bought three pairs a year. The response was, "Of course not! You have to be a big retailer to command a discount!" The point was finally made.

Hotel room rates are negotiated initially from the published or rack rates. Rarely, today, do customers pay the rack rate unless they are uneducated enough not to ask for the myriad array of other rates available, or are traveling during peak demand periods. From rack rates come corporate or commercial rates usually 10 to 15 percent lower than the rack rate.

As the business traveler became more savvy, the hotel industry began to violate the term *corporate rate*. Where once the corporate rate was offered to repeat customers to encourage brand loyalty, it is now offered to anyone who asks for it or presents a business card.

Hotels now negotiate individual corporate rates with individual corporate customers. Volume corporate customers recognize the widescale availability of corporate rates for anyone, and demand their own corporate rate relative to their volume. These rates can run 15 to 35 percent below the rack rate. This, of course, makes the rack rate a ridiculous pretension, so hotels raise the rack rate, say 10 percent, in order to raise the corporate and volume rates. With the few people who do pay rack rate, hotels thus manage to increase average rate about two percent each time.

The crux of the matter in this scenario is that corporate buyers have become much smarter (after all, their own company has been doing the same thing for years; who ever pays list price anymore?). The higher the rack rate, the more they argue for lower negotiated corporate rates on volume. The net effect overall has been higher rack rates and lower corporate rates, as well as desertion of many hotels, as new alterntives at far lower rates appear on the horizon.

Understanding Travel Patterns   The corporate organizational customer uses knowledge of corporate travel patterns to negotiate with hotel suppliers; the supplier responds in kind. For example, if the corporation has people traveling to a given city mainly when occupancy is already high, the customer will have far greater difficulty in negotiating preferred rates. On the other hand, if travel can be planned during low-occupancy periods, the customer may obtain not only high discount rates but also preferred availability during periods of high occupancy. The corporate customer tries to anticipate travel patterns, reserve in advance, and not just react to travel trends.

Controlling the Costs   When low room rates are negotiated, the corporate customer tries to ensure that they are used. If rates were negotiated on the basis of volume, then lack of volume may forfeit the rate. This stipulation is often inserted by the hotel. Of course, if lower rates are negotiated and company personnel don't utilize them, the cost savings are not realized.

Some companies develop policies to enforce their negotiated rates. The corporate customer might go into a marketplace and negotiate with hotels at various levels of product class and cost. For example, in Denver a company might have three preferred hotels: Holiday Inn, Sheraton, and Hyatt. Who stays at which depends upon the management level of the employee. To enforce compliance, the company may not reimburse hotel bills at alternative hotels unless the others are sold out.

Recently, there has been a trend by companies to hire intermediaries to handle this phase of the business. As rates for hotels and airlines become more complicated, along with the benefits of frequent traveler programs, the task of managing individual travel for corporations has become increasingly complex.

One solution has been the hiring of "in-plants" by companies with large travel budgets. An "in-plant" is a division of a travel agency that is located within the corporate offices of the organizational customer. The equipment and employees belong to the travel agency, but their utilization is dedicated to the one company's needs. These employees become the organizational customer, although they technically work for the travel agency. The in-plant receives either straight fees, commissions on bookings, or a combination of both for services rendered.

The in-plants offer unique resources to the corporation that would likely be inaccessible in any other way. Specificially, the in-plant can leverage its business with the one company plus other companies also served by the agency, to negotiate even lower rates. For example, XYZ company may have 500 rooms being used annually in Denver. This volume might justify a 10 percent discount off rack rates. The in-plant agency, however, might also represent four other companies with equal room usage in Denver. Thus, the in-plant can negotiate on the basis of 2500 room nights to receive a 25 percent discount for all.

The Corporate Meetings Market

The title *corporate meeting planner* includes a wide range of organizational customers. These people plan intimate meetings of 5 people for product introductions, or meetings for 1000 plus. This market represents over 700,000 meetings annually, with over $3 billion spent on hotels, food, and related expenses.[7]

To understand the needs of the meeting planner, one must review all the components of the organizational customer. In a nutshell, meeting planners need to "look good." They need to look good to their boss, to the person whose meeting they organize, and also to the hotel, if they want to continue to look good to the first two people. At least two hotels try to appeal to this need of meeting planners, as shown in Figure 7-2.

Meeting planners need to match the needs of the organization with the site of the meeting, and then feel confident that all of the arrangements that were discussed are executed. In the end, they need to evaluate their own organization, together with the performance of the hotel, to determine whether the meeting was a success.

What meeting planners do not need is for hotels to mislead them in regard to the capabilities of the physical plant and the personnel. The short-term nature of the hotel business sometimes lends itself to this type of misrepresentation, and eventual loss of the customer. With as much as a 70 percent annual turnover in many hotel sales offices, and bonuses based on room nights sold, the reward system essentially mandates how fast you can make your quota to increase your income or get promoted. Many other departments'

---

[7] *The Meetings Market,* study conducted by *Meetings and Conventions Magazine,* New York: Murdoch Magazines, 1983.

FIGURE 7-2   Ads appealing to the "look good" need of the meeting planner

people that service meetings are on a similar "fast track," often leaving the meeting planner in the hands of inexperienced new people.

Meeting planners need a professional conference coordinator to service the meeting. Meeting planners need a meeting room that will suit the purpose of the event. They also want a quiet room. Often, hotel ballrooms are divided by thin, movable walls that allow noise from the meeting next door to filter through. Employees are also a source of disruptive noise. While it is operationally convenient to have the kitchen right next to the ballroom, meeting attendees are disconcerted when the kitchen crew bangs pots and pans throughout the meeting. Doors that bang when people go in and out of meeting rooms are another source of high irritation.

The meeting planner needs an efficient front desk that will assign rooms to the right people: the V.I.P.'s in the suites and the attendees in the regular rooms. The billing needs to be right: Some rooms may be billed to the organization, some attendees may have to pay for their own. The meeting planner needs meeting rooms to be set up on time, and coffee breaks to arrive when ordered. The audiovisuals need to be in the meeting room at the right time, and in working order. The spare bulb for the projector should be on the cart, not locked in a closet at the other end of the building.

Meeting planners do not need excuses. It is not their problem that the banquet manager did not show up for work, or that the linen was supposed to be delivered at 10:00 A.M., or that they should not have scheduled the break so close to lunch time. The hotel staff assumes all responsibility for the "well-being" of the meeting.

In short, meeting planners expect all of the details to be handled absolutely professionally so that they look good. If a hotel is able to provide planners not only with what they think they need, but also with what they don't know they need, the planners will return. Figure 7-3 shows an ad for a hotel that apparently has run a few meetings right and received accolades for it.

From the hotel's side, there are problems with the corporate meetings market. While attendance at these meetings is compulsory, thus assuring the planned rooms and meal counts, cancellation of the entire meeting is often a threat. At the last minute, a corporation can cancel a meeting for hundreds of people that has been in the planning stage for months. Economic conditions, failure to develop a new product on schedule, or simply whim may provoke such a decision. Corporate meetings also have shorter lead times.

Corporate meeting planners may be spending only a small portion of their time on the meeting planning. They thus need as much help as they can get and may require a great deal of guidance in accomplishing their company's objectives. The hotel staff that provides that guidance will often secure the business. In fact, some corporate planners follow a salesperson when he or she changes jobs if they feel the planner does a good job for them.[8]

Conference Centers

Today there is a multitude of hotels from which meeting planners can choose. With this additional supply in most marketplaces, the need to attract meeting planners' business has

---

[8] Shaw, *Group Market*, pp. 13–14.

We've handled hundreds of successful meetings.

And what thanks do we get?

Simply the most outstanding praise any hotel could ask for. The prestigious Gold Key Award is given to the hotels that handle meetings and conventions best. In 1985 and 1986 we earned this national award. And we also won the 1986 Pinnacle and McRand awards. No other New England hotel has ever earned all three. What makes them extra special is that they are voted on by the groups themselves. Groups that hold meetings all over New England.

Why did they choose The Westin Hotel, Copley Place #1? Service. It's that simple.

Service that earned praise like, "The convention services staff is the most professional I've ever worked with," and, "The food, meeting rooms, and in-house audio-visual company are first-rate."

For your next meeting, call the hotel meeting planners call #1.

The Westin Hotel, Copley Place. Call our sales office at (617) 262-9600, or ask for the Group Desk at 800-228-3000.

THE WESTIN HOTEL
Copley Place Boston

(Courtesy of Westin Hotels and Resorts)

FIGURE 7-3   Rewards for "doing things right"

grown. Hotels that offered mediocre service in the past now find that there are willing competitors to match rates and offer service to win over and keep these customers.

One way the industry has responded to the unique needs of the meeting planner is by developing conference centers that are dedicated strictly to meetings, and that do an excellent job in specializing in this market. Some hotels claim to be conference centers by adding the words to their name—for instance, such and such resort becomes such and such resort and conference center. These hotels are not, however, conference centers in the pure sense: Pure conference centers book nothing but meetings. The needs of the meeting attendee are different from those of leisure guests or business travelers.

According to the IACC (International Association of Conference Centers) the big difference between a combined hotel-and-conference center and a pure conference center is not just technical services but *human* services. The IACC claims that the business of the typical hotel is 50 percent transients, limiting the attention and service it can give to every meeting, and that conference centers have a stronger commitment to conferences as essentially the only market they have. The attitude of the staff at a conference center, according to IACC, can be summarized as "we can."[9] Many hotels, however, are driven by financial pressures to try to be all things to all people.

In some cases, the combination of hotel and conference center works well when the markets are separated by time of the week or season. In other cases conflicts are created that can be detrimental. The ballroom that is ideal for weddings, or for trade shows, may be entirely inappropriate for meeting planners. For example, in the first case attendees would probably not hear noise going on in the kitchen. During a meeting sales presentation, however, those noises can break the concentration of the speaker and ruin the meeting.

The dividing walls of the same ballroom may be ideal for the separation of a cocktail reception and a dinner, while too porous for the holding of two meetings simultaneously. There are very few facilities that are ideal for all markets.

True conference centers attempt to serve one market only, the meetings market. They offer strictly meetings in controlled environments. With soundproof meeting rooms, dedicated audiovisual rooms with state-of-the-art equipment, and conference coordinators whose sole job is to faciliate the needs of the meetings, these properties offer a serious environment for conducting meetings. Most are located outside and away from major cities so that distractions are held to a minimum.

Many conference centers offer a full package rate that includes all the necesary services for one per-person price. These centers are dedicated to the needs of the meeting planners and serve them well. At the same time, some are having a difficult time making ends meet. Good occupancy occurs during selected time periods, but because these centers are unable (or, wisely, "do not desire") to attract other markets, the shoulder seasons incur very high costs without compensating revenues. Time will tell whether this reaction to the needs of the meeting planner will survive. Figure 7-4 gives an idea of conference center offerings.

---

[9] *Corporate Meetings & Incentives,* March 1988, p. 42.

FIGURE 7-4   Conference center solicitations

The Incentive Market

The incentive organizational customer has a unique problem (need) when compared with other customers of the hospitality product. The incentive customer has to provide not only for the accommodation of the group, but also for the group's idea of fun. This is a difficult task. When you think of your own idea of a good time, it is probably quite different from that of some people you know. This problem of disparity is one with which the incentive planner has to deal.

The incentive planner organizes travel as a reward for superior performance within a group. For example, the sales team of a computer manufacturer may have exceeded its sales quota by 30 percent. The reward is a trip to Bermuda for a week, with spouses.

Incentive trips are not limited just to salespeople. Managers of a retail store chain may be eligible for travel incentives if their profit margins are above a certain quota. The Society of Incentive Travel Executives, SITE, defines incentive travel as follows: "Incentive travel is a modern management tool that motivates salespeople, dealers, distributors, customers, and internal employees by offering rewards in the form of travel for participation in the achievement of goals and objectives."[10]

The incentive travel market generates over \$3 billion a year, including airfare and ground service. Over 50 percent is hotel related. Trip sizes range from 2 to 2000 people, with an average of over 100 people per trip. Most trips include spouses.[11]

Travel certainly is not the only method of incentive reward, but it is one that projects an image of excitement and relaxation away from the job. When this is done in the group format, teamwork and morale increase with the sense of accomplishment. Merchandise rewards, such as television, stereos, and cash bonuses, are the competition to travel rewards. Travel rewards are preferred by many companies, and managing that travel becomes an important task.

This has led to the growth of "incentive houses," companies that provide professional incentive planning and hope to assure no-hassle, successful, and satisfying trips. Because it is a reward, incentive travel always includes luxury and high levels of service demands.

Incentive Planners

The incentive planner often becomes involved in the development of criteria for incentive success. In order to have winners to send on trips, the framework of the incentive must be established. In order to have a successful incentive, the reward must be different and worth wanting.

Once the framework of the incentive has been developed, the incentive planner must formulate the appropriate travel prizes. Even if incentive planners do not specifically design the promotion, it is critical for them to have a full understanding of the composition of the group and its achievements. Incentive planners need to establish the perceived level of incentive, and plan accordingly.

---

[10] Quoted in Shaw, *Group Market*, p. 45.
[11] Lewis "Incentive Travel Market."

The Incentive Trip

The actual incentive trip can take three forms: pure incentive, incentive plus, and incentive weekends. The pure incentive trip is dedicated to having a good time without any business-related activities. These comprise about 15 percent of all incentive trips and almost always include spouses.[12]

The incentive plus is a more popular form of incentive trip and is used in over 70 percent of the cases.[13] Incentive plus trips combine pleasure with some form of meetings or new product introductions. In this way, companies maximize use of their incentive travel dollars. The company can disseminate valuable information without having another meeting elsewhere.

Incentive weekends are increasingly being used as rewards for good, but less than superior, performance. Companies recognize that while incentive trips are productive, they also take time away from the workplace. Three-day weekend incentives are more cost effective from a time management viewpoint.

The incentive planner has a multifaceted job when planning the actual trip. Specifically, all phases of the excursion must be minutely planned to enhance the end-user experience. This is different from planning corporate or association meetings, or conventions. In those cases, the planner plans the functions but leaves it to the individuals to get there and participate. The incentive planner, on the other hand, arranges for literally everything: air and land travel, hotel, food, excursions, sightseeing, entertainment, sports, and anything else that might take place during the trip. Each and every one of these categories can be critical to the success of the trip.

This is why incentive planners have almost always visited the site, and the hotels and restaurants at the site, before developing the package. They want to make sure not only that everything is up to par, but that every detail will be taken care of. Then they or their representatives go on the trip as a final security. This means that a hotel has a special challenge in booking and handling incentive travel. We know of one case, for example, when the planner ruled out a hotel on an inspection trip because the sand urns had cigarette butts in them and facial tissue was missing in some of the rooms. "If they can't take care of the little things, they'll never take care of the big ones," was this planner's comment.

Incentive trip planning also differs from that of other organizational customers in that the destination is of primary importance. The corporate customer or meeting planner may choose a facility because of the hotel itself or because of its proximity to business-related activities; for the incentive planner, the choice of hotel comes after the choice of destination.

Many companies are not large enough or skilled enough to develop incentive trips through their internal organization. A company may have a full-time corporate travel manager and a meeting planner, but the complexities of the incentive purchase are entirely different. Staying familiar with different destination areas and necessary ground arrangements is incredibly time-consuming, for example.

Incentive houses are a popular intermediary for the companies that need the dedicated attention of a professional. The incentive house is more than a travel agent; professional incentive planners help in all phases of incentive management. Broad

---

[12] *Successful Meetings*, November 1985, p. 105.
[13] Ibid.

The Inventive Incentive.

THE HARDER WORKING INCENTIVE
PROGRAMME, FOR YOUR HARDER
WORKING EXECUTIVES.
SHERATON FIJI RESORT.
STEPPING BEYOND THE USUAL
INCENTIVE BOUNDARIES.
OFFERING AN ACTION AND RELAXATION
PACKED BREAK IN THE WORLD'S
FRIENDLIEST ISLANDS.
SPORTING, SWIMMING, SUNNING.
SHERATON FIJI RESORT.
THE PRIME MOTIVATOR.

OPENING SEPTEMBER 1987

Ⓢ
**Sheraton
Fiji Resort**
The hospitality people of ITT

D E N A R A U　　B E A C H　　F I J I

THE
INCENTIVE
IN SINGAPORE

Take the charm and attractions of Singapore. Add the grandeur of truly world class hotels and you have the formula for a successful and memorable incentive programme. A programme built around Westin.
For a copy of our 'Meeting & Incentive Handbook' contact The Westin Stamford and Westin Plaza in Singapore Tel: (65) 338-8585, Telex: RS 22206 RCHTLS. Or in United States and Canada 800-228-3000.

THE WESTIN STAMFORD & WESTIN PLAZA
Raffles City
2 Stamford Road, Singapore 0617.

THE PEOPLE AND PLACES OF WESTIN.
Caring·Comfortable·Civilized.

WESTIN
HOTELS & RESORTS

The ultimate incentive now has a name.

Anyone who has ever been to Thailand never forgets the magic. And a lot of those people have never even been to Phuket! This glorious island is the ultimate incentive. From tropical jungles and hills to quaint, traditional architecture, unspoilt national parks, quiet villages and magnificent scenery. And the beaches! Long stretches of white sand and crystal clear water. And wherever you go, the wonderfully genuine hospitality of Thai people. Now Phuket has a superb hotel to match this unique location – Le Meridien Phuket. Located on its own secluded beach, Le Meridien has all the ingredients for a successful and memorable incentive. 470 rooms and suites, magnificent sea views, a choice of restaurants and bars, entertainment, sports facilities and a management experienced in handling incentive groups. Phuket is a dream island. And making those dreams come true is Le Meridien Phuket

Le
MERIDIEN
PHUKET

(Courtesy of Westin Hotels and Resorts, The Sheraton Corporation, and Le Meridien)

FIGURE 7-5　Ads aimed at the incentive travel market

experience with specialized organizational needs supplements seasoned knowledge in even first-time attempts.

Whether an incentive house or the internal organizational customer purchases the product, similar steps take place.

- The incentive is devised and established, and winners will be declared.
- The planner determines the budget based upon time constraints and the number of potential winners.
- The planner matches the needs of the group with possible destinations. The destination will be affected by the form of incentive.
- The planner, along with company officials, makes the decision on destination and facility. The choice of facility rests heavily on personal experience and references from other incentive planners. Hotel sales personnel may have considerable influence on inexperienced planners; experienced planners tend to rely more on their own sources and instincts. Coordinators at the site are also an important factor. The planner prefers veterans seasoned in handling incentive groups.
- The planning process begins. All details begin to flow from the group planner to the hotels, airlines, and ground services contacts.
- The trip occurs, usually accompanied by the planner or a representative from the incentive house to coordinate all of the details.
- The incentive is evaluated. The context of the promotion is evaluated along with the quality of the actual trip. The evaluation process influences the following years' incentive trips significantly. The same winners will most likely not be taken to the same place again. However, there may be winners in other categories or, for the incentive house, from other companies. For repeat winners, next year's effort will be to top the last one.

Overall, the incentive organizational customer has a unique job among hotel customers. The "fun" aspect of the planning can be anything but that. Hotels that want a greater share of the incentive market must be extremely flexible in their approach to this marketplace. Standardized approaches to capturing this market are likely not to be fruitful.[14] Ads aimed at this market are shown in Figure 7-5.

Association, Convention, and Trade Show Markets

Association and convention customers have similar needs, although they are somewhat different types of groups. Both tend to have large guest room and function space requirements. These organizational customers are, in many cases, full-time employees or executives of the associations they represent. With occasional exceptions, these planners in general are becoming more sophisticated and more professional.

The association and convention market represents about $35 billion annually spent in hospitality establishments. There are over 12,000 functions that fall under the jurisdiction of this organizational customer each year in the United States alone.[15]

---

[14] For more explicit details of the needs, wants, and satisfactions of incentive planners, and how to market to them, see Lewis, "Incentive Travel Market."

[15] "Association Meeting Trends," *Association Management*, April 1986.

An association meeting can comprise a group of people convening on a social basis. The Lions Club is an association of people that meet to elect officers, have social functions, and organize philanthropic endeavors, on a regional and/or a national basis. This category of organizational customer also tends to meet throughout the year in smaller groups, and social contacts are a major reason for attendance. There are, of course, innumerable professional (e.g., American Medical Association) and business associations (e.g., National Association of Manufacturers) that meet both regionally and nationally.

Conventions are more focused on annual activities, such as annual meetings of delegates for a political caucus. Other examples are union gatherings to decide policies for the coming year, or a fishermen's convention to plan lobbying efforts. The participants may or may not meet throughout the year, and dissemination of information, not social contacts, is the primary objective.

A convention solicitation showing all meeting space capacities is illustrated in Figure 7-6.

Finally the main purpose of trade shows is to sell products, as shown in the ad in Figure 7-7. Either booths or space is sold to purveyors, and attendees peruse the offerings under one roof. Although informational seminars may be given during the show, the main purpose of the event is to display products and take orders. The trade show organizer makes money from the booth or space sales. In turn, the purveyors hope to write enough business to make the expense worthwhile.

The hotel's task in booking trade shows is to provide the space, the access for products to be brought in, and the facilities such as electric power and lighting, to display the products. This requires a great deal of work, which can be disruptive to other guests. In addition, the hotel sells rooms and meals to exhibitors and those who attend. Exhibitors also make wide use of "hospitality suites" where they entertain customers. This puts heavy pressure on the hotel's room service division, albeit at high cost to the exhibitors.

While each of these three organizational customers (association, convention, and trade show) has a different reason for purchasing the hospitality product, the needs are similar. At times, an entire facility will be purchased for a two- or three-day period. Usually, the organizational customer arranges for guest rooms to be held, but reservations are made individually by the participants. The organizer will have a list of V.I.P.'s, but the majority of guest rooms are booked by direct calls or through the use of reservation cards.

Reservations cards are essentially order forms that are provided by the hotel and are designed specifically for the use of attendees. Attendees, of course, are always free to stay somewhere else if they prefer. Thus, the hotel sales department tries to make it conducive for them to stay there. Handling reservations in this manner can make coordination difficult. The hotel must be flexible to the needs of the attendees, many of whom are buying the hotel sight unseen. Strict inventory control is necessary. If, for example, the hotel accepts more king-size bedroom requests than it can accommodate, it may have many unhappy customers.

Food and beverage is also a unique proposition for hotels in these markets. The organizational buyer tries to be as precise as possible in the number of people who will attend meal functions, but the actual attendance can vary widely. If there are alternatives, as in a large city, many attendees will go out for meals. Attendance at different meal functions can vary widely even within the same meeting. The first night's award banquet

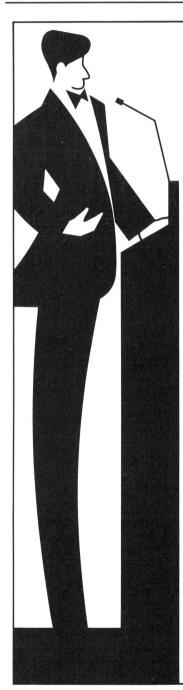

CONVENTIONS ARE STAYING HERE

In the new heart of downtown Montreal, a 4-star hotel par excellence – the elegant Hotel Meridien, with impeccable guest services and accommodations characteristic of Air France's hotels worldwide… a premier locale for both small conferences and large conventions.

Location. Downtown, part of sensational Complexe Desjardins (large shopping concourse enclosing a 1-acre public square). Linked by direct underground access to Montreal's Convention Centre and Place des Arts. 5 minutes from central business and commercial core.

Rooms. 601 deluxe rooms. Executive floor (Le Club Président) with special luxury as well as business services. All first-class amenities.

Dining and entertainment. Superb, gourmet-class dining in the Café Fleuri. Relaxing lobby lounge. Chic dinner theatre.

Recreation. Sauna and beautiful large indoor swimming pool, opening onto landscaped roof-top terrace.

Contact. Director of Sales, Hotel Meridien Montreal, 4 Complexe Desjardins, P.O. Box 130, Montreal, Que. (H5B 1E5). Tel: (514) 285-1450.
Toll-free reservations from other centres in Quebec, Ontario or the Atlantic Provinces: 1-800-361-8234. Elsewhere in Canada, or from the U.S.A.: 1-800-543-4300.

ROOM	SIZE	HT	CL'RM	TH'RE	BQ'T	RECEP.
Grand Salon	52' x 147'	18'	600	1000	800	1000
● Grand Salon A	52' x 43'	18'	120	220	250	260
● Grand Salon B	52' x 60'	18'	250	350	300	350
● Grand Salon C	52' x 43'	18'	120	220	250	260
Foyer	134' x 30'	9'	—	—	300	540
Salon Argenteuil	58' x 22'	9'	70	150	120	160
Salon Auteuil*	22' x 50'	9'	50	80	80	100
Salon Vaudreuil	25' x 22'	9'	20	25	30	30
Salon Touraine	23' x 14'	9'	12	20	16	20
Salon Lorraine	23' x 14'	9'	15	20	16	20
Salon Anjou*	23' x 37'	9'	35	70	60	80
Salon Picardie	30' x 51'	9'	80	160	140	180
Alfred Rouleau	195' x 35'	10'	225	400	650	850
● Section A	80' x 35'	10'	120	200	230	250
● Section B	57' x 35'	10'	90	140	180	200
● Section C	57' x 38'	10'			100	150
Foyer	1858 sq.ft.	—	—	—	—	150
Salon des Arts	26' x 60'	10'	50	80	—	100

*Salons Auteuil and Anjou can be divided

HOTEL **MERIDIEN** MONTREAL
TRAVEL COMPANION OF AIR FRANCE

FIGURE 7-6   Ad soliciting convention business

FIGURE 7-7   Ad aimed at trade show planners

might have close to 100 percent attendance. The following night might have a boring speaker and half the attendees will go elsewhere.

Association, convention, and trade show planners need extremely good coordinators within the hotel to execute all phases of the event. These coordinators are far more important than the salespeople in delivery of the final product. Technical details such as the voltage in the main ballroom, the delivery space for exhibits, and the audiovisuals for the speakers are all critical to the success of the function.

The hotel staff also needs to have good relations with the unions that are involved in handling large affairs. Not only are union members within the hotel utilized, but often there are members of other unions who set up booths, deliver products to the display area, and so forth. An organizational customer doing the planning from a distance will be unaware of the nuances of local unions. A mistake in procedures can ruin the set-up or break-down of a function very easily.

Delegates to these kinds of functions often will not stay for the duration of the meeting. They may book for three nights and stay two, and not give any notice of doing it. Many are small business people who cannot make definite plans for the future; others will simply feel they've had all they want and decide to leave.

Delegates to these functions also tend to be quite price-sensitive. The organizer, who wants to keep the delegates happy, looks for low rates and for low-cost or free meeting space. All three of these markets are tough to sell and tough to service, but they can represent lucrative business, especially if booked during slow business periods.

Summary

Organizational customers are unique to the hospitality industry in that they plan travel for others in groups, but not for themselves. These customers are responsible to the organizations they represent. They have to anticipate the wide variety of needs that members of these organizations represent.

Overall, the organizational customer is better educated and has more experience in the hospitality industry than the individual purchaser of the hotel and restaurant product. The single most important factor in their decision-making process remains the word-of-mouth of their fellow professionals. Second, references from someone in the organization help steer this customer toward a hotel choice. The contact coordinator at the hotel is probably more significant than the salesperson, in most cases, in creating and keeping customers. Advertising ranks low on the scale of influence. The organizational customer is a special case for the hospitality industry.

DISCUSSION QUESTIONS

1. What is the essential difference between the organizational customer and other customers discussed earlier in this book?
2. Why do hotel convention and conference coordinators play a more important role in the decision-making process of the organizational customer?

3. How do the corporate travel planner customer and the corporate meeting planner customer differ?
4. Describe the three types of different incentive trips. How would each of these affect the choice of destination and hotel?
5. Why is the postevaluation process critical for organizational customers?
6. Describe the differences between the association, the convention, and the trade show segments in terms of the end-users.

PART IV
Defining the Market

CHAPTER 8
Differentiation, Segmentation, and Target Marketing

In previous chapters we have somewhat casually talked about differentiation, segmentation, and target markets without really defining those concepts. It is time that we did so, since each is a vital and integral part of marketing. Accordingly, each deserves the extended treatment given in this chapter.

Differentiation, segmentation, and target marketing are each critical marketing concepts and tools that help us to understand and analyze the market. They are tools by which the marketer hopes to outflank the competition, seize marketing opportunity, maximize marketing efforts, and satisfy customer needs and wants. They are separate concepts and tools but, at the same time, they are highly interrelated—that is, rarely are all three not involved in the marketing of the same product. We will first define how they are different, then how they work together.

Product Differentiation

Product differentiation in its simplest form means differentiation of your product from those of others for the entire potential market. Wendell Smith calls it "the bending of demand to the will of supply."[1] This means you are distinguishing your product from that of the competition, so that demand will come your way.

The assumption is that the customer will perceive greater utility, better price value, and/or better problem solution in your product. Notice the use of the word *perceive*, a

---

[1] Wendell R. Smith, "Product Differentiation and Market Segmentation as Alternative Marketing Strategies," *Journal of Marketing*, July, 1956, pp. 3–8.

word that we expanded on at some length in Chapter 6; it is not necessary that there be an actual difference, only that the market perceives there to be one. It is just as important to note the converse situation: If the market does not perceive a difference, then for all intents and purposes it doesn't exist. It is clear, once again, how important knowledge of the customer is in marketing a product.

The objective of the marketer in practicing product differentiation is to convince consumers that a particular product is different, or better, so they will choose it over all others. There are numerous examples of this strategy in the hospitality industry, especially in advertising. (Refer again to the ads in Figure 1-3.)

For example, the Park Lane Hotel in New York City has run ads with the heading, "Soars 46 stories over Central Park," differentiating the product on the basis of the open view that very few hotels in New York City can claim. This is a true differentiation; the question for the consumer is, "Does it matter, especially if I get a room on the other side of the hotel?" The marketer hopes that the consumer's perception is that it does matter.

The Park Lane example of product differentiation in advertising demonstrates the use of appeals to selective buying motives rather than to primary buying motives. A view of Central Park will probably solve the problems of very few people staying at a hotel. It is not the reason most people buy a hotel room in a city. The same is true for Tara Hotels; a Sheraton franchisee, Tara developed its hotels with a castle theme to differentiate it from other Sheraton hotels.

Thus, the effort is, as Smith stated, to bend the demand to the supply. The appeal in the above cases, as you may recall from Chapter 6, is to the aesthetic needs identified by Maslow as cognitive needs, not specifically located on his hierarchy.

Bases of Product Differentiation

The bases for product differentiation are often minor product features. In themselves, they may be unimportant, but they can be very effective when (1) they cannot be duplicated, (2) they appeal to a particular need and/or want, and (3) they create an image or impression that goes beyond the specific difference itself.

Consider the Plaza Hotel or the Waldorf Astoria, both in New York City. Both are venerable hotels with a great deal of history behind them, which have been frequented in the past by people of international fame. These histories cannot be duplicated by other hotels in New York. This "product" has considerable appeal for consumers who like the old world and the feeling of blending with the past. Finally, there is an image or impression that these hotels, because of their past, will have great service and unmatched elegance. This may not be at all true, but for those who believe it is, demand is bent to meet supply.

In contrast to the Waldorf and the Plaza, consider the Marriott Marquis, which opened in 1986 claiming the tallest atrium lobby in the world. This subliminally suggests that the individual guest will be overwhelmed (Figure 13-2). Likewise, the Westin Stamford in Singapore advertised that it is the tallest hotel in the world. These are hardly insignificant differences in terms of grandeur, or "breathtaking" experience, but they may be totally insignificant in differentiating hotel services or core products. In fact, at least in the case of the Westin, the claim may be self-defeating. Many people purposely avoid higher floors in hotels for fear of fire or other catastrophe. Thus, these people might well avoid the Westin for fear of being stuck 40 stories up. (Westin would have done well to research its market before making its claim so loudly.) It can be seen, however, that these differences also fit the three criteria of effective differentiation.

If we assume, only for the sake of argument, that three of these hotels—the Waldorf, the Plaza, and the Marriott Marquis—are trying to attract the same consumer market, and that the rooms (those in the older hotels have been completely refurbished), the service, the food, and other hotel product elements are highly comparable, we can see the need for the use of differentiation strategies. In sum, companies that differentiate products must also face the need to instill an image in the minds of customers that distinguishes their products from others, and causes the customer to react more favorably toward them.

Some companies differentiate on brand name. Is Bayer different from other aspirin? Bayer would like you to think so, claiming, "It gets into the bloodstream faster," and "Doctors recommend it most." Is Burger King any different from McDonald's? After all, it is the "Home of the Whopper," where "We do it your way."

Differentiation of Intangibles

You can see that differentiation may be moot when it occurs within the same product class, especially when used in traditional marketing efforts. In the hospitality industry, most true differentiation occurs internally because, of course, that is where the product is used. If the service is poor or the product run-down, the final determination of differentiation may be negative, and age, history, or atrium will soon be forgotten.

Because the hospitality product is so largely intangible, differentiation in traditional marketing needs to center largely on "tangibilizing the intangible," an expression commonly used in services marketing to mean making a concrete representation out of something abstract, such as using an atrium lobby (concrete) to represent an "exciting" (abstract) hotel, as we also discussed in Chapter 6.

Some efforts to do this center on the frequent use of pictures of hotel buildings in advertising for purposes of tangible representation. When the hotel structure, however, is clearly little different from that of many other hotels, this tangibilization fails to differentiate. This obsession with hotel buildings is sometimes metaphorically referred to as an "edifice complex." It is demonstrated by the Marriott ad in Figure 1-3 and the Taj Hotel ad in Figure 8-1. At times, this complex may be as psychotic as the one attributed to Oedipus. Unless there is a substantial means of differentiating the intangible by virtue of the tangible, the effort may be a mistaken one.

It was mentioned earlier that what is differentiated may be totally unreal; the hope is that perception will make it real. Consider Loew's Hotels' ads of a few years ago. These ads featured the names of all Loew's hotels on a gold background with the caption, "The golden opportunity for the 80s." This caption was just as intangible as any hotel services and the differentiation from other hotels was totally abstract. The purpose, however, was to create a perception that these hotels were clearly differentiated from their competition. Whether or not they were is not demonstrated by the expression *golden opportunity*—in other words, nothing in that expression creates a perception of product differentiation.

The Desert Inn in Palm Springs, California, was even more blatant. Their ads

BOMBAY The Taj Mahal Hotel &
The Taj Mahal Inter-Continental

BOMBAY Hotel President

NEW DELHI The Taj Mahal Hotel

NEW DELHI Taj Palace Hotel

JAIPUR The Rambagh Palace

JAIPUR The Jai Mahal Palace Hotel

UDAIPUR The Lake Palace

BANGALORE Taj Residency

BANGALORE West End Hotel

GOA The Aguada Hermitage

GOA The Fort Aguada Beach Resort

GOA The Taj Holiday Village

MADRAS Taj Coromandel Hotel

MADRAS Connemara Hotel

MADRAS The Fisherman's Cove

BENARES Hotel Taj Ganges

OOTY Savoy Hotel

COCHIN Malabar Hotel

AGRA Taj-View Hotel

KHAJURAHO Hotel Chandela

CALCUTTA Taj Bengal (Opening mid—1988)

 THE TAJ GROUP OF HOTELS, INDIA

FIGURE 8-1 The "edifice complex"

simply stated, "We're the difference," and showed a picture of a hotel that looked like hundreds of others. In cases like this, consumers must really stretch their imagination to obtain the desired perception. As we showed in Chapter 6 in the section on personal constructs, consumers need tangible evidence to support intangible claims.

Differentiation as a Marketing Tool

Nevertheless, differentiation is an important marketing tool, whether the differences are real or only perceived. For one thing they help to create awareness and trial by the consumer. Atrium lobby hotels certainly did that for Hyatt, Ronald McDonald did it for McDonald's, boxcars did it for Victoria Station restaurants, and orange roofs and 28 flavors of ice cream did it for Howard Johnson's. Internally, personnel attitude has done it for the Opryland Hotel in Nashville, and cleanliness has done it for McDonald's.

As we shall see later in this chapter, sometimes the only thing we can do when we compete with others in the same market segment is attempt to differentiate the product. It is a world of limited opportunities, in this respect, when the product approaches commodity status and differentiation may occur only, as pointed out in Chapter 5, in the marketing.

Attempts to differentiate also have another aspect. When they are vulnerable to easy copying by the competition, there are two possible negative effects. The first is obvious and has already been mentioned: As in the case of extensive bathroom amenities, when the competition quickly follows suit, the differential advantage is lost, demand once again levels out, and the cost of the differential becomes a burden without producing additional revenue.

The second negative effect is the creation of expectation in the consumer, who comes to expect a differential even after the competition has done the same thing. This might be called the "what have you done for me lately" syndrome. The property is now caught in a cycle of being unable to fulfill expectations, and reality does not match expectation for the consumer. This is a Catch-22 phenomenon that the hotel industry got itself into with their amenities programs.[2]

There is a way out of this, however, and it lies in marketing in its true sense, rather than in essentially giving things away. This means, of course, going back to the customer. Consider the following two examples.

- The Shangri-la Hotel in Montreal added condoms to its amenities package in 1987 because, "Our first purpose was to come up with a practical amenity and *I think* [emphasis added] this one is more appropriate than anything else right now," according to the General Manager.[3] This may differentiate the hotel ("reaction to the news has been 'unbelievable,' with an estimated 98% of it being positive"); will it create a customer? Unlikely.
- Days Inn research revealed that guests prefer in-room coffee service over such basic amenities as shampoo, lotions, and shower caps: "87 percent indicated they would

---

[2] A Catch-22 situation is one in which something cannot happen until something else happens, but the something else cannot happen until the first thing happens.

[3] Tony Lima, "Updating Amenities to Meet Changing Lifestyles: From Computers to Condoms," *Lodging Hospitality*, June 1987, p. 108.

even pay an increased room rate if rooms were supplied with such a service. . . . 78 percent indicated . . . an in-room coffee system would influence their selection of a hotel the next time they traveled."[4] Will it create a customer? Very likely.

The difference between these two examples should be clear. Differentiation, to be effective, must be meaningful. There's still nothing like asking the customer.

Foodservice establishments actually have greater opportunity to differentiate than do hotels. Although some foodservice product classes may be somewhat close to commodity status, there is a wide variety of ways that restaurants can differentiate their product; in other words, it is much easier to be creative, economically, with a menu and decor in a restaurant than with a hotel room.

Hotel managements have also begun to realize this in the past few years. The traditional hotel always had a coffee shop, a fine dining room, and a lounge, often with little imagination or creativity and often not fulfilling customers' needs. Rather than be creative and seek new opportunities, it was simply accepted that food and beverage departments would operate at a small profit and there wasn't much that could be done about it. The frequent customer reaction was, "That's hotel food; let's go out to eat."

Although hotel restaurants today have more creative concepts, many of them still tend to ignore the customers' needs, as we have previously discussed. The situation is quite different outside the United States. Both in Europe and Asia it is not uncommon for hotel dining rooms to be the best restaurants in the city. Both hotel guests and the local populace patronize them heavily. In France, for example, one can find a two-star hotel with minimal rooms that includes a dining room superior to most in New York City.

One of the first to break this mold and take a different approach was Jim Nassikas when he opened the Stanford Court in San Francisco in 1971. Nassikas opened Fournou's Ovens restaurant within the hotel, but didn't tell the hotel guests. There was no mention of the restaurant in the guest rooms or within the hotel. To get there, guests were instructed to go out the front door and around the corner. In fact, one of Nassikas' favorite stories is of the hotel guests who hailed a cab in order to get to the restaurant. Nassikas' strategy not only added a mystique to the restaurant, it also differentiated it in the perception of nonguests who fastidiously avoided "hotel food." The result was a very successful, differentiated hotel gourmet restaurant now well established and no longer kept secret. Others have successfully used a restaurant to position a hotel, as with the Maurice restaurant at the Parker Meridien in New York City.

Today there are hotels with "fast-break" bars for juice, coffee, and rolls; restaurants for "grazing" (the somewhat pejorative term for eating less but more frequently), lounges with deli bars as well as liquor bars, and so forth. When the basic hotel room doesn't change much, these are excellent opportunities to differentiate in areas that are not as susceptible to copying and that, given the public's social propensity for these attributes, can offer unique and distinct advantages.

Differentiation—of Anything

The point that Levitt makes, as mentioned in Chapter 5, is worth reiterating. Levitt points out that goods manufacturers seek competitive difference through features that may be

---

[4] Ibid., p. 118.

(Courtesy of Beacon Hotel Corporation)

FIGURE 8-2 Segmenting the all-suite market

t　t we will need to locate those segments of the market with like needs and wants—in o　r words, we need to break the market down into smaller homogeneous segments. Our n　 is better served if we take this in stages, since there are a number of elements that we wi　eed to consider along the way.

eds and Wants of the Marketplace   In an oversimplification of the problem, we could 'uct a giant research survey in which we asked consumers what it was they wanted 　 hotel or restaurant. The complexity of this question is immediately apparent: Where? V.　2 With whom? For what purpose? At what price? It is clear that we will not get very far 　 his approach, so the first thing we will have to do is to set some parameters. Let 　 d with a hypothetical example.

We are considering 　 a restaurant in a city whose population is a million, including the environs. We have u　 fast-food restaurant but could be anything from an inexpensive family retaurant to a very e　urmet restaurant. We analyze what already exists and find that there is no high-quality French restaurant in the area. With this existing void, we could go this route and, without too much difficulty, clearly differentiate our restaurant from the competition, on French cuisine.

But what if no one wants French cuisine? We would be in serious trouble. Already we see the hazards of differentiating before segmentation. Instead, at this stage, let's ignore the competition and what already exists because, even if it exists, we really don't know if it is satisfying the needs and wants of the marketplace. Maybe it is not as successful as it looks; maybe it is successful only because there is no alternative.

So, let us set the parameters. To simplify the example, let's say we have found a location and we have decided to open for lunch and dinner. Otherwise, there are no restrictions. Now we can conduct our survey.

Assume that we can survey the entire population (actually, we would take a random sample, which will be discussed in the chapter on marketing research) of those with household incomes of $15,000 or more per year (50 percent of the population). The questions we could ask are almost unlimited but we will have to narrow them down: How often do you go out for lunch/dinner? Where do you go? What do you order? Are you satisfied with the offering? What would you like to have instead? How much do you spend? How far do you travel? Do you like the atmosphere? Would you like a different atmosphere? What? Where would you like to go? How often? How much would you be willing to spend? What would you order? and so forth.

Our survey shows that 6 percent of the population with family incomes greater than $15,000 would/do go to a gourmet restaurant with some frequency. They will go there an average of five times a month for lunch with an average of two other persons, and twice a month for dinner with an average of one other person. They would spend $12 per person for lunch and $24 per person for dinner.

Of course, the other 94 percent of the population is saying something else that, having open minds, we could not ignore. For purposes of illustration, however, let us concentrate on this 6 percent. This is a market segment: a relatively homogeneous segment of the market that likes, and will patronize, a gourmet restaurant. Armed with this information we proceed to step #2.

Projecting Wants and Needs into Potential Markets   This stage is called demand analysis. Demand analysis includes needs and wants plus willingness and ability to pay. Willingness and ability to pay are critical and we cannot afford to overlook them. For example, we may truly need a car to get to work every day, and we may truly want a Mercedes, but if we are unwilling to pay the price of a Mercedes, we are clearly not in the demand segment for that car. On the other hand, if we are willing but unable to pay, we are also not in the appropriate demand segment. Demand analysis means projecting needs, wants, and willingness and ability to pay into a potential market.

Our survey has shown that we have needs, wants, and willingness and ability to pay. What does this mean in terms of potential market? If we can believe the figures (again, this is an oversimplification to make the point), we can quickly calculate that 30,000 people in the area (6 percent of 500,000) would be interested in the restaurant. If we take the worst case and assume that those who would accompany them are also in the population surveyed, we calculate 50,000 [(30,000/3) × 5] lunches a month for a gross of $600,000 (50,000 × $12). For dinner we calculate 30,000 covers [(30,000/2) × 2] a month for a gross of $360,000 ($24 × 15,000). The total potential of this market is perceived to be approximately $1,000,000 gross per year. This appears to be sufficient, so we proceed to step #3.

Matching the Market and Capabilities   Recall that we had open minds about the type of restaurant when we surveyed the market. Now that we have found an effective demand, the question is, do we have the capabilities to meet that demand? In this case, because we are starting from scratch, we have to consider dollar resources and all the financial implications of a major undertaking; designing and equipping a gourmet restaurant is not the same as designing and equipping a family restaurant. But we also have to consider the expertise in the firm: Who will manage it? What is their experience? Is this our mentality or philosophy? Does it fit with other things we are doing? Do we need outside help? and so forth. It is important, but often overlooked, that a firm's capabilities be matched to the market it is trying to serve.

There are many examples in industry of failures due to lack of understanding of a different market. Two in the hospitality industry come quickly to mind.

Heublein was essentially a packaging and marketing company; in a sense they sold other people's products. Their greatest success was Smirnoff vodka. When they bought Kentucky Fried Chicken, Heublein was faced with a highly perishable product with many more variables in the purchase decision than in buying a bottle of vodka. In short, Heublein lacked the capability to handle this market, sales skidded, and eventually the Kentucky Fried Chicken division was sold to R. J. Reynolds, which had the expertise and turned the company around.

City Investing Corp. had purchased the Motel 6 chain. By exercising strong cost controls and positioning the property at the low-cost, no-frills, end of the budget motel market, City Investing succeeded where others had failed. It then took on Sambo's Restaurants and applied the same strategies and tactics, not recognizing the personal relationships of the restaurant business or the consumers' different perspective. In short, City Investing lacked the capabilities to operate restaurants, and Sambo's ended up in bankruptcy court.

If we have successfully passed the first three steps, we can proceed to step #4.

Segmenting the Market   We have determined the needs and wants of the market-place, projected them into potential markets, and matched them with our capabilities. But *gourmet* is a very broad category; in fact it is quite heterogeneous in composition. Not only does gourmet mean different things to different people, there are also many forms of gourmet. So we turn to further segmentation. To simplify the case, let's assume that we found a strong preference for French food in our survey; we decide to segment the market on those who have a high preference for French food. Now we have to go back through steps #2 and #3, and reevaluate the situation once more.

Selecting Target Markets from Identified Segments   Just as gourmet food is not all the same, neither is all French food. To take an example, this fact was learned the hard way by a restaurateur in a midsized New England city:

> This operator opened a French retaurant because "there weren't any around." He managed to build a small, loyal, steady clientele as well as an infrequent special-occasion following. When he closed, unsuccessful, two and a half years later his comment was, "The people in this city think French cuisine is quich Lorraine and Caesar Salad."

So we have to select specific target markets from the broader market segment. This will be discussed in more detail later, but we might target on occasion, on nouvelle French, on income bracket, on age, on business entertaining, or any number of other things.

Tailoring the Product to the Wants and Needs of the Target Market   Now we see the advantages of segmenting and target marketing in terms of the marketing concept. Let's look at these advantages more specifically.

- *We are better able to identify and evaluate opportunities in the marketplace.* By knowing our target market, we can track it, identify what is missing, find niches, and discover consumers' problems.
- *We can better mesh our product with the needs of the market.* Consider the survey we did of the entire population, an expensive and time-consuming chore. Now we can be more specific as to who the market is. We can ask more specific questions and get higher response rates because we now have people interested in the subject. We can identify better who those people are. We can have a much better idea of the acceptance of any innovation.
- *We can optimally allocate and direct our resources.* As in the case described above, we wouldn't build a fancy French restaurant for a market that wanted quiche, nor would we need the same level of manpower and expertise. Perhaps we could determine that there is a take-out market for quiche and develop that end of the business. In short, the potential for wasting resources is greatly decreased.
- *We can use relevant market intelligence to sense change and to change strategies.* Because we now have a smaller market and are closer to it, we can keep in touch with it better. We have more opportunity to "talk" to the customer. We are better able to determine cultural and reference group influences, to understand beliefs and attitudes, to recognize and influence perceptions, to use tangible evidence of intangible constructs, to understand the information processing of the consumer, and to give more "control" to both consumers and employees.

- *We have greater ability to tailor our behavior, promotion, logistics, distribution channels, and marketing mix to the market.* Essentially, this means we are better able to reach customers both by knowing where they are and by knowing what appeals to them, what they pay attention to, what they react to, and what media they use.
- *We are better able to be unique and to differentiate from the competition.* We can determine more readily what the competition is doing for this segment or target market. We know better what to copy, what not to copy, and what we do that will be copied. We have more opportunity to find competitive advantage and to exploit the weaknesses of the competition.
- *We are better able to determine strategies to develop and enlarge the core market.* Take again the example of take-out quiche. Initially we might not think this was a viable opportunity at all; by knowing our market we might learn that it was and start offering take-home quiche to our customers. Eventually we could expand this market by selling it to noncustomers—those who would not come to eat but would come to take it home.

Segmentation Variables

There is no one best way to segment the market but there is no shortage of different ways to do it. What's more, they are certainly not mutually exclusive. First, we will discuss some of the more commonly used segmentation variables and then we will take a look at how they overlap.

Geographic Segmentation

Geographic location is probably the original segmentation variable and one of the most widely used. It has its strengths and its weaknesses.

Geographically speaking, we can segment by country, city, town, part of city, or even neighborhood. The essence and the substance of geographic segmentation is that certain geographic locations are the major sources of our business. A hotel in San Francisco might draw most of its business from Los Angeles and New York. A hotel in Singapore might draw most of its business from Australia and Japan. A restaurant in New York City might draw most of its business from the upper East Side. A restaurant in Hartford, Connecticut, might draw most of its business from suburban towns.

If geographic segments can be pinpointed, then the problem of reaching those segments is greatly facilitated, especially if they are in concentrated areas. Both direct mail and media forms of communication are more easily specified. It is also possible to utilize available resources to learn more about the denizens of these areas.

The federal government defines large metropolitan areas in terms of supposed economic boundaries called *standard metropolitan statistical areas (SMSA)*—for example, the New York City SMSA. The government produces reams of data on these areas—population, ethnic mix, growth, income, discretionary spending, household size, occupations, and so forth. The use of SMSAs in hospitality marketing is probably greatest when the market is being segmented on certain demographic variables. SMSAs can be analyzed for the existence of these variables.

Another geographic division is the *designated market area,* or DMA, developed by the A. C. Nielsen research company. These designations are based on geographic areas served by television stations. Their data also include demographic characteristics that can be used for reaching specific audiences by television. Fast-food chains such as McDonald's and Burger King use these designations.

A final, widely used geographic designation is the ADI, or *area of dominant influence.* These designations are also based on television coverage but are used as well by newspaper and magazine media for distribution of their regional editions. Thus, one could use ADIs for print communication as well as television.

Geographic segmentation is the easiest segmentation to define but it is also the most fallible for the hospitality industry. The local neighborhood eatery doesn't have to employ SMSAs, DMAs, or ADIs to know where its business comes from. Broader-based operations draw from a wide variety of geographic locations and need to use more specific and economical means to reach their markets. In fact, one of the problems of individual restaurants is that they cater to numerous small segments that are difficult and prohibitively expensive to reach through traditional advertising media.

The other problem with geographic segments is that such definitions tend to arise largely after the fact. Once we have determined where our customers will or do come from, we then establish that area as the target of our marketing efforts. This may help in developing the area but may ignore other areas and does not necessarily influence buyers—that is, just because they are from that area does not mean they will come to our property, and does not tell us what their needs and wants are.

On the other hand, geographic segmentation can be very useful in concentrating resources. The tourism board of Bermuda knows that most of Bermuda's tourism comes from the northeastern United States, eastern Canada, and the United Kingdom, and their advertising dollar is concentrated in those three areas. The New York City restaurant that knows most of its business comes from the upper East Side can use direct mail to reach that market. Singapore can spend a major share of its marketing resources in Australia and Japan. Even the local neighborhood eatery can send fliers around the neighborhood to promote its specials.

While all this is both true and helpful, it helps us only to reach the market; it is not of much assistance in determining the needs and wants of the market, because geographic segments, unless they are very small ones, are still very heterogeneous in terms of consumer profiles, needs, and wants.

Demographic Segmentation

Demographic segmentation is widely used in almost all industries. One reasons for this is that, like geographic segments, demographics are easily measured and classified. Demographic segments are segments based on income, race, age, nationality, religion, sex, education, and so forth. For some goods, demographic segments are clearly product specific—for instance, children's clothes, lipstick, Rolls Royces, and denture cleaners.

For the hospitality industry, however, these segments may be somewhat moot.

Knowing that someone is 30 years old, earns $40,000 a year, is married, and has a child may not be too helpful in separating a truckdriver, a college professor, and an accountant. Each of these people will have different needs and seek different benefits, but for a large majority of hotels and restaurants the demographics will not distinguish between them.

There was a time, not that long ago, when this was not the case. You could open an expensive French restaurant, for example, and you didn't have to worry about what the customers' incomes were, what part of town they came from, what kinds of cars they drove, or whether they would wear coats and ties. Such a restaurant, by default, would define its own market segment.

This is no longer the case because demographic lines have, in many cases, become very blurred and fuzzy. Plumbers may have higher incomes than accountants with MBAs. Everyone wears jeans, regardless of social standing. Executives check into hotels on weekends looking as if they had just finished mowing the lawn. Some of the wealthy get wealthier by eating cheap, staying at budget motels, and fighting over the last nickel on their check. Even Lee Iaccoca eats at McDonald's. In fact, demographic lines have become so blurred that it is hard to tell what they mean anymore unless, of course, you operate something like a specific neighborhood ethnic restaurant.

For the hospitality industry today, one of the most useful demographic parameters may be age—age in the sense of attracting children who bring with them parents à la McDonald's, or age in the sense of senior citizens, a vast and rapidly growing market with distinctive needs and wants, not to mention discretionary income.

Another demographic variable that may be useful in some operations, particularly restaurants and resorts, is the family life-cycle stage. The cycle runs, of course, from the single young person, to the married couple, the married couple with children, the married couple with grown children, to the widow or widower. In between there are, increasingly today, couples who don't have children and both have incomes, divorced parents and nonparents, and second and third marriages. Each of these stages contains, for most people, its own level of discretionary income, personal time freedom, specific buying needs, and patterns of behavior. Marketers can tap into this information, as has been demonstrated by singles resorts, early-bird dinners, special tours, and packages.

Demographic market segments, like geographic ones, are also largely nonpredictive because they too are post hoc. We may know that older people with high incomes come to our property, but we still need to find out why; what needs and wants of these people are being satisfied or not? Age, income, education, nationality, and other demographic or sociodemographic characteristics are limited in informing us of the needs and wants of these segments.

Does this mean that demographics are an unimportant segmentation variable? No, it does not. It means that we have to understand the meaning of those demographics and how they relate to other segmentation variables. Demographics serve as gross parameters within which are found more specific subsegments.

Psychographic Segmentation

Psychographic segments are segments based on attitudes, interests, and opinions (AIO), self-concepts, and life-style behaviors. AIOs are personality traits and the word *psy-*

chographic actually means the measurement of personality traits. This view of segmentation is relatively new, having arisen mostly in the early and mid-1970s. Today, psychographic segmentation is very popular with some and totally disdained by others. There is good reason for both points of view.

First, we need to understand what psychographics are. According to Joseph Plummer, an advertising executive and one of the leading proponents of life-style segmentation, the concept is defined as follows:

> Life style as used in life style segmentation research measures people's activities in terms of (1) how they spend their time; (2) their interests, what they place importance on in their immediate surroundings; (3) their opinions in terms of their view of themselves and the world around them; and (4) some basic characteristics such as their stage in life cycle, income, education, and where they live [i.e., demographics and geographics].[10]

Life-style dimensions, as defined by Plummer, are shown in Table 8-1.

Those who are strong advocates of psychographic segmentation argue that life-style patterns combine, as can be seen in Table 8-1, the virtues of demographics with the way people live, think, and behave in their everyday lives. Psychographers attempt to correlate these factors into relatively homogeneous categories using classification terms such as *homebodies, traditionalists, swingers, loners, jet-setters, conservatives, socialites, yuppies,* and so forth. (The latest acronyms for certain couples are DINKS—double income, no kids or DEWKS—dual employed, with kids.) The classifications are then correlated with product usage, desired product attributes, and media readership and viewing.

The assumption is that product attributes can be tailored to psychographic segments and that the product will thus have special appeal to those segments. The greatest proponents and users of psychographics are advertising agencies, which use the classification elements to reach the segments via specific media, and to communicate the product attributes via the life-style factors. Life-style research provides advertisers with insight into the setting, the type and appearance of the characters, the music, the tone, self-perceived roles, and the rewards people seek.

Thus, we formerly saw on television the "typical" housewife, whose main concern was taking care of her family, standing by the washing machine extolling the virtues of a laundry detergent. Today, there is a different kind of woman, as well as man, washing clothes. As one example, they may be single. In response to this life-style, a more recent commercial shows a single man and a single woman meeting in the laundry room of an apartment building, where she helps him to pick the right detergent to get his clothes clean. Later, of course, after his clothes come out spotlessly clean, he asks her for a date.

Psychographics are, in fact, very useful in developing advertising messages but have been little used in the hospitality industry other than in broad categories such as "business traveler." Clear exceptions to this are national advertisers such as McDonald's and Burger King. Another exception has been Club Med resorts, which for years promoted a hedonistic and singles life-style for the swinger segment. More recently, Club Med has been trying to reposition for both family groups and conferences and has incorporated some life-styles of these segments into their advertising. In some cases,

---

[10] Joseph T. Plummer, "The Concept and Application of Life Style Segmentation," Reprinted from the *Journal of Marketing,* January, 1974, pp. 33–37, published by the American Marketing Association.

TABLE 8-1   Life-style Dimensions

Activities	Interests	Opinions	Demographics
Work	Family	Themselves	Age
Hobbies	Home	Social issues	Education
Social events	Job	Politics	Income
Vacation	Community	Business	Occupation
Entertainment	Recreation	Economics	Family size
Club membership	Fashion	Education	Dwelling
Community	Food	Products	Geography
Shopping	Media	Future	City size
Sports	Achievements	Culture	Life cycle stage

Source: Plummer, "Life Style Segmentation", p. 34.

however, it has been found that life-style variables themselves are more important than media exposure in planning vacations, and that media exposure alone may be inadequate influence.[11]

More commonly, however, hotel and restaurant advertising has stayed with the ubiquitous appeals of location, edifice, or a sterile picture of a man and woman in a hotel room. There may be good reasons for this, the greatest probably being that no substantial research has been able to classify hospitality customers in definitive life-style segments. Even resort advertising has not progressed far, when it pictures a beautiful woman in a bathing suit on the beach or by a pool. Presumably, these advertisers believe that this is the desired life-style criterion by which people choose a resort hotel.

In 1984 Hilton Hotels took what appeared to be a life-style approach to hotel advertising. This ad campaign featured assorted ads with one word in large print, such as *Ambition* or *Competition*. The illustrations in the ads were racing speedboats, single-pilot planes in an air race, competing racing cars, and so forth (Figure 8-3). The ads had little if anything to do with choosing or staying at a hotel. In fact, it was impossible to identify them with a hotel other than by reading the Hilton name. The assumption, however, was that people who vicariously yearned for this life-style would choose Hilton, which is also daring and risk-taking, a dubious assumption at best for a company considered by many to be one of the most conservative in the industry.

Plummer also lists other benefits of life-style segmentation.[12] For one, he stresses the simultaneity of many factors, both demographic and otherwise, which is not revealed when they are considered independently. Further, a new view of the market structure may be exposed that reveals clusterings different from those evident in a unidimensional view. Life-style information can be used for product positioning in terms of basic needs and how the product fits into one's life. Finally, life-style information can suggest new product opportunities as well as weaknesses in current products. For example, 1988 research by both Hyatt and Marriott revealed that resort goers were fantasy seekers and incorporated this into their marketing strategies.

[11] William R. Darden and W. D. Perreault, Jr., "A Multivariate Analysis of Media Exposure and Vacation Behavior with Life Style Covariates," *Journal of Consumer Research*, September, 1975, pp. 93–103.

[12] Plummer, "Life Style Segmentation."

It's the will to win.
It makes Hilton America's Business Address.

(Courtesy of Hilton Hotels)

FIGURE 8-3   Life-style advertising

Critics of psychographics will agree with most of the above, only they would add a great big "if." The biggest ifs concern whether these variables can be defined, are valid, and are stable. Life-style variables not only are difficult to define but also overlap greatly. Because of this there is considerable room for error variance in establishing the classifications. Furthermore, people change, and do so rapidly, in today's society: Today's life-style may not be tomorrow's.

It would not be too difficult to suggest even more user segments than those mentioned above. The point that has to be made is that each of these segments has some different needs and wants. They may also have many needs and wants in common, but it is catering to the different, special needs and wants that creates and keeps customers.

A given restaurant or hotel may well have every segment mentioned above as customers or potential customers. This is not as impossible a situation as it may at first seem; it is simply the nature of the hospitality business and demonstrates why paying attention to only broad segments such as business/pleasure or heavy user/light user may constitute falling into a trap. With few exceptions, a hotel or restaurant that wants to maximize its potential simply cannot afford to treat all people the same.

The Saturday night hotel guest is simply not the same as the Wednesday night one—*even when it is the same person*. Likewise, the Monday night restaurant customer is not the same as the Saturday night one. The anniversary dinner is not the same as the business dinner. One restaurant of one of the authors' acquaintance had a heavy weekday lunch patronage of businessmen but wondered why they never appeared for dinner or on weekends. Subsequent research revealed that these men found the restaurant convenient for lunch but did not find it satisfactory as a place to bring their wives for dinner.

There tends to be a heavy concentration in marketing circles on the so-called heavy user. This is probably advisable but at the same time it should not distract from the light user or, to coin a new phrase, perhaps, the "other-user." Hypothetically, let's suppose the heavy user represents 80 percent of an establishment's patronage while the other 20 percent represents a mix of various segments. That 20 percent may well also represent 5 more percentage points of occupancy or, in a volume-sensitive business, its spending may come 90 percent down to the bottom line. These are crucial figures that are too often unrealized. The airlines have increased volume by segmenting the light or nonuser and making special appeals to that segment.

User segments have an advantage over geographic, demographic, and psychographic segments. By their nature and narrowness they are more predictable. In other words, if we know what influences them (i.e., why they constitute a segment), the chances are good that they can be influenced. This is not necessarily the case simply because we know someone's age, income, sex, or geographic origin.

Benefit Segmentation

Benefit segments are based on the benefits that people seek when buying a product. Benefits are very akin to needs: comfort, prestige, low price, recognition, attention, romance, quiet, and safety are just a few of the possible benefits sought in a hospitality purchase. Like psychographic segments, benefits have the disadvantage of being more difficult to measure. Similarly, they are subject to whimsy and change. On the other hand, when measurement is reliable, benefit segments may be the most predictable of all segments and the ones to which we should pay closest attention.

The strength of this statement lies in the fact that benefits are also akin to need *satisfaction*. They are also a priori, i.e., knowing what benefits people seek provides a basis for predicting what people will do. Benefit segmentation is a market-oriented approach consistent with the marketing concept.

The classic article on benefit segmentation was written by Russell Haley in 1968 and has stood the test of time. In this article, Haley states:

> The benefits which people are seeking in consuming a given product are the basic reasons for the existence of true market segments. Experience with this approach has shown that benefits sought by consumers determine their behavior much more accurately than do demographic characteristics or volume of consumption.[15]

Haley suggested that market segments be determined first by the benefits people seek. From these segments can be derived other characteristics such as demographics, psychographics, usage patterns, and so forth; in other words, benefit segments can be used to identify relevant descriptive variables and consumer behavior.

Benefit segmentation is concerned with why consumers seek and purchase a particular product. In other words, benefits sought imply some order of causality and are thus better predictors of purchase behavior. Benefit segmentation, in the aggregate, is concerned with total satisfaction from a product rather than simply individual benefits. This phenomenon has been termed the benefit bundle and is the significant factor in segmenting markets by benefits. The sense of the benefit bundle is that people buy a product in order to receive a group of benefits rather than a single one.[16]

A group of Finnish researchers studied the benefit segments of Scandinavian hotel business customers. They found that business customers do not evaluate hotels homogeneously. Six distinct segments emerged, plus a seventh one that the authors called the "idiosyncratics". Benefits sought by the six different segments varied primarily on the use of business services, efficiency, friendliness, quiet, restaurants, image, clientele, interior decor, and location.

These benefit segments were related to background data for each segment: travel-related attributes, company-related attributes, demographics, geographics, hotel-related attitudes, and behavior. This study demonstrated both the power of benefit segmentation and the fallacy of treating business travelers as one homogeneous segment.[17] In fact, some of today's middle-tier hotel product is based on the business traveler's desire for facility, as opposed to service. In spite of industry claims, all travelers are not seeking better service.

In a study of restaurant benefits sought, different segment characteristics were distinguishable for three types of restaurants—gourmet, family, and atmosphere. The identified benefits were related to advertising appeals that could be used for each type of restaurant.[18]

Another example is a study conducted by the Canadian Office of Tourism to determine what appeals would be most effective for American vacation travelers in Canada. This study defined six segments and the benefits sought by each.

---

[15] Russell I. Haley, "Benefit Segmentation: A Decision-oriented Tool," *Journal of Marketing,* July, 1968, pp. 30–35.

[16] For an excellent and more detailed discussion of this concept see Paul E. Green, Yoram Wind, and Arun K. Jain, "Benefit Bundle Analysis," *Journal of Advertising Research,* April, 1972, pp. 31–36.

[17] K. E. Kristian Moller et al., "Segmenting Hotel Business Customers: A Benefit Clustering Approach," In T. Bloch et al., eds., *Services Marketing in a Changing Environment,* published by the American Marketing Association, 1985, pp. 72–76.

[18] Robert C. Lewis, "Benefit Segmentation for Restaurant Advertising That Works," *Cornell Hotel and Restaurant Administration Quarterly,* November 1980, pp. 6–12.

1. Visitors to friends and relatives, nonactive (29 percent). Seek familiar surroundings, visit friends and relatives, not seeking activity.
2. Visitors to friends and relatives, active (12 percent). Like segment 1, but also active in sightseeing, shopping, cultural events, and entertainment.
3. Family sightseers (6 percent). Seek new vacation places for enriching experience and treat for children.
4. Outdoor vacationers (19 percent). Seek clean air, rest and quiet, beautiful scenery. Includes campers, often with children.
5. Resort vacationers (19 percent). Seek water sports and good weather, prefer a popular place with big city atmosphere.
6. Foreign vacationers (26 percent). Seek places they haven't been before with foreign atmosphere and beautiful scenery. Money not a major concern but good accommodations and service are. Seek exciting, enriching experience.[19]

There are two important distinctions between benefit and other forms of segmentation. Benefits *are* the needs and wants of the consumer. More than that, benefits are what benefits do for the customer. Other segmentation strategies only assume a relationship between the segment variables and consumer needs and wants. We all know that McDonald's makes a special effort to appeal to children, a strong demographic segment. The next time you go to a McDonald's look around at the people and see if you can place them into a segment category. Chances are it will be a benefit segment; quick, clean, cheap.

Second, understanding benefits enables marketers to influence behaviors. (Consider the discussion of selective perception in Chapter 6 to see how it pertains to benefit segments.) Other segmentation variables are merely descriptive. The marketer can only try to appeal to what exists and its assumed relationship. Consider the singles category, a fairly large market segment: Is it relatively homogeneous, so that it can be treated as one major segment? Not at all, but break it down by benefits sought and you will find high degrees of homogeneity.

In summary, benefit analysis can be a powerful segmentation tool. Its best utilization lies in good research—research that can pay off in terms of understanding customers and what motivates them.

Price Segmentation

Price segmentation is no less than benefit segmentation, only more visible and more tangible. Ten years ago it would have been included in the benefits category. Because the hotel industry today essentially sees itself as segmenting on price, it now deserves separate consideration. There are two ways to look at price segments: One is within the product class, the other is between product classes.

To review our discussion in Chapters 4 and 5, when we talk about a product class, what we mean is all those products that more or less fit into the same class or category. Five-star hotels and budget motels are each a product class. Gourmet restaurants and

[19] Shirley Young, Leland Ott, and Barbara Feigin, "Some Practical Considerations in Market Segmentation," reprinted from the *Journal of Marketing Research*, August, 1978, pp. 405–412, published by the American Marketing Association.

fast-food restaurants are also separate product classes. The inference is that one product class does not truly compete with another on the same occasion, given the same circumstances. If we decide to go out to dinner we do not narrow our choices down to McDonald's and Chez Ritz; if we go to New York City we do not choose between the Waldorf Astoria and Days Inn.

Price segments within the product class, at least in hospitality, are limited. A lower price may increase the value of the benefit bundle, other things being equal, but customers will generally not make major trade-offs for a small gain in price; that is, they won't accept a poor location or poor service just to save a few dollars. It is difficult to develop segments based solely on price within the same product class, although it has been done.

Between product classes is a different story. The initial determination by the customer may be based on price range; it is the other elements of the bundle that will influence the final choice. As with Scotch whiskey and wine there are high-priced, medium-priced, and low-priced segments. These segments are based on expectation. No one rationally pays more for something without expecting to get more. In cases like these, markets are segmented within broad price ranges.

In the hotel industry, although there have obviously been shades of difference and exceptions, for many years the consumer had little choice other than top, middle, and bottom, and the expectation of what you got was fairly clear because there were definite lines of distinction. Today we have low budget, middle budget, upper budget, and luxury budget, and the same four classifications apply to the middle- and upper-tier categories.

Amazingly, with today's modern construction, the physical product is not all that different, within ranges, and in some cases neither is the price. In many cases lower prices have been obtained by lower construction and operating costs and through elimination of public space and food and beverage facilities. Surely as one moves up the ladder, the furniture gets better, the walls and the carpet get thicker, the atrium gets higher, and the bathroom (sometimes) gets larger and has more amenities. No longer, however, does the bed necessarily sag in a budget motel, or is the furniture necessarily scratched, broken, and torn, or the soap in the bathroom necessarily minuscule. In other words, the basic needs are still fulfilled. This is not the same trade-off as giving up Steak Diane for sauerbraten, or sauerbraten for meat loaf.

Why, then, are customers willing to pay more for relatively little more? And is this really market segmentation? Well, in many cases they are not, and in many cases it really isn't. Those cases when customers are willing to pay more constitute market segmentation. They are willing to pay more largely because of the intangibles that they receive in return: service, prestige, professionalism, and others. These, of course, are benefits and the net result is actually benefit, not price, segmentation. *Price* is the risk the customer is willing to take to obtain the benefits.

The success of putative hotel industry segmentation did not mean that customers suddenly joined a lower-priced segment; they simply found an alternative for expressing dissatisfaction with the high prices they had been paying. This brings us to the question of whether prices do indeed constitute market segments in the hotel industry.

The answer is somewhat ambiguous because, for most, price is a major consideration in any purchase, and varying price sensitivities will stratify any market. In the final analysis however, other than at the bottom of the market, it is rarely price alone that determines the segment. Price is only the risk that the willing and *able* buyer will take

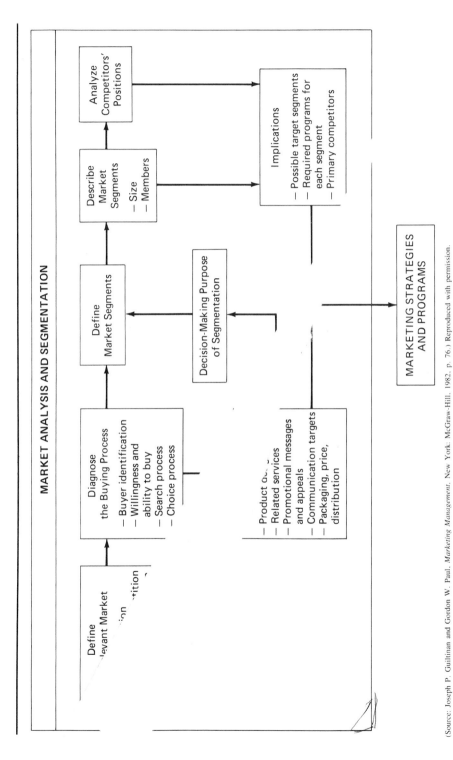

MARKET ANALYSIS AND SEGMENTATION

Define
Relevant Market
...tition

Diagnose
the Buying Process
— Buyer identification
— Willingness and
ability to buy
— Search process
— Choice process

Define
Market Segments

Describe
Market
Segments
— Size
— Members

Analyze
Competitors'
Positions

Decision-Making Purpose
of Segmentation

Implications
— Possible target segments
— Required programs for
each segment
— Primary competitors

— Product o...
— Related services
— Promotional messages
and appeals
— Communication targets
— Packaging, price,
distribution

MARKETING STRATEGIES
AND PROGRAMS

(Source: Joseph P. Guiltinan and Gordon W. Paul. *Marketing Management.* New York: McGraw-Hill. 1982. p. 76.) Reproduced with permission.

FIGURE 8-4 Relationship between market analysis and segmentation and marketing strategies and programs

227

Target Marketing

Target markets are drawn from segments. They might be called subsegments, but the word *target* has a more active connotation that is important. The same precepts apply as with segmentation, but they simply apply to more homogeneous markets that allow for more detailed analysis and evaluation of potential customers. This enables the creation of greater differential advantages.

Consider the very large business traveler segment. Hilton Hotels advertised themselves as "America's Business Address." This is extremely broad segmentation, which includes corporate officers, expense account travelers, salespeople, the self-employed, and conferences, to mention only a few. All of these have particular needs and wants and, in themselves, can be broken down into even smaller target markets. Target marketing means aiming specifically at one portion of a market.

One travel researcher found, for example, that the vacation market segment could be broken down into ten target markets. Each one represents an isolation of interests based on benefits, usage, demographics, and psychograpics. Each one has different needs and wants, and requires a different package, a different positioning, and different communication. These target markets and some of their specific characteristics are as follows:

- The carriage trade: desire a change of scene but not of style, secure in wealth and position, play golf and tennis year-round and when traveling, tend to vacation as a family.
- The comfortables: the largest group, insecure, seek social and psychological comfort, as in recommended restaurants, guided tours, and organized activities.
- The venturers: want to see new things, have a thirst for fresh ideas, information, and education; seek the new and the different; don't travel in groups; collect experiences.
- The adventurers: the venturer advanced one step—seek risk, danger, and the unknown.
- The inners: jet-setters, go somewhere because of who is there rather than what is there, they "make" destinations such as Acapulco, Majorca, Costa del Sol.
- The buffs: strongly subject-oriented, travel because of particular interest or hobby.
- The activists: not content to sit by the pool and bask in the sun, want constant activities.
- The outdoorsers: campers, hikers, birdwatchers, bicyclers, and other outdoor recreationists.
- The restless: travel for something to do, tend to be senior citizens, retired, widowed, collect travel experiences, travel all the time including off-seasons.
- The bargain hunters: can afford to travel but compulsively seek the best deal.

As with segmentation criteria, given above, there are criteria for choosing target markets. They overlap the segmentation criteria but are a little more precise.

1. What is the potential revenue and market share?
2. What are the demand characteristics? Are these customers able and willing to buy?
3. How are they currently being served by the competition?
4. Are they compatible with the objectives of the firm?
5. Are they compatible with each other?

At the same time, there is some tendency in the industry to try to be all things to all customers, rather than to determine what particular segments are to be served and how to serve them best, or to stick to the ones that were originally designated, especially when business gets bad. This tendency is a risky and usually unsuccessful one.

In Amherst, Massachusetts, a restaurant opened around 1983 with the motto, "Something for everyone." "Everyone" in Amherst includes students, faculty, business-people, social people, and out-of-towners. In the restaurant, there was a place for each— for instance, a downstairs rathskeller for students and an upstairs fine-dining room for out-of-towners. For the local cost-conscious there was the ubiquitous hamburger served on table linen. The result did not target the needs of any particular segment and created a confused image, as was supported by research findings. Management, however, didn't want to change. The restaurant never reached its expectation and closed four years later.

In Northampton, Massachusetts, the completely renovated Hotel Northampton claimed that its target market was the upscale corporate traveler and then eagerly sought bus tours to fill its rooms. Six years and four owners later, the hotel still has a confused image and is unsure of what segments it is designed to serve. The Embassy Row Hotel in Washington, D.C., an upscale hotel, also went after motorcoach tours when occupancy fell to 50 percent, partially due to a glut of luxury rooms, confusing its image in the luxury market.

The Omni Shoreham in Washington, D.C., promoted the concept of being "the only in-town resort in Washington!" Promotional literature described the features and benefits of a wonderful spa-resort concept in the heart of the city. Those who know the location and layout of the facility would be amused by this description; those who do not would be disappointed with their decision to stay there for spa-resort reasons. The Omni Shoreham, while a fine facility for associations and conventions, is by no means a "resort" facility, and for the hotel to target markets that were seeking those benefits was only counterproductive. Targeting markets other than conventions and associations was a logical decision. Targeting the leisure traveler seeking a destination resort was a bad segment-mix decision.

At the same time, it is important to realize that the same person can be a member of several target markets. A corporate business traveler during the week becomes a package consumer with spouse on the weekend. The trade show guest this week may turn up next month as a corporate group member. Different occasions find the same person having different needs. As an example, the express check-out service necessary for the business traveler at midweek may have little significance to the same person consuming a weekend package.

The successful marketing organization recognizes the needs of *realistic* and compatible target markets and provides the correct product at the correct price at the correct time.

An example of this occurred at the Sheraton Airport hotel in Philadelphia some years ago. This hotel was 100 percent corporate-market-oriented during the week, which left a void on weekends. The marketing team developed a product based on the proximity of the hotel to the Phillies' baseball stadium. After some test advertising, the product was purchased by many families for these sport weekend events. The entire complexion of the hotel changed every Friday. Businesspeople checked out in the morning and in the afternoon, families checked in for the weekend.

The mix was perfect, almost. While the hotel was full most weekends that the baseball team was in town, the restaurants and lounges were not receiving the business they normally received during a full house. The reason was obvious: The food and beverage product was still priced for the less price-sensitive corporate customers. Special "Phillies" menus were created and priced correctly to capture the weekend guests, who soon began using the food and beverage outlets. The menus were changed back on Sunday afternoon.

Buy Time

As mentioned in Chapters 7 and 8, it is also important to recognize that each segment has a different *buy time*. Each segment of customers purchases its hotel product at various stages of the decision-making process. A corporate traveler may make reservations two weeks in advance of an upcoming trip. The convention planner is booking business as far as ten years in advance. A weekend package user may buy on impulse within a few days or a few hours of check-in. The bus tour operator will have routes calculated a year in advance.

Knowing the timing of the purchase is important in selecting potential market segments. In order to maximize revenues, the ideal business mix of segments may include a variety of customers. With the different room rate potential of each customer grouping, managing the inventory becomes critical.

For example, a 400-room hotel may have an opportunity to sell 350 rooms to a midweek convention three years in advance at a rate of $75. At first glance, this would appear to be a good decision. The hotel will likely be sold out during this period, and the sales department can spend its time trying to fill other, less busy time periods.

More careful analysis, however, shows that this hotel has an average of 200 rooms per night occupied by business travelers during the week. The rate this year is $100, and in three years is expected to be at $125.

Few business travelers plan business trips three years in advance. These travelers will be calling the hotel about two to three weeks in advance for their room reservations, unaware of the convention that is being held there at that time. If all patterns hold, the hotel will lose $50 per room on the 150 rooms that it should have held for the segment that pays a higher rate, but books the shortest lead time. Mistakes like this are very subtle, because the hotel "appears" sold out, yet the revenues are decreased by $7500. The hotel may also alienate some regular customers who cannot get rooms. It does not take many miscalculations like this to bring home the importance of the lead time of market segments.

Another buy time variable is the use of a property at different periods of time. City hotels generally target business travelers during the week and pleasure travelers on weekends. The same variation occurs between summer and winter. Inter Nor Hotels in Norway issues a "Nordisk Hotellpass" for pleasure travelers during summer only, at close to 50 percent reductions. This strategy has accounted for large increases in occupancy for city hotels in rooms that would otherwise be empty.

Resort hotels have similar situations depending on the season of the year. At one time, many of these hotels simply closed during the "off-season." Today, more and more stay open year-round but seek different market segments. Palm Springs, California, for example, in the winter is a destination of jet-setters from all over the country and well-to-do winter golfers. Most hotels there used to close in the summer when the temperature exceeds 100° Fahrenheit; today, many stay open. The new market is families from the Los Angeles areas who come at much lower rates and have much different needs.

Segment mix and buy time decisions should be kept in mind as we proceed through the following discussion of broad segment categories.

The Business Traveler

The business traveler market segment is one of the most desirable for the hospitality marketer. It is not only the largest major segment, but it is also the least price-sensitive one. The business traveler is defined as a customer who is utilizing the product because of a need to conduct business in a particular destination area. While the hotel facility or restaurant may be used during business, the facility is not the sole reason for the buy. This segment differs from the corporate group market in that the corporate group meets within a hotel, utilizing meeting space and usually food and beverage facilities. The business traveler usually is alone or in small groups, and conducts business close to but not necessarily within the hotel.

This market is very large internationally, with over 33 million travelers annually in the United States alone.[1] On the surface, the needs of this market are simple; in practice, they are far more complex and not so simple to deliver. Broad-based, public research reveals that the most important factors in choosing a hotel for the business traveler are cleanliness and location. Although price does enter into the decision-making process, it comes after the abovementioned needs.

Much of this research, however, is misleading. In truth, the above factors are usually most important only when they don't exist—which presents a different perspective. Because this is such an important segment and the one that is researched the most, we will take some space to discuss it.

Business Traveler Needs

Perhaps twenty or so years ago, hotel or motel rooms in the United States were by and large undependable. Rooms were often small and cramped; plumbing, heating, and air conditioning did not always work; cleanliness was hit or miss and the bar of soap was minuscule. It was this kind of situation that Kemmons Wilson set out to correct when he opened the first Holiday Inn in Memphis in 1952.

Holiday Inns greatly improved the situation along the highways, but the real progress, especially in the cities, came a number of years later. Today, the unclean, cramped room and the minuscule soap bar are no longer the rule but the exception. Whereas travelers once complained loudly about the dirty shower and the soap bar, they now have other things to complain about. The industry has changed radically and so has the customer; the research has not.

Over the years Procter & Gamble, for one, has commissioned research on why

---

[1] Research conducted for *Travel Weekly* and *Hotel and Travel Index* by U.S. Travel Data Center, reported in *Lodging Hospitality,* January 1987, p. 13.

people choose hotels. The two top answers are always the same: location and cleanliness. Somewhere down the line come price, service, and other "minor" reasons. Such findings tell us nothing new and would seem to indicate that neither the customer nor the industry had changed in twenty years. This is simply not the case. The problem is in the research—the data collection, the analysis, the interpretation, and the assumptions drawn.

For example, in a 1976/1977 study, service (not service level) was a "weak sixth place in first-time choices" of a hotel.[2] Of course. How do you know what the service is if you haven't ever been there? If you were asked what was most important to you in choosing among hotels you had never been to and never heard of, and were given the choices of location, cleanliness, service, facilities, and price, how would you answer? Like everyone else you would say location and cleanliness (you're allowed to name as many as you wish).

Everyone wants a clean room and a convenient location. That's a given. If the location wasn't right you wouldn't even consider it. Now suppose you are told that the price of the room is $200: Would you like to change your answer? Or suppose you were told the location was great, the rooms were immaculate, and the price was low, but the service was terrible: How would you answer now?

More recently, we have two studies on the business traveler. A report of the first one states, "The study revealed that convenient location is, *by far, the most important consideration* [emphasis added] when business travelers select hotels, while clean, comfortable rooms, and room rates ranked second and third, respectively."[3] Given the choice of a great location and a dirty room, or a poor location and a clean room, which do you suppose the business traveler would choose, especially the 40 percent in the study who are women?

The same report also states, "Only 23% of business travelers stay at the same hotel on return trips." By inference, then, we should conclude that 77 percent of the stays either are bad locations, are dirty, or both—and much of this is at "luxury accommodations," which "44% of business travelers use."

The second study, commissioned by the Dial Corporation, reports similar findings on the frequent traveler. This study was broken down by user categories of economy, mid-price, and luxury. In all three categories, both in selecting a hotel for the first time and in returning to a hotel, the most important characteristics were clean/comfortable rooms and location.[4] As you might expect, given the sponsor, the study "implies" that all categories should have more amenities, "regardless of how often guests use them," to "increase guest satisfaction."[5] There is no basis for this conclusion.

The major problem with these studies (aside from the weakness and bias in the methodology) is that they ignore consumer behavior, as discussed in Chapter 6. No consumer, especially including the business traveler, makes decisions in this singular fashion. They make trade-offs: Do they want a large bar of soap in the bathroom? Yes, but there are about twenty other things that are more important.

---

[2] "Why Travelers Choose Hotels and Motels," *Lodging,* September, 1977, pp. 48, 50–52.

[3] "Frequent Travelers Often Switch Hotels: HTI Survey," *Lodging,* January, 1987, pp. 10, 82–83.

[4] Bonnie J. Knutson, "Frequent Traveler Study Perceptions of Economy, Mid-price, and Luxury Market Segments," E. Lansing: Michigan State University. Prepared for the Dial Corporation, 1987.

[5] Bill Gillette, "Dial Study Finds Travelers Expect Comfort, Safety," *Hotel & Motel Management,* August 17, 1987, pp. 2, 77.

When research respondents are allowed to check everything they consider important from a predetermined list, then any number of things become important. The items on the list are, of course, important because that's why they were chosen for the list. The surprising part of this research is not that 92 percent of respondents say that cleanliness is "very important," it's that the remaining 8 percent don't say it. Unless we change to a world of antiseptic sterility, cleanliness will always be very important to just about every traveler.

The second problem with this research is that it doesn't deal with the world as it is today. Let's say, to take an easy but not unreal example, that you are looking for a room in a major city. Within a five-block area you have a choice among Hyatt, Marriott, Sheraton, Hilton, Westin, and Four Seasons. Now we ask you what is important in choosing a hotel. Would your answer be cleanliness or location?

Contrary to the above research, price is a very important factor for most business travelers today. Today, in many but not all locations both in the United States and in some parts of Europe and Asia, there is an alternative to high prices, and it includes clean, comfortable rooms and good locations as well as security, prompt/courteous service, friendliness, and other factors. In understanding the business traveler, one has to understand the *role* of price: Its role lies in designating a price range and the benefits desired. Once that price range is determined, price is a relatively minor factor unless, of course, the same or better value can be found at a lower price, which is exactly what has been happening.

Darcy Acton, supervisor of corporate travel for Wendy's, says the company is definitely "trying to stay in less expensive hotels," but "not if it's a dump." With a $6 million annual travel budget, Wendy's employees are accountable for what they spend on lodging. Boeing Company has 9000 frequent traveler employees; one of the things they're "looking at very closely is the cost of a hotel room."[6]

An American Express Survey of Business Travel management found that 83 percent of industry have a formal travel policy on hotel use. On average, 41 percent require employees to stay at moderately priced hotels, and 45 percent require them to stay at hotels with which the company has special rates.[7] The effect of these actions has been not so much to move *on* the price curve, but to *shift* the price curve to the left. This concept is explained more fully in Chapter 14.

We have taken this much space to explain what business travelers *don't* do because there is so much questionable information in the trade press (through no fault of theirs; they just report it.) What do business travelers really do, on average?[8]

---

[6] Steven J. Stark, "Biz Travelers Increasingly Being Steered to Budget Hotels," *Business Travel News,* April 14, 1986, pp. 22, 24.

[7] "Business Travel Scrutinized," *Hotel & Motel Management,* January 12, 1987, pp. 1, 50.

[8] The comments that follow are based on a number of sources; one is extensive research on travelers at different hotels by the senior author, on what is salient, determinant, and important in deciding on, choosing, and staying at hotels. In this study, instead of just being given a list of items and being asked to name which were important, respondents were allowed to suggest their own factors. They were then asked to rate them (and others) on a scale of how important each one is. In analyzing the responses, statistical methods were used that related *all* the items—that is, all items were considered together rather than in isolation, as if each one were an individual and singular choice.

Second, proprietary research of others was consulted, including that done by research firms and that done or commissioned by two large hotel companies.

Third, extensive conversations by both authors have been held with numerous business travelers.

First, they consider location. If the location is inappropriate, it's out of the running. This rarely happens because they look at location first, and only then at what hotels are situated within that location.

Second, they look at rate ranges impacted by any company mandates or personal limitations. This is a determination by product class—that is, all hotels within the product class are assumed to be in the appropriate rate range, be it upscale, middle-tier, or budget. This is why the type of descriptive research described above does not indicate price as an important factor—that decision has already been made and is no longer a factor. Furthermore, price is a factor only relative to what is available. If the product class is Ramada and Four Seasons is the only other choice, price is the single most important factor in the decision, including location.

Third, they do not even consider cleanliness; they assume it exists unless they have had a previous bad experience. Almost never is cleanliness given as a reason for choosing a particular hotel at a particular time. What they want to know next is the reputation of the hotel or, barring that, the chain. This will come from their own personal exeriences or from conversations with others. (They have little if any faith in hotel ad claims unless there is a promise behind it that can be backed up.)

We are now at a level where the issues become myriad and idiosyncratic depending on the individual, but can be lumped together by target market. (Each hotel should do its own research on these aspects.)

One most important aspect, according to one hotel company's research, is covered by the question "Will they have what I ordered and have it on time?" This may include things like floor level, exposure, bedroom configuration, type of bed, working space, telephone location, lighting, and so on.

Other concerns are check-in lines, employee attitudes, deferential treatment, lighting, skirt hangers, mirrors, security, type of clientele, coffee makers, business services, noise (some business travelers avoid convention, atrium-lobby hotels), operational efficiency, hotel "rules," limousine service to the airport, and a host of other things.

On the whole, business travelers who are choosing a hotel do not consider bathroom amenities, shoe polishers, bathrobes, turndown service, chocolates on the pillow, and other such factors. These are nice "extras" but not critical, and customers have come to expect certain amenities, such as a decent size bar of soap. Goat's milk shampoo, herbal soap, and bubble bath are mostly "take home" items. Even when some are used, their absence wouldn't be considered serious. These travelers are more concerned with how the shower works. Bathroom amenities, in fact, have probably reached the stage of "overkill," as shown in Figure 9-1.

Most business travelers visiting cities do not consider the hotel's restaurants as a determinant factor, simply because there are usually numerous alternatives available. A good coffee shop is assumed; having other restaurants in a hotel is considered convenient, sometimes, but not totally necessary. A majority of hotel customers, at least in the United States, eat out. This somewhat contradicts the notion of convenient location. (This does not mean that an upscale hotel should not have good restaurants, but that they are not determinant in the choice of hotel.) Friendly, open lounges without loud, raucous music and without television that only the bartender and serving personnel watch are necessary for many.

FIGURE 9-1   Bathroom amenities—a state of overkill?

These are generalizations. As we have said, you have to know your own target market.

Dealing with the Business Segment

While the corporate office is saying, "Raise the rates," the local marketing team will frequently feel that lower pricing is the means necessary for capturing new customers, or for keeping existing customers. Naturally, if a hotel is significantly higher or lower in price than its competition, a choice may be made on price, but this alone is not the answer—and there is no one answer. What it is necessary to know is the appropriate price range, as we have said. This is not an arbitrary decision, as is sometimes assumed. An inherent conflict often exists, in this regard, between the local sales department and the corporate office of hotel chains.

For example, a 1400-room hotel in Toronto was undergoing a three-year, $100 million renovation program. This had caused considerable customer discontent and some serious loss of business, at the same time that the Toronto economy had turned down. Although hotel management felt that there was no problem in selling the 600 renovated rooms at a higher rate, there was a problem with the rest of the hotel and the disrupting construction.

The corporate rate for this hotel was $104. The corporate rate of the major competition was $99. The corporate office of this chain, in the midst of this situation, mandated that the Toronto property, for the forthcoming year, increase its corporate transient room nights from 60 to 65 thousand. At the same time, it mandated a corporate rate increase to $118, *while* the disrupting renovations continued. This mandate left the property sales staff in an impossible and weak competitive situation.

Most Business Travelers Are Price-Sensitive Today   We continue to emphasize this point because it seems that many developers, owners, and corporate offices of hotel chains are unaware of it—at least, they act as if they are. It is true, of course, that the business traveler who always stays at a Four Seasons or comparable hotel is probably not price-sensitive. In fact, all upscale hotels have some of these customers. The question is: Are there enough of them? (Refer, once again, to Figure 1-3. How many business travelers seek the "benefits" offered by these hotels?)

A new hotel opens; the corporate office says, "*Don't* discount." Three months later, at 45 percent occupancy, the corporate office wants to know why the hotel is not full. Here are some words, which we have heard many times, of a typical hotel sales manager of a major chain:

> I travel to Chicago, Los Angeles, and San Francisco. I spend days in these cities making sales calls. People say "we love your hotel, but your rates are too high." I go back home and tell my Director of Sales. He tells the Director of Marketing. He tells the General Manager. He tells corporate. I hear nothing. A month later, an edict comes from corporate, "Raise the numbers!"[9] I'm a good salesperson and I can sell anybody, but I can't make them pay what they won't pay.

The basic premise is simple: If a hotel is providing what the customers want at a reasonable price, then market share will be obtained.

The best consultants that any company has are the employees that deal with the customer. We know of one hotel chain that hired an outside consultant to improve its guest satisfaction index, primarily with business travelers. The consultant revised the method of rating and handling guest satisfaction. The company announced that management would now receive bonuses on guest satisfaction, as well as on the bottom line, which had been almost the sole criterion in the past. At least one General Manager now pulls the guest comment cards out of the guest rooms whenever he knows he has a "problem" group coming in; who knows what the others do? This is not to imply that there is anything wrong with basing bonuses on guest satisfaction; it only means that such a system has to start at the roots.

If this company had, instead, paid the consultant just to travel around the system and talk, confidentially, to front-line desk and salespeople about guest satisfaction, it would have obtained a million dollars' worth of information—and, incidentally, proceeded quite differently.

The hotel trade press is full of quotes from hoteliers about what their customer wants, and how "enthusiastic and confident" they are about providing it. What they mean

---

[9] Industry parlance for increasing occupancy *and* average room rate.

to say is, "This is the latest thing we've thought of. We *think* it might go over. We're not too sure, but we're going to give it a shot." Publicly, they make questionable, untested assertions similar to the following.

- Frequent traveler programs make a lot of sense because they create a brand franchise, a loyalty to the system, and expand the market.
- Programs are very expensive but produce tremendous profits and incremental business.
- Market research tells the kind of awards consumers want. We believe our new version offers them what they want.[10]

Sotto voce, it is rare (outside of Marriott) to find hoteliers who really agree and/or can back these assertions with hard evidence.

We (the authors) have talked also to hotel guests and hotel employees, like the employee who said: "They spend hundreds of thousands of dollars to have these big meetings and tell us how we have to satisfy the guest better. Back home they tell us they can't afford to give us a $1000 raise. How do they think guest satisfaction really happens?"

Or, the customer who said: "In X city I stay at Marriott, in Y, I stay at Sheraton, and in Z, I stay at Hyatt. It's still the individual hotel that counts. Besides, I get points at all of them so what difference does it make?"

Or, one could listen to Robert Hazard, Chairman of Quality International:

> You don't build business in a hotly competitive environment by discounts, giveaways and frequency programs, because the gains from these strategies are shortsighted and illusory. Instead, you build a better meeting planning network to attack the conference market; you employ new telemarketing techniques to solicit more group business; you freshen the product; you create a better price/value mix; you upgrade your image.
>
> You build market share by anticipating customer demands and tastes and developing innovative marketing programs that build business.[11]

The casual reader may think we have strayed far afield from our topic of dealing with the business segment. On the contrary, if you refresh your memory with chapters 1 through 3, you will find that we are right on target. The business market is the bread and butter of the hotel industry; all else is gravy. The only way to capture it is to serve its needs. Consider this case.

> The Sheraton Grand in Washington, D.C., by all reports, was in bad shape. Market share was off, occupancy was down, employee morale was low, and, it was said, "it was beyond hope." Corporate efforts failed to change the situation, yet this was the Sheraton flagship hotel in Washington.
>
> Kathy Ray was resident manager at the Sheraton Washington. She was promoted to General Manager at the Sheraton Grand. She did two things first: she talked to the employees and she talked to the customers.
>
> All line employees were gathered together for a meeting; management employees were barred. Ray put an organizational chart of the hotel on the wall. At the top of the organizational chart were the employees.

---

[10] Reported by Harvey Chipkin in "Frequent Guest Awards Advance Brand Loyalty," *Hotel & Motel Management,* March 9, 1987, pp. 3, 35, 66.

[11] Ibid., pp. 3, 35. *Authors' note:* Perhaps one of the reasons Quality Inns is so successful is because so few of Hazard's competitors are listening to him or practicing his ways.

A major account had booked substantial room nights every week. It went to another hotel because of the Grand's rates and no-discount policy. Ray called them up and said, "What do you need to come back?" They came back.

Ray practiced what she preached. She ate in the employees' dining room. Former GMs had never done that. She went into the kitchen to talk to the employees, not to have coffee with the chef or to have a special omelette prepared. She made her employees "believe"—and the customers noticed. It *can* be done in a chain hotel.[12]

For the restaurant industry, business travelers mean expense account travelers. Like hotels, a sizable number of restaurants would not be in business today were it not for these customers. In the past, this has led to the temptation by some for price-gouging: No one cared, it was all tax deductible. With the new tax law of 1986 this has changed somewhat, but not entirely. In the long pull, no business can go wrong by "treating the customer right."

The hospitality industry, world-wide, cherishes the business travel segment. The major competition in the marketplace is for this segment which, today, is simply not big enough to go around. The property that gets its fair market share, and more, will be the one that truly understands the needs, wants, and problems of this market. It will not be the one that tries to win it by giveaways and gimmicks. (Note Westin Hotels' approach in Figure 9-2.) The business traveler segment is not homogeneous. All of its members want location convenience and cleanliness. The irony is that some want price, some want service, some want room appointments (like a large desk with good lighting), and some want a number of other things. Separating the "somes" is the essence of target marketing.

Airline Crews

As the hotel industry faces increased competition to fill hotel rooms with a trailing demand, alternative target markets are needed to fill the guest rooms. To this end, the airlines have provided a reasonable alternative to traditional sources of business for many properties.

The airline market is defined as the housing of airline employees and crew members on a contract basis. Normally, when an airline flies its employees over a designated number of hours, as established by the Federal Aviation Agency, it has to provide a place for the crew to rest for a designated number of hours. In the past, hotels chosen for this purpose have been low-priced and located near the airport for reasons of reduced transportation costs.

Two factors have changed the traditional scenario: One is the supply/demand ratios in the hotel marketplace, and the other is the unions that participate in the bargaining process for their members.

In the first case, as more hotels have been built in relatively stable demand centers, the competition for customers has increased. This has put pressure on hotels to find new customers to fill their hotel rooms. In the second case, although airline unions have been

---

[12] This anecdote was contributed, without Ray's knowledge, by former Sheraton Grand employees who were there when this happened. It was confirmed through other sources.

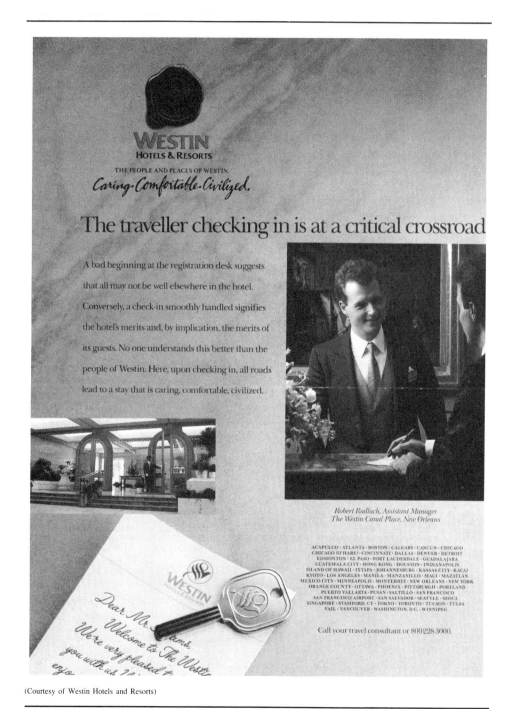

(Courtesy of Westin Hotels and Resorts)

FIGURE 9-2 A "caring-comfortable-civilized" approach to the business traveler

forced to accept lower wages after the deregulation of the industry, they have been sucessful in keeping and improving other benefits for their members, such as housing.

The net result has been that the airline station manager who negotiates for crew accommodations finds a number of better products to choose from, with pressure from the unions to make the best possible facilities available to their members. On the hotel's part, however, facilities alone will not hold the contract. Unless the hotel understands these customers and their unique needs, it will not deliver the product needed and will eventually lose the business to the hotel that understands the customers' problems.

Airline crew members have entirely different needs and problems from those of the corporate traveler or the weekend package guest. Due to tight flight schedules, there are sometimes as few as twelve hours available to rest between flights. Airline crews need to have all of their rooms available and assigned before they arrive. To ask each crew member for identification and credit cards would cut into twelve precious hours of rest. The captain is always in charge of the crew, even off the plane. All unusual situations need to be discussed with the captain before any decisions can be made.

Once in their rooms, airline crews do not prefer street views! Here is a market segment that would gladly take the rooms facing an inner courtyard or another building. Some airline crews have very unusual hours of sleep—for instance, some international flight crews check in at 8:00 A.M. and need to sleep immediately. Noisy, street-view rooms may be desirable for the corporate customer, but very impractical for the airline crew. Heavy black-out shades are also necessary to enable crew members to sleep during the day, a feature that would not affect most other customers of the hotel.

Coordination is needed in all phases of the operation. For the corporate client who is at a meeting, 11:00 A.M. may be the best time to have a houseman vaccum the hallways, but this is not true for the crew that checked in at 8:00 A.M. Wake-up calls are critical. Delayed flights can cost an airline thousands of dollars because an operator making $4.50 per hour forgot to make the wake-up calls at 3 P.M. There are numerous other seemingly small details that are critical for crew members, such as locating them away from elevators and ice machines, and not putting female crew members into connecting rooms that do not have their fellow employees next door.

Finally, integration of the food and beverage offerings needs to occur. Recognizing that crews are not on expense accounts, the lunch menu with an $18.00 average check will probably not be utilized by them. However, there is potential in these extra customers and special menu discounts can provide additional revenues and profits.

How much is too much? Airline crews tend to be contracted on a yearly basis for a set number of rooms. The rate can sometimes be very low in comparison to the printed rack rates, or even the corporate rates. Some managers shy away from airline business because of a low average rate and/or because they think it gives a negative image to a hotel. (Airline crews would certainly not be appropriate in the lobby of a Four Seasons hotel.) The real test of accepting airline business depends on the cash generated by the business and the compatibility with the segment mix.

To determine the profit margins of an airline contract, a displacement study needs to be done. First, management needs to determine how many nights during the year the hotel will run 100 percent occupancy. The number of sold-out nights becomes the basis for revenue displacement. In other words, how many nights could the guest room have been sold to a guest at a higher rate?

TABLE 9-1   Displacement Calculation for Airline Crew Contract

365	Nights available per year
−56	Sell-out nights
309	Nonsold-out nights
×40	Rooms of contract
12,360	Contract rooms
×$42	Contract room rate
$519,120	Total revenue generated
56	Sell-out nights
×40	Rooms of contract
2240	Rooms displaced
×$62	Difference between rack ($110) and contract ($48) rates
$138,880	Displaced revenue
$519,120	Total revenue generated
−$138,880	Displaced revenue
$380,240	Additional revenue
×68%	Rooms departmental profit
$258,563	Departmental profit

For example, a 400-room hotel has 56 sold-out nights a year when they can sell their rooms at a rack rate of $110. The airline contract in question requires 40 rooms per night at a rate of $42. Currently the hotel is maintaining a 68 percent rooms departmental profit. The displacement calculation is shown in Table 9-1.

Clearly, the hypothetical hotel in Table 9-1 should strongly consider this airline contract business. The calculation also does not take into account the peripheral revenues generated in the food and beverage outlets, telephone department, or gift shops. The marketing-driven manager would easily see that this business, despite its apparently prohibitive rate, is a profitable way to establish new customers. Until the number of sell-out dates increases dramatically, or the rate that the crews are willing to pay drops substantially, it would appear that this base of business would be feasible for the near future.

Overall, the airline business will be increasingly sought by hoteliers in the next few years. The organization that understands the needs of this new segment will get more than its fair share of what can be very profitable business.

The Package Market

This increasingly popular method of attracting customers during low-demand periods is becoming more crowded with offerings every day. In the *New York Times* Sunday Travel Section, hotels from the famous Ritz Carlton on Central Park and the Carlyle on the upper east side, to the convention-type Penta Hotel in the garment district and the Milford Plaza on Broadway are all offering weekend packages. The same is true in major cities throughout the United States, at resorts, and in London, Paris, Rome, Athens, Singapore, Bangkok, and just about any other place you look.

The hotel package market is defined as the offering of a combination of room and amenities to consumers for an inclusive price. While normally these packages are designed to boost occupancy during low-demand time periods, such as weekends and off-seasons, cases exist where packages are used to maximize revenues at all times.

An example of this might be a resort, where a package includes three nights' accommodations and breakfast and dinner daily. The purpose of this combined package is to ensure that while the hotel is full, the guests are required to make use of the food and beverage facilities. Also, the three nights are sold at once, ensuring their occupancy over the period. If sold individually, one night might sell out before the others, eliminating longer, more desirable bookings. Naturally, the hotel would have to forecast some significant demand to be able to force the customer to purchase that type of package.

We define a package as offering a combination of room and amenities, as shown in Figure 9-3, be it food and beverage or a welcome gift upon arrival. Often the term is debased to describe blatant discounting. Offering a guest room at a significant discount is nothing more than that; it certainly does not package anything for the consumer.

Once again, the needs and problems of the customer must be understood in order to succeed in developing the target package market. What works in one section of the country, or the world, may be completely foreign in another market. A good example comes from the Vista International Hotel, located in the Wall Street area of Manhattan.

Although this hotel enjoyed very high occupancies during midweek, the weekends were very problematic. All of the nightlife, theaters, restaurants, and museums of New York City are located in the midtown area, about fifty blocks away. The Vista, recognizing the need to fill the hotel during weekends while facing a location disadvantage diametrically opposed to their midweek location advantage, constructed packages that emphasized seclusion, romance, "getting away from it all," and doing what you want to do with someone you care about. They emphasized the pool facilities for relaxation, the signature restaurant, room service amenities, and the sophisticated ambience of the hotel. The graphics depicted scenes such as couples lounging in their hotel room, relaxing and exchanging banter about their wonderful stay.

The Vista spent thousands of dollars advertising and marketing this package, which was less than successful. For many hotels, this type of package is very successful. Why, then, did it not succeed better at the Vista International in New York City? Because it was not what the customer wanted for that geographic area. When a couple has had a busy week in downtown Boston or New York City, the opportunity to escape and be alone is appealing, and a hotel offering a product such as a "Romance Weekend" or the "Weekend in the Woods" may meet the needs of these customers.

In New York City the needs are totally different. Very few people go there to get away and spend the weekend in a hotel room! Instead, they want to get out and enjoy the sightseeing and museums, try the restaurants, and go to the theaters. Sitting in a hotel room for two days watching the excitement go by is not what the customer needs or wants. If the Vista had offered complimentary transportation to the midtown area to overcome the location disadvantage, the customer might have had more reason to buy the package.

FIGURE 9-3   Well-defined packages

Incidentally, the research done by Vista to develop this package was well done, but had the same failing as Coca-Cola's, which we discussed in Chapter 6. The research identified the weekend getaway problems and needs of working couples. The advertising was well executed to fulfill these needs and solve the problem, as shown in Figure 9-4. What wasn't measured was the attitude toward the act—that is, going to Wall Street for this purpose—or the subjective norms—for example, having friends say, "Why would you want to go to *Wall Street?*"

Once the needs of the target package consumer have been identified, the competition needs to be analyzed. As was mentioned earlier, there are very few places left that do not have a myriad of packages for the consumer to buy. Again, the key is the differentiation of the product to the target market. With so many different packages available, and plenty of availability on weekends, the creation must, to capture the market, clearly be better from an offering or price advantage.

From the customer's point of view there are four different advantages to packages, assuming the initial motivation is there from the needs and wants perspective. In other words, why buy a package when you can do the same thing on your own?

The first advantage is price. The implication with package prices is that the sum is cheaper than the individual parts. This is usually but not always true, and depends heavily on the quality of the parts. A low-rated, obscure room and an inexpensive split of champagne might have been bought cheaper on your own, but many people don't know this and either don't want or don't know how to take the trouble to find out, so they buy on price. Even when the price is not less, there is a *perception* of value in packages.

The second reason is that packages offer something that people want but probably would not request by itself—for example, breakfast in bed. "It's too expensive, but look, it's included." Or perhaps it's something like horseback riding: "I always wanted to do that but never would have thought of it." Packages remove the worry of "how to," and make it easier for the customer to do whatever it is.

The third reason, and sometimes the greatest, is that packages tend to be hassle-free. The customer doesn't have to make decisions about where to eat, where to dance, where to go to the theater, how to get there, and so on. This is particularly true for the inexperienced traveler. It is also why carefully thought-out packages can be priced at more than the sum of their parts. The package removes much of the hassle for customers, and they will pay for that, even though they probably think they are getting it cheaper. Packages make the multiple-purchase decision much simpler.

Club Med has become a master at this art by offering a total week's experience at their resorts, including airfare, ground transportation, all food, wine, and sports activities. All you pay for is drinks and you do that with poppit beads, for which you are charged on departure. In fact, Club Med is an excellent example of a marketing-oriented packaging company.

When Club Med was first conceived, packages appealed to the younger single set that wanted to get away and meet members of the opposite sex. There was a definite hedonistic overtone to the advertising messages. The market has since changed. Consumers are more conservative, and many of today's Club Med customers are older and married with children. Club Med's product has changed with them, offering a much more wholesome package.

Other companies have taken this one step further to what is called the all-inclusive

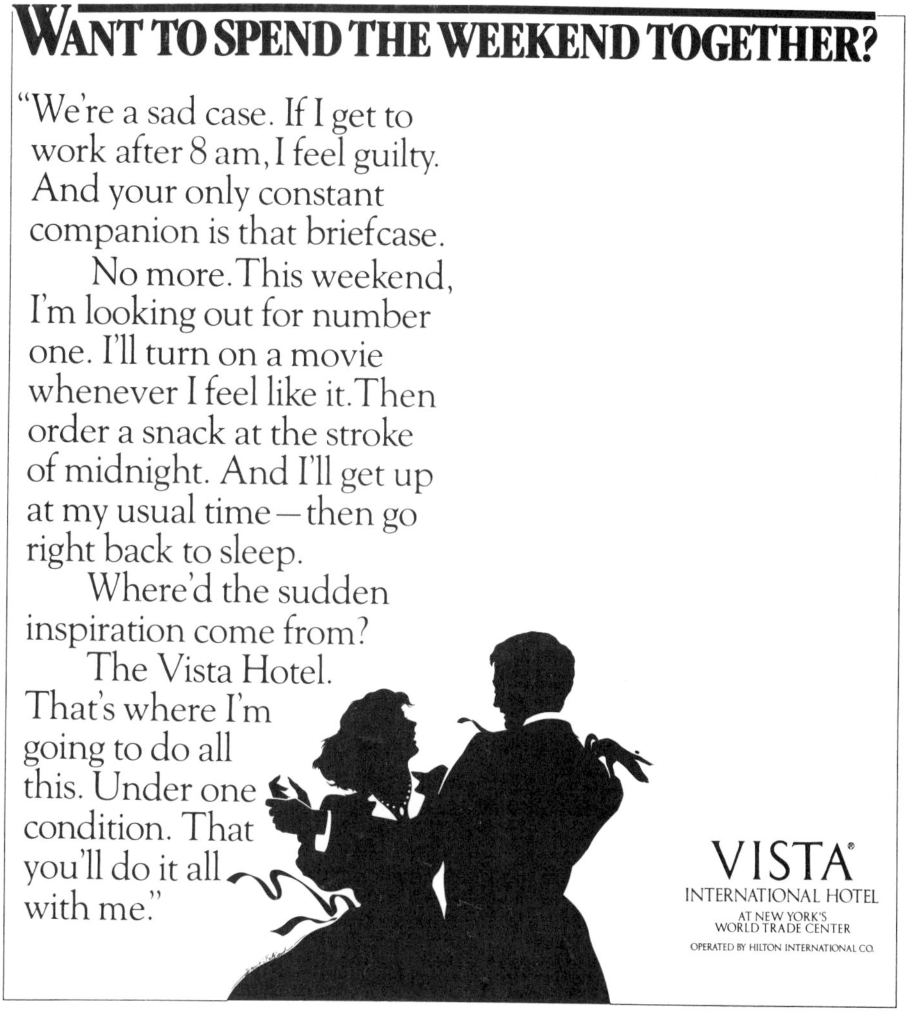

(Courtesy of Vista International Hotel, New York. Robert Mackey C.H.S.E., Director of Marketing. Agency: Albert Frank Guenther Law.)

FIGURE 9-4 A well-conceived package weekend

resort—for instance, Sandals in Jamaica (Figure 9-5). These packages don't include airfare but they include everything else—all you can drink, for instance, and cigarettes. The price is high but is paid only once. The customer feels that a problem is solved: "I can do whatever I want and don't have to worry about what it costs."

Figure 9-6 shows an ad for a successful package that offered both price and hassle-free benefits. This package was so successful that research was conducted afterward to determine why. Can you figure out what was found to be the primary appeal of this package?

FIGURE 9-5   An all-inclusive package

FIGURE 9-6   A successful short-term package

The fourth appeal of some packages is that buyers get something they would not get without the package. That something appeals to a particular interest. One example are the "murder weekend" packages that started in England and had mixed success in the United States. With these packages, a couple went to a hotel for the weekend and spent the weekend, with other couples, trying to solve a murder that was literally enacted before their eyes, with all the appropriate clues. With the package, of course, came room, food, and beverages. Other packages of this type are designed for "buffs." For example, there are rock buffs, seashell buffs, bird-watcher buffs, and others. Special activities are planned for these buffs, who know they will be sharing the experience with others of like interest.

There is an important caveat about packages that too often is violated: Provide what you promise in the package! This advice is obvious, but is not always followed, resulting in very negative feedback for the property. For example, we know one small city hotel that offered the usual weekend package. The main appeal of this package in the winter in New England was the indoor pool and lounge area. People from only a few miles away bought the package for that reason. More often than not, the hotel had a wedding party every Saturday afternoon that was held by the pool. Including set-up and break-down time, package customers could not use the pool for most of their stay.

Too often hotels do not deliver on the promises made with their packages. The main reasons for this seem to be that they do not plan for packages and consider them secondary, low-rated business. This is self-defeating and results in extremely negative word-of-mouth. Research done by the senior author on customer complaints has revealed a disproportionate number of complaints about package "promises."

The Tour and Travel Market

Under this umbrella segment lie two major subsegments: bus tour travelers and free independent travelers (FIT). Although these subsegments are somewhat different, they have similar buy decisions and rate expectations.

Bus Tour Travelers

In the United States, this market segment was traditionally set aside for the older travelers of the 1970s. In other parts of the world, however, where owning cars is not as prevalent, bus tours have long been a popular mode of getting around. As most of the trends in the industry indicate, things have changed in the United States. Many younger travelers are utilizing bus tour types of travel to see domestic sights inexpensively.

The bus tour market for hotels and restaurants can be defined as five or more travelers arriving at a hospitality establishment by motorcoach, as part of a total tour package. This market really has to be separated from other travelers arriving at the hotel by bus, simply because of their original reason for the purchase. A group of corporate businesspeople could arrive at a hotel by bus, yet their sole purpose for the visit would be a corporate meeting, making them a corporate group. A convention could have an entire delegation from a similar geographic area arrive by bus, but again the reason would be to attend the convention, not to visit local attractions.

The size of the bus tour market is ever expanding; almost 40 million passengers spent $3.5 billion on motorcoach trips in 1985. Although the majority of these trips were within one day, almost 40 percent stayed overnight in a lodging establishment. Nearly $750 million was spent in hotels and half again as much was spent on food and beverage.[13]

Motorcoach tours are arranged in two formats, series and ad hoc groups. A tour series is a prearranged link of stopovers, usually carrying a theme. For example, "Autumn in New England," marketed by Casser Tours in New York City, offers a motorcoach tour to see the New England foliage. Stopovers include country inns and landmark restaurants, with occasional visits to local museums.

An ad hoc group has a specific destination in mind; for example, Disneyworld. A group would arrange to travel there by motorcoach, and stay several nights to take advantage of the attraction. While ad hoc groups might also have another stopover, this is normally just a stopover and is not the reason for the trip.

When you are soliciting this market segment, responding to its specific needs makes the product more successful. Tours have tour leaders who are responsible for the well-being of the group as well as the satisfaction of its individual members. Tour leaders are also, in essence, sales representatives for the tour company. The hotel salesperson sells the hotel to the tour company, but the tour leader is the one who has to travel with the group and ensure their satisfaction. As with most other products, there are many similar tours available to the consumer, and often the tour leader develops a following of repeat customers.

The group requires special room key assignment, all being preassigned before the bus arrives. The keys are distributed by the tour leader, and the baggage is unloaded and tagged. The luggage is a critical need for this customer. It is unacceptable to have to wait over half an hour for luggage to arrive in the rooms, after a long day on the road and before an inflexible dinner time. Whether luggage is carried to the rooms by bellmen, or by the customer directly, this relatively simple yet unusual situation can, if not handled correctly, cause many dissatisfied customers.

Although the median age of motorcoach tour travelers is dropping into the 50s, generally such travelers prefer rooms that do not require the use of stairs. They prefer rooms with views, they like being close to each other, and they want the correct bedding configuration. Here is another opportunity to misunderstand a market. A weekend package user might ask for a double room, and be completely satisfied with a queen bed assignment. The same double room for the motorcoach guest indicates a need for two beds in the same room—and a roll-away is not an acceptable substitute.

Motorcoach tour groups are a viable market for many hotels; in fact, some hotels survive on them. The caveat here is the one we have mentioned before: They do not mix well with some other market segments, and special care is needed to see that this mix is not a problem. Bus tour groups are also low budget, for the most part, although there are exceptions. For example, for a very dear price one can tour through the vineyards of France, stay in chateaux, and eat at very expensive restaurants.

---

[13] Karen Rubin, *Tour Business Survey*, Lexington, Ky. March 1987.

Regardless of their budget, these travelers' needs come all at once. An average normal busload of 46 means 46 bags all at once, 46 luncheons all at once, and 46 breakfasts all at once. Staffing to handle this is critical, especially when these customers don't tip well and employees are not eager to serve them. Disgruntled tour groups make a great deal of noise!

Free Independent Travelers (FIT)

The FIT traveler is a "nonorganized" visitor who does not belong to a group. While these travelers may well participate in tours, or group activities, they essentially come on their own and do as they please. FIT travelers may also include business travelers although, because of that segment's importance, they are usually considered a separate segment. Hotels catering to the FIT market will usually set aside a block of rooms in advance, and fill them as reservations are made. The lead time may be three days to six months in advance. The hotel releases the unused blocked space according to its buy time schedule.

Both wholesalers and retail agents (who will be discussed in Chapter 18, on distribution) handle the FIT. This segment is normally willing to pay higher rates than group customers. However, a conflict arises with this situation. While the FIT is willing to pay a higher rate because of a lack of volume, the wholesaler and retailer are able to negotiate large discounts due to aggregate FIT bookings.

The resulting savings are not always passed on to the traveler. Therefore, the guest may pay a high price while the hotel receives a relatively low room rate. Often the FIT booked by an intermediary may get the poorest room in the house based on the rate being paid to the hotel. The traveler is at a disadvantage in these situations, and is surprised at the accommodations. This can hurt the hotel that is caught in the middle.

The remainder of the chapter provides a brief introduction to broad FIT segments, although members of any of these traveler segments may also travel in groups.

International Travelers

The international market is staggering in its size and complexities. Over 340 million people traveled outside their own countries in 1986, up 2.1 percent from the previous year. These people produced $115 billion in revenues for the visited countries. Overall, Asia experienced the largest percent increase from the previous year (6.8 percent), but the Americas hosted the largest influx of international travelers, with 55 million.[14]

The United States lags behind the rest of the world in promoting tourism abroad. The United States is rated thirty-seventh in the world by the United States Travel Data Center in terms of promotional expenditures on international travel. In fact, the federal government, which spent $11.5 million on tourism in 1986, was outspent by the individual states by 20 to 1.[15]

---

[14] "International Tourism Trends in 1986 and First Results for 1987," *World Tourism Organization, Feature 025,* March 1987.

[15] Alastair M. Morrison, "Selling the USA," *Travel and Tourism Analyst,* February 1987. Published by the Economist Publications Ltd., pp. 3–17.

Not long ago, most U.S. hospitality companies, both small and large, could disregard the international market unless they deliberately chose to enter it. This situation is changing quickly. To this day, foreign visitors to the United States can go to only a very few select hotels in major cities like New York and expect to find someone who speaks their language, apart from understanding their needs. The situation is even worse in restaurants; the only hope for a foreign speaker in this case is to go to a purely ethnic restaurant or hope to have an immigrant waiter or waitress who speaks the same language.

On the other hand, an American can travel almost anywhere overseas and find hotels and restaurants in which at least someone will speak English, or make an honest attempt at it. The overseas hospitality enterprise has long recognized the value of the American market. It is difficult for an American to travel anywhere and not be understood, even if rudimentarily. Even in some remote European or Asian villages it is possible for Americans to communicate basic needs and wants. Contrarily, foreign visitors to the United States are too often repulsed with a "Huh?" when trying to communicate in an American hospitality enterprise. This problem goes far beyond the problem of language difficulties; it extends into the area of basic consumer needs and wants. Because many foreign visitors to the United States are able to speak some English, Americans are relieved of the burden of understanding another language, but this does not relieve them of the burden of understanding the customer.

Overall, inbound traffic to the United States is over 50 percent represented by Canadian travelers. Mexicans are the second-largest body of foreign travelers, followed by the Japanese, the English, and the Germans, in 1986. Overall, $14 billion was pumped into the U.S. economy by these guests.[16]

Chapter 22 will discuss further the needs and wants of the international market. In general, however, international travelers do represent a segment of their own. To treat a foreign visitor like any other traveler could not only be a mistake, it could alienate this market from your business if it was one of your targeted markets.

The Resort Leisure Market

The resort leisure market is also unique from the consumer viewpoint. Business travelers stay at a hotel because they have business to do, and airline crew members are assigned to a hotel. Motorcoach tours stay at hotels on their way to, or from, somewhere. The resort leisure market, however, travels to resorts because it wants to be there, to get away from it all. Again, the wants and needs of these customers are different from those of the usual traveler.

Resort guests need to fulfill their idea of a vacation. Whether it be total, quiet relaxation or a sports/recreation schedule busier than their job back home, they must feel satisfied that their idea of relaxation was met.

---

[16] Ibid.

Overall, resorts have maintained a consistently high occupancy, relative to the rest of the hospitality industry. In 1986, this segment enjoyed a 66.2 percent occupancy, coupled with a $67.63 average rate. The 410,000 rooms categorized as resorts in 1986 are expected to grow to 460,000 by the year 1990.[17]

The complexion of resort guests is different from that of guests at commercial hotel. Fifty-seven percent are pleasure travelers, 29 percent are attending a conference or participating in an incentive junket, while merely 9 percent can be deemed business travelers.[18]

This varied market mix poses inherent problems. The hotel staff must be trained to deal with the diverse needs of the leisure traveler on vacation, at the same time that it executes complicated conferences with infinite details. The needs of the meeting planner and the leisure resort market come into conflict often. The hotel has to be prepared to serve them both.

For example, a major conference at the hotel may want to use the pool area for a cocktail reception, worth $10,000 to the resort. Should the manager shut down the pool area to leisure guests to accommodate the needs of the conference? This integration of diverse customers is more amplified in the resort setting. Often, the exclusive nature of the facility lends itself to these conflicts, as, for example, when there are so many conferees on the golf course that it is impossible for an individual to get a tee time. The marketing-driven manager will understand the needs of both customers, develop operating standards for both, and sell the facility so that revenues will be maximized without loss of guests.

The Pleasure Traveler

This target market, known too as the leisure market, is also part of some of the segments mentioned earlier in this chapter. Specifically, the leisure market comprises travelers that individually, in couples, or in small groups visit a hotel or restaurant for nonbusiness purposes. They may be traveling on vacation but often are not. Many, of course, are weekend, or other, package users. Others travel to cities for shopping, visiting friends, going to the theater, "just for a change," personal business, and various other purposes.

In the restaurant business, this segment includes a very large market of those who eat out just for pleasure. In many cities, both large and small, this is a powerful segment with many diverse needs and wants. Not as constrained as the business customer by having to "get back to the office," the pleasure diner tends to be more relaxed and casual. At the same time, since the primary purpose of being there is to eat and socialize, these diners have more time to be critically conscious of the product delivery.

Some pleasure travelers use the best hotels and visit the best restaurants. In recent years, however, there has been a growing trend toward short pleasure trips and frequent dining out at less expensive properties by those with limited budgets. This has consider-

---

[17] *United States Resort Lodging Industry 1986*, Laventhol and Horwath, 1987.

[18] Jerome Morrison, "The Resort Industry: Looking Good", *Lodging Hospitality*, October 1986, pp. 86, 87.

able impact on the hospitality industry both in expanding the industry and in the need to better serve this market.

The pleasure market is a high-growth potential market. While the business market remains relatively stable, traveling and eating out when it has to, a large portion of the pleasure market stays home and has yet to be developed. It *chooses* whether to travel or eat out. This is even more true outside the United States. Many countries have only recently seen a large growth in the so-called middle class with more discretionary income. Because they are not "big spenders," however, they are often closed out of a market that caters and prices to the expense account customer.

The airlines in the United States discovered the pleasure market almost by accident. For many years, the airlines were aware of a large untapped market that had never flown, or flew infrequently, in spite of efforts to get it on board. The change came when the airlines were involved in price wars after deregulation. Today, the percentage of Americans who have flown commercial flights is twice what it was 15 years ago.

The commercial hotel industry has been guilty of the same oversight. Perceived as a small market, "not worth bothering with" because it only represented about 10 percent of hotel business, the leisure market was priced right out of the system. Instead, the industry concentrated on the frequent traveler, who is actually a far smaller percentage of the market, but represents the vast majority of the business. While the industry urgently sought growth to fill its increased supply, it concentrated on the nongrowth segment. The inexperienced pleasure traveler who called a hotel for a room price was given the rack rate and often stayed home because of it.

This situation has changed rapidly in the recent past. In cities like New York, Chicago, and San Francisco there are now smaller, less elegant, and less pretentious hotels that have targeted the pleasure traveler. Additionally, of course, there has been a huge growth in the supply at the middle and lower ends of the market. Quality's McSleep (later called Sleep Inns) is a good example of this (Figure 9-7). In other countries this trend is just emerging.

For the top, exceptional hotels, the needs of the leisure traveler are simple—everything! When a guest checks into an upscale hotel and is paying the published rate for a four-night stay, there can be nothing that is impossible to get. Twenty-four hour room service needs to work perfectly, together with a valet department that can have pants pressed in a minute. Messages are not forgotten, but delivered promptly. The list goes on, but the service must be perfect. Figure 9-8 shows some differences between the pleasure and business traveler.

In the lower-tier markets, pleasure travelers are actually less demanding than customers in almost any other market. One reason for this is the lack of experience. Travelers may not realize just what is available and/or they may simply not know how to demand. (The exceptions, of course, are the business travelers now turned pleasure travelers.) They do, however, have long memories. These customers are prone to simply walk out of a bad experience without complaining, never to return. They also are more prone to spread negative word-of-mouth. They are and will become, however, more demanding as their travel experience increases.

There is a large market in pleasure travel, even if it comes in small pieces. The hotel that can segment and serve this market appropriately will reap the rewards.

What's A McSleep Inn?

The McSleep Inns guest room offers an 80" queen-sized bed, a 36" square desk, a large bay window and a unique, oversized shower.

They said it couldn't be done.

To claim you can build a 100-unit hotel with just over one and a half acres of land and as little as $2 million (including land costs), flies in the face of conventional wisdom.

To do it while offering a room that's superior to those of other budget chains has been flatly called impossible.

Because McSleep Inns don't have atriums, big lobbies, restaurants, swimming pools and meeting rooms, there's less money needed for development than traditional facilities. And there's more money

food service staff and no food theft. In fact, it takes as few as 11 full-time equivalent employees to run a McSleep Inn.

And that's just the beginning. Smaller rooms and standardized designs even cut your energy and maintenance costs.

Great room. Great price.

Obviously everyone wants a nice, comfortable room without paying for a lot of extras they don't need.

And that's what McSleep Inns offer. Every guest room has a queen-sized bed, king-sized desk, bay window and oversized shower.

Each room has a remote control color television and

McSleep Inns are what people crave.

After months of design testing and consumer research, we've come to what by now should seem like an obvious conclusion.

McSleep Inns are going to be very big. With a very big segment of the traveling public.

And not just because of the price. But because they offer consistently high

The new budget lodging chain that takes less and makes more.

McSleep Inns are a completely new budget concept in budget

lodging from Quality International that cost about two-thirds as much to develop (as little as $20,000 per room) as typical budget hotels, yet offer room features like upscale furnishings, queen-sized beds, king-sized desks, remote control color televisions, bay windows and unique oversized showers. All for an incredibly attractive room rate of around $25 per night.

But the real beauty of McSleep Inns is what they offer investors.

Like quick and easy construction that cuts development time and speeds positive cash flow.

And a design that can be built on very little land.

(Courtesy of Quality International)

to put into the rooms. Because you eliminate a lot of space, you can fit more rooms on less land. And since rooms generate revenue, you not only save money, you make more of it.

Even after it's built it keeps saving money.

Because of the low development cost, it's easy to finance a McSleep Inn. And because they can be built faster, they start producing revenue faster than any other concept in the hotel industry.

Then there are the operating costs. No pool means no pool maintenance and no insurance. No restaurant means no

VCR, rental movies and a telephone with a 15-foot cord. Adjoining rooms connect.

QUALITY'S RESERVATION SYSTEM

Behind McSleep Inns is Quality International's worldwide reservation system.

allowing guests to enjoy the suite experience at a very affordable price.

Every McSleep Inn is brand new—no conversions will be accepted into the McSleep Inn system.

And every McSleep Inn room has one more unbeatable feature. A room rate of around $25.

quality for a very low price.

McSleep Inns give you more options.

Because the front-end cost is so low, you have more development alternatives.

A multiple-unit investor can choose to cluster and dominate a given marketplace or spread the risk geographically. And a developer who could previously own only a single property can now enjoy the financial leverage of multiple-unit ownership.

McSleep Inns come with site-adapted, construction-ready plans, as well as completely specified FF&E packages. Designated "master builder" contractors will deliver McSleep Inns at a guaranteed construction price.

Every McSleep Inn gets the Quality touch.

Behind every McSleep Inn is the marketing power of Quality International. That means you have complete marketing and sales support, training programs, an international advertising campaign, problem-solving services and quality assurance.

Every McSleep Inn also has an appealing exterior design and signage with the familiar Quality look that is recognizable around the world.

But it also means you're tied into Quality's worldwide reservations system. A system that last year generated over 5.5 million reservation calls.

And you have the power and leverage of Quality International, the third largest lodging chain in the world. A chain with a remarkable track record for launching new products.

McSleep Inns offer exceptional features such as a 20" remote-control color television and a video tape player with movie rentals.

For example, today there are over 460 Comfort Inns. And only six years ago, Comfort Inns didn't exist.

Get your hands on an overnight success.

No other hotel concept offers so much for so little.

The McSleep Inn guest room is approximately 70% of the size of a standard hotel room. Customers even have the option of having adjacent rooms with connecting doors.

Budget hotels have been the fastest growing segment in the industry for the past three years. And McSleep Inns are the best concept yet in that segment.

No wonder we're projecting that over 200 McSleep Inns will be up and running by 1990.

Find out why. Call Fred Mosser, Senior Vice President, Development, and ask for franchise information.

Quality International

McSleep   Comfort   Quality   Clarion

Inns · Hotels · Suites · Resorts

10750 Columbia Pike · Silver Spring, MD 20901 · 301/236-5080

FIGURE 9-7 Product development for the low-budget traveler

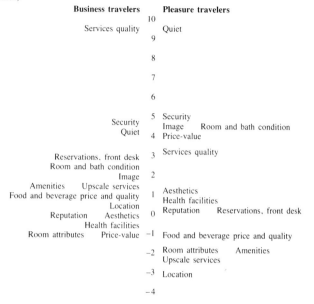

Comparison of determinance attributes for business and pleasure travelers (on a standardized ten-point scale after multiple regression of 15 factors derived from 67 attributes)

Business travelers		**Pleasure travelers**
	10	
Services quality		Quiet
	9	
	8	
	7	
	6	
Security	5	Security
		Image Room and bath condition
Quiet	4	Price-value
Reservations, front desk	3	Services quality
Room and bath condition		
Image	2	
Amenities Upscale services		
Food and beverage price and quality	1	Aesthetics
		Health facilities
Location		Reputation Reservations, front desk
Reputation Aesthetics	0	
Health facilities		
Room attributes Price-value	−1	Food and beverage price and quality
	−2	Room attributes Amenities
		Upscale services
	−3	Location
	−4	

Comparison of importance attributes for business and pleasure travelers (on a standardized ten-point scale after multiple regression of 14 factors derived from 67 attributes)

Business travelers		**Pleasure travelers**
	10	
Security		Services quality
	9	
Services quality		
	8	
Room and bath furnishings and condition		Restaurant quality and price options
	7	
	6	
	5	
Restaurant quality and price options		
Reputation Image	4	Building aesthetics
		Quiet
Location	3	Room and bath furnishings and condition
		Security
Quiet	2	Location
Amenities and conveniences		Amenities and conveniences
Price-value	1	Food and beverage service
Food and beverage service		Price-value
VIP treatment and extra luxury	0	
Health facilities		
Building aesthetics	−1	VIP treatment and extra luxury
		Reputation Image
	−2	
	−3	
		Health facilities
	−4	

(Source: Robert C. Lewis. "Predicting Hotel Choice." *Cornell Hotel and Restaurant Administration Quarterly.* February 1985. p. 91)

FIGURE 9-8   Relative differences in importance and determinant attributes of hotels for pleasure and business travelers

The Senior Citizen

The senior citizen market is another important growth segment for both the hotel and restaurant marketer. More than 30 percent of all adults in the United States are aged fifty-five and over (the usual classification for senior citizens), with the trend increasing into the twenty-first century. This segment is reported to travel extensively, spending over 50 percent more of its time away from home than the younger pleasure segments.

The senior citizen market is not homogeneous, as recent research has revealed. People aged fifty-five to sixty-four make up nearly one-half of the market; those aged sixty-five to seventy-four make up one-third, with the balance representing almost 25 percent. As these figures indicate, the highest growth in the next few years will come in the older age brackets, according to the Census Bureau. In fact, by the turn of the century the fifty-five to sixty-four age group will actually decline slightly.

The younger segment of the senior market leads all adult age groups in median income, about 8 percent above the median for all households. Additionally, discretionary income—that available for personal expenditure—is 16 percent higher than the national average.

This market is becoming more recognized by the hospitality industry. Some companies, such as Ramada, have done extensive research on the market and have developed products geared specifically to it. Restaurants also have increasingly developed menu items (in large print that can be read), early dining hour specials, and other amenities to attract this market.

The largest organization that represents senior citizens is called the American Association of Retired Persons (AARP). AARP has a full travel bureau that is managed by Olsen Travelworld, Ltd. This travel service offers a myriad of group and individual travel plans at significant discounts.

The needs and wants of the senior citizen market are different from those of other segments discussed in this chapter. It has often been reported that members of this market live longer, healthier, and more vigorous lives, are better educated, and have wider interests and activities. Their children are grown, their mortgages are paid, and they have the time, energy, and inclination to travel.

Hal Norvell, manager of AARP's travel programs, has noted, "They are seasoned travelers; more than 90 percent of travelers over age fifty-five are repeaters." The senior citizen travel market is growing each year. The latest trend is toward "soft adventures," defined as "participatory travel to gain insight into the culture, history, or natural history of an area, but without demanding excessive physical challenge of the tour participants."

The needs of the senior citizen are basically simple. They are not, as a group, a demanding one. They want rooms close to the lobby, they want help with luggage, and they want information. This market tends not to be rushed through their stay like conferees or business people.

Because most senior citizens are not traveling on expense account, it is their savings that are paying for the hotel rooms and restaurant meals. Their needs are different from those of the business person sitting next to them in the same restaurant. Too often their discount is loudly questioned in a check-in line or at a table. These customers should be treated as full paying guests, and staff should be happy to see them occupying rooms or restaurant seats that might have otherwise been vacant.

Senior citizens tend to travel outside traditional patterns, such as the businessperson's Monday through Thursday, or the weekend package guest's Friday and Saturday. They are also more flexible in rearranging their schedules. Senior travelers can often check in on a Thursday and stay through Monday, making their stay attractive to the hotelier.

The restaurateur can fill some seats early in the evening, since seniors tend to eat dinner earlier. In fact, "sunset dinners" or "early-bird specials" have become quite popular in attracting covers from 5:30 to 7:30 P.M., before the regular patrons arrive. These menu offerings normally include beverage and dessert at an attractive price.

Many hotel companies have developed specific programs designed to capture their fair share of this market. Marriott, for example, has a "Leisurelife Program," which when available offers a 50 percent guest room discount, a 25 percent food and beverage discount, and a 10 percent gift shop discount. Unfortunately for the senior citizens, the chain runs such a high occupancy that the discount is often not available. Other hotel companies have followed suit. Holiday Inns offers Travel Venture Club, Quality has Prime Time, and Days Inns has September Days.[19]

Summary

In this chapter we have reviewed the most common broad market segments that are encountered in the marketing of hospitality. There are numerous other segments, as well as more specifically defined target markets.

The most important point to remember is that market segments represent groupings of customers with similar needs and problems. Ideally, the scenario would be to operate a hotel that catered to one market segment year-round. Unfortunately, this is not often possible realistically. In fact, different segments will often be on premise at the same time, making service and execution of the product difficult. The marketing-oriented team responds to this challenge by truly understanding the needs of the customer, and communicating these needs to the staff that will deliver the product promised.

DISCUSSION QUESTIONS

1. Discuss the problems of oversegmenting and undersegmenting.
2. Buy time was presented as an important segment consideration. Discuss how you would use buy time to segment.
3. We have stated that, for the business traveler, price can be a "minor factor," and that most business travelers are "price-sensitive." How do you reconcile these two statements?
4. Why have Club Med's packages been so successful? Discuss the Club Med product. How would you define it in terms of the customer?
5. Distinguish the pleasure travel market. How might a hotel distinguish its product to appeal to this market segment?
6. Apply question #5 to the senior citizen market.

---

[19] The material in this section comes from various sources. Most of it was developed by Stowe Shoemaker, Restaurant Research Associates, Tustin, CA, who has written on the subject.

CHAPTER 10
Market Positioning

Market positioning is the natural follow-through of market segmentation and target marketing. In fact, it is upon those strategies that positioning is built because they define the market to which the positioning is directed. Essentially, market positioning means creating an image in the consumer's mind. By understanding the target markets—that is, those consumers—desired images and effective and efficient positioning strategies can be developed.

There are actually two kinds of positioning in marketing: objective positioning and subjective positioning, sometimes also called product positioning and brand positioning, respectively. We shall use the first two terms because they are more specific in what they represent. Each has its appropriate place and usage. Each is concerned with its position vis-à-vis the competition.

Objective Positioning

Objective positioning is concerned almost entirely with the objective attributes of the physical product. It means creating an image about the product that reflects its physical characteristics and functional features. It is usually concerned with what actually is, what exists. For example, let's take the statement "The car is red." We can all see that it is red and it will be a rare person among us who will disagree that it is red. If the company that makes this car makes only red cars, we might call it "the red car company." We would carry an image of these cars as opposed to those made by "the green car company."

That's a little simplistic so let's apply it to the hospitality industry. Motel 6 is a low-cost motel; the Cerromar Beach Hotel is on the beach; Ponderosa Steak House sells steaks; the Chicago Hilton is a big hotel. All of these businesses conjure up specific images based on their product. In two of the cases the image comes from the name itself.

Almost no one would argue with our image because it derives from an objective, concrete, specific attribute. If we know anything about the product, we know at least that much.

Objective positioning need not always be concrete, however. It may be more abstract than these examples. Mazeratis are not only red; they also go fast. The Ritz Carlton is a luxury hotel; the Chicago Hilton is a convention hotel; McDonald's is a clean place; Lutèce serves gourmet meals and fine wines. A few perhaps, but not too many, would argue with us on these images. Again, they derive from the product itself.

Objective product positioning can be very important and is often used in the hospitality industry, sometimes effectively and sometimes not. The so-called burger wars of 1984 were based on objective positioning. Burger King started it all by saying that their hamburgers were broiled—which they are, and no one can really argue that they are not. By implication, however, Burger King was also saying that their burgers were better than McDonald's or Wendy's. Obviously, many people can argue about that. They also implied that Wendy's and McDonald's fry their hamburgers, which is true. Wendy's countered by saying that their hamburgers are fresh (which they are) and therefore implying that their burgers were better. McDonald's countered by filing a lawsuit, a move they later regretted and withdrew. All of these actions, except the last, were attempts at objective product positioning—that is, saying the product is better because of its physical characteristics.

Hyatt Hotels have long been positioned on their atrium lobbies, which do exist. Howard Johnson's, early on, positioned on twenty-eight flavors of ice cream, which they did have. The Plaza Hotel in New York City positions on the important people who go there, who do go there.

You begin to get the picture—if your product has some unique characteristic or unique functional feature, that feature may be used to objectively position the product, to create an image, and to differentiate it from the competition.

Less successful objective positioning occurs when the feature is not unique. This is why many hotel ads with pictures of the hotel (the edifice complex) fail to create an image or to differentiate the product. Other unsuccessful approaches include a picture of two people in a hotel room that looks like six million other hotel rooms, or people seated in a restaurant, or, worse, a picture of an empty restaurant with tuxedoed waiters standing at attention, as shown in Figure 10-1. One of the first rules of effective positioning is uniqueness. We will come back to that, but first we need to explain subjective brand positioning.

Subjective Positioning

Subjective positioning is concerned with *subjective* attributes of the product or brand. Subjective positioning is the perceived image that belongs not to the product, but to the consumer's mental perceptions. These perceptions and the resultant image do not necessarily reflect the true state of the product's physical characteristics. They may simply exist in the customer's mind and it is possible that we could find many who would disagree with particular perceptions and images. What the marketer hopes is that the people in the target market will agree on a favorable image, whether or not the image is true. This is the test of effective subjective positioning.

FIGURE 10-1   Ineffective positioning

Hilton Hotels' former ad campaign, "When American business hits the road, American business stops at Hilton," and its slogan "America's Business Address" are examples of attempts at subjective positioning. The desired image, obviously, is that business people prefer Hilton Hotels. One reason that people might not accept this positioning is because it lacks uniqueness and does not differentiate from the competition. This failing is compounded by the pictures in the ads. For example, one picture is of an empty conference room with a conference table surrounded by chairs. These are objective product characteristics that clearly are no different from characteristics at hundreds of other hotels.

Tangible Positioning

There are two very important differences in the types of positioning when they are used in the hospitality industry. The first is the industry's product nearness to commodity status. We need to understand what this means for positioning.

Consider the ultimate commodity, salt. How would you use objective positioning to create a unique image and differentiate your salt from someone else's salt? Morton tries it with the positioning statement "When it rains, it pours." This is intended to imply that

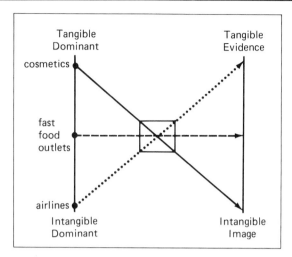

[Source: G. Lynn Shostack "Breaking Free from Product Marketing." Reprinted from *The Journal of Marketing* (April 1977, pp. 73–80) published by the American Marketing Association.]

FIGURE 10-2   Principles of marketing positioning emphasis

Morton salt is free-flowing even when the weather is damp, whereas other salts are not. It is not necessarily true that others are not, but if you buy into it you do so because you differentiate Morton's salt from other salts based on the physical characteristic of being free-flowing.

Salt is a very tangible good, or what Shostack calls "tangible dominant," as we discussed in Chapter 2.[1] As Shostack points out in her excellent article, the more tangible dominant the product, the more intangible the positioning needs to be. This notion is portrayed graphically in Figure 10-2. "Free-flowing" salt is not very intangible but the positioning is severely limited by the product. It would be difficult to argue that salt is exotic, tantalizing, or romantic.

Those arguments, however, could be made for cosmetics, and they certainly are, as we all know. Cosmetics are tangibly dominant. Their successful marketing is based on mental perceptions of intangible results. Consider the positioning of the fragrance Senchal by Charles of the Ritz Group Ltd.

> [They] have talked to women—not about what they want from a fragrance, but about what they want from life. Their answer: adventure, luxury and sex, especially sex. . . . Charlie, introduced in 1973, was intended for independent, carefree women. In 1975 there was Jontue for the romantic and Aviance for the housewife. Enjoli, for working mothers, came two years later. Now, there's yet another sort of female.
>   She's looking for some danger. She wants the passionate adventurous life. She's a connoisseur of luxury. . . . Or, as Senchal ads say: "She's not going to marry the boy next door."

---

[1] G. Lynn Shostack, "Breaking Free from Product Marketing," *Journal of Marketing*, April, 1977, pp. 73–80.

Because it's difficult for consumers to differentiate perfume scents, fragrance makers rely heavily on their ability to create an image that will attract prospective customers. What's in the bottle isn't as important as the bottle itself, the carton, the name, and the advertising.

. . . [In commercials, the] Senchal woman travels the world, posing in front of Egyptian pyramids, the Leaning Tower of Pisa . . . independent and adventurous . . . juxtaposed with photos of attractive, youthful men . . . she is bored [until] a more seasoned dashing fellow drives by in a sports car. . . . Senchal woman and her new mate caress on a beach. . . . The commercial concludes with a male voice: "I'm so glad you didn't marry the boy next door."[2]

This is an excellent example of targeting a specific market, determining the benefits and life-styles (at least fantasized) that are important to that market, and positioning on the intangible and highly subjective aspects of a very tangible good.

Now let's get back to hospitality and see if the same strategy will work with the hospitality product. If we are selling a near-commodity product that is tangible dominant, then we need to develop intangible mental perceptions that may or may not actually belong to the product. Thus arose the expression "Sell the sizzle, not the steak."

Consider again the hotel ad showing a picture of a couple in a hotel room. A hotel room is very tangible. It looks like thousands of other hotel rooms. As with salt, it is very hard to develop a mental perception of a hotel room that creates an image and differentiates from other hotel rooms. Two people in the room are also tangible. What's more, they are no different from two people in any other hotel room. Now you see the problem that hotel advertisers have been struggling with for years: How do you position a tangible product that has very little means of differentiation or intangibility? (No one has yet tried the Senchal technique, but perhaps there is a target market for that as well. See Figure 10-3 for how the French do this.)

It's difficult but not impossible. Hyatt has done it with some very creative advertising; refer back to Figure 6-7. People don't buy hotel rooms because of pears and light bulbs. These, of course, are highly tangible but in this ad they presumably carry an intangible mystique that is designed to create mental perceptions. In tangible positioning, we need to "intangibilize" the tangible.

There are other similar examples in the hospitality industry. What, for example, is more dull, plain, ordinary, and undifferentiated than a McDonald's hamburger? Is that the way you see a McDonald's hamburger? No? Why not?

Intangible Positioning

The second important difference in the types of positioning for hospitality products resides in the converse situation. What we are largely marketing is not tangible, it is intangible. Some would say that was nonsense, because what's more important than the room or the meal? They would be right, but that's what we're selling, and not what we're marketing. If we were selling rooms and beds, or steaks and salad bars, what difference would it make where the customer went, assuming a comparable level of quality? And that is an assumption we have to make within the same product class, so it doesn't get us very far.

---

[2] Bill Abrams, "Charles of the Ritz Discovers What It Is That Women Want," *The Wall Street Journal,* August 20, 1981, p. 29.

*L*orsque la nuit tombe, il fait bon
se retrouver dans un cadre douillet
et chaleureux pour vivre des soirées douceur
et se reposer d'une journée au grand
air ou puiser des forces nouvelles à l'issue
d'une réunion de travail.
Elégance, intimité, luxe... la nuit
passe comme un rêve.

When night falls, it feels good to be
in a cosy, warm setting to enjoy a quiet evening
and rest after a long day in the fresh air,
or to draw new strength at the end of a business
meeting. Elegance, privacy and luxury...
the night passes like a dream.

Wenn die Nacht fällt, findet man sich gern
in warmer und behaglicher Atmosphäre, um die
Annehmlichkeiten des Abends zu geniessen
und sich von einem Tag an der frischen Luft zu
erholen oder um nach einem Arbeitstreffen
neue Kräfte zu schöpfen.
Eleganz, private Atmosphäre, Luxus...
die Nacht vergeht wie ein Traum.

FIGURE 10-3   The Senchal technique at Le Relais Brenner, Paimpol, France

What we are marketing, of course, are intangibles. The tangibles are essential and necessary (facilitating and supporting goods), but as soon as they reach a certain level of acceptance, they become secondary. Because they are so difficult to differentiate, to be competitive we have to market the intangibles. Hospitality products are intangible dominant. Even when tangible (e.g., a steak) they have a measure of intangibility because they are consumed rather than taken home to be possessed.

If hospitality products are intangible dominant, we have to market them with tangible evidence. This is what is referred to as "tangibilizing the intangible." Recall from Chapter 6 the discussion on personal constructs supported by tangible evidence. That was theory, and positioning is one place we practice it. In the hospitality industry, the supporting goods elements of the product have a high degree of sameness. The intangible elements are abstract. To emphasize the concrete elements is to fail to differentiate from the competition. To emphasize the abstract (e.g., "escape to the ultimate") is to compound the abstraction. Thus, hospitality positioning should focus on enhancing and differentiating the abstract realities through the manipulation of tangible clues. Consider, for example, the intangibility of Merrill Lynch investment services to the tangibility of its bull literally walking through a china shop in television commercials.

Hyatt has done likewise with its atrium lobbies. People don't buy atrium lobbies; they buy what the lobbies tangibilize. We might not all agree, but some would say they are exotic, full of grandeur, majestic, or exciting. These are intangible images and nothing more than mental perceptions. The good part (for Hyatt) is that these perceptions carry over to the brand; ipso facto, subjective positioning. Hyatts are exciting, exotic, and majestic hotels; anyone can see that things happen here! Of course, check-in may be just as slow, and the rooms may be no different from those in other hotels, but the image is there, not just the physical characteristics. Today, many other hotels also have atrium lobbies but Hyatt got there first and the image is still maintained for many people.

Unfortunately, being aware of this need does not greatly ease the problem. It is still difficult to find meaningful tangible evidence that supports intangible constructs. What we want to do is create a "position" in the consumer's mind. You can see now why positioning follows so closely on target marketing—we need to know what mental constructs are held by the consumer in the target market, and what tangible evidence sustains them.

Return for a moment to the steak-and-sizzle argument. If we want to sell the steak, this argument goes, we need to market the sizzle. But our steak is just like all the others, so what we have to do is sell the sizzle, the intangible. How do we tangibilize the sizzle? If we knew we'd be millionaires. But you see the problem, and it is not totally insoluble. It is best explained by example.

There is probably no better example than what Jim Nassikas did at the Stanford Court Hotel in the 1970s. In fact, this was so successful in positioning the Stanford Court that Nassikas virtually stopped advertising and still ran one of the highest occupancies in San Francisco. Examples of the ads Nassikas ran are shown in Figure 10–4.

Note the positioning statement in these ads, "For people who understand the subtle differences." Note the tangible evidence in the picture. Finally, note the caption, "You're as finicky about choosing a fine hotel as you are about. . . . We designed the Stanford Court for you."

(Courtesy of The Stanford Court Hotel and Norman R. Tissian, Spiro & Associates, 100 South Broad St., Philadelphia, PA 19110.)

FIGURE 10-4   Ads that tangibilize the intangible

Now look at Leona Helmsley's ads in Figure 10-5. Notice the strong positioning of "Leona cares" obtained through the manipulation of tangible clues to represent the intangible construct of "caring."

For the restaurant business, note the ads in Figure 10-6. The positioning statement for one is, "An uncommon inn"; the graphics of the musketeer, the script printface of L'Armagnac, and the copy clearly tangibilize an intangible dining experience. In the other

FIGURE 10-5 Tangibilizing the intangible construct of "caring"

FIGURE 10-5 Continued

L'ARMAGNAC

AN UNCOMMON INN

(ROUTE 343) MILLBROOK, N. Y.

Named after . . .

the great Armagnac District of France --

home of Armagnac, the world's finest brandy,

truffles, foie gras, roquefort cheese and

D'Artagnan, Captain of the Three Musketeers.

FIGURE 10-6 Positioning restaurants with minimum graphics

ad the positioning is in the name, "Pistachio's: Courtyard of Contemporary Cuisine". Notice that these ads use a minimum of graphics. It is easier to create images with graphics, but not always necessary.

Positioning, then, is a relative term. It is not just how the brand is perceived alone but how the perceived image stands in relation to competing images. It is the consumer's mental perception, which may or may not differ from the actual physical characteristics. It is most important when the product is intangible and there is little difference from the competition on physical characteristics.

Effective Positioning

Our discussion so far has dwelled largely on image, the mental picture the consumer has of the product or service. We have also discussed the need for the image to differentiate the brand from the product class. These are two essential criteria for effective positioning, but there is one more.

This will take us back to the basic marketing concept, the notion of needs and wants and problem solutions—the promise we make to the customer. It also takes us back to Chapter 6, on consumer behavior in terms of the attitudinal disposition of the customer. Images and differentiation mean creating beliefs. Next we have to develop the affective reaction, the attitude toward the belief, and the action that will create the intention to buy.

Thus, effective positioning also must promise the benefit the customer will receive, it must create the expectation, and it must offer a solution to the customer's problem. And that solution, if at all possible, should be different from and better than the competition's. As Yesawich has pointed out, knowing what one's guests want is of little value if five of one's competitors are already serving those needs.[3]

Here are some better-known and successful positioning statements of the past with which many of us are familiar. As you read each one consider the image, the differentiation, and the promised benefit.

Seven Up—The Uncola
Avis Car Rental—We Try Harder (After Avis used this positioning statement for a while, they changed to a new one: "Avis is going to be #1." It failed. Why?)
Miller Lite—Everything you always wanted in a beer. And less.
Coca-Cola—The real thing.
McDonald's—We do it all for you.
Burger King—Have it your way.
Merrill Lynch—A breed apart.
Exxon—Put a tiger in your tank.
Hyatt—A touch of Hyatt; Capture the spirit; Wish you were here.
Marriott—Marriott does it right; Marriott people know how.

Most positioning statements are not so short and simple. Examine the La Quinta ad in Figure 10-7. This ad contains all the elements of effective positioning, which has been borne out by the success of the La Quinta chain. The image is there that you don't have to

---

[3] Peter C. Yesawich, "Marketing in the 1980s," *Cornell Hotel and Restaurant Administration Quarterly*, February 1980, p. 38.

Wake up to La Quinta.

La Quinta is checked into more and more by frequent travelers.

This growing popularity springs from a simple philosophy. We provide our guests with clean, comfortable, attractive rooms and friendly service in convenient locations at reasonable prices—about 20% less than other fine motor inns.

It's just that simple...and sensible.

No wonder 4 out of 5 of our guests are business travelers—the people who really know what to look for on the road.

No wonder 4 out of 5 of our guests are repeat customers.

Isn't it time for you to discover La Quinta? It's a nice way to go to sleep and a great way to wake up. Now in 24 states and growing.

For free directory, write La Quinta Marketing, Dept. **B3** P.O. Box 32064, San Antonio, Texas 78216.

Toll free reservations: 800-531-5900
(800-292-5200 from Texas)

La Quinta Motor Inns, Inc.

FIGURE 10-7   Positioning lodging with words

forsake the elements of a quality motel in order to obtain a low price: The ad differentiates La Quinta from similar properties; it gives you what they give you but at a lower price. Also, it promises a benefit—quality at a low price. This ad clearly positions to the target market: the self-employed or nonexpense account business traveler who wants a reasonable level of amenities without paying an arm and a leg for them.

Positioning's Vital Role

We have dealt with positioning so far in the context of advertising only because it is easier to illustrate that way. This is by no means, however, the only context in which positioning should be used. Positioning should be a single-minded concept, an umbrella from which everything else in the organization flows. Bill Dowling, a noted hotel marketer, states, "Properly targeted, single-minded positioning affects everything a hotel [or restaurant] does or stands for—not only advertising but also all of its promotions, brochures, facilities—even its decor."[4]

Dowling stops short, however. Positioning also affects policies and procedures, employee attitudes, customer relations, complaint handling, and the myriad of other details that combine to make a hospitality experience. Nassikas at the Stanford Court called these details "monumentally magnificent trivialities." He positioned the hotel "For people who understand the subtle differences." The positioning applied to the performance. If the positioning hadn't been made to perform then Nassikas would have had to look for another target market.

Positioning plays a vital role in the development of the entire marketing mix, which we will discuss in the next chapter. Hospitality services compete on more than just image, differentiation, and benefits offered. There must be a consistency among the various offerings of the entity and it is the positioning statement that guides this consistency. Likewise, although positioning can be applied for an entire chain, a given unit, or a specific service, chain operations should develop a consistency if the company desires to use one unit to generate business for another.

Kyle Craig, former president and CEO of S&A Restaurant Corp., a subsidiary of Pillsbury Company and operators of the Steak & Ale, Bennigan's, JJ Muggs, and Bay Street chains, says:

> When we talk about a marketing niche we are really talking about positioning. You must position your concept as offering a unique product or service. The key is to understand the consumer decision and then use it to your advantage to successfully stimulate sales. Once you understand what the customer wants and match that against what your chain has to offer, you have a better chance of success.
>
> . . . Finding a niche is tough but delivering the restaurant experience the niche demands is tougher. . . . Once the concept matches consumer needs there are two litmus tests. First, your position must be believable in the consumer's mind. Second, you must deliver on the promise on a consistent basis. [Craig also warns us to] watch out for a niche that is restaurant-driven rather than consumer-driven.[5]

---

[4] William Q. Dowling, "Creating the Right Identity for Your Hotel," *Lodging,* September, 1980, p. 58.

[5] Denise M. Brennan, "Niche Marketing," *Restaurant Business,* May 1, 1986, pp. 186, 189. Reprinted with permission of Restaurant Business Magazine.

Subjective positioning is a strategy for creating a unique product image with the objective of creating and keeping customers. It exists solely in the mind of the customer. It can occur automatically, without any effort on the part of the marketer, and any kind of positioning may result. Two very dissimilar products may be perceived as the same; two similar products may be perceived as different. What the marketer hopes to do is to control the positioning, not just let it happen. Failure to select a position in the marketplace and to achieve and hold that position, moreover, may lead to various consequences, all undesirable, as pointed out by Lovelock:

1. The organization (or one of its products) is pushed into a position where it faces head-on competition from stronger competitors.
2. The organization is pushed into a position which nobody else wants because there is little customer demand there.
3. The organization's (product's) position is so fuzzy that nobody knows what its distinctive competence really is.
4. The organization (product) has no position at all in the marketplace because nobody has ever heard of it.[6]

One may position in a number of different ways, all related to segmentation strategies. As discussed, positioning may be achieved on specific product features, product benefits, or a specific usage or user category. In sum, an effective position is one that clearly distinguishes from the competition on factors important to the relevant target market.

Repositioning

Repositioning, as the name implies, constitutes changing a position or image in the marketplace. The process is the same as initial positioning with the addition of one other element—removing the old positioning image. There may be a number of reasons for wanting to reposition.

One reason for repositioning may be that you are occupying an unsuccessful position in the first place. Another is that you may have tried and failed to fully achieve a desired position. Also, you might find that competitors, too many and/or too powerful, have moved into the same position, making it overcrowded. Another reason could be in perceiving a new niche opportunity of which you wish to take advantage.

All of these situations are relatively common in the restaurant industry, particularly when a new ownership follows one that has failed. A restaurant in Amherst, Massachusetts, now called The Gulfstream, for a year or more has been trying to reposition as a fine seafood restaurant. The previous two or three years were spent trying to reposition as a student bar and disco. Prior to that it tried to succeed as an Italian restaurant, and before that it was a steak house. All efforts so far have failed: The restaurant has not properly segmented the market, understood the segment, and positioned accordingly. With over 25,000 students within walking distance, plus a town of another 20,000 population, this restaurant has had five owners in eight years.

---

[6] Christopher H. Lovelock, *Services Marketing*, Englewood Cliffs, N.J.: Prentice-Hall, © 1984, p. 135.

Hamburger chains have tried repositioning as "gourmet" hamburger restaurants. Friendly's, originally an ice cream and sandwich chain, now owned by Hershey, failed in an attempt to reposition as a family restaurant. Howard Johnson's, among other things, tried repositioning from being only a family restaurant to being that plus a young adult restaurant with bar and live music. This served only to confuse an already tarnished image. Dunfey Hotels shed its weaker units and changed its name to Omni Hotels in order to reposition as an upscale hotel chain.

Here are some other repositioning efforts of national chains:

Bennigan's: After battling a decline in beverage sales for two years, gave up on its singles' bar image and repositioned as "the place to go to get great food, fun and good times. We . . . redefined what fun was. You don't have to drink at Bennigan's to have a good time."

Long John Silver's: "Ended the company's aggressive coupon and discount promotional program which had undercut the chain's high-ground market position as a premium-quality purveyor of fast food."[7]

Steak and Ale: Instituted a major overhaul of the dinnerhouse concept from menu and service to decor and ambience when surveys showed the restaurants lacked excitement.[8]

Repositioning might also be used to appeal to a new segment, to add a new segment while trying to hold on to an old one, or to increase the size of a segment. Another reason to use it could be that new ownership desires a new position or wishes to merge the position of a newly acquired property into that of other properties already owned. Finally, repositioning would be called for in developing a partially or totally new concept, or upgrading a property that has become distressed.

Examples of the first two statements immediately above are Holiday Corp. going into its upscale Crowne Plaza line, Ramada going into the upscale Renaissance line, and Marriott going downscale with the Courtyard line. Quality Inns introduced three product lines in place of the previous one, in order to increase the segment size, create a new position, and upgrade distressed properties. Developing suite hotels is an example of repositioning for a new concept.

Stouffer Hotels is a good example of a successful repositioning that took place because ownership wanted a new image. Stouffer hotels had been little more than a sideline for the Stouffer restaurant company. When William Hulett was brought from vice-president of operations for Westin to be president of Stouffer hotels, the owners, the Nestlé company of Switzerland, wanted to change that. Hulett established what the identity should be and defined the company's niche in the upscale market. Refurbishing followed, some properties were eliminated, including franchises, and a one-segment market positioning was instituted.

All of these situations call for repositioning. Another good example is the case of what had long been the classic hotel of Boston for many years. As was true of traditional hotels in those days, it was the central hotel of the city and the one where all the grand events occurred.

[7] "Turnarounds in '86: Mixing Luck and Pluck," © *Nation's Restaurant News,* December 1, 1986, p. F3.

[8] "Steak and Ale Launches Top-to-Bottom Overhaul," © *Nation's Restaurant News,* December 1, 1986, p. 1.

This was the Statler Hotel until Hilton took over the Statler chain and it became the Hilton Hotel. Many years had taken their toll. Rooms were small and dingy. Bathrooms were antiquated. Public facilities were limited. The entire property was tired and old. Hilton ran it for a few years, lost money on it, and decided to give up the ghost.

The hotel was awaiting the wrecker's ball when it obtained a last-minute reprieve from the Saunders brothers of Boston, who felt the hotel was too much of a landmark to be destroyed. They bought the hotel under the aegis of Hotels of Tradition, and completely renovated it. The marketing problem was one of repositioning, letting the public know that this was a "new" hotel, completely renovated and ready to compete in today's market.

The task of reaching travelers who come to Boston and had long since forsaken the hotel for more modern properties was monumental and very expensive. Wisely, the owners took a different approach. They marketed it to the "locals." The ad shown in Figure 10-8 demonstrates one way in which they did this. The locals told the visitors. This was a clever and successful repositioning effort.

Renovating old hotels has become a common practice today. As an example, Dunfey Hotels (now called Omni) based a strategy on this practice in buying, first, the Parker House in Boston, then the Ambassador East in Chicago, and finally Berkshire Place in New York City. These were all old, "classic" hotels that Omni refurbished and repositioned as historic, classic hotels in the upscale market.

Stephen Taylor does an excellent job of describing the problem:

Today an increasing number of hotel industry leaders as well as smaller owners/ developers are finding themselves with properties in distress situations. Even downtown luxury hotels, the workhorse giants of the business, are failing along with roadside independents. Fortunately for the industry, the art of repositioning is coming into its own. Repositioning, the economic [marketing] revival of troubled properties and the renovation and revitalization of old/outdated ones, can provide an alternative to the more traditional routes taken when hotels stop making good economic sense.[9]

Renovating old properties is not the only time for repositioning, as has been indicated. Since Taylor puts the case so well, however, we continue to quote from his article.

The task of repositioning is not as simple as creating a market slot for a brand-new hotel. A repositioner has to deal with two consumer images—the existing one and a new one that must be projected.

Repositioning is a two-pronged effort. In most cases, a negative image and consumer ill-will must be overcome before a new impression can be created. In some cases, the added burden of a market shift must be carried. . . .

. . . Winning back customers is a function of the type of expert marketing, promotion, and public relations procedures. . . . To achieve the goals which define the success of a repositioning effort . . . it needs to be finely tuned to fit the specific situation, and it takes thought, perceptiveness, and careful planning. . . . The successful repositioning of any hotel property begins with an intensive examination of the market the repositioner intends to enter.

---

[9] Stephen P. Taylor, "Repositioning: Recovery for Vintage and Distressed Hotels," *HSMAI Marketing Review*, Fall, 1986, pp. 12–15.

"Boston's grandest ballroom hasn't looked this good since... the night Millie and I danced till three in the A.M."

"Those were the days! Of course, we knew it as the Statler. Now it's the Boston Park Plaza. And they're changing a lot more than the name!"

The tone of elegance that greeted sophisticated Bostonians when the Statler first opened is back. In the fresh new Boston Park Plaza (and the adjoining Statler Office Building).

We're painting. Plastering. Carpeting. And refurnishing. Our restaurants and lounges are alive with new enthusiasm. Upstairs, we've got five hundred redecorated rooms for you and your out-of-town visitors.

The Boston Park Plaza is ready to host your next banquet, party, reception, or meeting in grand style. Just call us at (617) 426-2000.

We're not just putting the Boston back into the name. We're putting the Boston back into the hotel.

The Boston Park Plaza

Hotel, Towers, and Motor Inn
Arlington Street at Park Square
Boston, MA 02117
Earl G. Duffy
Vice President & General Manager

FIGURE 10-8 Repositioning an old hotel into a new one

The Art of Repositioning

Repositioning rests on a change of image. The appropriate procedure for doing this is as follows:

1. Determine the present position. It is essential to know where you are now, before you determine how you are going to get to where you want to go. In repositioning, this is absolutely critical because the consumer's image may not be at all what you think it is. Before trying to change a perception, you have to know what that perception is.
2. Determine what position you wish to occupy. This calls for thorough and objective research of both the market and the competition, as well as your resources and ability to occupy that position. One has to be very realistic at this stage and not simply engage in wishful thinking.
3. Make sure the product is truly different for the repositioning. Telling a customer that the product has changed, and is therefore now attractive, had better be followed through operationally.
4. Initiate the repositioning campaign based on the three criteria of effective positioning formulated from the research of the target market: image, differentiation, and promised benefits.
5. Remeasure to see if the position has significantly changed in the desired direction. This too is critical. It is naive to assume that perceptions have changed simply because you expected them to. Do not simply measure this in terms of sales or profits; changes there may be due to other causes. What you want to know is whether perceptions have truly changed.

The application of the first three criteria is evident in the effort of the Waldorf Astoria Hotel to reposition, as shown in Figure 10-9. The Waldorf was perceived as the hotel of U.S. presidents, royalty, and top business executives, and as being very expensive even though it was in the same price range as its competition. Management wanted to position to customers at the middle-management level. Research revealed life-styles of this level of the Waldorf's customers. The repositioning campaign emphasized these life-styles as well as the attributes and the affordability of the Waldorf.

There are pitfalls of which to be wary. The short-run effect may be a loss of sales while the repositioning is being accomplished. It may be a gain in sales only because people are "giving it another chance." There may be a sales drop because the new position was a poor choice and the market is too limited or already dominated by a competitor. It is important to find out why something has happened; it is never good business sense to assume that you know why.

Developing Positioning Strategies

Lovelock suggests the model shown in Figure 10-10 as appropriate for developing market positioning strategies. It can be seen that this model is no different from one that might be used for selecting target markets, and it needs no further discussion here. A major difference, however, would occur in the thrust of the research. In this case, however, we need to know a great deal more about perceptions, what they mean, and what they reflect. For example, a benefit is not a benefit unless it is perceived to be one.

THE WALDORF
REGULARS

Rick Strunck,
Market Planning and
Research Manager,
Royal Caribbean Cruise Line,
Miami, Florida

"Out in the country I'm on my own.
That's why I come here, for the quiet and
neat little surprises around every bend.
I can take care of myself out here, but when
I go to New York City I want somebody to
take care of me.

That's why I always stay at the
Waldorf=Astoria.

The rooms are the most comfortable
of all the hotels in town, and I've tried most
of them. What I like best are the big,
comfortable baths you hardly find
anywhere anymore.

I've been a Waldorf regular for some
time, ever since I found that the cost of a
double room can even be less than some
of the ordinary midtown hotels."

For reservations and information call
212/872-4534 or 1-800 HILTONS or call
your travel agent. The Waldorf=Astoria,
Park Avenue at 50th Street, New York 10022.

The Waldorf=Astoria
A Hilton Hotel

(Courtesy of The Waldorf Astoria and Kaufman & Maraffi, Inc., Agency)

FIGURE 10-9   Repositioning the Waldorf Astoria

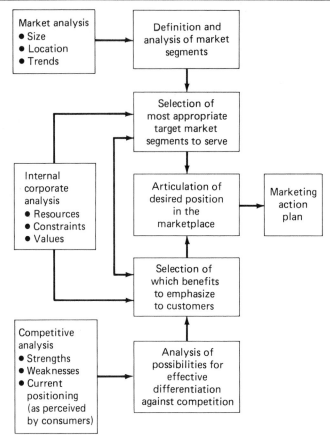

(Source: Christopher Lovelock, SERVICES MARKETING © 1984, p. 136. Reprinted by permission of Prentice-Hall, Inc., Englewood Cliffs, New Jersey.)

FIGURE 10-10   Developing a market positioning strategy

Consider a situation of positioning on price. We have already stated that price is not, by itself, a true segment category in many cases, particularly within the same product class. Between product classes, however, price can segment a market that is able to pay from one that is not able to pay. In either case, price is a powerful positioning tool because it is perceived to say a great deal about the product.

To use a simple and singular product example, many restaurant customers would perceive a $300 bottle of wine as an excellent bottle of wine. A wine connoisseur, on the other hand, might not agree and might be able to pick out a $50 bottle that was as good or better. Thus, we would need to know the perception of the target market vs. the benefit of an excellent wine list.

The power of price positioning is one reason that upscale hotel chains maintain high rack rates and then discount them severely. To lower the published price is perceived as lowering the image and positioning downscale. Of course, it works the other way as well: Potential customers who call reservations and are quoted only the highest rack rate perceive the hotel's position as out-of-reach and hang up, not realizing they could bargain for a much lower rate.

Once again, positioning is not in the product, in the brand, or even in the advertising; it is in the consumer's mind. It is definitely and positively not in management's mind. This is why it is so important for management to understand true positioning. It can be a perilous trap to assume that customers position in the same way as management.

Aaker and Shansby suggest that there are six major positioning approaches. These are listed below. A checklist for developing positioning strategies is presented in Table 10-1.

- positioning by attribute, feature, or customer benefit
- positioning by price/quality
- positioning with respect to use or application
- positioning according to the users or class of users
- positioning with respect to a product class
- positioning vis-à-vis the competition[10]

TABLE 10-1   Checklist for Developing Positioning Strategies

1. Company: What are strengths and weaknesses, resources, management capabilities, present market position, values, objectives, and policies?
   Where are we now? Where do we want to go?
2. Product/Service: What are facilities, location, attributes (salient, determinant, important), physical condition, level of service?
   What is it? What does it do, in functional terms? Why do/should people come?
3. Brand Position: What is awareness, loyalty, image? How does it compare to competition? What are the market segments? What are the perceived attributes and how are they distributed among the segments?
   Where are we positioned?
4. Customers: What are their segments and needs and wants? What benefits do they seek? What is the optimal position of attributes for each segment?
5. Competition: Who is their customer and why does he or she go there? What do they do or not do better? How are we differentiated? What positions do they occupy?
6. The Marketplace: Where is it? What are the segments? What is the generic demand? What is our market share? How are the segments reached?
7. Opportunities: What needs are unmet? Can we meet them? Can we improve on them? What innovations are needed? Are they worth going after? Are there new uses, new users, or greater usage?
8. Decision: What is the best overall position?

---

[10] David A. Aaker and J. Gary Shansby, "Positioning Your Product," *Business Horizons*, May–June, 1982, pp. 56–62.

Salience, Determinance, and Importance

There is another issue in regard to developing effective positioning that must be kept in mind. This is the issue of the differentiation among *salient, determinant, and important* product attributes or benefits. One might position on a salient benefit with poor results because those benefits are not necessarily determinant or important in the consumer choice process.

Salience

Salient attributes are those that are at the top of the mind. They are the ones that readily come to mind when you think of an object. Because of this, a list of strictly salient attributes obtained from customers may be totally misleading in describing how they make choices. If I say to you, "What is the basis on which you buy a shirt?" you might give cost as one answer. If I then assumed that the next shirt you buy will be the cheapest one you can find, I could be making a completely erroneous assumption. What really determines your choice could be the style of the shirt.

Salient factors might also be determinant factors, but they are not determinant when they are not the true differentiating factor the consumer is looking for, or when they are common throughout the product class. In the first case, let's go back to the Godiva chocolate on the pillow. This could be very salient and be remembered by customers, but it is doubtful that they would base their choice of hotel on a chocolate.

In the second case, an excellent example is location. Take a survey of almost any set of hotel customers and ask what is important to them in choosing a hotel. At the top of the list will almost always be location, as we have previously discussed and as descriptive, multiple-answer questionnaires will always reveal. Location is a very salient attribute, but if four hotels are within two blocks of each other, as is the case in so many cities today, location is not likely to be a determinant factor.

Determinance

In one study, 81 percent of respondents said location was salient in choosing a hotel, 82 percent said it was determinant, but only 18 percent said location was the reason they chose the hotel at which they were staying.[11] The frequency of consumers' naming an attribute does not necessarily indicate its relative determinance as the true differentiating factor in the choice process.

Determinant attributes are those that actually determine choice. These are the attributes most closely related to consumer preferences or actual purchase decisions—in other words, these features predispose consumers to action. These attributes are critical to the consumer choice process. The research problem, as indicated above, is that consumers do not always know exactly what it is that forms the basis of their choice.

An example here is the same one we have used before, bathroom amenities.

---

[11] Robert C. Lewis, "The Basis of Hotel Selection," *Cornell Hotel and Restaurant Administration Quarterly*, May 1984, pp. 54–69. Figure 9-8 in the previous chapter is also relevant to this discussion.

Bathroom amenities may not be very salient, but they could be quite important after we have become used to having them. Now, however, every hotel in the product class has them! Thus, they are hardly determinant any more, if they ever were. There is a caveat here, however: If we were now to remove the extended line of bathroom amenities, they might become negatively determinant—people might say, "I won't go there because they don't have good bathroom amenities." The implication is that perhaps hotels in this product class should now have the amenities, but promoting them or positioning on them would be to little avail.

This is also true of location and cleanliness, supposedly the main reasons that people choose hotels. People don't choose hotels simply because of location and cleanliness; they do choose against specific hotels because of their lack of location and cleanliness.

Importance

Importance attributes are those that are important to the consumer in making a choice, or after having made a choice. The example above of bathroom amenities demonstrated this. It is important that they be there, once the customer is accustomed to their being there, but they are still not determinant.

Salience, determinance, and importance are complementary concepts and they are all significant in the positioning effort. It is critical to understand the place of each. Recall the discussion in Chapter 6 of selective perception, selective acceptance, and selective retention. Salient factors may cause all three to operate. Determinant and important factors are more likely to cause selective retention, but only determinant factors are vital in the actual choice process. Much positioning that is done only on salient factors—for instance, location or atrium lobby—is less than successful when these factors are not determinant. The uses and interpretations of each concept depend highly on the nature of the target market.

Competitive Positioning

In developing positioning strategies, a critical element is the positioning vis-à-vis the competition. It is necessary first to examine extant images and positions in the product class. One should then try to anticipate the effects of the proposed positioning and the reactions of competitors. Examining strengths and weaknesses of competitive positioning can identify niches to enter, niches to stay away from, and areas of dissatisfaction where a new positioning could generate new customers or lure others from the competition. If the segment is expanding (e.g., suite hotels), this process could also identify a growth opportunity.

Focus groups (small groups of consumers gathered together for the express purpose of analyzing a product's image and gaps) can be very useful at this point of exploration. Similarly useful are *perceptual maps*. Perceptual mapping is used to place various competitive positions on a two-dimensional scale, along with an "ideal" position, in order to locate the gaps and niches or, conversely, the crowded areas. This technique may involve simple plotting on an arbitrary scale, or sophisticated statistical methods known as multidimensional scaling or discriminant analysis, which are far beyond the scope of the discussion here. A hypothetical output of the process, however, is shown in Figure 10-11.

The hypothetical perceptual map in Figure 10-11 shows the results of customer research and how customers position, in their own minds, various restaurants on the two dimensions of service quality and price. It also shows how they would position an "ideal" restaurant.

The "ideal" restaurant in this case has fairly high service quality and fairly high prices. There is no one restaurant that actually fits this ideal in the customers' minds. Restaurant A is perceived as having even better service but also higher prices. The customers' ideal would be to have less service that cost less. Restaurant E is at the other extreme, with low service and low price. Customers want lower prices than A, but they want more service than E has to offer at that price. You can compare these two, in the same manner, against restaurants B, C, and D.

Which restaurant has the best opportunity in this hypothetical situation? Probably B. If B can raise its service level, or the perception of its service level, just a little, it can raise its prices quite a bit (assuming, of course, that all other things are equal). On the other hand, to get closer to the ideal, A would have to lower its perceived prices, but could also give up some service refinements.

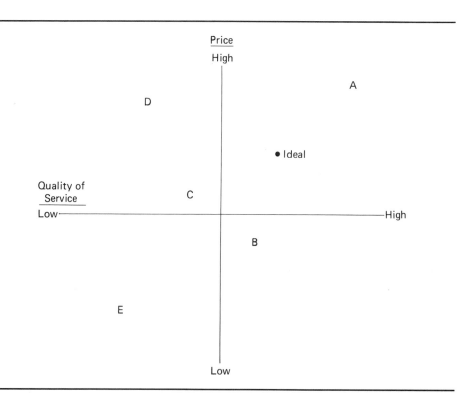

FIGURE 10-11   Hypothetical perceptual map of restaurant positioning on dimensions of service quality and price

In analyzing the position of the competition, marketers also want to be able to protect the position they hope to establish. This means interpreting possible competitive reactions and taking measures to reduce their impact. One method would be to use hard-to-duplicate product forms such as Hyatt's atrium lobby. As history has shown, of course, sooner or later duplication will occur, but getting there first can always be an asset.

In Figure 10-11, restaurant B could raise its prices "very cautiously" so that A would have to come down substantially to match them. If B knew its competitors, it might "know" that this is something A would be reluctant to do.

A case in point, in a general sense, is hotel restaurants, which for years have been perceived as overpriced. At the same time, they have been perceived as offering "hotel food." The current trend is to reposition hotel dining rooms by offering different food types. Consider the following.

> The days of ponderous and pretentious hotel dining are numbered. . . . the growing emphasis is on contemporary, upbeat concepts. . . . the major chains are working hard to recapture the hotel guest—a customer often lost to trendy and popular independent restaurants. . . . the traditional hotel dining room, with its reputation for being stiff and intimidating, is rapidly changing.
>
> Marriott . . . company research . . . targeted stuffy, overpriced restaurants as *passé.* . . . As a result, the company developed "theme" concepts which give greater flexibility than traditional restaurants.[12]

We recall reading many similar trade journal articles over the last ten years, often accompanied by such industry shibboleths as "getting back to basics." Although the change in hotel restaurant concepts is apparent everywhere, the change in the prices is not. In fact, it appears that customers are against paying almost the same prices for trendy food with less service that they used to pay for "fine dining" food. While hotel restaurants concentrate on the neighborhood customer, their own house guests continue to go out. In this sense, hotel restaurants, generically speaking, are positioned against nonhotel restaurants.

We recently had cocktails with the controller of a large, major hotel in New York City in a beautiful lounge that seated over 100 people, off the main lobby of the hotel. The hotel was full, but the lounge was empty and it was cocktail time. We discussed the problem as well as a similar problem with one of the hotel's dining rooms. "What are your liquor and food cost percentages?" we asked. "Fourteen percent and 24 percent," he proudly answered. This same hotel had a coffee shop in which one could obtain juice, coffee, and a roll for $7.95 plus tax and tip. Across the street, one could obtain juice, coffee, roll, two eggs, bacon, and hash browns for $1.79 plus tax and tip.

Obviously, there was a big difference between the two operations, although the waitresses were as surly in one as in the other, and both operations paid the same union wages. The $1.79 restaurant also had to pay its own rent, heat, light, and power. One was definitely cleaner and you had to wait for a hostess to take you to your table. But the food, for breakfast, was comparable. The example was a good case for positioning.

People who stayed in the hotel, mostly on expense account, surely could afford to

---

[12] Denise Brennan, "The Remaking of Hotel Restaurants," *Restaurant Business,* August 10, 1987, pp. 137, 148. Reprinted with permission of Restaurant Business Magazine.

have breakfast there, and many did. A great many also went across the street. This was not price segmentation, but benefit segmentation. Some liked the "benefit" of staying in the hotel in cleaner and more prestigious surroundings; others liked the "benefit" of feeling they got their money's worth. The two restaurants were subjectively positioned on benefits, and value was the positioning tool.

According to frequent trade press articles, hotels continually fight declining breakfast counts by "going back to basics." Perhaps what is basic, needs to be reanalyzed. As one GM said, "Then there's the guest who takes a suite, has rack of lamb and fine wine for dinner and goes across the street to Dunkin Donuts for breakfast."

In another hotel, in New York City, a new restaurant concept was designed to appeal to the local neighborhood. Seating 125, it averaged 40 to 50 covers a night and most house guests ate elsewhere. A quick look at the menu made one imagine a check average of around $35.00, although there were a few lower-priced items available. The actual check average was about $14.00, which should have told somebody something. To counter this, menu prices were raised! This is a case, as mentioned above by Kyle Craig of S&A Restaurant Corporation, where the positioning was restaurant-driven rather than customer-driven.

Some hotel restaurants have a major repositioning to go through. They not only need to be more realistic about current eating trends, but they have a major job in changing consumers' perceptions. Products must be matched with their market segments. Positioning makes a statement of what the product is and how it should be evaluated. True positioning is accomplished by using *all* the marketing mix variables. Not a single one can be ignored, because it is there whether or not a conscious effort is made to use it.

Once the positioning goal has been established, every effort must be made to be certain that the product or brand actually achieves the position. Even with all the necessary ingredients of good positioning there is no assurance of success until "share of mind" is achieved. This is where promotional strategy comes into play. Whether it is implemented through advertising or in-house, desired positions do not wait to be discovered. Success here means fruition of all positioning efforts. Table 10-2 provides a checklist for your positioning or desired positioning.

Multiple Brand Positioning[13]

Hospitality companies develop multiple brands for growth purposes. Sometimes this is through development of a new concept, sometimes through acquisition, and sometimes through both. Marriott, for example, in recent years developed the Courtyard (midprice) and Fairfield Inn (budget) lodging concepts to develop new segments, purchased Residence Inns for quick entry into moderate-price all-suite properties, developed Marriott Suites as luxury-tier products, and acquired Saga to expand its institutional feeding.

While development of multiple brands provide growth, they also provide protection from the competition against a single brand. Marriott saw other chains moving into lower-tier markets and threatening the middle-to-upper tier in which Marriott hotels were

---

[13] This discussion is also appropriate in Chapter 12 under the title of "Product Mix," and Chapter 20 under "Product Strategy." It is included here only for purposes of convenience.

TABLE 10-2   Positioning Checklist

1. Does it say who you are and what you stand for? Does it create a mental picture?
2. Does it set you apart and show how you are different?
3. Does it preempt a benefit niche and capitalize on an advantage?
4. Does it turn any liability into an asset?
5. Does it have benefits for the target market you are trying to reach?
6. Does it provide tangible evidence or clues?
7. Does it feature the one or two things that your target market wants most?
8. Is it consistent with strategy—for instance, does it expand or exchange usage patterns? Create new awareness? Project the right image?
9. Does it have credibility?
10. Does it make a promise you can keep?

positioned. Marriott felt it might as well steal its own customers, if that was to be the case, as let someone else steal them. It also realized that there were markets that the existing concept was neglecting.

Multiple brands, of course, are common practice in other industries; for instance, Procter & Gamble and General Motors. The restaurant industry has long had multiple brands, as in the case of Pillsbury, which owned not only Burger King but also Steak & Ale, Godfather's Pizza, Quik Wok, Key West Grills, Bennigan's, and Bay Street, a seafood restaurant chain. As the expression goes, "You can't tell who owns whom anymore."

The question here is one of positioning each brand. In the case of Pillsbury, positioning Bennigan's and Steak & Ale is not much different from positioning against an outside competitor in terms of positioning strategy, with one exception: It would be self-defeating for the parent company if these two chains cannibalized each other. What they want to do, instead, is to position to different market segments.

The different market segments may include many of the same people. They belong, however, to a different segment when they use restaurants for different purposes, in different contexts, or at different times. Thus, the positioning of each chain should be managed so that they do not steal from each other. With this one caveat, standard positioning rules apply.

This is easier to do when your chains are named *Steak & Ale* and *Bennigan's* and most people don't even know they belong to the same company, than when they are named *Ramada Inn, Ramada Hotel, Ramada Renaissance, Ramada Plaza, Ramada Suites,* and *Ramada Resorts.* As another example, note the various Howard Johnson brands (in itself a division of Prime Motor Inns) in Figure 10-12.

What Hazard started when he broke Quality Inns into Comfort Inns, Quality Inns, and Quality Royale (now Clarion) has led to a plethora of properties under the same or similar name, each trying to position to a different market segment. This is commonly referred to as brand proliferation.

Quality Inns states there is no question in its multiple brand line about the difference between the three brand names, which now also include suite concepts in each category.

FIGURE 10-12 An example of multiple brands

Most others claim the same, but the evidence seems to be that the customer is very confused. A *Cornell Quarterly* article contains some comments on this situation:

> Yesawich [president of the consulting firm Robinson, Yesawich & Pepperdine] said that the success of brands depends on creating a clear differentiation in the minds of customers. With only few exceptions, the advertising and promotion that has been initiated on behalf of new product concepts has failed to communicate clearly or convincingly the *basis* of the differentiation. Consumers are quick to discern the availabilty of free drinks or free breakfasts, but it takes much more to constitute a new product in consumers' minds. . . . If advertising doesn't communicate the perception of a new product, then maybe the product isn't really new at all.
>
> Some observers are concerned that consumers may be confused by a chain that has one name on a variety of hotels. Yesawich noted that chains pursuing diversification by introducing new products under different names have so far met with greater success.
>
> "In general terms, a brand name is an asset, as long as it stands singlemindedly for a specific package of value and benefits. Call it a personality," said Bloch [then senior vice-president for marketing at Four Seasons]. "Leaving a midprice brand name on an upscale property, as some operators are doing, may confuse some customres."[14]

Who has the right answer in this situation we do not know: We have seen no research that supports either case. Regardless, our point here is a different one. The problem is not in the name (only a possible cause of the problem), but in the positioning. This is best demonstrated by referring back to the example of Charles of the Ritz perfumes at the beginning of the chapter. There were Charlie, Enjoli, Jontue, and now Senchal, each positioned at different specific target markets with specific needs, and in a very intangible way.

Can hotel concepts under the same or similar names make the same claim? In other words, is each concept positioned to a different specific target market, each with specific needs that relate to the positioning? Second, if the first case is true, can these markets differentiate the positioning of each brand name so that they (the markets) know which one "belongs" to them? This is the case in point and is the concern of positioning any multiple brands, more so when the problem is compounded by similar names. If the answers to the above questions are no, then there will be a clear case of cannibalization.

To show that multiple brand positioning can be done successfully, we cite one example. Groupe Accor, a French firm, has developed lodging concepts called Formule1, Ibis, Novotel, and Sofitel. By French government rating these are one-, two-, three-, and four-star properties respectively. Each is based on the needs of a specific target market. Each is clearly differentiated from the other three; in fact, you could say that no customer would ever choose one when he or she wanted the other. Each is clearly positioned to its own market segment. This is true segmentation and true positioning in the hospitality industry.

---

[14] Glenn Withiam, "Hotel Companies Aim at Multiple Markets," *Cornell Hotel and Restaurant Administration Quarterly*, November 1985, pp. 39–51.

Internal Positioning Analysis

Perceptual mapping, mentioned above, helps to determine positioning strategies vis-à-vis the competition. There are also very useful methods for analyzing one's own position on a number of different attributes or benefits that relate deliverability with any one of the constructs salience, importance, and determinance. As has been said so often, internal marketing is critical in the hospitality industry. If this is true, then it is obvious that internal *positioning* is also critical.

Figure 10-13 illustrates another use of perceptual mapping. This is the case of an actual restaurant. Respondents were asked to rate the importance of certain attributes in choosing an upscale restaurant at which to have dinner. Some of these are shown in Figure 10-13. Respondents were also asked to rate this particular restaurant on a scale ranging from poor to excellent. No one rated it poor, but Figure 10-13 shows the quadrants in which are located those who rated it fair (F), good (G), and excellent (E).

In the same quadrants can be seen the reasons or attributes that were significant in determining the ratings. For example, those who rated the restaurant fair did so largely because it was intimidating. Those who rated it good saw it as a special occasion restaurant. Those who rated it excellent did so for the reasons shown, with the length of the lines (vectors) indicating how important each attribute was in the rating (e.g., quality of food and service were the most important determinants). While the last case is not totally revealing, the reasons for the fair and good ratings are very revealing. This information led the restaurant to initiate a campaign showing that it was not intimidating and was a place to go at other times than special occasions, and that it was indeed worth the price.

Internal analysis not only helps to determine internal positioning, but also indicates where the operation may be failing both internally and relative to the competition. Further, it aids in the best use of resources by indicating where they will count the most for the customer.

The hard questions that have to be asked are these:

1. What is important to the target market?
2. How does the target market perceive us?
3. How does the target market perceive the competition?
4. What should we differentiate on so as to make best use of our limited resources?

The reality of the matter is that if the target market doesn't perceive the image, it doesn't exist; if it doesn't believe that what you have to offer is a benefit, it isn't a benefit; if it doesn't believe that you can deliver the benefit, your promises are meaningless; if the benefit isn't important to the target market, it isn't important; if your benefit is not perceived as different from that of the competition, you haven't differentiated.

In short, images, benefits, and differentiation are solely the perception of the consumer, not management. We keep repeating these statements intentionally—they are the most often forgotten or neglected truisms of marketing. Let us also repeat, as a reminder, that these statements are especially pertinent to hospitality marketing because of the intangibility of the services offered and the simultaneous production and consumption of the offering, which permits evaluation only after the purchase is a fait accompli.

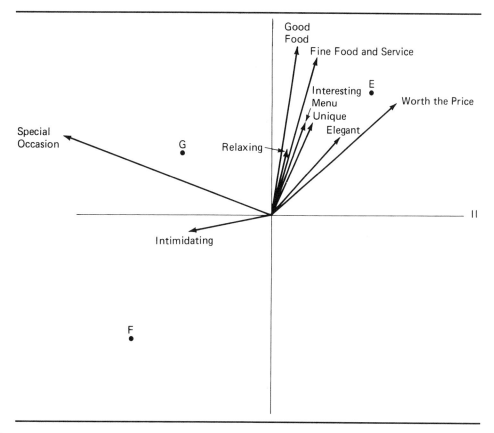

FIGURE 10-13   Perceptual mapping of restaurant attributes

Hospitality research too often fails to identify the vital elements of benefits. Comment cards, for example, ask customers whether they liked certain features of the property or operation. What those features do for the customer or how important they are even when satisfactorily rated is not revealed.[15]

The architecture of a property, the decor, and the furnishings are examples of attributes that may produce a benefit, or may be tangible surrogates for an intangible benefit, but are not themselves the benefit. The benefit itself is what the attributes do for the customer—for instance, give a sense of security, a sensation of grandeur, an aura of prestige, or a feeling of comfort. The credibility of these benefits may diminish rapidly if an expectation is not fulfilled. Decor is soon forgotten if the service takes an hour. The impression of security loses credibility if the guest encounters slovenly characters in the rest room. It is this fulfillment of expectations or lack of it that creates the perception of deliverability for the consumer.

---

[15] See, for example, Robert C. Lewis and Abraham Pizam, "Guest Surveys: A Missed Opportunity," *Cornell Hotel and Restaurant Administration Quarterly*, November 1981, pp. 37–44.

Finally, as previously mentioned, competing properties may be seen to offer the same senses of security, grandeur, prestige and comfort. The tangible surrogate attributes have lost their ability to differentiate and, at the same time, are no longer determinant in the consumer choice process.

Benefits, then, like positioning, exist in the mind of the consumer and are determinable only by asking the consumer. This information is essential to proper positioning analysis. A more sophisticated case of positioning analysis is presented For Further Study at the end of this chapter.

Summary

Market positioning is a valuable weapon for hospitality marketers. To position successfully requires recognizing the marketplace, the competition, and consumers' perceptions. Positioning analysis on a target market basis provides the tools to identify opportunities for creating the desired image that differentiates from the competition, and for serving the target market better than anyone else.

Positioning is the ultimate weapon in niche marketing. Stripped of all its trappings, positioning analysis answers the following questions:

1. What position do you own now (in the mind of the target market)?
2. What position do you want to own? (Look for positions or holes in the marketplace.)
3. Whom must you outposition? (Manipulate what's already in the mind.)
4. How can you do it? (Select the attributes or benefits that are salient, determinant, and important to the target market and that the firm can deliver.)

DISCUSSION QUESTIONS

1. What are the two kinds of hospitality positioning? Give examples of when you would use each one and why.
2. Discuss the problems a product can incur with a weak or undefined position.
3. Identify a hotel or restaurant you know that is in need of repositioning, and outline the steps needed to achieve the repositioning.
4. Discuss the salient, determinant, and important attributes of the same hotel or restaurant.
5. Develop a list of questions that you would pose to a focus group of customers of a cocktail lounge that seeks to establish a position in the marketplace.
6. How does competition affect the positioning of a product? Discuss.

FOR FURTHER STUDY

Internal Positioning Analysis[16]

The first step in positioning analysis is to identify those benefits that represent the range of possibilities for the target market in your type of property and that of your competitors.

---

[16] The rest of this section is drawn from Robert C. Lewis, "Positioning Analysis for Hospitality Firms," *International Journal of Hospitality Management,* Fall, 1982, pp. 115–118.

These can be culled from previous research, from focus groups, from personal interviews, and from management.

The second step is to quantify these benefits in terms of their importance to the target market. This consists of asking consumers to rate the importance of each benefit on a five- or seven-point scale. The resulting data can be handled in one of two ways. One way is simple, convenient and available to everyone; it consists of identifying as important (or salient, or determinant) only those benefits that have been rated by a majority of the respondents, preferably two-thirds or more, as being *very* important. Alternatively, one may simply plot the various scale positions of all respondents.

The second method is to use a multivariate analysis technique such as discriminant, factor, or regression analysis. The advantage of these methods is that they consider the ratings of all the benefits simultaneously and interactively, rather than one at a time. Discussion of these methods is beyond the scope of this text, but it is readily available in marketing research texts.

The next step in positioning analysis is to ask the same consumers to rate your property and those of your competition on how well they provide, or are perceived as providing, each benefit. This is also done on a five- or seven-point scale, and the same analytical procedures discussed above can be utilized.

The results obtained from both steps are measurements on two opposing dimensions. One is the target market's importance (or salience or determinance) measurement toward the benefits offered. The other is its perception of each of the properties on their ability to deliver the benefits. Plotting in "benefit space" is used to bring the two dimensions together in their marketing positions, and to see how each property is positioned against the others.

An Example   Guests of a 250-room motor inn (Hotel X) were queried in the method described above. Forty-one attributes were rated on their benefit importance during a stay at a motor inn, and on the respondents' perceptions of these attributes as being delivered by the motor inn and by two competing properties (Hotels Y and Z). The data were factor analyzed (a statistical method that collapses data along underlying dimensions for ease of handling) into ten categories. These categories are given general headings for demonstration purposes. The categories and their regression weights (weights derived from a statistical procedure that determines the relative importance of each attribute category) for Hotel X are shown in Table 10-3. Recall that this could also have been accomplished univariately by attribute importance level, as mentioned above.

A matrix is defined by the benefit ratings themselves by using the median of the importance and delivery ratings to divide the matrix into quadrants. The intercepts of the importance and delivery ratings are plotted on the matrix, as shown in Figure 10-14 for Hotel X.

The quadrants in Figure 10-14 can be interpreted as follows. Quadrant I indicates a solid position for all benefits located here. These benefits not only are important to the target market but also are seen as being delivered by Hotel X. In this case, Hotel X is perceived as excelling in room and bath facilities and comfort (A) as well as in convenient location and availability to other attractions (D). Benefits in this quadrant are optimally positioned and can be used to differentiate and create an image in the product class to the extent that the competition is not in the same quadrant.

TABLE 10-3   Regression Weights for Hotel X on Importance and Deliverability of Benefits

	Benefit	Importance rating	Deliverability perception rating
(A)	Room and bath facilities and comfort	0.22	0.20
(B)	Room service satisfaction	0.18	0.02
(C)	Sports facilities availability	0.12	0.12
(D)	Convenience of location and availability to other attractions	0.11	0.24
(E)	Room and bath maintenance and cleanliness	0.10	0.06
(F)	Professionalism and attitude of staff	0.09	0.10
(G)	Restaurant availability and service	0.08	0.08
(H)	Front desk service and attitude	0.05	0.13
(I)	Prestige and aesthetics of property	0.04	0.19
(J)	Prices—absolute and value	0.01	0.17

Note: Some of the importance ratings for Hotel *X* are counterintuitive. This appears to be due to the nature of the particular property. It demonstrates a contradiction between management's and consumer's ratings of importance benefits.

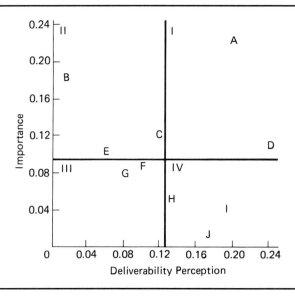

FIGURE 10-14   Positioning matrix for hotel X

Quadrant II contains those benefits that are important but are not perceived as being delivered by the property. If the competition is positioned in Quadrant I on these benefits, the property in Quadrant II is at a disadvantage. If the competition is also in the quadrant, no differentiation occurs but there may be an opportunity to reposition, change consumer perception, and gain an advantage.

Quadrants III and IV represent benefits that are not all that important to the target market. Benefits in Quadrant III lack both importance and deliverability perception. There will be minimal advantage in going to extra effort to increase favorable perception because these benefits are relatively unimportant.

The benefits in Quadrant IV are perceived as being delivered but there is no real need to use them for positioning, again because of their relative unimportance. Resources should be concentrated, instead, on benefits in Quadrants I and II. In Figure 10-14, positioning potency is weak because there are only two prime positioning benefit candidates. Marketing needs to be more efficient.

Figures 10-15 and 10-16 show the positions of the competition in Quadrants I and II. Hotel Y (Figure 10-15) has a positioning advantage in room and bath maintenance (E) but is perceived poorly in facilities and comfort (A). This creates both threats and opportunities for Hotel X. Housekeeping and maintenance departments need to be strengthened to at least nullify Hotel Y's position in this area.

On the other hand, Hotel X has the opportunity to position strongly on benefit A. A real advantage could be gained by increasing favorable perception of sports facilities and room service. The latter, however, might be short-lived since neither hotel in this example offered regular room service and Hotel Y could quickly follow if Hotel X instituted it.

Figure 10-16 adds emphasis to the fact that Hotel X had better make some strong improvements in room and bath maintenance. Hotel Z represents strong competition in its

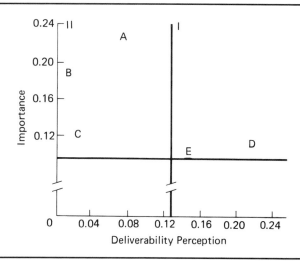

FIGURE 10-15   Quadrants I and II positioning for hotel Y

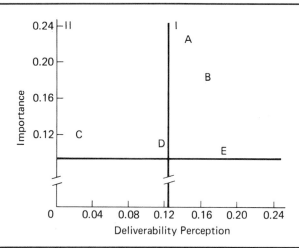

FIGURE 10-16   Quadrants I and II positioning for hotel Z

positioning potential against Hotel X. Again, however, an opportunity is available to Hotel X to differentiate on its sports facilities. Hotel X can also use its location to position against Hotel Z.

The utility of positioning analysis is evident from the foregoing discussion. It quantitatively analyzes what is important to the target market, how the target market perceives a property and its competition, and on what benefits a property's resources can best be spent to position against the competition.

Perhaps equally important, positioning analysis pinpoints those areas that constitute threats and weaknesses. Some of these may be unavoidable—for instance, when a location cannot readily be changed. Others, however, provide a strong message to management about areas where it needs to take action and make positive improvements.

Optimal positioning is tantamount to marketing effectiveness. By the same token, a positioning advantage should not be easily relinquished to the competition. Ideally, of course, management would like to see all important benefits located in Quadrant I. Conversely, if none are, or can be, located there it may be time to define a different target market.

PART V
The Marketing Mix

CHAPTER 11

The Marketing Mix

The last stage of the marketing philosophy model discussed in Chapter 1 is the marketing mix. As discussed there, the marketing mix is the stage of marketing management and strategy that directly affects the customer. It is the ultimate outcome of the company's philosophy and mission statement, and the final delivery of the company's offering to the marketplace. The marketing mix is, in fact, the culmination of everything we have discussed so far, including both traditional and nontraditional marketing.

The marketing mix is based, or should be based, on the needs, wants, and problems of the consumer (Chapters 3, 6, and 7). It derives directly from the opportunity and competitive analysis (Chapters 4 and 5), the segmentation and target marketing (Chapters 8 and 9), and the positioning in the marketplace (Chapter 10). It is because of this groundwork that we have left until now a full explanation of the marketing mix.

The Four Ps

The marketing mix was originally developed by Professor Neil Borden of Harvard in what have come to be known as the "Four Ps" through subsequent alteration.[1] The mix comprises certain marketing elements based on market forces. Borden decrees this mix as the combination of those elements that, at its best, leads to effective and profitable marketing. Borden's six original elements—product planning, pricing, distribution, promotion, servicing, and marketing research—were later reduced to four elements by McCarthy—product, price, place (distribution), and promotion.[2] Although we will quick-

---

[1] Neil Borden, "The Concept of the Marketing Mix," *Journal of Advertising Research,* June, 1964, pp. 2–7.
[2] E. Jerome McCarthy, *Basic Marketing: A Managerial Approach,* Homewood, Ill: Richard D. Irwin, 1975, pp. 75–80.

ly change the names of these elements to better fit the hospitality industry, it is well to understand the concept. Buell defines it as follows:

> The concept of the marketing mix suggests that the company resources devoted to product, price, distribution, and promotion (and the subsections thereof) should be mixed in varying proportions depending upon the industry category of the firm, its position in the market, and the competitive situation.[3]

What this definition suggests, and what we have alluded to in Chapter 1, is that the elements of the marketing mix represent a delicate balance of resources of the firm in providing the product, pricing it, getting it to the customer, and telling the customer about it. In effect, the marketing mix is the output of all marketing decisions. The target of the marketing mix is the customer.

Normally, the synergistic balance of the marketing mix will not be the same for any two companies. Just as each company, or hotel or restaurant within a company, has even a slightly different mission, target markets, and positioning, so too will vary the proportionate weight of each element of the marketing mix.

The problem that we have with the four Ps in hospitality marketing is not their concept, but the elements of the mix that are essentially based on the marketing of goods. Consistent with our previous arguments in Chapters 2 and 3, we construe that the marketing of hospitality services is different from the marketing of goods and thus requires a different approach to the marketing mix. The point in redefining the mix elements for this purpose is not to change their meanings—essentially, they remain the same—but to make the concept of the marketing mix more useful and applicable for hospitality marketing decisions.

The Hospitality Marketing Mix

The first attempt at developing a new marketing mix for the hospitality industry was undertaken by Renaghan.[4] The hospitality marketing mix, according to Renaghan, contains three major submixes: the product/service mix, the presentation mix, and the communications mix. To this trio we add back one of the original elements defined by Borden—distribution. Each element of the mix will be discussed in detail in the chapters to follow. Here, we only define the elements and their use.

The Product/Service Mix

> The combination of products and services, whether free or for sale, aimed at satisfying the needs of the target market. [p. 32]

Renaghan's definition of this element of the marketing mix is consistent with our discussion of the hospitality product in Chapter 2. An important addition here, however, is the word *free*. This, again, is an important distinction between the marketing of

---

[3] Victor P. Buell, *Marketing Management: A Strategic Planning Approach,* New York: McGraw-Hill, 1984, p. 22.
[4] Leo M. Renaghan, "A New Marketing Mix for the Hospitality Industry," *Cornell Hotel and Restaurant Administration Quarterly,* April 1981, pp. 31–35. This section draws heavily on Renaghan's article.

manufactured goods and the marketing of hospitality products. (On the other hand, manufacturers of goods often offer something "free" with their product that the hospitality industry normally does not. This is the warranty or guarantee and the ability to exchange the item or get your money back.) We can construe "free" as encompassing those supporting goods that the customer does pay for, but indirectly. In this category would be placed swimming pools, exercise facilities, free airport transportation, linen tablecloths, china and silverware, fresh flowers on the table, and so forth. These are items over which management has control, that thus become part of the offering decision process.

There are other "free" features over which management may have little or no control but that are part of the consumer's expectation. These items include such things as the sun, the moon, the stars, the ocean, the beach, and the view.[5]

An important feature of the product/service mix is the bundle purchase concept. This concept pertains to the entire submix. Consumers do not purchase individual elements of the offering; rather, they purchase a bundle or unified whole. If the elements of this mix change, the consumer's perception of the entire product/service may change. It is clear that a delicate balance exists in the mix and that management must be aware of how the various elements of the bundle interact. The product/service mix will be discussed in detail in Chapter 12.

The Presentation Mix

> All elements used by the firm to increase the tangibility of the product/service mix in the perception of the target market at the right place and time. [p. 32]

Renaghan describes the presentation mix as an "umbrella concept covering those elements under the firm's control that act in concert to make the total product/service offering more tangible to the consumer." He goes on to state, "The presentation mix is also the means by which the firm differentiates its product/service offering from competitive offerings." Hark back, again, to the section on intangibility in Chapter 2, or to the section on personal constructs in Chapter 6, to refresh your memory on the implications of Renaghan's statement.

Renaghan construes that there are five elements of the presentation mix that can be utilized to tangibilize the product/service mix and to differentiate from the competition. These elements include the physical plant, location, atmospherics, price, and employees.

Some argue that price does not belong in this mix but should stand by itself, as it does in the original four Ps. There is some merit to this argument and we will discuss it later. However, we concur with Renaghan and include it here because price is a highly tangible element that increases the tangibility of the product/service mix in the perception of the target market. For example, if you believe that the check average at a certain restaurant is $50, or the price of a hotel room is $25, you immediately construe an image relative to the product/service mix at those places. Because price is such a dominant factor in marketing, however, we will devote an entire chapter to it in Chapter 14.

There is one other element of the presentation mix that needs to be included—the

---

[5] An amusing and tongue-in-cheek perspective of this element was presented recounting the travails of a Vermont small resort owner in the long out-of-print book, *Does It Always Rain Here, Mr. Hoyt?*, publisher unknown. The title alone explains the book for anyone who has ever had a rainy vacation.

customers. In the hospitality industry, they too are an important tangibilization of the product. By this we mean that if you walk into a hotel or restaurant and look at the customers who are there, you will immediately get a tangible presentation of the type of facility that you have just entered. The level of quality, service, price, atmosphere, and a number of other factors, mostly intangible, will clearly stand out in most cases.

This is the area of nontraditional marketing that was discussed in Chapter 3. The presentation mix will be discussed in detail in Chapter 13.

The Communications Mix

> All communications between the firm and the target market that increase the tangibility of the product/service mix, that establish or monitor consumer expectations, or that persuade consumers to purchase. [p. 32]

Once again, we refer back to the section on personal constructs in Chapter 6 to explain the need for tangibilizing the intangible dominant products and services. This is the area of traditional marketing, albeit with some new twists due to the intangibility of the product. Except for these new twists, this part of the marketing mix is no different from the promotion element of the four Ps. The word *communication,* however, covers a far broader expanse than the word *promotion.* In fact, we will show that promotion is but one subset of communications. The communications mix will be discussed in detail in Chapters 15, 16, and 17.

The Distribution Mix

> All channels available between the firm and the target market that increase the probability of getting the customer to the product.

Renaghan's model construes distribution under the term *location.* This is an appropriate but limited application. The general concept of services, as opposed to goods, is that rather than the good being taken to the customer (e.g., through retail outlets), the customer must come to the service. Thus, a hotel or restaurant chain that has 500 locations nationwide is "distributing" the product so that the customer can come to it.

In this sense, the union of the customer with the product is part of the presentation mix because it addresses the inseparability of product and distribution (as location), which is the case in most hospitality marketing. This inclusion rectifies the problem of the four Ps approach, which typically assumes decisions relative to product design and distribution as largely independent of one another.

Renaghan's typology is useful in the above respect, but the network and complexities of selling the hospitality product, especially in the case of hotel rooms, through "800" telephone numbers, wholesalers, tour brokers, travel agents and others have become so confounded in recent years that location itself is no longer adequate to describe this phenomenon. Distribution has become an increasingly important part of the hospitality marketing mix. We will discuss it in detail in Chapter 18.

Summary

The marketing mix is the culmination of marketing in its direct interaction with the consumer. Most day-to-day marketing efforts take place in the implementation of this stage of the marketing effort.

The importance of the marketing mix is evident in the marketing of any good or service. Because of this, Borden's concept and McCarthy's popularization of it have made the four Ps everyday jargon in the lexicon of marketers. The reign of the four Ps has survived for many years and it has been difficult for marketers to break away from its constraints in terms of marketing services. Renaghan, however, has shown that traditional marketing-mix concepts have limited utility for hospitality marketers because they reflect strategies for marketing goods and ignore the unique complexities of marketing hospitality services. We strongly concur with that position and use it throughout this text to describe and discuss the hospitality mix.

It is sometimes helpful to both visualize and utilize the first three elements of the hospitality marketing mix in a matrix format in relation to customer utility. *Utility*, in this sense, means what something does for the customer. As we have already stated, it is the marketing mix which directly affects the customers; a matrix eases the task of understanding just how it does this.

Lovelock, working from basic economic theory, explains purchase behavior as it relates to services on the basis of consumer evaluation of *form* utility, *place* utility, *time* utility, *psychic* utility, and *monetary* utility.[6] We can construe these utilities as benefits from the customer's viewpoint, identifying the positive benefits to be emphasized, and the negative benefits to be minimized. By applying the tools of consumer behavior theory to create an image and using tangible clues to support that image, the marketer can translate the intangible benefits into realities that define the property for the appropriate target market.

The utility model and the hospitality marketing mix can be combined in a benefit matrix such as the simplified example for a hotel shown in Table 11-1. Marketers can easily complete their own matrix by noting the property's benefits, management's capabilities, and the market's perception of the property and its offerings. The benefit matrix can be used to identify the tangible clues that make the intangible benefits credible to the desired target markets.

Renaghan's model has not received wide acceptance in the literature, perhaps because his work has been read only by a limited audience. We hope to correct that oversight in this text for the reasons discussed in Chapters 2 and 3. The model undoubtedly needs further refinement, which goes beyond the limitations of this book. It is, however, an excellent starting point and we will embellish upon it in the next six chapters.

---

[6] Christopher H. Lovelock, "Theoretical Contributions from Service and Nonbusiness Marketing," in *Conceptual and Theoretical Developments in Marketing*, O. C. Farrell et al., eds., 1979, pp. 147–165, published by the American Marketing Association.

TABLE 11-1   Hypothetical Hospitality Benefit Matrix for a Hotel Combining Customer Utilities with the Hospitality Marketing Mix

Utility	(1) Product-Service	(2) Presentation	(3) Communications
Form	Food, room, pool, beach, lounge, room service, bed; performance	Physical plant (interior and exterior), employees, tangible presentations	Product-service; tangible attachments, tangible aspects of use and performance
Place	Convenience, ease of use, ease of buying, facilities, reservations	Location; nearby attractions such as business, shopping, arts; availability	Where available, where can be used, use- and performance-related aspects
Time	Convenient times; when needed, wanted, or desired	Pleasant use of time, time-saving, service level, seasonal aspects	When available, when can be used, use- and performance-related aspects
Psychic	Good feeling, social approval, prestige, reassurance, personal service, satisfaction, rest and relaxation	"Atmospherics": light, sound, space, smell; accoutrements	Tangible attachments to intangibles, dissonance reduction, nature of guests, prestige address, satisfied guests
Monetary	Cost, fair value, save money, how much	Price-value relation, easy payment, psychological effect, quality	Value perception, quality connotation, risk reduction

Source: R. C. Lewis, "The Positioning Statement for Hotels," *Cornell Hotel and Restaurant Administration Quarterly,* May 1981, p. 56.

DISCUSSION QUESTIONS

1. Discuss the virtues of the hospitality marketing mix against those of the four Ps. Do you think, as some do, that the four Ps are adequate for the hospitality market? Argue why they are or are not.
2. Discuss why and how customers are part of the presentation mix.
3. What is the value of the presentation mix as an extension of the product/service mix? Aren't they really one and the same? Discuss.
4. The various parts of the hospitality mix sometimes overlap. Give examples of this and explain how, why, and when it occurs.

CHAPTER 12

The Hospitality Product/Service Mix

In the previous chapter we used Renaghan's definition to define the product/service mix in general terms as the combination of products and services, whether free or for sale, aimed at satisfying the needs of the target market.

> The combination of products and services, whether free or for sale, aimed at satisfying the needs of the target market. [p. 32]

We need now to be more specific. From here on we will use the word *product* as a generic term to describe product/service or the offering of a hospitality entity.

> A product is an offering of a business entity as it is perceived by both present and potential customers. It is a bundle of benefits designed to satisfy the needs and wants, and solve the problems, of specified target markets. A product is composed of both tangible and intangible elements; it may be as concrete as a chair or a dinner plate, or as abstract as a "feeling." The utility of a product derives from what it does for the customer.

The key terms in this definition of product are *perceived* and *what it does for the customer*. Both are critical to the discussion that follows. *Perceived* means that if the customer doesn't see it, it isn't there; that is, something is not what management says it is, but what the customer perceives it to be. This notion is so critical and basic, yet so often overlooked, that one cannot be an effective marketer without grasping it. A simple example is the case of the restaurant that advertises "finest food." If that judgment is not consistent with the target market's perception, the advertising dollar is wasted.

What it does for the customer is an even more critical notion. We have covered this ground before but it bears repeating. Recall Levitt's analogy: "People don't buy quarter-inch drills, they buy quarter-inch holes." It is what the drills *do*, not what they *are*. Carry this thinking to the intangibility of the hospitality product; for instance, an expensive and beautifully decorated room. Such a room should make a hotel guest feel warm, comfortable, secure, luxuriant, or whatever. If the room doesn't actually do whatever it is supposed to do for the target market, then the decor and the cost are to no avail. Recall that we are in the business of solving consumers' problems, as abstract as they may be. Solving problems, then, is what the product does for the customer.

Designing the Hospitality Product

If, indeed, a product is defined in terms of what it does for the customer, then it becomes immediately obvious that the design of a product begins with what the customer wants done. In the case of goods, that is often easier to determine. People who buy tires want safety and endurance. People who buy stereos want good sound reproduction. People who buy Mercedes want prestige. But what do people want when they buy hotel rooms and restaurant meals? A comfortable bed and a good meal? Of course this is what they want, but we know that it goes far beyond those basic minimums.

As was stated in Chapter 11, people who buy the hospitality product buy a product bundle or unified whole. Every element of this bundle is an integral part of the product, which is why it is called the product/service *mix*. A change in one element can affect the perception of the entire product. Thus, it is useful to break the bundle down into its component parts: the formal product, the core product, and the augmented product.

The Formal Product

The formal product can be defined as what customers think they are buying. This may be as simple as a bed or a meal, or it may be as elusive as quality or elegance; it may be as intangible as environment or class, or as specific as location. The formal product, in fact, might be defined as what the customer can easily articulate. Because of this, it is easy to be misled by what the customer does articulate.

It has been noted that hotel and restaurant customers frequently name location and good food as their primary reasons for choosing a particular hotel or restaurant. In many cases, however, this is only because location and good food are elements that can be easily articulated. In fact, if these were really major reasons for choices we could dispense with the bundle concept and concentrate on these elements alone. Such, of course, is not the case and it would be a serious mistake to believe that it is.

The Core Product

The core product is what the customer is really buying. This usually consists of abstract and intangible attributes. Some examples of core products are experience, atmosphere, relaxation, celebration, and convenience. These are actually core benefits rather than product attributes. By now, of course, we know that what the customer is really buying is, in fact, benefits and not product attributes. In understanding the core product, we come closer to understanding problem solutions.

Understanding the core product—what the customer is really buying—means understanding the customer's problems. This has two very important implications. First, this is where product design should begin. Too often it begins, instead, with management's problems.

Consider, for example, the case of large banquet rooms that can be divided into smaller meeting rooms through the use of folding accordion doors. The innovation of doors of this kind came about some years ago because of a critical management problem: how to accommodate both large and small groups in the same space. The solution solved the problem for management, but caused one for the customer. In many hotels, even today, one can sit in a small meeting room and listen not only to what is occurring in that room, but also to what is occurring in the rooms on either side, not to mention the banquet kitchen. This is an aggravating and ongoing problem for meeting groups. Today, better folding or collapsing doors are built that almost eliminate this problem, but they can be found only in the newer and more expensive hotels.

Meeting rooms need doors that can be secured, but are safe for quick exiting. Architects solved this problem by installing large bar-levered doors with massive catches. Conference meetings often have frequent comers and goers. Each time someone comes or goes the door closes on its massive catch with a sound that resounds throughout the room, annoying almost everyone present. Lighting continues to bedevil hospitality customers. The ballroom is needed for both sales meetings and weddings. The lighting needs are entirely different. In many cases, neither customer is satisfied.

Although it may be true in some cases, not much has been written about meeting planners who "buy" the folding doors that separate meeting rooms, or doors that close meeting rooms, or lighting for ballrooms. The formal product, what customers think they are buying, is the meeting room and the seating capacity, and that's what the hotel is selling. The core product, what they are really buying, is a quiet, controlled, hassle-free, successful meeting. That's what the hotel should be marketing.

For another example, consider the case of a restaurant management that thinks the core product of the restaurant is its prestige, which is really the formal product. When a customer at New York City's Aurora Restaurant asked the waiter to split some entrees among his foursome, the waiter refused because the chef's "presentation" would be ruined. The rest of the story follows.

> [The waiter was asked] to present the food for all to appreciate—and then split the dishes; this led to a lecture from the captain about proper food presentation and, ultimately, a refusal to comply with the request or even to supply small plates so the guests could do the job themselves. "We ended up passing the plates around the table, . . . and when I left a meager tip, the captain actually came up and asked if anything was wrong."
>
> . . . the director of Aurora, acknowledges that the restaurant doesn't divide any dishes in the kitchen because that spoils their appearance. Combining portions on one plate can cause sauces to run together that don't mix well. And at a table for four, he says, it is too crowded to add extra plates. "We want the guests to have fun, but we like to preserve the integrity of the concept."[1]

These examples effectively demonstrate the complexities of the hospitality product. More important, they demonstrate the need for hospitality management to understand the product bundle, the customer's problems, and the design of the product.

---

[1] Kathleen A. Hughes and Laura Landro, "A Lot of Restaurants Now Serve Rudeness with the Rigatoni," *The Wall Street Journal,* November 12, 1986, p. 22.

The second important implication of understanding the core product is the awareness of what one should be marketing. Just about every hotel management in the world that has meeting facilities composes elaborate collateral describing and picturing the hotel's meeting facilities, sizes, and capacities. Rarely does one hotel differentiate substantively from the others in the same product class.

The formal product, of course, is the meeting space and unless it meets a minimum standard, it will be unacceptable. This is also the salient product. The core product, that which is also determinant and important, is how the entire facility deals with the meeting planner's problems. (This point was illustrated with ads from Atlanta hotels in Figure 1-3.) Likewise, the salient product at Aurora is the restaurant's prestige. This has little substance when the customer vows never to return and tells many others (not to mention making the front page of *The Wall Street Journal*).

The Augmented Product

The augmented product is the totality of all benefits received or experienced by the customer. It is the entire system with all accompanying services. It is the way the customer uses the product. The augmented product may include both tangible and intangible attributes. These attributes range from the manner in which things are done, the assurance that they will be done, the timeliness, the personal treatment, and the no-hassle experience, to the size of the bath towels, the cleanliness of the restrooms, the decor, and the honored on-time reservation.

It even includes the sun and the moon. As any resort manager can testify, there is nothing worse than three or four rainy days with all your guests locked inside on their vacation, or a ski area with unskiable conditions. The frequent effect is that customers go away mad over something management can do nothing about—or can it? For a marketing-oriented management the answer is yes. This is a customer problem that management anticipates and for which it prepares by developing alternative activities.

The augmented product is the total product bundle that should solve all the customers' problems, and even some they haven't thought of yet. In designing the product, it is critical to understand the augmented concept and its basis in consumer problems. This is different from simply augmenting for the sake of augmenting. Mints on pillows don't make up for poor lighting. Elaborate bathroom amenities don't make up for a businessperson's having no place to write.

The success of the all-suite hotel concept is based on the augmented product. This concept provides guests with a total living experience rather than simply meeting their basic needs. The success of McDonald's is based on the augmented product, which includes, among other things, cleanliness and fast service. In fact, the success of any hospitality enterprise begins with an understanding of the core product and its augmentation to solve consumers' problems.

The Complexity of the Product/Service

Now that we understand what a product is and what it does, it should be easy enough to go out and design a hotel or restaurant that will solve consumer's problems. Ah, if only life were that simple. Obviously, we have a multitude of consumers with a multitude of problems, and we can never hope to satisfy all the consumers or solve all the problems. We narrow the problem down, of course, by segmentation and target marketing, which is why these strategies are so critical to effective marketing. Even within these submarkets, however, we can never hope to be all things to all people.

It is clear, however, that we need to go beyond the basic and formal product when designing the hospitality product/service. Consider the following comment by Nelson Foote, former manager of consumer research for General Electric, a company widely recognized for its marketing acumen:

> . . . certain characteristics of products come to be taken for granted by consumers, especially those concerned with basic functional performance. . . . If these values are missing in a product, the user is extremely offended. But if they are present, the maker or seller gets no special credit or preference, because quite logically every other maker or seller is assumed to be offering equivalent values. In other words, the values that are salient in decision-making are the values that are problematic—that are important, to be sure, but also those which differentiate one offering from another.[2]

A hospitality property can offer a standard product, a standard product with modifications, or a customized product. Jain suggests two questions to answer when deciding which to offer.[3]

The first question is "What are our capabilities?" Without a clear perspective of the firm's capabilities, there is a danger of overidentifying them, which may mean that fullfillment will not be possible or will be inadequate. This can result in unfulfilled expectations and disappointed or irate customers. Recall, for example, our previous discussion of Howard Johnson's advertising caption, "If it's not your Mother, it must be Howard Johnson's." Probably no restaurant chain, much less Howard Johnson's at that time, has the capability of fulfilling such an expectation. The result was, as could have been anticipated, irate customers.

In some cases, the capability may exist but the execution is lacking. The result is the same.

> A hotel in Boston initiated a concierge floor at a time when it was quite fashionable to do so. A room on this floor had a rack rate of $40 more than the same room directly below it. Of course, certain additional amenities were added in order to "customize" the product for the expense account customer who was willing to pay the difference.
>
> One of these amenities was a lounge where continental breakfast was served and where concierge floor guests could go to have a quiet and relaxed drink without the undesirable features of a bar or cocktail lounge. The lounge closed at 11:00 P.M. Daily at 10:45 P.M., the "concierge" entered the room, turned the lights up to maximum capacity, and shouted, "Last call. Lounge closes at 11:00 P.M." In a flash, the customized product reverted to a standard product.

The second question to be answered is "What business are we in?" This is a strategic question that needs to be asked about any business, as we will discuss in Chapter 20; here, it pertains to the extent of the customization that we should hope to achieve.

---

[2] Cited in James Myers and Mark Alpert, "Determinant Buying Attitudes: Meaning and Measurement," *Journal of Marketing*, October, 1968, p. 14.

[3] Subhash C. Jain, *Marketing Planning and Strategy*, Cincinnati: South-Western Publishing, 1985, p. 657.

A successful example of customization in this sense was Burger King's "Have it your way" campaign. Burger King, as opposed to its archcompetitor McDonald's, was saying, "We know everyone doesn't like the same things on a hamburger. We'll make it the particular way you want it." The Burger King assembly line had the capability of providing this customization. Burger King management understood that it was in the business of providing an alternative hamburger to that of McDonald's.

There are other examples that were not so successful. Victoria Station restaurants thought they were in the business of selling beef at reasonable prices. They customized beef so the customer could have it in various ways. To the day of their bankruptcy filing, Victoria Station's management never realized that they were in the business of providing a total experience in dining out. The emphasis on beef and its customization was a large cause of their demise when beef prices rose drastically and they stuck to their initial strategy (and blamed their problems on the high price of beef).

Hotel developers and hotel managements make the same mistake. Instead of determining who the target market is—that is, what business they are in to serve that market—they sometimes decide that *they* want a particular class of hotel. The market doesn't buy it because it is the wrong product in the wrong market. This is true of many hotel signature restaurants, as we have mentioned.

Standard Products   Standard products have the advantage of providing a cost benefit derived from standardization. They are also more amenable to efficient national marketing. Holiday Inns' original motels are an example of a successful standardized product. No matter where in the country customers stayed at a Holiday Inn, they could just about find their way blindfolded to the front desk, their room, the lounge, or the dining room,

A problem with standarized products, however, and one that befell Holiday Inns, is the emphasis placed on cost-savings so that needed, and more expensive, variations in the product in certain markets are ignored. Eventually this results in a loss of customers who either want something different or want a more customized product. Even McDonald's, which has been incredibly successful with a highly standardized product, allows its franchisees to make variations on the theme. McDonald's does this because it is a marketing-oriented company; the effect has been a major contribution to their success.

Standard Products with Modifications   The standard product with modifications is a compromise between the standard product and the customized product. An example is the concierge floor of a hotel. In such cases, the scale economies of building and furnishing a standard room remain unchanged; the modifications are easily added to only those rooms requiring them, and an additional charge is extracted for them.

This strategy has one considerable advantage: The modifications, or added amenities, are easily added, removed, or changed as the market changes. Thus, the property maintains a flexiblity that in itself may be perceived as a desirable attribute because the property can more easily meet customer requirements and encourage new uses of the product.

In recent years, there has been a small but mounting trend in restaurants to offer different-size portions of their menu items. Such a policy has a high level of flexibility as well as the ability to cater directly to changing market needs.

Customized Products   Customized products are based on the premise of designing the product to fit the specific needs of a particular target market. Price is usually not a large consideration for the buyer of customized products, because he or she expects to pay a premium price to have it exactly the way it is wanted.

An example of a customized product in the hotel industry is the Four Seasons hotel chain. This is a top-of-the-line hotel chain that researches its market and then provides what the market wants. Unlike standardized hotel chains that will reduce payroll to cut costs when business is slow, and sometimes get caught short doing it, Four Seasons hotels are known for maintaining their staff and service level at all times.

The recent growth of all-suite hotel concepts has led to both modifications in the standard product and some degree of customization. Free breakfasts and free cocktail hours have been two of the modifications, while the perceived price/value of the suite is still maintained with rates in the $70–$90 range. One all-suite in San Francisco, however, charges $165 a night. This property stocks the suite with cooking and eating equipment, foods and snacks, liquors and wines, stereo, cassette recorders, and a VCR with a choice of movies and free exchange for other ones. The concept is customized to a very specific target market.

Making the Product Decision

Standardizing, modifying, and customizing are important marketing decisions in designing the hospitality product/service. Although the examples used here have been on a fairly large scale, these decisions also apply to all facets of the product. To illustrate this point, let's examine a relatively minor product decision in the light of the criteria that have been proposed.

If a restaurant has rack of lamb on its menu, or Dover Sole, or Caesar Salad, does it carve, bone, or mix these in the kitchen or at tableside? To do it in the kitchen is to standardize it. This provides cost efficiencies, and presumably the finished product offered to the customer is identical to the one offered when the work is done at tableside.

The decision, however, is a marketing one, not a cost one. To perform the work at tableside has elements of both the core and augmented product in it. First, we would have to identify the target market. Does this market expect, want, and appreciate the additional effort and cost to customize the product at tableside? Is it willing to pay an additional price for it?

What does the customized product do for customers? Does tableside service make customers feel better and more prestigious? Does it impress their guests, add perceived quality, or add romance or mysticism to the product?

What business are we in? Are we in the business of serving quality food at a fair price, or providing a dining experience? Are we providing elegance, flair, or entertainment?

Finally, do we have the capabilities? Is the staff properly trained, or can they be trained? If trained to do the carving, boning, or mixing properly, can they do it with flair and finesse? If not, we may defeat the entire purpose.

The hospitality product/service includes everything we have to offer the guest whether "free" or for sale. It contains the basic elements of what guests think they are

TABLE 12-1   Analyzing the Hospitality Product/Service

As Seen by the Target Market:

What is it in terms of what it does for the customer?
How does it solve problems?
What benefits does it offer?
How does it satisfy demand?
Who uses it? Why?
How does it compete?
What are the occasions for its use?
What are its attributes?
What is the perception of it?
How is it positioned?
Which attributes are salient? Determinant? Important?

buying, what they really hope to get, and the total augmentation of the product that constitutes the entire experience in purchasing it. From the budget motel in North Overshoe to the Bristol Hotel in Paris, from the hot dog vendor at Fenway Park to Freddie Giradeau's widely acclaimed restaurant in Switzerland, the hospitality product/service determination is a marketing decision based on the target market. The problem for the marketer is to determine the effective demand for the various product features and the total benefit bundle.

Table 12-1 provides a checklist for analyzing the hospitality product. This is a marketer's checklist for an existing product, because the answers will give the marketer the necessary tools to market the product. When applying the list, keep in mind the two critical definitions of a product: How is it perceived, and what does it do for the customer?

There is one more thing to be said about designing the hospitality product, which has been said before but bears repeating: No matter how successful your product is now, never forget that the customer changes. This, you will recall, is marketing leadership. The hospitality product requires constant evaluation and reevaluation. We will discuss this in more detail in the next section, on the product life cycle.

The Product Life Cycle

The concept of the product life cycle is basic to the marketing literature. It rests on the premise that a product goes through various stages during its lifetime, much as individuals do. There is the introduction, or embryonic, stage followed by the growth stage, the mature stage, and the stage of decline. Each stage calls for different strategies and tactics. The traditional and widely used perspective of the product life cycle, as illustrated by Kotler and applied to goods, is shown in Figure 12-1. However, Figure 12-1 must be interpreted carefully, since we have already seen that the marketing of hospitality products can differ considerably from the marketing of goods.

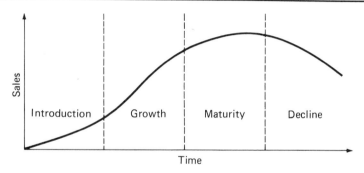

CHARACTERISTICS

	Introduction	Growth	Maturity	Decline
Sales	Low sales	Rapidly rising sales	Peak sales	Declining sales
Costs	High cost per customer	Average cost per customer	Low cost per customer	Low cost per customer
Profits	Negative	Rising profits	High profits	Declining profits
Customers	Innovators	Early adopters	Middle majority	Laggards
Competitors	Few	Growing number	Stable number beginning to decline	Declining number

MARKETING OBJECTIVES

	Introduction	Growth	Maturity	Decline
	Create product awareness and trial	Maximize market share	Maximize profit while defending market share	Reduce expenditure and milk the brand

STRATEGIES

	Introduction	Growth	Maturity	Decline
Product	Offer a basic product	Offer product extensions, service, warranty	Diversity brands and models	Phase out weak items
Price	Use cost-plus	Price to penetrate market	Price to match or beat competitors	Cut price
Distribution	Build selective distribution	Build intensive distribution	Build more intensive distribution	Go selective: phase out unprofitable outlets
Advertising	Build product awareness among early adopters and dealers	Build awareness and interest in the mass market	Stress brand differences and benefits	Reduce to level needed to retain hardcore loyals
Sales Promotion	Use heavy sales promotion to entice trial	Reduce to take advantage of heavy consumer demand	Increase to encourage brand switching	Reduce to minimal level

(Source: Philip Kotler, MARKETING MANAGEMENT: Analysis, Planning, Implementation & Control, 6e, © 1988, p. 367. Reprinted by permission of Prentice-Hall, Inc., Englewood Cliffs, New Jersey)

FIGURE 12-1   Stages of the product life cycle

The Nature of Product Life Cycles

Life cycles of products can vary widely in time span. Researchers have identified some as long as 100 years (Ivory soap) and some as short as six months (hula hoops). In retrospect, products with very short life cycles are usually referred to as *fads*. Life cycles also occur for a broad spectrum of product definition for either industry, specific company, or specific element.

For example, we could plot the life cycle of the fast-food industry, which is now considered to be in the mature stage, with its introduction having occurred in the 1950s. We could plot the life cycle of McDonald's, which started in the embryonic stage of fast-food. Many thought that McDonald's had peaked in the mid-1970s and would soon go into decline, but McDonald's accomplished what can be referred to as *reversing* the life cycle curve. We could plot the life cycle of Mexican fast-food, which is still in its growth stage.

Furthermore, product life cycles do not always follow the familiar S-shaped curve shown in Figure 12-1. The curve may be bimodal or strongly skewed. An example of a bimodal curve is the growth of the highway motel. This product had a fast growth period following World War II and the end of gas rationing. It then fell into disrepute (as well as disrepair) and went into decline, to finally emerge on a new growth curve as the motor inn with full hotel facilities. Today, there is another new growth curve in the motel life cycle caused by the boom in budget motels without full facilities. Of course, we could also call the budget motel a product by itself and plot its life cycle alone.

An example of a skewed life cycle curve is the all-suite hotel concept. The first all-suite hotel was about fifteen years old before the concept was duplicated by Granada Royale Hometels, followed by Guest Quarters. The all-suite hotel, however, remained in the embryonic stage until the early 1980s, when it entered a real growth pattern. An interesting exposition of the individual resort hotel life cycle is given in an article by Mike Leven that tracks the life stages of this kind of property.[4]

Hotel Product Life Cycles

As we have shown, the product life cycle can take many forms and can be applied in numerous different ways. To be certain that this is clear, consider a hotel property and just a few of the product life cycle concerns. There is the industry itself, which at this time is emerging from a strong growth period and is reaching maturity. There are geographic centers where it has peaked some time ago and now has serious occupancy problems, such as Singapore. At the same time, the industry is in the embryonic stage in China, and in a growth stage in various U.S. tertiary cities.

There are hotel brand names in various stages of the product life cycle. Wyndham Hotels was in the early growth stage at the first time of this writing (1986). By the time this chapter was edited the company had matured, sold off four properties to Stouffer, and was attempting to revitalize into a new growth stage. Marriott's Courtyard is in heavy growth. Hilton International is probably in the decline stage after having been sold twice

[4] Michael A. Leven, "The Hotel Life Cycle," *Cornell Hotel and Restaurant Administration Quarterly*, February 1985, pp. 10–11.

(Allegis and Ladbroke) in 1987. Lincoln Hotels (advertised with the self-fulfilling prophecy "The finest hotels you never heard of") was in the embryonic stage in 1986 and had a premature death in 1988.

There are types of hotels in various stages of the product life cycle. All-suites are in heavy growth, budgets are in moderate growth, conference centers are close to maturity, and Ma and Pa motels are in decline.

There are individual hotels in various stages. Dunfey Hotels (now Omni) resurrected the Parker House in Boston, the Berkshire Place in New York City, and the Ambassador East in Chicago, after these hotels had gone into total decline. Similar hotels in many cities are now in decline or are reemerging as apartment buildings or condominiums. The Marriott Marquis in New York City is in a growth stage, while the Waldorf-Astoria in the same city has been in its mature stage for years and is still holding.

Within hotels, there are innumerable individual product life cycles. Disco lounges had a fast growth, early maturity, and quick decline in the United States but are just maturing in Southeast Asia. Fern bars have matured and have started to decline. Dining room and cocktail lounge concepts grow, mature, and decline. "Grazing" restaurants are currently in the embryonic stage in hotels. Specific menu items (beef is in decline and fish is in growth), cocktails (margaritas are in maturity, wine coolers and bottled water are in growth, and martinis are in decline) also go through the various stages of the product life cycle. Even the 800 reservation number, which had a slow introduction, grew slowly, and is now in maturity, is said by some to be headed for decline. Further automation of the airlines reservations networks (such as PARS, Sabre, and Covia) may make telephoning obsolete.[5]

All these examples should make clear how products go through life cycle stages. How this relates to marketing is the issue that now needs to be addressed.

The Product Life Cycle Controversy

Actually, there are some who contend that the product life cycle (PLC) concept doesn't mean a thing in spite of its prominent place in every marketing textbook. The product life cycle has been criticized because of its lack of relevance and the absence of normative models to be used in its application. Others criticize it because of the lack of data to support it, and because of its subjective nature. Theodore Levitt has stated:

> The concept of the product life cycle is today at about the stage that the Copernican view of the universe was 300 years ago: a lot of people know about it, but hardly anybody seems to use it in any effective or productive way.[6]

Levitt made that statement over twenty years ago and many would still agree with it. In 1984, Hart, Casserly, and Lawless wrote:

> The PLC often constrains business thinking. . . . The result is often bad marketing decisions. . . . broad business concepts like the PLC are often unhelpful in any specific business situation because they do not reflect the unique characteristics of the situa-

---

[5] CONFIRM, a complete reservation system being jointly developed by American Airlines, Hilton and Marriott Hotels, and Budget Rent A Car, and scheduled to debut in 1991, will eventually provide a direct distribution system for consumers.

[6] Theodore Levitt, "Exploit the Product Life Cycle," *Harvard Business Review*, November–December, 1965, p. 81. Copyright © 1965 by the President and Fellows of Harvard College; all rights reserved.

tion. . . . the PLC is an idea whose strategic-planning time has gone. . . . The PLC is not useful as a predictive tool . . . for selecting a strategy to gain a competitive edge.[7]

Others, of course, have supported the concept. DeBruicker and Summe, for example, argue for its use in relation to customer experience with the product:

> The product life cycle concept is by now a familiar one. But how does a product's evolution toward maturity affect the buyer/seller relationship? . . . As the customers change, the benefits they seek change as well. . . . Sellers who understand and anticipate the customer experience factor can adopt any of several strategies to take advantage of the phenomenon.[8]

DeBruicker and Summe's argument is based on a specific use of the product life cycle concept. It is this argument—that the concept has valid and useful specific uses—that we will use here to support the case for the concept. In fact, we would argue that many of the failures attributed to its use are due to misapplication and adherence to the notion of the concept's broad generalizability. Most notably, we argue in accord with Jain:

> . . . the growth of a product is to some extent a function of the strategy being pursued. Thus, a product is not necessarily predestined to mature as propounded by the traditional concept of product life cycle, but can be kept profitable by proper adaptation to the evolving market environment.[9]

It is well to keep in mind that the introductory, growth, and decline stages of the product life cycle must at some point come to an end. The mature stage, at least theoretically, could go on for ever. Our argument, then, is that the mature stage is the most critical to the marketer. It is at this point, or at the stage of early decline, that the introductory and/or growth stage must be reincarnated if the product is to survive in some form.

One of the severest criticisms of the product life cycle concept, as noted by Hart et al. above, is that it is not predictive—that is, it does not predict when the product will move from one stage to the next. This is largely true as discussed above. It is our view, however, that this is not necessarily the highest and best use of the concept. In fact, it may be expecting too much. Perhaps what is most important, then, is to recognize the stage in which the product currently resides—for instance, to see that one's product is in the mature stage. Too often, management may be unaware of the product's stage, believing that growth will go on forever.

We point to the evidence of McDonald's, the Waldorf Astoria, the Greenbriar and the Homestead resort hotels, United Air Lines, or even the lowly baked potato, which now comes to us as "potato skin specialities."[10] These "products" have maintained mature status for long periods of time due to continuous new introductory and growth stages from

[7] Christopher W. Hart, Greg Casserly, and Mike J. Lawless, "The Product Life Cycle: How Useful?" *Cornell Hotel and Restaurant Administration Quarterly*, November 1984, pp. 58, 61, 63.

[8] F. Stewart DeBruicker and Gregory L. Summe, "Make Sure Your Customers Keep Coming Back," *Harvard Business Review*, January–February, 1985, p. 92. Copyright © 1985 by the President and Fellows of Harvard College; all rights reserved.

[9] Subhash C. Jain, *Marketing Planning and Strategy*, Cincinnati: South-Western Publishing, 1985, pp. 472–473.

[10] As an analogy, Crest toothpaste has been reintroduced several times: with fluoride, special plaque fighters, mint flavors, and a "new improved" dispensing cap.

product transformation, new product development, and/or new market exploration. We point, also, to Victoria Station and Howard Johnson's restaurants as examples of products that reached maturity without appropriate action by management, resulting in their decline and demise.

Stages of the Product Life Cycle

As can be seen in Figure 12-1, various stages of the life cycle have different implications for marketers. For hospitality products, some of the implications are contrary to those for goods.

The Introductory Stage   The very nature of the hospitality product often makes test-marketing prohibitive before introduction.[11] Ideally, then, the product should be developed on the basis of as much consumer research as possible. More frequently, however, this is not done and a new hotel or restaurant is opened on the conceptualization of the owner, developer, and/or management.

For hotels and chain restaurants, a prior analysis of the market and the competion is completed and the hotel or restaurant is built on the basis of forecasted demand. The new product may be simply a new hotel or restaurant not dissimilar to many that already exist, with possibly some architectural advances and technological innovations.

An exception was the Courtyard by Marriott concept introduced in 1984. Extensive consumer research was conducted before three Courtyards were built in the Atlanta area to test the concept before further expansion ensued. If the property is truly innovative, the marketer holds a two-edged sword: The product will be easier to differentiate, but may create more resistance to achieving trial and acceptance.

Whereas goods manufacturers will shroud their new products in secrecy as long as possible before introduction, hotels and restaurants do not have the same luxury. Construction time may be as long as three to four years and is often preceded by publicity due to zoning changes, financial arrangements, and other events that must occur long before the actual opening. This is considered an advantage to the property because it is all free publicity.

Whereas goods manufacturers may work with only two or three months lead time to promote the introduction of their product, hotels seek two to three years of lead time and restaurants may need up to a year. For hotels this is because groups, conventions, corporate accounts, and others must be solicited well in advance of actual purchase and usage. Thus, the property's marketing team arrives well in advance of the opening.

Introduction begins with a "soft" opening that may be a few days to a few weeks before the official opening. Word-of-mouth brings some customers, small groups (sometimes large ones) are booked, and various people, such as dignitaries, are invited to "test" the facility. This is the shakedown period, when management hopes to get a smooth operation going before the expected deluge.

---

[11] Our discussion here is concerned largely with physical properties or concepts. Products, of course, are also individual items such as a service or menu item. These may be test-marketed before systemwide introduction, an important phase of marketing a new product. In 1988, Burger King announced that menu and product research and development (R&D) would be incorporated into the marketing realm. Those functions had previously been part of operations. The change was long overdue in Burger King's ambition to catch up with McDonald's.

Looking back at Figure 12-1 we can see how the introduction of a hospitality product differs from that of a good. In fact, sales may, in some cases, be at their highest during the introductory stage. This is especially the case for restaurants. Customers have been anticipating the event for some period of time and everyone wants to try out the new hotel or restaurant.

Marketing's concern is very different with hospitality than with a manufactured good. The good has been built to specification and tested; so many units have been produced and distributed, and one hopes they will be sold.

Hospitality marketers have a different problem. Instead of producing just so many units to be sold, they must produce on demand. They hope they can "handle the crowds," that the staff is trained and ready, that everything has been thought of, and that there are no major snafus. Chances are that the product is not even totally complete since construction never seems to finish quite on time, and not quite all the furniture and equipment ever arrives on time. Hospitality products depend on repeat purchases. Business may boom initially; the question is "Will they come back?"

Initial hospitality customers are less innovators in the marketing sense than are new goods buyers, although initial hospitality customers may be more innovative with restaurants. More likely, people who try new hotels are variety seekers who want to try something different and may not be too willing to forgive when everything doesn't go right the first night. Also, competitors may be many, not few, and customers can always go back to where they came from.

The same factors apply, only to a lesser degree, to the introductory stage of a new cocktail lounge or restaurant concept. The lead times will be shorter, more publicity and advertising will be needed to create awareness, but the same concerns pertain. This is also true for a new service, menu item, or other smaller part of the product mix. Obviously, advance time is less, if it exists at all, and the risk is far lower, but the elements are the same.

The marketing objectives at this stage include creating product awareness and trial, as they do in Figure 12-1. The intensity of these objectives will vary, as has been pointed out, with the magnitude of the product that is being introduced. Another introductory marketing objective is to establish the property's position in the marketplace. When the property is part of a known chain this is easier to do than if it is an independent entity. However, brand name alone is insufficient to establish a firm position because of the often wide variations between properties, especially in the case of hotels. Research has shown that businesspeople, at least, judge far more by the individual property than by the chain name.

There is still a far more important marketing objective in the case of introducing the hospitality product; it points out the utility of recognizing the stages of the product life cycle concept. It is critical and essential that for a product to enter the growth stage, the customer must be persuaded in the introductory stage. Awareness and trial will come, relatively easily, through advance publicity, advertising, and word-of-mouth if the demand forecast is accurate. It is what happens to the customer during trial that determines the slope of the growth curve.

While there are obvious exceptions, the growth stage of goods depends more heavily than hospitality does on advertising and creating new customers. In some cases, especially low-priced items with minimal risk growth can be sustained for some time through the addition of new customers. New hospitality offerings, on the other hand, tend to depend more upon repeat customers and positive word-of-mouth.

This basic truism is too often forgotten or ignored. The marketing department is busy selling and advertising to get new customers, all of which, though necessary, is secondary to the critical need for relationship marketing.

Consider a case in point. A new large hotel opened in a southern city with existing ample competition and wholesale rate-cutting being practiced. The corporate office of the hotel company was so convinced that they had a winner and that there would be a deluge to stay at the new hotel that it issued orders not to offer discounts to get business. The sales staff was literally laughed at, and advance bookings remained minimal. After six months, corporate rescinded the order. The sales staff was laughed at again; they had alienated a major part of the market. The hotel survived because it was one of a large national chain with an excellent reputation but hundreds of thousands of dollars in revenue may have been lost in the process.

New product introductions rarely go perfectly, especially when they are major products such as a hotel or restaurant. This is the high-cost, low-profit stage of the life cycle. It is the stage when the customer has to be wooed and won at any cost. Failure to recognize this can be suicidal.

Strategies in the introduction stage (Figure 12-1) are also different for the hospitality product. The product must not be "basic," it must be "special" or customers will not return. Pricing must be in line with the competition. This is not the time for price skimming, a term that means using high prices to skim off the cream before the competition gets a foothold, and often used by companies like IBM in the introductory stage of a new product.

Distribution must occur through all possible channels. Advertising and sales promotion strategies shown in Figure 12-1 will, however, be similar to those for manufactured goods. The choices concern the breadth of the market that will be targeted. Most of all, the emphasis must be on internal and relationship marketing.

The Growth Stage   Many newly developed manufactured goods, in fact most, fail in the introductory stage and never reach the growth stage. This is not as true in the hospitality world, where there is large investment capital. If a new menu item, a new signature drink, or a new hotel service doesn't find acceptance, it can, like a manufactured good, be easily discontinued with minimal loss. If the new product is a $50 million hotel or a $5 million restaurant, it is more difficult simply to "discontinue" it. Generally, the property will find a new owner who buys it at the right price and has pockets deep enough to ride out the slow growth period. It may also emerge in a new form such as condominiums. There is an old saying in the restaurant industry that it is the third owner who succeeds, having bought it at the right price after two failures. But even the high rate of restaurant failures occurs mostly in the growth stage.

In 1987, the owners of the Hyatt Regency West in west Houston filed for bankruptcy. The hotel was built on anticipated demand (and a feasibility study), which never materialized after the entire Houston area was affected by the drop in oil prices as well as overbuilding of hotels. At the time the decision was made, many years before the hotel opened, there was a general movement in Houston for industry to move to the west end of the city. This area was so remote that even a ride from either of Houston's airports took well over an hour. The hotel never emerged from the introductory stage, and occupancies never averaged over 40 percent. In such cases, of course, the product is not simply discarded. It will, however, have to go through another introductory stage in some different form or at some different time.

In South Deerfield, Massachusetts, somewhat similar problems befell a Ramada Inn. It closed and lay fallow for three years before emerging as a highly successful budget Motel 6 property.

These examples, the Hyatt and the Ramada Inn, are not problems of relationship marketing. Rather, they are problems of targeting and positioning to markets that didn't exist. There is essentially no recall in such cases because there is no room for growth. Thus, once again, it is essential to understand the ramifications of each stage of the product life cycle. If the property is to survive, successful introductions must be followed by growth, and one must be certain that growth potential exists in the market.

Survivors of the introductory stage will proceed into a period of slow or rapid growth, or somewhere in between. This is where the previous relationship marketing pays off. Customers come back and they tell others. This is what the growth stage of a hospitality product is all about. Although, like goods, new customers are needed for rapid growth, the hospitality product depends far more on repeat customers. Good relationship marketing must, of course, continue. The hospitality customer is very fickle.

Unfortunately, success too often breeds contempt. Consider the following summation of a previously mentioned article on successful restaurants turned rude, where "bad manners go unchecked at places taking success and clientele for granted":

> So, what is to be done? If the evening is ruined and the dinner a disaster, if all the complaining—oral and written—is to no avail, the offended customer still might get some consolation from the certain knowledge that at least some of this month's most popular and crowded restaurants will, soon enough, be empty has-beens. "The trendy places take success for granted, and that hurts many of them eventually," says Paul Emmett, who manages Jake's Restaurant in New York. "You see places that were hot a year ago become lackadaisical, then sales drop precipitously and they fold."[12]

The growth stage is also the time of product refinement. Continuous customer research and feedback should result in both elimination of flaws and fine-tuning of the product to the target market. This is by no means a time to rest on one's laurels over the introductory stage having been a booming success. Product improvement should take place along with new complementary benefits, development of new target markets, addition of new distribution channels, selective demand stimulation, and careful pricing strategies. A frequent mistake made with hospitality products is for management to assume that initial fast growth gives them automatic license to raise prices. In the short term, this means higher profits; in the long term, it can mean disaster.

The growth stage of a hospitality product is the stage for building loyalty, not for gouging the customer. Here are some of the things that management can do to alienate the market after a successful introduction:

---

[12] Hughes and Landro, "A Lot of Restaurants Now Serve Rudeness with the Rigatoni," p. 22.

- charge for coffee formerly included with the meal
- raise prices of alcoholic beverages
- raise prices of menu entrees that are selling well
- stop taking reservations or fail to honor on time
- move tables closer together to get more people in
- refuse to serve arrivals who come at closing time
- not provide rooms requested
- raise room rates
- overbook and have to "walk" too many customers[13]
- dismiss complainants as a nuisance
- overcharge for small extras or room service items
- fail to honor special requests, such as for bedboards

Consider the above list. These are management or operational decisions and actions. It is management that makes these decisions 99 times out of 100, but you can see that they are really marketing decisions. Every one affects the customer. It is poor management that would make such decisions without a marketing perspective. Once again, we repeat, hospitality management is inseparable from hospitality marketing. Typically, instead, while these decisions are being made, management is exhorting its salespeople to "get out there and get more customers." And, believe it or not, when decline comes the only question management can ask is, "What happened?" Many will answer, "overbuilding," "too much competition," "everyone's going to Europe these days," "they rerouted the highway," or some similar platitudinous and/or pusillanimous excuse.

The growth stage of a product is the time for fortification and consolidation. It is the time to entrench the market position, go the extra mile for the customer, and increase market share. It is the time to plow back both money and good will, not take away; it is the time to sow not reap. It is the time to reward your good staff and to keep them enthusiastic and motivated. It is the time to listen to your customers and your employees for constant improvement of the product. It is the time to steal customers from the competition.

The marketing objectives at this stage are to solidify, to price for penetrating the market, and to keep customers. Every customer you keep at this stage will create other customers. This is the stage when you have to do things right; you no longer have the excuse of "getting the bugs out." This is the stage that will make or break the product. Finally, it is the time to start planning, if you haven't already, for extension of the mature stage.[14]

The Mature Stage   The mature stage of the product life cycle, as we have already said, can go for a long period of time. It can also end very abruptly. Once more, complacency is a bitter foe. If the product has successfully and correctly traversed the introductory and growth stages, the market should now be pretty well in place. The product's positioning should be established, its niche carved out, and its target market

---

[13] "Walking" a customer is industry jargon for not having a room available for someone with a confirmed reservation, forcing them to go elsewhere.

[14] For an excellent discussion on preplanning and extending the product life cycle, see Levitt, "Exploit the Product Life Cycle."

steady and loyal. There is a temptation at this stage to say, "We've got it made!" Nothing could be further from the truth. Never forget that fickle customer out there, the one who says, "What have you done for me lately?"

At the mature state, the product sometimes begins to get a little frayed around the edges—not just the furniture, carpet, and drapes, but also the concept and the execution. All elements need refurbishing. Too frequently, management thinks that a face-lift is all that is needed, and then wonders why business continues to slip.

Consider a 1400-room hotel in a large city, for years the largest hotel and the major convention property in town. Other chains started to move into the city with brand new state-of-the-art properties. Occupancy in this hotel began slipping. The corporate office's decision was to put $27 million into refurbishing the property. Two-thirds of the monies went into a new porte cochere. The hotel survives but never recovered its former position in the market.

This hotel essentially had the market to itself for a number of years with relatively little effort. It had stayed in the mature stage largely because there was no serious competition to stop it. It did need refurbishing, but probably could have done what was necessary for less than half the amount spent—but that wasn't the real problem.

The real problem was that management didn't communicate with the customer. It virtually ignored complaints or dismissed them with trite responses. It was notorious for snafus at the front desk—lost reservations, overbooking and walking, putting people in rooms not made up, making people wait until 5:00 P.M. to get into a room, long lines and waiting, incredibly slow room service, lost telephone messages, overpricing, and other related problems.

The hotel also had waited too long for refurbishment because management thought it had a captive market. Instead of building customer loyalty at the right time, according to many who stayed there, the hotel seemed to delight in alienating customers even to the point of refusing such simple requests as to split a bill on two credit cards. One large group that occupied a very sizable block of rooms four times a year had been complaining for years, to no avail, about both the services and the prices. This group, for one, moved en masse as soon as another hotel opened that could handle it.

The above example is a classic case of a management not understanding the ramifications of having reached the mature stage of its life cycle, of not having prepared for that stage, and of not taking the appropriate actions when it reached that stage. Even a customer research study showing that this hotel was perceived as the poorest in the city in its product class failed to daunt management. The hotel does and will survive because of its size, location, and membership in a large chain, but it will not fulfill its potential until management understands what business it is in.[15]

In the mature stage of the product life cycle, hospitality products must go head-to-head with the competition. Although Kotler's model (Figure 12-1) shows competitors beginning to decline in this stage, such is not the case for hotels and restaurants. More likely, competition has increased considerably. By contrast with manufactured goods, this is probably the most critical stage for survival.

---

[15] The general manager of this hotel through this period was moved to be general manager of another large property, in the same chain, that had been doing exceedingly well. According to reports, decline set in quickly. The GM was an efficient operator who could "make budget"; a marketing leader he was not.

The franchise boom of the 1960s saw literally dozens and dozens of fast-food concepts hit the ground running. Many of them soon became the "darlings" of Wall Street as sales soared and growth seemed to have no end. As both the concepts and the fast-food industry reached maturity, however, they began dropping like flies. Probably 90 percent are not around today. Of the largest four today—McDonald's, Burger King, Wendy's, and Kentucky Fried Chicken—only McDonald's has had no really serious problem in maturity. It is a strong marketing leadership company that knows how to compete.

In the mature stage, the product has to run harder just to stand still. Competition abounds, market segments have been tapped, and the product and product concept are old hat. The best defense at this stage is to have built the loyalty and fortification in the growth stage, but this alone will not be enough to contend with the newcomers on the block. One must also go on the offensive.

The best offenses are innovativeness, staying close to the customer, finding new markets, seeking and solving consumers' problems, and doing this better than the competition. McDonald's, for example, reached this stage around the mid-1970s. It developed the breakfast concept and Egg McMuffin. It researched its market to see what it could do better. It went overseas, into malls, office buildings, and other unsuspected places to find new markets. It developed new products such as styrofoam take-out containers to solve consumers' problems—and it did this all better than the competition.

You don't have to be a McDonald's to survive in the mature stage. You can be Joe's Bar and Grill down on the corner. The concepts, principles, and practices are the same; the difference is only a matter of scale. Sales growth slows down in this stage; that is to be expected. This is a maintenance stage, not of creating interest, but of maintaining it. This is a stage of developing new users and new uses, and new variations on the theme. It is a stage when product quality is paramount, and to slip now is to court disaster. It is the time for reevaluating the marketing mix. It is time to augment the product, and perhaps to give away a little something more without raising prices. It is a time when price promotions are common.

If the product is not maintained during the mature stage, it will enter into the decline stage. In some cases, this is a natural and appropriate thing to happen when the product was a short-lived fad and has run its course. Menu items lose their freshness, tastes change, the customer changes, and it is time to go on to bigger and better things. When the product is something like a hard piece of real estate, however, the situation is somewhat different. To avoid decline, sooner or later the product must be refurbished, renovated, reformatted, redesigned, repositioned, and/or remarketed. This is the time to reverse the curve before it heads south with abandon.

McDonald's did it with innovativeness and new markets. Burger King did it with head-on competitive advertising. Marriott is doing it with Courtyard and Fairfield, its budget chain. Omni wants to do it with franchising. The Chicago Hilton did it with refurbishing and repositioning. Holiday Corp. is trying to do it with all-suite hotels, downscale Hampton Inns, and upscale Crowne Plaza hotels. Other firms, like Marriott and Holiday, are also trying to do it with multiple brand positioning as discussed in Chapter 10.

Hyatt was not sure how it was going to do it, having publicly eschewed new market segments and frequent traveler programs, but the company has changed its mind on both.

The Greenbriar and Homestead Resorts in West Virginia and Virginia did it by targeting convention business instead of primarily the leisure market. Pinehurst Resort, in the golf capital of North Carolina, did it by repositioning from a golf resort to a family sport resort. Club Med is doing it by targeting families instead of singles and yuppies, as in the past.

Although all this may sound fairly easy, it is not. It takes real marketing leadership to know which way to go, to understand the market, and to take the risk involved. Often it demands a change in attitude, as with the case of the hotel discussed above. The main point is that the mature stage is the critical stage: Sooner or later it will end in decline if something isn't done, and done right.

Howard Johnson's failed because it waited too long, couldn't change its attitude, was too solidified in a negative position, and didn't understand the customer. Victoria Station failed because it waited too long, didn't understand what was happening, and didn't know what to do. Sambo's Restaurants failed because it took away management's incentive and didn't understand its employees. Many restaurants fail simply because they allow product quality to slip. Some hotels fail because management thinks the way to survive, when the product slips and business declines, is to raise prices and cut costs. These responses only serve to grease the skids.

The Decline Stage   Decline has a tendency to accelerate even faster than growth. Actually, some of the above examples of reversing the life cycle curve have occurred in, or very close to, the decline stage. Alert leadership does not wait that long; it knows when it is in the mature stage and that something has to be done. Even more alert leadership starts planning before it reaches the mature stage. We use the term *decline stage* here, then, to mean that the end is near. Although there may be a rebirth in some other form, for all intents and purposes the product, as we know it, is comatose. Howard Johnson's and Victoria Stations were both close to this state for a number of years. They live today in a reincarnated form.

Some products, of course, should die. They have lived their time and served their purpose. We may even push them into oblivion to make room for new products. Others, like the buggy whip, simply become extinct. When demise is not natural, not anticipated, and not desired, however, marketing has simply not done its job.

Locating Products in Their Life Cycles[16]

Another of the major criticisms of the product life cycle concept is that there is no real way to know what stage the product is in at any given time. Such an evaluation is highly subjective, prone to error due to irregularities in the S curve, and inconclusive. However, Jain suggests at least some guidelines. Personally, we believe that using these guidelines, along with good management acumen, marketing leadership, and willingness to objectively accept reality, makes determining the life cycle stage for hospitality products not as difficult as others might suggest.

The first step in locating a product in its life cycle is to study its performance, competitive history, and current position and match this information with the characteris-

---

[16] This section borrows heavily from Jain, *Marketing Planning and Strategy*, pp. 473–474.

tics of a particular stage of the life cycle. Past performance can be analyzed along the following dimensions:

- sales growth and market share progression in comparison with the best-fitting curve that one would expect for the particular product
- alterations and enhancements that have to be made to the product
- sales and profit history of similar, related, complementary, or comparable products
- casualty history of similar products in the past
- customer feedback
- repeat and new business ratios (heavy repeat business with declining overall business is a sign of maturity or decline)
- competitive growth and decline
- new competition and new concept introduction
- number of competitors and their strengths/weaknesses
- industry life cycle progressions
- critical factors for success of the product

Jain also suggests that, in addition,

> . . . current perspectives may be reviewed to gauge whether sales are on the upswing, have leveled out for the last couple of years, or are heading down; whether any competitive products are moving up to replace the product under consideration; whether customers are becoming more demanding vis-à-vis price, service, or special features; whether additional sales efforts are necessary to keep the sales going up; and whether it is becoming harder to [work through the distribution network].[17]

Such an analysis is not a task for amateurs; managerial intuition and judgment are critical. Because our thinking tends to be so strongly tainted or biased after the fact, a wise move could be to develop a model based on the above prior to introduction of the product. The model would then serve as a yardstick for future measurement.

Developing New Product/Services

It is clear by now that the development of a new product or service should start with customers' needs and wants and problems. This does not prohibit someone with a stroke of genius shouting, "Eureka, I've got it!" and coming up with just the right new idea that customers will love. It also does not necessarily mean that finding new ideas comes from asking customers what they want.

In fact, research has long shown that customers are really not very good sources for new product ideas if we ask them directly. Customers have difficulty articulating just what it is they would like to have in a new product. Nevertheless, it is around the customer that most new products should be developed.

Having said that, we must hasten to add that this is rarely the case in the hospitality industry. It is doubtful that anyone has ever asked customers whether they wanted a mint

---

[17] Jain, *Marketing Planning and Strategy*, p. 473.

on their pillow or their bed turned down. If they had, of course, the replay would no doubt be a unanimous "Yes." Why not? It doesn't hurt, and it's "free."

When the bathroom amenities "war" started, no one asked customers what amenities they wanted; management made that decision. Since then, it is true, customers have been surveyed as to which ones they use. Procter & Gamble, as mentioned before, found to no one's surprise that soap is the most frequently used bathroom amenity. No one has yet scientifically determined, to our knowledge, which of the amenities people take and use at home.

When frequent traveler plans are developed, how often are customers asked what should be included? When a hotel is built how many ask customers how they "use" it? (Actually, today, two or three chains do ask.) How often is the market asked what items it would like to see on a menu? (Some restaurant chains do ask.) Or how it would prefer the seating and lighting in a restaurant? Or whether it really likes that loud music in the lounge (often the preference of the employees who work there), especially when the lounge is empty most of the time?[18]

The point of all these questions is to emphasize that most new hospitality products emanate from the mind of someone other than the customer—yet their purpose is usually to enhance the product, increase satisfaction, create and keep a customer, and generally to fulfill the customer's needs and wants. With these objectives, it seems strange that the customer is not consulted more often. In fact, brand proliferation, as discussed in Chapter 10, is too often a result of "everyone else doing it" rather than being based on customer needs. There is, however, a definite emerging trend with more and more companies conducting or commissioning consumer research.

Those operators who do, in fact, introduce successful new products are usually those who have based the product on solving consumers' problems. Adding more fish to menus came initially from customers' problems with high cholesterol. No-smoking sections came from an obvious consumer problem even though, in most cases, it had to be mandated by law before restaurants would offer a solution. All-suite hotels came from consumers' problems of where to stay on extended stays. Directories in hotel rooms came from problems of wanting information, and keyless door locks came from consumers' problems with security.

But mints on pillows, turn-down service, the extravagance of bathroom amenities, and TVs in bathrooms (but not telephones) were ideas that emanated from management. Frequent traveler plans were designed to solve management's problem, not the customers'. The utility of all of these products in bringing the customer back, in many cases, is questionable at best. Perhaps the worst part of this kind of product development is that once the competition does the same thing, the differential advantage is lost, and what remains is a higher cost structure.

What we are saying is not that a new or improved product should not be developed to try and gain a marketing edge and differentiate from the competition. What we are saying is that products and services should be developed for the purpose of creating and keeping a customer, and that if you are in the new product development game, the best place to start is with the customer.

---

[18] An insight into new product development in restaurants, as well as an excerpt on the development of Courtyard by Marriott, can be found in Tom Feltenstein, "New-Product Development in Food Service: A Structured Approach," *Cornell Hotel and Restaurant Administration Quarterly*, November 1986, pp. 63–71.

What Succeeds?

Many new products fail, as we have previously said. What about those that succeed? Researchers have found the following factors most likely to be associated with successful new products:

- the ability to identify customer needs
- use of existing company know-how and resources
- developing new products in the company's core markets
- measurement of performance during the development stage
- screening and testing ideas before spending money on development
- coordination between research and development and marketing
- an organizational environment that encourages entrepreneurship and risk-taking
- linking new product development to corporate goals

New product development is a total company effort: McDonald's has proven that, if no one else has. Successful new products very often come from the bottom up rather than the top down. This is especially true in the hospitality business, because it is the bottom line of employees that is closest to the customer. It is often these people who can best tell you what the customer's problems are. Of course, you can always ask customers as well; do not ask what they would like to see, but what their problems are. In the final analysis, what succeeds is depicted in Figure 12-2.

Summary

The product/service mix is the basis of the marketing mix. It represents what the hospitality firm has to offer to the consumer, both tangible and intangible, both "free" and for sale. The product/service mix drives the other elements of the marketing mix; in some cases it may even drive the strategy of the firm. Accordingly, it is not just the marketer's job to "sell" the product/service. More important, it is the marketer's job to design in accordance with the needs and wants of the target markets.

A product/service has three elements: the formal element, the core element, and the augmented element. These elements are closely related to the concepts of salience, determinance, and importance discussed in Chapter 10. The astute marketer will develop products/services with these relationships in mind.

The product life cycle is concerned with the various stages of a product's growth in the marketplace. While some have argued that this concept is of limited value, it can demonstrably be a useful model of product behavior for planning marketing activities. The best use of the product life cycle is not so much to predict the future, but to recognize its existence and preplan for it, and to recognize the product's present stage and the appropriate actions necessary.

Product innovation is a characteristic of marketing leadership. The place to look for new product ideas is in consumers' problems. Too many new products are designed without considering the customer's real needs.

FIGURE 12-2 The relationship between product and need

DISCUSSION QUESTIONS

1. Take the augmentation of a hospitality product and discuss what it does for the customer. Given your discussion, how should the product be marketed?

2. The text has often discussed the proliferation of bathroom amenities and frequent guest programs. Discuss these "products" in terms of formal, core, and augmented product. Discuss them also in terms of standard, standard with modification, and customized products. How do these various factors relate? How do they drive the rest of the marketing mix?

3. Give examples of various hospitality products that are in various stages of the product life cycle. How do you define which stage they are in? What specific implications does this have for marketing them?

4. Discuss the following: Hospitality customers really have no choice in product determination. They can't articulate what they want until they have it. Therefore, there really is no alternative to determining the product for them.

5. Consider a common customer complaint—for instance, waiting for the elevator, waiting at the front desk, hearing the telephone ring fifteen times before the operator answers. Develop a new "product" that is economically feasible to solve these customers' problems.

6. Which part of the hospitality product is most important to the customer—the tangible or the intangible? Discuss.

CHAPTER 13

The Hospitality Presentation Mix

The second part of the hospitality marketing mix is the presentation mix. It is helpful to repeat the definition of the presentation mix given in Chapter 11:

> All elements used by the firm to increase the tangibility of the product/service mix in the perception of the target market at the right place and time.

First, we need to clear up what may be a source of confusion to some. Traditional marketers, or goods marketers, would be likely to tell us that this definition has done nothing more than embellish on the product/service mix. In a sense they would be correct. Discussion of the product/service mix in the previous chapter included some of the elements of the presentation mix. It would be difficult to argue that the physical plant, location, atmospherics, and employees are not part of the product.

In fact, it would be difficult to argue that price is not part of the product. Yet, traditional marketers establish price as a separate entity in the four Ps. Why this singular deviation? The answer is that price says something about the product. Price is a separate part of the marketing mix, or the four Ps, because it can be changed without materially affecting the formal, core, or augmented product itself. For this reason we include price as part of the presentation mix in recognition of the fact that it is a tangibilization of the product.

At the same time, we recognize that the development of pricing strategy, as a powerful marketing tool, deserves much fuller treatment than just as a tangible reflection of the product/service. To provide this fuller, albeit still limited, treatment, we devote all of Chapter 14 to further discussion of price.

In utilizing the notion of the presentation mix, we take the same license that traditional marketers take with price: You can change the presentation mix without materially affecting the formal product. The alert reader will immediately notice a problem with this statement. If, for example, location is the formal product (as we have indicated that it could be), it would appear that our rationale does not hold up.

Our response to that counterargument is that it is the exception to the rule. If what customers think they are buying is strictly location, then location is indeed the formal product. We would remove location from the presentation mix in this instance, and place it in the product mix. But what about the core product? If that is also location, and nothing else matters, then we can forget the entire presentation mix because there is no need for it: The customer is buying strictly location and nothing else.

In fact, in the above situation there would be no need for marketing at all. Once we have chosen the location and cannot reasonably change it, business would rise and fall relative to the merits of that one attribute alone. We have now come full circle and trust that the reader will see the point that we are making. The hospitality product is seldom, if ever, purchased because of one attribute alone; instead, it is the benefit bundle that is purchased.

The formal product part of the bundle is basic to needs and wants and is usually tangible. The core product, on the other hand, which the customer is really buying, is usually abstract and intangible. The customer cannot as readily grasp it with the senses. As discussed in Chapter 2, this presents real problems for consumers. How do they know, or gauge, what they will be getting? After consuming it, how do they know, or gauge, whether or not they got it? The answers, of course, are that they use tangible measurements to make the analysis. In this sense, we could really say that no hospitality customer *ever* buys location; what they really buy is convenience. Location is no more than a tangible presentation of that intangible attribute.

Where does the consumer get the tangible measurements? Recall from Chapter 1 that the prospective purchaser is seeking to build expectations and reduce risk. The human mind being as limited as it is, it seeks evidence to accomplish these tasks—tangible evidence. The architectural design of the hotel is not likely to make the bed any more comfortable, but it does tangibilize what one might expect to find inside in terms of feeling, comfort, service, and other intangible elements of the core product.

Thus, the hospitality presentation mix is the way we *present* the core product, or what the customer is really buying. It increases the tangibility of the product/service mix in the *perception* of the target market at the right place and time. This is not to say that there will be no overlaps between the product/service mix and the presentation mix; there will be, but that is irrelevant to our purpose.

Our purpose is not to develop nomenclatures or classification schemes so that we can do a better job of marketing. We do that only because these provide useful handles for mutual discussion. Our purpose, instead, is to provide marketing *tools* so that we can do a better job of marketing. Once we understand the mind and the decision-making process of the hospitality customer, we can see why the presentation mix is such an important tool in that task. It is also important that the successful hospitality marketer be able to conceptualize this distinction. This chapter will proceed with that understanding and will consider the six elements of the presentation mix: physical plant, location, atmospherics, employees, customers, and price.

Physical Plant

The term *physical plant* represents everything physical and quickly perceptible to the senses in the hospitality property. It is bricks and mortar, marble columns, potted plants, wallpaper and paint, chandeliers, flowers, gardens, lakes in lobbies, sand urns, and a vast multitude of other things. That should make life easy; all we have to do is hire a good architect and a good interior designer, and the problem takes care of itself.

What is so easy to forget (although we assume that after finishing this book, you will never forget it) is that all of this must emanate from the customer. Did you ever inspect a factory before you bought the stereo produced there? Did you care what the factory looked like after you bought the stereo? Of course not, but in hospitality things are different.

We will carry the analogy further because contrast aids in understanding this concept. Do you suppose the marketing department of the stereo company was consulted before building the plant? Why not? Because, of course, it has nothing to do with the customer.

Does this mean stereos are built without regard to the customer? Again, no; knowledge of what the target market wants in a stereo is taken back to the design team and the engineers. The stereo is built. If the research was well done, the marketing team can now take over. The job is relatively easy because the product has been built to the exact specifications of the customer. All that is needed now is basic traditional marketing and assurance to customers that this stereo does what they want better than the competition's. But because sound is also impalpable and cannot be seen, even the stereo company has to do some tangibilizing to create expectation and reduce risk. This is done with packaging. In the final analysis, however, the customer listens to the stereo, and judges by the sound before buying.

Developing the Physical Plant Package

The physical plant element of the hospitality presentation mix is nothing more than packaging, only in this case the customer has to largely consume and judge *after* buying. Packaging helps in attracting and creating the customer, and good packaging will help to bring the customer back; this is nontraditional marketing.

There are numerous examples of what we are saying. Atrium lobbies, elegant chandeliers, marble columns, luxurious bathrooms, and grand porte cocheres are all statements about a property and are tangible entities in the presentation mix. Rarely if ever are these decisions based directly on consumer needs and wants, nor would it be too feasible if they were. For example, we would never be able, even if consumers had the knowledge, to get a consumer consensus on the appropriate chandelier, wallpaper, or porte cochere. We have little choice but to rely on the expertise of architects and designers for these decisions. Their judgments, in turn, are strongly influenced by the owner's "gut feeling" and personal likes and dislikes.

When this happens, the consumer sometimes gets left out. Marketing plays little if any direct part in the physical plant decisions but is left with the job of selling the property in order to pay for the cost of those decisions. It is little wonder that a product orientation develops. (Remember the "lake in the lobby" story in Chapter 1?)

Although it is not feasible to ask customers to make all these decisions, it is feasible to ask, "What will this do for the customer? How will the customer use this property? What kind of tangible presentation does this make of what our product really is?" Architects and designers don't always ask these questions. Owners or developers, especially in the case of hotels, are probably even less knowledgeable. They only know what they like. In the case of some "grand" hotels, they may be consumed by an edifice complex and may hope to build what amounts to a monument.

Ignoring Marketing   Consider some examples. Although drawn from the "grand" end of the market, the principles are the same for a budget motel, a pizza parlor, or a McDonald's.

The New Otani Hotel in Singapore opened in 1983 with an $8 million waterfall that rises and falls to music. Occupancy remained low even with heavily discounted room rates. What did this waterfall tangibilize for the potential customer? Did it create customers? Did it keep customers? Or did customers look at it and say, "When you've seen one, you've seen them all"? Could $8 million have been used to better purpose?

At the Inter-Continental Hotel in Singapore there was a very, very expensive Maxim's of Paris restaurant, put there at the insistence of the owner and over the objections of management. It was probably the only restaurant in Singapore that required coats and ties. What did Maxim's and coats and ties in Singapore (where the weather is hot, and coats and ties are worn only for business in air-conditioned offices, never after dark) tangibilize for the potential customer? The covers on a good night in this restaurant were a dozen.

There was a relatively new hotel in a major U.S. city with a beautiful lobby and two-story waterfall. So as not to impose on the aesthetic sense, the front desk was tucked into a corner on the second floor. What did the lobby and waterfall tangibilize for the new customer who spent five to ten minutes wandering around trying to find the front desk?

There was another new hotel in the same city whose rooms had wall-to-wall windows covered by drapes about 2 inches too narrow. If the drapes were closed in the middle, they left a narrow slit on the ends, and vice versa. If you had a room on the east side on a sunny morning you never had to leave a wake-up call.

We know of any number of hotels targeting the business market that have desks in the rooms hardly large enough for two pads of paper, never mind the telephone, lamps with low-watt bulbs, and other paraphernalia. What does this say about the problems of the targeted business purpose?

A real-estate developer of our acquaintance decided to get into the hotel business. He bought a 300-room resort that was in the decline stage of its product life cycle, with plans to refurbish it. As sometimes happens, his wife became the interior designer and set up three beautifully refurbished rooms as prototypes. No one stopped to think how the guest would use the room. Here were some of the problems:

- The television was hidden in the bottom level of a console across from the end of the bed. It was impossible to lie in bed and see the television.
- The exquisite bedside lamps were about a foot tall. It was impossible to read in bed without leaning over the side to get enough light.
- The bed headboards were covered with a fine satin that absorbed hair stains, giving the appearance of uncleanliness.

On the same scale, consider The Stanford Court Hotel in San Francisco. Here too one could not readily find the front desk; in fact, there was nothing in the lobby to let customers know that they were in a hotel lobby. The decor deliberately said, "We don't want to look like a hotel." There was an antique Napoleonic clock in the lobby. There were always fresh flowers in both public places and bedrooms. The cocktail lounge and dining rooms were hidden away in corners. All of this made a tangible presentation that the highly repeat business target market loved.

It has been said that the greatest contribution Ray Kroc made to the success of McDonald's is not what you think: It was the large windows that surround McDonald's. For the first time, people could look into a restaurant and immediately see if it was clean. It took away the unknown; it reduced the risk. Kroc's windows are a tangible presentation of his concept.

On a smaller scale, the same principles apply. An incentive planner we know turned down a luxury resort hotel as a destination because when he visited there he found cigarette butts in the sand urns and empty tissue boxes in the bathrooms. He assumed that these were tangible evidence of how the hotel was managed and said, "If they can't take care of the little things, how can I expect them to do the big things right?"

We have cited almost entirely negative examples of the physical plant element of the presentation mix only because they make the point more clearly. In fact, there are thousands of examples for the physical plant elements making a positive presentation: lobbies, dining rooms, spacious seating, room arrangements, grounds, decor, space, lobby cocktail lounges, and so forth.

Considering Marketing   The point that we want to make, once again, is that the physical plant is an integral part of nontraditional marketing. When it "works," it makes a strong and positive statement about the property and the product it has to offer. When it doesn't work, it makes the opposite statement—in fact, it becomes a major source of customer complaints. Marketing should be involved in initial management decisions; management should be practicing marketing in subsequent operational decisions. There are always two lines of inquiry to be considered:

1.   What statement does the physical plant make to the target market—that is, how does it tangibilize the core product? Will it help to create customers?
2.   How does/will the customer use it—in other words, does it solve problems? Will it keep customers?

Pursuing these two lines of inquiry, we should make note that physical plants do not necessarily always have to be top drawer facilities. We have used those kinds of examples because they are more familiar and help to make the point. A physical plant can also say to the right target market, "Relax, don't worry; throw your peanut shells and your cigarette butts on the floor."

Location

Location is a limited but useful element of the presentation mix. Its limitation lies in three factors. First, location is inflexible once the property has been erected. Second, location is a minimum threshold attribute. By this we mean that location is in a somewhat black-or-white category with little gray in between. If the location is desirable, it then becomes secondary as a determinant or important factor, and other factors take over in the decision process. If the location is not desirable, other attributes may have little meaning.

The third limitation of location is that it tangibilizes only one attribute of the product—namely, convenience. There is no other reason for location to be a determinant factor in choosing a hotel or restaurant.[1] This truism means that location must play a smaller role in the marketing bag of tricks, if we accept the benefit bundle concept.

In spite of these limitations, location plays a major role in the minds of many hospitality marketers as well as hospitality customers. Exploring why this is so will provide some insight into the use of location in the presentation mix.

Location's Role

E. M. Statler, legendary founder of the Statler Hotel chain in the 1920s, is purported to have said that the three most important elements of a hotel were location, location, and location. No doubt that was true in the 1920s, when existing hotels may have been many blocks or many miles apart. Also, if one was staying at a hotel that was some distance from where one wanted to be, it was no easy task to traverse the distance in between. Today, of course, that situation is greatly changed and Statler's comment needs reevaluation.

The major role of location for hospitality customers derives from its salient nature. Almost any survey will show location as one of the most frequently mentioned attributes in choosing a hotel or restaurant. This response is strongly related to the tangible nature of location as well as its salience. When we think of choosing a restaurant or of staying in a city away from home, we immediately think of what is most convenient. That tends, in many cases, to become the first consideration. Whether it is the final consideration depends both on what else is available in relatively the same location, and what other of the multiple available criteria we choose to apply. Multivariate research, when a number of different variables are considered at the same time in relation to each other, has shown that location is a far less important variable than is indicated by its frequency of mentions. (Refer back to Figure 9-8 to see this relationship.)

The most important use of location in marketing is obviously in its initial selection relevant to target markets and competition. To build a hotel or restaurant where no one ever goes would not be too wise unless, of course, one could then get people to go there. Twenty years ago no one went to Cancun, Mexico, because there was nothing there but a large sandbar. Today, after a massive concentrated effort, there are thousands of hotel rooms and accompanying facilities, and Cancun is a major destination area for those who like to frolic in the sun and sand.

On the other hand, very few would ever go to Hot Springs, Virginia, or White Sulphur Springs, West Virginia, except for the hotels that are there, The Homestead and The Greenbriar, respectively. It is true that both hotels are in beautiful country settings, but it is also true that there are many other beautiful country settings in that part of the country. People go there specifically because of The Homestead and The Greenbriar; in

---

[1]There is, of course, an occasional exception to this rule. A location may be quite inconvenient but will be desirable as regards privacy, seclusion, vista, prestige, or other intangible elements. This, however, falls outside the common usage of the word *location*. We use the word here in its more common usage.

other words, location is not a strong tangible presentation of convenience for these hotels.

A similar but converse situation is the Banff Springs Hotel in Alberta, Canada. This hotel is also in beautiful countryside and people go to Banff because of that feature. While there, they stay at the Banff Springs Hotel because it is there. For the Banff Springs Hotel, location is a strong tangible presentation of convenience.

These examples are given to demonstrate the increasing or diminishing importance of location. Location today, as opposed to E. M. Statler's day, has been strongly affected by modern methods of transportation. Because of major expansion of air travel, for example, very few destination locations at this time can be considered "bad," as far as reaching them is concerned. While some are clearly more desirable, modern transportation has diminished location's importance.

The same thing applies within a city. Few go to the Vista Hotel in New York City for reasons other than its being the only major hotel in the Wall Street area. Those who go to the Waldorf Astoria on Park Avenue, however, have many other choices and choose the Waldorf for reasons other than location. In fact, some of them endure the long taxi ride to Wall Street by choice.[2]

We have a similar situation with restaurants. Fast-food restaurants tend to cluster on so-called fast-food rows. These rows are where the heavy traffic is and where the target markets for these restaurants prevail. Location is critical for fast-food restaurants because of the need for population density, which is why so many of them group together, giving the fast-food customer a choice in the same area. Many contend that all the good fast-food locations in the United States are now gone. Paradoxically, once established, location has little marketing value for a fast-food restaurant and one rarely sees it emphasized in their advertising.

Upscale restaurants face a different situation. To locate on fast-food row would probably be the kiss of death. Remoteness can well be an asset for these restaurants. In fact, there are many successful ones in the country in small towns that have no other claim to fame. In a city, the same thing applies.

One of the most successful restaurants in the United States is Anthony's Pier 4 in Boston ("You haven't been to Boston if you haven't been to Anthony's"). Although it is on the waterfront, that factor has little appeal once you are inside. Enduring the long wait for a table, when you get to it, will place you elbow to elbow with hundreds of others. Anthony's is also not that easy to get to from downtown Boston, and is situated among several abandoned warehouses. There are better restaurants in Boston with lower prices, better atmosphere, easier to find locations, and shorter taxi rides. Is location an important attribute for Anthony's? Not at all. Its target market doesn't much care where the restaurant is.

Location as a Marketing Tool

Let us go back now to the three limitations of location in the presentation mix to see when and how location can be an important attribute.

---

[2] At the same time, there is another location aspect that may be important only because it exists in the consumer's mind. For example, hotels in New York City may sell a location advantage as little as two blocks apart. A hotel on the east side of town traditionally commands higher room rates than those of comparable quality on the west side. It is unimportant that the east and west sides are separated by a street only 150 feet wide.

We said, first, that location is inflexible. This means that marketing must enter into the decision process at the first step, which, once decided, is irrevocable. The importance of the decision at this stage is directly related to the target market; if location is not important to the target market then it isn't important. The presentation element comes in "being there." As we have said in the case of fast-food operators, it would be of little use for them to promote location, but being in the right location itself makes the tangible presentation of convenience.

For the Banff Springs Hotel the situation is reversed. Its major attraction is its location. Thus, the location becomes the tangible presentation of the product/service, is a very important factor in its promotion, and should be used as a marketing tool.

The second limitation is that of minimum threshold. This limitation is more relevant to immediate competition. If you have a motel in North Overshoe, Maine, and the next nearest motel is 25 miles away, and your market wants to do business in North Overshoe, it may not matter too much what else you do. Location is your major asset and possibly the sole criterion in the choice of your motel—that is, it is a determinant attribute.

On the other hand, a hotel in Boston faces a different situation. Like business travelers in North Overshoe, people who go to Boston to do business in the downtown area don't want to stay at a hotel 25 miles away. Given, however, that a hotel is within a 5-mile radius in Boston, which would include twenty other hotels, it has passed the minimum threshold; for most it is "close enough." Location is salient but not determinant. This does not mean that if, for example, you intended to do business in the Prudential Center, it wouldn't be most convenient for you to stay at the Sheraton next door, or you wouldn't prefer to do that. It means that you would introduce other, more determinant, criteria in making your choice. In such cases, where competition possesses relatively the same location, location goes from being salient to being minimally determinant in the choice process.

The third limitation of location is its singular tangible presentation of the attribute convenience. To turn this to advantage, we again must examine the target market. If convenience is a determinant attribute for the target market, location should be stressed; otherwise, it has little appeal.

Location is a significant but somewhat overrated variable in hospitality marketing. While salient, it has limited use. Hospitality customers today have both many other choices and many other reasons for choosing a property. The strength of location in the presentation mix—the tangibilization of the product—lies in knowing when and how to use it in marketing, as shown in Figure 13-1.

Atmospherics

The third element of the presentation mix is a powerful one. While most of us are fully aware of this element—we often say that we like or don't like the atmosphere somewhere—marketers often do not take full advantage of it.

We have previously stated that hospitality customers buy a total bundle of benefits. One element of that bundle is the atmospherics. It is often the atmospherics that tangibilize all those intangible benefits that are sought—comfort, good feeling, excitement, serenity, contentment, romance, or any number of others. In the hospitality industry,

The 45-story Chicago Marriott stands just about where it ought to be – right in the middle of things.

The right hotel is never hard to find

The Marriott Hotel people have built their reputation on doing things right.

And one of the things they do most consistently right is to be, somehow, in just the right location for the business you want to conduct, in any given city.

In New York, for instance, Marriott's Essex House is right on Central Park. In Chicago? Right on Michigan Avenue (photo) – and also at O'Hare International Airport. In Kansas City, Cleveland, Miami, L.A. and Rochester, also conveniently right near the airport. In Philadelphia? Right at the edge of the Main Line.

Some cities already have several Marriotts.

Atlanta, four. Houston, three. Five in Washington, D.C. And new Marriotts are blooming worldwide. Marriott can now do it right for you in Saudi Arabia, Kuwait, Holland. Even right on the beach in resorts like Acapulco, Barbados, Santa Barbara, and Marco Island.

To reserve at a Marriott where you're headed, call a professional, your travel agent. Or dial toll-free 800-228-9290.

WHEN MARRIOTT DOES IT, THEY DO IT RIGHT. **Marriott Hotels.**

FIGURE 13-1   Emphasizing location in the choice of a hotel

atmospherics are a critical part of the marketing mix. In fact, the atmosphere itself may be the core product that consumers buy. If not, it can at least greatly influence the purchase decision. Kotler suggests that marketers can use atmospherics as consciously and skillfully as they use price, advertising, selling, public relations, and other tools of marketing.[3]

What Atmospherics Do

Kotler uses the term *atmospherics* to describe "the conscious designing of space to create certain effects in buyers. More specifically, atmospherics is the effort to design buying environments to produce specific emotional effects in the buyer that enhance his purchase probability" (p. 49). This could hardly be more true in any industry than it is in the hospitality industry.

Atmosphere is a quality of the immediate environment that is recognized by all the senses except taste, although taste can be influenced by the other senses. Thus, wine or food may seem to taste better when other atmospheric dimensions are positive.

Atmosphere constitutes a *sensory* experience, a by-product of many hospitality experiences. This is done in a number of ways. Visual sense is influenced by color, light, size, and shape. Hearing sense is influenced by volume and pitch, smelling sense by scent, and feeling sense by texture and temperature.

The hospitality customer learns to expect certain atmospheric conditions and often makes a purchase decision based on those expectations. A convention hotel is crowded, noisy, and boisterous; avoid it for a quiet weekend. A certain restaurant is dark and quiet, another is bright and happy. The task for the marketer is to create the atmosphere that will be perceived.

This is not as easy as it may sound, if only because of the individuality of customers. Many people will not equate the intended atmosphere with the perceived atmosphere simply because we all react differently to lighting, colors, sounds, and temperatures. Once again, this tells us that it is important to understand the target market.

The dimly lit restaurant is romantic for a young couple; for an older couple it makes reading the menu difficult. The air-conditioned restaurant is refreshing for the waitstaff, cool for the man with a jacket on, and freezing for those in short-sleeved shirts. The finely decorated restaurant is elegant for some; for others, it looks too expensive. The large hotel is "where things happen" for some; for others it is noisy and intimidating. Club Med is where many find that there is never a dull moment; others wonder "Why don't they shut up and leave me alone?" The more heterogeneous the customers, the more varied their perceptions will be. Knowing the target market becomes critical in this situation.

Atmospherics as a Marketing Tool

There are a number of situations where atmospherics can be particularly important as a marketing tool. The following pertain especially to hospitality establishments.

---

[3] Philip Kotler, "Atmospherics as a Marketing Tool," *Journal of Retailing,* Winter 1973–1974, pp. 48–64. This section borrows from Kotler's article.

1. In situations where the product is purchased and consumed on the premise
2. In situations where the seller has numerous design options
3. In situations where atmospherics help to create or increase the buyer's rate of consumption
4. In situations where there are a number of competitors, and atmospherics can be used to differentiate the product
5. In situations where the objective is to attract and hold a particular target market segment
6. In situations where product and price differences are small for essentially un-differentiated products
7. In situations where one wants to create a price difference for essentially un-differentiated products

Probably nowhere else in the presentation mix does a hospitality marketer have as much ability to manipulate tangible clues to increase the tangibility of the product/service mix in the perception of the target market at the right place and time.

The effect of atmospherics relates closely to the concepts of consumer behavior that were discussed in Chapter 6. Atmospheric qualities are designed into the product environment. Each buyer selectively perceives, attends to, and retains these qualities. The perceived qualities affect the belief and affective states of the buyer. The positively enhanced states lead to increased purchase probability.

Thus, atmospherics can be used to get attention, create retention, and manipulate perception. Accordingly, atmospherics are a message-creating medium by which marketers say certain things about the establishment. By this means they can communicate to the intended target market what they intend to offer. They can differentiate from other establishments. Affective states are enhanced by arousing sensations that create a desire for goods, services, and experiences. In this role, atmospherics help to convert behavioral intentions into actual buying behavior. Well-orchestrated atmospherics can move buyers into action.

Over approximately the last twenty years there has been a greater emphasis on restaurant atmospheres. Before that, restaurants tended to be quite plain and basic in their decor. Almost the total emphasis was on prices and the quality of food. There is no doubt that today, given a moderate level of food quality and the right price range, that atmosphere can often make or break a restaurant. Even institutional dining rooms have been caught up in the trend and few now look like the army dining halls they use to resemble.

There is a very important caveat here, however. Restaurants' atmospheres are likely to have a very fast growth period, early maturity, and quick decline. "Fern bars" (loaded with ferns just as the name implies), for example, which were extremely popular in the early 1980s, are becoming obsolete. The public is extremely fickle in this respect and today's "in" decor is tomorrow's "out" decor. Most vulnerable seem to be those restaurants that are also called theme, or even atmosphere, restaurants. In these restaurants the decor follows a particular theme such as nautical, western, or early American. Victoria Station restaurants were an early example of this, with their boxcar theme.

Atmospheres must be continually reevaluated in relation to the changing market, new possibilities, and competitive developments. Effectiveness also declines because of imitation or changing styles. Management must be constantly alert to the need for refreshing or revising atmospheres.

Using atmosphere as a marketing tool for restaurants thus becomes a tricky proposition. This is one area where you really cannot go out and ask customers what their needs are because they can tell you what they like only after they see it. One very successful practitioner in this respect is Richard Melman, president of his own company, called Lettuce Entertain You. It is worth following his career briefly to get a feeling for the marketing of atmosphere.

> It's nearly noon in Chicago, and hordes of people are making that big decision—where to *do* lunch? These days, the place to be is Ed Debevic's Short Orders Deluxe, the newest creation of restaurateur Richard Melman.
>
> Ed Debevic's? The joint with the neon sign perched atop an 11-ft. Coke bottle proclaiming "Eat at Ed's"? Where the waitresses are named Blondie and Bubbles? With the plastic flowers and Ed's bowling trophies on the wall? Yeah, Ed's. The unabashedly tacky 1950s-style diner that has buttoned-down corporate types, punk rockers, and North Shore dowagers waiting to get in.
>
> Ed himself doesn't exist, but Rich Melman is for real. By taking chances with off-beat concepts and relying on his uncanny sense of what the public wants, Melman, 42, has built his company—Lettuce Entertain You Enterprises Inc.—into one of the most creative forces in the industry. Melman is no flash in the pan. His 18 one-of-a-kind Chicago eateries—boasting such names as Lawrence of Oregano, Fritz That's It and R.J. Grunts—have been so successful that large, publicly held restaurant companies are lining up for his consulting services.[4]

In restaurants today, quality of food is necessary but not sufficient.

In hotels, a prime example of the use of atmospherics is the atrium lobby. In Chapter 1 and elsewhere we have mentioned Hyatt and atrium lobbies; here's the story.

The Hyatt Story   The use of atmospherics in hotel public spaces began with Hyatt Hotels and the atrium lobby. The story of Hyatt is an excellent, albeit not typical, example of the power of atmospherics as a marketing tool.

> John Portman, a relatively unknown Atlanta architect, designed the first modern atrium lobby hotel with open air space, glass elevators, and the accoutrements that are relatively common today. Portman tried to peddle his idea to a number of the large hotel chains. No one bought, and one reason was the cost of heating and cooling such a physical plant.
>
> At the time, Hyatt was a very small chain going nowhere. The chain started when the wealthy Pritzker family of Chicago bought the Hyatt Motel at Los Angeles International Airport. A few subsequent purchases were of similar mundane properties. When Portman approached the Pritzkers, they had both the capital and the imagination to support the potential.
>
> The first Hyatt atrium hotel opened in Atlanta to "rave reviews" and international press coverage. Others soon followed and Hyatt was on its way to being a major force to be reckoned with in the hotel industry. Unfortunately for Hyatt, they didn't "own"

[4] "Rich Melman: The Hot Dog of the Restaurant Business," *Business Week*, February 11, 1985, pp. 73, 76.

Only one hotel can take you to such heights.

A glass elevator ride takes you through the world's tallest atrium—into New York's most spectacular and unique hotel experience. The New York Marriott Marquis. A marvel on Broadway. Convenience and excitement that combine to offer you the best of the Big Apple. Where the city's only revolving rooftop restaurant and lounge brings you Manhattan as it's never been seen before. The New York Marriott Marquis. We'll make you feel on top of the world. For information and reservations call 800-228-9290 or 212-398-1900.

Marriott People know how.

NEW YORK **Marriott**.
MARQUIS

1535 Broadway at 45th Street New York, NY 10036-4017

(Courtesy of Marriott Corp.)

FIGURE 13-2   Physical plant and atmospherics

342

Portman and Portman didn't own a patent on atrium lobbies. He was soon designing hotels all over the world, as were others who copied the idea. In 1985 the tallest atrium lobby hotel, the Marriott Marquis, opened in New York City as a joint project of Portman, Marriott, and others (Figure 13-2). Inevitably, in 1987 the Portman Hotel opened in San Francisco.

Although atrium lobby hotels are a great success story, in some cases they may have gone too far and forgotten the customer. Some of these hotels have tremendous noise problems due to the reverberation of sound throughout and across the atrium. Some developers seem to think that atrium lobbies are what it takes to get and keep customers, and have sometimes neglected some of the basic tenets of hospitality marketing.

Atmosphere Planning

There are numerous other facets of atmospherics that the reader should have no problem identifying, including music, color, lighting, and design. We need, however, to take a more general approach to discussing the marketing elements of atmosphere planning.

If atmospherics play an important role in the buying process, then we need to apply the same regimen to their planning that we would to any other consumer behavior process. What atmospherics do, of course, is create a feeling; that is, the best atmosphere is one that makes the customer "feel good." Feeling good, of course, can take on many dimensions depending on the purpose and the use—for instance, it can mean exciting, romantic, or relaxed. Our first criterion, then, as usual, is to recognize who the target market is. We need to ask the following questions identified by Kotler:

* What is the target market seeking from the buying experience?
* What atmospheric variables can fortify the beliefs and emotional reactions the buyers are seeking?
* Will the resulting atmosphere compete effectively with competitors' atmospheres?

These are necessary questions but not easy ones to answer. It is often for lack of answers to these questions that some "great" atmospheres fail that were considered great by the owner or management, the architect, the designer, and often their spouses and friends. Even customers come in and say, "Boy, is this great!" But somehow it doesn't capture the right feeling, create the right emotional reactions, or compete effectively with the competition.

Also, it just may not suit the target market. This is not a very excusable mistake given today's marketing consciousness. Probably the most frequent reason for this occurring is that the marketing department had minimum input into the decision and/or no one takes time to fully analyze the target market.

A fairly typical case is the one we have mentioned before of a hotel in New York City. The new management team refurbished the hotel, including what had been a coffee shop. The F&B vice-president developed the concept of an authentic French brasserie, with menu prices at least double what they had previously been. Although the conception was good, the restaurant turned out to be totally out of touch with the hotel's market and did poorly.

As in any type of marketing planning, the more homogeneous the target market the easier it will be to design the appropriate atmosphere, and the more heterogeneous the market, the more difficult the task. With more than one target market, as is often the case, there is always the risk of pleasing one while alienating another.

A good example of this is provided by the smaller hotel properties, such as Holiday Inns and Ramada Inns, that have only one lounge. Often these lounges have had dark lighting, small tables, low banquettes, waitresses in skimpy uniforms, and a live music group playing the latest musical rage with maximum amplification. This pleases a particular target market, often the locals who come there for entertainment. Members of another target market—for instance, business travelers, especially women—who are staying in the hotel at $80 plus per night find that there is no place to have a quiet drink, quiet conversation, or enough light to do a little reading while relaxing, not to mention that the existing atmosphere is intimidating.

It is important to keep in mind that hospitality customers are not just buying, they are also consuming on-premise. "Living" with an atmosphere for two or more hours can provoke very different reactions than those from simply walking in and out. After a period of time, noise can seem louder, colors can be annoying, and decor can be distracting. Thus, one must recognize what experience the customer is seeking not only immediately, but over a period of time. It must also be recognized that emotional reactions can change over the same period of time.

Pretesting and Research   It would be nice if one could construct an "atmosphere" and pretest it on the target market. Although scale models are recommended, they are not overly effective for pretests simply because one has to live with an atmosphere in order to experience it realistically. Some hotel companies, notably Marriott and Holiday Inns, have constructed full-size models of prospective hotel rooms and have utilized actual customers to provide feedback on the rooms' utility, not so much for atmospherics as for room content, design, and arrangement.

Although full pretesting is usually prohibitively expensive for individual units (not necessarily for multiple units of the same theme, such as hotel rooms or multiple restaurants), and customers are unable to articulate what an atmosphere should be, it would be a critical mistake to ignore customer feedback. Presenting a new atmosphere should be followed by immediate research on customer reaction, rather than waiting until the concept has failed. Small changes such as lighting or sound can often turn a disaster into a triumph.

In one example, a restaurant chain hired a research firm to survey its customers before and after a major change in decor. The research firm planned to conduct the "after" survey in the first two months after the work was completed. The chain's management, however, disagreed and said, "Let's wait six months and let them get used to it." Of course, by that time the people who liked the change would still be there, those who didn't like it would be long gone, and the research would have lesser value.

Kotler reports the example of a major motel chain that uses a standard decor for its motel offices, one of the features of which is soft lighting. Research revealed that travelers felt that the soft lighting made the motel look lifeless. They preferred another chain where the bright lighting of the offices as seen from the road suggested a busy, cheerful place.

Atmosphere is always a factor in a purchase situation, whether it be at the local pub, a ski lodge, or the fabulous Dolder Grand Hotel in Zurich. It is not only a presentation of the offering but also a powerful competitive tool. More research is needed to understand just how different atmospheric elements work and what messages they communicate. Atmospherics call for conscious, not casual, planning because they represent tremendous potential for differential advantage when there are few other ways to achieve it.

Atmospherics also represent tremendous potential for marketing mistakes. Consider two new concepts introduced in 1988. Marriott developed Allie's restaurants, as a conversion of its Big Boy units, after spending $200,000 to research 10,000 families over a 2 year period. Howard Johnson developed Herbie K's, a 1950s diner concept, as a conversion of its Howard Johnson restaurants next to its motels, because the cost of conversion was found to be the least expensive alternative. Which do you suppose will be the most successful?

Employees

It should be more than obvious that employees are an important part of the presentation mix. In some cases they may be the most important part. The hospitality industry is one in which management, the entire property, the service, and the quality of the product can be judged in the consumer's mind by employee contact, sometimes even by a single incident.

In Chapter 3 we discussed the important concept of internal marketing and the notion of "selling" the job to employees. We will not repeat that discussion here although it is pertinent to the subject. Instead, the thrust of the topic here lies in the definition of the presentation mix: the tangibilization of the product/service mix at the right place and time.

The initial tangibilization is in the presentation itself—the appearance of employees. Not much argument is encountered when one says that public contact employees in a hotel or restaurant should be neat, well groomed, personable, and attractively dressed or uniformed. This is paramount. Customers arriving at the front door of an establishment are no longer looking at the architectural design. What they see is the employees who greet them: the doorman, parking valet, bellhop, desk clerk, host or hostess, waiter or waitress.

On the other hand, as with the physical plant and atmospherics, there are many times when the staff's being well groomed not only is unnecessary but also is not expected. A guest at a budget motel doesn't really expect to see a smiling "Hyatt girl" in uniform behind the desk. A family-run neighborhood restaurant gains much of its charm from family members working in various forms of dress. Tangibilization sets no standards; it simply implies the presentation, in whatever form, of the desired product to the target market.

What this means is that employees should "fit" the presentation mix. For example, the French brasserie, in the hotel example given above, was staffed with fifteen-year veteran union coffee shop employees. The staff didn't fit the concept or the intended market.

These people immediately become, if only temporarily, the product itself. They are the physical manifestation of what the establishment has to offer, and most people accept this premise. What many don't realize is that it is not just that employees should "look good," it is also that they are part of the marketing team, and this means they should also "look right." Looked at this way, employee appearance takes on a slightly different perspective and should receive more attention than it does in some cases.

What about casual or noncontact employees such as maids, engineers, servicepeople, maintenance workers, chefs and cooks, and so forth? How does their presentation affect the tangibilization of the product? This may be a weak analogy, but the case of airline cockpit crews makes the point.

> Few airline passengers see the cockpit crew except for a goodbye when deplaning or when walking through the terminal. The crews almost always look neat and well groomed and have all the other desired qualities. So far, so good.
>
> Now, suppose you stopped for dinner at a restaurant on the way home. While waiting in the cocktail lounge you see an airline captain—neat, well groomed, and all the rest—sitting at the bar having what looks like a double martini on the rocks. How would you feel? Chances are you might never fly that airline again. Perhaps he is only on his way home as well; perhaps he is only drinking ginger ale while waiting for someone. It wouldn't matter, would it? The tangibilization of airline safety just became something else. This, of course, is why airline crews are forbidden to be in cocktail lounges when in uniform.

The point made by this analogy is the same one we have made numerous times before. It is the perception that counts, not the reality, because for the consumer, perception *is* the reality. Think back to a hotel or restaurant situation. It is with perception that we are concerned. Every single employee is part of the marketing team. Some managements allow employee appearance to slip when business gets bad. They want to save on the cost of uniforms as well as laundry and cleaning. The man who comes to fix the TV is in jeans and a torn shirt, and the maids slough around in old slippers: These are signs of the beginning of a downhill slide.

"Smile training" plays a role in the presentation mix as well. Greeting guests, calling them by name, offering to help, and all the rest that goes with generally accepted public contact behavior is important. It is not always easy to extend this practice to noncontact employees. Frequently these people are of strong ethnic backgrounds and may speak no or limited English. Also, they are not always happy with their jobs (internal marketing). But people smile in every language in the world, and often that is all it takes. Although it may seem like a worn-out cliché it is still nothing short of amazing what a smile can do for a tired, irritable, unhappy, or discontented customer. While not sufficient, smiling is a necessary requisite in employee presentation.

Employees are one of the most powerful parts of the presentation mix and can be used to tangibilize the product, as shown in Figure 13-3. This is commonly accepted wisdom in the hospitality business. The only problem seems to come in its execution. Management needs to be constantly aware of this critical aspect of the marketing concept and to understand the motivations of employees.

In one not atypical case, a waiter received the "employee of the month reward" because he came in during a snowstorm, slept in the hotel, and worked long hours to compensate for the shortage of other employees. When asked privately why he did this, he said, "I knew there would be a shortage of help and I could make lots of money. I made $600 in two days."

FIGURE 13-3   Emphasizing the employees' part in the presentation mix

In another case, an uneducated maid with three children and an absent father, who had trouble paying the rent, also won the employee of the month award. Her reward? An IBM Selectric typewriter!

Understanding employees' needs is every bit as important as understanding customers' needs!

Customers

Customers—how can customers constitute a marketing tool? Think about it—when you go into a restaurant or bar, do you look to see who else is there? Of course you do, and not just to to see whether there is someone you know. You look at the type of people, how they are dressed, how they behave, and how they look.

This is an area where hospitality truly departs from manufactured goods. We buy goods without too much concern for who else is buying them, unless we want an opinion on a major item like a computer. When we buy a hospitality product we are concerned because we share space, noise, atmosphere, and other elements with people who are there to consume the same product or service.

Consider two extreme cases to make the point. The Ritz Carlton hotel in Boston did not allow in its dining rooms or lounges men without coats and ties, or women in slacks. In fact, it was about all you could do to walk through the lobby without the designated dress without feeling out of place. The Ritz Carlton wanted only a certain class of people in its hotel. One of their means of discriminating was through clothing requirements.

The other extreme is at the opposite end of the scale, a blue-collar bar. If a man goes there in a three-piece suit he will surely feel out of place. Those who are regular patrons will look at him in a way that will make him feel out of place, if he doesn't already.

In between there are many variations on the theme. No longer, in the vast majority of places, do hospitality establishments discriminate by dress. People who wear jeans drive Mercedes, and people who wear three-piece suits may not be able to afford them. So we use other means to judge the patronage and to see if we "belong." In effect, *the customers become part of the product.* They are a tangible manifestation of the product/ service being offered. We can tell a great deal about that product/service by looking at the people who use it. In effect, we are asking, "Are we in this target market?"

Positioning the Customer Mix

Does this mean we "kick out" those who don't fit the right image? Of course not. What it means is that by our positioning, the level of the product/service, or the target markets we designate, we establish the types of customers we expect to come to our establishment. Would you expect to see a bus tour unloading at a Four Seasons hotel as you were checking in yourself? Consider the following incident.

> A couple went to the Eleuthera Island Club in the Bahamas for their honeymoon. They chose this destination because the brochures had pictured it as a quiet, remote place on the ocean, with individual bungalows and a romantic setting. When they arrived they found 85 percent of the rooms occupied by a tour group that was drinking heavily, carousing most of the day and night, and making an incredible amount of noise. When they went to the dining room for dinner they found that it looked like a university dining hall. They had to wait an hour before reaching the front of the line. They were then told they would have to share a table with a couple from the tour group. It is not surprising that they checked out the next morning and found another resort.

Today, except at the highest and lowest ends of the scale, we are accustomed to seeing people of all kinds in hotels and restaurants. Yet it is a task of marketing to attempt to sort out these groups so as to establish specific target markets and cater to their needs and wants. It does this, in fact, by catering to the needs and wants of the specific target markets and not to those of the other customers.

A business traveler's hotel doesn't feature cribs, baby-sitters, or entertainment for children, although it may have them available for select instances. A family hotel doesn't feature conference rooms. A gourmet restaurant doesn't offer children's portions. McDonald's, at least in the United States, doesn't serve alcoholic beverages.

At the root of market segmentation is the question of what sorts of customers should be served. Although many hotels and restaurants would like to cater to one customer segment, economics dictate other action. If the property is unable to obtain enough of the most desired target customers, a decision must be made: either accept other customers or don't pay the mortgage.

Regardless, the customer mix is an issue that must be addressed if the establishment hopes to avoid conflict between market segments, as in the honeymoon example above. The hospitality industry is a high public contact business, where even the customers interact and share services. The customer base is readily apparent by the means mentioned above as well as many others. These customers contribute to the *atmosphere* of the establishment. As such, they should be aware of some of the *rules*—regarding dress, decorum, behavior, and courtesies. Management cannot mandate these rules, but it can create awareness by careful selection of the target markets.

Refusal to admit people is today both unethical and illegal. That is the way it was done in the old days. Today it is done by good marketing that identifies to the marketplace the positioning of the property and the kinds of people who go there (see Figure 13-4).

This takes careful planning. Fully homogeneous market segments are not likely. Most properties have to respond to two or more different segments, which may or may not mix well. When they do not mix, it is wise to keep them separated. For example, a hotel might have primarily business customers during the week and families on the weekend, with children who love to run around the hotel.

Sometimes it is possible to separate by different sections of a restaurant. Some hotels try to separate by using different floors. This doesn't always work because sooner or later the two groups are likely to come together in the public spaces. Pricing is another, and simpler, method to separate groups, as long as it doesn't lead to the alienation of a desired segment.

The best customer mix, sometimes called the ideal business mix, varies from one establishment to another. The important point is that it shouldn't be allowed to just happen. For example, Omni Hotels says that this is the profile of the Omni Hotel Customer:

- 97 percent attended college
- 83 percent earn $50,000 or more per year
- 53 percent have postgraduate degrees
- 79 percent stay 10 or more nights per year
- Well-traveled. Affluent. Loyal.[5]

---

[5] From an Omni Hotels ad soliciting franchisees, Figure 18-1.

(Courtesy of The Sheraton Corp.)

FIGURE 13-4 Emphasizing the "quality" of the customer

Hospitality marketers need to be concerned about who their customers are because customers help to define the character of the organization. Selective targeting is mandatory for the most potentially successful operation. The customer is tangible representation of the product/service.

Price

Prices are the most visible and the most flexible part of the presentation mix. This is of critical importance. Flexibility means, at least in the United States, where prices are not regulated, that prices can be changed at any time—on a whim, in response to competition, to make a deal, or just to fill more rooms or sell more steaks. Visibility means that the use of price to influence the consumer is rapid—in some cases, instant. This flexibility and visibility provides management with a very versatile and useful sales tool.

The flip side is that price flexibility can lead to misuse. Using price flexibility strictly as a revenue generator or a financial tool ignores the fact that pricing is best used as a marketing tool. The visibility of prices makes them the most tangible aspect of the presentation mix. Prices undeniably say something about the product. Prices are a critical factor in the risk/return trade-off and the value/expectation relationship discussed in Chapter 1. This means that prices should invariably be consumer-based according to the target markets.

The development of pricing strategies will be discussed in Chapter 14. Here we extract only minimally from that discussion to place pricing in its appropriate place in the presentation mix. What we need to keep in mind is that the ultimate objective of pricing strategy from a marketing viewpoint is to present the desired tangible surrogate of the product/service. Chapter 14 deals with how we go about doing that, along with the financial ramifications of pricing. The discussion here deals only with the end result.

One of the objectives of pricing concerns how we want to influence the customer—that is, what tangible presentation we wish to achieve. Because customers use price to make judgments too readily when other information is unavailable, price is a potent force in creating perception. That perception represents reality to consumers until they learn otherwise. Because price is so visible it may be the only variable on which a judgment is made. If that judgment is negative, there is a good chance that consumers will go no further and will not buy, and that their negative judgment will be a lasting one. Our first decision, then, is what it is that we want price actually to say to the marketplace.

In the above sense, price is a potent force in positioning either a product or a brand in the marketplace. Because of this, the hotel industry, as discussed in Chapter 8, has segmented the market by price. What this strategy says is that there are segments of the market that buy hotel rooms based on price. This is a product-oriented strategy seeking a market. Thus, if price says something about product, the effect is to position a low-priced property as an inferior product.

No one, admittedly or intentionally, buys an inferior product. Contrarily, if instead we utilize price as a tangible surrogate and as consumer-driven, we really want it to say something different about the product, perhaps something like "bargain" or "good value." This is the appropriate use of price in the presentation mix. Instead of segmenting by price, we segment by benefit bundle and use price to represent that bundle. This is a fine but important distinction: It is the difference between being product-oriented and marketing-oriented.

Another customer objective of pricing is to use it to differentiate the product from that of the competition. This is something more than price segments because it assumes that the competition is competing for the same market segment. Customers use price to make a judgment about value; they use price to develop expectations; they use price to assess risk. All these uses are part of the trade-off decision process of the consumer. Realizing this, marketers or price-setters have a complex situation on their hands. The tools for dealing with this situation are discussed in Chapter 14.

Summary

The presentation mix of the hospitality product makes a statement to the marketplace. Especially where the product is abstract and intangible, as it is with services and as it is with customer experiences, the presentation mix may be all the customer has to "hang on to." As with products, the presentation mix is the hospitality marketer's major tool for communicating with the customer in the sense of nontraditional marketing. Using tangible aspects to communicate with the customer in the sense of traditional marketing falls under the rubric of the communication mix, which will be discussed in future chapters.

DISCUSSION QUESTIONS

1. How is the physical plant different for hospitality presentations than for consumer goods? Give some examples from personal experience.
2. Discuss the limitations and roles of location in the presentation mix.
3. Define and discuss how atmospherics would influence your choice of a restaurant.
4. Decribe how the customer integrates with the product/service mix. Give positive and negative examples.
5. What is the role of pricing in the presentation mix?
6. Establish the advantage of recognizing the customer in the design of the physical plant of a hospitality product.

CHAPTER 14
Pricing the Hospitality Product

Price is of unique importance to marketers for a number of reasons. It is the matching of resources and supply to demand so that financial objectives can be achieved. It is also a powerful force in attracing attention and increasing sales. As such, price must be based on a thorough decision-making process that results in value that will communicate the seller's estimated worth of the total offering; a worth that is consistent with the market's perception of the offering's value. The importance of price in the marketing mix has been stated by Martin Bell as follows:

> Price is a dangerous and explosive marketing force. It must be used with caution. The damage done by improper pricing may completely destroy the effectiveness of the rest of a well-conceived marketing strategy. . . . As a marketing weapon, pricing is the "big gun." It should be triggered exclusively by those thoroughly familiar with its possibilities and dangers. But unlike most big weapons, pricing cannot be used only when the danger of its misuse is at a minimum. Every marketing plan involves a pricing decision. Therefore, all marketing planners should be equipped to make correct pricing decisions.[1]

Bell made that statement in 1971. Many others have made similar statements since. How far have we progressed? Kent Monroe, a prolific author on the subject, recognized as a leading pricing authority, said in 1979: "Of all the marketing variables that influence demand, price is the one that has received the least amount of attention from *marketing* professionals [emphasis added]. Essentially, pricing practice remains largely intuitive and routine."[2]

---

[1] Martin L. Bell, *Marketing: Concepts and Strategy*, Boston: Houghton Mifflin, 1971, p. 857.
[2] Kent B. Monroe, *Pricing: Making Profitable Decisions*, New York: McGraw-Hill, 1979.

Perhaps nowhere are these two statements more true than in the hospitality industry. Product and price decisions are inseparable because of the importance that buyers place on price in relation to value. The buyer uses price to estimate value received even when competitive prices are the same. This means that there is a real opportunity to enhance the product's acceptance with the proper pricing decision.

We have said it before and we'll say it again: Without customers, nothing else matters. If the customer won't pay the price, it makes little matter how high or low your costs are or what your profit goals are. Price, like product, flows from the consumer; the integration of product and price is critical. Notice how this is done in Figure 14-1.

Setting prices is a complex exercise, with any number of strategic and tactical implications. For example, sometimes it seems to work in reverse—that is, from the product rather than from the customer. By contrast with manufactured goods, the hospitality industry has fixed physical plant products and locations. Sometimes we have to work with the product we have and set prices accordingly. In other words, rather than set the price to the target market we may have to find the target market that will accept a given product at a given price. The given price is the price we have to charge to meet the financial requirements.

This is called product-driven pricing, but it is still the customer who will determine the acceptable price. In the final analysis, pricing, like product, is consumer-driven. It is this thesis that we will pursue in this chapter. First, we will set the stage by discussing recent pricing history in the restaurant and hotel industries.

Pricing Practices

Restaurant Pricing

The concept of consumer-driven pricing has sometimes been ignored in the hospitality industry. The first to learn this was the restaurant industry. When inflation became rampant in the 1970s, the restaurant industry responded by continuously increasing prices. Whenever the cost of staples of the industry (e.g., butter, beef, sugar, coffee) went up, restaurant prices quickly followed suit. The result was that the consumer eventually said, "Whoa!" and turned to other alternatives.

The fast-food segment of the industry owes much of its success and rapid growth in the 1970s to the raising of restaurant prices. Foodservice in convenience stores owes a good part of its growth to the raising of prices in fast-food restaurants. Even supermarket business increased because of the raising of restaurant prices. Consumers traded down and down until many, and not just those at the lowest level, decided to stay home and eat. Many who preferred higher-quality restaurants maintained that quality level by eating better at home.

Eventually, the industry caught on after being urged by industry leaders and trade journal editors to "get smart." It found new ways to do things, new items to put on menus, new ways to prepare menu items, and new ways to serve them (e.g., the salad bar) to cut labor costs. The consumer is the final decision-maker on prices; in the restaurant industry the reaction can be very swift, if only because it is relatively simple for someone else to enter the market with a new idea and/or a better price.

FIGURE 14-1   Emphasizing savings without loss of product class attributes

The paradox of that situation occurs at the upscale end of the restaurant industry, where prices tend to be sometimes exorbitant and unrealistic. This makes the point about the importance of target markets. Upscale restaurants have been almost totally supported by expense account customers who don't seem to care what the prices are; the companies that pay the expense accounts are the ones that foot the bill.

When the 1986 tax bill was being considered in Congress, the National Restaurant Association and owners of upscale restaurants went on the attack. It was forecast that hundreds of thousands of restaurant jobs would disappear, tax revenues would be lost, and bankruptcies would occur if the tax bill passed allowing only 80 percent of these expenses to be deductible (which the final version of the bill did).

The argument was faulty for three reasons. As clearly came out in congressional testimony, the American businessperson is not going to take the chance of losing a "deal" over 20 percent of a restaurant check. In the second place, if worst came to worst people would simply trade down to a reasonably priced level (the owners of these lower-priced restaurants weren't saying much, but stood to benefit). As this tier of the business grew, so too would it absorb more employees. In the third place, the everyday American taxpayer had been supporting these exorbitant restaurants for too long and the time was overdue for these restaurants to get their comeuppance. In fact, two years after the bill was passed, its effect on restaurant business was largely unnoticeable.

The point of all this is that, once again, the customer has the final say. Eventually, even government support erodes and each and every businessperson has to make it on his or her own. This is the law of the free market in a capitalistic society.

Hotel Room Pricing

The hotel industry fell into the same trap. Throughout the 1970s and 1980s, average hotel rates increased at a pace considerably exceeding the increase in the inflation rate or the consumer price index (which more or less paralleled operating costs).[3] Rack rates have increased even faster, average rates being held down only by heavy discounting. The industry complained about the need to discount as well as about lower occupancy rates. Blaming lower occupancy on "overbuilding" seemed to ignore the fact that there is a correlation between rates and occupancy.[4]

Yet, there was ample warning. Once again, as in the case of the restaurant industry, the seers and pundits sounded the horn.[5] Most of this occurred at the upscale end of the market, which dominated the hotel scene for a considerable period of time.

---

[3] According to Laventhol & Horwath National Trend Reports, for the 74 months from January 1983 through February 1988, room rates increased 73 times and occupancy decreased 46 times from the year earlier period.

[4] "Overbuilding" is a very frequent complaint of the industry that was disputed by an exhaustive study by Albert Gomes, Senior Partner at Pannell Kerr Forster, an industry accounting firm (now with Arthur D. Little Company). Gomes reported that there were about the same number of hotel rooms per capita in 1986 as in 1930 and that people are "confusing competition with overcapacity." See *Hospitality in Transition: A Retrospective and Prospective Look at the U.S. Lodging Industry*, New York: American Hotel & Motel Association, 1985.

On the other hand, a major factor is operating that, for the moment, we are ignoring: the demand by owners, who are rarely hoteliers, for greater profits through higher prices. Due to highly favorable tax laws before the 1986 tax act, many hotel owners today are almost totally financially oriented. This has had considerable impact on hotel pricing and has severely strained its relationship to marketing.

[5] For some of the more recent warnings, see, for example, Stephen W. Brener, "Lodging Industry Needs New, Efficient Facilities," *Hotel & Motel Management*, August, 1985, p. 69; John J. Rohs, quoted in "Domestic Lodging Industry Showing Signs of Weakness," *Business Travel News*, September 30, 1985, p. 45; Robert C. Lewis, "The Basis of Hotel Selection,"

The big names in the industry were publicly proclaiming that they were after the top 10 percent (or 2 percent, or 5 percent) of the market. This market, of course, was the high expense account customer. When industry leaders were asked privately or publicly—for instance, at industry conferences—about the future impact of budget motels or suite motels, the answer was usually something akin to this: "They're just a fad with little if any growth potential."

History is doomed to repeat itself. It was 1960 when Ted Levitt said, in his classic article, that businesses fail "*not* because the market is saturated. It is because there has been a failure of management" that makes the following mistaken assumptions:

- There is a never-ending, ever more affluent population that will sustain increasing demand for an industry's major product.
- There is no competitive substitute for a product.
- There is preoccupation with a product that lends itself to improvement and cost reduction.

Worse than the restaurant industry, the hotel industry did more than pass on its cost increases, and then some, to the customer. It also started practicing "reverse economics": When business goes down, raise the prices.[7] Many companies automatically raised rack rates quarterly or semiannually regardless of occupancy ratios or business trends. In the wake of this practice, what followed was a multiple discount process that was, at best, unsophisticated, naive, confusing to the customer, and, in the final analysis, self-defeating. We have already related the common story of the hotel salesperson who reports that the market "won't pay the price," and the response from corporate: "Raise the numbers." Here's another example from a regional director (RD) of sales and marketing for a major hotel chain, responsible for the marketing of some thirty properties.

> Rarely, if ever, am I consulted by corporate on pricing policies within my region. Pricing edicts are communicated directly to the property managements from the corporate office. More likely, I receive a phone call from a general manager that goes like this:
>
> GM: Do you think I should raise my rack rates 10 percent?
> RD: How's your occupancy?
> GM: Terrible. We're barely doing 50 percent.
> RD: How many of your guests pay rack rate?
> GM: About 2 percent.
> RD: If you raise your rack rates, how many of your customers do you think will pay them?
> GM: About 1 percent.
> RD: Then why do you want to raise your rates at all?
> GM: Corporate tells me I have to.

Hotel and Restaurant Administration May, 1984, p. 61; Steven J. Stark, "Biz Travelers Increasingly Being Steered to Budget Hotels," *Business Travel News,* April 14, 1986, pp. 22, 24; *Consumer Reports,* July 1986, pp. 472–478, a report on hotel ratings by 150,000 subscribers.

[6] Theodore Levitt, "Marketing Myopia," *Harvard Business Review,* July/August 1960. Reprinted in Theodore Levitt, *The Marketing Imagination,* New York: The Free Press, 1986, p. 141, 147. Copyright © 1960 by the President and Fellows of Harvard College, all rights reserved.

[7] See, for example, "U.S. hotel prices rose 5.5% in the first half of 1985 . . . say Laventhol and Horwath, industry accountants. . . . Reduced occupancy rates and sluggish volume at hotel restaurants prompted price increases," *Wall Street Journal,* September 12, 1985, p. 1; and "Standard U.S. hotel rates will go up—despite the many empty rooms. Reason: the hotels are trying to recoup their losses from business discounts and flat convention rates," *Bottom Line,* October 15, 1985, p. 7.

The upscale end of the hotel industry literally forced the growth of the middle-tier properties and spawned the growth of the budget and all-suite chains. In 1985, Stephen Brener, noted hotel financial expert, stated,

> The hardest area of segmentation to comprehend is the pricing strategies being used . . . and the rate differentials being offered in the various categories within the "rate sensitive/limited service" segment. . . . It is fair to assume that the largest percentage of hotel users fall into the "mid-price range," and the smallest in the "high price," and that between these sizes lies the rate-sensitive hotel guest. . . . All groups in the rate-sensitive categories appear to be growing, including senior citizens, budget-oriented vacationers and price-sensitive commercial travelers.[8]

One only had to look back at the airline industry to see what was happening. The first class section of airplanes had shrunk from 80 percent to less than 10 percent, as more and more companies mandated that their employees fly coach.[9] Today, the budgets, the middle tier, and the suite segments of the hotel industry are growing fast. The only thing holding back their expansion is the difficulty of finding places to build. Even poor locations are stealing business from the "big boys." The big boys, meanwhile, are practicing the old adage, "If you can't lick 'em, join 'em," as we have previously discussed.

Once again, customers have their say.[10]

The Basis of Pricing

The marketing discipline grew out of the economic discipline. The basic theory of economics, simplistically stated, is that the economy responds to the consumer. The basic theory of marketing is that the consumer calls the shots. When it comes to setting prices, these basic theories need to be remembered. Prices need to be established with the long-term customer, not the short-term margin, in mind.

The case on which we will follow up is well stated by Elliot Ross of the well-known consulting firm, McKinsey & Co.:

---

[8] Brener, "Lodging Needs New Facilities," p. 69.

[9] Judi Bredemeier, "Leisure Trips Outnumbered Business Trips in 1986," *Business Travel News,* December 1, 1986, p. 20.

[10] Ironically, it appears that the industry is determined to shoot itself in the foot once more, according to participants at an all-suites lodging conference in 1988, as reported by Roseanne White, "High-End Competitors Are Escalating All-Suite Rates," *Tour & Travel News,* April 11, 1988, p. 17:

> The entry of high-end hotel chains into the all-suite lodging market is pumping up amenities and prices, and many suppliers say this may be defeating the original purpose of all-suites: to offer a lodging segment with more space for a slightly higher price than traditional hotels.
>
> According to [Ted Mandigo, a partner in Pannell Kerr Forster] customers do perceive a better price-value relationship at all-suite properties. "All-suites have a more stable rate structure with less discounting because of that perceived value. They are able to get closer to rack on a more consistent basis than traditional hotels."
>
> There is "amenity creep" among all-suite hotels, with companies adding back some of the things they took out to maintain price value, said John Jorgenson, Quality International's development vice president in charge of all-suites.
>
> Radisson Hotel Corp. operations vice resident Jay Witzel agreed that the current trend among all-suites toward increased amenities could be damaging to the all-suites concept. "As we escalate it and begin to layer in more amenities that are labor-intensive, the price-value relationship is going to go away."

. . . improving pricing performance without the risk of damaging market repercussions [rests on understanding how the industry's pricing works and how customers perceive prices, based on] information about market and customer characteristics, competitor capabilities and actions, and internal capabilities and costs. . . . Proactive pricers . . . time price changes to the anticipated reactions of customers and competitors rather than to . . . their own analysis of costs.[11]

Sophisticated and integrated marketing and pricing strategies must be developed on a supply and demand basis. Pricing decisions should be based on solid "market research and thorough understanding of the economics of price changes," rather than "intuitive judgments of what the market will bear."[12]

The reverse situation is also true. When business is bad it is folly to simply follow a knee-jerk reaction and lower prices. Again market research and understanding of the economics of the marketplace are necessary. Singapore is an excellent case in point.

> Overbuilding and a decline in foreign arrivals seriously affected the Singapore market in the 1980s, causing hotels to drop their rates drastically. As one did, others quickly followed suit until who could charge the lowest price almost appeared to be a game. This began in the early 1980s. Building continued as construction proceeded that was already on line when the market appeared to be booming, although some hotels were never opened or were converted to other uses. Prices continued to decline.
>
> In the mid-1980s the Singapore economy turned sour, even business traffic slowed, and hotel prices decreased further. By 1987 one could obtain a room in a five-star deluxe hotel for US $40 or less. The Singapore government attempted to persuade hotel managements to close off entire floors until demand caught up with supply, but the industry resisted the pressure. The result was low occupancies, some as low as 20 percent in brand new hotels, at very low prices. Some hotels that were more market-ing-oriented and understood their markets better did much better than others. But even these properties were forced to severely discount because the traveler simply had too many equal choices.

Some discounting in the face of this situation was certainly necessary; prices had been set too high in the first place and had caused disintegration in the market even before overbuilding became rampant. But the other extreme was not the answer either. For example, six months after the Inter-Continental opened in 1982 with rack rates of $135, it was quoting prices of $35 a night. This had only a slight effect in increasing occupancy. The unanswered, and presumably unasked, question was, "At what point do lower prices fail to attract additional business?"

For the business traveler, such as those affected by the downturn in the economy, it didn't matter. The price of a hotel room did not alter the need to go to Singapore. For the leisure traveler, of course, room rates at a destination area can affect the choice of a destination. But how many who will make the expenditure in time and money will go there for a $40 room as opposed to a $60 room, or an $80 room, in a deluxe five-star hotel? Apparently not too many: Occupancy in Singapore did not improve in any direct

---

[11] Elliot B. Ross, "Making Money with Proactive Pricing," *Harvard Business Review,* November–December, 1984, pp. 145–155. Copyright © 1984 by the President and Fellows of Harvard College, all rights reserved.

[12] James Abbey, "Is Discounting the Answer to Declining Occupancies?" *International Journal of Hospitality Management,* Vol. 2, No. 2, 1983, pp. 77–82.

relationship to the drop in prices—that is, the perceived price elasticity (a concept we will discuss later) simply did not exist.

In Manila there was a similar but slightly different situation in 1987. Hotel prices were very low, as were restaurant prices. A suite at the famed Manila Hotel was $75, a bargain in any language. Manila suffered from a poor image due to the political unrest following the downfall of President Marcos. It was perceived by many to be an unsafe place. While the Philippines were probably as safe a place for foreigners as most countries, lowering hotel room prices was not going to persuade travelers to go there who thought they might get shot at. There were some bargain paradises on some of the Philippine islands going begging. The task was to change perception of safety, not of prices.

There are five major categories to be considered in developing pricing strategies: pricing objectives, costs, competition, market demand, and customers. We will discuss each in turn, but will not go into depth on those areas that are traditional financial concerns, mainly because this chapter is not on pricing per se, but on the role of pricing in marketing. Financial concerns receive heavy treatment in economics and traditional marketing texts.

Our light treatment is not intended to indicate that financial concerns are insignificant. To the contrary, they are critical. We maintain, however, that the role of pricing must be, first and foremost, consumer-based. Cost and profit considerations follow under the heading of "Can we afford to do it?" as has been indicated earlier. Recall that profit should be the test of the validity of management decisions, not the cause or rationale for them.

Pricing Objectives

Objectives are what we want to accomplish. Without them it is hard to determine where we are going or how we are going to get there. Pricing objectives fall into three major categories: financial, volume, and customer objectives.

Financial Objectives   Financial objectives are probably the most dominant, omnipotent, ubiquitous, and enduring pricing objectives in the hospitality industry. Although absolutely essential to success, or even survival, the heavy emphasis on financial objectives tends to overwhelm all other considerations. In some cases this can actually lead to failure; in others, even in successful firms, it can lead to the inability to maximize potential.

Financial objectives take different forms, all interrelated. Profit is the one that usually comes to mind first. We call this pricing for profit maximization, whether the emphasis is on gross profit or net profit. The first problem with the heavy emphasis on profit in pricing is that it tends to ignore a multitude of other considerations—in particular, the marketplace. The second and related problem is that built-in profit determination can be very elusive in the hospitality industry.

In other industries, the relationship among cost, price, and profit is more direct and obvious. In the hospitality industry it is indirect and vague. Widget makers can calculate very closely both their variable and indirect costs. From that basis they can add on a profit margin per widget and are left only with the problem of estimating supply and demand ratios. If they are good forecasters they will do well because the widget they don't sell today they will sell tomorrow, even if they have to discount it and reduce their profit margin.

In hotels and restaurants, the room or the seat not occupied tonight cannot be sold tomorrow even at a discount.[13] Yet a large part of the fixed and semivariable cost of selling that room or seat exists, regardless. Even with these problems, there are tools for calculating desired profit margins, which go beyond the scope of this section.

Instead, we are more concerned with the setting of prices based on the thesis that the higher the price, the greater the profit. That thesis will hold true if the price has no effect on patronage. For example, airline terminal bars are notorious for overpricing and operating with an under 15 percent of liquor cost to sales. It is doubtful that this egregious practice has much effect on volume given the nature of the captive market. In most other instances, however, this will not hold true.

High prices alone will reduce volume in most cases. Thus, after setting high rack rates, hotels discount to get back the volume at a lower price. From a marketing point of view, something else occurs in the process—the hotel loses customers who are turned off by the high prices, don't know how to negotiate a discount, or simply don't like being gouged. These customers not only don't come, or don't come back, but they also tell many others. It is because of this common practice by upscale hotels that we say that they have spawned the growth of the middle- and lower-tier properties.

The airlines learned this lesson even though it was forced upon them. A 1986 survey showed that a record 72 percent of adult Americans had flown on a commercial airline, up from 49 percent in 1971. Additionally, 54 percent of air travelers were on pleasure/personal trips. The study showed that business trips no longer predominate, not because of a decline in business travel, but because of a significant increase in pleasure travel.

What happened was that low fares induced many people to fly who had never flown before, and others to fly more often, and the airline industry had increased its customer base. In a business in which the variable cost is so low, as in hotels, this is a significant factor for the long term and a lesson to be learned by the hotel industry. Essentially, pricing for profit maximization by maximizing prices ignores marketing forces.

Other financial objectives in pricing are target return on investment (ROI), stabilization of prices and profit margins (to preclude price wars), internal rate of return (IRR), and cash flow pricing (to maximize short-run sales to generate cash). All of these objectives have their place in pricing and, in fact, are necessary. In the hotel industry today, with its absentee ownerships, these are common predominant objectives. Problems arise when one of them becomes the sole pricing objective. The effect is similar to that of profit maximization.

Volume Objectives   Volume objectives are a second set of pricing objectives and take a number of forms. These objectives are particularly prevalent in the hotel industry because it is such a highly *volume-sensitive* business—that is, fixed costs are high but

---

[13] This is, as previously noted, referred to as the perishability of the product, widely proclaimed as the nemesis of hoteliers and restaurateurs. To counteract this, prices are set accordingly. This practice, unfortunately, ignores the seldom mentioned and also previously noted perpetuability of these products—the unique ability to sell the same product over and over. To do so means, among other things, setting the price correctly the first time.

variable costs per room can run as low as 15 percent to 25 percent of departmental income. Once fixed costs have been surpassed, a small gain in volume supports a large increase in profit, as with the airlines. In the restaurant business, a *price-sensitive* business (i.e., a small increase in price supports a large increase in profit), variable costs can run as high as 35 percent to 55 percent of sales. Both industries, of course, seek volume (with some noted exceptions, where high prices are designed to promote exclusivity). Lower variable costs, however, provide hotels with the ability to discount deeper to promote volume while, contrarily, much of the restaurant's variable cost can be sold the next day. Hotel restaurants also have this advantage as well as the unique position of "paying no rent," by contrast with their freestanding competitors.[14]

One major and commonly used measure of volume is market share. Alternatively, this objective may simply be stated as the desired sales growth rate. The same considerations apply.

Market share was described in Chapter 5, so we will mention here only that it is the percentage or dollar volume share of the total business of that type in a given market area. Market share has been shown in other industries to be a leading prognosticator of profit. It also measures how well one is doing vis-à-vis the competition and also how well in terms of one's own fair share.

To increase market share, a property has to do something better than the competition. This can be a better product, better service, better location, or better perceived value. One can also be "better" by lowering prices. This may or may not be self-defeating. For a restaurant, a quickly calculated break-even analysis can indicate at which point increased volume will overcome the lost revenue due to lower prices. For a hotel, it is more likely and more quickly possible that competition will follow suit and market share will soon return to where it was before. It is probably foolish in most cases in the hospitality industry to lower prices for the sole purpose of increasing market share.

Another volume objective is to build business by increasing the customer base, as occurred in the airlines case above. With this strategy, prices are usually lowered, either temporarily or in special promotions, to attract more customers with the hope that they will become permanent customers. This also can backfire, as it usually does with restaurants that run "twofer" promotions (two meals for the price of one). The reason it backfires is that many consumers who take advantage of the promotion will never return to the property when they have to pay the regular price.

There can be much merit, however, to using price to build the customer base when doing so will build customer loyalty, especially during normally slow periods. For hotels, more customers in the rooms can also mean more customers in the food and beverage outlets.

Another objective is to increase occupancy or seat turnover. This is really no different from talking about increasing sales by lowering the price. Higher occupancy or seat turnover helps to cover relatively fixed labor costs and overhead. Again, for hotels it

---

[14] This creates an interesting paradox in many hotels that is counterproductive. The following scenario is common. A sales manager books a large group at a favorable (to the hotel) room rate. To do so, she had to "give away" the meals. The food and beverage manager and the chef scream—the prices will ruin their food cost percentage—oblivious to the overall profit to be gained from the booking. Some hotels counter this "F & B mentality" by assigning a portion of room revenues to F & B revenues.

can mean more customers in the food and beverage outlets. Hotel management personnel are also judged on their occupancy ratios and are often rewarded accordingly, so there is high incentive to price with the objective of increasing occupancy.

A final volume objective is the contribution to fixed costs that is made by any incremental business. If the variable cost of a meal is $3 and the meal is sold for $4, the contribution to fixed cost is $1. This is better than zero if the meal is normally sold for $8 but can't be sold. The high fixed costs and volume sensitivity of hotels make this objective even more viable.

This observation is even more apt when one considers the disadvantage that hotel restaurants incur contrasted with their freestanding competitors. This disadvantage is the fixed costs incurred because outlets must be kept open for guest convenience. Local restaurants can close on days when business is slow; hotels do not have the same option. Many hotels must also offer room service in spite of its unprofitability.

Volume and profit objectives in pricing often go hand in hand, but this is not always the case. Volume objectives tend to be more oriented to the long term and, when done wisely, to building the customer base.

Customer Objectives   The term *customer objectives* as used here means influence of the customer in a favorable way. This is truly the marketing objective of pricing. There are many ways that pricing can be used to do this simply because it is the most visible part of the presentation mix. We will suggest a number of those ways.

One customer objective is to instill confidence in the customer by price stability. In these days, who hears of a price going down? All they ever do is go up! Well, not always. McDonald's is an example of a company that tries to hold prices level and in some cases has lowered them. McDonald's recognizes its customers' high sensitivity to prices. This is also true of a number of other members of the restaurant family, except at the upscale end of the market, where there seems to be a sense by many that there is no price sensitivity. In some cases this is true; in others the result is lost customers.

In the inflationary times of the 1970s, the public became accustomed to continuously increasing prices. It also learned to trade down when it felt it was being taken advantage of. A major portion of the hotel industry, once again, appears to believe it can still ride the waves of inflation even when inflation doesn't exist. This has destroyed a great deal of consumer confidence and has built business for those properties that don't follow the practice.

While hotels discount rampantly, they almost never lower rack rates; in fact, like the American automobile industry today, they raise prices and then discount. This is a strange phenomenon. In Europe and, in limited cases, in Asia we have seen rack rates lowered followed by a commensurate increase in occupancy. In the United States, contrarily, both the automobile and the hotel industries have succeeded in increasing the competition through their self-defeating policies.

However, the hotel industry is not completely oblivious to this fact. It has used pricing to provide stability through what are known as "corporate rates." In some cases this has been done on a broad scale except that these rates, too, increase on a regular basis. On a more narrow scale, hotel companies have negotiated rates with other corporations that remain constant for some period of time. The rates are usually based on the guarantee of a certain number of room nights during the same period. This allows corporations to better budget their travel expenses when they are confident of a stable price. It has done nothing, however, for the pleasure/personal traveler—the same one who is now flying in airplanes. Lack of confidence in hotel rates may have scared many of these people out of the market, at least at the upscale end.

Another customer objective is "inducement to try." Restaurant twofers are designed for this purpose, as are other special promotions. Restaurants run *loss leaders* (items on which they take a loss or lower margin with the hope of making up the profit on other items) just as retail stores do. "Opening specials" represent a specific case of inducement to try pricing. Individual and new menu items may also be priced lower for this purpose.

In practice, new hotels often open at the highest price they think the market will bear and avoid initial discounting on the assumption that natural demand will fill the rooms. The objective in this situation, rather than inducement to try, is another customer objective called "enhancing the image." The attempt is to make the property appear so special, new, and different that it is worth the higher price. Unless that is really the case, the net result is often lost customers in the long run.

At times hotel managements seem not to understand that in most marketplaces, new demand is not created because a new hotel is opened. The meetings or business traveler market already exists, in another hotel. Opening pricing is extremely important; the idea is to get existing customers in competitors' hotels to try the new product, not to scare them away.

The practice of initial high pricing is also called price skimming. The term derives from the notion of skimming the cream off the top, before the competition comes in and forces prices down. Price skimming is sometimes profitable when a company introduces a new product into the market. For hotels and restaurants, it usually creates the negative, and often lasting, image of being overpriced, and is to be avoided.

"Enhancing the image" is better used when the product is truly unique and special. Four Seasons is a hotel chain that follows this practice. The Helmsley Palace in New York City has the same strategy by establishing high rates and generally not discounting, except in off-season. The Stanford Court in San Francisco did likewise and maintained some of the highest average rates and occupancies in the city. Some very special restaurants also successfully price high for the same reason, under the philosophy that "If you have to ask the price you shouldn't be here." These are excellent examples of tangibilizing the product through pricing, but there are very few of these opportunities in the marketplace. When these practices are based on ego rather than reality, they are self-defeating.

Another consumer objective in pricing is to "desensitize" the consumer to the price. Outstanding examples of this practice are Club Med and the all-inclusive resorts of Jamaica (Figure 9-5). Club Med started the trend with its "one price covers all" policy, sometimes even including airfare. Alcoholic drinks and incidentals are extra, however, but you "pay" for them with colored beads that you buy (they go on your bill) at the front desk and wear as a necklace. You are desensitized until you check out, but it works.

The all-inclusives have no extra charges; everything is "free" after you have paid one price (substantial) per week. An example of attempts to desensitize in restaurants is the use of prix fixe menus, with one inclusive price.

A good price/value relationship is another pricing objective that is a policy for many hospitality companies. This is another form of image enhancement, since the market is generally conceded to be very price/value sensitive, except for the high expense account customer. Restaurants in the middle to lower price ranges use this technique all the time in their advertising. Hotel companies are frequent proponents. In 1986, for example, the "new" Howard Johnson, then a new division of Prime Motor Inns, announced the opening of its first Howard Johnson Park Square Inn. The announcement was accompanied by this statement:

> "It's a unique product. It's something no one else can offer." . . . The target is between $45 and $60. Bean [vice-president of franchising] says that Howard Johnson's competitors, who are geared for the midpriced segment, have lost focus. "I see us as being in that very niche to a more sophisticated traveler, and to a businessman who wants a quality room and is still looking for price and value in a room."[15]

Whether these statements are true or mere wishful thinking remains to be established, however.

Two other customer objectives are worth mentioning. One is using pricing to differentiate the product, usually with higher prices. If the product appears essentially the same, then price can be used as a consumer perception mechanism to differentiate one product from another: The 12-ounce prime New York sirloin for $16.95 certainly must be better than the same item for $12.95 somewhere else. Another objective in the same vein is to introduce or promote added services and/or physical facilities. Concierge floors in hotels are priced in this manner, as are flambé desserts at tableside in restaurants. While it is difficult to justify the price differences for these services in the formal product, other core elements such as "prestige" may justify the cost to the buyer.

Cost Pricing

Cost-oriented pricing comes in a number of versions in the hospitality industry. Most popular among these are cost plus pricing, percentage or markup pricing, break-even pricing, contribution margin pricing, and $1 per thousand pricing. We will cover each of these briefly.

Cost Plus Pricing   This method involves establishing the total cost of a product, including overhead, plus a predetermined gross profit margin. Its common use in pricing food and beverages is to relate the gross profit margin to the selling price. Thus, if cost was to be 40 percent with a 60 percent gross profit, a $4 item would be priced at $10. Each product or product line is allocated an appropriate share of every type of expense as well as its own variable cost. The intent is that every product should be profit-generating.

The method ignores the notion that total income is a combined effort in which some products will not generate profit but will contribute to the whole. It is also subject to misallocation of costs such as depreciation, maintenance, and so on. Cost plus pricing does not allow for flexibility in pricing decisions nor does it take into consideration consumers' perceptions of a product's value. It is totally cost-oriented and ignores

---

[15] "Howard Johnson's New Market," *Restaurants & Institutions,* December 10, 1986, pp. 122–123.

demand. Attempts to apply different gross margin percentages to different menu items to account for different labor costs have done little to overcome the deficiencies of this method.

Cost Percentage or Markup Pricing   This method is heavily favored by the restaurant industry. It features either a dollar markup on the variable ingredient cost of the item, or a percentage markup based on the desired ingredient cost percentage, or a combination of both. A bottle of wine that costs $10 might be subject to a $5 markup, making the selling price $15. The markup percentage would be 50 percent of cost or 33⅓ percent of selling price. If, on the other hand, a 50 percent wine cost was desired, the bottle would be marked up 100 percent to make the selling price $20. A combination of both would be to mark the wine up 100 percent plus $2, making the selling price $22.

The foodservice industry appears to be enamored of this method of pricing. Food cost and liquor cost percentages become the standard by which results are measured. The major fallacies of this method are (1) that it ignores consumer perceptions of value, particularly in times of widely fluctuating costs; and (2) that it tends to price high-cost items up to a level that customers are unwilling to pay.

Break-even Pricing   Break-even pricing is used to determine at what sales volume and price a product will break even. It distinguishes between fixed costs and variable costs. The break-even point is graphically plotted for several prices using the same fixed and variable costs. By also plotting the quantity demanded at various prices, a revenue line is drawn so that a comprehensive picture of profit can be created at various demand levels.

Figures 14-2(a) and 14-2(b) demonstrate the process. Figure 14-2(a) shows a hypothetical break-even analysis for *price-sensitive* restaurants. In this case fixed costs are relatively low and unit varible costs are relatively high. Because of these factors, sales quickly pass the fixed cost line but the profit margin remains relatively narrow regardless of the quanity sold. This leaves relatively little room for discounting for purposes of increasing volume.

Figure 14-2(b) demonstrates a break-even analysis for *volume-sensitive* hotels. The fixed cost line in this case is higher and it takes longer for the sales line to pass it. Once past it, the profit margin widens quickly as variable costs remain a relatively small percentage of unit sales. There is more room for discounting to increase volume once the fixed and variable cost lines have been passed by the sales line.

Break-even analysis is a fairly efficient method of determining profit margins at various price levels if—and this is a big *if*—sales volume can be accurately predicted at the different price levels. To predict this volume, knowledge of consumer perception and demand is still needed.

Contribution Margin Pricing   This method is depicted in Figure 14-2(c). By contrast with (a) and (b), a variable cost line is interjected into the plot at the same place as the sales line, starting at the zero intersection. This demonstrates the concept of "contribution," showing that if the product sells at a higher price than its variable cost, then it makes a contribution to fixed cost even when sales are not high enough to produce a profit.

The technique is very useful for hotels in soft periods of demand. Room prices can be discounted substantially, if that is what it takes to have them occupied. Even though no

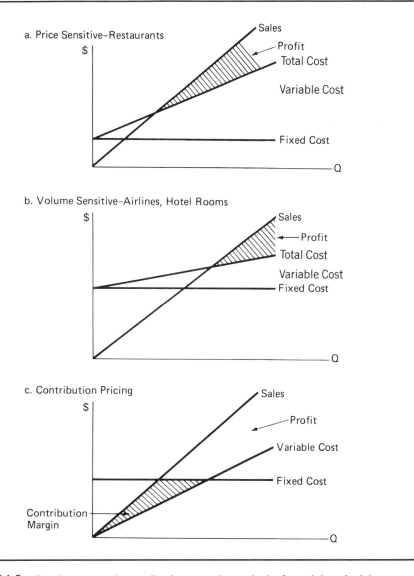

FIGURE 14-2   Break-even and contribution margin analysis for pricing decisions

profit results, a portion of the fixed cost will be covered that would occur even if the room was not occupied. The success of this technique depends on the demand generated eclipsing the regular rated customers' new-found discount. (See Figure 14-3.)

Contribution margin pricing is also another version of markup pricing that can be used beneficially in pricing food and beverages to overcome the problem of overhigh prices on high-cost items. For example, a $50 cost bottle of wine could be priced with a contribution margin of $25 for a selling price of $75. Wine cost percentage would then be

FIGURE 14-3　Discounting prices to maintain contribution margins

67 percent, a very high and forbidding percentage by industry standards. However, the contribution margin would be higher than on two $10 bottles sold at $20 each with a 50 percent wine cost.

$1 per Thousand Pricing   This is a method unique to establishing the selling price of hotel rooms. Although it should serve strictly as a rule of thumb, it is a widely proclaimed measure in the hotel industry. The rule is that the average room rate in a hotel should be $1 per every $1000 of construction cost per room. Thus if a hotel cost $80,000 per room to construct and furnish, the average selling price of the rooms would be $80.

This rule of thumb is somewhat archaic in today's world and totally ignores consumer perception and demand. It should be used more as a starting point than anything else. After the hotel is built, the rates are adjusted according to other factors.

Competitive Pricing

One of the most direct methods of determining price is to base it on what competitors charge. One has little choice but to stay in line with other properties offering *the same product in the same product class*. It is difficult to get higher prices, and lower prices will probably be met by competitors. Competitors' prices, both published and actual, are readily available, making it easy to use them as a benchmark.

Competitive pricing is viable as long as there is no consumer perception of significant differences among the entities, as long as one's cost structure allows pricing at that level, and assuming competitors' prices are set right at the beginning. This means that the market must be willing and able to buy at that level or, better, it means determining what the customer thinks is a fair value for the price.

For example, a new upscale hotel will price its rooms competitively with existing upscale hotels. That seems to work fine as long as the demand exists. If, however, present upscale hotels are running at low occupancy and the market has largely traded down, this may be sheer folly. It might be advantageous to position by pricing somewhere in between the two tiers, with the advantage of a better product than one and a lower price than the other. If existing upscale hotels react by meeting this lower rate the consequences will be the same. A positive effect, however, would be that at least the upscale properties together might take business back from the lower tier.

The other side of competitive pricing is that the *augmented* product is rarely ever the same, even in the same product class. This will make little difference—unless the customer perceives it to be so. One way to create that perception is with pricing as a tangible aspect of the product/service mix. When one prices above the direct competition, a statement is made that a better product is being offered. The reverse is true if one prices below. In the final analysis this is only a starting point; the market will make the final decision. Thus, it is inherently foolish to attempt to win the customer with pricing if the product is not there to support it.

A good example is a hotel in New York City that was running an average room rate of $86. New ownership and management took over and decided to go upscale after moderately refurbishing the hotel. Rack rates of $149 and $169 were posted. The market quickly perceived that the refurbishing was inadequate to justify this kind of price increase, and occupancy dropped. Not until rates were dropped to $109 did the hotel regain its market share. The same situation can also work in reverse: The same company opened a refurbished smaller hotel in a different location, and priced rooms at $95. The market saw an incredible value, because comparable hotels in the area were already at $125.

In restaurants there is far more variation in the product relative to the same product class. Atmospherics are probably more important, along with the menu items, the chef's preparation, the quality of food and drinks, and other variables. The need to maintain a strong pricing relationship with competitors is less acute. Restaurants have more opportunity to differentiate their product and should price accordingly, provided the market perceives that differentiation and is willing and able to pay for it.

Restaurants, more typically than hotels, will set lowball prices initially to create awareness and trial, steal customers, and build volume. This strategy is called penetration pricing because it is designed to penetrate the market. Once the business is established, it is not unusual for prices to be increased. Sometimes this works, and sometimes it backfires and business is lost, at which point it is far more difficult to lower prices and recapture the business. The image of being overpriced or having poor price/value is an enduring one with the consumer.

In setting prices, the marketer must always make conscious predictions about competitive reactions. Will they meet the prices? What will be the effect if they do/don't? What will undoubtedly become a classic textbook case is the case of People Express Airlines. By drastically reducing airfares, People captured enormous market share until the bigger carriers met them at the same price levels with a superior product. This eventually led to the demise of People.

Another classic case that demonstrates both an end run around the competition and the use of price to tangibilize the quality of the product is that of Smirnoff vodka.

> Vodka, by law in the United States, is essentially a commodity, an undifferentiated product. Smirnoff, through clever promotion, had captured major market share and led sales of all liquor brands in the United States.
>
> Wolfschmidt vodka was introduced by means of an advertising campaign that pictured a bottle of Wolfschmidt next to a bottle of Smirnoff. The caption stated that the only difference was the price and that Wolfschmidt was priced $1 below Smirnoff. Smirnoff was faced with the following dilemma: Maintain its price and lose market share, or lower its price and lose revenue.
>
> Smirnoff's wise decision was to do neither. Instead, Smirnoff raised its price and positioned as the premium brand worth the difference. It then brought out a new brand, Relska, priced at the same level as Wolfschmidt, and another brand, Popov, priced below Wolfschmidt. Although Wolfschmidt is still around, not many have heard too much about it since. There is a caveat in this story, however. Smirnoff was able to create the perception in the consumer's mind that its product was superior to Wolfschmidt's when, in fact, there is essentially no difference between them. If it had not been able to do this, the strategy would have failed.

The decision of whether to meet, ignore, or undercut a competitor's price moves is a situation-specific one. We can only caution here that the marketer should conduct a thorough analysis of the complete situation—the product, the market, and the competition—before establishing prices or reacting to the prices of others. This is not a time

TABLE 14-1   Competitive Information Needed for Pricing Strategy

1. Published competitive price lists and advertising
2. Competitive reaction to price moves in the past
3. Timing of competitors' price changes and initiating factors
4. Information on competitors' special campaigns
5. Competitive product-line comparison
6. Assumptions on competitors pricing/marketing objectives
7. Competitors' reported financial performance
8. Estimates of competitors' costs, fixed and variable
9. Expected pricing retaliation
10. Analysis of competitors' capacity to retaliate
11. Financial viability of engaging in price war
12. Strategic posture of competitors
13. Overall competitive aggressiveness

Source: Jain, 1985, p. 715
Subhash C. Jain, *Marketing Planning and Strategy,* Cincinnati: South-Western
Publishing, 1985, p. 715. Used by permission of the publisher.

for seat-of-the pants judgments, because the wrong decision can be near-fatal, as it was for Wolfschmidt. Jain suggests that one should have the information contained in Table 14-1.

Our discussion has centered on restaurant menu and liquor prices, and on hotel rack rates. For hotels, this is an inadequate discussion because of the rampant discounting that occurs. Because this practice deserves extended discussion on its own, it is covered in For Further Study at the end of this chapter.

For the moment, the emphasis is on the rack rate, because that is the published and most visible rate to the consumer. Thus, it is the most readily tangible presentation by price of the product. The share of the market that pays rack rate—1 percent to 90 percent, depending on the property—is nevertheless a critical share for those seeking to expand the market. Perhaps more critical are those customers who seldom enter the market because the rack rate is the only perception they have. For these, either the price/value/risk trade-off is not justified, or they are unwilling or unable to pay the price.

Market Demand Pricing

The term *market demand* covers a broad range of factors to be considered in any pricing decision. The appropriate term for the consideration of all these factors is *demand analysis*. Demand analysis should be a major portion of any feasibility study because it is the most critical element in selling a product. Demand analysis means more than demand for a product; it means, instead, asking whether there is a market sufficient in size that is willing and able to buy this product.

Sufficient demand means that there is a large enough market that wants the product. Let's simplify the problem and say the product is a Rolls Royce automobile. *Willing to buy* means that not only does the market want it, but there are sufficient number that are actually willing to buy it. For a Rolls Royce, the market is now considerably smaller. *Able to buy* means that those who are willing are also able—that is, they can afford it. Now we have a very small market.

With this information (and much else, of course) the makers of the Rolls Royce can make a pricing decision. The target market is very small so large quantities will not be sold, eliminating economies of scale. To make a reasonable profit or return on investment, the car will have to be priced considerably higher than its variable cost. Will the target market pay this inflated price? The willingness and ability exist. In fact, for this market, another $10, $20, or $30 thousand is not going to make much difference. The car can thus be priced at the appropriate level.

The same process applies to steak dinners, lobsters, flambé desserts, vacations, hotel rooms, suites, or any other product that is put out to market. If there is not sufficient market willing and able to buy, the product is doomed to failure. It doesn't matter what the costs are, what ROI is expected, how much advertising you do, what the guarantee is, or anything else. The critical question is simply, "What is the market acceptance level of price?"

The answer is not the simplest to find. Many don't find it until after the product has been marketed, for better or worse, but a careful analysis of the market beforehand can make life a great deal easier when the pricing decision is being made. The example was given above of a hotel in New York that tried and failed to price above the market. This is the same hotel described in the discussion on atmospherics in Chapter 13 as having made the same mistake in putting in a French bistro restaurant. In these cases the market was relatively easy to identify, but management chose to ignore it and go with its own whim.

There is another concept of demand analysis that is called demand or price elasticity, which was mentioned at the beginning of the chapter. The concept is covered fully in economics texts so it will not be discussed in detail here.[16] Suffice it to say that, generally speaking, elasticity means that the higher the price, the lower the demand; for instance, for the Rolls Royce. There is nothing pure about this concept, however, as we saw in the case of Smirnoff vodka. In the case of the Rolls Royce, we could say that *within* the target market, the product is inelastic—a few thousand more dollars is not going to affect demand.

Nevertheless, we cannot ignore the elasticity concept and we cannot ignore that this concept must be applied to the appropriate target market. This is especially true in the cases of hotels and restaurants where there are numerous alternatives. Alternative options increase the elasticity of the product. This is exactly why hotel rooms are subject to major discounting in order to obtain sufficient business.

The above point is demonstrated in a study conducted on hotel attributes as perceived by hotel guests in six major hotels in an eastern city. In this study, 19 percent of business travelers and 31 percent of pleasure travelers at one hotel (small, upscale) indicated that price was a determinant factor in choosing a hotel. At another hotel (large, convention type), 51 percent of business travelers and 72 percent of pleasure travelers said

---

[16] The simplest and most common equation for elasticity is percent change in price divided by percent change in quantity sold equals degree of elasticity, that is, the proportionate change in demand relative to the change in price represents the degree of elasticity.

that price was a determinant factor. Yet, and this is an important yet, only 1 percent of all travelers at the first hotel and only 9 percent of those at the second hotel said that price was the reason they chose that specific hotel.[17]

There are a number of other points in regard to market demand that affect pricing that we will not discuss in detail, but will mention briefly. The list is not all-inclusive but only suggests elements of the identified and appropriate target markets that must be considered.

Usage. How is the product used? Business purposes, pleasure, or personal? What are the users' life-styles? Do they use it because it is convenient or do they make a special effort to come here? Do they buy on price? Do they shop for the best price? Is it the main usage in this area or an alternative? Do they use it regularly or just for special occasions? Do they use the whole product or just part of it? Do they use it seasonally, cyclically, at certain times, on certain days, during certain periods? Are there different target market differences? How many are on expense accounts? Use credit cards? Come through agents who receive commissions from us?

Alternatives. What are the competitive options? Upscale, downscale? Other locations? What are nonprice alternatives such as staying with friends or staying home?

Demand satisfaction. Is there unfulfilled demand or is the market saturated? What is the market acceptance level? Is the quality level satisfied? What is the generic demand as opposed to the brand demand? Are the available product/service mixes appropriate? How many customers are in the market? Is the number increasing or decreasing? Do demand differentials reflect differential costs?

Economic conditions. Good? Bad? Inflationary? Is promotional and discount pricing in vogue? Will we have to compete?

Customer Pricing

Here again we refer to the target market. Because we have discussed the customer in some detail already we will not reiterate all the elements that need to be considered in pricing the product. The reader knows by now that in using any marketing tool, such as pricing, the customer is the first consideration. The short treatment here is not intended to cast any doubt on that notion.

Price/Value In establishing prices, some elements are particularly pertinent in regard to the customer. The first of these is the perceived price/value relationship, as it is commonly called. Given that the customer is willing and able to buy, this is the first price consideration in a purchase decision. It may not be articulated in exactly those words, but by whatever words and by whatever criteria, it is this element that will establish the correct pricing levels.

There are many criteria to serve the customer in the price/value appraisal. Each customer will make different trade-offs such as location for price, prestige for price, service for price, quality for price, and so forth. All will evaluate in terms of the quality of

---

[17] Robert C. Lewis, "The Basis of Hotel Selection," *Cornell Hotel and Restaurant Administration Quarterly,* May 1984, pp. 54–69.

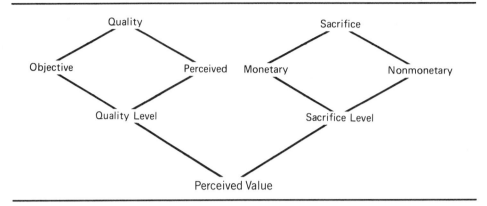

FIGURE 14-4   The relationship between quality, sacrifice, and value

the entire experience (i.e., the total product), but each will evaluate the benefit bundle by different criteria.

The hospitality industry places special emphasis on the price/value relationship. It is not at all uncommon for an executive or a manager to state, "We give price/value," or "Our distinction is the price/value we give," when asked to identify their marketing strength. Often, however, the concept of price/value is in the mind of management or in the product quality level (e.g., bathroom amenities) rather than in the mind of the consumer.

Price/value is a complex consumer construct that needs to be better understood, because it includes a number of other constructs. These constructs include both objective and perceived quality, both monetary and nonmonetary sacrifice, and value—the perceived relationship between quality and sacrifice. This relationship is shown in Figure 14-4.

In practice, quality is most often operationally or physically defined by management, and is objective in nature, giving rise to such statements as "Our service is the best," "Our food is excellent," or "Our atrium lobby is the highest in the world." In essence, these are cognitive beliefs attributed to objects, as discussed in Chapter 6.

Perceived quality by the consumer, on the other hand, is more likely to be affective and/or experiential, especially in the case of hospitality services. The objective quality of the atrium lobby may be negated by the perceived quality that is experienced from the noise that resounds across the atrium. Thus the objective price established by management may differ considerably from what the perceptive price should be to the consumer. In fact, a rude desk clerk or waiter can, instantaneously, change a "fair" objective price to an "unfair" perceived price.

Sacrifice is both monetary and nonmonetary, as with inconvenience, time, and experience. Thus, the meal or room, and their respective objective qualities, may justify the monetary price. The perceived quality, on the other hand—such as an experience with a rude employee, a noisy atrium, a long wait for the elevator, the raucous music in the lounge, or the menu with print too small to read—may well not justify either the monetary or the nonmonetary (experience) sacrifice.

The implication of this discussion and the model in Figure 14-4 is that the so-called price/value relationship is actually something more complex. The ultimate objective of management should be to increase perceived value. If management can truthfully say, "Our unique difference is greater *perceived* value" (at any price), then and only then has the ultimate objective been reached. This means, as well, that management recognizes that perceived value is a function of objective and perceived quality, monetary and nonmonetary sacrifice, as shown in Figure 14-4.

There is much talk in the hospitality industry about quality, as we have previously discussed. Too often, however, quality is not measured by guest perception. Only by using guest perception as the standard—and matching objective quality to perceived quality—can management establish the right price that results in the right so-called price/value relationship. This in turn will lead to information on how to add value, in a true sense, that increases the price/value relationship and/or truly justifies the raising of prices.

Expectation Pricing   As we know from Chapter 1, consumers purchase problem solutions based on expectations. Let's turn that around and say that consumers also have in mind a price they expect to pay for a given solution. Reactions to prices will vary around this expected price. This is an important concept to grasp.

We know from the research on customer satisfaction that satisfaction occurs when the actual experience is equal to or greater than what is expected. Thus, consumers would be most satisfied when the price paid is the same or less than what they expected to pay. The old adage "You get what you pay for" has been proven incorrect too many times but, nevertheless, still forms a basis for consumer expectations. Satisfaction occurs when customers feel they got what they paid for.

Research has also shown that consumers, in some arbitrary fashion, establish an upper price level at which they deem a product to be too expensive, and a lower price level below which the quality of a product would be suspect. In between is the "indifference" price, the price perceived as normal for that product in a given market. The "normal" price will vary according to previous experience, self-image, societal expectations, and the context of the purchase, depending upon the item and the consumer. This concept is called price sensitivity.[18]

Clearly, there are certain hotels and restaurants in both the same and different areas at which we would expect to pay different prices. When we are "surprised" by an unexpected price, we may tend to become somewhat irate. Thus, it behooves the price-setter not to surprise the customer.

Expectations should be built into the pricing decision. Research can determine what the market thinks the product should cost. This can be especially useful in the pricing of services where a cost basis is lacking for developing an expectation. Findings may indicate that the service can be priced higher; contrarily, a lower-than-expected price may offer competitive advantage.

---

[18] See, e.g., *Price Sensitivity Measurement*, Los Angeles: Plog Research, Inc.

Knowledge of price expectation can help avoid both overpricing and underpricing, such that the quality is suspect, or that the product is positioned as "cheap" and retains that position later when the price has been increased, thus later appearing overpriced. People do change their expectations to adjust to changes in pricing levels (e.g., the cost of gasoline from 39 cents a gallon to $1.39 a gallon and back down to 99 cents a gallon over a twelve-year period). The current heavy discounting in hotel rooms suggests that the consumer has actually not adjusted to the continuous rate increases of recent years.

Psychological Pricing   Prices cause psychological reactions on the part of consumers just as atmospherics do. As noted, high prices may imply quality and low prices may imply inferiority. Thus, higher-priced items may sell better whereas lower-priced items may sell poorly, in defiance of the standard economic model. Psychological reactions, however, do not necessarily correspond to reality, and it is not unusual for consumers to learn that they have made a mistake. When reality is juxtaposed with perception, psychological pricing can succeed in both creating and keeping a customer.

This is especially true in the hospitality industry because of the "visibility" factor. Being "seen" at an upscale restaurant or hotel is very important to some customers. For example, a businessman might buy inexpensive furniture for his apartment and drink Gilbey's gin in his martini at home. This same businessman, trying to make an impression on peers and customers, will rave about the antique furniture in the hotel lounge and the Beefeater gin in his martini—in other words, he wants to be seen with the product that offers the highest affordable visibility factor.

Buyers and nonbuyers of products also have different perceptions of price. This contrast can be demonstrated best with the case of upscale restaurants. Many such restaurants are perceived by those who have never been there to be far more expensive than is actually the case. For increasing market share, it is important to understand the price perceptions of nonusers as well as users.

Another psychological pricing technique is called price-lining. This technique clumps prices together so that a perception of substantially increased quality is created. For example, a wine list might have a group of wines in the $8–$10 range and have the next grouping in the $14–$16 range. The perception is a definite increase in quality, which may or may not be the case.

Still another version of psychological pricing is called odd numbered pricing. This is a familiar tactic to all of us. Items sell at $6.99 rather than $7.00 to create the perception of a lower price. Sometimes this is carried to an extreme, as with a computer that sells for $6,999.99. This tactic is most commonly used in menu pricing. A study by Kreul of 242 restaurants showed that 58 percent of menu prices ended in 9, 35 percent ended in 5, and only 6 percent ended in 0.[19] The effectiveness of this technique is questionable but, nevertheless, it is widely used.

All these differences in consumers' perception might seem to make pricing an impossible task. Perhaps that is why so often hotels and restaurants tend to ignore the customer and to price according to other factors! Consumer-based pricing is not impos-

---

[19] Lee M. Kreul, "Magic Numbers: Psychological Aspects of Menu Pricing," *Cornell Hotel and Restaurant Administration Quarterly,* August 1982, pp. 70–75.

sible, however. It is the virtue of target marketing that relatively homogeneous markets are pinpointed and that the product and the price are designed for those markets.

The marketer should also be aware—very aware—of how the customer uses price to differentiate competing products and services. This is a key to positioning with price. Value perception is always relative to the competition, whether the value perceived is real or imagined. The simplicity or complexity of the customer decision process will find a way to sort all this out. It is the marketer's or the price-setter's job to understand this process.

As an example of what we have just said, consider the case of a major hotel chain that conducted price research in one of its major market areas. Following are some of the findings and conclusions of the research.

> The research revealed a steady loss of regular-rated room nights and revenue—that is, there was enough increase in discounted transient room nights to make published rack rates virtually meaningless. Moreover, many of these rooms were being sold at rates below the corporte rate. This trend had led to declining average rates overall, with almost half of the room nights being sold at deep discounts. Although published and corporate rates had increased dramatically, discount rates had remained flat. In regard to customers, this research also had some interesting findings. For one, the pricing strategy was building loyalty and repeat business with the "wrong" target markets. Customers were found to have a high degree of rate awareness that influenced their value perception and intention to return; corporate- and regular-rate customers felt the hotels were overpriced. The indifference price was found to be as much as $25 lower than the regular or corporate rates being charged. For discount customers, however, it was slightly higher than what they were paying. In addition, corporate- and regular-rate customers gave the hotels lower value ratings, and the higher the rate they paid, the less likely they were to return. Market share of high-rated customers was being lost to competitors. Furthermore, reservation incentive systems designed to obtain higher rates from customers were, in fact, damaging long-term profitability by alienating customers. One important conclusion of these findings was that by reducing high rates and raising discount rates, the market mix could be changed so as to produce increased profits in the long run.

Common Mistakes in Pricing

The following list summarizes the most frequent pitfalls of pricing. Because pricing is the most flexible part of the presentation mix, it requires constant evaluation. Those who evaluate their pricing should check their pricing strategies against this list.

1. Prices are too cost-oriented. They are increased to cover increased costs and don't allow for demand intensity and customer psychology.
2. Price policies are not adapted to changing market conditions. Once established they become "cast in cement."
3. Prices are set independent of the product mix rather than as an element of positioning strategy. Integration of all elements of the marketing mix is essential.

4. Prices ignore the customer psychology of experience, perception of value, and the total product. These are the true elements of price perception that will influence the choice process.
5. Prices are a decision of management, rather than marketing.

In the final analysis, the best price is the one that makes the best overall contribution.

Summary

Pricing is a complex marketing tool but it is, first and foremost, a marketing tool. Thus, by definition, pricing is customer-based and customer-driven. Pricing is also a tangible aspect of the product/service offered. As such, it can be utilized to change and manipulate customer perception. The effective marketer must understand this process.

The first step in establishing prices is to identify the target market objectives in terms of financial objectives, volume objectives, and customer objectives. The marketing mix strategy should be based on these objectives and the customers' needs and wants. Cost and competitive pressures establish constraints. Finally, it is the market demand and the customers themselves that will determine the appropriate pricing strategy and actual setting of the pricing schedule.

DISCUSSION QUESTIONS

1. Discuss the three types of pricing objectives, how they are different, and how they overlap.
2. Why is using only cost percentage pricing methods not recommended as a marketing-driven option, especially in the hospitality industry?
3. Research two competitive hotels or restaurants and analyze their pricing in conjunction with the competitive pricing section.
4. Discuss your personal pricing elasticity in terms of restaurants; that is, at what point in the price/value mode will you trade down?
5. Discuss how psychological pricing can make a product seem to have a higher price/value relationship.
6. Choose two common mistakes in pricing and apply them to a real-life hospitality establishment.

FOR FURTHER STUDY

Special Issues in Hotel Pricing

This section pertains particularly to hotels. Although restaurants also discount and quote prices, treatment of their practices will be covered in Chapter 16 under the topic of promotions. Such discounts are normal operational practices. So too are discounts for urban hotels on weekends, for resort hotels in off-seasons, and other hotels during slow periods. This is logical and rational business practice designed to create the perception of value and create new business when it is needed.[20]

Hotel pricing and discounting, as will be discussed here, deal with the universal practice of recent years, in the upper end of the market, of periodically raising rack rates beyond the level of reality (above the consumer price index and the inflation rate, and in the face of declining or static occupancy rates) with the full knowledge that most rooms will be sold at a discounted price. The practice of discounting has been subjected to both criticism and praise.

The second issue discussed in this section is price quoting. This has been discussed by others under the guise of "selling up," "selling down," and "what price do you tell the customer?" These are all marketing issues that warrant insight.

Special Prices and Discounting[21]

There are two major justifications given by hotel management for pricing high and then discounting. The first is that if rooms were not priced so high there would be no room for discounting: "Because everyone wants a discount, we have to price high enough to be able to give it to them." The second justification is that if rack rates were at a lower level, "the 10 percent who don't know any better and pay the rack rate would pay a lower price, so what do we have to lose?"

Both arguments have inherent weaknesses, as is supported by empirical counterevidence. Counterevidence can be found in the automobile industry, which currently follows the same practice and is at a loss to understand the quandary it is in, and in the airline industry, which has followed the opposite practice (for whatever reason) and has increased its customer base dramatically by doing so.

At the time of this writing, the upscale hotel industry in the United States is undergoing the same trauma that the Japanese caused the automobile industry. The "Japanese" in this case are the budgets, the middle tier, and the all-suites properties. The surviving airlines, at this time, are poised on the threshold of a new era of opportunity, although badly damaged from years of price wars.

The Ills of Discounting   Much has been written about the ills of discounting hotel rooms. Authors such as Sumner, Buttle, Greenberg, and Abbey have gone to considerable length to explain the woes and deficiencies of discounting hotel rooms. They have

---

[20] Although some hotel managements seem to underestimate the power of perception. In Bermuda, the slow winter season is called "Rendezvous Season: All of Bermuda without the crowds and the high prices." The normal discount of hotel rooms from in-season rates was 20 percent. Thus, a $240 room cost only $192. Occupancy on the island at this time was fairly consistent year after year at around 27 percent. Palm Springs, California, had the same problem in the summer. Hotels there discounted rooms 50 percent and more. Occupancies ran over 50 percent in the off-season, more than covering operating costs and maintaining employee payrolls. See Robert C. Lewis and Thomas J. Beggs, "Selling Bermuda in the Off-Season," in *The Complete Travel Marketing Handbook*, Andrew Vladimir, ed. Chicago: National Textbook Co., 1988, Chapter 11, pp. 101–108.

[21] Much of this section is taken from an article by the senior author. See Robert C. Lewis, "Customer-Based Hotel Pricing," *Cornell Hotel and Restaurant Administration Quarterly*, August 1986, pp. 18–21.

carefully explained the amount of increased business necessary to compensate for the discounting.[22]

Janet Carroll of Laventhol & Horwath also contends that discounting "may not be the most profitable way to fill hotel rooms."[23] She shows that the average discount at resorts was 28.1 percent in 1984 and 23.5 percent in 1985; for center-city properties it was 20 percent and 23 percent; for airport properties it was 28 percent and 24 percent, respectively. Overall, the industry discounted 19.9 percent in 1985. According to Carroll, "Discounting is apparently damaging to the bottom line."

The general tenor of these works is that "discounting doesn't pay," but none of the authors offer a solution as to what to do when you don't discount and the customers stop coming. Whether or not the industry is overbuilt—and that is a moot question, as we have already stated—the fact is that the industry is where it is in the current marketplace. To survive, one has to do something better than the competition.

The same situation occurred concurrently in the computer industry. Although weaker companies lost out, the industry as a whole lowered prices, increased its customer base, and went about improving its product. Why is the solution for the hotel industry to raise prices? Barring illegal collusion on prices, what would the hotel bottom line look like if they had refused to discount? The dissenting authors mentioned above tend to ignore the alternative. As someone once said, "Growing old isn't so bad when you consider the alternative."

The Real Problem   We have no conceptual disagreement with the arguments against discounting. Our argument instead takes a different position: The problem is not one of the sagacity of discounting; the problem is the artificial establishment of rack rates at astronomical levels in the first place. In essence, at least the upscale end of the hotel industry is killing the goose that lays the golden eggs.

Hotel rack rate increases of recent years have been almost totally driven by the bottom line and by the mental disposition that the way to increase profits is to raise prices and cut costs. Yet the bottom line doesn't seem to get much better, as Carroll points out. No price is too high when there are people willing and able to pay it; when they aren't, the pricing needs another look. When corporate dictates "raise the numbers" (rates and occupancy), and one goes up while the other goes down, the time seems overdue for someone to take another look at the hotel customer.

In October 1986, a front-page news item in the *Wall Street Journal* stated the following:

---

[22] J. R. Sumner, *Improve Your Marketing Techniques: A Guide for Hotel Managers and Caterers*, Sussex, UK: Northwood Publications, 1982, pp. 82–83; Francis Buttle, *Hotel and Food Service Marketing: A Managerial Approach*, London: Holt, Rinehart and Winston, 1986, pp. 266–267; Carol Greenberg, "Room Rates and Lodging Demand," *Cornell Hotel and Restaurant Administration Quarterly*, November 1985, pp. 10–11 (this article states that "overall, lodging demand is relatively 'price-inelastic'—in other words, an industry-wide cut in prices will simply reduce lodging-industry revenues," a statement that is contrary to what is happening in the industry); James Abbey, "Is Discounting the Answer to Declining Occupancies?" *International Journal of Hospitality Management*, Vol. 2, No. 2, 1983, pp. 77–82. Abbey is probably not in total disagreement with us when he states, in conclusion, "Certainly the room rates of many properties may need to be reevaluated considering the piece-meal treatment received during their rapid rise prior to the recent recession."

[23] Janet D. Carroll, "Focus on Discounting Hotel Rack Rates," *Cornell Hotel and Restaurant Administration Quarterly*, August 1986, p. 13.

Travel costs become a prime target for a growing number of businesses. Steadily rising travel expenses prompt more companies to apply standard purchasing procedures to "what was once a very personal, private activity." . . . The tax act, which limits travel-cost deductions, will provide many companies with a good excuse to crack down further. . . . Standard Oil Co., for example, uses its clout to negotiate hotel rates 25% lower than usual corporate rates.[24]

This is only one of many similar news items in both the trade and business press over the last few years, yet the warnings have been largely ignored.[25] Most of the industry (there are notable exceptions) see this as an industry problem. It is not. It is a consumer problem; consumers don't want to pay the price being asked for what they are getting! There are also a multitude of news items that make this point, like the following:

During the course of my career [as an investment banker], I probably logged over a million miles on the road. I got really tired of standing in long lines to check into my room and of staying in hotels that were cold and lonely and charged you $150 a night.[26]

What has happened is this. The hotel industry has interpreted the demand for quality accommodations as a mandate to raise prices and add services and amenities of questionable value. Lines at front desks are just as long in spite of computers. Guests are no cleaner, nor do they smell any better, in spite of all those bathroom amenities. Chocolates on the pillow don't compensate for noisy rooms, lengthy van waits, "guaranteed" reservations that aren't, poorly staffed desks, unmanned special check-in stations, poor attitudes, or sloppy service.[27] Service aspects of frequent traveler programs give a few customers what all customers, those paying for the programs through higher room rates, should be receiving.

The hotel industry's position seems to be this: "Pay your money and see what we can give you in return." The historic attitude of customers is the opposite: "Offer me value; if you do, I'll pay the price." As Ted Levitt noted in the retrospective written some years after his classic article,

To be sure, sellers said, "We have to provide service," but they tended to define service by looking into the mirror rather than out the window. They *thought* they were looking out the window at the customer, but it was actually a mirror—a reflection of their customers' situations.[28]

Thus, customers demand hotel discounts just as they do for overpriced automobiles. They always will, too, because that is the natural reaction of customers when they don't believe the product is worth the price. Is this just because there is overbuilding? No, it is also because customers now have alternatives spawned by overcharging in the first place, just as Levitt warned in 1960.

---

[24] *Wall Street Journal,* October 23, 1986, p. 1.

[25] See, for example, Steven J. Stark, "Biz Travelers Increasingly Being Steered to Budget Hotels," *Business Travel News,* April 14, 1986, pp. 22–24.

[26] Maria Lenhart, "Smaller Hotels Are Providing Cozy Alternative in S.F.," *Business Travel News,* July 27, 1987, p. 30.

[27] This list is taken from the "litany of gripes heard from hotel guests," in "Hotels and Frequent Flyers: The Changing Relationship," *Frequent Flyer,* August, 1986, p. 69.

[28] Levitt, "Marketing Myopia."

The Rate-Sensitive Customer   Rate-sensitive guests, the vast majority today,[29] either find a discount price, book at a lower-priced property (to heck with location!), or don't use a hotel at all—and this includes many travelers on expense accounts. In essence, it would be foolhardy to pay rack rate for an upscale hotel room unless a convention or some other situation has filled up the destination.

One hotel executive, when asked if the 10 percent of his market that paid rack rate wasn't getting a bad deal, replied, "We don't care about them." Can you imagine the airlines saying that? Overbuilding? Perhaps in some areas, but a basic economic tenet is being ignored: When you increase supply you have to increase demand. You don't increase demand by raising prices, or by giving customers "extras" that they don't need or want. You do it by *solving customers' problems*. (Refer to our discussion of the pleasure traveler in Chapter 9.)

Let's take that one step further, into other areas of hotel pricing. Assume you go to a hotel and pay the rack rate of $160. Now what? You order a bottle of scotch. Across the street in the package store it's $12; from room service it's $45 plus a 15 percent service charge. You want a hamburger and it's anywhere from $8 to $12. In the morning, you decide room service is too expensive so you go to the coffee shop, where you pay $15 for juice, coffee, an egg, and a Danish—plus tip, for a waiter you had to hunt for to get your coffee cup refilled. Note the following trade press item.

> After scaring off breakfast patrons with high prices, hotel restaurants are attempting to lure back guests and local customers by featuring more unusual and healthful foods, speeding up service and positioning themselves as meeting sites. ". . . even if the food were free [in New York], a hotel would still have to get at least $12 just to break even on labor [for breakfast]."[30]

Across the street the same breakfast sold for $1.79. Somewhere, someone is missing the boat. Somewhere there is an opportunity, and it's not in "breakfast pizza, bagel benedict and quiches, waffles and pancakes covered with fresh fruit," as one hotel cited in Romeo's article is offering. A menu like that does not solve the customer's problem. Albert Kelly, regional vice president and then managing director of the Hyatt Regency Grand Cypress, Orlando, said it this way:

> I see hoteliers and restaurateurs who, when faced with declining profits, respond in a knee-jerk manner rather than to the conditions that caused it. . . . The manager . . . usually will choose the well-traveled managerial route. . . . The product will be of lesser quality, and the sales figures will reflect customer displeasure. . . . The manager's response again will be to streamline the operation . . . and so on and so forth . . . until labor costs collide with lack of sales. . . . The solution is to adjust prices upward in order to produce the desired margins.

---

[29] At least 74 percent of the market according to recent research. See "Business and Pleasure Use of Lodging Segments." *Lodging Hospitality,* June 1988, p. 18.

[30] Peter Romeo, "Hotels Work to Justify High Cost of Morning Fare," *Nation's Restaurant News,* February 17, 1986, p. F19.

The resulting customer response will be one of the following:

A. To tolerate the initial increase;

B. To order the less expensive dishes, or;

C. Not to frequent the establishment at all.

As the scenario is repeated, more customers choose options B and C until, finally, the restaurant loses its market.[31]

Once again, listen to the customer:

> One thing consistently bugged me during our four-day stay [at a five-star hotel]. Every time we asked for something—ice, extra towels, an iron—. . . I felt obliged to lay a couple of bucks across somebody's outstretched hand. I know that sounds cheap, but when you're spending $200 for a night's stay, I think service people should be falling all over themselves to do whatever I ask them to do. How else can somebody justify asking those prices?[32]

Whether to discount is not even the question in these situations. Discounting is a promotional tool for slow periods or for getting rid of merchandise you don't want anymore. The answer is setting rates and prices based on the customer as the focal point. Set prices fairly, stick to them, and tell customers what they'll get for their money—the solutions to their specific problems . . . and make sure they are delivered. You can pay $5000 more for a different grill and have the same car called a Rolls Royce instead of a Bentley, if that's something you really need, but you have the option!

Solving the Problem   Robert Hazard, CEO of Quality International, is one hotel executive who seems to understand the problem. He states,

> The secret to success in the lodging business will be to provide guests with higher quality and better value at reasonable prices. Those who improve their price-value perception will tap into a nearly inexhaustible supply of new guests. Those who ignore it will choke on an ever-expanding supply of empty new rooms.[33]

The general industry reaction has been to choke, while sitting around and moaning about overbuilding.[34] Others sit around and have executive brainstorming sessions about what else to offer customers "to accommodate their every wish." ("How about *two* chocolates on the pillow?" or, "Better frequent traveler prizes?" or, "Condoms in bathroom amenities packages?") Very few are talking to the customer, or talking to the front-line employee to find out what the customer's problems really are. To paraphrase George Bernard Shaw, "There are two kinds of people: Those who accept the world as it is, and those who try to change it. Progress is made by the second kind." The hotel industry seems to be ready for more of the second kind.

Actually, not quite everyone is complaining about overbuilding. Some hotel operators aren't saying a thing; they are too busy finding out what the customer wants at which price. These are the operators who will still be around after the industry shakeout is over.

---

[31] Albert J. Kelly, Jr., "Band-Aids Are No Remedy for Bottom-Line Diseases," *Hotel & Motel Management*, April 7, 1986, p. 102b.

[32] Michael DeLuca, "What I Did on My Summer Vacation," *Hotel & Motel Management*, August 17, 1987, p. 6.

[33] Robert C. Hazard, Jr., "Bracing for the Changes Ahead in the Hotel Industry," *Business Travel News*, May 13, 1985, p. 26.

[34] See, for example, "The State of the Industry," *Cornell Hotel and Restaurant Administration Quarterly*, May 1986, pp. 20–27.

Hazard of Quality International, quoted above, and Michael Leven of Days Inn (who calls for an end to frequent user programs and putting the money back into the physical and human product, or even lowering the prices as an alternative[35]), are well known dissenters of the "give 'em more and raise the prices" syndrome that pervades the industry. "But they're not in the upper tier of the industry," say the proponents. Listen then to Pecco Beaufays, vice president, sales and marketing, for Kempinski International, a luxury German-based hotel chain now entering the United States with its first hotel in Dallas. Within a year of its takeover of the former Registry Hotel, Kempinski increased occupancy from 45 to 56 percent in a so-called overbuilt city suffering from decreasing occupancy rates.

> We want business travelers to know that when they stay at a Kempinski hotel they will receive the best possible service available. We don't try to sway them with the promise of extraordinary amenities and better service if they book a room on the concierge floor at a higher rate. We have no differentiation: our entire hotel is a concierge hotel—each guest receives the same special service and amenities.
> . . . these are amenities that Kempinski hotels have always offered their guests— not new promotional inducements aimed at luring away travelers from the competition.
> . . . we are so attuned to their needs and pay strict attention to detail. . . . We anticipate their needs and treat each one as a VIP—it's a type of hospitality that most Americans aren't accustomed to.[36]

Recall from Chapter 3, the 1986 study that showed only 2 percent of business travelers consider a frequent traveler program in choosing a hotel, and only 6 percent belong to these programs. A 1988 study by ConStat Inc. shows that only 10 percent of customers bother to take advantage of these programs, but 86 percent are dissatisfied with room service—a service many hotels consider necessary but unprofitable, and thus often inadequately staff or plan.[37]

There is progress in sight. Hilton's new 1988 senior vice president of marketing, Michael Ribero, plans to use in-depth research "to get to the bottom of what business travelers are looking for on a business trip." This is a far cry from a former Hilton marketing vice president who, when asked how Hilton profiles its guests, replied, "We ask the desk clerks."

Marketing is a customer-focused practice. Pricing is a marketing tool and should be used with the long-term customer in mind. The industry needs to develop more sophisticated, integrated marketing and pricing strategies that respond to supply and demand. It must learn to sell rooms on a demand basis with a "flexible rate system that will generate new traffic and produce a greater overall yield to the hotel."[38] The hotel industry should woo rate-sensitive customers before they are lost completely, and the effort begins with customer pricing and value.

---

[35] Paris R. Wolfe, "A Sharp Point About Point Systems," *Lodging Hospitality*, June 1988, p. 118.
[36] Quoted in J. Herbert Silverman, "The Foreign Factor," *Hotel & Resort Industry*, June 1988, pp. 72–73.
[37] Howard Riell, "The Hard Facts Shaping Our Industry," *Restaurant Business*, July 1, 1988, p. 2.
[38] Hazard, "Bracing for Changes."

Price Quoting

The issue of how to quote hotel room prices when a customer calls and asks for a rate is an old one. Many authors of books on the industry, but not all, recommend that hotels should quote the highest rate first and then come down only if they meet buyer resistance. Other authors talk about "up-selling"; quote a low or middle rate but immediately try to up-sell the advantages of a room at a higher rate. Various hotel companies have various policies and practices, including practices that are different from their own policies.[39]

Policies and Practices   All of the literature and almost all of the companies' policies are aimed at maximizing room revenue, a laudable aim. For example, Quain and Hermann contended that "good business sense would dictate [quoting] the higher-price rooms first, and marketing the lower-price rooms only if the higher rates were unacceptable to potential guests" (p. 73). While this may make good business sense, we are not convinced that it makes good marketing sense, because it ignores the customer.

Following up on the previous discussion on excessive rack rates, quoting higher priced rooms first may actually lose the customer. In many situations that we have tracked and with many hotel customers we have talked to, we have found that the hotel reservationist does *not* "market the lower-price rooms" when resistance is met. Often this is because the reservationist makes no attempt to do so. More often it is because they never get the chance; the customer hangs up and the room sale is lost forever. Here's an example:

> A friend of not considerable means wanted to take his wife to Boston for a weekend. He called a major hotel and was quoted the rack rate of $140. He hung up and went, instead, to a Holiday Inn at less than half the price. It was later learned that the first hotel had a 40 percent occupancy that night and a weekend package at a considerably lower and acceptable price.

In the body of Chapter 14 we discussed consumer price expectations. Let's accept that business travelers, frequent travelers, and in fact most hotel guests know what to expect in a room rate. They also know how to ask for corporate discounts or weekend package rates. Let's assume, for the sake of argument, that these people will find their own level of room rate regardless of what is quoted first.[40]

Telling the Customer   Who is left? No one but that same 10 percent to 20 percent who "don't know any better"—the same people who learned to fly commercial airlines after the tariffs came down. These are also the same people whom hotels need to expand their customer base, and the same market that Levitt calls a "growth opportunity." This is the first problem: rack rates are so high that the easiest way to lose customers is to quote the highest rack rate and lead them to believe that that is the only rate available.

---

[39] See William J. Quain, Jr., and Peter W. Hermann, "What Happens When Guests Call," *Cornell Hotel and Restaurant Administration Quarterly,* May 1982, pp. 70–73; and Robert C. Lewis and Christopher Roan, "Selling What You Promote," *Cornell Hotel and Restaurant Administration Quarterly,* May 1986, pp. 13–15. Much of this section is drawn from the article by Lewis and Roan.

[40] In fairness, recent changes in some hotels' practices have recognized this trend. At least on 800 lines, many are switching from the traditional top-down approach, that is, quoting the highest price first and coming down only if the customer shows resistance. Most of these changes are to quote middle rates first. In some cases, in slow time periods, the lowest rate is being quoted first.

Even more common and more self-defeating is the second problem: discounting the rack rate and not telling the customer about it! Consider the following example:

It was June 20, 1986. I had to be in a certain city from Wednesday to Sunday in early August. In a full-page ad in *The Wall Street Journal,* I saw a national hotel chain's offer of a special summer rate of $69 for its property in that city. I called the 800 number and had the following conversation:

Me: I'd like to book a room in August. Could I have the special rate of the association I belong to?

Hotel: Rooms are available, but not at that rate.

Me: Why is that?

Hotel: Each hotel decides for itself, and we are fairly busy at that time.

Me: What rate is available?

Hotel: $135 per night.

Me: Is that all?

Hotel: Yes.

Me: What happened to the $69 rate advertised on a full page of *The Wall Street Journal?*

Hotel: I don't know anything about that. What did it say? [I retrieved the ad and read it.] Oh, yes, we have those. Those are class D rooms but they're all gone.

Me: How come you didn't know about these rooms before I mentioned them?

Hotel: It's because they come up on a different screen. I was looking at the screen for the rate for Friday and Saturday?

Me: How about a weekend rate for Friday and Saturday?

Hotel: Yes, we have a special weekend rate of $84. That's a class E room but none are available.

Me: Is a class E room smaller than a class D room?

Hotel: Right.

Me: So my only choice is $135?

Hotel: Right.

Me: [I had stayed at that hotel before, and it's not worth $135.] Thank you, but I will look elsewhere.

Hotel: Thank you and have a good day.

The rest of this story is that the person who told it had a friend who worked at the front desk of the hotel in question. Out of curiosity, he found out what the occupancy was on the days of his proposed stay: 72, 68, 58, and 45 percent for those four days, respectively.

At the same time as the incident described above, three other major chains were nationally advertising similarly low weekend rates at all their hotels. Phone calls to these chains' 800 numbers requesting the advertised rate at randomly selected properties revealed that 12 of the 18 selected hotels were sold out. We can only assume that, very suddenly, 67 percent of these chains' hotels were full on weekends.

If we assume that these rooms would otherwise be vacant, a good case can be made for discounting. In fact, however, those chains that continued the program applauded its success in increasing occupancy by 10 percent, which would mean that occupancy had been 90 percent before the promotion, a condition we know not to have existed.

The research by Lewis and Roan indicates, in fact, like the above example, that hotels are very reluctant to admit that weekend discounts exist, even when asked about them and even after spending hundreds of thousands of dollars promoting them.

Two hundred phone calls were made to request weekend reservations, both direct and by 800 number, at 100 hotels belonging equally to five middle-tier and upper-tier chains. In 64 percent of the cases where a weekend rate was available, the special rate was never mentioned until it was *specifically requested*.

For the five upper-tier chains this was true in 76 percent of the cases. Of the 100 properties, 23 had no weekend rate, but 12 of these did have a rate lower than that first quoted. In none of these cases was the lower rate quoted voluntarily. In some cases a weekend rate could, with persistence, be obtained through the 800 number but not through the hotel direct, or vice versa.[41]

What Happens   When customers call for hotel reservations, they have an idea of what they would pay to stay in the hotel. Those who don't know how to play the discount game may simply hang up when they are quoted a hotel's top rate. Some will stay home, some will stay with friends, and some will stay with a competitor whose opening quote is lower. Another customer is lost, not to mention those who do pay the higher rate and learn later that there was a lower one. (The greatest discrepancy in the study between quoted rate and lowest rate available was $121.)

Again, there is a lesson to be learned from the airlines. If you're trying to lure customers with a special rate, it only makes sense to tell them about it.

Yield Management

In 1988 some players in the hotel industry introduced a pricing concept called yield management.[42] This concept was copied from the airlines, which, it is claimed, change rates as many as 80,000 times in a single day through central computer reservations systems.

Under the yield management system, discount prices are opened and closed based on fluctuating demand and advance bookings. Like airline passengers, hotel customers under this system pay different prices for the same room depending on when their reservation is made. Through the sophistication of a central computer, different prices are set depending on demand, day by day or hour by hour.

For example, when demand is soft, discounts requiring advance bookings remain available or are reopened for sale shortly before the dates that are not fully booked. When demand builds, the discount rates are removed so that customers then booking will pay higher rates. In other words, all levels of pricing are controlled by opening and closing them almost at will with any variation in demand.

It has been said that the competitive advantages available through yield management are enormous.

---

[41] Lewis and Roan, "Selling What You Promote." In 1987 some hotel companies, including one of the major perpetrators in the research cited, began actually publishing lower weekend rates instead of "hiding" them as in the cases above. We applaud this action and recommend the practice to others.

[42] For a detailed discussion of yield management from an earlier date, with and without computers, see Eric B. Orkin, "Boosting Your Bottom Line with Yield Management," *Cornell Hotel and Restaurant Administration Quarterly*, February 1988, pp. 52–56.

Yield management can dramatically increase revenues; maximize profits; greatly improve the effectiveness of market segmentation; open new market segments; strengthen product portfolio strategy; instantly improve cash flow; spread demand throughout seasons and times of day; and allow management to price according to market segment demand.[43]

Obviously, the first users of yield manangement are and will be those chains large enough to afford the computer systems. Not all companies, however, are in favor, since they fear alienating customers who pay the higher rates. The success of these systems remains to be seen at the time of this writing. It appears, however, that the potential exists to revolutionize hotel room pricing. The effect could be disastrous for the small company without matching facilities. It will become even more essential to differentiate on benefits other than prices.

Summary

Pricing practices in the upper end of the hotel industry appear to be unscientific, self-defeating, myopic, and not customer-based. This has been true in most major cities around the world, much of it being led, however, by American-based hotel chains. In Paris, for example, in the spring of 1987, four-star luxe hotels (as they are designated by government) were quoting minimum rates of 1500 plus FF ($250 plus) and were running occupancies in the fortieth percentile. Three-star hotels at 400 to 800 FF were running occupancies in the seventieth percentile, and many were selling out during the week.

Likewise, bars and restaurants in Paris were busy, but hotel outlets in the upper-scale category approached being empty much of the time. We saw the same phenomenon occurring in other European cities. By contrast to the United States, however, there has been some reduction in rack rates both in Europe and in Asia. The Concorde Lafayette in Paris, in fact, took steps to downgrade to three-star status so it could offer fewer amenities, charge lower prices, and charge lower sales taxes than those required by the government in four-star properties.

Prices are the most flexible part of the marketing mix, as we stated in the body of Chapter 14, and they are the most visible. Confusing the customer with high pricing and steep discounting, and keeping prices a secret represents some kind of boondoggle. It ignores the customer. Instead of using prices as a marketing tool, it uses them as a financial weapon. The end result is counterproductive.

DISCUSSION QUESTIONS

1. Discuss the two issues raised in this For Further Study. Take a side and argue for or against these practices.
2. Discuss the consumer's role in the pricing of hotel rooms and other hotel services.

---

[43] James C. Makens, "Yield Management: A Major Pricing Breakthrough," *Piedmont Airlines* (in-flight magazine), April 1988, p. 32.

CHAPTER 15

The Communications Mix: Foundations and Advertising

The third part of the hospitality marketing mix is the communications mix. This is what we have come to know as traditional marketing. Again, it is useful to repeat the definition given in Chapter 11:

> All communications between the firm and the target market that increase the tangibility of the product/service mix, that establish or monitor consumer expectations, or that persuade customers to purchase.

Some elements of this definition need further explanation. Note the phrase "between the firm and the target market": This tells us that communications are a two-way street. It is not simply what the firm does to communicate, but it is also the feedback from the target market that tells the firm how well it is communicating and how well it is doing.

Second, the definition says that communications "increase the tangibility of the product/service mix." As we have seen, the presentation mix does the same thing. The difference is that the presentation mix did this with tangible physical evidence of the product. Communications do it with words and symbols, not facets of the product itself. We are thus dealing at a different level of abstraction.

Third, communications "establish or monitor consumer expectations." This phrase places communications in both an initiation and a regulation mode. Not only do they create expectations, but communications also provide warning when expectations change or are not being met.

Finally, marketing communications "persuade customers to purchase"—we hope. Although interim communications, particularly in advertising and public relations, may have other specific purposes such as to create awareness, enhance a corporate image, and so on, the ultimate goal of all marketing communications is to induce purchase.

This may happen in strange ways. For example, a very effective (in terms of increased sales) advertising campaign was television's Mr. Whipple and his "Please don't squeeze the Charmin." Research showed the commercial to be obnoxious and repugnant to many consumers. The recall factor (how well something is remembered by the consumer), however, was so strong for the average consumer that it had a very positive effect on sales.

Word-of-Mouth Communication

What is missing in the definition of the communications mix? The alert reader has already raised that question. The most powerful form of communications, especially in the hospitality industry, is word-of-mouth. In some cases this is believed to be 100 times more powerful than any other form of communication. This is particularly true of many individual restaurants that do not formally use any portion of the communications mix.[1]. How, then, can we ignore it?

We don't ignore it; we simply don't control it through the communications mix, although we may very well affect it. Elements of the communications mix can, of course, influence word-of-mouth behavior. We may see an ad, read or hear publicity, or talk to a salesperson, and from any one of those experiences develop a perception and expectation. We may then communicate that perception to someone else via word-of-mouth even though we really have no actual experiences with the product.

In this sense, the communications mix does affect word-of-mouth and, indirectly, may persuade someone to purchase or not to purchase. This is a by-product and we include it under the appropriate element of the mix that causes it, so we have not really ignored it.

By and large, however, word-of-mouth behavior originates in actual experience or the word-of-mouth of others who have had an actual experience. Thus, we control behavior more by what we do (relationship marketing) than by what we say, and do not include it as a separate element in the communications mix that we can control. This is not to ignore the power of word-of-mouth, as we will reiterate throughout the next two chapters.

The Communications Mix

The communications mix contains five elements: advertising, promotion, merchandising, public relations and publicity, and personal selling. We will discuss each of these in turn. First, we relate a fictitious anecdote to demonstrate the elements of the mix.

> Jim and Paula Johnson saw a news item in the paper that a new restaurant was going to be created in a long-abandoned, historic, old stone mill down by the river. "It's about

---

[1] A Gallup national survey of 1015 adults found that the average restaurant patron tried a new restaurant 3.2 times over a twelve-month period. In 44 percent of those cases, a recommendation was cited as the reason for the visit. Curiosity was cited by 20 percent, "went with someone who was going there" by 10 percent, "just happened to be there" by 8 percent, and location by 7 percent. Only 6 percent said they had seen a newspaper ad, and only 2 percent went because they had a discount coupon. Reported by David Zuckerman, "Word-of-mouth is Top Draw," *Nation's Restaurant News*, August 11, 1986, p. 159.

time," they thought, "that this town had a new restaurant. This one sounds intriguing. Any restaurant in an old stone mill has to be an exciting concept and it would have to have good food."

Jim and Paula forgot about the restaurant, except when someone mentioned it during a bridge game or in casual conversation, until about six months later. Then they saw a half-page ad in the newspaper. The ad announced the grand opening of the Old Stone Mill restaurant on Friday night. They couldn't go Friday, but immediately made reservations for Saturday night, when the grand opening special drink prices and hors d'oeuvres would still be featured.

On Saturday night they drove with some friends to the restaurant. They had difficulty finding it because the roads down by the river were confusing and not clearly marked. They finally found the restaurant but couldn't find any nearby parking spaces. It was a clear night with almost a full moon, however, and they found the walk to the restaurant invigorating. They looked forward to a great meal and a great experience.

When Jim and Paula got to the restaurant they found a long line waiting to get in. Because they had reservations, they passed by the line and went into the cocktail lounge. They had come early to take advantage of the special offer. They found the lounge packed, with no seating space available. The special hors d'oeuvres had all been devoured. They tried to find someone to take their drink order, to no avail, so they went looking for the hostess. They were 30 minutes early for their reservation, but the hostess told them there would be an hour and a half wait for their table. "What the heck," they said, "it's always this way on Saturday night anywhere," and decided to wait. They were seated an hour and 45 minutes later.

They waited a long time for a waiter. The waiter suggested a menu item that he said was a special and a unique creation of the restaurant owners. Jim and Paula both decided to order it. They then waited a similar length of time until they were served. The waiter explained that the special dish required extra care and time to prepare. On the table, however, was a table tent featuring a carafe of house wine and some shrimp canapés at a special price. They ordered this to have while waiting for their dinner and it came quickly. By the time the meal came, they were filled up on the canapés, salad, bread, and cheese, and were not very hungry. The meal was delicious but they had lost their appetites. They wanted to have another wine with dinner, but were never brought a wine list so didn't order it. Later, they were just as happy that they hadn't. They didn't complain but, as they left, vowed never to go there again and to tell their friends what kind of experience they had had.

A few weeks later, the ad rep from the local paper visited the same restaurant to solicit some advertising. The owners were glad to see him because they were having real problems. The restaurant had opened to rave reviews. At first, it was so busy that they couldn't keep up. Lately, however, business had dropped off dramatically. There had been very few complaints; in fact, almost everyone praised the food, the decor, and the concept. The owners figured that what they needed now was a good advertising campaign.

This anecdote presents an example of the kinds of problems that arise in marketing communication. The Johnsons felt frustrated because they were not satisfied with the restaurant. They wished they had complained to the management. In that wish, they were typical of consumers who feel reluctant and frustrated in not communicating their true feelings to business organizations.

The restaurant owners also felt frustrated. Apparently people were not returning to the restaurant and there had to be some reason why. On the other hand, the owners knew their food was superior and their atmospherics were unique. They wished that they had spent more time talking to their customers to see what they liked and disliked about the restaurant. In that wish, they were typical of business owners who feel they could do a better job of communicating with their customers.

The anecdote illustrates a lack of effective marketing communication. The restaurant has frustrated its customers by not being responsive to their needs. Customers complain to each other by word-of-mouth, but don't communicate their feelings to the restaurant management. Both parties would like to have a favorable relationship with the other but don't know how to go about it.

The anecdote also demonstrates all the elements of the communications mix: publicity, advertising, promotion, personal selling, and merchandising, as well as word-of-mouth. As once said in a classic movie line, "What we have here is a failure to communicate." If the restaurant owners had understood communications, they might have made the necessary adjustments and prevented the business drop-off. The lack of communication in business causes conflicts with employees and consumers. This chapter will explore those conflicts and their resolution.

Communications Strategy

Communications strategies are concerned with the planning, implementing, and control of persuasive communication with customers. Strategies are the plan and tactics are the action, as we will discuss in Chapter 20. This is an important distinction because it is very easy, in implementing marketing communications, to get bogged down in the tactics. When this happens, it also frequently happens that our communication tactics are not consistent with our strategic objectives.

For example, in personal selling we might call on a client hoping to convince him to book his next group meeting at our hotel. Knowing when his next meeting will be held, we might try to persuade him to book that period. That's a tactic. But he has already reserved at another hotel for that meeting. The result is no sale, and we will have to go through the same maneuver for his subsequent meeting.

Instead, we might use strategic persuasion. Our strategic objective is to persuade the client that our hotel, of all hotels, can best serve his meeting needs and solve his meeting problems. We don't mention dates, we don't "sell" our product; we address his needs. Instead of a "no sale," we receive this response: "I've already booked our next meeting, but I'll get in touch with you for the one after that." If our persuasion has been successful, he will.

In advertising, the same concept applies. We really like the ad copy, but what is its objective? What will it accomplish? Does it address the needs of the target market? Take a familiar example we used previously: The ad copy illustrates a beautiful, well-proportioned woman in a bikini lying by a pool. What is the objective? What needs does it address? We're sure you could think of lots of them, but are they the needs of the target market? Are they what we expect the ad to accomplish? Will they persuade the customer to buy?

The first step of our communications strategy is to decide what our objectives are and what we hope to accomplish. These are broad objectives that will serve as an umbrella for all our communications efforts; that is, they will permeate our advertising, selling, promotion, merchandising, and public relations. Some, or all, of these elements may also have subobjectives but they will all be subsumed under the main objectives. Similarly, we may have more than one objective at a time. In any case, we want the objectives to be congruent and not in conflict with each other.

There are many possible main objectives. Here, we list just a few: to create an image, to position (both objectively and subjectively), to create benefits, to offer problem solutions, to create awareness, to create belief, to stir emotions, to change attitudes, to create expectation, and to move to action. These are all strategic objectives and it is that strategy that guides the entire communications process.

The communication process has five broad stages. The first of these stages is "what to say." Remembering our strategic objective, this stage sets the guidelines in terms of theme, featured attributes, concept, positioning, benefits offered, promises made, and so forth. Consider two different hotel ads for the purpose of relating the communications process to an actual strategy. Figure 15-1 is an ad for one specific hotel, the Helmsley Palace. Figure 15-2 is an ad for a chain of hotels, Omni Hotels. Each ad has a different strategic objective. Before reading further, look at each ad. What is the message you are receiving—what do you think they are trying to say other than, of course, to buy? Now see if the message you receive is the same as the objectives of the ad.

What to Say

The "what to say" strategic objective of the Helmsley ad is to position the hotel as a top-of-the-line, first-class property. Without looking at the ad, consider the many different ways that this might be accomplished. Pretend that the ad does not yet exist. Given the objective and the creative minds of the advertising agency, the marketing department, and no doubt Leona Helmsley, go to work.

The objective of the Omni ad is quite different. The intent is to create a picture of uniformity, albeit "classic" and first class, among all Omni Hotels. Omni hotels are quite different in physical characteristics: Some are brand new and modern; others are older, renovated properties with more traditional atmospheres. Omni's theme is to persuade the market that even though these hotels are different, the same "classic" service prevails throughout. Again, there are many ways that this could be said.

Whom to Say It To

The next stage is to define the target market. Assuming that the appropriate research has been done and the needs and wants of the target market have been clearly identified, this sets parameters on implementation of the objectives. For the Helmsley Palace, the target market is the traveler who has "made it" and wants nothing but the very best. This traveler is the full and unlimited expense account executive or the wealthy business or social traveler. This person not only wants the best but can afford it and, furthermore, expects to pay for it.

For Omni, the target market is the upscale business traveler—educated, on expense account, but probably more businesslike, more cost-conscious, and looking for good, but

It's the only Palace
in the world
where the Queen stands guard.

Peruvian lilies, freesia, and tulips — that's the order of the day.
And Leona Helmsley, proprietress of the Helmsley Palace,
sees that each petal is in place throughout exquisite 100-year-old lounges.
What better way to please her royal family. You. Her guests.

It's The Helmsley Palace

455 Madison Avenue (at 50th Street), New York, N.Y. 10022
For reservations, call toll-free: 1-800/221-4982.
In New York, 212/888-1624. Or see your travel agent. TELEX 640-543

The Leading Hotels of the World.

FIGURE 15-1   Ad with objective of positioning

FIGURE 15-2   Ad with objective of creating product quality uniformity

not necessarily elegant, service. This traveler, it is hoped, can be persuaded to be more brand-loyal once convinced that the same level of service is available at different locations.

How to Say It

Once the first two stages have been absorbed, the creative juices of everyone involved start flowing. This is the copy, the appeals to the customer, the execution stage. There are many, many options; which one will work best? Which one most precisely accomplishes the objectives consistent with the identified target market?

Leona Helmsley says it by telling the reader that she, personally, is right there to make sure everything goes absolutely perfectly—not a manager, not a franchisee, but the proprietress herself. The staff, of course, is excellent. How so? Because she "stands guard." Why does she do this? Because you are her guest, her "royal family." This ad creates a very high expectation level at a high risk (cost) to the customer. Consider, for yourself, the problem solutions offered and the price/value relationship as discussed in Chapter 1.

The Helmsley ad is very clear in carrying out the communications objectives. The Omni ad is not so clear. An attractive woman in a tuxedo and bow tie, holding a bowl of flowers, can say a number of different things to a number of different people. For example, some might interpret the service as not only "classic," but also very formal. If so, does this fit the needs and wants of the target market? Does it fit the Omni Nassau Inn on the Princeton campus? Some have interpreted this ad as indicating that the service is cold and haughty. Some have perceived it as artificial (including the flowers). Whether or not it achieves the objective of depicting uniformity is unknown, although perhaps Omni research indicates that it does. Consider, again, the consumer trade-off model in Chapter 1: How does the ad fit this model? What expectations does it create, what problems does it solve, what is the price/value relationship and the risk?

Consider both the Helmsley and the Omni ads in terms of the definition of the aims of the communications mix:

- establish communications between the firm and the target market
- increase the tangibility of the product/service mix
- establish or monitor consumer expectations
- persuade consumers to purchase

Have these things been accomplished? Consider the ads also in terms of selective perception, selective attention, selective comprehension, selective acceptance, and selective retention. (We already did some of this for the Helmsley ad in Chapter 6.)

How Often to Say It

The next stage is both a consumer-driven and a budget-driven one. Repetition has been shown to aid selective retention. It has also been shown to increase "wear-out," that is the tendency of the consumer to ignore it after having seen it so often. Therefore, this stage requires careful consideration of when to say it (e.g., television times, newspaper placement, in-flight magazines), as well as how often, which will always have a budget limitation.

Another "how often" involves the ad copy itself. The Helmsley Palace campaign used the same theme over an extended period of time but frequently changed or alternated ad copy and graphics. The first three strategic stages remained constant, but in a slightly changed format. Omni, on the other hand, used almost identical copy repeatedly over a period of years.

Where to Say It

Where, as used here, applies to the various components of the communications mix. The examples used above were advertisements, but only for ease of illustration. It might also be decided to carry out the first four stages through personal selling, promotion, merchandising, and public relations—any one or all five. The important thing is that the strategy should be consistent throughout; one medium must not contradict another.

To demonstrate this very important point, consider again the Helmsley Palace objective in each context. For advertising, the selection of media would be critical; the appropriate medium would be that read by the target market. This ad was used extensively in the magazine section of the Sunday *New York Times* and in *Business Week* magazine; you wouldn't expect to find it in *Sports Illustrated* or *Time* magazine.

Hotels are also heavy users of collateral or brochures. These are used in mailings as well as by travel agents and other distribution outlets. The Helmsley Palace would not be heavy users of this medium, especially as compared to Omni with its chain of hotels, because of the nature of its select, small, unique target market.

In personal selling, the same theme must be portrayed. It is doubtful that Helmsley salespeople would say to their clients, "It's the only palace in the world where the queen stands guard," but they would stress the special attention, the excellent staff, and perhaps even the perfectionism of Leona Helmsley herself.

Merchandising (on-premise selling) and sales promotion (sales incentives), terms we will explain in more detail in Chapter 16, would not seem particularly appropriate for the Helmsley Palace. People do not come here for special deals and they don't want to be "pushed" to buy, once they are there. Contrarily, however, the Helmsley Palace does run ads pushing special rates and packages for weekends and during the summer. These ads, however, have very different objectives—in other words, the first four stages are different. Different copy is used, and the ads are run in the *New York Times* travel section.

Public relations would be important for the Helmsley in carrying out the theme. News items would be "planted" about the King of Timbuctoo and people of his ilk staying there. Grand events in the ballroom, dignitaries' meetings, and so forth would be given as much publicity as possible. Public relations and publicity are especially important for upscale properties.

Target Markets

As with everything in marketing, target markets are integral in developing the communications mix. There is not much more to say except this: "*Know* your target market."

There are three basic rules of persuasion, and they were laid down by Aristotle centuries ago.

Logos—logic and reasoning (e.g., "where your meetings run like clockwork")
Pathos—emotions (e.g., "where a waterfall cascades down through the lobby")
Ethos—source credibility (e.g., Leona Helmsley is the president herself)

Which one(s) will persuade your target market? We will not discuss these rules and all their offshoots here because they consume chapters in advertising texts and their proper treatment is too extensive for this book. For the marketer, however, they represent commonsense treatment in communicating with the target market. Logos, pathos, and ethos are a refinement in stage three of communications strategy, how to say it—that is, what is the most effective means of persuasion for the target market?

The other thing we need to know about the target market is what "stage" it is in. Lavidge and Steiner suggest that people move up through a series of seven steps to actual purchase of a product.[2] The steps are not equal: Some may be climbed quite rapidly, or even simultaneously, but when there is more psychological and/or economic commitment involved in the purchase, it will take consumers longer to climb the steps, and each step will be more important. The steps the consumer progresses through, as suggested by Lavidge and Steiner, describe the consumer's state of mind; they are as follows.

1. Has complete unawareness of the existence of the product or service
2. Has mere awareness of the existence
3. Knows what the product has to offer
4. Has favorable attitudes toward the product
5. Has preference for the product over other possibilities
6. Has a desire to buy and is convinced that it would be a wise decision
7. Actually purchases the product

An adapted version of the Lavidge and Steiner model is shown in Table 15-1. This model points up the need to know the existing stage of the target market.

Analyzing the target market in terms of this model is critical to development of communications strategies. Good strategies may prove useless if they address the market at a stage other than the one that exists.

Another model that is useful in planning communications strategy is called the "adoption process model." This model of consumer behavior contends that adoption, or purchase of a product, is a process. The process starts with awareness, because obviously consumers cannot buy something if they are not aware of it. Awareness can develop simply from walking down a street and seeing a restaurant entrance. It can also develop from seeing a billboard on the highway and, of course, from word-of-mouth. Apart from word-of-mouth, awareness in the hospitality industry is usually created by advertising.

Once the consumer is aware, the next step in the process is "interest." If consumers are interested they seek further information and details about the product, such as the quality, the cost, how to buy it, and so forth. This information may, and often does, come via advertising. In many hospitality cases, however, it may come through the consumer's

---

[2] Robert J. Lavidge and Gary A. Steiner, "A Model of Predictive Measurements of Advertising Effectiveness," *Journal of Marketing,* October, 1961, pp. 59–62, published by the American Marketing Association.

TABLE 15-1   A Model of Consumer Stages and Their Impact on Communications Strategy

Consumer Stage	Effect Stage	Strategy
Cognitive: the stage of thoughts/beliefs	Create awareness, beliefs, interest; differentiate	Provide information, get attention
Affective: the stage of emotions	Change attitudes and feelings, get involved, evaluate	Position, create benefits and image, stir emotions
Conative: the stage of motivation and intention	Stimulate and direct desires, adopt	Move to action, reinforce expectation

Adapted from Lavidge and Steiner, "Model of Predictive Measurements."

own initiative—that is, consumers will pay to use the telephone or mail to obtain more information on their own. Personal selling also plays an important part in providing information when marketing to groups and meeting planners.

The third step of the model is "evaluation." At this stage consumers ask themselves a number of questions: "Does this fulfill my needs? Does this solve my problems? Does it do it better than someone else's product? Is it worth the risk?" Advertising, personal selling, and public relations can play important roles at this stage. If the evaluation is favorable the consumer moves on to the next stage, trial.

As we have seen in Chapter 2, trial of the hospitality product usually means the same as purchase; there is really no other way to try it. The promotion and merchandising parts of the communications mix are often used to induce trial, beyond that induced by the other mix elements.

If the trial is favorable, consumers "adopt." They become repeat customers and tell others, thus becoming sources of awareness, information, and evaluation for others who are at various stages of the process. Marketers can influence adoption only through performance and relationship marketing, which is why the quality of these two factors is so critical to successful marketing.

As with the Lavidge and Steiner model, marketers should know at what stage of the adoption model their target market is. This knowledge will strongly influence the communications strategy and objectives.

Research for the Communications Mix

If we have to know the target market in order to develop the optimal communications mix and strategy, it follows that the best results will be obtained through research. In the long run, good research will save communications dollars.

We recognize that many properties, particularly individually owned restaurants, will not have such involved communications mixes as those described here. Even these properties, however, will most likely engage in merchandising, promotion, and some advertising, if not personal selling; and good public relations can be used by any business. Research is done both internally and externally. The following guidelines apply to even the smallest business, if in somewhat modified form.

Communications are designed to establish and monitor consumer expectations and to persuade consumers to purchase. To accomplish this, we need to know not only about the target market but also about our property and how we are perceived. Research is one form of communications that comes the other way. There are five major questions to be answered.

Where Are We Now?

This means not what we ourselves think, but what the target market thinks. In other words, how are we perceived? Examples might be "expensive," "luxurious," "good service," "good food," "full facilities," "atmospheric," or any number of other things.

We seek to understand perception through the eyes of the target market, but more than one research effort has revealed that the market segment being reached is not even the one that management thought it was reaching. Thus, the first thing we may need to learn is who our actual target market is.

Here are other questions to be asked:

How do we compare with the competition?
What do their customers think of us?
Are they aware of what we have to offer?
Have they tried us? If not, why not? If so, do they return? Why? Why not? What are their attitudes and feelings?

In short, the research question at this stage is, "How are we seen now?" Our management may believe that we have the finest food in town, but if the market doesn't believe this, it really doesn't matter whether we do or not. It is hard to go anywhere if you don't know where you are starting from.

Why Are We There?

This research step calls for an evaluation of the product and previous communications efforts. To embellish on the example above, suppose analysis shows that our food is really not that good. If the objective is to be perceived as having the finest food in town, the product will have to be altered and a new communications effort initiated. If, in fact, we do have the finest food in town, then the communications objective will be to change perceptions.

Besides product evaluation, here are other aspects to be researched:

Are prices too high or are they perceived as too high?
What is the real quality level of our service?
Is the competition doing the same thing, only better?
Are our attributes and benefits what we think they are?
Do we really solve consumers' problems? The right ones?

What puts us in this position?
What are our strength and weaknesses?
What are the users' dissatisfactions?
What is the profile of users?
What is the usage pattern of users?
Have we communicated what we want to communicate?

The research questions at this stage are "How is our product perceived? How is it used?" If where we are now is not where we want to be, then we have to find out how we got there. Even if it is where we want to be, we still need to know how we got there. There is nothing like knowing what you are doing right and why.

Where Could We Be?

If where we are now is not where we want to be, then were could we realistically be? Answering this question takes even more critical self-assessment. Let's say we are not perceived as having the best food in town, but that is where we would like to be: Is that realistic? Do we have the right staff in the kitchen? Can we afford to buy the finest ingredients without raising prices? Would we have to raise prices to achieve the "finest food" objective? Is there a market for it?

That's the product point of view. Perhaps we do have the finest food in town, just what we want to be, but the market doesn't see it that way. Then we would have to ask whether it is realistic to believe that we can change perceptions that, in this case, would be vis-à-vis the competition. Here are some other issues in this stage:

What market position could we achieve?
Are there new buyers and users out there?
Can we increase awareness?
Can we change beliefs or create new ones?
Can we increase benefits and solve other problems?
Do we have the right target markets? Are there others?
Can we create new target markets?
Can we steal from the competition?

The major research question at this stage is "What unmet needs, wants, and problems are there that we have the capability of fulfilling?" The answers to these questions will establish our communication objectives.

How Can We Get There?

Now comes the creative thinking. When this is based on good, solid research, it comes easier and is more likely to work. The first and most obvious question is "What do we have to change?" This could be any part of the product/service mix, or of the presentation mix that is tangibilizing the product/service to the marketplace. Thus, we might have to change the product, the service, the price, the atmospherics, the facilities, the employees, or, if we can, the location. We might also have to change the distribution network, or the target markets.

Once we have the product right, and not until then, we can commence with what we have to change, via the communications mix. The Howard Johnson's[3] case in Chapter 1 gives an example of trying to persuade with communications before the product is corrected. Howard Johnson's ad campaign, "If it's not your mother, it must be Howard Johnson's," stretched consumer credibility to a limit that very few restaurants could hope to achieve. Such actions are often fatal; the customer doesn't like to be fooled twice.

Some years later, after Marriott had bought Howard Johnson's and resold the lodging properties to Prime Motor Inns, another communications campaign took place. We will use this to illustrate all of the above points.

Where Are We Now?   Prime Motor Inns conducted research to answer this question. According to the trade press, Prime's research determined that the negative image accorded Howard Johnson was due solely to the restaurant division; the lodging division was perceived as having a positive image.

We are not familiar with the actual research, but let's consider what it should have done. First, go back to Lavidge and Steiner's seven steps. Awareness was not a problem; just about everyone knew Howard Johnson. Step three is knowing what the product has to offer. Howard Johnson's early motel units were notorious for thin walls, noise, poor maintenance, dark and depressing lobby, and other negative factors. This generates a research question: Does the consumer now know that at least some of the properties do not fit this image?

Step four is favorable attitude toward the product. If the answer to step three, knowing what the product has to offer, is no, then the answer here is no. If the answer to step three is yes, then the question is "Do some units with positive conditions create a favorable attitude toward the entire product line?" If the answer was no, then the first step of the campaign would be to create a favorable attitude—after the problems were corrected, of course.

This would mean repositioning. Recall from Chapter 10 that repositioning can mean removing negative images while creating positive ones. One way to help do this would be to change the name and paint Howard Johnson's famous orange roofs another color.

Prime's research answer, as we have indicated, was "yes"—some units with positive conditions created a favorable attitude toward all units. Prime therefore retained the name, and, the last time we looked, the roofs were largely still orange (although at least one franchisee was planning to paint his roofs in late 1988). Frankly, we doubt the validity and reliability of this finding. We think that Prime had some doubts about it too because, as we will soon see, they went to great effort to change the image. The task could have been far easier if they had also changed the name.[4]

From this point, the research should address the issues in Lavidge and Steiner's steps five to seven—that is, how do we actually create preference, the desire to buy, and the actual purchase? If Prime had believed what they said they believed, this is where they would have commenced the communications campaign, in stage three, the conative stage

---

[3] The apostrophe s in the name Howard Johnson's was dropped in the mid 1980s. The correct name today is Howard Johnson.

[4] Another good example of this kind of situation is in the airline industry. U.S. Air, now a respected carrier, formerly carried the name Allegheny Airlines. Most travelers who were forced to use it referred to it as "Agony Airlines." New management helped to expedite the change in image with a new name.

of the Lavidge/Steiner model in Table 15-1. Instead, they commenced it in the affective stage.

Why Are We There?　　Howard Johnson's had a long history that provided many answers to this question. Even given a favorable answer to "Where are we now?" however, fresh research would prove very enlightening. If a favorable answer to "Where are we now?" was, in fact, an incorrect answer, this fact would have come out at this step and caused a change in direction. If that answer was, in fact, correct, we would learn at this step why it was correct. This could form the basis of the new communications campaign.

Where Could We Be?　　The answers to this question for this example deal largely with positioning. What position could Howard Johnson fill? Did it have to change beliefs to do that? Did it have the right target markets, and so forth? This stage of research is designed to bring realism to the campaign, as opposed to wishful thinking.

How Can We Get There?　　This is the ultimate question, the answer to which will drive the communications campaign. For Howard Johnson, in our opinion, it meant a total repositioning aided by a name change. In Prime's opinion, apparently, it also meant repositioning, but with the same name and without any real effort to destroy any previous negative image; in other words, they said, "Believe us when we tell you that we have 'turned Howard Johnson upside down,' " as shown in the ad in Figure 15-3.

Here's what a Howard Johnson spokesman said about the estimated $5 million advertising campaign:

> Howard Johnson wants to inform the public that the company has changed dramatically . . . to position itself solely as a lodging chain. "What we're saying is, 'Hey, folks, we've got a really good product here and don't be discouraged by what we were in the past. Now we're strictly in the hotel business. If you try us, chances are you're going to like us and want to come back.' . . . We wanted a campaign that would cut through all the clutter out there. We wanted our customers to know that something is changing at Howard Johnson."
>
> The new ad campaign is based on research that indicated . . . "A lot of the negative image of Howard Johnson *is* related to the restaurants."[5]

Another company, Holiday Inns, went through a somewhat similar crisis. In the late 1970s, Holiday Inns had instituted an advertising campaign that headlined "The Best Surprise is No Surprise." When you went to a Holiday Inn, the message was, you got what you expected; there were no surprises, at least not negative ones. Unfortunately, the campaign raised expectations that were not fulfilled. Customers found all kinds of surprises, including some they might never have noticed before the campaign.

Holiday Inns had a difficult time getting customers back; consumer attitude was "once was enough." Its ad campaign, designed to do almost the same thing as Howard Johnson's, took a different approach. Unlike Howard Johnson, Holiday Inns literally made a promise to the consumer, as shown in Figure 15-4. If you found a "surprise" now, it was made right or you received your money back. Which campaign do you think worked better?

---

[5] Steven J. Stark, "HoJo 'Dusts Off' its image with a $5M Ad Campaign," *Business Travel News,* June 9, 1986, pp. 1, 50.

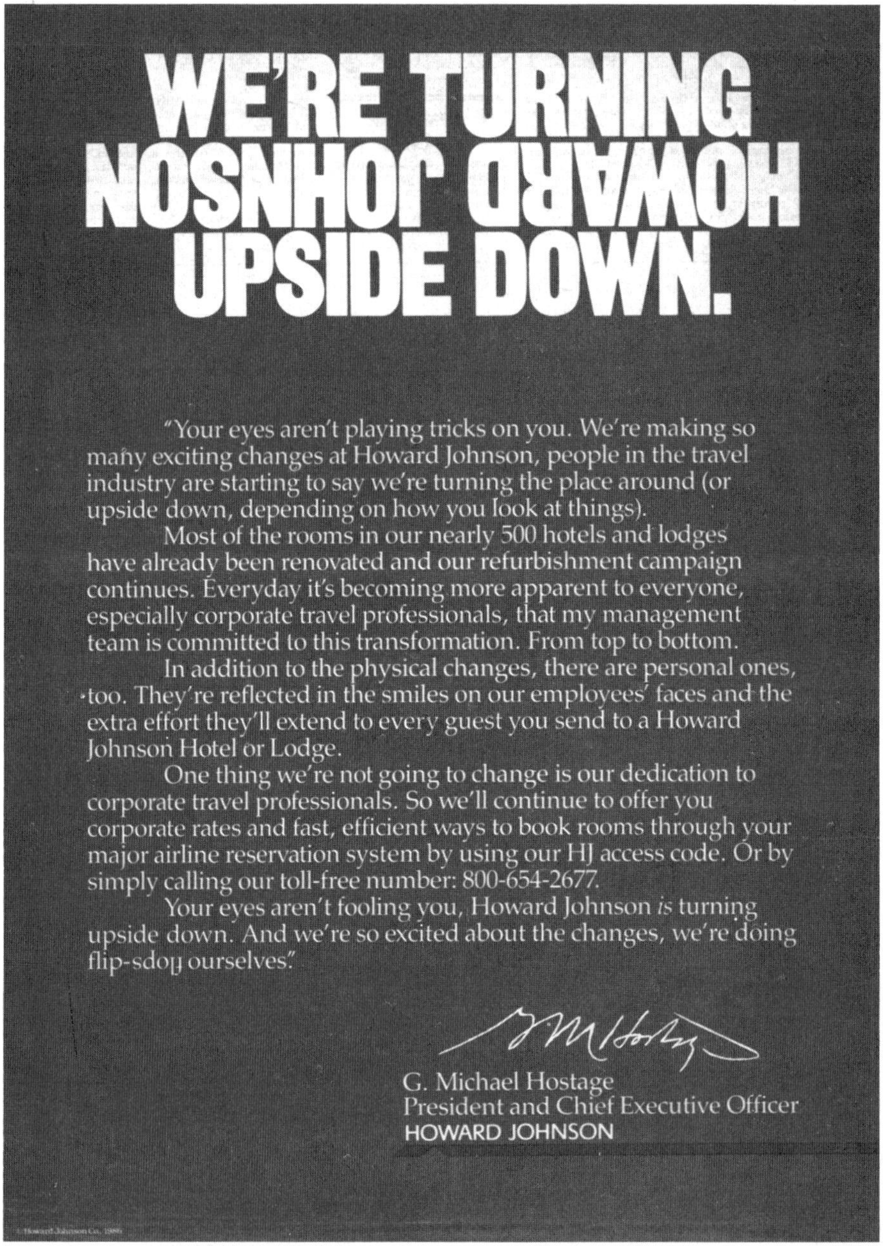

WE'RE TURNING HOWARD JOHNSON UPSIDE DOWN.

"Your eyes aren't playing tricks on you. We're making so many exciting changes at Howard Johnson, people in the travel industry are starting to say we're turning the place around (or upside down, depending on how you look at things).

Most of the rooms in our nearly 500 hotels and lodges have already been renovated and our refurbishment campaign continues. Everyday it's becoming more apparent to everyone, especially corporate travel professionals, that my management team is committed to this transformation. From top to bottom.

In addition to the physical changes, there are personal ones, too. They're reflected in the smiles on our employees' faces and the extra effort they'll extend to every guest you send to a Howard Johnson Hotel or Lodge.

One thing we're not going to change is our dedication to corporate travel professionals. So we'll continue to offer you corporate rates and fast, efficient ways to book rooms through your major airline reservation system by using our HJ access code. Or by simply calling our toll-free number: 800-654-2677.

Your eyes aren't fooling you, Howard Johnson *is* turning upside down. And we're so excited about the changes, we're doing flip-sdoʃ ourselves."

G. Michael Hostage
President and Chief Executive Officer
HOWARD JOHNSON

FIGURE 15-3 Ad with objective of converting negative image to positive

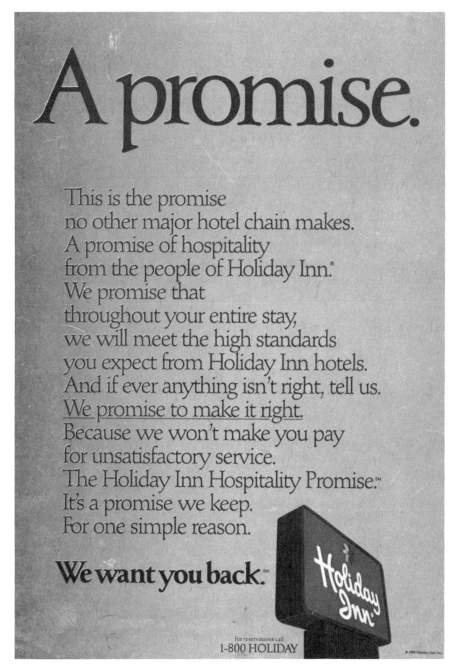

(Courtesy of Holiday Inns, Inc.)

FIGURE 15-4   Ad with objective of inducing retrial

As we have just shown, the communications mix questions up to this point are the same ones as those at the beginning of this chapter: what, whom, how, how often, and where. Are the target markets in the cognitive, affective, or conative stage? In what stage of the adoption process are they? What perceptions do we have to change, and so forth?

Are We Getting There?

This is probably the most neglected stage of communications research. It really means starting over again at the beginning, except that now the field is narrower because we know what we are looking for. This is research to measure results. It asks, "What have we, or haven't we, changed?"

Whether we are "getting there" cannot be measured in just dollars or increased patronage. Taking those as the sole criteria is a mistake that can be fatal, as we have shown earlier in the cases of the early Howard Johnson's and Victoria Station. The trade press offers many similar examples. Dollars and patronage are a by-product of what we hoped to achieve. If the objective was to be perceived as having the best food in town, are we now so perceived? The campaign may have brought people, which can be temporary and misleading, but what we want to know is whether we have changed perception, which will have a long-lasting effect. For Howard Johnson, the question is "Do people believe us?" For Holiday Inns, it is "Have we kept our promise?"

Thus far we have looked at the communications mix from a broad, overall view. Both the thrust and the synergism of the mix are vital to success in communicating to and with the marketplace. In this and the next two chapters, we will now look at each of the five parts of the mix individually.

Advertising

Advertising is mass communication that is paid for. It is the most visible element of the communications mix. It has the broadest potential reach of all the components of the communications mix—that is, it can reach the largest mass of people. It can also be the most expensive component. The question is, how effective is it? That is a question that researchers, especially those connected with advertising agencies, have been trying to answer for years. It is an especially pertinent question in the hospitality industry, where word-of-mouth is such a potent force.

We include in advertising all those things that are part of the public media, such as newspaper and magazine ads; television and radio commercials; billboards; airplane streamers; train, bus and taxi cards; and so forth, as long as those are paid for by a specific sponsor. We also include collateral, such as hotel brochures, flyers, and pamphlets, and direct mail, which are not exactly public media but fit into the same genre.

The Roles of Advertising

Advertising, of course, performs the same general role of all communications as a whole: it informs, creates awareness, attempts to persuade, and reinforces buying behavior of present customers. It also can play a major role in positioning, as we have shown.

Advertising is subject to the same guidelines that we discussed in the first part of this chapter; the major difference is that it is paid mass communication.

For the hospitality industry, the most important objective function of advertising may be to create and maintain awareness of the property or some particular component of the property, such as a new addition or a new service. The most important subjective function is to position the property, as was pointed out in connection with the Helmsley Palace ad.

See, for example, The Portman ad in Figure 15-5. This ad, run seven months before the hotel was scheduled to open, certainly had the creation of awareness as its objective. However, it does not stop there. The ad also promises benefits aimed at the meeting planner, and is intended to position the hotel at the top of the line for meetings.

Advertising also informs, although much hospitality print advertising is not very informative because its constant sameness often fails to differentiate one property from another in the same product class. One of the greatest informative uses of advertising concerns location. If consumers are aware of a particular hotel or restaurant chain, or even an individual property, and are favorably disposed toward it, then the next thing they want to know is where it is.

Figure 15-6 shows a Dunfey Hotels (now Omni) ad expressly designed for that purpose. There is no positioning in this ad, no differentiation, and no real attempt at persuasion; we would have to presume that the designated target is already aware of Dunfey Hotels. Many hotel and restaurant chains use advertising for this purpose, although locations are usually only part of the copy.

Another example of informative advertising of single-minded purpose is what was a long-running campaign by Sheraton featuring only their 800 reservations number, as shown in Figure 15-7. However, whereas the Dunfey ad functioned more in the cognitive stage, creating awareness, the Sheraton ad functions in the conative stage, the stage of motivation. The strategy behind the Dunfey ad is to provide information; the strategy behind the Sheraton ad is to move consumers to action: "Call Now!"

What Advertising Should Accomplish

Major advertising campaigns in the hospitality industry are conducted only by very large companies with large resources. In the restaurant industry, we are all familiar with the television commercials that emanate from McDonald's (one of the largest advertisers in the country), Burger King, and other fast-food chains.

On the other end of the continuum are the individual restaurants or motor inns that do almost no advertising. In between these two extremes lies a vast group of hospitality operators who do limited advertising on very limited budgets. For these operators, the "more bang for the buck" principle is especially appropriate: Advertising dollars have to be carefully allocated to where they will do the most good.

To do the most good, the ideal hospitality advertisement will accomplish five things:

1. It will tangibilize the service element so the reader can mentally grasp what is offered.
2. It will promise a benefit that can be delivered and/or provide solutions to problems.

May we request
a minute of your time?

START | Opening May 1987, The Portman, San Francisco will be an unforget-
1 ONE THOUSAND · 2 ONE THOUSAND · 3 ONE THOUSAND · 4 ONE THOUSAND

table hotel. Because the service will be unprecedented. With a fleet
5 ONE THOUSAND · 6 ONE THOUSAND · 7 ONE THOUSAND · 8 ONE THOUSAND

of Rolls-Royces. Personal valets to meet your every need. And
9 ONE THOUSAND · 10 ONE THOUSAND · 11 ONE THOUSAND · 12 ONE THOUSAND

complete business services to make your stay as enjoyable as your
13 ONE THOUSAND · 14 ONE THOUSAND · 15 ONE THOUSAND · 16 ONE THOUSAND

meeting is productive. Productivity that begins when you book your
17 ONE THOUSAND · 18 ONE THOUSAND · 19 ONE THOUSAND · 20 ONE THOUSAND

meeting. You'll work with one Conference Services Director from
21 ONE THOUSAND · 22 ONE THOUSAND · 23 ONE THOUSAND · 24 ONE THOUSAND

start to finish. Unique in San Francisco is our Executive Conference
25 ONE THOUSAND · 26 ONE THOUSAND · 27 ONE THOUSAND · 28 ONE THOUSAND

Center, a totally dedicated and enhanced learning environment with
29 ONE THOUSAND · 30 ONE THOUSAND · 31 ONE THOUSAND · 32 ONE THOUSAND

continuous refreshment pantry, adjacent dining, Conference
33 ONE THOUSAND · 34 ONE THOUSAND · 35 ONE THOUSAND · 36 ONE THOUSAND

Concierge and complete privacy. And if you call (800) 225-1491*
37 ONE THOUSAND · 38 ONE THOUSAND · 39 ONE THOUSAND · 40 ONE THOUSAND

before Dec. 31, The Portman will guarantee a rate today for any
41 ONE THOUSAND · 42 ONE THOUSAND · 43 ONE THOUSAND · 44 ONE THOUSAND

meeting tentatively or definitely booked through 1989. All in all, the
45 ONE THOUSAND · 46 ONE THOUSAND · 47 ONE THOUSAND · 48 ONE THOUSAND

meeting you plan with The Portman will be time well spent. | FINISH
49 ONE THOUSAND · 50 ONE THOUSAND · AND WE'VE LEFT YOU TIME TO CALL RIGHT NOW**

Near Union Square...

THE PORTMAN
SAN FRANCISCO

FIGURE 15-5   Ad to create new product awareness

408

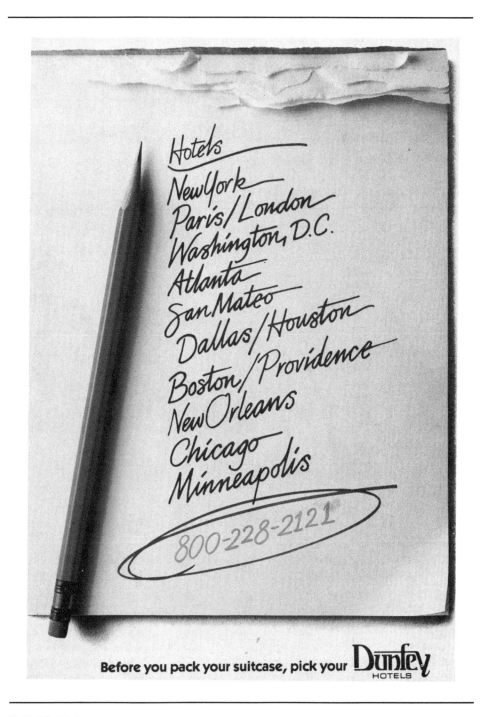

FIGURE 15-6 Ad to create location awareness

FIGURE 15-7   Ad to compel consumer action

3. It will differentiate the property from that of the competition.
4. It will have positive effects on employees who must execute the promises.
5. It will capitalize on word-of-mouth.

We can demonstrate these accomplishments by referring to the Marriott ad in Figure 15-8. Marriott is a national advertiser, but the same principles apply even if you are only advertising in your local newpaper.

The Marriott ad promises a benefit and a solution to one of the most common complaints of hotel guests, slow room service. It differentiates from the competition by promising that room service will be on time, a promise that few hotels make. The ad also says that Marriott will keep that promise because (1) there's Bill Marriott himself putting his name on the line, and (2) if they don't keep the promise, you don't have to pay for the breakfast.

"At Marriott, breakfast arrives in your room on time. Or it's on us."

"That's right. You enjoy a delicious, wholesome breakfast when you want it...or we eat the cost. *Guaranteed.*

How do we do it? Simple. Just order from our *Guaranteed Breakfast Menu* at any participating Marriott Hotel or Resort. Check off your order and the 15-minute time period during which you'd like to have breakfast. Then hang the menu on your doorknob before you go to sleep.

The next morning, as sure as the sun rises, you'll enjoy a piping-hot room service breakfast delivered within the 15-minute time period you selected.

We guarantee it.

Room service breakfast when you want it. Guaranteed reservations. Quick check-ins and check-outs. Superb accommodations. Marriott's high standard of service. All add up to an enjoyable, hassle-free stay.

After all, I have to make sure we do things right. It's my name over the door."

President, Marriott Corporation

800-228-9290

Marriott
HOTELS·RESORTS

FIGURE 15-8   Ad demonstrating the five major accomplishments of good hospitality advertising

The ad also tangibilizes the service. It shows the room service cart arriving and it shows Bill Marriott checking his watch. The reader has no trouble conceptually grasping what the benefit will be. The ad has a positive effect on employees because it makes a commitment from the president of the company that he is prepared to back up what he says, thus creating an inspirational effect.

Finally, the Marriott ad capitalizes on word-of-mouth. Even though a reader may not have yet experienced the service, he can talk about it: "Hey, did you hear Marriott promises your room service on time or you don't have to pay for it?" Of course, this word-of-mouth will be even more positive once the actual experience has occurred.

Note that the Marriott ad is also informative and creates awareness (of a new service). It reinforces the Marriott image for present customers ("See, we're always doing something to make your stay with us better"), without coming right out and saying it. Many ads strain so hard at doing this that they lose credibility. The ad also positions Marriott as service-oriented, as always trying to do something more for its customers. Finally, the ad is persuasive. It addresses an issue of frequent concern and says, "We've taken care of that particular problem for you." Figure 15-9 is one of a Ramada series and another example of addressing a common consumer problem. Concurrent with this series, Ramada ran another headed, "What Makes Madden Glad."

It is seldom easy to get all these elements into one advertisement; often we have to settle for less. Even then, however, one should strive to get away from the sameness that characterizes so many hotel and restaurant ads. A typical hotel ad, for example, shows a picture of the hotel. Unless there is something visibly unique about the hotel, this kind of ad fills none of the requirements given above. There may be ways to do this, however, as can be seen by the ad in Figure 15-10. This might be called "breathing life into a hotel building."

Another typical hotel ad scene shows a couple in a room, usually with the woman sitting on the bed and the man standing in a sliding doorway, or they may be in a swimming pool or at a golf course. While the room, the pool, and the golf course are all part of the product, they do not differentiate from other hotels in the same product class. They don't position the property, they promise no special benefit or problem solution, they don't tangibilize the service, they don't provide reinforcement, they don't have positive effects on employees, they don't generate positive word-of-mouth, they are not very informative, and they hardly persuade the consumer to choose this hotel.

So much for graphics—how about copy? The same rules apply. Ads that simply list the physical facilities of the property (e.g., number of rooms, pools, restaurants, bars, etc.) also do not fulfill the criteria we have given. True, it may sometimes be necessary to provide this information, depending on the target market. Perhaps it does need to be included, but this does not exempt the remaining copy from saying something different.

Note the Trump Plaza ad in Figure 15-11. Apply the same criteria to the copy in this ad: Does it do the job?

The Use of Advertising Today

Advertising is traditional marketing. It is so traditional that it has lost much of its creativity. If you cannot make an impact upon the market with advertising, other than to

FIGURE 15-9   Ad showing consumer problem solution

(Courtesy of Royal Garden Hotel)

FIGURE 15-10   Ad that breathes life into the hotel building

414

Picky! Picky! Picky!

Good meeting planners are tough to please. They want every base covered and every promise delivered. They want a full-service convention staff at their every beck and call. We understand all this. We're pushovers for picky planners. Which is why more and more meetings are being planned at Trump Plaza.

Featuring 586 ocean view rooms and suites • 28,000 square feet of meeting space (all on one level) • Eight marvelous restaurants • Five lounges to unwind in • Posh pool and health club • A showroom full of stars • A new $30 million transportation center • The most exciting casino on the boardwalk.

So, pick on us! Call 609-441-6760 or 800-441-0909.

SUCCESSFUL MEETINGS
PINNACLE AWARD

TRUMP PLAZA
Hotel and Casino • Atlantic City's Centerpiece

Mobil
Travel Guide
1987

The Boardwalk at Mississippi Avenue   Atlantic City, New Jersey 08401

FIGURE 15-11   Ad that lists physical facilities but also has copy that fulfills other criteria

create awareness and provide information, it might be better to save your dollars and put them to better use (for instance, in the product or in lower prices, which will generate positive word-of-mouth, a far more powerful force than most advertising). See, for example, the ads in Figure 15-12 which seem to lack all the essential criteria.

The consumer today is constantly bombarded with advertising messages from all directions. The human mind is not capable of paying attention to all these messages. Instead, the mind will selectively perceive, attend to, comprehend, accept, and retain that to which it is most responsive. What the mind is most responsive to are those things we have just outlined.

Product parity is common: Your competition is selling the same thing, unique niches are harder and harder to find, services are easy to copy, and aggressive competitors are using innovative positioning strategies. These things mean that it is difficult to gain advertising advantage. In many cases, it may be too expensive to achieve effective awareness and persuasion levels.

All this means that advertising must be approached with extreme care. Successful advertising is not just copy and graphics, not even just clever copy and graphics, but it derives from a well-planned strategy. Yet there is a strong tendency for management to look just at the copy and ignore the strategy. Many copy decisions in all industries, in fact, are based on what the president likes and/or what the president's husband or wife likes. It

FIGURE 15-12 Ads that beg the question "Why would you want to stay here?"

FIGURE 15-13   Contrived setting in hotel brochure

is no wonder they say that only half of advertising is effective but no one knows which half! Like everything else in marketing, there is only one criterion for measuring advertising effectiveness—the customer.

Incidentally, although we have not specifically addressed it here, the same rules discussed above also apply to collateral, direct mail, and any other form of advertising. We do not reiterate them here, but because collateral is such a common form of advertising for hotels, we recommend reading material prepared by Jane Maas on this subject. An expert in the field, Maas discusses this much better than we could. You will see that the principles are the same.[6] We add a commentary, however: some hotel print advertising has progressed considerably in the past few years beyond the stereotyped ads we have described. Hotel collateral, on the other hand, has progressed only in rare instances and consists of essentially contrived, unreasonable depictions and standardized copy, both dull and boring. We guess that if you changed the name, address, and picture of the hotel, in at least 75 percent of all hotel brochures you couldn't tell one hotel from another. See, for example, the contrived and artificial setting shown in Figure 15-13.

[6] See, for example, Jane Maas, "Brochures That Sell," *Lodging*, October, 1981, pp. 49–52. Also, Peter C. Yesawich, "The Execution and Measurement of a Marketing Program," *Cornell Hotel and Restaurant Administration Quartely*, May 1979, pp. 41–52.

Tara Hotels
THE FLATLEY COMPANY

Fifty Braintree Hill Office Park • Braintree, Massachusetts 02184 • (617) 848-2000

Richard E. Chambers
Vice President, Marketing and Sales

January 4, 1987

Dear

After a very busy holiday season, you deserve a relaxing weekend for yourself. A Merry Weekend at one of our Tara Hotels may be just the reward you need. To make sure you have enough time to completely relax, Tara Hotels is offering a Complimentary Night's Stay in addition to your Merry Weekend!

Our Tara Hotels offer the finest accommodations, many with new, state of the art health clubs. The Upper Crust Restaurants have been awarded the prestigious People's Choice Award in a survey conducted by the Greater Boston Restaurant Guide. Overall, Tara Hotels offer a unique opportunity to spend a luxurious long weekend.

Between now and March 31, 1988, our Complimentary Night's Stay coupon is redeemable at any Tara Hotel listed on the enclosed brochure. The Complimentary Night's Stay coupon is valid for either Thursday or Sunday night in conjunction with the normal Friday and Saturday night Merry Weekend. The coupon is not redeemable for cash, and is based on space availability. Reservations must be made in advance, by asking for the Complimentary Night's Stay Merry Weekend.

I sincerely hope you enjoy Tara Hotels' offer of a relaxing, extra night on your Merry Weekend.

Sincerely,

Richard E. Chambers

REC:sc

P.S. Redeem this coupon in our newest addition to the Tara Hotels, the Sheraton Tara at Monarch Place in Springfield, MA and receive a free gift!

Massachusetts: Braintree • Danvers • Framingham • Hyannis • Lexington • Springfield
Maine: So. Portland • **New Hampshire:** Bedford • Nashua • **New Jersey:** Parsippany • **Rhode Island:** Warwick (Airport)

(Courtesy of Tara Hotels)

FIGURE 15-14   A direct mail special promotion

Direct mail is another special form of advertising and/or special promotion. In many instances direct mail can be a far more influential medium than print advertising. The reason is that one is much better able to directly address its target market. This is especially true for single-unit restaurants which have limited market reach.

Direct mail is also easier to track. While "image" advertising can develop awareness, a direct-mail piece with a "call for action," such as redemption of a coupon, can provide almost immediate feedback for the campaign.

Much has been written in recent years, including entire books, on direct mail for all industries. As there is not room to discuss this here we refer the reader again to a special source that discusses direct mail for restaurants. Again, the principles are the same.[7] Figure 15-14 illustrates a direct mail special promotion.

For the same reasons we have not discussed trade advertising here. That subject is well covered in an article by two experts on the subject, which is highly recommended to the interested reader.[8]

Summary

In this chapter we have discussed the foundations of the communications mix and its probably most visible component, advertising. The foundations prevail throughout the entire mix; they establish the strategy for all parts of the mix that must be integrated. We have shown this applies in advertising. We have also shown how their successful implementation depends so critically on knowing the target market and conducting the appropriate marketing research.

In small firms, all the parts of the communications mix will often fall within the domain of one person, or one department, thus easing their coordination. In larger firms, there may be both an advertising and public relations firm on retainer, with only personal selling handled mostly in-house. In these cases, a special effort is needed to be certain that all the elements of the communications mix are synchronized. In either case, the mix should emanate from the marketing need of the firm and be consistent with its overall marketing strategy.

In Chapter 16, we continue with the communications mix and two of its other elements, merchandising and promotions. In Chapter 17, we will finish this section with a discussion of public relations and publicity, and personal selling. The discussion of these elements in separate chapters in no way removes them from the constraints of the same umbrella, nor does the brief treatment given them in this text, which is limited by available space.

DISCUSSION QUESTIONS

1. Discuss word-of-mouth communications and how they are affected by the communications mix. Give specific examples. How does this affect the need, or lack of a need, to advertise?

---

[7] See, for example, Robert T. Reilly, "Rediscovering Direct Mail: A Primer for Hospitality Firms," *Cornell Hotel and Restaurant Administration Quarterly*, May 1982, pp. 46–51.

[8] Peter Warren and Neil W. Ostergren, "Trade Advertising: A Crucial Element in Hotel Marketing," *Cornell Hotel and Restaurant Administration Quarterly*, May 1986, pp. 56–62.

2. Spot the five elements of the communications mix in the anecdote given in the beginning of the chapter. How could the restaurant have communicated better? How could the couple? Is the answer to the restaurant's problem now to advertise? Discuss.

3. Evaluate the Omni ad in Figure 15-2. Discuss the strategy and tactics of this ad and how they are/are not implemented.

4. Leona Helmsley has received much criticism for her advertising. Examples are shown in Figures 3-6, 10-5, and 15-1. The criticism is usually directed at her ego, since she always has a picture of herself in her ads. Discuss this criticism. Is it warranted? What is the impact from the view of the ads' effectiveness?

5. Why is it so critical to understand the target market before developing the communications mix? Discuss this in detail, with specific examples.

6. Some companies hire their advertising agencies to conduct research before and after running advertising campaigns. What do you think of this policy? What are the pros and cons? Discuss.

CHAPTER 16

The Communications Mix: Merchandising and Promotions

This chapter will discuss two more elements of the communications mix: merchandising and promotion. While reading this chapter, the reader should keep in mind the definition and discussion of the communications mix umbrella from the beginning of Chapter 15, as well as that relating to communications strategy and research.

Principles and Practices of Merchandising

Merchandising is primarily in-house marketing designed to stimulate purchase behavior through means other than personal selling or purchase of time or space in media. In a sense, merchandising is marketing to the captive customer once the customer comes into the hotel or restaurant to purchase a room or a meal. Many customers will buy nothing other than the basic product. The goal of merchandising is to stimulate sales of related or auxiliary products and services. Additionally, this chapter will introduce a method to merchandise the guest room product through inventory control.

The Goal of Merchandising

The goal of merchandising, however, should not be just to stimulate sales; it also has a more long-term goal of increasing customer satisfaction. When the pastry cart is wheeled to the restaurant table at the end of the meal, the goal is to have customers order pastry and increase the check average. It is also to have customers feel even more satisfied because they have finished their meal in a very pleasing manner. If hotel guests order room service, they add to their overall bill. Also, we hope, their stay has been made just a little bit better and we have a few more satisfied customers.

As with everything else we have discussed in this book, then, we approach merchandising from a marketing perspective—fulfilling customers' needs and wants and solving their problems. If we are able to do this, the higher check averages and the larger bills will follow as night follows day. If, instead, we put all the emphasis on the increased revenue we are likely to fall into the same old trap of forgetting about the customer.

To make this point even more strongly, let's take a simple but all too typical example: the wine list in a restaurant. The wine list is a great merchandising tool but in most restaurants receives too little attention, in four ways.

The first way is in the development of the list. Too many wine lists are designed without any thought for the customer. In many cases, the task is handed over to a wine distributor, who is more than happy to print the list at no charge to the restaurant. Of course, the list will include all the wines carried by that distributor, which he or she naturally wants to sell. These wines may, and often do, have little to do with the menu, the target market, and the appropriate price range. Instead of the restaurateurs marketing to their customers, the wine distributor is marketing to the restaurateurs.

As an alternative to the above situation, the restaurateurs themselves, or someone they designate, develop the wine list. Although this provides a better possibility that the wines will complement the menu, often that is still not the case. The wines are chosen for themselves rather than as food complements and, especially, without regard to the target market and its pocketbook. Wine lists notoriously include overpriced wines including one, two, or a few in the $50 and above range, which are intended to add "prestige" to the restaurant. Frequently, these wines do not match the menu price range and rarely sell.

Some restaurateurs we know wonder why their inferior house wines sell so well when they have such a "great" wine list. In order to maintain a 35 percent wine cost, the $4.00 house wine is priced at $11.50, with a contribution margin of $7.50. The $8.00 Bordeaux is priced at $22.75 with a contribution margin of $14.75, provided the customer buys it. The customer is far more likely to buy the Bordeaux if it is priced at $17.50, which would provide a $9.50 contribution margin, or two dollars more than that of the house wine. Of course, the wine cost on that bottle is now 46 percent so the price remains at $22.75. The result is that the house loses $2.00 but, more important, it has failed to maximize satisfaction for the customer. A merchandising opportunity has been lost.

The second way that wine lists fail to merchandise satisfactorily is when the customer doesn't get the wine list. Any self-respecting restaurant that hopes to maximize wine sales should deliver the wine list to the table at the same time as the menu. In fact, many people today order their dinner around the wines they have chosen. Further, every person in the party should receive a wine list even though only one may do the ordering. This helps to get and keep people interested in wine.

In the worst case, however, no wine list is delivered unless it is requested. Those with only a mild interest in wine will not bother to make the request. Those with a greater interest may never get the list or may receive it only after repeated requests. Another merchandising opportunity has been lost.

The third way that the establishment fails to meet the needs of the customer is to have untrained help serving the wine. If the customer was lucky enough to be presented with the list, the entire merchandising effort can be sabotaged by an unknowledgeable waiter or waitress. Although it is unrealistic to expect each server to have the knowledge of a sommelier, the fundamentals of the wine on the list should be understood. In addition, someone on the staff at the time should be prepared, upon request, to discuss the details of the offerings. The service delivery of the merchandising is critical for success.

The fourth way that the restaurant can miss the merchandising potential is to be out of the wine that was selected. All of the table tents, wine lists, and trained staffs cannot deliver a product that is not there. When a selection that is requested by a customer is "86'ed" (a restaurant slang term for being out of an offering), the expectations are immediately reduced, and the rest of the guest experience is in jeopardy.

The Basic Rules of Merchandising

The point of this example is not to emphasize the merchandising of wine lists, but to illustrate the principles of merchandising *anything* in a hotel or restaurant. There are two basic rules to merchandising. The first rule is that any merchandising tool should be designed with the customer in mind, including prices, and that it should complement the rest of the product/service. What is being merchandised (e.g., wine) is actually part of the product/service; the merchandising of it is no more than a communication to customers that is designed to influence their purchase behavior.

The second rule of merchandising is that the merchandising tool should be readily available to, or readily perceived by, the customer and should make it easy for the customer to buy. If you are going to lead a horse to water, you should make it easy for it to drink if that is what it chooses to do.

There are many examples of merchandising in hotels and restaurants that violate these rules. One is the case of room service liquors and wines by the bottle in hotels. These are notoriously overpriced, and the practice is totally contradictory to normal consumer purchase behavior. Customers learn to bring their own rather than pay $45 for a bottle. But consider this situation:

> In a new hotel of a major chain, a customer who was booking a meeting asked the sales manager about the cost of room service liquor. Proudly, the sales manager stated the wisdom of management in pricing room service liquor at the reasonable retail price. The customer commended the chain for being one of the first to finally take a new approach to the pricing of room service liquor.
>
> When the customer checked into his room, he told the bellman that he wanted to order some liquor, since he understood that the prices were reasonable. At the same time, he checked the room service list and saw that the Scotch that he wanted to order was $22—much better than normal, but hardly retail. The bellman, without hesitation, suggested that the customer go to the liquor store in the lobby where he would find the prices lower.
>
> The lobby store had the same Scotch for $16. The customer asked another bellman where the nearest liquor store was located. The response was, "Across the street," where the customer eventually bought the Scotch for $11.

In relating this story, which is not atypical, the customer told us that he would have been happy to pay $15 for the bottle delivered to his room, plus a service charge, just for the convenience. The hotel would have had a 100 percent markup over its cost of $7.50; instead it got zero. More important, the hotel would have had a satisfied customer, instead of one who felt he was being taken advantage of.

There is an age-old adage to this story in merchandising: "You can fool all the people some of the time, some of the people all of the time, but you can't fool all the people all of the time—especially hotel customers."

Examples of Good Merchandising

Examples of good merchandising techniques abound. One case in point is the emergence of "business centers" within *some* hotels. These business centers offer a variety of secretarial support services such as typing and dictation, together with copying, and in some cases computer terminals. The business centers are usually located somewhat off the lobby, with a separate room in which to work. These services cost money for the guests and hotels can make a profit on them. More importantly, they fill a need of the traveling businessperson and create a better guest experience.

Another example of good merchandising in a business-related restaurant is the offering of a "45-minute guaranteed lunch" to cater to the limited time of working people. While no additional charge is made for this service, the restaurant has differentiated itself from its competitors by satisfying a need through merchandising.

The emergence of pizza on finer hotels' room service menus is a merchandising opportunity that fills a need of many customers. Many people do not want a full, heavy meal in their room. Some just want to watch television and have something "fun," as if they were at home. The pizza (merchandised often with beer) fills the need of the customer while putting money into the hotels' cash registers.

This type of merchandising can only increase revenues. Rarely would you find a customer ordering a lower-priced pizza instead of a steak. Price does not become the deciding factor; instead, the product becomes the reason for the purchase. Those customers who really wanted pizza in the first place might have called for a delivery from outside or gone out of the hotel; either way, the money would have been spent outside the hotel or not at all. More important, once again, you have satisfied a customer by fulfilling a need.

Too much merchandising is designed to "get the buck" rather than to satisfy the customer. In fact, there are too many cases where it "gets the buck" once, but loses the customer. This seems to happen most often with price gouging. The customer pays but never returns, or never buys again.

The inclusion of "minibars" in guest rooms both is satisfying to customers and increases hotel profits. Minibars are self-contained units that have beer, wine, mixed drinks, and soft drinks together with snacks for the guest to eat. An inventory is taken of the unit's contents before the guest checks in, and all items consumed are posted to the bill. The probability is low that a guest would call room service for one beer. With a minibar in the room, customers can lean over while watching television or reading, and open a beer at their convenience. The hotel and the customers both benefit from this merchandising opportunity. Again, however, too many minibar contents are overpriced, sales from them are not maximized, (even in Paris they seldom contain wine) and customers are not particularly pleased when they have to pay the high prices. Instead, many buy outside and use the minibar as a refrigerator.

Merchandising is marketing to the "captured" customer. Unless your hotel or restaurant is alone on a desert island, don't translate capture into captivity. Even on a desert island, you may never see that customer again. Instead, translate capture into opportunity: "Here's an opportunity to make the customer even more satisfied."

Merchandising Caveats

The opportunities for merchandising in a hotel or restaurant are almost endless and are limited only by the imagination. A spate of ideas is available in other sources.[1] There are, however, a number of caveats that affect all merchandising and we will discuss some of them here.

Purpose   As with everything we do in marketing, all merchandising should have a purpose. The commonly expressed purpose—"to increase sales"—is true, but not sufficient. Instead, let's say that the overall purpose is to increase customer satisfaction. Of course, we could also say the purpose is to fulfill needs and wants and solve problems. Much of merchandising does that, but in this case we go a little bit beyond the basic marketing concept.

Sometimes just knowing that something is available, and can be had if wanted, will establish the need or want and/or increase satisfaction even when that thing is not consciously needed or wanted. A good example is the year-round swimming pool in an urban hotel. Proportionally, very few guests use these pools, but research has shown that they like the idea that the pools are there to use if they wish. A positive, however, is turned into a negative when the pool is not open at reasonable times that people want to use it, as so often seems to be the case, usually for operational convenience.

The same sense of availability may be true of pastry carts in restaurants for all those people "on a diet." It is human nature to want to feel that we can have something if we want it; merchandising creates that feeling and increases satisfaction.

The other reason we go beyond the basic marketing concept is that merchandising is much involved in the *creation* of wants. Marketing does not do a great deal to create basic needs, but it can create wants. Restaurant diners might feel a need for chocolate after dinner (might even want it, in fact), but repress that need because it's "fattening." Along comes the pastry cart with all those chocolate goodies; now, they really want it! The same is true of after-dinner drinks and flambé desserts. Restaurants have tremendous merchandising opportunities. The most powerful one, sometimes neglected, is the menu itself which can range from the mundane and blasé to exciting and provocative.

By the same token, hotel guests do need to eat; merchandising can make them want to eat in one of the hotel's restaurants. Cards are put up in the elevators, signs in the lobby, and information on the desk in the room. Today, in many hotels, guests also see and hear about the in-house restaurants on the television in their room. In many European hotels, merchandising is practiced upon check-in when the desk clerk asks if the guests would like a dinner reservation made for them.

---

[1] See, for example, William P. Fisher, "Marketing and Merchandising in a Foodservice Enterprise," in *Creative Marketing for the Food Service Industry*, W. P. Fisher, ed., New York: John Wiley, 1982, pp. 19–38; and Francis Buttle, *Hotel and Food Service Marketing*, London: Holt, Rinehart and Winston, 1986, pp. 393–397.

The misdirected conceptualization of so many hotel restaurants, as we have discussed, represents a tremendous merchandising opportunity lost. In other words, merchandising doesn't begin with "telling the customer that it's there"; it begins with designing the product that the customer wants.

The vast majority of hotel F&B outlets are conceived by F&B managers, directors, vice-presidents, consultants, or those of similar title. It is our frank opinion, except in the not usual situation of their being marketing-oriented, that these people should be kept at a distance in the conceptualization process. It should be the marketing people who, armed with the appropriate research, should do the conceptualization. At times, they might "go wild." That's not a problem. They will have to argue, and support their arguments, before the architects, designers, and F&B people until a compromise is reached between what the customer wants and what is feasible to do. The greatest failures in lounges and restaurants have been those concepts developed by F&B people without a marketing orientation, rather than by marketers.

The reason F&B and other non-marketing people are more likely to fail in this process is because they are not in touch with the market. Even the usually "marketing-wise" sometimes make this mistake. Marriott (or the developer) put a half-million dollars into a dated disco in its new hotel in Copely Place, Boston. When Alain Piallat became GM he found that hotel customers wouldn't go near it, "the music was too loud, the people were too punk, and it never made money." The replacement Piallat came up with, Champions Sports bar, is now showing up in other Marriott hotels. "Most important," says Piallat, "It fits with my hotel."

The above statements are not made to derogate F&B people. Everyone has his or her own special training. What we are saying is that you don't call in cosmetic surgeons to do your brain surgery; they are consulted after the essential needs have been established.

All merchandising ploys need to have their purpose understood. One purpose, as we mentioned, is to create the feeling, "If you want it, we have it." Another might be to create excitement, as with an exotic drink, a flambé dessert, or a "spinning salad bowl," which, corny as it was, made Don Roth's Blackhawk Restaurant in Chicago famous. Another purpose might be entertainment, such as that provided by in-room movies, or even sensuality, as provided by the late-evening adult movies. Other possible purposes are convenience (room service), relaxation (aperitifs), contentment (after-dinner cognac and cigars), or information (in-room directories).

Notice that most merchandising increases the tangibility of the product/service mix and establishes consumer expectations, as well as persuading customers to purchase. Merchandising is designed to boost sales, increase check averages, and do all those other good things, but its purpose should be based on the consumer. What will it do for customers to make them feel more satisfied? If it does that, they will spend the money; if it doesn't, forget it, no matter how great an idea you thought it was.

For an example of good hotel merchandising with a purpose, refer back to the Marriott ad in Chapter 15 (Figure 15-8) where Bill Marriott promises the guest breakfast room service on time or "it's on us." This theme carried out in the hotel is excellent merchandising of room service as well as the creating of customer satisfaction.

Another merchandising technique used by Marriott in some of its hotels, which can also be used in restaurants, occurs when you are first seated at your dining room table. A waiter or waitress immediately approaches with a basket of house wines, offered by the glass. The customer has immediate service, and a need identified by the customer has been served. Even if there is a delay in ordering the meal, instant satisfaction has been created. Marriott also uses the same approach at breakfast, as do Le Meridien in Paris and others: You are immediately greeted by a server with a pot of coffee in one hand and a pitcher of fresh orange juice in the other.

Compatibility and Consistency   Merchandising efforts should be compatible and consistent with the rest of the marketing effort in terms of quality, style, tone, class, and price. They should reinforce the basic product/service mix, since these efforts themselves are part of the augmented product. "Way-out" offerings are confusing to the customer and distort the image.

Perhaps under this category falls the affected "Hello, my name is Linda. I'm your waitress tonight," syndrome. This practice was started by someone who seriously wanted to make the customer more comfortable. The intent was marketing-oriented; the failure was in not checking on customer reaction. While this may be appropriate in some places, it is not appropriate in many and, in the category of trivia, is the bane of many restaurant customers. (One friend, anticipating this, greets the waitress with, "Hello, my name is Steve. I'm your customer tonight.")

Practicality   The rule here is if you can't do it right, don't do it. Failure to follow this rule results in lost customers, not satisfied ones. One of the most flagrant abuses of this rule in hotels is room service. Room service is highly merchandised by most hotels that offer it, but those that cannot handle the service properly and expeditiously do themselves a disservice. The staff and method should be in place before a service or product is offered. A good example is the free morning newspaper for "honored" guests. These guests never expected it until it was promised; now they complain when it isn't delivered.

Visibility   Let the customer know about it and how to get it. Elevator cards merchandising restaurants often fail to say where the restaurants are or what hours they are open. In today's modern hotels, where restaurants might be anywhere, it can literally be a mind-boggling experience to find one. Management seems to assume that everyone else knows what it knows about the hotel's layout.

In-room directories get hidden in bottom drawers. Once found, some are so confusing that the guest either turns to the telephone or gives up. We have even seen directories with full pages on the swimming pool and health club facilities but no indication of how to get there or what to wear on your way. Many people don't use pools simply because they are too embarrassed to go there in a bathing suit and don't want to change in dressing rooms. The Royal Garden in Trondheim, Norway solved this customer problem by identifying a "swimming pool/health club" elevator specifically for that purpose. The Stouffer Orlando Resort has done likewise.

On the other hand, visibility doesn't mean total clutter. Some restaurant tables, or hotel desk tops, have so many table tents, flyers, and brochures on them that there isn't room for anything else and it is too confusing to find what you want.

Simplicity   Make it easy to understand and easy to obtain. Make it clear how much it will cost, how long it will take, when it is available, or any other information that will

If you haven't been to our Upper Crust Restaurant, here's an additional lure.

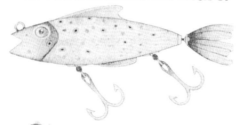

Now you can get a taste of sunny Florida this winter without ever leaving the hotel. Because right now, our restaurant is featuring fresh Florida seafood. Including Gulf Shrimp, Red Drumfish and Stone Crab Claws. Flown in fresh. And delicious. So call for reservations. We think you'll find that one bite and you'll be hooked.

The Upper Crust

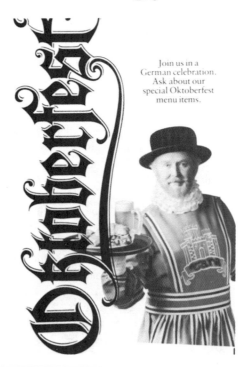

Join us in a German celebration. Ask about our special Oktoberfest menu items.

FIGURE 16-1   Examples of hotel in-room merchandising

make it unnecessary for the customer to have to make additional inquiry. Customers tend to just give up when they have to go through too much rigmarole.

Knowledgeable Employees   Make sure everyone knows about it, what it is, how it works, how you get it, what you do with it, and so forth. Nothing is more aggravating to a customer than repeatedly to ask the same question of a number of people, all of whom should have the answer and none of whom do. As we saw in the example earlier, all of the steps of good merchandising can be in place, but if the waiter or waitress doesn't know the wine being served, everything is lost.

Merchandising is just one more marketing tool for creating and keeping customers. It is also a communications tool because it says to the customer, "Here is what else we can do for you." Wisely used, merchandising is a powerful tool; it is a revenue-producer and, more important, a customer-satisfier. Too often, it becomes a "customer-annoyer." Figure 16-1 shows examples of hotel in-room merchandising.

Merchandising Through Inventory Management

A somewhat different twist to merchandising is merchandising the guest room product through inventory management. There are thousands of travelers today using a variety of different hotel products. Trying to influence their choice of hotels is a very difficult task.

While advertising, public relations, direct mail, and so on are all employed to convince a guest to stay in a particular hotel, it is increasingly difficult to get the message across in these traditional media. Research indicates that the average consumer is exposed to 450 to 500 different commercial messages daily through radio, television, newspapers, billboards, and point of sale.[2]

The result, ironically, is that as media become more available to influence the customer, the customer is so overwhelmed that the message is more likely to get "tuned out."

Even when customers are bombarded with advertising messages, what convinces them to try the product? Traditionally, the sales office of the hotel is charged with the task of personal persuasion but can reach only a small percentage of the market. Only 25 percent of business travelers are influenced by or utilize travel agents or corporate travel departments.[3] This leaves a tremendous number of travelers who never receive a sales call and who are increasingly less influenced by media.

An alternative method for getting a new customer to try your hotel product is through inventory management. Let us first examine a typical business traveler's decision-making process, as shown in Figure 16-2

As we follow the decision-making process, we see that the customer's primary need is to travel to a destination to conduct business. The customer's secondary need is to stay at a hotel. If the customer's first choice is not available, there is the option of cancelling the trip altogether or choosing an alternative. In the case in Figure 16-2, the Westin Hotel received the next call and booked the reservation.

[2] Peter C. Yesawich, "The Marketplace Beyond 1985," *Lodging Hospitality*, May 1986, p. 30.

[3] "Hotel and Travel Survey," *Hotel and Motel Management*, December 15, 1986, pp. 2, 47.

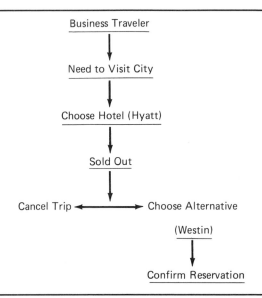

FIGURE 16-2   Business traveler's process in choosing a hotel

Experience shows that customers will continue to call various hotels until they have to leave the product class to get a reservation. For example, if customers called and found a sold-out situation in the upscale product class until the only option was a Red Roof Inn, they might well then cancel the trip. A similar analogy would follow for Red Roof Inn customers. If they called all alternatives in that general price range, and had only a Four Seasons product to choose from, they might cancel the trip.

The merchandising situation is this: Unless customers have had an unsatisfactory experience at their hotel of choice, they will be unlikely to try a competitive product unless they cannot purchase their favorite hotel because it is sold out. It is difficult to convince satisfied customers to switch products. Even if customers are not satisfied, how do you persuade them to try your hotel over all the other choices in the marketplace?

The key to exposing your product to those customers using a competitor's product is through rooms merchandising. At the same time, saving the right number of rooms for potential new customers is a tricky proposition. To illustrate, consider the simple hypothetical example in Table 16-1.

The timing of the buy decision of the transient guest tends to be relatively short-term. In order to maximize revenues, the Clarion Hotel would normally book 600 group-related rooms and save the remaining 200 rooms for regular business travelers. Groups and conventions normally book six months to five years in advance, small corporate group customers may book 30 to 90 days in advance, while individual business travelers book one to three weeks in advance.[4] If each hotel merely sold to groups the number of rooms it needed to sell out, and saved the remaining inventory for the business

_____

[4] Ibid.

TABLE 16-1   Hypothetical Rooms Merchandising Situation in Cincinnati, Ohio

Hotel	Number of Rooms	Number of Rooms Used Daily by Business Travelers
Clarion	800	200
Omni	600	200
Hyatt	500	300
Westin	500	300
Total	2400	1000

traveler, the market would remain stagnant. Each customer would get his or her first choice of lodging facility.

However, there are far more exceptions to the perfect market than there are compliances. For example, the Clarion and Omni together might commit 1200 rooms to a major convention. This is an opportunity for Westin and Hyatt to hold open an increased number of rooms. Clarion's and Omni's regular business travelers will still be planning to come to Cincinnati, unaware that their first-choice hotel will have a rooms shortage.

As we demonstrated above, customers will continue to call for a reservation until they find or don't find a similar product. In this case, the Westin and Hyatt hotels have a chance to merchandise their inventory and to expose their product firsthand to potential new customers. What better way to show the business traveler your service than by having a room available when they cannot book their first choice. If their experience with you is better than at the current hotel, they will become part of your new customer base.

Rooms merchandising through inventory management is not a simple task. However, given the alternatives, it can give a marketing-oriented management an edge over competitors. It is a tool for recognizing customers' buying habits, understanding how the competition operates, and providing the service necessary to steal business travelers away permanently when they really have a problem.

A great deal more can be said about rooms merchandising that is beyond the scope of this text. Essentially it involves two elements. The first of these, as in the above special situation, is deciding what rooms to sell when. For a simple example, do you book a low-rated group of 300 rooms three years away, when you might get higher-rated business in some percentage of those rooms? This might better be called rooms-juggling. It is a necessary practice for all hotels to maximize revenues.

The other merchandising practice is the one of upgrading customers to higher-priced rooms. This does not mean forcing customers into higher-priced rooms until they resist. It means trying, very tactfully, to sell a better product at a better price, a practice common in all retailing.

Principles and Practices of Promotion

A better title for this subject perhaps, and one used by several authors, is *sales promotion*. That title differentiates the subject from the generic term *promotion*, commonly used as one element of the four Ps to represent the entire communications mix. By either name, as used here, the promotion we are talking about is marketing communications that serve specifically as incentives to stimulate sales on a short-term basis. Promotions are superbly used to stimulate trial purchases. In hospitality, they are as frequently used to stimulate business during off-periods when the normal business flow is inadequate to maintain maximum patronage.

When General Motors offers $500 rebates on certain models of its cars, that's a promotion. When Palm Springs hotels offer 50 percent off during the summer months, that's a promotion. When restaurants offer twofers, that's a promotion.

One of the most common forms of promotion in the tourism and hotel industries is the package,—a bundling of any combination of travel, rooms, meals, sightseeing, and so forth in one all-inclusive price. These kinds of packages, however, are directed at specific market segments. For that reason and no other, because it would be just as appropriate to discuss them here, they are discussed in Chapter 9 under the general heading of specialized market segments.

Promotion involves the development of creative ideas aimed at producing business, or creating a customer, in support of the total marketing effort. Promotions must be in tune with overall objectives and must complement other elements of both the communications mix and the marketing mix. Promotions are designed to fulfill a marketing need.

We usually think of promotions as short-term, of the moment. The frequent traveler programs that many hotel companies have instituted, however, are largely designed to be long-term—that is, to keep the customer coming back. In this sense, frequent traveler programs are part of the augmented product, albeit they are also promotions. Regardless, the principles of promotion as discussed here apply just as well to frequent traveler programs.

We have discussed frequent traveler programs in previous chapters. Here we look at them more analytically, because there are lessons to be learned that apply to the general category of promotions, and because they are the biggest promotion going on in the hotel industry today.

The very concept of the promotion genre in business is short-term. Short-term promotions may succeed in the long-term, for instance, may develop repeat business. Long-term promotions, however, rarely succeed in the long-term. The reason for this is simple: long-term promotions become part of the product—that is, they are no longer promotions as originally intended. They become, instead, something you are forced to give customers, meaning that customers must pay for it whether or not they want to. Such practices can be dangerous, especially if they do not fill customers' long-term needs.

Frequent Traveler Programs

Most hotel frequent traveler programs are tie-in promotions that offer benefits both inside and outside the hotels, such as free room stays, car rentals, and airline tickets. The car rental companies and the airlines reciprocate. Other plans give away U.S. savings bonds, console pianos, or selections from a full gift catalog. Most plans award "points" to obtain these benefits. (See Figures 3-3 and 3-4.) These are true promotions that, at best, fill short-term needs.

Other programs are more simply termed "corporate rate programs" and offer guaranteed and preferred rates, guaranteed rooms, speedy check-out, express check-in, free room upgrades, complimentary cocktails and newspapers, free stay for spouse in room, and other amenities. These programs are benefit marketing and do not come under the category of true promotions. They fill long-term needs.

There is much overlap between the two types of programs, resulting in much of the confusion. From a marketing viewpoint they should be separated. The purpose of both programs is, purportedly, to cultivate the loyal customer, the one who will return to the same property or chain. That is a justifiable purpose for corporate rate programs, but not for long-term frequent traveler programs, which is why they are not truly promotions and are self-defeating in the long term.

Promotions, by definition, while they should increase customer satisfaction, are not likely to build long-term customer loyalty in themselves. Obviously, there is nothing wrong with them if they do; it is just that they rarely work that way.

Consider, for example, that Sears department stores have a warehouse sale on appliances—returned merchandise, slightly damaged goods, and so on—a true promotion. You go buy a refrigerator for half-price. Do you now feel compelled (loyal) to go to Sears to buy a microwave oven at the regular price? Isn't the same thing true of a special weekend rate at a hotel at one-third the regular rate?

Sears also guarantees that you can return any merchandise for any reason, no questions asked. Sears customers pay for that privilege, although the cost is hidden in the purchase price. It is not, however, a promotion; it is a policy designed to build customer loyalty, and it does.

Now suppose that Sears has a permanent warehouse sale "promotion" on all merchandise. All other things being equal, you go to Sears. Now Penney's, K-Mart, and fifteen other large chains do likewise. Where is your "loyalty" now?

The airlines have been at it longer so it is easiest to explain what we are saying by looking at their programs. Although the airlines' plans have been touted as great successes, it is difficult to know whether that is really the case. Pan American World Airways reported losing $45 to $50 million after some colossal blunders when its plan was first inaugurated. *Business Week* reported that "most carriers lose as many fliers to rivals' programs as they attract to their own."[5] However, airlines that have tried dropping the plans have felt an immediate loss in business and have had to reinstate them. The largest carriers with the biggest route systems (e.g., American and United) will probably win in this war, but even they have begun to feel the repercussions.[6] For other carriers, it is a purely defensive measure—"Do it or get killed."

Will the same thing happen with hotels? The answer is probably yes. Tony Carpenter, Vice-President for Operations for Hilton International's American-based Vista Hotels, reports,

> I think everyone in the industry would agree that the jury is still out on the subject of frequent guest programs. We ran a pilot project with our Vista Hotel in Washington, D.C., and we really haven't decided whether or not it was profitable. The great

---

[5] "Does the Frequent-Flier Game Pay Off for Airlines?" *Business Week*, August 27, 1984, pp. 74–75.

[6] See, for example, "Frequent Flyer Rules Get Tougher," *Successful Meetings*, May, 1987, pp. 87–89; "Frequent Crying," *Time*, May 4, 1987, p. 39.

unknown factors are how much of the business would you have gotten anyway? And how much loyalty is generated?[7]

In the same article, Mark Lomano, director of leisure-time industry research for Laventhol and Horwath, states, "Once you start giving something to a hotel guest, it's very difficult to take it away," i.e., it has become part of the product offering. This is the dilemma that the hotel industry faces. We believe that long term "promotions" of this kind may not work for hotels for four major reasons.

In the first place, hotel guests have many more options than airline flyers. This means that they can belong to everyone's program and still stay where they want depending on the city where they are at any given time. Very frequent travelers will build up credits in everyone's program and still stay where they would have stayed anyway, only at more cost to the hotel. Less frequent travelers will switch back and forth so that everyone wins and everyone loses, and the net gain or loss remains the same.

Furthermore, the hotel guest is far more fickle than the air traveler and is known to choose hotels by individual property rather than by chain. This, of course, is what the programs are designed to overcome, but they don't help much when the benefits are similar everywhere.

The second reason is that for hotels, different factors pertain. While the airlines are running their programs they have also engaged in fare wars resulting in lower prices. This has attracted many new flyers into the market. These new flyers do not fly very often, and thus are more prone to stay with one or two airlines, build up their points, and take free flights that they would not take otherwise.

The hotel industry has done the exact opposite. Not only has it continued to increase rack rates, but the cost of these programs will cause it to increase them even more. Thus, instead of expanding the market, the hotel industry is shrinking it or pushing it into lower price brackets. A 15 percent discount means little when the rack rates were just raised 15 percent. Infrequent and unsophisticated travelers, the only real hope for growth other than normal population growth, are squeezed once again and they don't like it. Hotels end up with the same market base, perhaps even losing some of it, plus the high cost of running the programs.[8]

The third reason is that the hotel industry, in large part, has a problem understanding its market. The heavy sales orientation is more prone to giving customers what they don't necessarily want, rather than finding out what they really do want, or not providing the flexibility to give it to them when they ask for it (e.g., pool hours). The airlines have been researching flyers for years and know them pretty well. Only relatively recently have

---

[7] Reported in David Martindale, "Hotels and Frequent Flyers: The Changing Relationship," *Frequent Flyer*, August, 1986, pp. 67–68.

[8] "[M]ost chains refuse to provide specifics about expenses for competitive reasons." However, Marriott's program is estimated to cost between $27 million and $54 million a year. Jeff Hershberger, "Fighting for Free-quent Guests," *Lodging Hospitality*, June 1988, p. 118.

There is another problem when hotels can't, or won't, deliver on their promises. In 1988, hotel chains began to impose blackout periods whereby bonus points cannot be redeemed at certain times and/or at certain locations. Complaints resulted and "the number of the disgruntled are likely to grow. Since many hotel plans are a year old, the number of guests taking awards is only now mounting." *The Wall Street Journal*, March 7, 1988, p. 19.

On the other hand, hotel firms are not as vulnerable as the airlines to future rooms liability because many of the awards in the hotel programs are for gifts, airline travel, and other nonhotel awards.

some hotel companies started to do some serious consumer research. Other companies will be left playing "me too."

The fourth reason is that staying in one hotel or another is very different from flying one airline or another. The elements of product and service vary far more in hotels than they do in airplanes, not to mention the duration of stay. The frequent hotel customer is far more prone to choose a hotel because it fills specific needs than to choose an airline where schedule is the main determining factor. The frequent hotel traveler is also, most likely, a frequent flyer who already has more travel points than time to use them, including free hotel stays.

As a group, the hotel industry is giving away something to get the customer it already has while trading customers with other frequent guest programs, winning some and losing some, and spending millions of dollars to do it. At the same time it punishes the vast market it doesn't have (90 plus percent of the market) by making it pay the bill. It flies in the face of reality to construe this as a successful promotion.[9]

Notice the Hilton ad in Figure 16-3. Hilton said that the purpose of this promotion was to lure more occasional travelers, say "thank you" to its infrequent guests (an estimated 30,000 a night who would participate in the program), and create a list of travelers that could be converted to a longer term program.

"We're doing something unique. Nobody has anything else that compares to it," said Joseph Smyth, then Hilton senior vice president of marketing, and the same man who inaugurated the somewhat overkill program for Inter-Continental that gave a free round-trip flight to Europe for five nights stay in an Inter-Continental hotel.[10]

This is certainly unique but look at the cost. The million dollars a day is estimated at retail, so call it a 50 percent cost, or $60 million for the duration of the program. Add $4 million to advertise it and $10 million to handle it, and you have a total cost of $74 million. Divide that by 30,000 travelers per night for the 109-day duration of the program and you could cut the room rates by $22.63 a night at the same cost. How many travelers would rather pay $22.63 less per night instead, or even $10.00 less?[11] Regardless of its virtue, the Hilton four-month program does fall into the category of a promotion.

Marriott, after carefully studying the Hilton giveaway, devised its own promotion for similar reasons—to appeal to infrequent travelers, those who don't bother to join frequent traveler programs, and to stimulate trial and exposure to the Marriott product. This promotion is show in Figure 16-4. Marriott estimated that during the six-month

---

[9] "I've always been a Marriott user, and when they announced the program, it just made me even more loyal," said one business traveler (Hershberger, p. 116). Perhaps the most telling comment in this article comes from Jim Burba of Pannell Kerr Forster (PKF), "They're not just marketing the product anymore, they're marketing their marketing programs" (p. 115). Representatives of PKF and Laventhol & Horwath, hotel consulting firms, are quick to commend these programs but have not offered hard data to support their claims.

Proprietary research conducted by the senior author in 1988 at two hotels of a major chain with a strong frequent guest program reveals the loyalty impact of their program. A random sample taken over a four-week period indicated that 44 percent of guests belong to the chain's program, 10 percent chose these hotels because of their chain loyalty, and less than 3 percent chose them because of their frequent traveler program. Extrapolating from these figures it can be shown that 41 percent did not choose the hotels because of the awards, but received them anyhow, and 97 percent of the customers paid the costs of the hotels' obtaining the 3 percent.

[10] Steven J. Stark, "Hilton Hotels Introduces Free Gift Program for Travelers," *Business Travel News,* November 17, 1986, p. 18.

[11] "Hilton officials estimated the total giveaway will surpass $1 billion." George Taninecz, "Hilton Giveaway Hits High Gear," *Hotel & Motel Management (H&MM),* January 12, 1987, p. 29. We don't know how Hilton arrived at that number but, if true, the daily per person payout would equal $305.81. Either Hilton or *H&MM* need to invest in a new calculator.

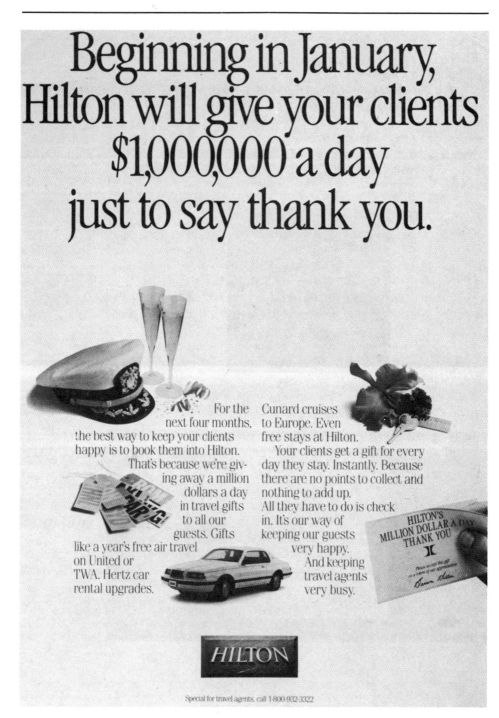

(Courtesy of Hilton Hotels)

FIGURE 16-3 Ad promoting "give-away" program

(Courtesy of Marriott Corp.)

FIGURE 16-4   Selling hotel rooms like selling soap

promotion, it would attract an additional 250,000 customers who would generate 325,000 room nights and spend $2.6 million.[12] It didn't even come close.

Both the Hilton and Marriott plans are true promotions—they are short-term vs. the long-term of these companies' frequent traveler programs. But they will not build customer loyalty. One has to question whether both short- and long-term effects might not be more positive if the monies spent were converted into lower room rates.

We don't have the answer to that question but would be willing to guess at it, not to mention the question of the new customers that would be attracted to hotels more often. The hotel industry needs to do some serious research before they give and price themselves away into oblivion. One thing is certain: Giving away the store is not the true sense of promotion or marketing. There is another thing that we firmly believe: selling hotel rooms is not the same as selling soap, the promotional direction in which the industry seems to be headed, as seen in Figure 16-4.

Promotions and Marketing Needs

Promotions, we have said, are designed to fulfill a marketing need. It follows, then, that the first thing to be done is to define that need.

There are any number of needs for promotions. To create new business, to create awareness, and to create trial purchase are common marketing needs. Some others are to increase demand in slow periods, to take business from the competition, or to meet the competition in its own promotional efforts. Whatever the reason, there is one major caveat in regard to promotions: they should be tied to something positive such as a new or better facility, a new product, or a special time or offering.

Promotions tied to negative features—for instance, lack of business when it is expected to be good—tend to backfire. An example of this is restaurant twofers. Twofers are designed to generate business by bringing in new customers. In the best situations they succeed in doing this, but the customers they bring in are not from the designated target market and few of them ever return.[13] Although there may be a temporary increase in business, it is obtained at a cost: If food cost percentage is 35 percent, it is now 70 percent. At the same time, regular customers who would normally pay the full price are also dining at half-price. The net gain is minimal, if not negative. This does not mean that twofers can not be useful for other purposes, such as creating awareness or trial purchase. Usually they will work best at low-priced, family or fast-food restaurants, rarely at upscale restaurants. Feltensein states,

> The trick is to discount in such a way that you do not sabotage the integrity of your menu. Disguise the lure so that it's perceived as something other than an attempt to discount mainline items.
>
> . . . In the consumer's mind, there is always a correlation between product and price. . . . But over time, discounting is bound to raise questions in the consumer's mind about the integrity of your pricing structure. . . . If you must discount . . . [and]

---

[12] Steven J. Stark, "Marriott Launches Gift Giveaway Promotional Campaign," *Business Travel News*, October 26, 1987, p. 3. These numbers work out to $8 a room night. Either Marriott or *Business Travel News* need to invest in a new calculator.

there are times when discounting is a sound promotional technique—then put together a separate package to your regular offering, that will engender no recognizable negative effect on your customer's perception of the value and price of your menu.

...once you get the customer in the store, remember it is going to take more than a cents-off coupon to bring him or her back.[14]

Promotions at upscale restaurants tend to be more sophisticated. Intense competition has forced "prominent fine-dining restaurants across the country to take a hard look at some new promotional strategies," according to an article in *Nation's Restaurant News*.[15] This article reported on comments of restaurateurs at the 1986 *Travel-Holiday* Fine Dining Awards Reunion.

"We have to be more astute in our promotions today. The business has become so competitive. We're all finding that we're not the only guy on the block anymore." "Not many restaurants can get away without promoting themselves anymore."

A number of those present said, for the time being, at least, they are examining promotions such as direct mailings, special dinners, and advertising brochures to combat the current and pervasive decline in customer counts. While most accepted the need for some form of promotion, it was widely agreed that the wrong type of short-term promotion can do long-term damage. Discount couponing, in particular, was decried by many of the participants as a dangerous strategy to adopt. Tim Gannon of Copeland's restaurant in New Orleans likened couponing to the "death rattle" of a restaurant. "We have to be more aggressive, ... but I'm against these two-for-one types of promotions. It becomes part of a restaurant's image—and often one which can't be erased."

For the most part, it was concluded that any promotion a restaurateur attempts to implement should be closely tailored to the restaurant's image. [p. 97]

An important criterion of any promotion is to be able to deliver what you promise. If you do not, your success will be short-lived. Also, promotions should not be used as an obvious way to get rid of something you want to discard, if you are looking toward the long term.

An example of this principle is one mentioned before—what Bermuda calls its rendezvous season, the slow winter season. The emphasis of this promotion is that Bermuda, and what it has to offer, is the same—just quieter, more peaceful, less hectic, less crowded, and, of course, lower-priced. The fact that you will probably be unable to sunbathe on the beach is ignored; the emphasis is put on the activities, the shopping, and the charm of the island without the intrusion of a multitude of tourists.

This is an intriguing promotion. Unfortunately, it is less than successful because during this season Bermuda is actually not the same. Even without the sunbathing, the offerings of the island are greatly decreased and the prices are not. The word gets around fast, and Bermuda hotels during rendezvous season run, on average, less than 30 percent

---

[13] See, e.g., "Fine-Dining Coupons Flop," © *Nation's Restaurant News*, June 13, 1988, p. 1, 7, which states, "Fine-dining operations across the nation are complaining that coupons and restaurant profits mix like horseradish and heavy cream. 'It's a mistake,' operators said, 'thinking that frugal coupon diners can be converted to regular, upscale patrons.' "

[14] Tom Feltenstein, "How to Discount Your Product Without Sabotaging Your Image," © *Nation's Restaurant News*, November 9, 1987, p. F20.

[15] Paul Frumkin, "Independents Boost Promotion Strategies," © *Nation's Restaurant News*, October 20, 1986, pp. 1, 97.

occupancy. In other words, Bermuda rendezvous season does not deliver what it promises.

Sheraton Hotels classifies promotions by the results they generate into three major categories: revenue-producing promotions, advertising trades or barter deals, and publicity-generating and image-building campaigns. According to Sabina Noering, Director of Transient Marketing for Sheraton:

> Promotion is a vital ingredient in the recipe for marketing success, and Sheraton promotions are designed to give our hotels the competitive edge as well as to supplement corporate and individual advertising and publicity campaigns to gain a greater reach without spending "real" dollars. Getting the Sheraton name in front of the public with popular, upscale projects is the major thrust of our promotional publicity endeavors. This past year we have succeeded in generating national, and often worldwide, publicity and public awareness for Sheraton Hotels.
>
> When putting together promotions, [this] key element should be remembered: Is proposed promotion reaching a market that is also your target market? If not, do not participate. . . . Promotion is a great tool for producing image, publicity, and most importantly, revenue. Use this tool wisely, often, and always to your best advantage.[16]

Guidelines for Promotions

There are some general guidelines for promotions that should apply to most cases. The first of these is to define the real purpose of the promotion. That seems obvious enough, but often this guideline is violated. The result is that, after the fact, it is found that even the successful promotion does not meet its objectives.

Be Single-minded   It is well to keep the purpose single-minded and not try to accomplish too many things at one time. Is the purpose to create new business, awareness, or trial; to increase demand in a slow period; to take away business; to meet the competition; or to sell specialties? Trying to do more than one or two of these things tends to diffuse the promotion, confuse the market, and accomplish none of them.

Define the Target Market   Is it first-time users, heavy users, nonusers? What benefits does it seek? What are the demographic and psychographic characteristics? The promotion must specifically focus on the needs of the target market.

What Specifically Do You Want to Promote?   This is not necessarily the tangible item that you may be promoting. For example, you may want to promote a new decor or atmosphere in the lounge, but the promoted tangible item could be a new or a free drink. A hotel might want to promote its rooms on weekends; the tangible promotional feature could be free breakfast in bed with champagne.

What Is the Best Way to Promote It?   It is not positively necessary to just give something away. You may even want to promote higher quality at a higher price. You could offer an additional service, a package price, a future incentive. Before you give something away, think carefully about what you will get in return.

---

[16] Sabina Noering, "Selling Sheraton Through Promotion," presentation made at the University of Massachusetts, January, 1986.

Make Sure You Can Fulfill the Demand   This is a critical point. Many customers are alienated and lost forever—the exact opposite intention of the promotional objective—by failure to deliver on the promotion. If you are promoting lobster dinner specials, don't run out of lobsters even at the risk of having to let some spoil. If you're offering weekend packages, provide the rooms even if you have to upgrade. The worst thing that can happen is that you'll have a happier customer. At a minimum, do as the retail stores do and provide rainchecks; then, when customers collect on them, give something better, just to compensate for the inconvenience. Too many promotions end up losing customers rather than winning them, because management forgets why it is having the promotion in the first place.

Make Sure Reality Meets Expectations   Do this for the same reasons as those just mentioned. Grand-opening promotions that aren't "ready" lose customers instead of winning them. Don't embellish on what you have to offer; stick to the facts. If you don't have it, don't say it. Also, don't be "picky" on other items. Some managements try to make up for what they are losing on the promotion in other ways, only to create an upset customer.

Communicate Your Promotion and All Related Aspects to the Market   Some promotional literature or ads are so confusing and/or presume so much knowledge on the customer's part that the customer ignores the ad or gets irritated. Specify clearly all pertinent information such as price, quality, procedure, place, dates, time, and any other necessary detail. When customers ask for "it," give it to them; don't play games and say, "There are no more of those left." If you're promoting "children free in the same room," don't hassle with the customer as to whether the child is under 16 or not—that's a no-win situation. The airlines seem to get away with some of these tactics; for hotels and restaurants the situation is different.

Communicate It to Your Employees   This is critical. Promotions break down so often over failure to do this that it's absurd. Management runs an ad in the local paper about a forthcoming promotion and simply assumes that the employees who have to implement it will know exactly what it's all about and how to handle it. A restaurant we know once ran a promotion of free movie tickets with certain special dinners. None of the waiters or waitresses knew anything about it when diners asked for their tickets, and management was "out of town." The result was a disaster. Front-desk clerks at hotels have the same problem with weekend specials, not to mention reservationists at 800 numbers, who often don't know what it is they are supposed to be selling.

Finally, Measure the Results   Do this not just in terms of bodies or of dollars. Did the promotion meet its objectives? What were the benefits, gains, losses? Will it work again? If it didn't work, why didn't it? Will there be a lasting effect, or was it a one-shot deal? Some of the best promotion results are nothing more than good will, which will pay off in the future.

Promotions can be communicated via advertising, direct mail, tent cards, publicity, personal selling, telephone selling, and various other means. Promotions can be persuasive marketing tools when used wisely and appropriately.

Developing Promotions

The use of promotions in the hospitality industry centers on creation of demand. A promotion is the development and execution of an event outside the normal day-to-day business.

The purpose of a promotion is twofold: to increase the satisfaction of the guest while increasing revenues for the hospitality establishment. If the guest is extremely satisfied with a promotion but the costs were so high that money was lost, then the promotion was unsuccessful. Simultaneously, if the hotel or restaurant made a great deal of money but the customers felt slighted, then the promotion was equally unsuccessful.

Normally there are two types of promotions, those centered around established events and those created entirely on their own. A promotion created around an established event might be a Mother's Day brunch, a Bastille Day food offering, or a hotel package for Valentine's Day. In these cases hospitality establishments have an opportunity to create excitement for customers, and to build their volumes. Participation can vary from flying in a French chef to cook for Bastille Day to placing a corned beef sandwich on the menu for St. Patrick's Day.

The second type of promotion—that created independent of an established event—is more difficult to develop and execute. A very good example of a successful promotion came from the Plaza Hotel in New York City in the mid-1970s. The hotel decided to create a strawberry promotion. The execution was flawless, and the entire staff was walking and talking strawberries. All signs in the hotel pictured strawberries, everyone wore a button with a strawberry, special menus were designed to sell strawberries, and the food displays in the restaurants featured strawberries.

The consumption of strawberries increased 500-fold during this promotion. The customers entered a fun, light-hearted atmosphere that was conducive to eating strawberries. In this case, both the customers and the hotel were beneficiaries of an excellent promotion. (A similar promotion using asparagus, which failed, is discussed in Chapter 22.)

Murder Mystery weekends are a good example of independent promotions that sell hotel rooms. Guests spend two days experiencing a choreographed "murder," complete with all the clues for solving the mystery. At the end of the weekend, a suspect is identified and confronted by the participants. Figure 16-5 shows a hotel ad for a murder weekend, and Figure 16-6 illustrates promotions designed to fill slow weekends.

Another successful promotion for hotel rooms has been a "suitcase party" where dinner customers come to the hotel with their suitcases packed for a weekend. During the evening, an exotic weekend away from the hotel is awarded randomly, and the couple is whisked away to their destination. The remaining couples already have their bags packed, and have the option to check into the hotel at a reduced rate.

An equal number of bad promotions have occurred in our industry. Hilton Hotels created a "Tootsie" promotion in the early 1980s to capitalize on the success of the film of the same name. Soon after the movie was released, a generic "Tootsie" salad was to appear on all menus in Hilton Hotels. This "Tootsie" salad was a recreation of a menu item that Dustin Hoffman had ordered in an obscure scene of the movie. The promotion was a failure because the customer was unable to identify the significance of the menu item with the movie. The staff was equally confused, and the item was eventually removed.

FIGURE 16-5 Example of a special feature, independent promotion

FIGURE 16-6   Promotions to build business during slow periods

Hilton ran another restaurant promotion that did poorly. This one was a "fitness" menu, and ads featured Frank Shorter, the Olympic runner. The trade press gave it much publicity in the industry but the customer never bought it; it was a management conception rather than a customer one.

There are many, many variations of promotions. In fact, the number is limited only by the imagination. Figure 16-7 describes five different promotions reported by an industry newsletter.

Designing the Successful Promotion

What, then, are the steps that need to be taken to ensure a successful promotion?

Identify the Gap   The purpose of the promotion from the management perspective is to increase revenues. It makes sense to plan promotions when the facility is not at capacity; the idea is to create new demand. A promotion should be designed to build revenues during slack times or sell products that are traditionally in low demand. A promotion can be held in conjunction with a busy period, such as the strawberry festival, when the goal is increased consumption of a menu item that is in slack demand.

Design the Promotion   There are two areas to address when designing the promotion, that of the customer and that of time. Normally, the customer should be considered before putting any type of promotion together. However, management might design a promotion because of excess inventory. Perhaps some wine was bought in too large a quantity, and needs to be sold. A wine promotion is created, regardless of the needs of a customer, but the promotion itself is designed to satisfy needs.

Promotions do not always "transfer" from one place to another. The suitcase party may be a big hit in California, but in a more conservative state such as Alabama the local customers may feel uneasy with the promotion.

The promotion must be consistent with the positioning of the restaurant or hotel. A disco promotion at the Ritz is not in keeping with the positioning of the hotel. Similarly, a caviar promotion in the local diner is equally inappropriate.

The second important aspect in the design of the promotion is the timing and planning. For example, we have seen a restaurant manager decide, the week before Thanksgiving, that a turkey promotion is needed to get business. Last-minute flyers are produced, an advertisement is hurried to the newspaper, and a menu is created. Servers are warned as they come to work that day, and the entire promotion is executed in an unprofessional manner.

The proper delivery of a promotion includes the integration of a variety of items in the communications mix. Advertising, merchandising, and public relations all need time to be coordinated. Those promotions that do not have the proper timing and planning are usually a failure.

Throughout the design of the promotion, a clear and concise message must be put forth to the customer. While this may not be as necessary for promotions centered around established events, promotions that are attempting to present a novel concept have to be clear. A St. Patrick's Day promotion can be easily understood by most customers because the event carries with it a certain level of expectation; a novel promotion, as we described in the "Tootsie" example, needs to be clear and concise. The customers cannot be left to guess about the promotional tie-in.

Chocolate and Ice Cream Lovers Sweeten Weekend Sales at Upscale Florida Hotel

The First Annual Ice Cream & Chocolate Lovers Hyattfest may have ended Tampa's July quiet forever. Jennifer Regen, PR director of the 525-room Hyatt Regency Tampa, calls it a smash. *"We had over 2,000 people in the hotel over three days;* we sold over 250 room nights," reports Regen. On Sunday, the public got into the Taste Fair for $3 and 1,500 attended. The package, $69 for one night or $99 for two, included admission to the Taste Fair both days. Regen invited Muhammad Ali's new chocolate chip cookie firm to take a booth, and Ali himself attended, providing publicity punch. *The event made a rare first-year profit.*

Free Harbor Cruise Tickets Help New England Lodge Fill Rooms on Sunday Night

Unless your property is different from most, Sunday night business is usually the slowest of the week. In West Yarmouth, Mass., the Tidewater Motor Lodge offers guests who either stay or check in Sunday night free Hyannis Harbor Cruise tickets. *"It definitely increases activity,"* says manager Don Lake. Ads appear in The Boston Globe and require that the ad be presented to get the bonus. *In summer, Lake estimates that 10 to 15 guests per week take advantage of the offer.* And, Lake pays only for the tickets that are used. The cruise operator tallies how many rides his guests have taken and he receives a bill.

Beach Hotel in Mexico Wins Rave Reviews, Publicity by Offering Cooking Classes

Last year, the 1,020-room Acapulco Princess Hotel began offering cooking class packages to a limited number of 20 guests during low summer season. *It has proven so successful that there's now a waiting list* of those who want to book this year. Public Relations Manager Judy Blatman reports that enrollees learn how to prepare red snapper Mexicana, carne asada Tampiqueña and Kahlua truffles, among other dishes. The package also includes tours of the hotel kitchen and a trip to Acapulco's fish market. The hotel has also reaped free publicity—*articles on the classes appeared in 75 newspapers and magazines.*

Downtown Hotel Carves Weekend/Holiday Niche by Appealing to Culture Seekers

The 107-room Juliana Hotel in downtown San Francisco has built up a strong business clientele, but like many properties needs to fill in around the weekend and holidays. It found the solution by deciding to become identified with the arts and cultural community. Last December, *the hotel sold 75 packages with 2-for-1 tickets to the S.F. Ballet's "Nutcracker,"* and began promoting weekend packages for "second tier" (lesser known) music and stage groups. The groups mention the Juliana in their mailings and program. *Weekend/holiday occupancy is up about 15%,* reports Sales Manager Kathy Hansen.

Local Radio Broadcasts From Your Property Can Help Boost Room Sales, Catering

It pays to have radio broadcasts air from your property. There are two shows originating from Atlanta's 521-room Stouffer Waverly Hotel, one named Big Band Friday Night and the other a remote disc-jockey session from the lobby during Sunday brunch. *About 40% of the hotel's business is locally oriented* and its marketing director, Bill Maguire, estimates the broadcasts contributed toward *weekend occupancy gains of 10% a year since the radio shows began* three years ago. In addition to boosting room sales, Maguire believes the broadcasts help local residents remember the hotel for weddings, parties and gala receptions.

(Source: The Newsletter Group, Inc., 1552 Gilmore St., Mountain View, Cal. 94040)

FIGURE 16-7   Promotional ideas

Analyze the Competition   Competition should be analyzed before a promotion is developed. If all of the restaurants in town are offering a turkey dinner for Thanksgiving, what will make this promotion different? If a suitcase party has been held successfully across town, would it be wise to copy the format, or to develop a new promotion to attract customers? A close watch on competitive activity can give the promotion designer a head start on potential problems.

Allocate the Resources   No promotion will be successful if customers are unaware of the activity. A major reason for the failure of a promotion is underestimating the resources needed to bring in customers. Just putting the corned beef sandwich on the blackboard of the restaurant may not be enough exposure to have a successful St. Patrick's Day promotion.

All parts of the communications mix should be evaluated for their ability to bring customers to a promotion. Public relations, advertising, and even direct sales can be used to get the message to potential participants. Direct mail can be a cost-effective way to deliver the promotion. In hotels, traditional merchandising methods such as table tents, signage in the elevators, and employee buttons can carry the theme of the promotion.

Establish Goals   How should success be judged? If a promotion is to satisfy both the customer and the manager, how many extra rooms, or covers, or strawberries can reasonably be expected to be sold? Goals should be set in advance for evaluating the promotion at the conclusion of the event. Goals need to be realistic, and a measurement form should exist before the promotion takes place.

Understand the Break-even Point   It is imperative to understand the economic consequences of the promotion before its execution. In following the steps outlined above, there may be too many resources allocated to the promotion to ever make meeting the goals financially feasible.

A promotion might use a $500 full-page advertisement in the local paper to reach the maximum number of potential customers. If the promotion was slated for a Thursday evening in a restaurant that normally sells 75 covers, a realistic goal for a successful promotion might well be 125 customers on the night of the event. However, if the average check for the event is planned at $15, with a profit margin of $4.50, the additional profit would be $225, obtained at a cost of $500. Many so-called happy hour promotions in restaurants fell into these no-win situations.

Break-even analysis should be conducted early in the promotional planning. We saw one supposedly great promotion developed by a hotel team that at its most successful point—and success was widely anticipated—would have lost $100,000. The greatest "success" of this promotion, had it been carried out, would have been its failure. Both overallocation and underallocation of resources must be carefully analyzed in relation to the success of the promotion.

Pricing is an important factor in promotions and not just because of profits. Is the promotion so expensive to the customer that there will be little demand for the product, or is it so inexpensive that the market will be apprehensive of the quality?

Execute the Promotion   This stage of the promotion is as important as all the others. Execution includes delivery of the product to the customer in the framework of the created expectation. Promotion delivery is more critical than normal delivery because the customer is excited and anticipatory. The promotion has created a demand. Demand has created a special reason to use the product, and customer expectations are unusually high.

Proper execution includes employee participation. The entire staff needs to understand the promotion and its specific involvement. When a bartender shows up for work in the middle of an Oktoberfest without knowing the service steps involved, trouble can be anticipated. Employee involvement, perhaps even in the design stages of the promotion, will increase the chances for optimal delivery of the correct product.

Execution also means maintaining the proper inventory of goods to be sold. If the restaurant runs out of bratwurst during the Oktoberfest and has to substitute hamburgers, the customers' expectations will not be met. Part of the planning process of the promotion is the development of goals. Purchasing should be based on the attainment of these goals, at minimum. It is more desirable to have some waste than to not fulfill expectations.

Evaluate   All promotions should have an evaluation mechanism installed. Were the goals met? Were resources optimally allocated?

While these questions are certainly relevant and necessary, they constitute only half the equation designated for success. The second half consists of the following questions: Were the customers satisfied? Were there any unusual complaints? Do comments reflect any information that might be useful for future promotions? All of these questions should be addressed in the evaluation process to allow a total assessment of the event.

When all feedback has been analyzed, the next stage is formulating the next promotion. Perhaps this particular promotion can be held monthly, or yearly. What other promotions can be developed to fill in gap periods or to sell slower-moving products? The process of promotional development begins all over again

Summary

It should be clear that these two parts of the communications mix, merchandising and promotion, are not simple to orchestrate. While it is easy to employ merchandising and promotion techniques, it is difficult to do so successfully. A management that does not recognize this and performs them carelessly is asking for trouble.

There is a common theme in the development of both merchandising and promotion, that of the customer. In both cases success depends upon the needs of the customer. While the needs of management are used as a benchmark for financial success, it is the customers' experience that should be enhanced by the experience to ensure its success.

This chapter offers a foundation and a methodology for successful execution of merchandising and promotion programs. The most common reason for failure in delivering these subsets of the communications mix is lack of planning. If merchandising and promotions are poorly planned, there is little hope for success. Part of the planning process in both instances includes assessing the needs of the customer, and then providing the product to the customer in a cost-effective manner. With a strong planning process in place and a good evaluation mechanism, both revenues and customer satisfaction can be maximized.

DISCUSSION QUESTIONS

1. Discuss the basic rules of merchandising using a real-life example.
2. Develop an example of good merchandising for a hotel or restaurant using at least two of the other communications mixes.
3. Discuss the individual traveler model (Figure 16.2) in terms of a specific geographic area, for instance, Boston or Los Angeles.
4. How are promotions fundamentally different from merchandising?
5. Develop a hypothetical promotion including all of the steps outlined for a successful promotion.
6. Why is it important to balance the expectations of customers and owners/managers in the development of merchandising and promotions?

Chapter 17

The Communications Mix: Public Relations, Publicity, and Personal Selling

This chapter will discuss the last, but not least, elements of the communications mix: public relations, publicity, and personal selling. While reading this chapter, once again the reader should keep in mind the definition and discussion of the communications mix umbrella described at the beginning of Chapter 15, as well as the discussion of communications strategy and research.

Public Relations and Publicity

Public relations is becoming an ever-increasing force in the area of marketing communications. Some companies are now putting more than 50 percent of their "advertising" dollars into public relations (PR). Ten years ago this figure would have been more like 15 to 20 percent. The main reasons for this change are that PR is more measurable and may have greater impact than advertising.

Public relations and publicity are actually two different items. We group them together because of their commonality, which is the "free" use of the media, but we will also discuss them separately. Instead of buying space in a newspaper or time on a radio, the organization obtains it gratis provided the media think the organization is newsworthy or of interest. In that sense, the organization does not control the placement of the information. Effective public relations is the management tool to present the product to the media in the best light.

Although publicity can derive from public relations, the difference is that publicity constitutes only the information the media choose to use. This can bode well or ill for the organization. Public relations, on the other hand, is the attempt by an organization to control publicity, and to "plant" information in the press or to create a favorable image for reasons other than its formal product.

That is the normal and most frequent concept and use of public relations. Public relations also occurs through word-of-mouth. While much of this may be started by the media, other aspects may be spontaneous. For example, a restaurant makes a special effort to employ disabled people. This fact may never strike the media, but the word gets around and the restaurant is looked at as a "do-gooder." This reflects positively on other aspects of the restaurant.

A Sheraton franchise owned by the Flatley Corporation opened in Springfield, Massachusetts, in 1987. The owner of the company, Thomas J. Flatley, came to Springfield to participate in the ceremonies shortly after a Flatley employee had been killed in an accident outside the workplace. In the past, if this had happened, there were only limited benefits to the employee's heirs. Quite spontaneously, Mr. Flatley announced at the opening ceremonies that henceforth if this ever happened to a Flatley employee the family would receive two full years of that employee's salary. This announcement created very positive public relations for the new hotel.

Public relations creates preopening publicity for hotels and restaurants by developing news releases that the media will carry. It makes sure that the grand opening, or "ribbon-cutting," is attended by the press. It invites dignitaries who make news and in whom the press and the public are interested. It sends out news releases about who slept or ate there. On an ongoing basis, it keeps the press and hence the public, informed as to what is happening at your property or with your firm. Figure 17-1 is an example of a PR news release.

To the listening public, public relations and publicity may be the most believable forms of the communications mix. A salesperson pitching a product, or a slick advertising campaign, may be subject to skepticism from consumers. When an independent source, such as a newspaper, writes about the product in an unbiased setting, credence is lent to the message unmatched by any other communications format. A potential customer for a restaurant is more likely to try the veal specialty recommended by a restaurant reviewer than to try the same dish touted by a full-page ad proclaiming its excellence.

Public Relations

Public relations today however, for the most part, is the planned management of the media's perception. Although the press certainly cannot be told what to publish, a public relations effort can steer the story toward the best features of the product and away from negative images. Public relations efforts are designed to create stories that capture writers' attention with the hope that the writers will, in turn, communicate "the good news" to the desired readers, or target market.

Publicity is different from public relations in that events are created, in a situation analogous to the difference between promotions and merchandising. Public relations "tells the story" of the product, while publicity "makes a story" for the product. In essence, publicity is a subset of the overall public relations effort.

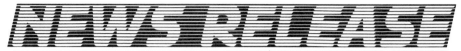

TARA HOTELS THE FLATLEY COMPANY   FIFTY BRAINTREE HILL OFFICE PARK • BRAINTREE, MASSACHUSETTS 02184

CONTACT: Richard Maple, General Manager   RELEASE DATE: Immediate
Upper Crust Restaurant
One Gateway Place
Newton, MA   02158
617/969-3010

NEWTON, MA, October 28 -- Thomas J. Flatley today hosted the opening
of the Tara Newton's Upper Crust Restaurant, part of his extensive
renovation of the Howard Johnson's property.

Among the civic and business leaders attending the reception were
Mayor Theodore D. Mann and Director of the Newton-Needham Chamber
of Commerce Lewis Songer.

The Mayor presented The Flatley Company with a citation welcoming
the new restaurant to Newton and honoring its contribution to the
economy.

The property will be managed by Richard Maple, formerly of the Sheraton
Tara in Braintree and the Parker House in Boston.

The restaurant is open for lunch and dinner. Its feature entrees
are fettucine pancetta, shrimp & linguini pesto and veal pommeroy,
which are also specialties of the other Upper Crust Restaurants located
in the New England area.

The Upper Crust's unique hors d'oeuvres offering, "tapas" include Enoki
and woodland mushrooms marinated in white wine and olive oil, red
peppers stuffed with seasoned crabmeat, sweet sausages served with
sweet and sour figs, and strips of duck breast stewed in garlic, tomato,
pepper and olive oil.

The other Upper Crusts are located at the Sheraton Tara Hotels in
So. Portland, ME; Nashua, NH; Lexington, MA; Danvers, MA; Framingham,
MA; Braintree, MA and Parsippany, NJ. The most recent addition
to the Upper Crust Restaurants came in Springfield, MA at the new
Sheraton Tara.

Tara Hotels   **Massachusetts:** Braintree • Danvers • Framingham • Hyannis • Lexington • Springfield • **Maine:** So. Portland
THE FLATLEY COMPANY   **New Hampshire:** Bedford • Nashua • **New Jersey:** Parsippany • **Rhode Island:** Warwick (Airport)

(Courtesy of Tara Hotels)

FIGURE 17-1   A public relations press release

We can demonstrate these points with some examples. A few years ago, a walkway above the atrium lobby of the Hyatt Regency in Kansas City collapsed, killing a number of people and injuring others. The immediate reaction of the national press to play up the disaster resulted in negative publicity for Hyatt. Obviously, this was the type of press that Hyatt didn't want, so their public relations team went to work.

Although public relations could not kill the story it could lessen the negative effect. Hyatt did this by emphasizing its concern for the victims, for safety, and for future preventative efforts. Although the walkway collapse was not the fault of Hyatt, but in the construction of the hotel, the public tends to relate situations like this to those who can be most easily identified. It is difficult for the media or potential customers to differentiate between Hyatt as the operator of the hotel and XYZ Construction company as the builder of the hotel. Some people might react to this kind of situation by saying, "I'll never stay at a Hyatt again." Public relations is used to overcome such attitudes.

Another example is that of McDonald's, a company widely acclaimed for its public relations efforts. For McDonald's, public relations is a major part of the marketing strategy. Ronald McDonald homes for homeless children are nationally famous. When disaster strikes anywhere near a McDonald's some of the first people on the scene are McDonald's employees with coffee and hamburgers for the unfortunate, and for workers on the scene. When a man went berserk a few years ago in a McDonald's in California and shot and killed customers, McDonald's immediately closed the store and provided financial aid to the victims' families. When the company wanted to reopen the store a few months later, the townspeople strongly opposed it. McDonald's quickly complied by closing the store permanently. McDonald's, in essence, "created" these stories and gained a great deal of positive publicity from its public relations efforts.

In such cases and more often in less serious situations, publicity or public relations is used to formulate an image in the consumer's mind of what the company or product represents. Publicity enabled McDonald's to capitalize on a possibly negative image. Having Ronald McDonald homes for homeless children has nothing to do with the production of hamburgers. The story is "created": the company cares for children (and perhaps, one thinks subliminally, has the same care while preparing the food?). McDonald's is a "good guy" in a bad situation.

Doing Public Relations

Negative public relations happens as a result of bad publicity. Other public relations—the good kind—we try to make happen. Because the public views the editorial press as more credible than paid advertising, PR can be far more effective. Robert McGrail, when Senior Vice-President of Marketing for Lincoln Hotels, stated:

> I can't think of any aspect of the marketing discipline that can be as cost-effective for hotels as public relations, and yet, of all of the marketing tools available to us, it is the most misunderstood, misused, and underused. It is time we got away from the hokey, contrived "events" and started developing meaningful publicity plans. We need to employ PR professionals, either in-house or consultants. The publicity business is no place for amateurs.[1]

---

[1] Quoted in C. W. Hart and D. A. Troy, *Strategic Hotel/Motel Marketing*, E. Lansing, MI: AH&MA Educational Institute, 1987 p. 174.

McGrail believes that public relations is not there just to deal with negative happenings or simply to create positive happenings. Instead, public relations is an ongoing task and an important part of marketing planning.

In this capacity, public relations plays the following roles:

> . . . improving awareness, projecting credibility, combating competition, evaluating new markets, creating direct sales leads, reinforcing the effectiveness of sales promotion and advertising, motivating the sales force, introducing new products, building brand loyalty, dealing with consumer issues and in many other ways.[2]

Public relations also creates images for the local, public, and financial communities as well as for the firm's employees. It creates favorable attitudes toward a firm, its products, and its efforts.

Public relations creates preopening publicity for hotels and restaurants through news releases that the media will carry. The result is that the press attends a grand opening, or "ribbon-cutting." It invites dignitaries who make news and in whom the press and the public are interested. It sends out news releases about who slept or ate there. On an ongoing basis, it keeps the press, and hence the public, informed as to what is happening at the property or with the firm.

Large companies or properties usually have their own public relations firms, which are hired on monthly retainers to maintain favorable publicity for the organization. Even these large companies, however, as well as smaller ones that cannot afford PR agencies, must practice PR in-house on an ongoing basis. Doing this involves employee relations. It also involves relationships with taxi drivers and local police, attitude toward the press, competitive relationships, members of the distribution channels (such as airlines, travel agencies, tour operators), purveyors (who can be excellent carriers of good tidings), shareholders, bankers, and all manner of other publics with which the firm interacts.

Hotel and restaurant managers should belong to the local Rotary, Chamber of Commerce, community task forces, and other groups with which the firm interacts, that will reflect on the firm's relations with the public. One could almost say that everything management does has some aspect of public relations in it. Even the employees of the firm may be excellent public relations elements; in fact, for some firms they may be the most important of all. What your employees say about you and the way you operate reflects heavily on the image that will be created in the public's mind. PR serves well in times of need as a defensive weapon; more importantly, it is a continuous and on-going offensive weapon.

Planning Public Relations

The same rules apply in planning public relations efforts that govern the rest of the communications mix. These include purpose, target market (in this case it may not be the customer at all, but might be the financial community, the industry, employees, intermediaries, etc.), setting of tactics, integration with the product service and the firm's overall marketing efforts (positioning), and so forth.

---

[2] R. Haywood, *All About PR*, London: McGraw-Hill, 1984. Excerpted from Francis A. Buttle, *Hotel and Food Service Marketing*, London: Holt, Rinehart and Winston, 1986, p. 400.

Purpose   The purpose of a specific public relations effort must be established before any further planning occurs. The purpose must be definitive and quantifiable. For example, a restaurant might be under a new management that has to overcome a perception in the marketplace of slow service. In this case, it is unlikely that an advertising campaign would really convince anyone that the service was better. Improving the customers' perception of the restaurant's service would be the purpose of the public relations campaign. The quantifiable measurement, as in advertising, would be the increased number of covers. The subjective measurement would be the change in perception of the service.

A hotel might have a perception in the marketplace of being too expensive for the local customers, and might thus be unused by them. The purpose of the public relations effort would be to dispel the perception by improving the price/value relationship image for the local marketplace. The success of this program can be measured by increased usage of guest rooms by local customers, or in increased restaurant or lounge business outside of usual occupancy trends.

In both these situations, market research, as discussed in earlier chapters, should be used to correctly evaluate customer perception, both before and after. Only then can the public relations effort be correctly focused. Too often the manager of the restaurant or hotel hears three comments from associates in the community, and extrapolates this hearsay into a marketplace perception!

Target Markets   When planning public relations, one must consider the benefit to the customer in the target market. Choosing a target market for a public relations effort is as important as choosing the correct market for any advertising campaign. You must ask, "How will the target market be influenced to perceive the product?" This involves not only short-term benefits, but long-term ones as well, because hotels and restaurants are a major part of the community in which they exist. They are the most public of all commercial enterprises, so much so that they often become "public places" where people meet. It is these same people, as well, who answer such questions from out-of-towners as "Where should I stay" or "Where's a good place to eat?" Public relations will influence local responses even when the people themselves have never stayed or eaten at the property. Public relations creates an image in the mind of the consumer and reinforces that image in many ways. After the purpose and quantifiable measure have been established, gaining an understanding of the needs of the customer (target market) is the next step.

Jessica Dee Rohlm, a leading public relations expert in the hospitality industry, sums up this phase of the process as follows:

> Traditional marketing studies for the travel industry have focused on the who, when, where and hows of the travel habits while ignoring the why. Rather than cost, season, and means of transport, the marketer should look into the mind of the consumer—his attitude about traveling, the image he identifies with, the psychodynamics behind his choice to take a vacation rather than buy a new car. Does he seek culture, pleasure, family fun, night life, status, shopping, sports, an event, or a rest? Targeting in on his motives is the way to reach today's consumer.[3]

---

[3] Jessica Dee Rohlm, "Public Relations or Advertising?" *Selling Travel Magazine,* September 1978, pp. 10–13.

The restaurant or hotel has to have a clear target audience in mind before the plan is designed. Additionally, the motive for the customer to purchase the hospitality product has to be understood.

Choosing Targeted Media   Along with identifying a target audience comes the task of reaching these customers. While geographic location of the customers needs to be understood, the correct media to reach that geographic area must be analyzed as well. While a computer trade journal may appear to be a good place to advertise for a corporate meeting, this is not where a potential vacationer would be reading an article on the benefits of staying in a hotel.

Rohlm mentions how a well-placed article in *Prevention Magazine* drew more response for her health resort client than a similar article in *The Boston Globe*. The latter publication has a greater readership, but if most of the readers have no interest in the product, the public relations effort is wasted. Many advertising firms have large staffs that do nothing but analyze media for the placement of advertisements. A well-planned public relations effort will have some definite publications identified as well.

While "selling stories" may sound unusual, good public relations experts will have a network of editors to whom they can do just that by calling upon them personally. This relationship with decision-makers of a media channel can be critical to breaking a story. For this reason, public relations is becoming more of a science, and less of a "hit or miss" type communication effort.

The public relations expert will push a story much as a salesperson sells a product. Calls are made to the editors, they are wined and dined, and thank-you notes and flowers are sent in appreciation of the placement of the story or press release. A press release is a document giving the salient points of a story in a generic industry-wide format. A press release usually contains the contact name of the public relations professional who wrote the story, background information on the facility, and the body copy of the story. The press release is directed to the editor of a publication.

Personal contacts are what differentiates a good public relations firm from a poor one. Anyone can write stories and send them to papers and broadcast media, but only a true professional has the contacts to follow up until the article is printed.

Positioning   A cohesive message must be developed before a public relations campaign is launched. Ideally, the public relations message will integrate with the other forms of the communications mix. If the advertising message is telling customers that service is the main advantage of the product, the public relations stories should also center on that theme. If food quality is the spearhead of the marketing effort, stories on the chefs and their background will augment this effort.

The positioning must also be kept within the framework of the purpose of the public relations effort. If a public relations effort is undertaken to change the customer's perception of slow service, then the positioning should also follow this generic format. It is very easy to get distracted during a public relations campaign and begin many activities unrelated to the purpose or positioning of the product.

Developing Tactics

Before the P.R. subset is employed, it is important to begin to develop stories on the product itself. Creating a story is usually much more expensive than presenting the existing product to the editors. The following subject titles represent good starting points in a public relations campaign.

Personnel   Numerous stories can be submitted based upon the employees who work every day in a hotel or restaurant. The Omni Parker House in Boston was very successful in getting a major article in *The Boston Globe* when a bellman retired who had been working in the hotel for twenty-five years. A story line was developed, centered on all of the famous people whom this bellman had helped to their rooms. Cute anecdotes on past celebrities and politicians were used, together with pictures of the hotel and the employee.

The hotel wanted to reach the local community by showing a caring attitude toward its employees. The desired thought process for a potential reader went like this: "A person must like working in that hotel if he stayed for twenty-five years. If an employee likes his job, he probably gives good service. Good service is a reason to stay or eat at a hotel." The hotel conveyed an image to the customer in a very cost-effective and believable manner.

For restaurants, a background on the chef can provide an interesting story. If the chef has won any awards or trained outside of the country, the local media are often willing to convey the story to their readers.

Customers   Sometimes customers become a story in themselves. A honeymoon couple from thirty years back checking into the same room can generate empathetic interest. A customer who has eaten lunch in a restaurant every day for ten years conveys an image of consistency that might cause readers to try the product. When celebrities or politicians dine in a restaurant or stay in a hotel, the public has a natural curiosity. The Ramada story told previously of the 59-year-old "child" staying free in the same room created favorable public relations nationwide.

Positioning becomes an important element in using customers as a lead story for a hotel or restaurant. Be sure, however, that the customer being featured is the right representative for the desired target market. Publicizing that the rock band Led Zeppelin is staying at the Pierre Hotel in New York could drive away customers who were seeking to have a quiet and inconspicuous stay in Manhattan.

History   A story line developed about the building, neighborhood, or owner's or manager's background can also provide a format of interest to the public.

Publicity

When "natural" stories like those above have been fully developed, other methods need to be employed to keep the press interested in the restaurant or hotel. Publicity now needs to be "created" so that editors will continue to have something to write about.

The creation of events is not as simple as it may sound. The purpose of the event needs to be established together with a target medium, and an evaluation of the event needs to follow. Publicity, in this sense, is like promotions, except that publicity is aimed specifically at the media to generate public relations. Promotions can be held without publicity; publicity is best held with promotions.

Publicity differs from promotions in the preparation for the event. Targeted audiences (readers) are researched, and the appropriate editors and radio or TV station managers are invited. Again, the personal relationship developed by the public relations expert is critical for successful attendance by the right people.

The event must be organized so that everything goes perfectly. If a promotion is not executed well, the hotel or restaurant is at risk for all of the patrons exposed to the event, plus any other potential customers who hear of it by word-of-mouth. While this might be catastrophic, it is nothing compared to the potential lost business that one editor could produce by writing in a newspaper with a circulation of 100,000 readers.

At the event, press releases with background information are made available to the press. A prepared press release will answer questions such as the number of seats available in the restaurant, the name of the manager, and so on. The public relations professional will "work the event" by attending and selling the points personally to the attendees. The end of the actual promotion signals the beginning of the placement work for the public relations effort. Thank-you notes and flowers are sent to remind the attendees of the importance of the event. Follow-up calls are made to cajole the writers to place the story in the best light, and to the editors for the actual placement. Having a story placed in a newspaper or on radio/television is not the only measure of success. Where the placement occurs is also vital to the maximization of the readership. The physical placement of the story is as important as getting the story into the media.

After all of this work is finished, the last stage of the public relations effort is the evaluation. Have more customers been generated? Was perception in the marketplace altered to the satisfaction of the management team? The evaluation process is as important as any other phase of the publicity effort. Restaurant covers and rooms sold can be tracked at the property, but changes in customer perception are more difficult to measure. Further market research should be employed to better understand the impact.

Caveats

There are additional caveats to public relations suggested by another PR expert, Joe Adams, president of the Adams Group Inc., a national PR firm.[4]

- P.R. is not free. This is the most common mistake hotels make. If you don't budget, don't expect results.
- Use top P.R. talent. P.R. titles are often bestowed on people who have no training or experience in public relations. You can usually buy the services of a good P.R. firm for what it costs to hire one experienced individual.
- Have a written plan. If you can write it down, you can make it happen.
- P.R. people must understand your marketing plan. You can't expect results unless you let them in on your plans and objectives. Make sure they understand that P.R. is a marketing tool.
- Demand regular reports on P.R. results. A consistent, on-going P.R. program should provide consistent, on-going results.
- If it doesn't sell it's not creative. It takes innovative ideas to get deserved P.R. coverage.
- Remember: Great public relations depends upon creative management.

---

[4] Joe Adams, "Good P.R. Plan Can Be Potent Marketing Tool for Hotels," *Hotel & Motel Management*, June 8, 1987, p. 60.

Personal Selling

The direct sales effort or personal selling (which are one and the same) for a restaurant or hotel is another important portion of the communications mix. Personal selling may be one of the more challenging aspects of the communications mix because it relies heavily on an individual's ability to meet with a customer face to face. Public relations communicates through stories and the media, advertising communicates through copy and artwork, and merchandising communicates through in-house promotions and selling. The salesperson communicates through direct oral presentation to the customer.

Personal selling is not just "selling"; rather, it is marketing carried directly to the customer. Because sales efforts are a major subset of the total marketing effort, personal selling has become an incredibly important marketing tool for the hotel industry. Bob Bloch, former Senior Vice-President of Marketing, Four Seasons Hotels, says, "Sales is 50% of our [external, visible] marketing effort."[5] For the restaurant industry, because of its fragmentation, personal sales as a formal activity is less used but nevertheless important in many instances.

The nature of the hospitality product lends itself to a heavy emphasis on the personal selling effort. Table 17-1 shows how the product offering predicates the need for a sales force.

Emphasis on Personal Selling

In each of the four subheadings of Table 17-1, the application to the hospitality product can be seen to lend itself to the direct sales portion of the communications mix. Buying the product requires a major commitment on the purchaser's part. A meeting in a suburban hotel of thirty people for three days can easily exceed a $10,000 expenditure. Assistance is necessary in application, and personal demonstration and trial are common. The price for meetings and group bookings is normally negotiated. Distribution channels, as outlined in Chapter 18, are short and direct. Advertising is inadequate and too expensive to reach and fulfill the needs of the buyer. Finally, the marketplace sees the salesperson as an integral part of the product.

All the rules of the communications mix apply to sales. The only difference is that they are carried out personally and directly. The direct sales effort is a sizable portion of the marketing plan. Management decides what customers it wants (target market), and the sales or marketing director develops the appropriate strategies consistent with the overall marketing strategy.

Personal selling is the only part of the communications mix that permits direct feedback from the customer. This is true regardless of whether it takes place in an organized fashion through the sales staff or through direct communication with the customer by management or employees. Once again, personal selling is a subset of the total marketing plan that creates images, offers benefits, and differentiates from the competition.

A good example of customer feedback through direct sales was evidenced by the repositioning of a large hotel in New York City. The original marketing plan designated a

---

[5] Comment to one of the authors, November 1986.

TABLE 17-1   Characteristics of the Marketing Mix That Support Emphasis on Personal Selling

---

Personal Selling is generally a significant tool when . . .

Product

The product requires that the customers receive application assistance (e.g., with computers and pollution control systems).

The product requires that the customers receive personal demonstrations and trials (e.g., with private aircraft and totally new products).

The product purchase decision requires a major commitment on the purchaser's part.

Pricing

The final price is negotiated, not fixed (e.g., with real estate, automobiles, and many industrial goods).

The final price and quantity purchased allows an adequate margin to support selling expenses (traditional department stores vs. discounters).

Distribution

Distribution channels are short and direct.

Channel intermediaries require training and assistance.

Communication

Advertising media do not reach the intended markets effectively.

Information sought by potential customers cannot be provided entirely through advertising and sales promotion (e.g., with life insurance).

The size and dispersion of the market make advertising too expensive.

The firm's promotional budget is small and sales per customer are high.

The market sees personal selling as an essential part of the product.

Source: William Lazer and James D. Culley, *Marketing Management*, p. 752. Copyright © 1983 by Houghton Mifflin Company. Used by permission.

target market consisting of primarily individual midweek business travelers. All of the appropriate direct sales strategies were developed and executed. Through sales calls to customers, it was learned that this target market preferred smaller hotels at this destination—a need the hotel could not fulfill. The strategy was changed, and the sales team was redirected toward a more productive base of business. It would be difficult to measure this type of customer response to advertising; direct sales allows for a more immediate feedback mechanism.

The Sales Process

Once a target market has been identified, the sales team must have a clear understanding of the needs of the customers to whom it will be selling. A sales call solicits a current or new customer for business. It can take place in person or over the telephone. The features and benefits of the products are matched to the needs of the customer, which are carefully extracted through a series of questions during the sales call. Product attributes and customer needs are matched. Salespeople should know their product well in order to present it in the best relation to the needs of the customer. "Closing" takes place when the customer makes a commitment to buy.

Probing

Probing is a method to determine the needs of the customer through a series of inquiries. Questions such as "What is important to you?" or "What made your last meeting a success?" are examples of probing customers for their perceived needs.

Not all customers are especially cooperative in the inquiry process, and their responses need to be channeled. This is done through the use of "open" and "closed" probes. An open probe is a question that is phrased to encourage a customer to speak freely. Customers who appear receptive to sales calls should be approached with open probes. The two example questions in the previous paragraph are open probes.

Closed probes are used to direct customers who may not be aware of their needs or cannot express those needs well. Some examples of closed probes are "Is a pool important for your meeting?" and "Is a ballroom that can seat 500 people too large for your reception?" In these examples, both questions elicit a yes or no response. A closed probe is usually first answered by yes or no. One hopes that once customers have responded, more of their needs will surface.

Features and Benefits

Once the needs of the customer have been established through a series of probes, the customer is introduced to the product features. A feature is a tangible or intangible subset of the product the customer will buy. It is also important to recognize those features that differentiate the product from that of the competition. These distinctive features should be especially emphasized if they are important to the customer.

The most important thing to remember is that customers do not buy features; they buy benefits. A benefit is the reason that a customer needs the feature or product. Unless the benefit is clearly explained, the customer may not understand why the feature is important.

As an example, a pool is a feature. The benefit to the meeting planner is that conferees will have a place to relax and unwind after a busy day of seminars. All hotels claim to offer good service, but what is the benefit to the customer? In this case, it is problem-free meetings. Why is express check-out important to a meeting planner? Because it allows conferees to leave the hotel without waiting in line, making the final experience at the facility hassle-free.

To sell the potential customer on buying the product, the good salesperson will attempt to match the features and benefits to the customer's needs. Features that may not provide any benefit to the customer should be excluded from the presentation. A primary mistake made in direct sales is to misunderstand the needs of the customer, while simultaneously presenting features and benefits of the product that are unimportant.

The same pool that is so attractive to the meeting planner for conferees would probably have no impact on a bus tour planner who has a group of senior citizens coming to the hotel for a quick stopover. The reason is that the two customer sets have different needs. Similarly, dining service facilities will not matter to the tour operator who wants to book a group out of the hotel for their meals. Introducing the ballroom to a meeting planner wanting to book a group of twenty is obviously poor selling.

Closing

Throughout the sales call, the needs of the customer should be surfacing and the appropriate features and benefits should be emphasized. At some point the salesperson tries to "close." A close is merely an attempt to gain a commitment from the customer. While a definite booking at this point would be ideal, the best commitment may be to get the customer to decide to visit the facility. The hard sell often doesn't succeed in the hospitality industry.

The customer may reject the close by not making any commitment. The salesperson may then try to find a need that hasn't surfaced previously, and introduce new features and benefits.

Closing becomes more difficult as the customer becomes more knowledgeable and sophisticated. Organizations such as Meeting Planners International host a variety of educational seminars that provide meeting planners with information on the negotiating process. Additionally, the supply-and-demand situation of the marketplace often gives the customer more choices. The need to say yes to a sales pitch is less immediate to a more knowledgeable customer with many similar options.

The disciplined, cohesive sales effort following the steps outlined above should consistently produce results. The customers who are called upon will give the feedback necessary to make the correct marketing decisions.

Prospecting

Prospecting is the term used for finding new customers. Prospecting means making sales calls on customers who are not currently using the product. Prospecting is more difficult than calling on existing customers because new customers don't know the product, although they may certainly have some perception of it. New customers need to be convinced that the product they are currently using does not satisfy their needs as well as your product would.

It is highly unlikely that a meeting planner will "create" a meeting just because of your facility. The meeting either will already exist, having occurred before at a competitor's hotel, or will have been partially developed and waiting to be placed in a facility.

New customers are the competitors' existing customers (and vice versa!). In direct sales, the most common way to get new customers is to take them away from competitors. In almost all cases, new customers are currently using a competitor's product and have to be convinced (sold) to use yours.

With this in mind, direct sales prospecting tactics should be targeted at competitors' customers for maximum results. Sales representatives, through the sales call process, identify at the beginning of the sales process clients who use the competition. The other steps of the sales process remain the same.

Cold Calls

Using lists of potential clients to make cold calls (i.e., calls with no advance contact) is called nontargeted prospecting. A cold call might consist, for example, of entering an office building without an appointment, walking into the office, and asking to see the person in charge of making hotel arrangements. This tactic has been popular in the past but is awkward for both the salesperson and the customer. Additionally, it is not an efficient use of time. Telephone solicitation of lists is similarly nonproductive in the same way.

Customers should first be qualified to determine whether they even have a need to use a hotel. Qualification of customers is no more than finding out their needs. Through the use of probes, the qualification process determines the reason that customers buy the product (such as price or location) and the expected quantity needed (number of room nights or covers). There are numerous specific techniques for identifying competitors' business that will produce logical and focused solicitations for new customers, although these go beyond the scope of this book.

Sales Management

The management of an effective sales force means integrating a variety of skills. The proper allocation of resources, development of personnel, and motivation of the workforce all combine to make a sales team efficient.

Allocation of Resources   The size of the sales force is determined by the number of sales calls that should be made on a yearly basis. Each customer is assigned a call frequency; customers who use the product more frequently are called more often than smaller accounts. Also, sales calls are needed to find new customers through prospecting. If a hotel has not yet opened, all sales calls are dedicated to finding new customers. If the hotel has been open for over two years, it will have a mix of old and new customers, and the mix of finding new customers balances with the calling of current customers.

Staffing the sales office should result from a mathematical calculation of sales calls needed to satisfy current customers and those needed to find a reasonable amount of new customers. This is different from the practice in which a salesperson is added only when sales are down, and is eliminated when sales are up. In these situations, resources may be overallocated or underallocated, and sales will swing downward.

Once staffing guidelines are established, salespeople are usually organized by territory and product line. For example, in terms of potential customers for a hotel, the city of Cleveland can be divided into the east and west side. In order to keep the sales process orderly, one sales representative may be assigned to the east side while another is assigned to the west side.

The product lines are assigned by the type of service within the hotel that the salesperson represents. There are three types of product offerings sold through direct sales: group, transient, and catering. The group product line is for customers who purchase a number of rooms at the same time. The group salesperson may or not sell the function space simultaneously. For example, a bus tour would be considered a group but would have no need for function space. IBM might have the same number of guest room requirements as the bus tour but have extensive meeting space needs. Depending on the size of the hotel, there may be more than one group salesperson; for example, there may be a need for an exclusively bus tour salesperson if this is a major market for the hotel.

Transient salespeople sell to customers who have a need to book guest rooms on an individual basis. The *catering* salesperson normally handles meetings and social events like weddings that don't require a large number of sleeping rooms. This person sells the function space with food and beverage, if possible.

It takes a very disciplined effort to keep an effective sales organization on a focused track. The director of sales needs to cue salespeople as to when business is most needed. For example, weddings may book a ballroom a year in advance. Large groups, such as an Elks Club convention, may also want the ballroom for the same weekend, but also will reserve a large portion of sleeping rooms. If a wedding with a few overnight rooms was already booked for the ballroom, the Elks Club business might be lost. Conversely, if the wedding was turned away and the Elks Club did not choose the hotel, the ballroom might be empty on that date. Such decisions are made on a daily basis.

Development of Personnel   The development of personnel is critical to the success of a sales organization. If the wrong people are hired, customers will become upset and choose another facility. If good salespeople leave to go to a competitor, there is additional opportunity to lose business. If a position remains open for any length of time, necessary sales calls to existing and new customers will not be made. Turnover in the sales departments of major hotel companies is well over 50 percent annually. Companies need to be conscious of this problem and address the reasons for it.

Development of an effective sales staff begins with recruitment. There should be an ongoing effort to locate and know the best salespeople in the marketplace. While new talent can be solicited at the college graduate level, there is still a void at the experienced salesperson level. Organizations such as Hotel Sales and Marketing Association International are good forums for getting to know the better salespeople in an area.

Training is critical to the development of salespeople. Although there are many existing sales training programs, the challenge is to use them. At least one month of training is necessary for new salespeople to minimally learn the product and understand the needs of customers. Even seasoned salespeople need to be constantly trained through role-playing and sales meetings, to keep their skills sharp. Training also indicates the level of commitment that the company has toward the individual development of a salesperson's career.

Motivation   Salespeople need to be consistently motivated to be effective. While this may be true of all job categories, it is especially true of salespeople, who represent the product on a daily basis.

Unlike their counterparts in the operations aspect of the hotel business, salespeople are paid on commission. Normally, the operations people are paid a bonus based on the financial progress of the property and, one hopes, customer feedback. Salespeople are paid on their productivity, based upon quotas. Quotas are developed based upon the territory and the product sold. This quota is normally derived from the budget that the hotel has set for the sales office that year. Once quotas are established, the salespeople are paid for progress over and above the quota. Some incentives are paid monthly, and others quarterly or yearly. It is likely that the more immediate the gratification, the more motivated the salesperson will be.

Other forms of motivation, such as incentive trips and merchandise, are becoming part of the motivational toolbox of sales organizations. These are also based upon quotas, and may be used when there is a short-term sales gap that needs to be filled.

Product Line Management   Most hotel sales offices are structured to sell the three distinct products that we have discussed. These are transient programs for the individual traveler such as Marriott's Honored Guest, Sheraton's S.E.T., and Omni's E.S.P. programs; the group product that offers the customer the opportunity to purchase both sleeping rooms and function facilities for a meeting; and the catering product for the customer who needs function or meeting space without guest rooms (the term for this last type of business is *free-standing*).

Many customer accounts have a need for more than one product, and in some cases a need for all three. For example, a planner at IBM might need transient guest rooms, group space, and free-standing function space in the same hotel for the same or different occasions. Present methods divide the sales effort and provide for three different salespeople to represent the three products in the same hotel.

Most other industries do not operate in this manner. For instance, you can buy an entire range of automobiles or insurance coverage from the same person. Why, then, does the hotel industry make the same IBM customer talk to three different representatives to buy very similar products in the same location? The industry has been slow to react to the customer in this regard. The problem is also compounded by the fact that a majority of customers experience turnover within a sales office at least twice a year.[6] The customer experience of trying to purchase various hotel products from the same hotel can easily mean negotiating with six to seven salespeople in one year.

Research has shown that customers clearly want to change the way they are purchasing the product.[7] The product line approach to sales, in which one sales representative services all three products for the same customer, is the recommended method to gain competitive edge over sales offices organized in the traditional format.

This is not to say that the current transient salesperson should be out selling weddings—that would result in utter chaos. It means that customers who have a need for more than one hotel product should be handled by the same salesperson in order to offer continuity to the customer during the sales process. Those customers who have only a need for one product (e.g., a wedding) should be handled in the regular manner, by the catering salesperson.

Sales and Operations

"Sales sells and operations provides" is an expression that describes what is often seen as the relationship between sales and operations. That relationship is a critical one and needs

---

[6]Richard Chambers, Christine Dipré, and Erica Schwartz, "The Product Line Approach to Sales." Presented at World Hospitality Congress III, March 10, 1987.

[7]Ibid.

some explanation here, because a conflict between sales and operations can be incredibly damaging to a hotel's relationship marketing effort. In fact, this is a case of a real need for internal marketing. The situation has been described by Venison:

> Nowhere in the universe of hotelkeeping can the interdepartmental chasm be so wide as it often is between sales and operations people. There often seems to be a natural barrier between operations and sales personnel. It is, of course, not difficult to see why—for are not the sales personnel the unruffled well-dressed ones, always wining and dining on the company's money and on the fruits of the labor of the rest of us; are not sales personnel the ones who always promise the impossible but are rarely around to make sure that the impossible is achieved; are not sales personnel the very ones who after the event is all over arrive with all the trifling little complaints?[8]

Knowledge of the product and the capabilities of the organization is essential to successful selling. Constant and continuous communications between sales and operations are imperative to effective marketing for a hospitality organization. It should suffice to say that if what the salesperson sells cannot be delivered, the hotel will in most cases eventually lose the customer. It is natural for a salesperson to want to make promises in order to make the sale.

A thorough knowledge of the product and the capabilities of the organization will go a long way toward keeping these promises from creating unreasonable expectations for the customer. If the salesperson is not sure that the hotel can deliver, then he or she should confirm with operations before making the promise. This not only provides a confirmation, it also gets operations into the act so that there is more likelihood that someone will follow through.

It is not uncommon for operations people to find salespeople's requests "impossible." Although this may often be true, in many cases a little imagination, creativity, and willingness to adapt to the situation will often change impossible to possible even if some modifications are necessary. If both parties are truly tuned in to solving the customer's problems, and each party fully understands the problems of the other, satisfactory resolution is most always possible. This is both internal and relationship marketing practiced at their best. It is the marketing and management leadership of the property or the company that should make sure that it happens.

Many times the operations team has little knowledge of the difficulty of facing customers after a problem develops. The salesperson must go back to dissatisfied customers and ask for their business once more. The front office manager or steward may never face the customer again.

Summary

It is evident that the public relations effort of a hospitality entity is a very effective element of the communications mix. It may be the most effective element in that it is the most believable for the consumer. A potential customer reading or hearing a third party's praise for a product is more likely to be convinced by that than by an advertising campaign.

---

[8]P. Venison, *"Managing Hotels,* London: Heinemann, 1983, p. 119.

The public relations campaign should be focused and quantifiable, within targeted positioning and purpose objectives. Publicity remains a subset of the public relations umbrella, to be utilized after all natural stories are highlighted for the press to cover. Understanding the customer is the core both of the public relations effort and of marketing in general.

A sales organization needs to have a clear definition of the markets that it wants to attract, and a recognition that it needs to penetrate competitors' business in order to increase its own. Additionally, the organization has to be knowledgeable about its goals through the sales organization, and be prepared to sell the customer with appropriate features and benefits. The sales office that allocates its resources carefully and develops and motivates its people effectively will be the most productive. As the marketplace absorbs more new hotels and demand remains stagnant, the competitive fight for the same business will intensify. Those who establish a strong plan based on the components discussed in this chapter will have the competitive edge necessary to win fair market share.

DISCUSSION QUESTIONS

1. What are the components of a good public relations plan? Discuss how you might apply them to a local restaurant.
2. Discuss the similarities and differences between merchandising and promotions, and publicity and promotions.
3. Contrast public relations and publicity and discuss the implications of each.
4. Many hotel salespeople are selling essentially the same thing as their competitors when making sales calls. Discuss how you as a salesperson would deal with this, using hypothetical or real examples.
5. Compose a features and benefits chart for a hotel and discuss how you would use it to address a specific target market.
6. Discuss the needs and difficulties in organizing a sales force by territory and by product offering.

Chapter 18
Channels of Distribution

By definition, channels of distribution are a set of independent organizations involved in the process of making a product or service available for use or consumption.[1] Most companies that produce goods or services need assistance in distributing their products to the end user, the consumer. Goods-producing firms such as Procter and Gamble, Ford Motor Company, and Coca-Cola must somehow arrange to distribute their product—that is, get it to where the consumer can buy it. It is unlikely that consumers would go to the bottling plant each time they wanted a drink of soda. Similarly, traveling to Detroit to purchase a car from the plant is clearly impractical for most.

In the same sense, hospitality companies like Sheraton, McDonald's, and American Airlines need distribution systems through which their customers can find their product. There is a growing need in the hospitality industry to utilize channels of distribution as never before. When the demand for hotel rooms and restaurants exceeded the supply, customers managed to find their way to the product offered. This is not the case today, with the proliferation of new hospitality products all vying for the same customer.

How Distribution Channels Work

In a usual manufactured goods situation, the producer of the goods uses a wholesaler or a broker to assist in the distribution of the product. A wholesaler is a business unit that buys, or takes on consignment, merchandise from the producer and sells it to the retailer. A broker serves a similar function but may or may not actually acquire the merchandise. The

---

[1] Paul S. Busch and Michael J. Houston, *Marketing, Strategic Foundations*, Richard D. Irwin, Inc.: Homewood, Ill. 1985, p. 476.

retailer is the point of sale where the consumer can purchase the product. Wholesaler, broker, and retailer are all part of the distribution system.

Companies have found it necessary to utilize these separate channels of distribution if only because of the prohibitive costs of developing owned distribution systems. Ford Motor Company, for example, distributes through its retailers, the local car dealerships, which sell Ford cars to the public. To purchase the real estate, construct the facilities, staff the organizations, and market the cars would be a tremendous burden on Ford's resources.

Procter & Gamble, on the other hand, works through brokers and wholesalers to get its product to the retailers, of which there are tens of thousands, worldwide. Coca-Cola distributes through franchisees who buy syrup in bulk, make and bottle the final product, and deliver it to innumerable retailers. Variations of such distribution systems are endless. Some systems are vertically integrated: In these, retailers are owned by the manufacturer and sell only that company's products. An example would be Tandy Corporation, which owns Radio Shack, the only stores that sell its product.

In conventional distribution systems, however, the retailer carries many brands, including those of competing companies. Control of the channel lies in the strength of the product being sold. If an item is in very high demand, the producer of this product may be able to set the terms of the channel. If the producer is offering a very strong product, it may manipulate the retailer into carrying and merchandising other and weaker products as well. When the product is weak, the wholesalers and retailers will dictate the terms of the channel to the consumer.

Although the principles are the same, the channels of distribution for the hospitality industry differ significantly from those used for manufactured goods. For one reason, the hospitality product is normally not "moved" to the consumer like a bottle of soda or a tube of toothpaste. For another, the product is often sold in conjunction with another product, such as airline tickets or charter tours. Finally, because of the unusually high perishability of the lodging product, many traditional channels simply would not work. In distribution channels of the hospitality industry, a separate wholesaler or retailer rarely takes physical possession of the product to be marketed and delivered to the end consumer at a later date. In hospitality, the manufacturer is not only the retailer, but manufactures and sells the product simultaneously. The problem, then, is not how to distribute the product to the retailer, but how to distribute the customer to the retail outlet. Thus arises the need for a different kind of distribution system to broaden the base of customers and sell the product more efficiently.

We will first discuss distribution systems that are similar to those used by manufacturers: company-owned/-managed, or franchised properties. We will then discuss some more unusual distribution channels used in the hospitality industry.

Owning and Managing

Hospitality companies either own (wholly or partially), manage, or franchise the properties that bear their name or, in some cases, someone else's name. In any case, the major issue of distribution is where to be. In the owning and franchising categories, there is an additional issue of optimal deployment of direct financial resources.

Owning

It is critical to the successful distribution of a brand name to be in the right geographical areas. These are often defined as primary, secondary, and tertiary markets. There are fifteen so-called primary cities in the United States, including Boston, Los Angeles, and Denver. Secondary markets include Hartford, Salt Lake City, Portland, Oregon, and San Antonio, Texas. Finally, there are tertiary markets such as Des Moines, Iowa, Lexington, Kentucky, Boise, Idaho and Spokane, Washington. The ranking depends on the size of the market and its buying power. There are also, of course, many smaller or even isolated market areas.

The same is true internationally. Primary international destinations are Paris, London, Tokyo, and Singapore. Secondary ones are Brussels, Amsterdam, and Stockholm. In the tertiary category are Cologne, Marseilles, and Düsseldorf.

Resort destinations likewise abound, from the Rocky Mountains to Honolulu to Bali, to the Côte d'Azur in France and the Costa del Sol in Spain. Having a property in Switzerland may be as important to a hotel company as it is for a fast-food chain to have a position on the New Jersey Turnpike.

Upscale hotel chains usually strive to be in the primary markets first, and then move into the other markets. Restaurant chains may do it the other way around. Certainly McDonald's is in about every level of market conceivable. The point, of course, is to distribute the product to the right markets—first, by being there and second, by being able to capture the same customer in another place. In order to increase the number of customers in the distribution system, it is necessary to offer the product in a variety of marketplaces where the customer either is or goes. Having a presence in the correct marketplace is critical to the success of a distribution channel.

A case in point is the Marriott Marquis Hotel in New York City. As an entity in itself, the hotel will probably never be a major profit producer because of the cost of land and construction. Why, then, would Marriott have engaged in the project? Because of the importance of New York City in the company's channel of distribution for major conventions.

Marriott wanted to capture large conventions from the existing network of Hilton and Sheraton hotels. Major convention planners could buy the Hilton or Sheraton product in New York City, Chicago, and Las Vegas, among others. The Marriott product had a market presence for the smaller, corporate-oriented business, and was a late entry into the large convention marketplace. The Marriott Marquis in Atlanta was the first step into this distribution system. No major player in the convention circuit can maximize its customer base without a hotel in New York City. Thus, the individual profit and loss statement of the New York City hotel is not as important as is that hotel's overall contribution to the Marriott convention network nationwide.

Owning provides the brand name with the best integrity, from a product delivery point of view. If a company both owns and manages a facility, the product has a better chance of being consistently maintained and presented to customers in the network. Expansion, however, comes harder when one firm owns and manages all facilities. Capital monies are spread thin, and the importance of expansion may overtake the need to own and deliver the product. From a distribution standpoint, the need to expand the name brand identity usually outstrips the financial resources of the company.

There are two good examples of companies that chose to expand their channel of distribution by not owning or managing their expansion outlets. The first, McDonald's, has thousands of stores neither managed nor owned by the parent company, yet it has been very successful in maintaining a consistent product worldwide. Quality control is so effective that the distribution system has been expanded without sacrificing the integrity of the product.

The second example, Sheraton Hotels, has been less successful. (The same is true of Hilton, Holiday, and some other hotel companies that franchise.) There can be a large product difference among Sheraton properties. One hotel may be clean, modern, and well managed; another may be older, unkempt, and disappointing. This difference in product quality is apparent and confuses the customer. The customer who happens upon the well-managed Sheraton leaves happy, and most likely will stay at another property in the distribution system. The customer who happens upon the other type of property is not as inclined to make the same choice again.

While both Sheraton and McDonald's own and manage properties within their channel of distribution, there is very little difference in a McDonald's product system-wide. There is a clear difference between company-owned Sheratons and some noncompany-owned, i.e., franchised, Sheratons. The hotel product, of course, is far more difficult to control than the fast-food product.

Every hospitality company that wants to expand its product offerings geographically must eventually decide either (1) to make slower progress by owning (at least partially) and managing each unit, (2) to manage without owning, or (3) to franchise. Companies that take the last option should take heed of the quality control systems of McDonald's.

Managing

Managing is next best to owning and managing for maintaining the quality standards of the product name in the channel of distribution. In many cases, companies manage for a fee while the physical property is owned by others. The fee, however, is not always the sole objective of the managing company. As discussed above, being in the right places in the distribution channel can be equally or more important. For example, Westin or Inter-Continental hotels' presence in Singapore, at the time their new hotels were built, would probably have been sheer folly from an ownership perspective. Westin moved into a poor position in Stamford, Connecticut simply because it wanted a presence in that market.

Currently, by contrast with the recent past, lenders usually require some sort of equity position on the part of the management company. The reason for this is the increasing risk factor of hospitality enterprises. In the past, tax laws were so advantageous for the investor that the cash flow or actual business value of the facility was not as important as the tax breaks.

This situation was mutually beneficial for some time. The investor would provide the money for the facility, anticipating large tax write-offs in the short term and watching the value of the real estate grow in the long term, exclusive of the actual performance of the hotel. Simultaneously, management companies found a way to increase the presence of their brand name in important marketplaces without utilizing their own capital.

As with all "good deals," the economic laws of supply and demand eventually took over. Many marketplaces were overbuilt, with too many hotel rooms or restaurant seats in the same product class available for a marginally growing demand. Denver, Miami, and Singapore are examples of locales with too many hotel rooms for too few customers.

In addition, the tax advantages of such relationships were largely eliminated in the United States by legislation enacted in 1986. Taxes and oversupply combined have all but eliminated the no-equity management of hotels. (By no-equity deals, we mean the management of a hotel without significant capital investment on the part of the managing company.) Typically, the management company is paid a fee based on gross sales of the facility, with bonuses applied for performance over a mutually agreed-upon profit margin. These constraints will slow growth of new hotels in the future and, eventually, allow the demand for the product to rise to meet the supply.

In the next few years, there will be a tremendous shake-out of current management contracts. With management companies at little financial risk, investors may be saddled with nonperforming assets in overbuilt markets. Capital monies will be less available, compromising management companies' ability to keep some products in their portfolios.

For example, there may be a Hilton Hotel in a tertiary marketplace such as Lexington, Kentucky. A group of local investors may have provided the money to build the facility; Hilton manages the operation. As the marketplace becomes overbuilt and the tax incentives dry up, cash flow stagnates or dwindles. As the product becomes older in its life cycle, refurbishment becomes necessary to keep it competitive. The original investors can no longer depend on the asset itself to be self-supporting. Even if the hotel is covering its mortgage payments, it is unlikely that additional money has been set aside from operating funds for necessary refurbishment after the normal five- to six-year life cycle.

Hilton would now have to make a decision. Although its name is on the facility, and Hilton customers are becoming less satisfied with the product, the owners may be unable or unwilling to fund the necessary renovation. If the hotel is important enough to the Hilton distribution system, Hilton may choose to provide the funds itself, and wait until the supply/demand imbalance corrects itself and the hotel again becomes profitable. Hilton's other option is to withdraw from the contract and forfeit this marketplace in its distribution system. While the loss of a hotel location in Lexington might not in itself be earth-shattering to Hilton, the big picture around the United States tells us otherwise. There are thousands of Lexingtons waiting to happen, nationwide, for all of the large chains such as Sheraton, Marriott, and Hyatt, each with a somewhat different scenario and timetable. The decision scenario above will occur time after time in the next ten years.

At the same time, some management companies have become even more aggressive. For example, AIRCOA, the largest independent hotel management company in the United States, moved out of ownership into management on a fee-for-service basis. In 1988, AIRCOA operated a mixed bag of 121 hotels, ranging from tiny independents to convention properties and representing 15 different franchise companies, and the company was targeting an expansion of 26 properties a year.

Franchising

Franchising is a commonly used method for a hospitality entity to increase its distribution network, both to create more revenue and to obtain the geographic presence discussed above. Franchising is also a common method of distribution for nonhospitality companies from Avis Rent-a-Car, Midas Mufflers, and Manpower Temporary Services to H&R Block tax services and 7-11 convenience stores. Coca-Cola and Pepsi Cola franchise by allowing bottling plants to utilize their mixtures and then distribute their product. This method of distribution has been in common usage since what was called the franchise boom of the 1960s.

Franchising is the usage of a name by someone else for the purpose of selling that product or service. Briefly, a company creates a product or service. It then offers other companies or persons the opportunity to use the name to market the offering in a variety of geographic areas. The amount of control a franchisor (the parent company) has over the franchisee (the company that buys the name to distribute the product or service) varies as widely as the franchising options available.

There is normally a license agreement between the franchisee and franchisor that outlines the terms of the relationship. Items such as marketing support, revenues to the franchisor (usually determined as a percentage of sales), and duration of the agreement are covered. Territorial rights are also negotiated at the same time. A franchisee might obtain rights to a two-mile zone, five-state area, or an entire country, in which no other franchisee of the same product or service can operate. For example, separate franchisees in India have acquired exclusive rights to the Days Inn, Quality International, and Sheraton names in that country.

The leader in franchising for hotels has been Holiday Corporation, although Days Inn and Quality International are catching up fast; in fast-food the leader is McDonald's, followed by Burger King, Wendy's, and Kentucky Fried Chicken. These companies and many others recognize that their ability to distribute their products' name and identity throughout the country and the world is limited by the amount of capital available. Methodically, they have offered their name and their service to potential franchisees.

Major companies need to expose their products to more customers, in effect creating brand-loyal consumers who will buy their product wherever it is available. The rationale is that the more places the customer can buy the product, the more often that customer will become a new customer of the same product in another marketplace. This distribution of the brand name by franchising has become integral in the growth of many major restaurant and hotel chains. There are, however, notable exceptions, such as Stouffer and Westin Hotels, Courtyard by Marriott, and TGI Friday restaurants.

From a distribution standpoint there are two main advantages to being a franchisee. First, it automatically positions the hotel or restaurant in the marketplace where customers already have an image—for instance, McDonald's or a Days Inn. Without a known name, customers have a more difficult time determining the position and eventual product delivery of the facility. Second, for a lodging property, franchising often provides an immediate reservations network.

Traditionally, the franchisor provides the following services with its name affiliation.

Technical Knowledge   Each franchise operator does not have to reinvent the wheel. Although there are vagaries in each local marketplace, many of the components of a business are generic. The franchisor provides the procedures for the business.

Managerial Techniques   In some cases, the franchisee lacks management skills. Although procedures may need to be adapted to the local situation, they need not be developed from scratch each time a franchise is sold. Training and procedure manuals are made available by the franchisor. Some franchisors provide full mandatory training programs for their operators. Examples of these include Holiday Inn University and McDonald's Hamburger University.

Marketing Support   Clearly the phrase "the sum of the parts is greater than the whole" can be applied here. Franchisees pay a percentage of revenues toward the franchisor's marketing efforts. Each franchisee may market his or her product locally, but being part of a larger organization enables penetration into many cost-prohibitive geographic areas. Local marketing may have to follow guidelines to provide continuity with the rest of the product lines.

Financial Support   Connection with a successful franchisor is sometimes the key to obtaining financing for a business. Lending institutions are more willing to lend money to a project with national affiliation than one of a local entity. The ability of a local operator to obtain business from outside marketplaces is greatly enhanced by a national or regional affiliation.

Safeguards   This broad-based category is a catch-all for the support services offered by the franchisor to the franchisee. It includes such things as legal matters, safety regulations, and insurance issues.

Auditing   Most franchises have specific guidelines for operation of their businesses. Some are more stringent than others. The level of service needed to maintain a Days Inn franchise is different from that of a Marriott franchise. Normally, there is a systematic evaluation of the franchise to ensure that the customer is receiving the appropriate product and service.

Reservation System   For hotels, a major advantage of franchising is the reservations network. Being a member of a nationwide chain can make the difference between a 50 percent occupancy and a 70 percent occupancy. The franchise affiliation automatically positions a hotel in the local marketplace. Simultaneously, it exposes the hotel to brand-loyal customers.

Traditionally, in the United States, a toll-free 800 number is provided for the benefit of the customer. This is a great advantage for other intermediaries such as travel agents, as well as the individual customer. Perhaps the best-known toll-free number belongs to Sheraton. By continually advertising this number (see Figure 15-7), accompanied by an easy jingle that the customer can remember, Sheraton's 800 number has obtained at least some "top of the mind" awareness for potential and existing customers.

Hilton, on the other hand, made a grave error in first establishing their reservations system. Instead of one number to call for all Hilton hotels, there were over twenty regional offices, each featuring a different toll-free number. The original concept was to have a regional office that understood the needs of local customers better than an impersonal central reservations system. The result were quite different. A Hilton traveler had to know all of the numbers in order to place reservations in various parts of the country. The customer became frustrated and many switched to other hotels' systems. Hilton has since changed to a central reservations number.

In terms of room nights, good reservations networks can make a major difference in a hotel's daily business. For example, there are millions of brand-loyal Sheraton customers traveling daily who need a place to sleep. While they may have some local favorites, when they travel to a different destination chances are that they will purchase a product with which they are familiar. This is a tremendous potential market. Of over 33 million business travelers alone, 60 percent will go to an unfamiliar domestic destination at least once a year.[2]

Internationally, franchising has yet to catch on as it has in the United States. There are some franchise networks emanating from American companies such as Holiday Inns (which is usually positioned as an upscale product in the overseas marketplace), but the American franchise system in hospitality remains essentially American.

Other marketing support from a franchise relationship may include a national sales force that sells the product name to large consumer markets. These salespeople provide coverage in marketplaces where it would not be cost-effective for the local property to enter. The purpose is to sell all of the hotels in the chain to customers who have a need for more than one location.

For example, the accounting firm of Peat Marwick Main may need to have training meetings in Dallas, Tulsa, and Jacksonville. Because Peat Marwick Main is based in New York City, it is more cost-effective to have a member of a hotel chain's national sales organization call on this customer, representing all three locations (which may be managed by three different hotel companies under the same franchise umbrella), than it is for the individual hotels to send their own sales representatives. In many instances, the customers also prefer to deal with one sales representative rather than having to listen to three different sales pitches.

Franchising companies are recognizing the need to provide greater services to their franchisees. As the competition increases for expansion, it is critical to maintain the expansion of the number of franchises. To do this, additional services such as special toll-free numbers for travel agents, one-stop shopping for group bookings, and centralized commission disbursement for travel agents, all attempt to differentiate the franchise in the eyes of customers and investors.

Franchising also provides immediate positioning for a restaurant. Pricing, quality of food and beverage, and general ambience are all preconceived by the sign outside the establishment. Restaurant franchises are usually regulated by the franchisor more than their lodging counterparts. Variation in quality of product in fast-food stores such as Denny's, McDonald's, or Dunkin Donuts are rare. There are, however, a myriad of product and service experiences for travelers at Holiday Inn or Sheraton franchises.

Most customers cannot differentiate between the corporate-owned and -managed hotel or restaurant, and that of a franchise. A sales representative of a franchisee in the east is somewhat at the mercy of another franchisee and different management company in the midwest or Europe. Often, sales representatives meet resistance because of problems encountered by customers using the franchise in a different location and managed by a different company.

Philosophies of Franchising   Hospitality companies have different philosophies of franchising. Marriott, for example, franchises a relatively small amount of hotels for a

---

[2] *Mastercard International Frequent Business Traveler Study,* presented at the American Hotel and Motel Association Convention on November 14, 1983.

(Courtesy of Omni International)

FIGURE 18-1   Soliciting franchisees for a defined target market

FIGURE 18-2   The competitive battle for franchisees

company its size. Only about 25 percent of Marriott hotel properties are franchised. Contrarily, Holiday Inn has franchised over 88 percent percent of its hotels; Hilton follows with 81 percent and Sheraton with 71 percent.[3] There are also some companies, such as Hyatt, Four Seasons, Stouffer, and Fairmont, that do not franchise at all. The philosophy of these latter companies is that the level of service they are attempting to deliver can be maintained only by direct control.

A newcomer may obtain initial success in the distribution network through franchising. Radisson Hotel Corporation, operating with a relatively unknown name, was quickly able to amass a network of close to 100 hotels with about 50 percent of them franchised. By marketing the chain as a "collection" of hotels, Radisson was telling the customer up front that the physical product might be different upon check-in, while the services inside were presumably the same.

By adopting this concept, Radisson directly addressed one of the pitfalls of franchising, namely, that the product is not always the same. This is different from the confusion created by Omni Hotels. Omni offered a wide range of physical products under the same name. From the Omni Nassau Inn, a country inn located on the campus of Princeton University, to the megastructure of the very commercial, middle-tier, 1450-room Omni Park Central in New York City, to the high quality of the Omni in Atlanta, the Omni customer could only be bewildered by the differences in the product line. In the distribution process, this can be self-defeating.

The power of franchising in distribution strategies cannot be overestimated. Figures 18-1 and 18-2 are ads by two major players in the hotel industry for the purpose of attracting franchisees. The Omni ad represents a decision to go into franchising to expand the company's distribution. The Days Inn ad, on the other hand, is only one of a number that articulated a direct attack on competitors. Using subtle innuendos in this ad series, Days Inn insinuated that a franchise with them is better than a franchise with numerous other companies, in this case Holiday Inns. Some attacked this ad campaign as unscrupulous; such attacks have not intimidated Days Inn management.

Consortiums

A consortium of hospitality companies is a loosely knit group of independently owned and managed properties with a joint marketing distribution purpose. Examples of consortiums include *Preferred Hotels,* which represents a number of very upscale hotels, and *Logis and Auberges de France,* which represents almost 5000 family-run hotels of varying sizes in the one- and two-star categories (logis) and ungraded smaller properties (auberges) in France. What ties these properties together is a joint marketing effort aimed at similar target markets at different times and places. What also ties them together, and differentiates them from strictly reservations networks, is that there is also some measure of control placed upon the membership.

The purpose of the consortium is to open a channel of distribution by maximizing combined marketing resources while retaining individual and independent management and products.

---

[3] 1986 Business Travel Survey, *Business Travel News-Annual Business Survey,* May 1986, pp. S22–S30.

The Preferred Hotel Group, headquartered in the United States, is a consortium of about 60 independently owned and managed hotels in North America, Europe, and Asia. Preferred has a central reservations number and provides regional sales assistance in key cities. The advantage to the property represented is its ability to retain individuality while obtaining worldwide representation. Customers, in turn, realize that they are not buying a standardized product line. The Preferred Hotel Group maintains very high standards within its membership grouping, and the traveler need not be wary of the potential experience. In 1984, Preferred received 173 requests for membership information and 12 actual applications; it accepted only 3 hotels as new members.

The Preferred consortium benefits include not only referrals, but also large savings in joint advertising costs, a reduced 3.25 percent credit card fee from American Express, a toll-free reservation number, and inclusion in airlines' computerized reservations systems used by travel agents. Figure 18-3 illustrates Preferred's Advertising for its members.

Many people consider Best Western a hotel chain. In fact, this worldwide organization is a consortium of over 3300 individually owned properties in 2150 communities, under a common umbrella. The variety of product offered to the customer is significant. The overall theme of the consortium is the price-value relationship of the hotels. Best Western, in any marketplace, will tend to offer a clean room for the lowest price. The Best Western consortium is a very successful channel of distribution. Although standards are lower than those for up-market counterparts such as Marriott and Radisson, the strong sense of value in all marketplaces keeps customers coming back. Best Western, the largest such organization in the world under a common name, constantly seeks to add new members worldwide. It does not hesitate, however, to drop members who fail to live up to established standards.

The primary objective of consortiums is to combine the marketing efforts of independently owned hotels. The examples are far more abundant in Europe than in the United States. As an example, consider Inter Nor Hotels in Norway, which operates somewhat differently than Preferred.

Each of the twenty-eight Inter Nor hotels is independently owned and managed. It is doubtful, however, that many people know this. The collateral of each hotel carries the names of the other twenty-seven. Most promotions take place in all hotels simultaneously. Reservations are easily made from one to the other. Each hotel is labeled an Inter Nor hotel as if it were, in fact, a member of a unified chain. There is a "corporate" office in Oslo, which suggests and administers marketing programs for the "chain," evaluates the performance of each unit, arranges seminars to improve marketing and management, and, in general, acts in many ways like the corporate office of a hotel chain.

This type of consortium doesn't end there; it hooks-up with other consortiums both to provide interchange reservations systems and to broaden the entire network. Inter Nor, for example, hooks up with Danway hotels in Denmark, Arctia Hotels in Finland, Icelandic Hotels in Iceland, and Sara Hotels in Sweden. These arrangements provide a distribution network of over one hundred hotels that not only reserve with each other but also combine on promotions.

The "art" of consortiums is far more refined in Europe than it is in the United States. Relais & Chateaux is a Paris-based consortium with over 400 members in thirty countries, including the United States. Its 1987 collateral listing members, published in several different languages, describes the consortium as follows:

Life has a different rhythm at Preferred Hotels all over the world. It's a celebration of enduring style and quality. It's prestigious. Private. And personal. Always unhurried, and filled with a quiet comfort and beauty all too rare in the world today.

UNITED STATES
ALEXANDRIA, VA/
WASHINGTON, D.C.
• Morrison House
ANCHORAGE
• Hotel Captain Cook
ATLANTA
• Colony Square Hotel
AUSTIN
• La Mansión Hotel
BEVERLY HILLS/
LOS ANGELES
• Beverly Wilshire Hotel
BIRMINGHAM
• The Wynfrey Hotel at
Riverchase Galleria
BOSTON
• The Colonnade
CARMEL, CA
• Quail Lodge
CHARLOTTE, NC
• The Park Hotel
CHICAGO
• The Barclay Chicago
DALLAS
• Hotel Crescent Court
• The Mansion on Turtle Creek
DENVER
• The Brown Palace Hotel
DETROIT
• Hotel Pontchartrain
FT. LAUDERDALE
• Pier 66 Hotel and Marina
GRAND RAPIDS
• Amway Grand Plaza Hotel
HONOLULU
• Halekulani
HOUSTON
• The Warwick

INDIANAPOLIS
• The Canterbury Hotel
KANSAS CITY
• Alameda Plaza Hotel
KEYSTONE, CO
• Keystone Lodge
LAS VEGAS
• Desert Inn Hotel & Casino
LOS ANGELES
• Hotel Bel-Air
LOUISVILLE
• The Seelbach Hotel
MEMPHIS
• The Peabody
MILWAUKEE
• The Pfister Hotel
MINNEAPOLIS
• Marquette Hotel
NEW ORLEANS
• The Pontchartrain Hotel
NEW YORK CITY
• Grand Bay Hotel at
Equitable Center
NEW YORK CITY/
LONG ISLAND
• The Garden City Hotel
ORLANDO
• The Peabody Orlando

PALM BEACH
• The Breakers
PORTLAND
• The Heathman Hotel
RALEIGH/DURHAM
• Hotel Europa at Chapel Hill
SAN ANTONIO
• La Mansión del Rio
SAN DIEGO
• U.S. Grant Hotel
SAN DIEGO/LA JOLLA
• La Valencia Hotel
SAN FRANCISCO
• The Stanford Court Hotel
SEATTLE
• The Sorrento Hotel
STAMFORD/
GREENWICH, CT
• The Inn at Mill River
TUCSON
• Tucson National Resort & Spa
WASHINGTON, D.C.
• The Embassy Row
• The Watergate Hotel
WILMINGTON, DE
• Hotel duPont

CANADA TORONTO
• Park Plaza Hotel
• Hotel Plaza II
• The Prince Hotel
CARIBBEAN
BRITISH VIRGIN
ISLANDS
• Peter Island
AUSTRIA VIENNA
• Hotel Im Palais
Schwarzenberg
ENGLAND LONDON
• The Dorchester
FRANCE PARIS
• Hotel Le Bristol
GERMANY
BADEN-BADEN
• Brenner's Park-Hotel
COLOGNE
• Excelsior Hotel Ernst
DÜSSELDORF
• Hotel Breidenbacher Hof
FRANKFURT/
WIESBADEN
• Hotel Nassauer Hof
MUNICH
• Hotel Bayerischer Hof

ITALY ROME
• Ambasciatori Palace Hotel
NORWAY OSLO
• Holmenkollen Park Hotel
SPAIN MADRID
• Palace Hotel
SWITZERLAND
GENEVA
• Le Richemond
LUCERNE
• Grand Hotel National
LUCERNE/VITZNAU
• Park Hotel Vitznau
ZURICH
• Hotel Baur Au Lac
• Dolder Grand Hotel
ISRAEL TEL AVIV/
HERZLIA-ON-SEA
• The Daniel Hotel and Spa
HONG KONG
• The Peninsula
JAPAN
OSAKA
• Royal Hotel
TOKYO
• Imperial Hotel
KOREA SEOUL
•Hotel Lotte
PHILIPPINES MANILA
• The Manila Peninsula
SINGAPORE
• Goodwood Park Hotel

Preferred Hotels WorldWide

Possibly the last of the great private collections.

For reservations call your travel planner or from all
50 states and Canada call toll-free **1-800-323-7500.**
In Chicago call **(312) 953-0505.**

For a free 1987 Directory, write to:
Preferred Hotels Worldwide
Suite 220, 1901 S. Meyers Road
Oakbrook Terrace, IL 60148

© 1986 Preferred Hotels Worldwide. All rights reserved.

FIGURE 18-3   Consortium consumer advertisement

480

Our objectives and procedures do not correspond to a fashion (fashion becomes outdated) but to a need—yours—we have no desire to change except for the better. . . . "The Relais & Chateaux do not form a chain, but a product." . . . our clients are not interested in a chain. They look for a product with clearly defined differences, even if the presentation differs from one place to another.

A major problem with consortiums—as with franchises only more so, because the only direct control is the right of membership—can be the disparity among properties, both physically and in the way they are managed. Although properties are carefully screened for membership and there is really no desire for look-alikes, problems still arise.

Within Inter Nor, for example, there is a disparity both among physical plants and among marketing approaches. The Royal Garden Hotel in Trondheim is a unique, new, architectural property where management seems to bend over backwards to accommodate the customer. This hotel backs up its architecture with its service. The historic, elegant, and excellent but different Grand Hotel in Oslo falls into the same category.

At the Park Hotel in Sognefjord, however, the experience belied the claims of the hotel's brochure: "exclusive, yet unpretentious . . . guest rooms . . . emphasize discreet elegance . . . and our staff is fabulous too!" We found the hotel to be common, pretentious, and neither discreet nor elegant, and to have a staff so callous and indifferent that we wondered whether we were checking into a hotel or a boarding house—at $150 for a single room! This hotel slapped a $50 ticket on your car if you exceeded the 30-minute limit in the parking lot in front of the hotel, instead of going into the hotel's parking garage. If one's only experience at an Inter Nor hotel was at the Park Hotel, one might seriously wonder about the other properties. Is it any wonder that the parking lot in front of the hotel (where guests can't park) was largely occupied by tour buses whose passengers were the primary hotel occupants, at one-third the room rate?

These differences among properties are not, of course, unique. Many chains, as well as consortiums, have them. The franchise systems of Hilton and Sheraton, as previously discussed, are full of them, as are Holiday, Ramada, Wyndham, and many others. This is also true of Ponderosa, Bennigan's, and Friendly's restaurants.

The problem that arises, in any case, is the one of customer expectations and perceptions. While the consortium network is a powerful one in the distribution system, it is also one that must be treated with great care. A chain can blame only itself if one of its units breaks down; a consortium, on the other hand, outside of flagrant protocol violation, must suffer its "wayward children." Such sufferance can be difficult. Conversely, the consortium distribution system represents the maintenance of individuality in a world of chain "sameness," with the advantage of chain marketing clout.

Reservations Networks

Reservations networks are central reservations systems that serve multiple companies or properties. There is much overlap between consortiums and reservations systems. By contrast with consortiums, however, there are essentially no entry requirements other than, perhaps, that the properties be within a certain product class range. A charge is assessed by the reservations system for each reservation made. Further, there is no significant central control that polices the properties.

FIGURE 18-4   A reservations network

Steigenberger Reservation Service (SRS) in Frankfurt is a case in point. SRS has almost 200 members worldwide, all of which are in the "prestigious" hotel class. They are linked by a sophisticated reservations network and thirty global sales and reservations offices. Sales offices supply detailed information concerning all affiliated hotels.

Supranational is another example (Figure 18-4). Supranational's purpose is to unify the reservations network without sacrificing the identity of the individual property or chain. Supranational represents a hotel company in each country in which it has a presence (300 hotels in thirty-four countries). Thistle Hotels in the United Kingdom, Reso Hotels in Sweden, and Omni Hotels in the United States are members of this system. The selling point for customers is that by calling the local hotel or any of the member chains, they can book reservations directly anywhere in the world in any of the member chains' properties. A customer in Sweden can call a Reso Hotel in Stockholm and make a reservation at the Omni Hotel in New York City. Additionally, Supranational provides sales support in some countries. Each member of the system attempts to market its counterparts, in hopes that the counterparts are doing the same for them.

Many chains, of course, operate their own reservations networks. Among the largest and most successful are Holiday's Holidex and the systems of Sheraton, Hilton, Marriott, and Hyatt. For the small chain or independent hotel, however, it is usually more cost-effective to hook up with a network system, or use it to supplement its own system.

Affiliations

Some companies affiliate with other companies for joint marketing and distribution endeavors. An example is the Ashok Group of India. (Figure 18-5). Radisson Hotels, which has no properties in Europe, affiliates with Mövenpick Hotels International of Switzerland and SAS International Hotels of Oslo. These affiliations may include joint sales and advertising efforts as well as marketing and reservations connections. Even Mövenpick restaurants throughout Europe carry listings of all Radisson Hotels in the United States and Mexico.

Quality Inns affiliated with Clarion Hotels, a division of AIRCOA, in order to gain quicker identification in the upscale market for its Quality Royale product line. Research determined that Quality's powerful reservation system did not have the customer base to drive reservations into upscale hotels. Its customers were used to paying $40 and $50 a night, and were unlikely to pay $110 regardless of the quality or location of the product. The decision made was to change the name to Clarion, which already had an upscale customer base and name. Clarion brings prestige to the Quality Royales, now called Clarion, and Quality brings marketing clout and an excellent reservations system to Clarion.

We need to emphasize that there is frequent overlap among distribution categories. For example, an organization that fits all of the categories mentioned so far—owning, managing, franchising, consortiums, reservations networks, and affiliations—is Golden Tulip Hotels, a subsidiary of KLM Royal Dutch Airlines (Figure 18-6). This kind of conglomerate is becoming more and more common in the hotel industry.

FIGURE 18-5   Affiliations

484

Where can you book unpretentious elegance for a friendly price?
In 350 Golden Tulip Hotels around the world.

Golden Tulip World-Wide. Perfecting a tradition for international travellers. And adding an extra dimension to hospitality. It's Golden Tulip's world of unpretentious elegance. At 350 hotels. In 200 cities. On 5 continents.

And KLM's Corda Computer System is your instant passkey to Golden Tulip's global network. Making world-wide reservations easier than ever before. A fine opportunity to sample our world of unpretentious elegance.

Some affiliated Golden Tulip Hotels

Golden Tulip SEURAHUONE, Helsinki

Golden Tulip BARBIZON CENTRE, Amsterdam

Golden Tulip BARBIZON, New York

Golden Tulip GOODWOOD PARK, Singapore

Golden Tulip ARUBA CARIBBEAN, Aruba

Golden Tulip MIGUEL ANGEL, Madrid

GOLDEN TULIP HOTELS
WORLD-WIDE HOSPITALITY

Information: Head-office, P.O. Box 619, 1200 AP Hilversum, Holland. Tel.: (035) 284588. Telex 43651.

Reservations: USA Toll Free (800) 3441212, UK (01) 5689144, Japan (03) 2160771, Holland (035) 232390, Germany (069) 290401, France (01) 47425729, Sweden (08) 231350 or your local KLM Royal Dutch Airlines office.

FIGURE 18-6   A conglomerate of distribution categories

Representative Firms

A representative (rep) firm is a channel of distribution that brings a hotel to a marketplace. These companies basically market a hotel to a customer base for a fee and are hired to act as sales organizations for independent properties that don't have sales or reservations networks of their own. Major chains may also use rep firms to enhance their regional sales efforts. Rep firms have their own sales forces and represent a number of hotels through regional offices in different geographical areas.

Once a representative firm has been engaged, it uses all of the normal communications mix, such as direct sales, direct mail, advertising, and public relations, to get customers to buy certain hotels. Sales calls are the most utilized form of the communications mix, followed by direct mail. Utell International is a firm that represents 3500 properties in 133 countries, and maintains thirty worldwide sales offices (Figure 18-7).

A good rep firm also offers services to consumers, such as meeting planners, in prescreening hotels to be sure they will meet the consumers' needs, checking for space availability, negotiating the most attractive rates, and providing other information about hotels.

Representative firms differ from travel agencies in that they are primarily group-oriented and sell specific hotels, or packages, to the customer. Travel agents, on the other hand, are usually given a destination and make the choice based on the needs of the customers.

Representative firms either operate on a retainer basis or are paid a fee when the group checks out of the hotel. Once a hotel has retained the service of the representative firm, the firm prints a brochure on the facility and markets it in clusters with other hotels in its network. Sales representatives of these companies operate in much the same way as a hotel's sales department. They maintain a client base and files, and make sales calls to convince customers to use a facility in their portfolio rather than an alternative. Having a franchise does not preclude the use of representative firms. Some operators like the opportunity to have as many people selling their hotels as possible.

A representative firm can be more cost-effective for a hotel company than establishing individual sales office in feeder cities. (A feeder city represents a geographic area from which business is derived, but where a company may or may not have a property of its own. For example, Chicago is a major feeder city for New York City, as are Los Angeles, Paris, and London.)

If Chicago was a major feeder city for a hotel in Phoenix, it might not be cost-effective for the Phoenix hotel to have a sales representative make frequent sales trips. Also, setting up a regional office to call on customers can be very expensive. Instead, a representative firm is retained in the feeder city and makes local calls, as the most cost-effective method to build the channel of distribution.

Representative firms differ from normal wholesalers and retailers in the consumer goods channels of distribution in that they do not take possession of the goods. These firms do not buy blocks of hotel space and then resell. The client hotel does not pay for what it doesn't receive, but inventory can go unused if the representative firm is not successful.

UTELL
INTERNATIONAL
The world's largest hotel representation company

UTELL
INTERNATIONAL
at the service of the

TRAVEL TRADE

The Utell International computerised Hotel reservation system is designed to provide you, the Travel Agent with an ideal service, and guaranteed commission.

IN USA:
800 44 UTELL
IN NEBRASKA
402 493 4747

IN CANADA
FROM TORONTO:
416 967 3442
FROM ONTARIO:
800 268 7041
FROM QUEBEC:
800 268 7041
FROM VANCOUVER:
604 873 4661
FROM ALBERTA & BC:
800 663 9582
FROM MANITOBA
AND EAST COAST
800 387 1338

OR CALL ANY UTELL
INTERNATIONAL
OFFICE

A completely free service to you the Travel Agent.

Full commission on all bookings.

Full information on all hotels (3500 in 133 countries on 6 continents)

Hotels offered at normal published rates.

Immediate 'yes' or 'no' on room availability.

Printed, mailed confirmation.

Your Travel Agent's name and address on each confirmation.

Paytell – we can even pay the hotel bill for you

UTELL
INTERNATIONAL
at the service of the

HOTELIER

The Utell International computerised Hotel reservation and Marketing system provides you, the Hotelier, with easy access to the world's major travel markets, supported by sales promotion.

AMSTERDAM
AUCKLAND
BANGKOK
BOGOTA
BOMBAY
BUENOS AIRES
CARACAS
DUBAI
DUBLIN
DUSSELDORF
HELSINKI
HONG KONG
JOHANNESBURG
LONDON
MADRID
MANILA
MEXICO CITY
MILAN
NEW YORK
OMAHA
PARIS
RIYADH
SAO PAULO
SINGAPORE
STOCKHOLM
SYDNEY
TOKYO
TORONTO
VANCOUVER
ZURICH

Worldwide representation by 1 company only. (Utell has 30 offices)

Centralised worldwide Travel Agent's commission payment system.

Toll-free telephone reservation services.

Offices and sales staff in each location, not just a telephone number

Co-operative world-wide TradeShow programme (52 annually to choose from)

In-house advertising agency offering market research, scheduling and production.

International airlines/ hotel reservations interfacing.

A unique guaranteed reservations and payment system – Paytell

FIGURE 18-7   Ad for a representative firm

On the surface, representative firms, which are usually located in major metropolitan centers, seem to offer a lucrative support system to the marketing distribution effort. This is usually the case. Sometimes, however, there are disputes as to where the booking originated. For example, a hotel might have an IBM account in its file system when the representative firm uncovers a piece of business from the same company but from a different contact. The question arises as to whether the firm should be paid for the booking. Details like this need to be worked out before the representation agreement is consummated. If handled properly, this channel of distribution can be an effective addition to distribution efforts.

Incentive Houses

Incentive houses are an excellent example of a strong channel of distribution. These are companies that specialize in handling strictly incentive reward travel. As discussed in Chapter 7, many organizations and firms have incentive contests to reward top-performing employees, salespeople, dealers, or retailers. Travel rewards are a popular form of incentive.

Major corporations often have their own in-house travel departments or individuals to handle incentive arrangements. Many companies have used travel agents. More and more, however, both large and small companies are relying on incentive houses to organize their trips.

The reason for this is that incentive travel is a special case. For companies that use this kind of reward frequently, there is a constant need for destinations that are new, different, and exciting—in other words, that offer a real incentive. Second, there is a real need for the trip to be letter-perfect. Keeping up with all this, on a worldwide basis, is expensive and time-consuming.

Incentive houses, because of their collective accounts, can partial out the costs of their expertise. Almost always, someone will have visited and thoroughly inspected the destination, the hotels, the restaurants, and the ground services before putting together the incentive package. The incentive house then "sells" it to the company and helps the company to "sell" it to those who will seek the reward.

For upscale hotels, particularly in resort areas or foreign destinations, it can be a real boost to the distribution channel to be on the incentive houses' lists. In these cases, a property (and incentive planners deal with individual properties as opposed to chains to be certain of the product) does not simply buy an incentive house's services. In effect, it earns them by doing things right. By contrast with consortiums, reservations networks, rep firms, and travel agents, the incentive house's service is paid for by the customer, not the hotel.

In these situations, each channel member is integrally dependent on the others for performance. The incentive house has the corporate customer base. If customers are dissatisifed with the trip, they may choose another incentive house for the next program. Each channel member has to make sure that everything goes as promised. For example, if the ground transportation is an hour late in picking up a group at the airport, the entire trip can be spoiled. Future business may be lost not only to another incentive house, but to another destination.

Travel Agents

A travel agent is an intermediary in a channel of distribution who makes reservations for a variety of hospitality needs. The travel agent is compensated in the form of a commission, usually based upon the rate of the service purchased. As a rule of thumb in most cases, a 10 percent commission is paid to travel agents who book cruises and hotel rooms, while airlines and rental car firms pay a lesser rate.[4]

As a channel of distribution, the travel agent is second to none. At this point there are some 200,000 plus individual travel agents located in 27,000 different locations in the United States alone.[5] According to a survey of 3600 business travelers in the United States conducted by the U.S. Travel Data Center, 44 percent of frequent business travelers use the services of travel agents, and nearly half the time the agent participates in the hotel selection. In a rating of agent services in the same survey, 87 percent reported that "finding the right hotel" was an important travel agent service.[6]

In the less recent past, the travel agent was primarily oriented toward the individual traveler, be it for business or pleasure. This practice has been changing, and agents are handling more meetings and group itineraries each year. The travel agent also is more of a full-service channel, whereby the hotel booking may be incidental to the airline and ground transportation already arranged. Because of this, travel agencies are actively soliciting corporate meeting accounts, especially when they have previously handled the company's individual business travel. By promising more clout in negotiating rates, agencies' role in meeting planning is bound to increase.

The travel agent is faced with a blizzard of changing conditions in the marketplace. Airlines, collectively, are reported to change fares as many as 80,000 times a day. To recommend a hotel, the agent needs knowledge of location, rates, amenities, dining, entertainment, parking, ground transportation, recreation facilities, and more. The technology of the industry is changing at a furious pace in an attempt to keep up with all this information.

Agencies that were on manual systems only a short time ago, now have sophisticated data-base equipment to manage their bookings. These automated systems are, in fact, reservation terminals provided by the airlines (e.g., Apollo, by United Airlines, and Sabre, by American Airlines), creating a direct link between travel agents and the airlines controlling this distribution channel.

Rates change at a rate unparalleled in the history of travel. The proliferation of hotels offering thousands of packages, incentives, and varying rate structures to varying people at varying times make booking a difficult task at best.

The rental car industry has followed suit with the airlines and hotels, offering special promotions and incentives every day. Many of these promotions have conditions attached to them, such as booking an airline seat thirty days in advance with cancellation penalty clauses. Add to all this the overlapping frequent traveler awards (and the traveler's

---

[4] Travel agencies also form consortiums, using the strength of many individual agencies to combine marketing and negotiating clout as a channel member. A good example is the Boston-based Woodside Travel, which has member agencies worldwide.

[5] *Hotel and Travel Index, A Special Report,* Fall 1985. Hotel & Travel Index, Secaucus, NJ.

[6] Ad of *Hotel & Travel Index* in *Cornell Hotel and Restaurant Administration Quarterly,* February 1987, p. 1.

perplexity among taking airline, hotel, or car rental points) and you have an impossibly complex problem for the ordinary traveler. A good travel agent tries to ease this burden and may well earn the commission on this basis alone.

For some time, travel agents were considered necessary evils by both the airline and hotel industries. Managers felt that commissions were being paid for bookings that would have been received regardless. Supply-and-demand changes in the industry have brought a new significance to the role of this intermediary.

The travel agent needs clear, concise information on the product, and cooperation with the delivery of the product. The hotel company that can provide the least complicated products to the travel agent, and deliver them to the customer, will get the most bookings. The more agents have to decipher very difficult booking procedures, the less likely they are to recommend the facility in the future.

All rates and information furnished to travel agencies on a property need to be as current as possible. Travel agencies have their own customer bases, and will be blamed by their customers for poor service at a facility that they recommended. As one example, the fact that a pool has been closed for lengthy renovations should be communicated to the travel agents before they hear it from their customers. The short-term loss of revenue from the agents' not booking the facility during the renovation period will appear small when compared with the possible customer dissatisfaction and loss of future bookings.

Cooperation with the agent consists also of paying commissions on a timely basis. The agency has performed the desired service of bringing the product through the channel of distribution. For that service, it needs to be paid. Because most agencies are small, cash flow is very important to their survival. A company or hotel can very quickly get the reputation of being slow or of not paying on commissions. Agencies will go out of their way to avoid recommending the property if they are not receiving their commissions. Contrarily, agents are quick to recommend those who pay commissions promptly.

Further, cooperation with travel agents includes upgrading their important clients at no extra charge, offering complimentary stays to allow them to experience the product firsthand, doing special promotions to gain their loyalty, and, in general, working with them in every way possible. To fail to do this is to bite the hand that feeds you. Hotel companies today often market directly to the travel agent (Figure 18-8).

The hospitality company that does the best job utilizing this channel of distribution will be the one that gets the lion's share of their business. A familiarization trip (commonly referred to as fam trips) is a popular method used to expose the hotel product to intermediaries in the channel of distribution. A fam trip is just that; the hotel has a group of travel agents visit the facility to familiarize them with the features and benefits. Word-of-mouth advertising is the most believable form of communication. If travel agents are impressed with a facility during a fam trip, they will convey their enthusiasm to customers, and bookings will increase.

Travel agents are as important worldwide as they are in the United States. In major destination areas such as Singapore, Hong Kong, and Manila, many agents operate as "inbound" agents—that is, they deal primarily with people coming into the country as opposed to those going out. This means setting up ground arrangements, hotel bookings, local tours, and so forth.

In the United States, travel agencies are becoming fewer in number but larger in size. This is because size is needed to handle the large accounts and negotiate the best

You're Finally Getting Through To Us.

800-777-7800
Just For Travel Agents.

Travel agents, we hear you. Now you can call for reservations on your own private, toll-free line. That means you can get confirmed rates and reservations even faster than before.

This one number puts you in touch with over 100 Radisson Hotels in North America, including our plaza hotels, suite hotels, inns, airport hotels and resorts.

It also connects you with our overseas affiliates: SAS International Hotels in Scandinavia, Concorde La Fayette Hotel in Paris and Mövenpick Hotels International in Switzerland, Germany and the Middle East.

Of course, you still get top priority on special requests and bookings, all of them guaranteed. And you still have the option of booking rooms through SABRE, APOLLO, SYSTEMONE or PARS systems.

You see, when you want to talk to Radisson about reservations, we're all ears.

The Radisson Hotels

© 1987 Radisson Hotel Corporation

(Courtesy of Radisson Hotel Corporation)

FIGURE 18-8   Marketing to the travel agent

arrangements, a necessary ability for being the agent of choice. Further, by banding together in consortiums, groups of agencies have been able to bargain collectively with travel suppliers to gain access to preferred rates or other customer benefits. These are subsequently used as enticements to lure and retain commercial clientele, who could not obtain the same benefits. Through the control of information, agents exert great influence in all segments of the travel market.

Approximately 85 percent of all U.S. agencies possess automated ticketing systems, but process only about 10 percent of their room reservations via those systems. However, this percentage is increasing as the speed of a transaction becomes increasingly critical to an agency's profitability.

Ironically, the technology that allows agencies to have access to an increasing volume of information is the same technology that threatens their existence. Once the technology is refined for easy adaptability on personal computers, the channel of distribution will become increasingly direct to the consumer. All this, concludes Yesawich, will result in attempts by many to circumvent established channels of communication. More, "it will yield new thought on how best to identify, communicate with, and satisfy the guests of the next decade."[7]

Tour Operators

Tour operators differ from their counterparts in channel management options in that they actually take "possession" of the hotel inventory to sell it to the public. Tour operators also take possession of the food and beverage product, by making reservations in a number of outlets at anticipated destination points.

There are two types of tour operators—wholesalers, or tour brokers, and "ad hoc" tour operators. The wholesaler or broker blocks space in hotels and restaurants, and then use various combinations of the communications mix to market the facilities to individual and group consumers. Direct mail is one of the most popular methods. The wholesaler prints a brochure featuring the tour and all related accommodations, and mails it to existing and potential customers. Advertising in the print media is also a common practice to attract tour customers (Figure 18-9). Destination points and length of tours run the gamut.

The wholesaler market includes people using a variety of transportation options. The wholesaler negotiates with the airlines, railroads, hotels, and bus companies to develop travel options to be resold as a total package. Groups come from every realm of the spectrum, from a high school hockey team to an upscale corporate trip to the Super Bowl. Wholesalers negotiate the lowest possible rates from the suppliers, and then mark up the price to include their profit margins.

International wholesalers exist both domestically and abroad. Domestic wholesalers under the umbrella of, for instance, "Visit USA" are called inbound operators; they handle tours and groups organized overseas, and manage their travel needs while in the United

---

[7] The foregoing discussion on consortiums and technology is extracted from Peter C. Yesawich, "The Marketplace: Beyond 1985," *Lodging Hospitality,* May 1986, pp. 30, 32, 34.

FIGURE 18-9   Ad for a tour operator

States. Their outbound counterparts handle the reverse travel internationally. This is true of all countries serving international markets.

Ad hoc groups are organizations that are already formed and want to book a tour to a previously visited or new destination. An example of an ad hoc group would include a Lions Club tour to the Ozarks in Arkansas, or an archaeology club to Mexico. The tour operator again takes possession of the inventory of hotel rooms and restaurant seats, but the risk is much lower because a solid booking is in place.

Although there are many examples of tour operators worldwide, a very good one, and the largest, is American Express. This company operates in both wholesaler and ad hoc categories, and as a travel agent.

The tour operator needs the full cooperation of channel members to be successful. Ad hoc groups are the simplest to administer. The wholesale tours, on the other hand, are very risky; some hotels and restaurants have strict cancellation guidelines, and if the tour doesn't sell, the wholesaler can end up holding a large perishable inventory.

This is where good channel management can work both ways. If a wholesale tour broker is attempting to coordinate a tour series to a destination, the hotels and restaurants should remain flexible to help in the development of the distribution network. The fall foliage season in New England may not be the time to help a channel member create a new series, since demand for the hotel product at that time exceeds the supply of hotel rooms. If the wholesaler is attempting to bring in business in a less busy time, such as spring, every attempt should be made to encourage the effort. Short-term decisions regarding cancellation clauses could prejudice an active channel member in the future.

The other side of the coin is that, in times when business is slow, the tour operator will wield clout to obtain the lowest possible rates.

Strategies for Distribution Channels

There are two major strategies for increasing usage of the product in a distribution channel. These are the "push" strategy and the "pull" strategy. In the pull strategy, inducements are offered to make the consumer want to "pull" the product down the channel. Examples of pull strategies in the hospitality industry are the frequent traveler programs. With these promotions, the customer presumably has an increased desire for the product and seeks the appropriate distribution channel.

The push strategy acts in the opposite way, by giving the incentive to the channel member (e.g., the travel agent) to sell the product to the consumer. An example of a push strategy would be to offer a 20 percent commission on all bookings made during a low-demand time period. At twice the normal commission, the travel agent has a reason to push the product over another that may be offering a lower rate. Certain incentives, such as free rooms, free airfare to destinations, and in some instances cash bonuses, have come into use. As competition for channel members' business becomes more intense, we expect the incentives of the push strategy to increase proportionately.

Promotional Tie-ins

This category of strategies is the catch-all for the burgeoning attempts of the industry to expand its market base through intermediaries. Under this umbrella lies the couponing utilized by restaurants and hotels alike. The numerous dining clubs sprouting up through-out the country present a good example of the promotional tie-in channel of distribution. In this method, a number of restaurants participate in a dining club, whereby the intermediary organization prints, markets, and distributes the coupons representing every-thing from a free dessert to a two-for-one dinner offering. Hotel companies have been represented by various coupon organizations, primarily selling a 50 percent discount to their members on weekends and slow periods.

Another area of tie-ins for hotels are the airlines. A majority of airline customers eventually become hotel customers. Hotels work with the airline to arrange specific marketing packages to mutual destinations. Now, the channel of distribution grows longer. After the hotel enters an agreement for distribution with an airline, a second channel member, the travel agent, moves in. Each intermediary, while offering new customers, takes a commission.

Hotel and rental car companies are increasingly integrating with the airline reserva-tions systems. By combining technology, these channel members present a unique opportunity to the customers (in this case, travel agents) to take advantage of "one-stop shopping." Through direct access to airline computers, agents can make the flight arrangements, get a rental car, and book the sleeping room without ever using the telephone.

None of this channel participation is without cost. An independent operator of a franchise can pay a commission to the airline system, the travel agent who booked the reservation, and the franchise system that delivered the booking! Without constant supervision and evaluation, channels of distribution can sometimes become cost-prohibitive. For example, "super-saver" room rates could indeed bring in less than the cost of the channel of distribution. At $49, the commissions paid to the airline network, the travel agent, the contribution to the advertising, the contribution to the frequent traveler plan, and the franchise fee could bring the net revenue to below the cost of providing the service!

Pitfalls of Channel Promotions

One of the major problems in the hospitality industry's attempts at channel distribution lies in the execution of promotional tie-ins. In essence, the burden of execution may be on the most unlikely candidate, the employees. Think for a moment of a supermarket. Within the confines of the store there are at least five thousand different items available for purchase. Many of the strongest channel managers in the world are represented there—Procter & Gamble and Pepsi Cola, to name just two. Most of the products have made their way down some channel of distribution to be on the shelf, available for purchase.

Once in the store, there are hundreds of different promotions on a daily basis. Some soap companies are offering two bars for the price of one, a cereal maker offers trips to Ireland, and a barbecue sauce company offers a free grill if you participate. The supermarket clerk does not need an M.B.A. to be qualified to handle these promotions. Somehow, the consumer goods industry has offered thousands of promotions and give-aways under one roof, yet the check-out clerk has no direct participation. Check-out lines are rarely encumbered with questions on different promotions. Most of the administration of the programs is handled at the host companies' designated places of redemption.

Now, think how the hospitality industry has done the exact opposite. When a hotel company distributes coupons or has giveaways or special promotion programs, the desk clerk is the one that has to decipher all the different options and be prepared to encounter a myriad of customer inquires. For example, a desk clerk in one day must handle the frequent traveler program that the hotel sponsors; administer a 50 percent discount program that the sales office has arranged; be knowledgeable about the award levels of the airline with which the hotel has a tie-in on a fly/stay package; understand group, corporate, and other discount rates; try to upsell to higher priced rooms; deal with the amenities offered those in the hotel's "club" plan; and, in his or her spare time, check in the lonely guest who is not associated with any of the above. We have not mentioned "and keep smiling"—yet this clerk is one of the lowest-paid employees in the hotel who, when you look at it closely, may be the one most responsible for guest satisfaction.

Poor channel management compounds this problem. To publish a booklet outlining the procedures for each program currently in place, and to expect each concerned employee to be able to remember and handle them is a simplistic and myopic answer to a bigger problem. Additionally, the tremendous turnover in the front office staff of most hotels makes prohibitive the training involved to keep each clerk cognizant of the programs.

The answer lies in shorter, simpler channels of distribution for the promotional tie-ins that are simultaneously managed at a location other than that of the point of sale. The use of coupons in the supermarket business is formalized and is understood by both the customer and the unit level grocery store. All coupons and programs are handled in the parent company's facilities (be they leased out to an independent agent or handled internally). The supermarket clerk merely handles the transaction as if it were money, and proceeds on to the next customer.

Front office clerks, besides all of the above, may have to stamp, validate, and hand out coupons for breakfast to some, and coupons for drinks to others, while offering free parking to weekend guests and not to midweek guests. The industry has left the critical execution of its promotion programs to the lowest-paid and least-trained employee in the organization. Think of the time and money spent on the development of a promotional tie-in channel of distribution; if the clerk is overwhelmed by the complexity of the programs, the entire promotion may be a failure.

Selection of Channels

The choice options for intermediaries in the hospitality industry having been described, a process needs to be established to select the correct member(s). Frequently, a corporate marketing department will develop a great promotion and give it to an airline, and the channel begins. If the plan is not well thought out, the program can roll out of control. Eventually, the customer is disappointed by the confusion and lack of delivery. Also, the local units of the company become frustrated by the myriad of options and the lack of information to help execute the programs.

Set Objectives   To begin, a set of distribution objectives needs to be established by the company. One way to phrase the question would be, "If we were successful at the end of this channel, what would the results be?" The overall objective of any channel of distribution should be to create a customer. More specifically, the objective might be to have a larger share of airline customers.

The next step is to determine the influences on the channel strategies. What airlines can or will we do business with? The decision process might be narrowed down by the number of flights that go to cities where the chain has hotels. A thorough analysis of competitive hotels' channels would be needed to determine what they offer to both the channel member and finally the customers themselves.

Influences on Channels   Included in the influences on channel strategies is the corporate organization. Who is going to monitor and evaluate the programs offered? Is there need for additional staffing, or perhaps a combining of departments, to ensure that the channel is working as smoothly as possible?

At this point, it is necessary to realistically assess the strength of the product or promotion being driven through the channel. If the product is weak or redundant to other similar products, potential channel members such as travel agents and airlines may not be anxious to distribute the product, or at the very least, may not put forth a strong effort to make it successful.

For example, if a hotel develops a fly/drive/stay package with an airline and rental car agency that is not differentiated from the hundreds of other similar products in the marketplace, the intermediaries (in this case, the airline and rental car agency) would really not have any reason to aggressively market the package. If a competitive hotel was offering its corporate rate to an airline's customers, would the same offer be enough to differentiate the product in the eyes of the channel member? Would there be enough of an incentive for the airline to aggressively market the offering? If not, the product needs to be enhanced enough to get the support of the airline and to provide a productive channel. Being clearly superior to the competition will make the success of any channel more probable.

Selecting the Channel of Distribution   Selecting the distribution channels is the next step. The length of the channel needs to be analyzed. In no uncertain terms, shorter is better; the longer the channel of distribution, the more potential problems arise for the management of that channel.

By short or long we refer to the number of intermediaries in the channel. Each intermediary has to make a profit and each one involves some measure of coordination. Therefore, the fewer middlemen involved, the more profit and the less chance for errors. At some point there may seem to be a need to add on channels. If the new intermediary can be reasonably expected to bring in more customers at a profit for the originator, the channel should probably be expanded. If the channel member cannot deliver the needed number of customers and the profit, the decision should be negative.

Vertical Integration   When a company becomes its own supplier of products, it becomes vertically integrated. This type of distribution needs a large amount of capital to be successful, and this strategy should be considered only if the potential for success is somewhat assured. Examples in the hospitality industry include the former Allegis Corporation and Radisson Hotels.

In 1987 Allegis attempted to become the largest and most complete hospitality entity in the world through vertical integration. United Airlines acquired Westin and Hilton International Hotels and Hertz Rental Cars. The company was renamed Allegis to connote its all-inclusive nature. The concept was to develop an "all-Allegis" customer, each piece of the network feeding customers to the next. Other problems ensued, however. This resulted in the resignation of the CEO and conceptualizer of the idea, Richard Ferris, and the break-up of the company. Many had felt the idea would not have worked because of the basic lack of customer loyalty to any one company.

Radisson Hotels' vertical system was less wide-ranging. Carlson Travel Agencies was organized to feed reservations to Radisson hotels. All customers of the Carlson Travel Agencies were aggressively encouraged to stay in Radisson Hotels in all of the viable destinations. If the customer had a firm preference for an alternative hotel, the travel agency would certainly book the reservation. In a vertically integrated channel of distribution such as this, the company becomes its own source of business.

Channel Management

Good channel management stems from the formulation of a good working relationship among channels from the start. All agreements pertaining to the workings of the channel should be in writing and should be updated as conditions periodically change. There is rarely an all-win situation. If a channel member is not deriving some reasonable value from the network, that member will not participate actively and distribution will eventually become more difficult and more costly.

For example, a hotel could develop a good working relationship with a representative firm for marketing of the property. The representative firm then markets the hotel through sales calls, brochures, direct mail, and so on. A booking results, and a commission becomes due. If the hotel begins to dispute the validity of the origination of the bookings, or becomes lackadaisical or arrogant about the payment, the relationship within the channel of distribution becomes ineffective. The representative firm will not be anxious to market the facility in the future, and will spend its time selling more cooperative hotels. This becomes a no-win situation. The hotel is dissatisfied with the productivity of the channel member, and the representative firm will move on to more lucrative endeavors.

While each channel member seeks to create customers for a profit, without some give-and-take on a regular basis by all channel members the system becomes tedious and disruptive. The hospitality firms that have carefully selected their partners and are managing them well will be consistently increasing their customer base while others are looking for new channel members.

Evaluation of the Channel

This step is critical for the continued success of any program. If a hospitality entity is unable to tell how many bookings a representative firm produced, or how many coupons were turned in from the dining guide, then intelligent channel management is impossible. Often, channel members can report the statistics. The large travel agency Woodside

Travel is currently state-of-the-art from a reporting standpoint. It produces monthly documents showing productivity by rooms sold, dates of stay, and so on. If unit management is unable at least to spot check these numbers, when it comes time to negotiate the next agreement, the channel member will be in control.

In the example above, the hotel that engages in a channel agreement with an airline sets an objective. The objective needs to be set in a quantitative format, to be used in the evaluation process. For example, the success of the channel of distribution might be defined as raising the productivity of the airline reservation service from 100 rooms per month to 120 per month.

It is also beneficial to understand the break-even point of the channel. In the above example, it would take an additional 10 rooms per month to cover the additional commissions and some combined advertising costs. After a predetermined amount of time, the channel is evaluated. If it is producing less than 110 rooms per month, careful consideration might be given to either increasing the marketing support for the program or dropping the channel member completely.

Evaluation is more than just a tally of dinner covers or room nights. A channel may be driving the volume, but if the customer is unhappy, the effort is not only short-sighted but dangerous.

A dining guide can market a two-for-one dinner promotion in a number of different ways. If customers expect two lobsters for the price of one when making reservations, and find out the promotion applies only to chicken, they will be sincerely disappointed. If the hotel guest was expecting deluxe accommodations, and agreement with the channel member was to offer a run-of-the-house room, the guests who get the inferior rooms will not be happy with their purchase. They may not be unhappy enough to complain, but still worse, they may be unhappy enough not to come back.

The marketing-driven company with good channel management skills will ensure their customer satisfaction throughout the process. If a channel member is producing customers that are consistently unhappy it would be better never to have used that distribution method in the first place.

Motivation and Recruitment of Channel Members

During channel management, two ongoing factors are needed to ensure continued success. These are motivation and recruitment. For motivation, it must be recognized that most channel members are carrying many similar products into the marketplace. Travel agents have a variety of hotels and airfares from which to choose. The representative firms have several hotels in their portfolio that match the needs of their customers. The number of promotional tie-ins available to both the consumers and the channel members are mind-boggling. Franchising options for the developers and independent managers are plentiful.

Motivation   Some type of motivation must be continuously offered by the channel leader in order to promote continued success. Unless the product offered is so desirable that there are several channel members bidding on the rights to carry it, motivational techniques are necessary.

The push strategies mentioned earlier are the primary source of motivational support for channel members. Incentive trips for outstanding travel agents or the best franchisee in the system will go a long way toward smoothing operating channels of distribution. Many companies in the consumer goods and industrial products industries have full-time staff members who do nothing but organize and implement channel incentives in order to keep members interested in their products.

Incentives need not be in the form of travel. Consumer goods such as appliances and televisions can make the bonus system easier to attain, and provide short-term gratification for participants. The drawback of the magnificent incentive trip to Europe may be that it takes a year to win, and only a very few employees will ever have a chance to collect the prize.

Although the motivational options available are almost unlimited, an area that also needs attention is that of top management. All of the sales representatives can win trips and toasters, but the president of the company is often ignored. Travel agency owners do not need toasters and trips; what they need is the personal attention that allows their views to surface to someone important. An invitation to dinner by a senior executive of the hospitality company would buy more loyalty than 1000 toasters. Too often, in the rush to motivate a channel member, the owner of the business is left out of the process.

Recruitment   The second ongoing task for the channel manager is to recruit potential new channel members. If this task is not organized and planned, the channel is in perpetual danger. Unfortunately, the danger is subtle because a company may not realize that it is exposed until a member drops out. For example, a travel agency may be one of your best producers in the Florida market. It sends an unusually high number of guests to your hotel because it has done a good job marketing your facility, and has built up a good clientele.

One day the travel agent calls and says it is dropping your facility in favor of your competition down the street. Immediately the reservations slip and business starts falling. This scenario is very realistic for a number of managers: First, the competitor had a good recruitment program in place and replaced its channel member with yours, thereby improving its distribution network overnight. Second, without having had a good recruitment program of its own, your hotel now has to begin the process of finding a strong replacement channel member. As you are now in dire need, the negotiations will swing in favor of the potential new channel member.

There will always be times that a channel member leaves and/or needs to be replaced. This is part of doing business. However, a good channel manager will have alternatives ready and prescreened according to the criteria mentioned earlier in the chapter.

Recruitment is also necessary to provide alternatives to channel members who are not performing satisfactorily. It is far easier to deal with an unsatisfactory situation once you have other options than to have to recruit channel members when at a disadvantage.

Summary

Channels of distribution are an underutilized and misunderstood method of marketing a hospitality entity. Many of the programs in effect are complicated and costly, and lack a full evaluation process in place to maximize their effectiveness.

The backbone of any channel of distribution is channel management. In many cases this management is nonexistent or operates as an afterthought. The distribution method of marketing that has been so critical and successful for the consumer and industrial goods industries has new significance for the hospitality industry.

Any marketing-driven organization will take the time to evaluate its current distribution system and organize a cohesive plan for improvement. A competent channel manager should then be assigned to monitor and consistently reevaluate the network to obtain the maximum benefits to the company. This channel manager may take the form of the Director of Sales, the General Manager, or the Resident Manager at the unit level of the hotel. The corporate marketing office should assume responsibility for the chain-wide agreements. Finally, the satisfaction of the consumer is the true test of a channel's success. Without this, none of the steps outlined above are productive or needed.

DISCUSSION QUESTIONS

1. Discuss the advantages and disadvantages of franchising as a method of increasing the channels of distribution.
2. Discuss the similarities and dissimilarities among consortiums, reservations networks, affiliations, and representative firms.
3. Why are channels of distribution inherently different for the hospitality industry than for goods industries?
4. Describe the difference between a push and a pull strategy. When might it be best to use one instead of the other?
5. What are the most important criteria for choosing a channel member and why? Discuss the ramifications.
6. Describe ways and means of motivating channel members and their significance.

PART VI
Managing the Marketing System

CHAPTER 19
Marketing Intelligence

Good intelligence is the basis of good marketing decisions. This is not to say that some good decisions have not been made on intuition alone. Anthony Athanas owns and operates the very successful Pier IV restaurant in Boston, which grosses about $14 million a year, as well as a number of other restaurants. Anthony Athanas is a millionaire who likes to tell how he arrived from Albania as an emigrant with 21¢ in his pocket. Ask him if he ever did any marketing research and he responds, "Of course not, that's a waste of time and money; I just knew it would work."

That's the kind of success story we love to hear in America. We don't like to hear (and seldom do) of the tens of thousands of others who also "knew it would work"—only it didn't. Those kinds pass quickly. The world today is not what it was when Anthony Athanas started his restaurant. Today's world is far more competitive, far more "dog eat dog," and hunch decisions usually don't go very far in open warfare.

There's another reason marketers need better intelligence today. The world is changing much faster than it used to, and so is the consumer. Also, that consumer has many more choices. This means that marketers too have many more choices. Choices mean decisions, and making more decisions means acquiring more information, even if only to verify intuitive thought. Today, virtually no one in business makes a decision without acquiring information of some kind. The quality of the decision depends on the quality of the information and how it is used.

The last sentence warrants elaboration. All the information in the world will not lead to the right decision, if it is not properly interpreted and used. In the early 1980s Holiday Inns decided to go "upscale."[1] It defined its mission as being a provider of hospitality services. Intrigued by the higher profits in the upscale market (as many hotel chains were at the time and still are), Holiday Inns decided that its traditional middle market was saturated. On the basis of its situation analysis, and after analyzing sales by

---

[1] "Holiday Inns Opens Doors for the Upscale Traveler," *Business Week,* April 25, 1983, pp. 100ff.

geographic market, by business and pleasure-traveler segments, by traveler brand awareness, by guest satisfaction, and by room and facilities conditions, the company inaugurated a new upscale chain called Crowne Plaza.[2]

While Crowne Plazas have not been a failure, only one or two have reached projection levels in the U.S. marketplace. What Holiday Inns did was to enter an already saturated market and draw their attention away from the market that was swelling—the middle-tier and budget markets. In 1988, the company was trying to recoup with budget Hampton Inns and Embassy all-suites. In the meanwhile, Holiday failed to acknowledge that customers had changed and it hadn't, left itself vulnerable to takeover, recapitalized, sold all its European properties and some others, gave up its rights to develop hotels outside North America to obtain much-needed cash, and increased its debt burden. At the same time, franchisees started deserting for such names as Days Inn and Park Inns.[3] Holiday either had the wrong information, misinterpreted it, or misused it, which put Holiday in a weakened rather than stronger position. Today, Holiday is selling assets to reduce debt and becoming primarily a management company.

Marketing intelligence flows from many directions. The trick is to get it routed in the right direction and in a form that is accurate and most useful. At the same time there is the problem of information overload—that is, being bombarded with so much information that it is difficult to sort out what is relevant and what is not. In this chapter we will discuss information sources, as well as their relevance to marketing decisions.

As with many other subject areas in this text, marketing intelligence is not restricted to one chapter. In fact, much of the discussion throughout the text has been about the use of information that is needed to make marketing decisions or to handle marketing problems. In particular, one of the best sources of marketing intelligence comes from the customer. That topic was covered in Chapter 3 as an important area of nontraditional marketing.

Environmental scanning, discussed in Chapter 4, is another area where intelligence flows from many sources, and is obviously very critical to marketing decisions. Chapter 5 dealt with the use of intelligence for competitive analysis. Chapter 18 pointed out the importance of intelligence received through distribution channels. Both strategic planning and developing the marketing plan, as discussed in Chapters 20 and 21, also are framed in the context of intelligence sources.

In this chapter we will deal more specifically with intelligence needs and their acquisition. Essentially, we can break down the sources of marketing intelligence to three major areas: the external environment, the internal environment, and formal marketing research. First, we will discuss the need for such information.

Information Needs

Hotels

The most complete and recent articulation of information needs in hotel companies comes from research conducted by A. Neal Geller.[4] Geller personally interviewed seventy-four

---

[2] "Room at the Top?" *Forbes,* March 12, 1984, pp. 58–61.

[3] "The Holiday Inns Trip: A Breeze for Decades, Bumpy Ride in the '80s," *The Wall Street Journal,* March 5, 1987, pp. 1, 23.

[4] A. Neal Geller, *Executive Information Needs in Hotel Companies,* Peat, Marwick, Mitchell & Co., 1984.

TABLE 19-1   Alphabetical Listing of "Wish List"
Items Frequently Cited by Hotel Executives

Better ways to measure consumer satisfaction
Computerized complaint system
Daily sales information
Day of the week sales and occupancy
Demand forecasts
Exception reporting
Guest history information
Marketing information
Qualitative information
Repeat business information
Turndown/sales backlog information

Source: A. Neal Geller, *Executive Information Needs in Hotel
Companies,* Peat, Marwick, Mitchell & Co., 1984, p. 35.

executives in twenty-seven hotel companies, including some with as few as three properties and others with hundreds of properties. In addition to rating the usefulness of common information that every hotel information system should provide (e.g., occupancy, average room rate, and sales), the executives also completed "wish lists" of information they would like to have. The items on that wish list that apply directly to marketing are shown in Table 19-1.

It is interesting to note that every item on the wish list, with the possible exception of marketing information (which is not explained) is information that can be obtained internally. Those interviewed were "at the minimum, each company's chief executive officer, chief operating officer, and chief financial officer. In some cases . . . [they were] the chief development and marketing officers."[5]

Although those interviewed by Geller were not primarily marketing people, it is somewhat surprising that neither the list in Table 19-1 nor Geller's own compiled list included any mention of market share, information on competitors, market segments, market trends, prime accounts, moving trend lines, channel distribution ratios, product mix, product/service quality, customer expectation, customer perception, marketing expenditures, marketing research, advertising effectiveness, or many other critical marketing input data. Geller does state, however, that negative comments made by these executives about their information systems "focused on the lack of marketing and competitive data, and especially on the need for the information systems to be more predictive."[6]

Clearly, information systems are needed to fulfill not only the wish lists of these executives, but also the marketing input data that we have just mentioned. In fact, three items mentioned—market share, product/service quality, and marketing ex-

---

[5] Ibid., p. 12. As Geller states, these are information needs only of top executives at multiproperty hotel companies. "Future phases, to be conducted . . . will investigate information needs at the hotel property level, at staff levels, and for middle management." We trust that this new research will show greater desire for information on the market, the competition, and the customer.

[6] Ibid, p. 34.

penditures—have been shown to be among the six factors of primary importance in terms of impact upon profitability in just about every major industry.[7]

Since we are concerned here with marketing information, it is worthwhile to note Geller's findings when the executives were queried as to the effectiveness of the information systems currently in place at the hotel companies.

> The general conclusion is that in the traditional areas of historical operating statistics and financial statistics most hotel executives are satisfied with their [information system]. In the future-oriented or predictive types of information, particularly marketing, most hotel companies lack the sophisticated systems necessary to produce the information most desired by management.[8]

We can only add that until there is a recognized need for certain specific information, it is highly unlikely that a system will be created to provide it. Thus, at this point we have to conclude that marketing information systems in the hotel industry are very poor in providing critical marketing information that is useful for understanding the customer, developing product, marketing plans, or strategic planning. Geller adds an emphasis to this point:

> For any management technique to work it must be fully supported, and must include the information necessary for design, implementation, and monitoring. As businesses become more sophisticated, they employ new and more complex management tools and techniques. If the information systems and data bases necessary to support the innovations do not keep pace, the innovative techniques themselves will fail. The evidence gathered in this study indicates that in hotel companies, information systems often lag behind new developments and new techniques. The evidence is particularly indicting in the two areas of greatest concern to executives, marketing and personnel. If hotel companies are to keep pace with progress, they will have to reverse this trend and place the development of information systems on the same priority as other innovations.
>
> . . . the hardware and software necessary to produce and maintain the systems should be a result of the design of the systems. They should support the systems, not drive or prescribe them. In other words, they should follow, not lead, in information system design. The evidence of this study tends to show the opposite.[9]

Restaurants

We know of no study similar to Geller's that queries restaurant executives as to their information needs. However, Reid suggests that marketing information is needed by foodservice management for making decisions in regard to market segmentation; advertising and promotional efforts; capital investment and expansion or construction of units; changes in menu offerings; identifying sales opportunities; hours of operation; changes in

---

[7] As determined by an ongoing program under the name of Profit Impact of Marketing Strategy (PIMS). The PIMS program originated in connection with Harvard Business School in 1972. Today it is conducted by the nonprofit Strategic Planning Institute in Cambridge, Massachusetts. The program is a computerized cross-sectional study based, in 1987, on about 200 pieces of data supplied by more than 450 companies in more than 3000 businesses. The program has invariably shown that the profitability of a business is affected by 37 basic factors that explain more than 80 percent of the profitability variation among the businesses. Six factors have proved to be of primary importance: investment intensity, market share, product/service quality, marketing expenditures, research and development expenditures, and corporate diversity. For a brief explanation of PIMS, see Subhash C. Jain, *Marketing Planning and Strategy,* Cincinnati: South-Western Publishing, 1985, pp. 898–911.

[8] Geller, "Executive Information Needs," p. 4.

[9] Ibid., p. 5.

design, decor, and atmosphere; and market position.[10] It is worth noting that much of Reid's list is externally derived information.

Clearly, these needs, as well as internal information needs, are little different from those of hoteliers excluding, of course, hotel-specific data such as room occupancy. Strangely, however, we know of restaurateurs who have only vague ideas of their customer count, seat turnover, average check, food and beverage ratios, or repeat business, not to mention market share, market segments, or customer perception.

Much of the reason for this lack of information is due to the entrepreneurial nature of the business and the lack of sophistication in both management and marketing techniques. These people base their information needs largely on gross sales and profit. By the same token, however, many restaurant entrepreneurs are closer to their customers and have a good realization of the level of customer satisfaction, unscientific as it may be. A problem occurs if business begins to decline with no apparent explanation and some good, solid information is needed. Larry Reinstein, vice-president of operations for the company that operates six Souper Salad restaurants in the Boston area, states, "Over the past 11 years our company has made some outstanding decisions and some terrible ones concerning locations. The biggest lesson we've learned is that knowing your market is at least as important as knowing your business."[11]

Restaurateurs also seem to have a good idea of how their competitors are doing. For one reason, they eat at their competitors' restaurants and pay the bill. This way they can judge not only the volume of business, but also the menu, the check average, the quality of the food, and other customers' reactions. (Hoteliers, on the other hand, tend to stay at their own hotels or get VIP treatment from their friends, making it difficult for them to make objective evaluations.)

Large restaurant chains, in many cases, have far more sophisticated information systems than their hotel counterparts. Companies such as McDonald's, Burger King, and Wendy's maintain sophisticated computerized information systems, as well as conducting frequent customer research for perception, satisfaction, test marketing, and new concept development.

Large restaurant chains are also more prone to subscribe to data services that track consumer trends. The best known of these is probably CREST (Consumer Reports in Eating Share Trends), conducted by a division of NPD, Inc., a marketing and research firm. Companies that subscribe to this service and others receive regular reports on expenditures and behavior in the commercial foodservice industry by type and classification of restaurant and by meal period. Essentially, this report tracks broad trends (useful for environmental scanning), but for individual companies it can provide specific information on their product as well as market share percentages.

Information Aquisition

External Information

External information flows through distribution channels, competitors, suppliers, and various local, state, and national agencies and associations, as well as the marketplace.

---

[10] Robert D. Reid, *Foodservice and Restaurant Marketing,* New York: Van Nostrand Reinhold, 1983, p. 66.
[11] Quoted in "How to Tackle Expansion," *Restaurant Management,* March 1988, p. 65.

Some of this is simply statistical data gathering; some goes under the name of research. The question is what is relevant. Apart from information needed for environmental scanning, which was discussed in Chapter 4, there is often a mass of external or secondary data (that is, collected for some other purpose) available.

Distribution channels that can provide information include travel agencies, reservation systems, credit card systems (for example, American Express can provide expenditure and market share data for a particular area but only relative to people who charge with American Express), tour brokers, wholesalers, and so forth.

Competitors themselves are a source of information. In at least some U.S. cities, hotels nightly exchange occupancy information from which market share can be quickly calculated. Some hotel managements, as you might expect, refuse to participate in this program. In Singapore no one wants to tell anyone else anything (but everyone knows it anyway). In Kuala Lumpur, some information is exchanged but "we all lie." So-called networking, however, often provides the solution wherever you are, and so too do cocktail parties. Some hoteliers read others' reader boards, call for room rates and/or reservations, and even go so far as to book rooms.

At least one hotel in New York City has its sales reps spend two nights each per year in competitive hotels. Each hotel is rated on eight different attributes, plus or minus relative to the sales reps' hotel. The individual scores for each of the eight attributes are tallied for each hotel. These figures are used to determine the price/value relationship for each competitor hotel. The analysis is used to develop pricing and positioning strategies. The more you know about your competitors, the more you will know about your potential new customers.

Customers can also reveal a great deal of information about the competition. Marketing people should be alert to this when they call on customers who have current data on competitors' products and services. People in the company outside of marketing may also have sources they can tap. As Jain states the case,

> Competitive intelligence includes information beyond industry statistics and trade gossip. It involves close observation of competitors to learn what they do best and why, or where they goofed and why. No self-respecting business will admit to not doing an adequate job of scanning the competitive environment. What sets the outstanding companies apart, however, is that they watch their competition in such depth and with such dedication that [often they know about competitive moves even before the management of that company knows it].[12]

Suppliers are a great source of information, especially in the individual restaurant business. Both food and liquor salespeople have firsthand knowledge about how well various restaurant operations are doing. Of course, one must always keep in mind that what they are telling you they are also telling your competition.

Finally, there are government agencies and trade associations. Municipal, state, and federal governments and/or tourism boards of any one of these all collect readily available information in the form of restaurant or hotel expenditures; tax receipts; lists of airport arrivals, out-of-state visitors, countries of origin, purpose of travel, length of stay; or whatever.

---

[12] Jain, *Marketing Planning and Strategy,* p. 159.

In the United States there are state and national associations that collect data from their members. These include the National Restaurant Association, the American Hotel & Motel Association, and their state counterparts. Similarly the accounting firms Laventhol & Horwath and Pannell Kerr Forster publish annual reports drawn from their clients on trends and financial data. Unfortunately, these are usually published so late that the information is ancient history before anyone receives it.[13] In other countries there may be similar organizations, associations, or, instead, travel agent associations.

Information from government agencies and trade associations is broad and may or may not be useful. The same is true of private firms that do research for open publication. Knowing that adults who dine out often are more likely to eat dessert, that 72 percent of people are likely to select tomatoes on salad bars, or that 30 percent of restaurant customers always eat mints when available, for example, may not be too helpful to the restaurateur in East Podunk, Iowa, who would like to make some important decisions.[14] Knowing that German arrivals are up 22 percent in Singapore, on the other hand, can tell both hoteliers and restaurateurs something about market segments and market demand.

Internal Information

The hospitality industry as a whole has access to more information about its customers than perhaps any other industry in the world. Thus, it is somewhat surprising how little is known about those customers. Of course, there is the standard information that most operators gather: occupancy, average room rate, average check, number of covers, frequently ordered menu items, and so forth, but the opportunity to know more about the customer is too often left unseized.[15] This is particularly true considering the huge data bases acquired by some companies through their frequent guest programs. These data bases, probably the most commendable part of frequent guest programs, are widely underutilized.

Here is some information that can be learned from customers. Holiday Corp., which had a twenty-eight-member research staff with an annual budget of more than $2 million, developed room concepts from prototypes that were evaluated and actually used by guests. Amenities such as thicker towels, glass tumblers instead of plastic, larger bars of soap, and massaging showerheads were added as a result of these studies. They also learned that business travelers work in their rooms about 50 minutes each night and that 20 percent of guests take baths rather than showers.

Rodeway Inns developed profiles of their business travelers along with information about travel habits and awareness and perception measures. Marriott studied individual motivation of different groups and learned that most important to its guests were whether things were "as ordered" when they arrived.

Internal information obtained by most hotels from their guests, however, is obtained by comment cards placed in rooms (Figure 19-1) or, as also used by restaurants, on

---

[13] E.g., *Foodservice Industry: 1985 in Review* was published by the National Restaurant Association in July 1987. By that time it was hardly of more than passing interest.

[14] "Gallup Report," *Independent Restaurants*, July, September, October, 1985, pp. 16, 28, 16.

[15] In recent years, more and more hotel chains are researching their customers to learn more about them. While this effort is laudable, in many cases the research findings are of limited reliability and validity because of the research techniques used. This issue will be addressed more fully in the research section of this chapter.

512

OMNI ✿ PARK CENTRAL
7th Avenue at 56th Street, New York, New York 10019

GUEST EVALUATION

1a. Was your room reservation in order upon arrival at hotel? ☐YES ☐NO

1b. If NO, was the problem handled to your satisfaction? ☐YES ☐NO

2. How well did our staff meet your expectations in terms of their hospitality and efficiency?

(Please circle appropriate number)

	Below Expectations				Exceeds Expectations
A. Reservations Staff	1	2	3	4	5
B. Door/Valet Parking Staff	1	2	3	4	5
C. Front Desk Receptionist	1	2	3	4	5
D. Bell Staff	1	2	3	4	5
E. Housekeeping Staff	1	2	3	4	5
F. Concierge Staff	1	2	3	4	5
G. Telephone Operators	1	2	3	4	5
H. Room Service Staff	1	2	3	4	5
I. Engineering/Maintenance Staff	1	2	3	4	5
J. Front Desk Cashier	1	2	3	4	5

3. Please give your assessment of the following:

	Below Expectations				Exceeds Expectations
A. Check-in process	1	2	3	4	5
B. Cleanliness of room upon arrival	1	2	3	4	5
C. Cleanliness and servicing of your room during stay	1	2	3	4	5
D. Comfort of your room	1	2	3	4	5
E. Telephone Message Service	1	2	3	4	5
F. Parking	1	2	3	4	5
G. Check-out, speed and efficiency	1	2	3	4	5
H. Value for price paid	1	2	3	4	5

4a. Was everything in your room in working order? ☐YES ☐NO

If NO, please tell us what was not in working order.
☐ Room Air Conditioning
☐ Room heating
☐ Bathroom plumbing
☐ Television
☐ Light bulbs
☐ Other (please specify)

4b. Was the problem corrected promptly for you? ☐YES ☐NO

5. Please rate the food and beverage facilities you used during your stay:

A. Restaurant (please specify name):

MEAL: ☐Breakfast ☐Lunch ☐Dinner

Were you greeted quickly? ☐YES ☐NO
Was your greeting friendly and proper? ☐YES ☐NO
Was your order taken promptly? ☐YES ☐NO
Was your food served promptly? ☐YES ☐NO

	Below Expectations				Exceeds Expectations
Service	1	2	3	4	5
Quality of food	1	2	3	4	5
Menu variety	1	2	3	4	5
Value for price paid	1	2	3	4	5

B. Room Service

Prompt Delivery	1	2	3	4	5
Service	1	2	3	4	5
Quality of food	1	2	3	4	5
Menu variety	1	2	3	4	5
Value for price paid	1	2	3	4	5

C. Cocktail/Lobby Lounge

	Below Expectations				Exceeds Expectations
Service	1	2	3	4	5
Quality of Drinks	1	2	3	4	5
Ambiance/Atmosphere	1	2	3	4	5
Entertainment Offering	1	2	3	4	5
Value for price paid	1	2	3	4	5

D. Banquet/Meeting Event

Service	1	2	3	4	5
Quality of Food	1	2	3	4	5

6a. On an overall basis, how did our hotel meet your expectations? 1 2 3 4 5

6b. Overall, how welcome did our staff make you feel? 1 2 3 4 5

7. What was the primary purpose of your visit?
☐ Pleasure
☐ Attending convention/meeting/banquet (in the hotel)
☐ Attending convention/meeting (outside the hotel)
☐ Business (outside the hotel)

8. Have you stayed at this Omni Hotel previously? ☐YES ☐NO

9. Have you stayed at other Omni Hotels previously? ☐YES ☐NO

10. When in the area again, what is the likelihood that you would return to this Omni Hotel?
☐Very likely
☐Somewhat likely
☐Not very likely
☐Not at all likely

11. Would you stay at other Omni Hotels in the future as a result of your experience at this Omni Hotel? ☐YES ☐NO

12. Your Sex: ☐ Male ☐ Female

13. Your Age:
☐ 18-24
☐ 25-34
☐ 35-49
☐ 50-64
☐ 65+

OTHER COMMENTS: _____

_____

_____

PLEASE PROVIDE THE FOLLOWING INFORMATION: (optional)
(Please Print)

Departure Date: _____

Length of Stay: _____ days Room number: _____

Name: _____

Home Address: _____

Company or Organization: _____

Business Address: _____

FIGURE 19-1   A better hotel comment card—a widely used internal information system of limited value

restaurant tables. These cards have their best use in spotting operational breakdowns and complaint trends. Due to the fact that in many hotels, returned comment cards come from less than 1 percent of the occupied rooms, their use for drawing clear conclusions is quite problematic.[16] In the For Further Study to this chapter we discuss a major hotel chain's reaction to this situation.

As previously noted, most information that hotel executives say they want is internally derived. The same is true of restaurateurs. Think what Procter & Gamble has to go through to find out whether people like Crest toothpaste or Ivory soap, or what Coca-Cola had to go through to find out whether people preferred the new Coke (around 200,000 blind taste tests). The hospitality industry has its customers right under its roof and still knows very little about how they use a hotel room, or what they expect from a restaurant.

Why should hotel executives have "wish lists" about customer satisfaction, daily sales information, day-of-the-week sales and occupancy, guest history, repeat business, or turndown information, when all this information is readily, easily, and cheaply available right in their own house? Why should restaurateurs have to wonder about what items will sell, what their repeat customer ratio is, or why people don't order dessert when it's all right there in front of them? It is clear that information systems in these areas are lacking.

Jerry Hamilton, director of marketing research for Ketchum Advertising in San Francisco, says "With demographics such as age, income, and sex we were only able to sketch an outline of consumers. Now we've filled in the sketch. We know who consumers are, how they live, what they buy—and more important, why they buy it." Says Mark Albion, marketing professor at Harvard Business School, "Mass marketing is no longer the most effective or cost-efficient way to sell. Most companies have to aim their products at more discrete segments of the population. To do that right, you can't know too much about the consumer."[17]

If you aren't impressed yet, read this:

No one knows you better than Mom. But does she know how many undershorts you own?
  Jockey International Inc. does.
  Or the number of ice cubes you put in a glass?
  Coca-Cola Co. knows that one.
  Or how about which you usually eat first, the broken pretzels in a pack or the whole ones?
  Try asking Frito-Lay Inc.

Or, how about applying this one to restaurant choice:

---

[16] In spite of this well established fact, these comment cards have much force in the reward system for management. In many cases, this is counterproductive because complaints are "covered up" instead of brought out into the light where they can be remedied. For one commentary on comment cards and their failings, see Robert C. Lewis and Abraham Pizam, "Guest Surveys: A Missed Opportunity," *Cornell Hotel and Restaurant Administration Quarterly,* November 1981, pp. 37–44. The Omni card in Figure 19-1 is one of the better ones because it measures expectations on a one to five scale. Many, if not most, comment cards ask perfunctory questions with dichotomous answers, e.g., "Did the doorman greet you? Yes__ No__."

[17] "Wizards of Marketing," *Newsweek,* July 22, 1985, p. 42.

We almost always tell survey takers the most important thing about a shampoo is how well it cleans. Yet when researchers show us samples, the first thing we do is smell the fragrance.[18]

Geller states it this way:

The guest is *in* the hotel [restaurant]. He or she made a reservation (or walked in), registered, provided credit evidence, is beginning to accrue charges, and will eventually settle the bill and check out. The idea is to use all these processes to obtain the marketing data needed, and to do so in a way that creates the smallest amount of inconvenience to the guest. The high technology of today provides the mechanical tools necessary to do the job. It is simply a matter of forethought, redesign, and reeducation for the employees.[19]

It is clear that there is a tremendous amount of information that can be accumulated on the internal guest of any hotel or restaurant. Although not always completely objective, the front line employees who have contact with the customer can provide invaluable information, yet seldom are they asked (or listened to).

Designing the Marketing Information System[20]

The first steps in developing a marketing information system are to define the goals and critical success factors of the particular organization, and to identify the information needed to make the decisions to reach those goals. This provides a vehicle whereby management is forced to think about and isolate those areas most critical to it. Identification of critical areas will enable the further identification of the information needed to measure progress in those areas, and the need to establish a system to provide that information.

A good information system should encompass the following:

- The information provided should satisfy user needs.
- The information must be accurate and objective.
- The information must be summarized to be relevant and to be reduced in volume. One way to do this is to report variance from forecast or exception from expectation, rather than a massive set of all-inclusive data.
- The information must flow quickly and smoothly within the organization and be routed only to those to whom it is pertinent.
- The system must be flexible and capable of being changed as critical factors change.

A seven-step program for accomplishing this is as follows:

1. Establish a project team and steering committee. In a small organization this could, in reality, be one person.
2. Document business plans and goals.

---

[18] John Koten, "You Aren't Paranoid If You Feel Someone Eyes You Constantly," *The Wall Street Journal*, March 29, 1985, pp. 1, 22.

[19] Geller, "Executive Information Needs," p. 7.

[20] This section continues to borrow from Geller (ibid.), pp. 38, 39, 52, because he has stated the case so well.

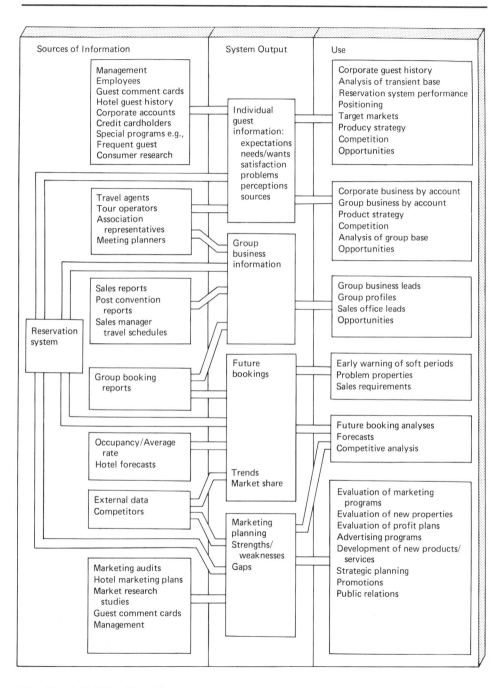

Sources of Information

Management
Employees
Guest comment cards
Hotel guest history
Corporate accounts
Credit cardholders
Special programs e.g.,
Frequent guest
Consumer research

Travel agents
Tour operators
Association
  representatives
Meeting planners

Sales reports
Post convention
  reports
Sales manager
  travel schedules

Reservation
system

Group booking
reports

Occupancy/Average
rate
Hotel forecasts

External data
Competitors

Marketing audits
Hotel marketing plans
Market research
  studies
Guest comment cards
Management

System Output

Individual
guest
information:
expectations
needs/wants
satisfaction
problems
perceptions
sources

Group
business
information

Future
bookings

Trends
Market share

Marketing
planning
Strengths/
  weaknesses
Gaps

Use

Corporate guest history
Analysis of transient base
Reservation system performance
Positioning
Target markets
Producy strategy
Competition
Opportunities

Corporate business by account
Group business by account
Product strategy
Competition
Analysis of group base
Opportunities

Group business leads
Group profiles
Sales office leads
Opportunities

Early warning of soft periods
Problem properties
Sales requirements

Future booking analyses
Forecasts
Competitive analysis

Evaluation of marketing
  programs
Evaluation of new properties
Evaluation of profit plans
Advertising programs
Development of new products/
  services
Strategic planning
Promotions
Public relations

(Adapted from A. Neal Geller, 1984, p. 53)

FIGURE 19-2   A desirable hospitality marketing information system

3. Define the critical success factors of the business.
4. Analyze the information that will be necessary to bring about and to measure the critical success factors.
5. Define the system necessary to provide those information needs.
6. Install the system to be efficient and effective.
7. Monitor the system and its fullfillment and performance, and update as needs require.

A schematic drawing of a marketing information system for hospitality companies is shown in Figure 19-2. One part of that system is the formal research. We move on to discuss that area in greater detail because it is the stage of creating information rather than collecting information, which has been the focus of most of the discussion thus far.

Marketing Research

Formal marketing research—and we use the word *formal* to distinguish it from the haphazard collection of data such as that provided by comment cards—is the objective and empirical collection of information about consumers. In this same sense, it means *primary* data as opposed to secondary data. Secondary data are those collected for some other purpose that may be useful to our purpose. What was discussed above under the heading of external data is largely secondary data. Primary data, on the other hand, are data collected for a specific purpose and constitute what is called formal, or primary, marketing research.

Data are not necessarily *information*. This point is important because research is only as good as its interpretation. There is another important point about business research: Its purpose is to provide information to make decisions; if it doesn't serve that purpose it is a waste of both time and money.

Consider, for example, what is called the "Gallup Monthly Eating-Out Monitor," briefly mentioned earlier in the chapter. This is ongoing research conducted by the Gallup organization, a large research firm, that reports on eating-out trends. The findings are reported in trade journals. Although the sample is representative and the data collection is scientific, one could not reasonably base a local business decision on the information reported.

A Gallup report, for example, stated that salad bars are on the wane—the national survey showed a slightly declined interest in salad bars. Such data may, but probably do not, portend a trend.[21] If so, put this information in the category of environmental scanning. Unfortunately, Gallup will not query this issue again for some time (they query a different one each month), so there is no way of knowing if in fact it is a trend or simply an aberration during the month they collected the data. Even if it were a trend you could not use it to make a decision: salad bars might be "hot" in California and "cold" in Maine. What is the restaurateur in Iowa to assume?

Another Gallup study queried a very important subject, whether people "prefer to eat in the hotel restaurant rather than going someplace else." Once again, unfortunately,

---

[21] A statement made sometime later by Gallup in a promotional brochure asserted, "The majority of diners prefer a salad bar to being served a salad at their table."

the reported results are meaningless.[22] Gallup's question, posed to a "nationally representative sample of adults," asked: "When I stay at a hotel or motel, I usually prefer to eat in the hotel restaurant rather than going someplace else. Would you say the statement is very true, somewhat true, somewhat untrue or very untrue of your opinion?"

Our own answer (the authors') might be as follows, depending on the hotel or motel, its location, and the reputation and prices of its dining room: for breakfast, very true; for lunch, very untrue; for dinner, somewhat untrue—all depending, of course, on why we are there, whom we are with, what we are doing, and so forth. How do you interpret our answer? Gallup just lumps everything together, apparently on the assumption that the meal period, time, context, company, and numerous other variables have no bearing on the response. Thus, as we have stated, the report is meaningless.

Here's another by Gallup: "I expect a hotel or motel to provide me with complimentary toiletries such as shampoo. Would you say the statement is very true, somewhat true, somewhat untrue, or very untrue of your opinion?"[23] We leave the discussion and interpretation of this one to the reader.

There is a problem, as just demonstrated, of so-called averages in research. In fact, they can be dangerous to interpret unless they come from homogeneous groups or market segments. One way to remember this is to keep in mind the following example: Four women are seated around a table. One is pregnant. On average, therefore, each woman is 25 percent pregnant. Basing serious business decisions on averages of heterogeneous samples is not recommended.

Public Domain Research

There is a major problem, also, with what is called "research in the public domain." It is to be perused with interest but utilized with extreme caution. In a previous chapter, we mentioned the research by the U.S. Travel Data Center that indicated (as reported in the trade press) that, by a large margin, the most important reason people choose a hotel for the first time is location. More sophisticated research (and reporting) has shown that while location is extremely salient in hotel choice, it is a "minimum threshold" attribute. It is of first importance *only* if many other things also exist, and even then is important only largely in a negative sense—that is, a poor location will determine a negative choice.

Such situations abound, which is not to say that the same flaws cannot show up in proprietary research because, in fact, they do. By and large, however, research conducted by trade journals, by trade associations, and even by noted research firms such as Gallup for the public domain are of little use for decision-making purposes or even for drawing specific conclusions.

We don't say this for the purpose of criticizing these organizations but to advise that generalized research data that are collected and analyzed without proper controls can be very misleading. Such information is also not likely to be situation-specific. This is a problem with public domain research. Such research may, however, be very useful in environmental scanning when one wishes to observe broad trends.

---

[22] "Hotel Dining: Likes and Dislikes," *Lodging Hospitality*, October 1987, pp. 32, 34.

[23] "Do Consumers Expect Amenities? It's a Toss-up." *Lodging Hospitality*, February 1988, p. 24.

To make this point, because we think it is an important one, we will demonstrate with an annual "study" done by the business publication *Business Travel News*.[24] These studies seek to find out which are the best hotel chains in the view of "corporate travel managers and travel agents." In the 1985 survey, for example, there were 462 responses from possibly over 100,000 distributed questionnaires. There was no control over who received the questionnaire or who the respondents were.

Respondents to this survey were first asked to check off, from a list, which of 66 hotel chains they had corporate rate programs with. They were then asked to list the three best of these companies in a number of performance categories (best facilities, best food, best looking, etc.). Marriott, Hyatt, Hilton, Sheraton, and others with a large number of units were the usual top "winners" for obvious reasons—by their sheer number and the fact that they had more corporate rate programs, were visited more frequently, were better-known names, and in some cases were in a different product class. Frequency of use, or even personal experience, was not measured, nor is it known on what basis the attributes were rated. The effect is that if 100 respondents had programs with Marriott and 50 of these rate Marriott best (50 percent), Marriott would achieve a higher score than Four Seasons, where perhaps only ten respondents had programs, all of whom rated it best (100 percent).

The lack of control demonstrated above is an inherent danger in all research, which will be discussed later on in this chapter. It is particularly prevalent in public domain research and special caution is advised in using such research for drawing any specific conclusions or making any specific decisions.

Proprietary Research

Proprietary research is research conducted for a particular organization for the particular use of that organization as opposed to a general use. It may be conducted by the organization itself or by an outside "supplier," a firm commissioned to do the actual data collection for another firm. In the hospitality industry, very few companies conduct their own research. Even Marriott, which has its own research department and is the hotel leader in research, contracts with outside suppliers to actually conduct most of its research and, at least, to collect the data.

Regardless of who conducts it, the research requirements are the same. Absolute rigor and control are necessary for the findings to have validity and reliability. There are two broad categories of research—qualitative and quantitative. Both have their place; the important thing is to know what that place is.

Qualitative Research

Qualitative research is concerned with obtaining information on consumer attitudes and behavior on a subjective basis. It is largely exploratory in nature and the findings cannot

---

[24] *Business Travel News*, November 5, 1984; November 4, 1985; November 7, 1986. Other publications print similar research results based on similar types of data collection. See, for example, "Hotel of the Year Awards," *Executive Travel*, June 1987, pp. 16, 96. One of the awards, which go to hotels worldwide, granted by this publication is for the "hotel with the most comfortable beds" (the Dorchester in London). Since 1987 *Business Travel News* has made some changes and some improvements in conducting this study.

be generalized to a larger population. Its purpose is usually to learn more about a subject, to understand how consumers use a product, to test a new product concept, or to provide information for developing further quantitative research.

The most common form of qualitative research is the focus group. A focus group is six to ten people "typical" (a judgment obtained by screening in their selection) of the type of people expected to use the product. These people are brought together in a room where a skilled moderator leads the discussion.

As illustration, suppose a restaurateur was considering a radically new menu. He has a mock-up of the menu made but before he goes ahead with the change he wants to see how his customers might react. He invites eight of his customers on each of four different days of the week to have a free dinner if they will agree to participate in a two-hour focus group. He hires a skilled moderator (he would not do this himself because of his lack of skill and potential bias) who leads the group in discussion. The moderator not only asks questions but also attempts to build a rapport with the group and spends a great deal of time probing. The relationship between the moderator and the group is important, because a reluctant group will not provide thorough information.[25]

It is not uncommon to audiotape and/or videotape focus groups. Thus, more complete analysis is possible after the session is over. Also, while the session is being conducted, the restaurateur and some of his staff may sit behind a one-way mirror and observe the proceedings, watching for special nuances and signs that the moderator might miss.

The other common form of qualitative research is the personal interview. This constitutes an unstructured exchange in which the interviewer probes for specific comments and reactions.

There are a number of pragmatic reasons for using qualitative research; for example:

- It can be executed quickly in a short period of time.
- It is relatively economical.
- The environment can be tightly controlled.
- It permits direct contact with consumers.
- It permits greater depth by probing for responses.
- It permits customers to "open up."
- It develops new creative ideas.
- It establishes consumer vocabulary.
- It uncovers basic consumer needs and attitudes.
- It establishes new product concepts.
- It interprets previously obtained quantitative data.

The major problem with qualitative research is that you cannot generalize from it. The best you can say is that this is what these particular people say. It does, however, help in getting inside the consumer's mind. It helps to define problems and it forms the basis for quantitative research to follow. Sometimes we think we understand the problem but we really don't; we are unable to put ourselves into the consumer's perspective.

---

[25] For further discussion in this area see, Joe L. Welch, "Focus Groups for Restaurant Research." *Cornell Hotel and Restaurant Administration Quarterly*, August 1985, pp. 75–85.

Other times we simply don't know just what the problem is. Comment cards may be positive, customer comments are good, and everything looks rosy, except business is declining. Through qualitative probing it may be possible to uncover some problems that otherwise would never reveal themselves.

Quantitative Research

Quantitative research deals with numbers. It measures quantitatively what people say, think, perceive, feel, and do. *Descriptive* quantitative research is the kind with which we are most familiar. It tells us how many, how often, and what percentage, such as how old people are, their sex, their income, their education, or whether they like or dislike something. It then tells us frequency and percentages—for instance, there are 362 females in the sample (48 percent), they ate in a restaurant 2.3 times last week, and 36 percent of them have at least a college education.

Descriptive data tell us who and what but they don't tell us why. They might tell us how many persons in each age bracket ate out how many times and the relative percentages. From this information we could also determine, statistically, if any differences in eating-out patterns by age category were likely to have occurred by chance. But these data wouldn't tell us how these factors interact—for instance, does the age of an individual predict how many times that person will eat in a restaurant in a given week?

As an example, from a comment card we might learn that an individual thought the food and service were fine but we wouldn't be able to predict if that meant that the person would return. Or, in the example given previously of the importance of location in choosing a hotel, the descriptive research conducted would not tell us the interaction of location with the price one would be willing to pay.

Descriptive research tells us one or more things at a time, but it does not tell us if there is an implied causal relationship between them. Descriptive data don't identify the real reasons consumers behave as they do and make the decisions they make. The frequency of consumers' naming an attribute—for example, location—does not necessarily indicate its relative determinance in the choice process, especially when subjects are allowed multiple responses.

Allowing multiple responses on limited choice questions introduces a bias problem that is particularly common in both public and proprietary descriptive research, and often destroys the validity of the findings. When the question choices are also biased, it can be seen why some people say, "You can prove anything you want with research." From poker parlance this is called "stacking the deck."

We mentioned this problem in Chapter 9. Because the practice is so common and is to be avoided or treated with suspicion when done by others, we will discuss here the research aspects with a previously mentioned example.[26]

The makers of Dial soap commissioned a study on frequent travelers. The questionnaire provided limited lists of items to be rated by the respondents on the degree of

---

[26] Bonnie J. Knutson, "Frequent Traveler Study Perceptions of Economy, Mid-price, and Luxury Market Segments," E. Lansing: Michigan State University. Prepared for the Dial Corporation, 1987.

importance or expectation of each of the items when staying at a hotel. We will discuss here one such list called "Services Expected in Hotels."

This list had 29 items in it, one of which was a "Bar of Soap." Respondents evaluated each item. Thus, it is conceivable that all 29 items could be rated as being expected. It is difficult, at least in the United States, to conceive of anyone given 29 items to choose from who would not expect to find a bar of soap in their hotel room. Apparently, however, that is not the case, because only 96.2 percent of the luxury hotel respondents indicated they expected to find a bar of soap. As this was the highest percentage of all items, the conclusion of the study was that the most important service expected in a hotel is a bar of soap and that hoteliers should put more personal care items in their rooms. From a research perspective, such an interpretation is invalid for two reasons.

The first reason is the factor of multiple responses. As was pointed out in Chapter 9, being allowed to name as many items as desired with no rank ordering or choices to be made, very salient items like soap will almost always be mentioned.

The second reason is the bias of the list. Under the category of services, besides the bar of soap which is not a service, were items like wake-up call, direct dial phone, cable TV, check cashing, free newspaper, tennis courts, swimming pool, fresh flowers in the room, all of which are either services or augmented products. None of the 29 items, with the singular exception of soap, is offered by *all* hotels. Because soap is *always* present and expected in a hotel, and the other items are not, the results of this research were preordained, i.e., it was a no-lose situation for Dial.

To doubly emphasize the point, let us carry it one step further. Suppose, now that we know that only 96 percent of guests expect soap, that we wanted to prove that soap was *not* the most expected item. We could very easily do so. In our limited choice list, besides soap, we would include the following: bed, sheets, pillows, blanket, chair, lamp, toilet, hot and cold running water, and carpet. With this list we would likely "prove" that in fact soap was 10th on the list of expected items.

You may think this somewhat absurd, and this case is a particularly blatant one, but this type of research and reported findings are particularly prevalent in the hospitality industry.

Inferential quantitative research is a horse of a different color. It allows us to generalize to a larger population based on the findings from a probability sample, in which each person in the population being studied (e.g., business travelers) has an equal chance of being selected. Since it is rarely feasible to survey everyone in whom we might be interested (called a population), we have to select a few people from the larger group (called a sample). With inferential statistics, it is possible to draw conclusions about the population on the basis of the sample data.

At the same time, inferential methods enhance the multivariate analysis of interaction effects which requires probability sampling as an underlying assumption. An example would be measuring various effects in studying why members of a particular market segment might choose a particular restaurant. A sample from the segment could be surveyed and asked to rate the importance in their decision of food quality, service, ambience, location, and price. In *multivariate* analysis, each of these attributes would interact with the others. The analysis would then reveal weights—that is, the respective weight of each attrribute in choosing the restaurant. This would reveal both the relative relationship of the various attributes and the predictive capability of each in choosing the restaurant.

With the findings from the above, assuming we had surveyed a representative sample of all people who choose that restaurant, we could generalize to all those people (the population) as to why they make that choice. This would tell us what is important in influencing people to choose the restaurant or, perhaps, why they would not choose it. Thus, inferential data are far more powerful and useful than descriptive data. They are also more complex, take more skill to obtain, require the use of a computer, and are more expensive both in collection and analysis. Further, while more powerful, inferential and multivariate data are also more susceptible to misinterpretation.

The Decision to Do Marketing Research

For some, *research* is a scary word. It conjures up visions of spending lots of money, of academic eggheads, of esoteric symbols, of computers, and of undecipherable reports. Although each, and perhaps all, of these may occur in some research situations, they are hardly typical in the business world, nor need they be.

More important, perhaps, marketing research is the only way to really get to know your market. Marketing research is a relatively new phenomenon in the hospitality industry. Already, however, a number of foodservice and hotel companies, not to mention tourism organizations, have research departments or commission out research. Ten years from now there will be no major players in the market that are not either conducting or commissioning research. Why is this so?

That's a good question, which goes beyond the obvious competitive situation, yet it is the competitive situation that largely drives the need for research. As creating and retaining a customer becomes ever more difficult, it becomes more and more necessary to know and understand that customer. Because of this, marketing research is necessary, among other things, to accomplish the following:

- lessen uncertainty
- replace intuition with facts
- stay current with the market
- determine needs and wants
- locate segments and target markets
- plan strategies and tactics
- act in advance for the future
- make business decisions

Some of the areas of marketing research that need to be pursued to accomplish the above are:

- customer perception
- customer awareness
- need for new products and services
- dated products and services

- price sensitivity
- communication strategies—image, media, targets, frequency, content, appeals
- product strategies—service, quality, price, needs and wants, renovations, amenities
- market segments—demographics, psychographics, users, benefits, volume, motivations
- consumers—opinions, beliefs, attitudes, intentions, behavior
- demand analysis
- competitors' strengths and weaknesses

This list could easily be continued at some length but that is not necessary here; you will find many additions to it in the preceding chapters. The important point, however, is not the list but the identification of why you are doing the research. It is the answer to that question that leads to good research design.

Research Design

Developing the research design may be the most important part of all research. This is because perfectly executed and analyzed research is virtually worthless if it is not based on the appropriate design. The design is what guides the research from beginning to end, as shown in Figure 19-3. Whether you are conducting research, commissioning it, or reading it, you should understand the requirements of the research design. For that reason we will go through it step by step. The first four steps are the most critical ones for building the research foundation. They include specifying the research purpose, defining the research problem, establishing the research objectives, and determining what we expect to find out.

The Research Purpose

Research design begins with establishing the purpose of the research, which derives from the management problem. To the uninitiated, this may seem very obvious and the purpose itself may seem very obvious. In truth, that is not necessarily the case. For example, you might say the purpose of a research study is to find out why business is declining, which is actually the management problem. You might learn that it is declining because three new competitors have come to town and your former customers are going to them. That would be interesting but it wouldn't tell you what to do about it. What you want to know is how to *stop* business from declining.

The purpose of research is what you intend to do with the findings—that is, what kinds of business decisions you plan after you have the results. You might want to develop an advertising campaign, change your menu, refurbish your decor, run a special promotion, or any number of other things. Simply knowing that you had new competition, which you probably knew anyway, would not help much in making these decisions. Knowing your purpose will lead to obtaining the information you need to fulfill that purpose. The purpose of the research establishes the parameters of everything that follows in the research design. The first of these is the research problem.

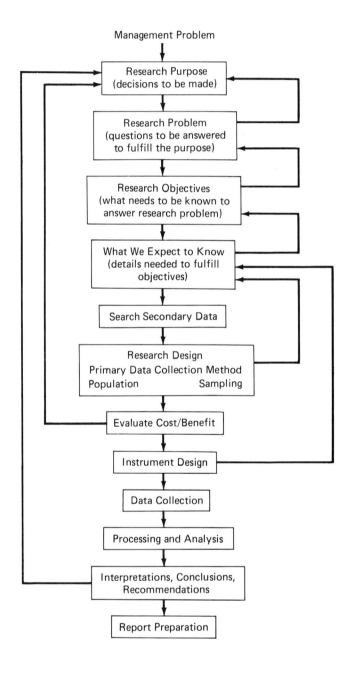

FIGURE 19-3 A flowchart of the research process

The Research Problem

The research problem means exactly that, the *research* problem. It doesn't mean the management problem; the existence of the management problem explains why you are doing the research in the first place. The research problem is how to provide the information that addresses the management problem.

We can utilize the same example as before—business is declining. That is the management problem. The research problem is to answer the question "What is causing business to decline?" or, as in the example above, "Why are our customers going to the competition?" The answer to this question will tell us what to do to stop it from declining—that is, how to fulfill the research purpose. These first two steps are so important in designing research that we will elaborate further.

Suppose we had said that the purpose of the research is to find out why business is declining and that the problem was to find out why it was declining. We discover that the answer is that our customers are going to competitors so we have the answer to the problem and we have satisfied the purpose. Instead, let us say that the research purpose is to develop a marketing strategy to stop the decline in business. That leads us directly to the problem: What needs to be done to stop the decline in business?

We now know that learning that our customers are going to new competition is not enough. We need to know why they are going there, or perhaps, why they are not coming here anymore—that is, we need to know what has to be done to stop this desertion. This, in turn, guides the rest of the research design. In fact, it is often useful to state the research problem even more specifically in the form of a question: What needs to be done to stop the decline in business?

Objectives of the Research

These are the specific objectives—what we want to find out. To follow from the research problem ("What needs to be done to stop the decline in business?"), it is obvious that the sample that we survey is not going to provide the answer directly. We will need to infer that from the information we collect. The research objectives, then, might be to find out what people do and why, for instance:

- What are present eating-out habits?
- What are perceptions of our restaurant?
- What do customers look for in a restaurant?
- What would they like to see in a restaurant?

The objectives are to obtain the information we need to address the problem. From the objectives flow the answers to the question "What do we expect to know after the research is completed?"

What We Expect to Know

What we expect to know is all the pieces of information that are necessary to fulfill the objectives, for instance:

- Where do they go now?
- How often do they go there?
- Why do they go there?
- How much do they spend there?
- What do they order there?
- Why do they dine out at all?
- What do they think of us?
- What do they seek that they can't find?
- What would persuade them to go to a different restaurant?

It should be clear now that if we simply deal with the issue of why business is declining, we might not come up with answers that would be very useful in changing the pattern. That is why the above four steps are so critical to good research, and why each one must flow from the previous ones. What each step does, in turn, is simply to narrow the parameters of the research so that it focuses directly on what is needed to make management decisions. This process continues. The first four parameters will establish who the population is, the sample that is needed, the questions that need to be asked, and whether the research should be qualitative, descriptive, inferential, or some combination of these.

Research Method

The remainder of the research design is called the research method. This includes establishing the sample, the sample size, the method of data collection, the questions asked, and the type of analysis that will be applied.

Population The *population* is all those people in whom we are interested. This might mean all present customers, all potential customers or both. It might mean all people who eat at restaurants in this area, or all those who come from another area. It might be all businesspeople, or leisure travelers, or those who eat beef, or those who don't. It might be all those who use a certain restaurant category (fast-food), or a certain restaurant brand (McDonald's).

In the broadest sense, the population is all those people who might spend money to buy our product. The important criterion is that the population be as homogeneous as possible—that is, that its members have similar characteristics along the dimensions we wish to measure. Consider the following example.

> The operator of a restaurant wishes to determine the opinions of a particular group of people concerning her restaurant operation. The populations involved could be classi-fied in the following ways.
>
> - all people who eat out
> - people who like to dine out in the type of restaurant operated by this restaurateur
> - people who have an opportunity to dine at this type of restaurant
> - people who know about this particular restaurant, and
>   -have never dined there
>   -have dined there in the past but do not dine there now
>   -dine there now on an irregular basis
>   -dine there now on a regular basis

Sample The sample is derived from the population. Because we can't survey everyone, we will have to survey only a few. From these few we hope to learn the characteristics of the many. Selection of the appropriate sample and sample size is beyond the scope of this book. There are prescribed methods for doing this that may be found in any research text. Our main concern here will be with the type of sample.

A probability sample is one in which every member of the population (or the sample frame, which is a subset of the population when the population is very large) has an equal chance of being selected. This means that the sample is collected randomly without any bias as to who is selected. A simple method of randomly selecting a sample group of fifty might be to put all the names in the population in a bowl, reach in, and pick out the fifty names one at a time.

Statistically, it can be shown that a random sample will closely approximate the true characteristics of a population. This is why we can infer from a sample. It can also be shown that we can say with a certain degree of confidence anywhere up to 99.99 percent that, given a certain error tolerance, what we have learned could not have occurred by chance. Demonstrating these points mathematically is also beyond the scope of this book. Suffice it to say that the larger the sample, the higher the level of confidence and the smaller the possible margin of error.[27] It is only with probability samples that one can legitimately use inferential analysis. This is true because of the statistical controls that are possible with this kind of sample.

A nonprobability sample obviously means just the opposite—that is, everyone in the population does not have an equal chance of being selected. This is called a convenience sample, in which people are selected simply because they are convenient. We might choose to sample the first fifty people who check out of the hotel one morning. This does not allow us to generalize our findings to anyone else who stays at the hotel. People who check out later, or on another day, might have very different characteristics from these first fifty.

Another kind of nonprobability sample is called a judgmental sample. In this case, it might be decided that some specified variation is needed such as a mixture of sexes, age groups, travel purpose, and method of arrival at a hotel. We might choose the first ten of each category who check out. Judgmental samples are often used for focus group selection because focus groups are usually specifically selected to represent certain characteristics. In these cases, subjects are first screened to be certain that they meet certain criteria such as demographics or usage. For example, in the example given above, if we wanted to ask people which hotel had the most comfortable beds in the world, we would first screen them to be certain that they had slept in all the hotel beds in the world.

A common method of creating judgmental samples is what is called a mall-intercept. This means, essentially, that we go to a shopping mall and intercept people. If they will respond (many won't), we screen them, by asking, for example, "Do you eat dinner in a restaurant two or more times a week?" If the answer is no, we move on; if it is yes, we proceed with further questions.

Of course, all so-called mall-intercepts don't take place in malls; they may take place in airline terminals, restaurant entryways, or hotel lobbies.

---

[27] Large sample sizes do not, however, overcome sample biases, or aberrations in the sample that will distort the data and the findings. In fact, in nonprobability samples, larger sample sizes will only magnify the bias and distort the data even further. Further, very large samples are almost always likely to produce statistical significance.

How large, then, should a sample be? Many variables affect that answer. An extensive discussion is beyond the scope of this book, but can be found in any good research book. We will only add that bigger is not necessarily better, and statistical confidence levels should be employed to arrive at the correct answer.

Another type of nonprobability sample is composed of the people who fill out guest comment cards in hotel rooms. This is a biased "default" sample. Although you could argue that everyone who stays in a hotel has the same opportunity to fill out the comment card, this does not constitute a probability sample because the researcher has no means of controlling the probability. This results in a default selection. The bias comes from the fact that the sample would represent only those people who are prone to fill out comment cards. These people may differ drastically from people who never fill out comment cards.

Data Collection   The data collection design comes next. However, data collection was clearly in mind when the sample was selected because the two are closely interrelated and must be coordinated. Already decided as well would have been whether the research was to be qualitative, quantitative, or a combination of the two.

Regardless of the form of data collection, some written preparation is required beforehand. If focus groups are to be used, a moderator's guide is prepared. This will be needed first to screen the potential participants to be certain that they fit the criteria established. If we wanted to ask questions about eating out, for example, we would screen to be certain that participants were people who did eat out.

The main use of the moderator's guide is during the group process. Although focus groups are generally unstructured, guidelines are used to keep the conversation on course and to be certain that the appropriate and important items are discussed.

In other forms of qualitative research such as personal interviewing, the interviewer will also use a guide for the same reason. Additionally, it may be desirable to ask specific questions and write down specific responses for later analysis.

In quantitative research, a questionnaire is prepared, whether the data is collected by telephone, personal interview, or mail. A mailed questionnaire will require more care in its preparation in terms of format, design, appearance, and other factors that will both induce respondents to complete it and make it easier for them to do so. It is also important that the data collected be easy to tabulate or feed into the computer for analysis.

Questionnaire design is not as simple a task as it may sometimes seem. Questions must be clear and unambiguous. Each question should, as nearly as possible, have the same meaning for all respondents. This means that if an abstract term such as *quality* is used, the word *quality* should be defined so that everyone interprets it in the same way.

The subject of questionnaire design is covered in research textbooks and will therefore not be discussed here. We only caution of the hazards involved, because if you are not measuring what you think you are measuring, you will obtain invalid data and findings. For this reason, too, it is always necessary to pretest the questionnaire. This means trying it out on people who will not be included in the sample in order to get feedback on the wording, the time it takes, the clarity, the understanding of terms, possible omissions, and other factors that might confuse respondents or invalidate the findings.

The decision as to whether to use personal interviews, focus groups, mail, telephone, or other distribution methods (such as comment cards or individual intercepts) is an important one in the research design. Each one has its trade-offs in terms of time and money. While the budget is always a limiting factor, the most important criterion is the method that will provide the most reliable data for the problem at hand. There is no one answer to this because each case is individual and must be weighed on its own merits.

Analysis   The data obtained must, of course, be analyzed very carefully. The method of analysis will have been decided beforehand, including whether it will be done by hand or by computer. Also, the analytical techniques to be used should be pre-determined, since these will affect the way questions are asked, the type of response solicited, and the scale that is used to measure them. Inferential data used in multivariate analysis, for example, require responses to be collected on a scale (e.g., 1 to 5) instead of simple yes/no or rank-ordered data, or multiple-choice responses. Such data also require a dependent variable—that is, a measurement such as "likelihood to return" that can be used as an overall scale to measure the impact of the other (independent) variables. Data analysis is also beyond the scope of this book; instead, we refer readers to any good marketing research text.

Figure 19-4 includes a minicase and a very brief research design to illustrate the points that have been covered.

Reliability and Validity

The research design, the sampling, the data collection, and the data analysis must be all rigorously controlled when doing research. Each step is critically important, none more or less so than the others. Two supreme tests are applied to research findings: reliability and validity. Because these tests are so critical we will discuss them further.

Reliability   Reliability in research means that the findings can be projected to a larger population if it is one of the intents of the research to do so. It means that if we took a similar sample from a similar population we would get similar results. It means that if we asked the same questions in a different way that we would get similar results. Even if reliable, the findings may or may not be valid.

Validity   Findings must be reliable if they are to be valid. They cannot be valid if not reliable, particularly if we intend to project the findings beyond the groups of people being researched. Validity means that the data must support the conclusions. The conclusions must be valid in that they are based on whether the research actually measured what it is presumed to have measured. Some of the critical forms of validity are as follows.

Face validity—Is the instrument (questionnaire) measuring everything it is supposed to measure? Is the sample representative of the behavior or trait being measured?

Construct validity—Is the construct being measured the one we think we are measuring? For instance, if we want to find out why people choose a restaurant and they tell us that the most important factor is quality of food, are they really telling us that this is the reason they choose a given restaurant?

Internal validity—Are the findings free from bias? Are they true or are they an artifact of the research design—for instance, are there intervening, interactive, additive, or spurious effects that affect the responses and are extraneous to the causal relation-ship? An example of this is the research on "best" hotels previously mentioned. If 100 people are asked their opinions of a hotel and 50 have been there and 50 have not, then having been to the hotel is an intervening variable—that is, it "intervenes" in their opinion. Such variables must be controlled. In this case, we would control

TACO GOURMET

A successful restaurateur decided to start a Mexican fast-food chain offering "gourmet" tacos and other Mexican foods, to cash in on the latest fast-food trend but at a higher level of quality. His pilot effort was called Taco Gourmet. The food quality was superior because he used only the best ingredients. He priced his items about 30 percent higher than the competition for the same items.

Business was excellent the first month, then started falling off. After three months it was only half of what it had been the first month. The owner noticed that few of his customers were repeaters. He inquired among his friends to see if they had heard complaints. The only complaint that seemed to appear was about the prices. The owner decided to conduct some formal research. After analyzing the situation, a consultant developed the following research design.

Purpose of the research: To determine product and pricing strategies.

Research problem: What is the market looking for in a Mexican fast-food restaurant?

Objectives:
1. To determine quality perceptions of Mexican fast food.
2. To determine the price/value relationships of Mexican fast food.
3. To determine market demand for Mexican fast food at different price/quality levels.

What we expect to find out:
Do people know and appreciate the difference between quality and ordinary Mexican fast food? If yes, what is the difference based on?
How much are they willing to pay?
How frequently do they eat it?
Where do they go now? How often? How much do they spend?
What is the present awareness and trial of Taco Gourmet?
What is the present perception of Taco Gourmet?
How much more, if anything, will people pay for "different" Mexican fast food?

Population: All people over the age of 16 within a five-mile radius who eat Mexican fast food at least once a month.

Sample: Assuming 50 percent of the population appreciate the difference in quality, with a 5 percent margin of error and a desired confidence level of 95 percent, a sample of 384 is required.* With an expected response rate of 25 percent, a probability sample of 1600 names will be drawn from street listings.

Data collection: Four focus groups divided by sex and age will be convened. Data collected from these groups will be used to develop a written questionnaire to be mailed to the sample.

Data analysis: Frequency statistics will be derived and data will be cross-tabulated by demographics. Regression analysis will be used to predict intention to purchase Mexican fast food at various price/quality levels.

---

*The computation of sample size is done here using the proportional method which is described in research texts.

FIGURE 19-4 Minicase illustrating the research design process

by asking if they had or had not been there. We could then compare the responses from each group to see if they differed.

Without validity, research findings projected to a larger population are meaningless. Anyone who wants to use research for decision-making purposes should always verify its validity first. Lack of validity is the most common cause of faulty research. Other common faults of research projects, presented, more or less, in order of the frequency of occurrence and importance, are contained in the following list.

1. lack of construct validity
2. failure to control for intervening variables
3. unwarranted conceptual leaps, unsupported conclusions, and presumptive judgments
4. failure to apply tests of statistical significance
5. errors in sample selection
6. failure to identify the issue, problem, or purpose of the research
7. failure to capture the richness of the data (whether because of poor research instruments or poor statistical analysis)
8. failure to define or limit variables
9. poor writing
10. failure to notice spurious relationships[28]

Toward More Useful Research[29]

Despite its importance, marketing research will never compensate for bad management, a bad product, poor service, or a product that has no market. Assuming none of these conditions, marketing research is appropriate when you don't know for certain:

- why people choose your property
- why people choose another property
- who your real competition is
- how many of your customers come back
- how many don't
- how people "use" your property
- what trade-offs your customers make in choosing
- how to gauge acceptance of a new concept
- price sensitivity and how much to discount to gain competitive advantage
- whether your product and pricing strategy are in tune with your market
- who your target market is
- if your thinking is the same as that of your customers
- what the persuasive appeals are for each market and each type of customer

[28] Robert C. Lewis and Abraham Pizam, "Designing Research for Publication," *Cornell Hotel and Restaurant Administration Quarterly*, August 1986, p. 57.

[29] This section is excerpted from Robert C. Lewis, "Getting the Most from Marketing Research," *Cornell Hotel and Restaurant Administration Quarterly*, August 1985, pp. 97–99.

- whether you are keeping up with changes in your customers' needs and wants
- whether your customers are truly satisfied
- whether you are keeping or losing customers with complaint handling
- whom your advertising is reaching and affecting, if anybody
- how your advertising is positioning your property in the market's perception
- if you are ahead of market trends or running to catch up
- many, many other things about your market

Marketing research forms the basis for decisions, but it does not make them for you. It should be designed to provide specific information to answer the questions to which an operator needs answers. This is not a simple matter. Too much research is conducted without full undersanding of what management hopes to learn. On the other hand, too much research is conducted to confirm decisions already made or to feed an ego. When the decision fails, the research is blamed.

The results of valid research should be accepted and used, even if they refute existing beliefs. Too much research ends up buried in a file drawer because it did not agree with someone's prior assumptions. Regardless of what management believes, it is customers' perceptions that count.

Summary

It is difficult to overemphasize the importance of marketing information systems in the hospitality industry today. Whether it is environmental scanning, internal data, competitive analysis, or consumer perception and behavior, the time has come when management will no longer survive, except in rare cases, by intuitive decisions only. Management at every level of a hospitality organization needs information not only to manage effectively but also to act in advance for the future. It is not as easy as it seems to set up the systems that will provide the information, nor will the systems come until management fully understands what its needs are and demands the systems to fulfill them.

On the other hand, the problem may be one of having too much information. Computer technology and information services provide an abundance of information too unwieldy for ready digestion. The additional problem, then, is one of selection. Effective marketing information systems will come only after defined and selective informational needs are established.

Marketing research is an area of the marketing information system just coming into its own in hospitality. In an industry that is physically closer to its customer than most, the hospitality industry is one that knows the least about its customer. The result has been both the loss of customers and the winning of customers by default. Essentially, this has resulted in the "trading" of customers. For the firm that wants to keep customers, it is simply going to have to know that customer better.

There is a myth that marketing research is used only to make big decisions and has little to do with daily operations. While this argument might have some merit in, say, manufacturing tires, it bears little weight in an industry where brand loyalty is fleeting and every product unit has a personal relationship with the individual who purchases it. The value of research is tied more to the level of uncertainty than to the level of risk in the decision.

DISCUSSION QUESTIONS

1. Why are management information systems and marketing research more important today than they were ten or fifteen years ago?
2. How is the hospitality industry unique in its ability to gather internal information? Give some examples of how this can be done. Make a list of things you would want to know about your customers if you managed a hotel or restaurant. Discuss how this information would help you make management decisions.
3. Describe how inferential quantitative research is different from descriptive research. What implications does this have for understanding the hospitality customer? Give examples of situations in which you would use each or both.
4. Describe the difference between a probability and a nonprobability sample. Be prepared to discuss when you would use each and why.
5. Discuss validity, its different versions, and reliability.
6. You, as manager of a hotel, have run a unique weekend package promotion for six weeks. It was an unqualified success. You wonder why and decide to commission some research to find out. Define the research purpose, the research problem, the objectives, what you would expect to know when done, the population, the sample, data collection, and analysis (in general terms).

FOR FURTHER STUDY

The Sheraton Customer Rating Index[30]

In 1987, Sheraton made a major move at the corporate level to get closer to its customer. One part of this move was the development of a "Customer Rating Index." In a decided departure from reliance on the standard guest comment card, this index is based on a research design that follows many of the principles we have outlined in this chapter. To our knowledge, Sheraton and Westin are the first hotel companies to move so strongly in this direction.

The objective of Sheraton's program was to provide management with a comprehensive, cost-efficient, easy-to-implement customer satisfaction monitoring system as a tool for making better-informed business decisions.

Through research of guests at a number of Sheraton properties, approximately twenty attributes were designated as those most important to guests in rating a hotel's performance. Utilizing these attributes, a questionnaire is randomly distributed to guests upon check-in (Figure 19-5). Analysis of responses is completed to produce the following (hypothetical examples only are shown in the figures):

- A gap analysis chart (Figure 19-6): attribute importance plotted against attribute ratings;
- Comparative analysis (Figure 19-7): attribute mean ratings for each hotel against market segments, all Sheraton hotels, and national norms;
- Demographic analysis (Figure 19-8): ratings across demographic segments;

---

[30] This section is used with the courtesy and permission of Sheraton Hotels.

I. Please let us know how we measured up to your expectations...

	Below Expectations			Exceeds Expectations			Did Not Apply
Your expectations of our employees...							
Hotel has friendly/hospitable employees	1	2	3	4	5	6	X
Hotel employees perform job quickly and efficiently	1	2	3	4	5	6	X
Staff at front desk are courteous and helpful	1	2	3	4	5	6	X
Service staff are courteous and helpful	1	2	3	4	5	6	X
Staff shows that they want me to come back	1	2	3	4	5	6	X
Hotel staff are problem solvers when necessary	1	2	3	4	5	6	X
Friendly greeting upon arrival	1	2	3	4	5	6	X
Hotel employees answered my questions	1	2	3	4	5	6	X
Hotel employees anticipate my needs	1	2	3	4	5	6	X (10)
Overall expectations of our hotel...							
Cleanliness of room	1	2	3	4	5	6	X
Everything in the room is in working order	1	2	3	4	5	6	X
Beds are comfortable	1	2	3	4	5	6	X
Fast/efficient check-in	1	2	3	4	5	6	X
Room lighting is sufficient for my needs	1	2	3	4	5	6	X
Feel safe and secure in hotel	1	2	3	4	5	6	X
Fast/efficient check-out	1	2	3	4	5	6	X
Wake-up call service	1	2	3	4	5	6	X
Value of hotel as a whole	1	2	3	4	5	6	X
Hotel is consistent within its chain of hotels	1	2	3	4	5	6	X
Hotel provides first class quality service, facilities and staff	1	2	3	4	5	6	X (29)

III. We would also like to know about you ..

1) Is this your first stay at Sheraton?
 Yes □ 1
 No □ 2 (36)

2) When in the area again, what is the likelihood that you would return to this hotel?
 Very likely □ 1
 Somewhat likely □ 2
 Not very likely □ 3
 Not at all likely □ 4 (37)

3) What is the primary purpose of your visit?
 Business □ 1
 Pleasure □ 2
 Convention/Conference □ 3 (38)

4) How many nights did you spend in hotels while traveling during the past 12 months?
 1 - 5 □ 1
 6 - 10 □ 2
 11 - 20 □ 3
 21 - 50 □ 4
 over 50 □ 5 (39)

II. Please indicate the following characteristic(s) the hotel staff demonstrated during your stay by giving a plus (+) for service which "exceeded your expectations" and a minus (-) for service which "fell below your expectations" ...

	Courteous	Friendly	Helpful	Perform job efficiently	Perform job quickly	Enthusiastic	Took a personal interest in me	N/A
Front Desk								(30)
Bellman/Doorman								
House-Keeping Service								
Room Service								
Restaurant Staff								
Telephone Operator/Message Staff								(35)

5) When traveling for business, how is your hotel selected?
 Company policy □ 1
 Travel agent □ 2
 Make selection yourself □ 3
 Recommendation □ 4
 Other: □ 5
 Do not travel for business □ 6 (40)

6) Your age:
 Under 25 □ 1
 25 - 34 □ 2
 35 - 44 □ 3
 45 - 54 □ 4
 55 - 64 □ 5
 65+ □ 6 (41)

7) Your sex:
 Female □ 1
 Male □ 2 (42)

8) To which of the following hotel frequent traveler clubs do you belong?
 Holiday Inns Priority Club □ 1
 Hyatt Hotels Gold Passport □ 2
 Marriott Honored Guest □ 3
 Ramada Business Card □ 4
 Sheraton Club International □ 5
 Other: □ 6
 None □ 7 (43)

534

FIGURE 19-5 Research questionnaire

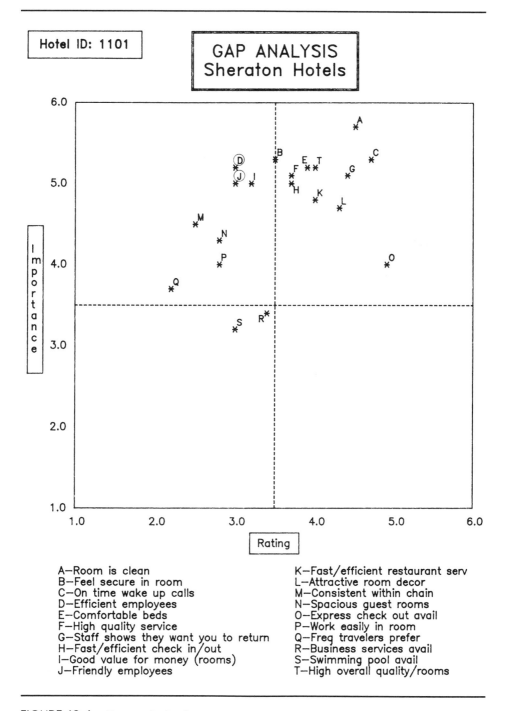

FIGURE 19-6   Gap analysis chart

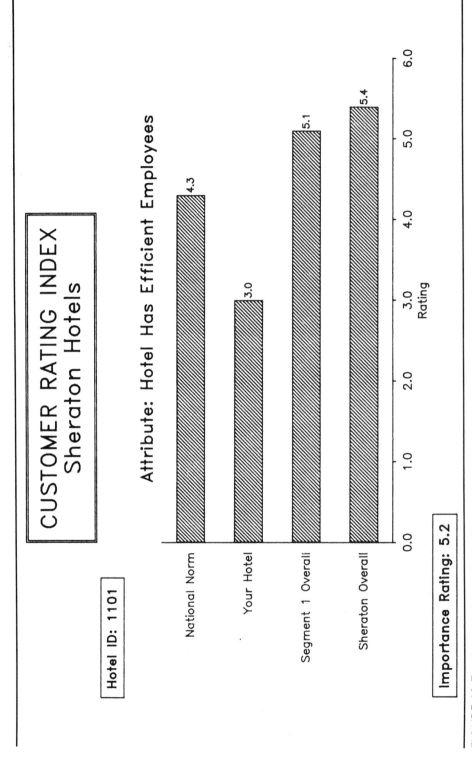

FIGURE 19-7 Comparative analysis chart

CUSTOMER RATING INDEX

******************SHERATON HOTELS**QUARTER 1**(HOTEL ID 1101)**************************

HOTEL HAS FRIENDLY EMPLOYEES

	TOTAL	--SEX---		/TRIP PURPOSE-/			/-OCCUPATION--/			1ST VISIT/		/--TRIPS/YR---/		
		MALE	FE-MALE	BUS	CONFR	LEI-SURE	PROF	MGR	OTHR	YES	NO	< 7	7 +	NOT SPEC
(1)DOES NOT DESCRIBE HOTEL AT ALL	410 36%	313 35%	97 40%	291 46%	75 27%	44 19%	81 37%	90 33%	239 37%	97 40%	313 35%	141 22%	255 69%	14 11%
(2)	78 7%	63 7%	15 6%	42 7%	20 7%	16 7%	15 7%	22 8%	41 6%	15 6%	63 7%	58 9%	11 3%	9 7%
(3)	187 16%	144 16%	43 18%	97 15%	51 18%	39 17%	32 14%	56 21%	99 15%	43 18%	144 16%	129 20%	46 13%	12 10%
(4)	100 9%	79 9%	21 9%	46 7%	27 10%	27 12%	21 10%	19 7%	60 9%	21 9%	79 9%	68 11%	15 4%	17 14%
(5)	245 22%	205 23%	40 17%	72 12%	82 29%	91 40%	53 24%	58 21%	134 21%	40 17%	205 23%	171 27%	2 1%	72 58%
(6)DESCRIBES HOTEL PERFECTLY	112 10%	88 10%	24 10%	76 12%	25 9%	11 5%	18 8%	28 10%	66 10%	24 10%	88 10%	75 12%	37 10%	-
UNSPECIFIED	2 *	2 *	-	2 *	-	-	1 *	-	1 *	-	2 *	1 *	1 *	-
RESPONDING CUSTOMERS	1134 100%	894 100%	240 100%	626 99%	280 100%	228 100%	221 100%	273 100%	640 98%	240 100%	894 100%	643 101%	367 100%	124 100%
MEAN	3.0	3.1	2.9	2.7	3.3	3.6	3.0	3.1	3.0	2.9	3.1	3.5	1.9	4.0

IMPORTANCE RATING = 5.0

FIGURE 19-8 Demographic analysis chart

537

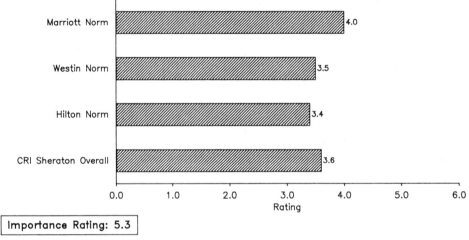

FIGURE 19-9   Competitive analysis chart

- Competitive analysis (Figure 19-9): competitive position vis-à-vis other hotels in the product class.

We applaud Sheraton for this effort and predict it will be a forerunner of other similar efforts. (In fact, we know of at least two others in the works.) In the customer questionnaire, Figure 19-5 respondents are asked about their expectations, not satisfactions, as discussed in Chapter 1. It is possible, as well, to accomplish more powerful analysis with the data than that described above and done by Sheraton.

For example, the question of "likelihood to return" can be used as a dependent variable to determine the interactive impact of each of the "expectations" ratings in combination with all the others. This would tell Sheraton which combination of met or unmet expectations predict the likelihood to return.

An even better, or additional, dependent variable would be one that measured "overall expectations met." This would have higher construct validity and would tell each hotel just where to put its emphasis for its own particular target markets.

Using dependent variables, as was just suggested, in multivariate analysis would no doubt change the findings since none of the twenty attributes behave independently. It would also change the gap analysis chart (Figure 19-6) for the same reasons. We would

How Reliable Are Guest Surveys?

The Customer Rating Index vs. The Guest Comment Card

The service sector of the world economy has changed dramatically. Customer expectations for delivery of improved services are increasing. Less tolerance for mediocrity and more choices in all service areas has put the decision squarely back on the customer.

Improving your competitive position in this market requires vigilant monitoring and reliable measurement of changes in customer satisfaction with the delivery of your service.

The **Customer Rating Index** was developed to provide an ongoing customer satisfaction monitoring system which *is representative, reliable, and projectable ... which guest comment cards are not.*

■ Respondents are randomly selected to participate, which gives every guest an equal chance of being selected ... this provides a *representative* sample of your total customer base.

■ A guest survey is considered *reliable* when it presents an accurate reflection of the customer's experience ... the same customer would again give the same rating.

■ Data collected from a representative sample using a reliable survey provides *projectable* data -- consequently, from a small number of observations (200-300), management can confidently make decisions regarding future actions.

In contrast, the **Guest Comment Card** is a necessary communication medium enabling guests to respond to immediate extremes of satisfaction and dissatisfaction. Due to the self-selected nature of the respondents, though, guest responses *cannot be used as representative, reliable or valid evaluations* against which service standards could be established.

On recruited interviews, research has shown that hotel guests who had completed an interview gave similar responses two weeks and three months later. When hotel guests who had filled out a Guest Comment Card were contacted two weeks after checkout and asked to rate the hotel again, over half revised their opinion ... to a more positive stance.

Therefore, the Guest Comment Card should be viewed as a vehicle used to highlight problems requiring immediate attention. The Customer Rating Index should be implemented as a reliable measure of customer satisfaction. Together, both programs provide you with a comprehensive customer feedback system.

FIGURE 19-10   Research vs. comment cards

also suggest quantifying Part II of the questionnaire, which now provides only pluses or minuses on staff characteristics.

Finally, respondents are instructed to mail the completed questionnaire to the CEO of Sheraton, or return it to the front desk. As we have previously pointed out, returning it to the front desk can be fatal, because negative ratings will probably never reach their intended destination. It has also been found that using the chief executive officer as the designee lacks credibility. Goods-producing companies have found that using a title such as "vice-president—guest relations" adds credibility. It also says, "There's someone up there who cares about us."

Figure 19-10 is a copy of a print-out distributed to Sheraton management regarding the program. It addresses comments that we have made throughout the text on the need for greater reliability in customer ratings.

DISCUSSION QUESTION

1. Analyze the Sheraton guest questionnaire. What other ways would you suggest to use it or to alter it, in order to capture richer data and analysis and to provide more practically useable data?

CHAPTER 20

Strategic Marketing

Throughout this text we have frequently used the word *strategy*. Strategy is a commonly used word and thus we have proceeded on the assumption that the reader had no particular difficulty with its usage. In fact, however, the word has different meanings for different people.

We have also discussed a number of aspects of strategic marketing: environmental scanning; opportunities, threats, and competitive analysis; segmentation and positioning; and marketing intelligence systems. Thus, you will find some overlap between previous chapters and this one, as well as the next one on marketing planning.

In this chapter we will clarify the use of the word *strategy* in the marketing or management context. We will then enlarge upon the process and implications of strategic marketing planning and demonstrate its importance in any marketing context. Most important, we will present a strategic framework to be used in developing marketing strategies, which will demonstrate how all of the various elements fit together.

The Concept of Strategy

We begin with the standard textbook definition of strategy vs. tactics, which is directly derived from the military: Tactics are the way to win the battle; strategy is the way to win the war. In a simplistic example, we could demonstrate this as follows:

Objective: Surround the enemy
Strategy: Take one area at a time
Tactic: Use armored tank divisions

Actually, marketing is not much different. Strategy is the way to gain and keep customers; tactics are the step-by-step procedure of how to do it. For example:

540

Objective: Be perceived as the hotel of choice.

Strategy: Give customers better value.

Tactics: Always have their reservation and room (table) ready; call them by name; make sure they receive their wakeup call; have full-length mirrors and good bathroom lighting in their rooms; offer fresh-brewed coffee as soon as they sit down for breakfast; have room service delivered on time; have the print on the menu large enough to read; offer a selection for those who are light eaters; and so forth.

From this example it can be seen that tactics flow from strategy. That means that the first thing we have to do is develop the appropriate strategy. It is the strategy that drives the firm and specifies the direction in which it is going.

If that is the case, you might ask, if no strategy has been developed then what drives the firm? The answer is that there is always a strategy, in one way or another. If there is no explicit strategy, then there is an implicit one. In fact, too often strategies exist by default. Here's a simple example.

> One of the basic tenets of marketing strategy is segmentation. Suppose no one has even given it a thought, much less developed a strategy. The result is that "we'll take any customers we can get." The strategy, by default, is to take anyone as customers. Along comes a bus tour; we take it and it fills the lobby. Our corporate customers say, "What's going on here? We thought this was a peaceful and quiet hotel. Let's go somewhere else next time."

The default strategy in this case is counterproductive. That is why strategy should never be left to chance. It should be both planned and executed very carefully.

The Concept of Strategic Planning

The essence of *strategic planning* is "how to get from here to there." Although it is not quite that simple in execution, it is that simple in comprehension, and you should keep that in mind. It naturally follows that there are two things inherent in such a statement: If you want to get from "here" you have to know where "here" is; if you want to get to "there" you have to know where "there" is. In strategic planning, the first is called a "situation analysis," or "where we are now"; the second is called "objectives," or "where we want to go." Strategic planning fills the gap: How do we get from where we are now to where we want to go?

In a more formal sense, strategic planning is concerned with the setting of business objectives, the match between products and markets, the choice of competition, the allocation of resources, and the proactive planning to reach the objectives. Although some people would put strategic planning on an esoteric plane, it does not belong there at all; it is an everyday, basic concept. We'll explain this with another simple example.

> Consider a high school graduate. Where is he now? Seventeen years old, no real skills, no profession, and certainly little chance for professional growth in a solid career path. Where does he want to be? A solid candidate for a good job in a firm that will offer opportunities for growth and advancement. Strategy? Get a good education and enhance his capabilities and potential in the business world. Tactic? Go to college.

Although most strategic planning is done at the higher levels of a business organization, this should not necessarily be the case. *Strategic marketing planning is appropriate at any level*. We emphasize this because of the common perception to the contrary. In fact, this has been one of the major failings of strategic planning: it often takes place only at higher levels and doesn't filter down to *strategic management* that focuses on implementation of the strategic plan and the search for long-term, sustainable, competitive advantage in serving the needs of the target markets. Actually, *strategic thinking* is an asset at any level of management, and the best strategic marketing occurs when the decision process is primarily bottom-up.

To use the same example as above, giving the customer better value can be a strategy at any level. If this is the actual corporate strategy of a 300-property hotel chain, let's see how it translates down to the strategic management of a coffee shop in only one of those 300 units.

> The manager, a recent college graduate, thinks, "If that's the corporate strategy, then how does it affect me—how do I give better value?" She looks around and says, "Right now (situation analysis) we're just another coffee shop. What we'd like to be (objective) is the best coffee shop in town. The answer is (strategy) giving the customer better value. How that is done (tactics) is always to have fresh orange juice and fresh-brewed coffee, offer coffee as soon as a customer is seated for breakfast, never close off the most desirable part of the dining room no matter how slow it is, don't "push" customers so we can turn the tables over, don't put singles next to the kitchen door, and be sure that prices are competitive.

In contrast, a fast-food operation works on volume. The objective is to maximize patronage and turnover. The strategy is to give the customer every reason to move on quickly. The tactics are to have food all ready, accept pay for food when it is picked up, and minimize table setting so the table can be ready for another party almost immediately.

This, then, is the concept of strategic planning: decide where you are now, decide where you want to go, and develop and manage the strategy that will get you there. From that strategy, let flow everything else that you do, including all tactics.

In this sense, strategic planning is the tour de force behind all decision-making. It is the deployment of company resources to their best advantage. It concentrates on the markets to be served, the needs and wants of those markets, and the competition for those markets. It is planning for the long-run advantage; strategy specifies the direction. Jain states it as follows:

> Marketing strategies should devise ways in which the [business] can differentiate itself effectively from its competitors, capitalizing on its distinctive strengths to deliver better value to its customers. A good marketing strategy should be characterized by: (a) a clear market definition; (b) a good match between [business] strengths and the needs of the market; and (c) superior performance, relative to the competition, in the key success factors of the business.[1]

The strategic marketing planning and management process is hierarchical in nature and requires a systems perspective. The strategic framework for this perspective is illustrated in Figure 20-1; we will discuss it step by step.

---

[1] Subhash C. Jain, *Marketing Planning and Strategy*, Cincinnati: South-Western Publishing, 1985, p. 43.

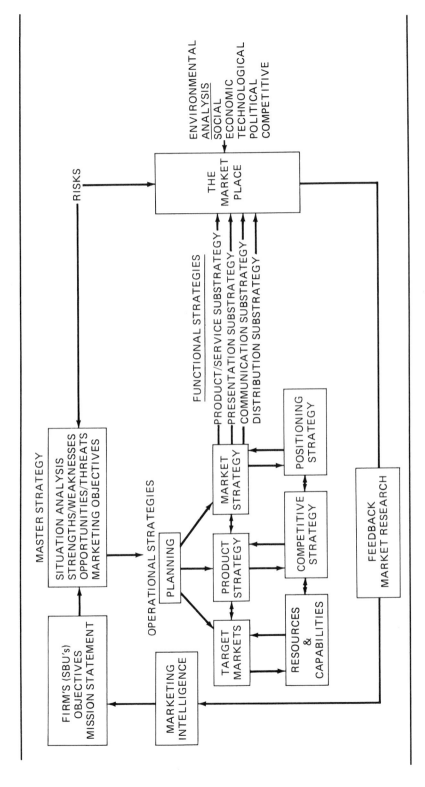

FIGURE 20-1　The strategic marketing systems model

543

The Strategic Marketing System

Any strategic planning process begins with the firm's objectives and mission statement. This is true whether you are IBM or Joe's Diner. Both IBM and Joe have specific objectives and missions. IBM's may be put together by an executive committee of senior vice-presidents. Joe may carry his around in his head and, if you asked him, might be unable to articulate them. It doesn't matter; they are still there and they will guide the operation of the diner every bit as much as IBM's will guide the operation of that giant company. Objectives and mission statements go hand in hand so we need to analyze them.

Objectives and Mission Statements

Any firm has certain financial objectives and we will not dwell on those here, keeping in mind that profit is the test of the validity of decisions. In addition, the firm has competitive objectives, consumer objectives, and company objectives, all of which are related. These objectives are brought together in what constitutes the business mission statement.

The business mission statement delineates the total perspectives or purpose of a business. It states why we exist, who we compete against, who our market is, and how we serve our constituents—those who have an interest in what we do. These include customers, employees, owners, financial backers, and the local community.

Objectives and mission statements obtain not only at the corporate level, but also at the level of every strategic business unit (SBU) within the firm. Thus, as IBM corporate has objectives and a mission statement, so too does the personal computer unit (an individual SBU). Strategic business units are units of a business that have a common market base. Every SBU serves a clearly defined product-market segment with its own strategy, but in a manner consistent with the overall corporate strategy, its own mission, and its own identifiable competitors.

As Marriott Corporation has its objectives and its mission, so too should the Courtyard by Marriott division, the restaurant division, and the institutional feeding division. The same is true of the Marriott Long Wharf and the Marriott Copley Place, both in Boston. These hotels not only have their individual competitors but also compete against each other, not to mention three other Marriotts in the Boston area. By the same token, the restaurants and lounges at the Marriott Copley Place should each have their own objectives and mission, and their own identifiable competitors.

The key to the success of this planning, of course, lies in its execution. Mission statements and objectives in fancy binders lying on credenzas and gathering dust, while management continues to operate by "the seat of the pants," will have little strategic impact.

The strategic business unit has developed as an alternative to the profit center concept. The profit center concept emphasises the short-term and optimization of the profit center. The SBU, on the other hand, while identifying its own competitors and customer groups, battles for its own resource allocations within the role it must play in the total business framework. In a manufacturing company, a product line or a group of product lines might constitute an SBU for the purpose of strategic planning. In the hospitality industry, a hotel or restaurant may constitute an SBU of a particular chain.

A good example of this occurring is at Hyatt International hotels. In 1986, this chain started a conversion of new and some old hotels to the SBU concept of F&B outlets. Under this concept, a restaurant in a hotel would have its own manager and its own chef who would operate the outlet as a strategic business unit, in contrast to the usual arrangement by which an executive chef and an F&B manager of the hotel oversee all outlets.

This strategic change has considerable merit. One reason is that people tend to exert their energies in the areas that they enjoy most. Executive chefs, for example, have far more interest in the "gourmet" restaurant than they do in the coffee shop, which is often where the real profits are.

It is the corporate mission statement, however, from which all other mission statements in the organization flow, as shown in Figure 20-1. Figure 20-1, on the other hand, can be applied just as well to any strategic business unit. Thus, in the case of Marriott Copley Place, we could replace "Firm's" objectives with "Hotel's" objectives. By the same token, we could replace "Hotel's" objectives with "Restaurant's" objectives. The notion that strategic planning occurs only at the corporate level is obsolete; it occurs at every level where a strategic business unit exists. We should bear that in mind as we discuss the remainder of the strategic marketing systems model.

A firm's (or SBU's) objectives may include growth, ROI, IRR, profit, leadership, industry position, status symbol, or other determination. These are included in the mission statement. Thus, developing the mission statement is a crucial assignment. Before entering into that task we note one crucial and often violated caveat.

Mission statements indicate the purpose of the business; they are a statement of why the business exists. As such, they drive all subsets of the business. When, instead, mission statements reflect wishful thinking, grandiose hopes, or pie-in-the-sky fantasies that do not reflect the realities of the business climate or the company's resources, they are counterproductive. For a mission statement to say, as some do, that "we will be known as the leader in the hotel industry" when such a possibility is not realistic only leads to confusion at lower levels of the organization.

The mission statement should be something that all employees can believe in. It sets goals and it urges everyone in the organization to meet those goals. Properly, it is communicated throughout the organization for all to follow. That, in fact, is one of its purposes—to unify the organization. When the response at lower levels is "Who are they kidding?" the entire effort becomes a meaningless and self-defeating endeavor.

An effective mission statement, which is nothing less than an overall strategy statement, should do the following.

1. It states what business the company (or SBU) is in, or will be in. This goes considerably beyond being in the hotel, restaurant, or food business. Instead, it is more specific and states how we serve our customers and specifies who they are. For example,

    Motel XYX is in the business of providing the traveling and price-sensitive public with modern, comfortable, and clean accommodations at a very reasonable price.

Accordingly, it recognizes the basic needs of travelers as well as the need for a pleasant and hassle-free experience, but without the amenities for which this market is unwilling to pay. Motel XYZ wants to be known as the best buy at the moderate price level, satisfying all essential needs for the motoring public.

You can see that this statement has numerous ramifications such as how, what, when, and where. These are enumerated later in the strategic plan, but the answers will be driven by the mission statement.

2. It identifies the special competency of the firm and how it will be unique in the marketplace.

    Motel XYZ is and will continue to be a leader in its field because of its special identification with the budget-minded traveling public and its needs. By continuous communication with its market and regular adaptation to the changing needs of that market, Motel XYZ will maintain its position as the motel of choice of its customers.

    Again, it can be seen that the mission statement has committed the firm to a definite course of action. Its competency and uniqueness is special knowledge of the target market and a committment to maintain and implement that knowledge.

3. It defines who the competition will be—that is, it actually chooses whom it will compete against and does not leave this to chance.

    Motel XYZ's niche in the market will be between the full economy, highly price-sensitive market that chooses accommodations almost solely by price, and the middle-tier market that will pay $20 more for additional amenities and services. Accordingly, XYZ competes only tangentially against ABC and DEF, on the one hand, and GHI and JKL on the other hand. XYZ competes directly for the same market against MNO and PQR as well as other companies that choose to enter this market.

    As Burger King knows it has to beat McDonald's and Pepsi Cola knows it has to beat Coca-Cola, XYZ knows it has to beat MNO and PQR and will watch these competitors very closely.

4. It identifies the needs of its constituents.

    Customers: XYZ will conduct ongoing research of its customers needs, both at the corporate and unit levels. It will continuously seek to satisfy those needs within the constraints of its mission.

    Employees: XYZ recognizes all employees as internal customers with their own varying needs and wants. Accordingly, it will attend to those needs and wants with the same attitude it holds toward its paying customers and will maintain an open line of communication for that purpose.

    Community: XYZ recognizes its position in the economic, political, and social communities. Thus, it will maintain a role of good citizenship in all endeavors and efforts.

Backers: XYZ has committed itself to a 15 percent ROI for its investors as well as a positive image of which they can be proud. XYZ will function both in the market-place and in its operations to maintain these committments.

5. It identifies the future.

Motel XYZ will develop and expand through controlled growth in suitable locations. Its strategy will be to develop regional strength as a gradual development toward national strength, with the objective of reaching that goal by the year 2000.

Figure 20-2 contains the 1986 mission statement of Radisson Hotels as published in its internal magazine for employees. It is probably somewhat shorter than the actual mission statement and is designed to define the Radisson mission for all employees. The purpose is to gain total committment at all levels. You should evaluate this mission statement in light of the previous discussion.

Master Strategy

Developing the master marketing strategy is the next stage in the strategic marketing system, as shown in Figure 20-1. The master strategy is designed to be long-term, not short. This does not mean it will never change; if conditions change, then so too should the master strategy.

Consider, for example, Holiday Inns, which had defined itself as being in the travel business and had diversified into buses, steamships, casinos, and numerous other businesses that it hoped would funnel customers into its inns. The strategy did not work well and change was commenced in 1979 under a new CEO, who stated in 1980:

> We are in the process of reshaping Holiday Inns into a different company. Holiday Inns is actually a "hospitality" company—a concept that will limit its scope to food, lodging, and entertainment. . . . In the future the company will get into as few businesses as possible, and only those that have good growth, high returns, and are synergistic with our main business—hotels.[2]

As we noted in the previous chapter, Holiday Inns also changed its middle-of-the-road master strategy in 1983 when it entered the upscale hotel market. This was contrary to its previous strategy, which stated that the company would offer moderately priced, full-service facilities in a manner that gives the customer the best price/value in the industry.

The intention, however, is that the master strategy will endure for some time. This means that it takes a long-range perspective of the environment as opposed to the short-range perspective of the marketing plan (discussed in the next chapter), even though many of the issues are the same.

The master strategy shapes objectives after developing and weighing alternatives. It specifies where the firm is going and thus is the framework of the entire marketing effort. Derived from the mission statement and objectives, the master marketing strategy turns to the marketing emphasis to fulfill those missions.

---

[2] Roy Winegardner, Holiday Inns President, quoted in "Holiday Inns: Refining its focus to food, lodging—and more casinos," *Business Week*, July 21, 1980, p. 104.

RADISSON HOTEL CORPORATION MISSION STATEMENT

The Radisson Hotel Corporation is recognized as a dynamic growing hotel company, and by 1990 this will be further evidenced by the presence of managed hotels in prime business locations in targeted major cities. Radisson hotels will be acknowledged as the industry standard for personalized service to the guest. Radisson hotels will also be noted for outstanding food and beverage products, service and facilities. Each Radisson hotel will be the best of its type in its served market and will be one of the top choices for guests.

The greatest potential for attaining this position lies in:

• "Yes, I can," a system-wide program and mentality, that extends from corporate through each hourly position

• The profitability and success of each hotel

• The Radisson management and/or franchise as the first choice of developers and owners

• Expansion of Radisson Marketing Association and the 800 number

Due to the effectiveness of its operations, Radisson Hotel Corporation will assure results for its constituents as follows:

• *Owners*: Increased return on capital from their investments

• *Guests*: Highly personalized service in hotels staffed, equipped and designed to satisfy their requirements

• *Employees*: Opportunity for professional growth and development while making a contribution to the success of the company

• *Franchise Management*: Systems and programs to insure/promote the success of their Radisson hotels

• *Development*: Radisson hotels, plazas, inns, resorts and suite hotels in operation in the numbers and locations targeted by the company

(Courtesy of Radisson Hotel Corporation)

FIGURE 20-2 The 1986 mission statement of Radisson hotels

To continue with the hypothetical Motel XYZ, its mission statement noted that it wanted to be perceived as the best buy at the moderate price level. The master marketing strategy, then, would deal with that accomplishment to make it happen.

The master strategy begins with a situation analysis, again asking the questions, "Where are we now?" and "Where do we want to go?" It is the "where" of the strategic marketing system that shapes objectives and overrides all decision aspects. A master strategy deals with such issues as new markets, growth sectors, customer loyalty, repeat business, quantity vs. quality, cheap vs. expensive, best vs. biggest, high or low markups, quick turnover, product/service range, building brand name, consumer awareness and perception, and a host of other things that will guide the operational strategies. Marketing objectives are identified in the master strategy in these contexts.

To address these issues it is clear that one must first know their current state. We begin with the environmental analysis, looking especially at the long-range trends and effects. As this was discussed in Chapter 4 and will be discussed again in the next chapter on marketing plans, it will not be reiterated here.[3] There is clearly an overlap between developing a master strategy and developing a marketing plan that also contains strategic elements. The major difference lies in specific application to the short term in the case of the marketing plan.

Situation Analysis   The situation analysis involves a number of other elements as well. The major ones are listed below.

Internal
Organizational Values
> What are the values that guide us? What is the corporate culture? What drives us in a real sense? Do these limit alternatives?

Resources
> What are our distinctive capabilities and strengths? What do we do particularly well? How do these compare to the competition? What are our physical resources? Are there any conflicts among our resources, our values, and our objectives?

Objectives
> Where do we want to go? What do we want to accomplish? How do we want to be perceived? What are the long-/short-range considerations?

Policies
> What rules do we have now? How do we operate? What guides us? Are any rules conflicting?

Organization
> How are resources, authority, and responsibility organized and implemented? Do we proact rather than react? Does the organization enhance the strategy or does the organization need to be changed?

External
Generic Demand
> Why do people come here and why do they use this product? Where else do they go? What do they need, want, demand? Are there unmet needs? What do users/ nonusers look like? What are the segments for this product category? What are the alternatives? What are the trend patterns—cyclical, seasonal, fashionable? What complementary product categories exist or are needed. What is the relationship with ours? Where is the product class in the product life-cycle?

---

[3] The discussion of environmental planning is placed in Chapters 4 and 21 for purposes of convenience in the flow of the text. This should not diminish their integral importance in strategic planning.

Brand Demand

Who is our customer? Why? What is our position? Who are our market segments and target markets? To which do we appeal the most? What use do they make of our product/service? What benefits do we offer? What problems do we solve or not solve? What are the levels of awareness, preference? Are we a convenience, shopping, emotional, or rational purchase? What is our market share? Where are we on our brand life-cycle?

Customer Profile

What do they look like—demographically, psychographically, socially? Are they heavy users or light users? How do they make the decision? What influences them? How do they perceive us? What do they use us for? Where else do they go? What needs and wants do we fulfill? What are their expectations?

Competition

Who are they? Where are they? What do they look like? How are they positioned against us? In what market segments are they stronger/weaker? Why do people go there? What do they do better/poorer than us? What is their market share? What are their strengths and weaknesses? What are their expectations?

Product/Service

What is it? What benefits does it offer or problems does it solve? How is it perceived, positioned? What are the tangibles/intangibles? What are our complementary lines? What are our strengths and weaknesses?

From the situation analysis, the marketing strategist analyzes the strengths and weaknesses, opportunities and threats of the firm or SBU, and establishes the strategic marketing objectives.

Strengths and Weaknesses, Opportunities and Threats   We have discussed these areas previously; here, we review them with a more strategic perspective.

The distinctive competency of an organization is more than what it can do; it is what it can do particularly well.[4] It often takes a great deal of self-analysis to understand this caveat and to abide by it. The objective situation analysis is the tool to lay bare the facts. Abiding by it is sometimes more difficult. Holiday Inns learned this when they diversified into over thirty different businesses in which they lacked strength or distinctive competency. In many cases, failure to recognize strengths and weaknesses results in targeting the wrong markets. Strategically speaking, a firm should do only what it has the competency and resources to do well. Ignoring this fact may result in a colossal strategic error.

Stevenson analyzed six companies in terms of the process of defining strengths and weaknesses for strategic planning. Among the difficulties these firms had in being objective in the process were the lack of situational analysis, the need for self-protection, and the desire to preserve the status quo. Stevenson suggests that defining strengths and

---

[4] Kenneth R. Andrews, *The Concept of Corporate Strategy*, Homewood, Ill: Dow Jones-Irwin, 1971, p. 97. An interesting example of which most readers are probably unaware is American Air Lines (AAL). AAL got into the hotel business in the 1950s when it was faddish for airlines to do so (and still is). It soon recognized that this was not its competence, and got out to concentrate on the airline business. This has allowed it to avoid the turmoil of United Air Lines, which got into hotels at about the time that American got out.

weaknesses aids individual managers in accomplishing their tasks. Critical areas for examination should be tailored to the authority and responsibility of each individual manager.[5]

King suggests even further difficulties in strength and weakness analysis relative to strategic planning:

• They are made judgmentally or using a mechanistic rating scheme.
• They are primarily indications of past performance and are unlikely to produce assessments that are indicative of future opportunities.
• They may be "staff studies" by individuals who lack a practical feel for the realities of day-to-day operations and make assessments within the rational frameworks with which they themselves operate, and thus lack credibility with line managers.
• They may be too objective, that is, they may overlook things that cannot be substantiated.
• Contrarily, they may "leave nothing out" by not making significant choices as to what is crucial.

King suggests the following ways to improve strength and weakness analysis:

• Involve the managers who are in charge of strategy and who make the final strategic choices.
• Make strength and weakness assessment an integral and useful element of strategic planning.
• Explicitly test alternative strategies against the strengths and weaknesses of the firm.
• Evaluate strengths and weaknesses in terms of their strategic significance.
• It is more important that strengths and weaknesses be perceived than that they be proved.
• Evaluate strengths and weaknesses in terms of the future and strategic opportunity, and relative to the competition.
• Separate weaknesses to guide strategic decisions from simple "problems to be overcome."
• The final output should be a concise list of the most significant strengths, on which the future of the business should be built, and the most important weaknesses, which should be assiduously avoided as underpinnings of strategy.[6]

Solid strength and weakness analysis may be the most neglected phase of strategic planning in the hospitality industry. Without a doubt, this lack was a major contribution to the failure of Howard Johnson's. Consider the following chronological excerpts:

[1979:] Daiquiris, discos and candlelight dinners: that's what Howard Johnson's is serving up these days. . . . The bastion of the highway travel market is out to change its image. . . . Says Johnson, "We know where our operations will be in the 1980s, but the question is 'will we be in the right spot?' " . . . "I still don't think the food business

[5] Howard H. Stevenson, "Defining Corporate Strengths and Weaknesses," *Sloan Management Review*, Spring, 1976, p. 66.

[6] Reprinted by permission of the publisher from "Integrating Strength-Weakness Analysis into Strategic Planning," by William R. King, *Journal of Business Research*, II, pp. 475–487. © 1983 by Elsevier Science Publishing Co., Inc.

is a marketing business." . . . "I'm sure that we're making the right long-term moves."[7]

[1983:] The wraps are slowly coming off a new strategic business plan at the Howard Johnson Co. Key to the sluggish giant's assault on its problems is a carefully planned, major reorganization of the way the company manages and markets its restaurants and lodges. . . . "It's just a case of reorienting the thinking under new leadership."[8]

[1983:] "Everybody has a theme restaurant, but I think Ground Round [a restaurant concept division of Howard Johnson's] has a unique niche among them. Both families and singles are comfortable with us. We have done the one thing older chains have failed to do: marry the family trade with strong liquor sales."[9]

[1984:] Bettering the chain's infamously undependable service has suddenly become a priority.[10]

[1985—after the fall:] Howard Johnson's restaurants had become overpriced and understaffed purveyors of pallid food, hamstrung by outdated ideas. . . . Howard Johnson's troubles [were blamed] on everything but incompetent management. . . . Howard Johnson stood fast with a diversified menu while it was being "segmented" to death. . . . for two decades, what an opportunity was blown![11]

Perhaps if Howard Johnson's had heeded the following advice of Michael Porter, the outcome would have been different. Strength and weakness analysis is certainly one of the most critical stages of strategic planning and direction.

[The] strategist's goal is to find a position in the industry where his or her company can best defend itself against these [competitive] forces or can influence them in its favor. . . . The strategist, wanting to position his company to cope best with its industry environment or to influence that environment in the company's favor, must learn what makes the environment tick. . . . The first approach [to positioning the company] takes the structure of the industry as given and matches the company's strengths and weaknesses to it. Strategy can be viewed as building defenses against the competitive forces or as finding positions in the industry where the forces are weakest.

Knowledge of the company's capabilities and of the causes of the competitive forces will highlight the areas where the company should confront competition and where avoid it.[12]

Opportunity analysis is the matching of strengths to opportunity while counteracting, when possible, the threats caused by weaknesses. Many opportunities and threats spring from the changing environment, as we saw in the case of Howard Johnson's, as well as from consumers' problems, as discussed in Chapter 6. Strategic competition is the "studied deployment of resources based on a high degree of insight into the systematic cause and effect in the business ecological system."[13]

We will illustrate the points made above with excerpts from the strategic marketing

---

[7] "The Howard Johnson Team: Razing the Orange Roof," *Restaurant Business*, February 1, 1979, pp. 123–134.

[8] "Hojo Unveils New Strategy to Overcome Sluggish Sales," *Nation's Restaurant News*, January 17, 1983, p. 1.

[9] "Welcome Back, Howard Johnson's," *Restaurants and Institutions*, December 28, 1983, p. 88.

[10] "Howard Johnson: Is It Too Late To Fix Up Its Faded 1950s Image?" *Business Week*, October 22, 1984, p. 90.

[11] "The Sad Case of the Dwindling Orange Roofs," *Forbes*, December 30, 1985, pp. 75–79.

[12] Michael E. Porter, "How Competitive Forces Shape Strategy," *Harvard Business Review*, March–April, 1979, pp. 137–145. Copyright © 1979 by the President and Fellows of Harvard College, all rights reserved.

[13] Bruce D. Henderson, "New Strategies for the Global Competition," *A Special Commentary*, Boston: Boston Consulting Group, 1981, p. 6.

plan of a hotel in Asia. The reader is urged to evaluate these excerpts in light of the foregoing. Without enclosing the full situation analysis that forms the basis of the strategy, we have placed some key questions in brackets.

Marketing Objective

> To be perceived as a premier super deluxe hotel marketed to the connoisseur consumer.

Master Marketing Strategy

> To create an image of exclusivity and uniqueness with premium quality facilities and services.

Strengths

- Personalized and professional service
- Prime strategic location
- Part of chain which has already made its mark
- High standards of food and service
- Newly refurnished outlets
- Renowned shopping arcade on premise
- Wide variety of excellently appointed suites

[Do these strengths represent unique competitive differences perceived by the customer that build defenses against competitive forces or find niche positions in the market?]

Weaknesses

- Higher room and F&B rates make it difficult to secure international conference business
- Market sensitivity that we are more pro-foreigner and have less identification with local community
- Lower percentage of national clientele
- Marketing is more product-oriented than customer-oriented
- Lack of exclusive executive club
- Absence of well-located properties in chain that reduces chain utilization

[Are these weaknesses or problems that need to be solved?]

Opportunities

- The commercial market in the city is very active and our location is strategic.
- Development in this area is strong and has strong affiliation with our hotel.
- Entrepreneurial market is growing and most are locating in this area.

[Is this a matching of strengths and competencies to opportunity?]

Threats

- Foreign traffic will be dependent on political stability of the country.
- Corporations are developing own facilities to encourage privacy and reduce expenditures.
- Renovated rooms at biggest competitor.
- Some corporations are moving to suburbs.

[Are these threats caused by weaknesses? Can they be avoided? Can resources be better deployed?]

Operational Strategies

Referring back to Figure 20-1 it can be seen that the next stage in strategic marketing, and one flowing from the master strategy, is the planning stage, or what are called the operational strategies. Operational strategies are the "how" of strategic marketing—that is, "how" we're going to get from "here" to "where" we want to go. Strategies at this point are more easily measurable and may have time and performance requirements.

This is the stage at which the organization acts in advance, rather than reacts, by planning for change. It is here that the organization shapes its own destiny. Strategy here provides an even better sense of direction and cohesion as it coordinates efforts. It is the planning stage that attempts to minimize risk, maintain control, and allocate resources to keep in focus and reach the strategic objectives.

The planning stage is also the stage of specific matching of the product to the market, of dealing with changes in the product life cycle, of understanding where the business is going to come from, of developing new products and services, and of influencing demand. Its success is measured by market share, penetration, and increased sales and volume. As you know, we have covered these areas before so we will deal with them only briefly here, including further excerpts from the marketing strategy of the Asian hotel used above. You should take special note of the interrelationship among the various elements of the operational strategies.

Target Market Strategy   Target market strategy clearly depends on, among other things, resources and capabilities. To target a market with homogeneous needs and wants, and other necessary criteria (Chapter 8), is grossly insufficient, if not fatal, when the resources and competencies are not there to serve that market. The appropriate strategy is to target not just markets that appear to have the most opportunity, but also those that the firm can serve best, and, one hopes, better than the competition.

A common failing in this respect are hotels that target the top end of the market and price accordingly, but don't have the resources and capabilities to sustain an advantage. Such strategies are suicidal; they always fail unless the customer has no alternative. To compensate, the hotel accepts lower-rated business while management continues to vehemently maintain that it is in the upscale market. The result is a confused image and failure to fulfill potential. Such strategies are usually built on egos and wishful thinking rather than introspective analysis.

Another area of weakness in target market strategy is targeting too many different markets—a strategy of providing something for everyone, which results in confusion for anyone.

Target market strategy means defining the right target market within the broader market segment. Jain makes the point that

> The corporate direction of all successful companies, without exception, is based not only on a clear notion of the markets in which they will compete but also on specific concepts of how they will sustain an economically attractive position in those markets.[14]

The strategy of the Asian hotel we have been discussing is to target the following market.

Age: 35 plus
Income: High
Lifestyle: Result-oriented, professional business person, aristocratic with a modern
        outlook on life, respected in the community, voices an opinion, a leader, an
        active socializer

---

[14] Jain, *Marketing Planning*, p. 358.

Desired consumer response:

> Rational—I like staying here because the rooms are spacious and beautiful. I like the computerized telephone exchange with its automatic wake-up call and direct international dialing. The executive club with computers and word processors is time-saving, smooth, and trouble-free. Check-in/check-out is fast and efficient. Because the hotel is so exclusive I don't encounter undesirable people. Service is smooth, courteous, and efficient.
>
> Emotional—I like staying here because everyone knows me and takes care of me. I feel very much at home with the room service and restaurants. They know my likes and dislikes and make it a point to remember. It is so exclusive, I like to be seen here.

Product Strategy   Product strategy deals with the benefits the product provides, the problems it solves, and how it differentiates from the competition. It also is concerned with the offering of different products and services to satisfy market needs. Product strategies should be directed at opportunities and their contributions to objectives.

At the operational level of strategic planning, product strategies will involve such issues as number and size of meeting rooms, number of bedrooms, number and kind of F&B outlets, overall ambience and atmosphere, lobby bars vs. enclosed lounges, and similar long-term decisions that are based on market needs.

Contrarily, we often find that such decisions are not strategic in nature. Rather, they are based on owners' or managements' concept of what the product should be. For example, it is quite common in southeast Asia for upscale hotels to have as many as five formal dining rooms. These will inevitably be Chinese, Japanese, and French, plus one native to the country. The other is likely to be Italian or American. The reasoning, of course, is that all these geographic markets are served by the hotel. Each room usually seats 100 or more and in most cases is fortunate when it is 50 percent occupied.

The low patronage does not occur because there is no market need. Demand exists for all these ethnic foods, but at varying levels. Further, there are numerous free-standing restaurants in the city also filling these needs—at least the Chinese, Japanese, and native. Instead of strategically analyzing the market and the competition, owners simply insist on the variety of restaurants.

When the New Otani, a Japanese-owned and -patronized hotel, opened in Singapore with an American (albeit Polynesian format) Trader Vic's restaurant, it simply defied the logic of the marketplace. Such decisions are purely tactical and without strategic substance.

We also know of a hotel in Bangkok that expanded from 175 rooms to 630 and targeted the traveling family market, much of it American. Ignoring the trend toward double-double, king and queen size beds, or even single-double, all 630 rooms were furnished with twin single beds. This tactic represented a product strategy inconsistent with the target market strategy.

Conversely, negotiating a potential joint venture plan to develop properties in India for the middle-tier Indian market, an American corporation refused to alter its concept of all double-double rooms, regardless of room size, which does not suit this market or the cost restrictions. The venture failed to materialize. Instead Quality International, more flexible in their approach, beat the first company into a vast potential marketplace.

A different kind of example of product strategy is illustrated in Figure 20-3. Although Quality International, from whom this exhibit came, calls this segmentation strategy (as does most of the industry), it is actually product strategy, as previously pointed out in Chapter 8. More specifically, it is multiple brand strategy, or differentiated strategy.

The implication of multiple brand strategy (and the distinction from segmentation) is that the firm goes after the whole market. Long practiced by such companies as Procter & Gamble and automobile manufacturers, this strategy is aimed at presenting a broad-scope product across segments. The important strategic concern in these cases is that the products do not cannibalize each other. That is what happens with five ethnic restaurants in southeast Asian hotels.

These are just a few examples that point out why there are two-way arrows in Figure 20-1 between the various operational strategies. It is often product strategies that dominate the overall strategy, as well as the company mission, and address the threats and opportunities of the firm.

This is especially true in the hospitality industry and, in particular, the hotel industry. The reason for this is that the basic product is not readily changed—that is, it cannot suddenly be decided to produce square widgets instead of round ones because that is what the market wants.

The crux of marketing is to design the product to fit the market. When, however, the product already exists, the situation is reversed: the market must be found that fits the product. A good example is renovated hotels that try to position "upscale," when the product simply does not fit the upscale market or compete effectively against newly

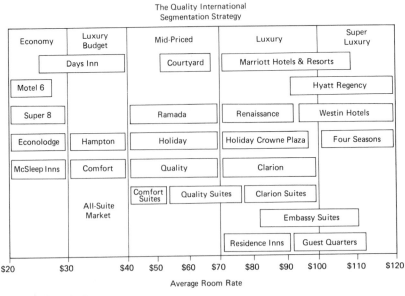

(Courtesy of Quality International)

FIGURE 20-3   The Quality International segmentation strategy (1988)

constructed upscale hotels. In such cases, Jain recommends that the desired position for a product be determined by the following procedure.

1. Analyze product attributes which are salient to customers.
2. Examine the distribution of these attributes among different market segments.
3. Determine the optimal position for the product in regard to each attribute, taking into consideration the positions occupied by existing brands.
4. Choose an overall position for the product (based on the overall match between product attributes and their distribution in the population and the positions of existing brands).[15]

In the case of the Asian hotel example we have been using, product strategy is specified as follows:

> Three features have to be emphasized: an ambience of total sophistication and classi-ness; a unique mixture of Victorian elegance, and all modern amenities and business aids for the business traveler; premium quality facilities and services.

Competitive Strategy In developing competitive strategy, the firm actually chooses its competition and when and where it will compete. At first glance that may seem a little cavalier. In truth, however, it is totally realistic provided the choice is realistic, but not if it is based instead on delusions of grandeur.

Restaurant managements usually seem to have a pretty good idea of whom they are competing against. Hotel managements are not necessarily of the same ilk. We never cease to be amazed by the hotel managements that state, blithely, "We have no competi-tion." The reason the "other guy" is running an occupancy 10 percentage points higher is because that hotel is taking business that we don't want (but, secretly, would love to have).

Let's turn to another industry for an analogy. Texas Instruments made a fortune on inexpensive, mass-produced, production-line calculators. Timex did the same with watch-es. Did they choose to compete against Hewlett-Packard on calculators or Rolex on watches? Obviously not, yet that is the questionable choice that so many hotel companies make. Holiday Inns wanted to compete against Hyatt with Crowne Plaza hotels. Ramada wanted to compete against Marriott with its Renaissance hotels. Howard Johnson's wanted to compete against Crowne Plaza with its Plaza hotels. In New York City, the Parker Meridien wanted to compete against the Helmsley Palace. All of these efforts to compete against the "leader" were less than successful.

When competing against leaders, it is usually folly to attack them head-on. The end-run or "attack the flanks" approach is usually more successful as, for instance, the cases of Pepsi Cola vs. Coca-Cola, Avis vs. Hertz, Burger King vs. McDonald's, and Nike vs. Adidas, have evidenced in the past.[16]

Perhaps the best example of poor strategic planning is choosing the wrong com-petitors to compete against with the wrong product. As we have said repeatedly in this book, and as Michael Porter and many others have said, the secret to competitive

---

[15] Jain, *Marketing Planning*, p. 639.

[16] For an excellent discussion on when and how to attack an industry leader, see Michael E. Porter, *Competitive Advantage*, New York: Free Press, 1985, pp. 513–536.

marketing strategy is to find the defensible niche or the sustainable economic advantage. When Omni took over the New York Sheraton and refurbished it, management chose as its competition upscale hotels such as the Essex House and the Parker Meridien, coming not even close to offering a comparable product. Gross operating profit doubled when, in 1986, it chose instead to compete against the lower-scale hotels in the marketplace.

At Quality International, it has been stated as follows:

> In today's segmented marketplace, what type of product you choose to build can be just as important as where you put it. And how you plan to market that hotel can just as easily be the final determinant of your success.
>
> . . . the first step in the development process must be to determine where a void exists in the market:
>
> • Seek a concept which can accommodate the traveler or price segment which is underserved.
> • Find a product that competes with those hotels that are vulnerable because of dated facilities or inequitable price/value.
>
> . . . Once the most opportune niche is identified, then the nuts and bolts of site selection come into play.
>
> . . . with all else being equal, the key to your competitive edge will lie in choosing the brand name that best positions the product in the market.[17]

When you have an existing product, unlike Procter & Gamble, which can far more easily develop a new product, you have to find the niche in the market for that product. Aiming for the stars without the launching rocket to get you there results in a dull thud, if not a mighty crash, when you return to earth.

Successful competitive strategy represents the essence of putting the product, the resources and capabilities, and the positioning together with the target market to define a niche in the marketplace. Consider examples on both ends of the spectrum.

Four Seasons Hotels has positioned at the top of the market. Their product is "top drawer" and it is *never compromised*. They maintain a full staff and nearly always deliver the product they promise.

Days Inn, under its president Mike Leven, has positioned between the budget and the middle-tier markets, and very successfully. When Days Inn went into the New York City market because it wanted a presence there, it maintained its position instead of trying to go upscale, as many others have tried. These companies and others—such as La Quinta, Marriott, The Stanford Court, Red Roof, Groupe Accor (France), Peninsula (Asia), SAS (Scandinavia), or McDonald's, Lutèce, and TGI Friday's—have been successful because, among other reasons, they chose their competition, stuck to it in the marketplace, and were realistic about the choice. This is the essence of formidable competitive strategy.

We return to our example of the Asian hotel whose strategic plan describes one of its competitors as follows.

> This hotel discounts heavily to increase occupancy and trial. They have diverse clientele and very aggressive marketing with gimmicks such as secretary incentives

---

[17] Joseph E. Lavin, Vice-President, Development, Quality International, "Product Selection Is as Critical as Site Selection," Quality International *Portfolio*, Summer 1986.

and food festivals. They get a large share of executives on fixed expense accounts. They have leverage through their chain system and have done well with their executive floor/club. We will compete with them only against the executive floor.

Market Strategy   Market strategy is concerned with reaching the market with the product. In the final analysis, if you can't reach the market, the best product and the most well-defined strategy will fail. Some hotels, hotel companies, and restaurants have failed or done poorly for just that reason.

For the hospitality industry, reaching the market can be looked at in two ways. The first is taking the product to the market; the second is bringing the market to the product. By contrast with manufactured goods, taking the product to market is a major commitment and, in some cases, a major capital investment. (We say "in some cases" speaking from the hotel company's point of view. Today, hotels have been built all over the world and are managed by hotel companies with little or no equity investment.)

For multiunit hotel and restaurant companies, taking the product to market is part of the distribution system. This is the area where location becomes a major factor. The strategy involved concerns the appropriate markets to enter. We'll start with a single unit example.

> The Stanford Court Hotel was opened in San Francisco in 1972. Its president, Jim Nassikas, and his backer considered a number of American cities. Nassikas wanted to build his dream hotel based on European concepts of service. There were few markets in the United States that would support such a hotel—that is, the market strategy was critical. After a rough start, the Stanford Court became a very successful money-maker.
>
> Nassikas started to wonder where he could duplicate the concept. He considered that perhaps only Washington, D.C., Beverly Hills, Chicago, Boston, New Orleans, and New York City would be viable markets, and then only in special neighborhoods. Because these markets are very expensive to enter, and afraid that he would not be able to maintain the same level of quality, Nassikas' strategy was to stay where he was and do what he did best.

Some might call this a location decision; actually, it is a market strategy decision of which location represents a part of the implementation. Le Français restaurant in Wheeling, Illinois, a very successful five-star restaurant, was, as the expression goes, in the middle of nowhere when it first opened, yet it drew heavily from the Chicago market some distance away.

The same is true of another five-star restaurant, Harrald's, in Stormville, New York, a town that does not even appear on most maps. This restaurant draws from Westchester County and New York City. Doesn't the market come to the product in these cases? Yes, but the market strategy is to be where the right market can reach it. In other words, choosing the location is not the major issue; choosing the market to serve is.

For example, there is the case of Mamma Leone's, a very successful New York City restaurant. A duplicate restaurant was opened in Boston, which has a large Italian population and upscale trends. It folded within a year because the market it chose to serve was not the right market for its product.

For multiunit companies that seek growth, the case is the same, only multiplied many times. Ignoring for the moment the issue of distribution and referral advantages (e.g., "no viable upscale hotel company can *not* have a hotel in New York City"), the market strategy revolves around the market to be served, potential demand, time of entry, and existing competition.

When McDonald's saw its growth limited in free-standing drive-up stores, it changed its market strategy. Soon McDonald's appeared in inner-city locations, office buildings, universities, and almost anywhere else one looked. It then headed overseas to both the European and Asian markets. In Singapore, on the main road of the city and right next to the Hilton International, sits what became the highest-grossing McDonald's in the world. Market strategy has been a major factor in McDonald's success.

Four Seasons Hotels has a *single-market* strategy at the top end of the market, where it seeks to find a unique niche, avoid confrontation with large competitors, and dedicate itself to serving the one market. Quality Inns has a *multimarket* strategy, serving four segments of the market.

Groupe Accor of France has a *total-market* strategy, with hotels distinctively aimed at every level of the market. Accor has six different hotel brand names, each with a different market strategy and aimed at different market segments. Accor has done the same with its foodservice division. Holiday Inns, Ramada, and Howard Johnson's (before the fall and again in 1988 with an announced expansion of its upscale Plaza line—see Figure 10-12) have *confused* market strategies—it's hard to tell just where they are aiming (except that Ramada definitely aimed downmarket when it bought Rodeway Inns in 1987).

In the restaurant area, Howard Johnson's, as we have already shown, totally confused its image for lack of a well-thought-out market strategy. Victoria Station did the same when it changed to a total-market strategy aimed at just about every segment of the population, but all with the same product. Both these companies began, and became very successful, with single-market strategies. When things started to get "tough," they lost sight of strategy and tried to be all things to all people. This was not the cause of their downfall; rather, it accelerated the downfall because they reverted to tactics that were not strategically based.

Contrarily, TGI Friday's has done well sticking to its single-market strategy of "yuppies." Because yuppies are now growing up, it has to reevaluate its strategy. One hopes that TGI Friday's will not make the same mistake as Victoria Station and Howard Johnson's.

Using geographic market strategies, Burger King hopes it will gain a big lead on McDonald's by being first in the Russian market. Sheraton trumpets its entry as the first American company in the Chinese market. Hilton International's market strategy was to be in major capital cities throughout the world. Inter-Continental aimed for cities where Pan American Airlines, its former owner, flew. Oberoi Hotels started in India but built its strength in the Middle East before going into full development in the Indian market.

For its top-of-the-line brand, Sofitel, Groupe Accor's market strategy in the United States has been to enter secondary cities such as Minneapolis first. (This has been a difficult strategy to implement. Travelers in secondary cities are more likely to stay in brand name hotels rather than take a chance on an unknown entity.) On the other hand,

Meridien Hotels, a subsidiary of Air France, chooses to enter primary cities like Boston, New York, and San Francisco. Marriott likes to saturate an area with multiple units, as it has done in Boston and Washington, D.C. La Quinta slowly built a solid base of ubiquity in the southwest before expanding out slowly as an extension of the same travel circuit. Days Inn, long a southern chain, sought nationwide then international growth as its market strategy and has signed agreements in Europe, India and the Pacific Rim.

We list these examples simply as evidence of market strategies practiced by different companies. Not all are solid, well-based strategies but all are related to the markets to be reached. Some, in fact, are based on little more than prestige-seeking or greed for growth. Victoria Station restaurants, for example, had a market strategy something like "we'll go anywhere with a large enough population" (originally set at one million and later lowered). The company grew rapidly to about 100 units in less than ten years. In 1988 they were down to 11 units and were in bankruptcy court. Victoria Station's founders and officers got ready for growth and, with a high-flying start, felt they could do no wrong. The result was they never developed a solid market base.

Getting the market to the product involves a new set of strategies. It means reaching out to the markets, wherever they are. When resources are scarce, as they usually are, the market strategy must designate where to expend those resources. There are many, usually too many, choices.

A restaurant may choose the surrounding neighborhood and concentrate on word-of-mouth. McDonald's, on the other hand, uses national television to cover the entire United States, as well as other countries. The Stanhope Hotel in New York City uses the *International Herald Tribune* in Europe to attract the European market. The Stanford Court in San Francisco, in its early days, wrote letters to the wives of executives; later it depended on word-of-mouth. Hyatt concentrates heavily on airline magazines, meeting planner journals, and travel agent indexes. Marriott concentrates on its frequent traveler program.

Some companies choose single markets to reach, others choose multiple markets. Some companies choose broad market segments (business travelers), while others choose geographic segments (Bermuda). Some route through travel agents with advertising support to back them up (Club Med). Some use push strategies, some use pull strategies.

Again, these are strategic marketing decisions. How does a hotel in Asia with limited resources reach the broad international market? Consider the case of our Asia hotel example, which has a market mix as follows:

North America	13.5%	Domestic cities:	
Latin America	0.5%	1. 50.5%	
Western Europe	23.3%	2. 22.5%	
Eastern Europe	0.5%	3. 12.0%	
Southeast Asia	3.2%	4. 4.3%	
Far East	10.6%	5. 3.2%	
West Asia	16.4%	6. 3.2%	
Africa	2.3%	7. 2.3%	
South Asia	1.6%	8. 2.0%. . . .	26.5%
South Pacific	1.6%		

One strategy could designate the major markets: domestic, North America, Western Europe, Far East, and West Asia. But think of the difficulty of covering any one of these alone, apart from the expense. Another strategy might assume that the major markets are "natural" markets, and therefore concentrate on building up the others. The solution, of course, but not an easy one to find, is to concentrate on the market(s) where you can "do the most good for the least amount of dollars." This requires analyzing natural demand, potential demand, and cost.

For many, such as small local restaurants, there is no choice at all—word-of-mouth is the only alternative. Regardless, it is a strategic decision that needs to be made.

One market strategy of our Asia hotel is as follows.

> The executive club will be marketed as an extremely exclusive businessperson's club within the reach of only a privileged few. This will be very effective in drawing business because once the CEOs and diplomatic heads begin visiting a hotel their overseas counterparts follow suit. About 75 percent of the members will be local corporate leaders. The club will provide unique and classy facilities and services. Members will be automatically upgraded in hotel rooms, if available.

Positioning Strategy   The last, but by no means least, of the operational strategies is the positioning strategy. Positioning strategy, and why it is last, is no less than the culmination of the product strategy, directed at the target markets, consistent with the resources and capabilities of the firm, aimed at specific markets, vis-à-vis the competition.

Positioning was thoroughly discussed in Chapter 10 and needs no further elaboration here. What is most important is to note its relationship vis-à-vis the other operational strategies, as shown in Figure 20-1. As we have said many times, trying to position to markets that you can't properly serve is sheer folly.

The strategic plan for positioning the Asia hotel to its market is specified as follows.

> The hotel will be positioned as a super-deluxe property for the "up" market. It will be positioned to image-conscious elitists and high-flying business executives. All marketing will be geared to the top-brass higher-echelon bracket of both the social and business circles, for whom facilities, specialties and personalized attention are the main criteria for selection. The exclusive executive club, the businessman's club with business equipment, and the rooms with antiques, objets d'art, and special butler service, will symbolize luxury plus.

Functional Strategies

Functional strategies (refer again to Figure 20-1) are the "what" of the strategic system— that is, the "what" we are going to do to get "where" we want to go. You will recognize, of course, that these are the marketing mix strategies that have been discussed in previous chapters and will be discussed further in the next chapter on marketing plans.

The important thing to remember is that these are still strategies, not tactics, which come immediately afterward. It is this set of strategies that flows directly to the consumer. For example, in the Asian hotel situation the communication strategy might be to portray luxury, the pricing strategy to price exclusively, the product/service strategy to render personal attention (e.g., butler service), and the distribution strategy to use exclusive referral systems and select travel agents. The functional strategies are the substrategy implementation of the operational stategies.

Product/Service Substrategy   Strategies at this level of the hierarchy represent shorter-term and more flexible strategies. Four Seasons Hotels has a top-of-the-line product strategy at the master and operational strategy levels. At the functional strategy level, strategic decisions must be made on the level of service to offer, and when and how to offer it. The same criteria, of course, apply: What is important to the target market? What does the target market expect? What problems does the target market have?

Let's say the product/service substrategy is to provide luxury. This would be a natural derivation from the master strategy and the operational strategies. The question is how to put it into practice. These are the tactics. Consider terry-cloth bathrobes in each room—is this important to the market? Does the market expect it? Does it solve a problem for the customer? For Four Seasons the answer may be yes, and the customer is willing to pay the additional cost. For most other hotels the answer is probably no.

If the strategy is to provide luxury and the customer is paying for luxury, then we have to provide luxury. Terry-cloth bathrobes in hotel rooms symbolize luxury—even if they aren't used! To most guests robes aren't important, they aren't expected (at least initially), and they don't solve problems. What is important, is expected, and does solve problems is luxury. Ipso facto, the hotel with this strategy provides symbols of luxury.

The Oberoi Hotel chain in India changed its master strategy in 1986 and decided to aim at the luxury market. Into the rooms went antique desks, personalized stationery, beautiful brass ashtrays, and terry-cloth bathrobes, among other things. The rooms themselves weren't much different; it was the symbols of luxury that made the difference and the presentation strategy had to change. Many other changes were also made in the hotel's marketing mix to carry out this strategy.

Oberoi had a well-defined strategy and the product and the market and the prices to go with it. In the United States there are also hotels putting terry-cloth bathrobes in the rooms even though they do not target the luxury market. The rooms, however, are otherwise pretty standard. In fact, the bathrobe may be the most luxurious thing in the room. Rack rates are discounted to the traveling businessman, who has become somewhat price-sensitive. We ask the same questions: Is the robe important, expected, or solving problems? Probably not.

Then why put it there? That's a good question. Does the guest appreciate it? Of course. He goes home and says, "You ought to see the bathrobe that was in my room! And, oh yes, look at all these shampoos and soaps and bubble baths I brought you!" Everyone is very happy and we have a satisfied customer. The only problem is at the hotel—those bathrobes and amenities are expensive, so they decide to raise their rates. When the same customer has to return to that city, he is asked: "Are you staying at Hotel X again?" "No, it's too expensive. The company is on our backs to cut travel costs." The robe and amenities are long since forgotten.

This hypothetical situation may be a little exaggerated, but it reflects typical consumer behavior and reaction that we have run across many times in our research, and it is perfectly logical if you think about it. It is taken for granted that we should meet customer expectations, satisfy needs, and solve problems. It is folly to think you can exceed expectations in unimportant areas, charge more for it, and capture customers. Such tactics derive from ill-founded, nonexistent, or poorly executed strategies. They are decisions made by the "seat of the pants" rather than flowing from well-thought-out strategies.

At General Motors a cost savings of 25¢ per car can amount to a savings of $1,000,000 a year. Whatever other problems General Motors has, do you think they would put leather seats on your Chevrolet because it would make you more satisfied—and raise the price accordingly?

Hyatt Hotels once had a policy that every dish that went out of its restaurants must have fresh fruit on it; strawberries showed up in the strangest places but the tactic, at least, was consistent with the strategy of fresh quality. This was also the communications strategy at that time and ads portrayed fresh fruit (tactic). In other situations this is not the case. The Sheraton Towers in Boston had a product/service strategy of exclusiveness and provided bathrobes, but didn't open the pool until 9:00 A.M., and all the light bulbs in the rooms were only 67 watts. Marriott's Courtyards didin't open the pool until 10:00 A.M., in spite of the people trying to get in at 8:00 A.M. The Southampton Princess Hotel in Bermuda emphasized service, convenience and told you that its coffee shop was open until 1:00 A.M., but closed it if no one happened to be there at 10:00 P.M. It also closed its lobby restrooms and waterfront pool and bar in the slow season to keep down costs, but maintained expensive bathroom amenities and high room rates in the largely empty rooms.

The Americana Dutch in Orlando offered nightly dancing but only disco and only "locals" went. The hotel was full of families, its target market. The Holiday Inn in Kuala Lumpur offered fresh orange juice but not before 10:00 A.M. and targeted Americans. The Asia hotel in Bangkok, catering to an American and European market, had minibars in the rooms but no wine in them. The Harbour Castle Westin in Toronto had "Do Not Disturb" signs to hang on your door knob. The maid knocked at 8:00 A.M. anyway.

The Marriott Copley Place in Boston had drapes that didn't close all the way to shut out the morning light, no pull-out clotheslines in the bathroom because they're "too much trouble," and a restaurant with coffee shop decor, appointments, and service, but fine dining room prices. The Park Hotel in Sognefjord, Norway, billed itself as the finest hotel in Norway, charged $200 for a double room, had tiny soap bars (albeit in a fancy box) reminiscent of the early American motels.

The same principles apply in the restaurant business although restaurateurs do not seem as inclined to giveaways as their hotelier counterparts. One reason is that they know they can't pass on the cost too easily. In Paris it is traditional in the better hotel restaurants, not necessarily elegant, to have a place setting of five to seven pieces of silver that continuously gets changed throughout the meal. While some people may know what to do with all that silver, our observations have been that at least half of it goes to the dishwasher unused. Should this cost be passed on to the customer who doesn't expect or need it?

These examples demonstrate that product/service functional strategies concern the level of product and service offered consistent with higher-level strategies. Because higher level strategies must be built around the target markets and the product, so too should the functional strategies that flow from them and the tactics that are implemented. As we have just shown, this is sometimes not the case in practice.

Presentation Substrategy   The same rules apply to this strategy as to the product/ service strategy. Recall that the presentation part of the marketing mix is to tangibilize the product/service. Much of what we have said above could also be applied here—that is, this strategy is no less than a carryover of the previous one.

Physical plant and atmosphere must be consistent with the product/service. This means they shouldn't be overdone or underdone. There are many beautiful hotels and restaurants that remain largely empty because they were built and designed without an underlying valid strategy that emanated from valid master and operational strategies.

Employees must be hired and trained accordingly. Certainly we expect a bigger smile and quieter maids at a four-star than at a two-star hotel, and better service at a three-star than at a one-star restaurant. But we expect something more—an emphasis on the customer rather than on the service. This difference, in fact, is why Four Seasons does so well at what it does. The reverse is also true, at McDonald's we expect the service consistent with the product strategy.

The customer mix strategy is very important. In some four-star luxe hotels in Paris and London you don't get in the door without a coat and tie. At other places you may be an "oddball" if you have them on. There is a basic strategy here that really applies in almost all cases: don't mix incompatible markets if you can possibly help it; if you have to deal with incompatible markets, keep them separated in both time (e.g., seasonally) and space (e.g., separate dining rooms).

Pricing strategy, in our experience, represents the greatest potential incongruity in the marketing mix. In too many cases, in fact, there seems to be no strategy at all. Prices seem to be set totally independent of all other strategies and without regard to their interrelationship. We have already presented a number of examples: dining room prices in a coffee shop product, deluxe room prices for a standard room hotel, $45 for a $10 bottle of liquor from room service, breakfast prices in hotel coffee shops. Here's another: Courtyard by Marriott was designed and priced for the price-conscious traveler, but in the lounge charged $3.50 for an undistinguished four ounce glass of wine. This is the same price charged in many of its higher-priced hotels, where the wine is already over-priced.

Nothing tangibilizes a product more than price to everyone except the totally price-insensitive, which includes the Sultan of Brunei (reputedly the richest man in the world), but does not include Sam Walton (reputedly the richest man in America). Nothing creates expectations more than price. If I tell you that you can have a room that costs $50 or one that costs $150, how would your expectation change between the two? Consider the airline passenger who pays $2000 to fly first class vs. the one who pays $600 in economy. They leave and arrive at the same time and travel at the same speed. What does $1400 tell you? That's an easy one. What does $100 in a hotel room tell you? Or $80, or $50, or $30, or $10?

McDonald's operates with a very carefully thought-out pricing strategy. So does Quality International. So do Four Seasons Hotels and many restaurants at all levels of the spectrum. For many others it seems as if the strategy is, "What can I get today?" Because we have already spent an entire chapter on this subject it will not be belabored here. Suffice it to say that pricing is both a powerful and a dangerous strategic tool.

Following is the pricing strategy for the Asia hotel example. Take particular note of the last line.

The following points have been considered in developing the pricing strategy:

1. The special features of the product
2. The spending power of the market
3. The traffic movement of the market
4. The possibility of losing regular users of high-rate rooms to lower-rate rooms
5. Pricing of the competition
6. Management policy to avoid discounted business, group business (especially low budget), and any upgrading to the new rooms
7. The rates will be raised in three months.

As Jain states,

Increase in price should be considered for its effect on long-term profitability, demand elasticity, and competitive moves. While in the short run a higher price may mean higher profits, the long-run effect of a price increase may be disastrous. The increase may encourage new entrants to the industry and competition from substitutes. . . . an increase in price may lead to shifts in demand which could be detrimental. . . . before the price-increase strategy is implemented, its long-term effect should be thoroughly examined.[18]

All of the possibilities mentioned by Jain have happened in the hotel industry in the last ten years, both in the United States and in Europe.

Communication Substrategy   The issue here is obviously the strategy to be used to communicate all of the above to the marketplace. The strategic issue is what to say, not how to say it. The "how to say it" requires exceptional creativity in many cases and is often best left to those with that kind of expertise. The "what to say," however, is a strategic management decision and should not be left for advertising agencies to decide. That is not their job.

Management's failure to clearly articulate its strategy will not stop the agency from being creative. But it could, and often does, result in advertising that is only tangentially related to what management should be communicating. Actual copy, the "how to say it," should always be checked back against the strategy to be certain that that is what it is really saying.

An example is Hilton International's advertising when they introduced hotels in the U.S. marketplace under the name Vista International. According to company executives the strategy was to create awareness of Hilton's presence in the U.S. and its adaptation to American tastes. One two-page ad was about 80 percent ocean waves and 20 percent copy. The message: "No longer must you cross an ocean to stay at a hotel operated by Hilton International." Another two-page ad with the same space proportion illustrated bushels of ripe red apples. The message: "You can choose from a whole menu of authentic American dishes . . . at Vista International." In relatively small print at the bottom was "Vista International."

The strategy behind these ads was well-founded but the message was lost. Although the graphics were excellent and eye-catching, an informal survey showed that readers did not identify the ads with a hotel company, much less Vista. The creativity got away from the strategy.

---

[18] Jain, *Marketing Planning*, p. 731.

A contrasting example is a Holiday Inn campaign. Headlined, "A promise" with a bottom line, "We want you back," the copy promised that your stay would be "right" or you wouldn't have to pay for it. The presumed strategy here was to get customers back who had had bad experiences. The copy (Figure 15-4) was believable and executed the strategy.

Advertising, of course, is not the only part of the communications mix strategy. The strategy will also dictate the methods of communication. Under the umbrella of the overall communications strategy and what to say is the mix of personal selling, public relations, promotion (including frequent traveler programs), merchandising, and direct mail. The strategy will indicate where the emphasis and proportion of budget will be placed on each. An excerpt from the strategic plan of the hotel in Asia follows.

Objective:
   To creatively highlight the uniqueness of the product.
Strategy:
   To convince customers, especially the FIT and corporate segments, that we have a unique hotel in terms of its being traditional in decor, equipped with the most modern business aids, and a greater accent on personalized service.
   To create awareness of the new F&B outlets.
Mix:
   [This is followed by an extensive list including advertising media, in-house materials, sales materials, direct mail, publicity materials, brochures, sales trips and blitzes, research, personal invitations, travel agencies, and other strategic and tactical plans.]

Distribution Strategies   Strategies for distribution deal with channels and, in the case of most hospitality services, how to move the customer physically to the product. Relevant categories, as discussed in Chapter 18, are travel agents, tour brokers, wholesalers, referral services, reservations systems, airlines, travel clubs, and so forth. Strategies involve the emphasis placed on each (or none) as well as the channels used.

Destination hotels and resorts will place special emphasis on utilizing these channels. Distribution systems have become increasingly complex in the hotel industry and for many companies consume far more attention today than they did ten years ago.

Club Med presents a somewhat unusual situation. The Club Med vacation is generally all-inclusive, sometimes including airfare. Accordingly, they tend to act largely as their own travel agent. This strategy was less than optimally effective in penetrating the American market. The revised strategy was to cultivate specific and select travel agencies. Club Med personally trained these agencies in the "Club Med concept" and made them "Club Med specialists." This strategy established a special distribution channel that turned out to be very effective.

Restaurants are generally not as involved in distribution channels. There are special cases, however. Cattlemen's Restaurant in New York City had a horse-drawn hansom that traveled through the city physically bringing customers to the premises.

We predict that distribution strategies will become increasingly important in global markets. They must, however, be consistent with higher level strategies. For example, upscale master and operational strategies do not lead to pursuance of price conscious tour groups as, in practice, is sometimes the case.

Feedback Loops   There are two feedback loops in the strategic marketing systems model in Figure 20-1. One is the risk loop. Feeding back to the master strategy, this loop questions the risks if the strategy is pursued. Some of the risk questions to be asked are "What can happen? Will it work? What if it doesn't? How will competitors react? What are the economics? Does it meet objectives? Does it match capabilities? Does the organization support it?" These are critical questions that must be asked. If answers are negative, reevaluation must take place. This is far better than following hunches that often end in failure.

The second loop is the feedback on whether the strategy is working once it is in place. Market research is fed into the marketing intelligence system that contains all the information discussed in the previous chapter. This is the control that warns management to act before the possibility arises of the system's being out of control.

Strategy Selection

As we have progressed through the strategic marketing systems model illustrated in Figure 20-1, we have probably raised more questions than we have provided answers. That is because there is no single right marketing strategy for any situation; there are simply right alternatives. The situation analysis, if done objectively, should lay bare the facts. The environmental analysis and future prognostications provide the bases for assumptions. From these sources, the strategic planner develops alternative courses of action. Which one should be chosen?

That is a simple question that has no simple answer. When you consider that there are also alternatives at every step of the strategic planning process, you find that you have dozens, perhaps hundreds, of choices to make. That seems like a formidable task and it may well be. Some are better at it than others. Good common sense, wisdom, judgment, and intuition still have their place. Interpreting information, while objective, is not mechanical.

At the same time, we want to mention once again that all strategic thinking and planning need not take place only at the corporate or higher levels of management. Unit managers have to be involved in strategic planning, as has been pointed out. We have given numerous examples of what happens when strategic planning is not done, or is done poorly, or is poorly executed. At the least, every manager should be thinking strategically at every level.

Strategic planning may occur only at the functional level following the strategies set forth at the higher levels. It may occur for a 60-seat coffee shop or a 20-unit motel. Regardless, it is strategy that drives tactics and that, when done and executed properly, will optimize marketing performance. Even Joe at Joe's Diner will sell more hot dogs when he plans strategically.

The functions of strategic planning are to define objectives in terms other than profit, to plan ahead, to influence and not respond to change, and to inspire organizational commitment. They also include understanding the customer's role in the process, to wit,

A business is . . . defined by the want the customer satisfies when he buys a product or service. . . . To the customer, no product or service, and certainly no company, is of much importance. . . . The customer only wants to know what the product or service will do for him tomorrow. All he is interested in are his own values, his own wants, his own reality. For this reason alone, any serious attempt to state "what our business is" must start with the customer, his realities, his situation, his behavior, his expectations, and his values.[19]

Drucker's statement is the beginning of strategic marketing planning. The only other side to strategic planning is the competition. If you can adhere to Drucker better than "they" can, you'll have no problem.

Once your strategy has been formulated, it should be evaluated. Here is a checklist for that purpose.

- Is it identifiable and clear in words and practice?
- Does it fully exploit environmental opportunity?
- Is it consistent with competence and resources?
- Is it internally consistent, synergistic?
- Is it a feasible risk in economic and personal terms?
- Is it appropriate to personal values and aspirations?
- Does it provide stimulus to organizational effort and commitment?
- Are there indications of responsiveness of the market?
- Is it based on reality to the consumer?
- Is it workable?

Problems with Strategic Plans

The best-formulated strategy in the world can fail if it is badly implemented. There are a number of reasons for this happening. In some quarters, strategic planning has acquired a bad name because of these failures; it is better to understand the reasons for failure than to blame the process.

Gray conducted research with business executives to find out why strategic planning failed. Although these executives complained about problems of implementation, Gray attributed most of the failures to preimplementation factors. His list follows, along with brief descriptions of suggested cures to prevent implementation problems.[20] We have added comments of our own and others.

1. Poor preparation of line managers.
    Cure: Prepare line managers for this role; strategic planning is a line management function. Propose strategic planning as a better way to manage rather than a burden from above. Focus on managers' real problems so as to see the troubles in their current strategic context.
    Comment: The major emphasis in the hospitality industry is on the bottom line. Most management people have learned, no matter how often they are told otherwise, that

---

[19] Peter F. Drucker, *Management: Tasks, Responsibilities, Practices,* New York: Harper & Row, 1974, pp. 79–80.

[20] Daniel H. Gray, "Uses and Misuses of Strategic Planning," *Harvard Business Review,* January–February, 1986, pp. 89–97. Copyright © 1986 by the President and Fellows of Harvard College; all rights reserved.

this is how they will be rewarded. Like any sensible person, they manage accordingly. Four Seasons Hotels is an exception: They reward managers $\frac{1}{3}$ on customer
evaluation, $\frac{1}{3}$ on employee evaluation, and $\frac{1}{3}$ on bottom line. The results are evident
when you stay at a Four Seasons.

We regularly hear types of comments from line managers like this actual one:
"They don't want my opinion even when they ask for it. Sometimes they listen
politely; sometimes they don't even do that. The emphasis remains on short-run
objectives. Owners' demands become the compelling decision process. Nobody
makes budget—unrealistic expectations produce a no-win situation. The basic belief
is in service to the financial statement. All hotels in the system are perceived as
'top-market' and untouchable; we know differently but they won't listen. The
emphasis is on long hours, hard work, and limited vacations. How do you think
long-term when you're trained, rewarded, in fact pushed, to think short-term?"

2. Faulty definition of business units.

Cure: Organization comes after strategic planning. The main purpose of organization
is to support the development and execution of strategy. Organizational units already
in place may be the wrong way to do this.

Comment: Renaghan has previously pointed out the need for a "marketing organization" in hotels as opposed to the more common "functional organization."[21] His
argument is that functional organizations are not consumer-oriented, lead to friction
between departments, are reactive rather than proactive, do not lend themselves to
operational efficiency or timeliness in decision-making within and between units of
the organization, and do not have a strategic orientation. Hayes notes,

> the role of top management is not to spot and solve problems as much as to create an
> organization that can spot and solve its own problems. . . . Entrepreneurship at the
> bottom cannot be 'ordered' from the top—particularly when, as usually happens,
> top-down, staff-dominated planning and control systems have caused most of the
> entrepreneurs to leave. . . . most strategic planning focuses primarily on financial
> wherewithal, ignoring the capabilities of the organization. . . . Rather than trying to
> develop optimal strategies that assume a static environment, [the company should
> seek] opportunistic improvements in a dynamic environment. . . . In such organiza-
> tions *everybody* is assumed to be responsible for the organization's prosperity. Its
> success rests on its ability to exploit opportunities as they arise, its ingenuity, its
> capacity to learn, its determination and its persistence. . . . As the 'counters' gain
> ascendency over the 'doers,' the best doers are likely to become counters. Or they go
> elsewhere, where they can do it their way.[22]

Comment: Organizations need to determine whether they have the right organizational structure to implement the preferred strategy. Internal operating policies must
guide strategy implementation and be workable, practical, consistent, and efficient.
Strategy dictates the organizational structure, processes, and policies. As the market
changes, so too do the ways of serving the market. As strategy adjusts, so too must

---

[21] Leo Renaghan, "From Sales to Marketing: The Design of Effective Marketing Organizations for Hotel Firms," in *The
Practice of Hospitality Management, II,* R. Lewis et al., eds., Stamford, Conn.: AVI, 1986, pp. 337–345.

[22] Robert H. Hayes, "Why Strategic Planning Goes Awry," *The New York Times,* April 20, 1986, pp. 2f.

the organizational structure to fit the strategy. Schaffer provides examples of three strategic postures in the hotel industry and their appropriate organizational structures:

Defender strategy: Concentrates on efficiency, tight cost and overhead controls. Organization specifies behavior of managers. Avoids deviation from policy. Centralizes control in detailed, formal policies. Limited decision making at lower levels. Deviation authority required from corporate. Product: consistent, non-innovative. Example: Marriott. Analysis: highly centralized structure fits strategy.

Prospector strategy: Searches for innovative market opportunities. Experiments. Responds to environmental trends. Create change and thrive on uncertainty. Focus on product innovation vs. efficiency. Employees given broad authority. Organization informal to encourage innovation. Example: Hyatt. Analysis: loose, decentralized structure matches competitive strategy.

Analyzer strategy: Aim for particular segments or geographic markets. Strategy based on serving particular market well. Management works to achieve differentiation. Watches competitors, adapts their ideas. Highly trained management with low cost, no frills approach. Example: La Quinta. Analysis: tight, controlled structure fits strategy.[23]

Comment: Marriott, Hyatt, and La Quinta are generally acknowledged to be successful companies. Whether you like their strategies or not, the point is their successful implementation through structure. Following are some statements made to the authors by a middle-level executive in a hotel company where the structure doesn't fit the strategy:

The company is trying desperately to change the way it does business. There is a tremendous shift towards decentralization from a strong centralized system. The result has been turmoil and confusion for the past two years. Specifically, the shift came before the correct personnel were in place to execute.

...units were given autonomy with leaders who were used to being told how to do everything from the home office. In addition, many of the home office personnel were reluctant to relieve themselves of their former responsibilities. The emphasis still remains on short run objectives at the property level.

... Traditions that underlie the corporate culture: defensiveness, operations emphasis, financial emphasis. The culture is becoming consistent with the strategy. The culture dictates more activity as a sign of success. As the budget becomes more elusive, the solution becomes "add more tactics," thereby dispersing the concentration of effort even further. You are a failure if you do not have a list of 100 items to be completed by Friday, instead of doing three things that will make a difference.

The culture does not adapt to the economic environment. Budget is basically set at 10% above the past year performance, bar all historical trends.

The hotels "poo poo" any competitive threats, lose significant market share and then retrench in a "hold on to what we have" mentality. The other option is to cut costs in payroll/other expenses, making the product less competitive!

The organization does not adapt to the changing social environment. For example, it is a major surprise to most managers that liquor sales have slipped. In view of

---

[23] Jeffrey D. Schaffer, "Structure and Strategy: Two Sides of Success," *Cornell Hotel and Restaurant Administration Quarterly,* February 1986, pp. 76–81.

significant changes in public perception of drinking habits, alternative revenue sources should have been analyzed and new products introduced.

Top management has seen very little change over the past ten years. There have been no top level management changes. Losers appear to be nurtured past all reasonable sense of time. Rewards are clearly placed for cost-cutting. Rules are tacit. The employees see the real priority as cost cutting, continuous under-staffing, and lack of materials to do their job.

A formal organization does exist. The communication appears open, while the structure is not.

Comment: The mission statement of this hotel company clearly states that the company is "market-oriented, people-oriented, and plans for change."

3. Vaguely formulated goals.
   Cure: Move beyond general goals.
   Comment: "Planning's top-down orientation has emphasized the development of grandiose strategic leaps, rather than the patient step-by-step improvements that are difficult for competitors to copy. . . . Goals that can be achieved within five years are usually either too easy or are based on buying and selling something."[24]

4. Inadequate information bases for action planning.
   Cure: Make more detailed action plans.
   Comment: "The cure for half-baked strategy is action detailing. . . . Planning in detail should be used as a further test of a strategy's feasibility. . . . Good action detailing requires the participation of middle and lower management and the work force. Top management knows the direction; those below know the terrain. Not only is lower level participation essential to working out practical steps, but it is also highly desirable. . . . The alternative, which is to try to push strategic planning out into the organization and down through the ranks by exhortation and other forms of one-way "communication," has only minimal effect."[25]

5. Badly handled reviews of business unit plans.
   Cure: At this stage, units' plans are force-fit into the corporate plan. Focus is on the numbers rather than on the strategies. Numbers are altered so as to close the gap without any discussion of the need to revise the risk assessments, competitive reactions, probability estimates, and other problems lying beneath the numbers. "The force-fit . . . is an invitation to play games and a clear signal that scrupulous planning is considered a waste of valuable time."
   Comment: Trade-offs to obtain consensus in this type of situation are counterproductive to strategic planning.

6. Inadequate linkage of strategic planning with other control systems.
   Cure: "A strategic planning system can't achieve its full potential until it is integrated with other control systems such as budgets, information systems, and reward systems. . . . Strategy is what makes a fact relevant or irrelevant, and a relevant fact significant or insignificant."

---

[24] Hayes, "Planning Goes Awry."
[25] Gray, Uses and Misuses.

Comment: Strategic planning takes organizational structure into account. Strategic planning is a way of thinking about a business and how to run it.

Summary

Strategic planning is a difficult but essential process. At the highest level of the firm, it drives the firm. At the lowest management level, it drives day-to-day activities. It is not a mystical activity but an essential phase of management and marketing leadership.

Good strategic planning rests on knowing where you are now and where you want to go, and finding the best way to get there. Its success rests on objective analysis, knowing what business you are in, understanding markets, integrating within the firm, and creating an organizational structure that will provide the implementation. In essence, there is no substitute for strategic planning and execution in today's competitive environment.

DISCUSSION QUESTIONS

1. Discuss the key differences between strategies and tactics. List three examples of each as they apply to the hospitality industry. Do the tactics flow from the strategies?
2. Discuss why a mission statement and objectives are needed at the highest and lowest levels of management.
3. How is product strategy different from target market strategy in strategic planning?
4. Discuss the functional substrategies and how they flow from the master and operational strategies.
5. How does pricing strategy present an incongruity in the hospitality marketing mix?
6. What are the most critical factors in strategy selection? Discuss why.

CHAPTER 21

The Marketing Plan

The marketing plan is the working document that the hospitality enterprise develops for action during the forthcoming year. It is the written and specific plan of how the mission and the strategy will be accomplished in the short term. Although sometimes marketing plans are written for future years, and in fact often give at least some brief mention to the next two to five years for the sake of consistency, they are usually written for just one year at a time.

Just as strategic marketing and the mission statement of the business unit flow from corporate strategy and the corporate mission statement, the marketing plan of the business unit flows from its own strategy and mission statement. Many firms practice marketing management without first doing strategic planning, at least at the business unit level. Strategic planning is often left to the corporate level, as we mentioned in the previous chapter.

Of course, in many hospitality firms the "corporate" level and the business unit level are one and the same. This does not negate the need for strategic planning. On the other hand, many hospitality firms do not develop annual marketing plans either. Marketing plans are quite common in chain hotels, airlines, large travel agencies, and large restaurant companies, but not so common in smaller companies or individual properties, especially restaurants.

We believe failure to make a marketing plan is a mistake, just as it is a mistake not to do strategic planning. Perhaps people omit these tasks because both sometimes seem incredibly imposing, yet they need not be. Marketing plans that run into the hundreds of pages usually disappear into filing cabinets, never to be seen again. Instead, we believe in short plans that are both concise and precise.

Although this chapter will appear to favor the longer document because of the need to cover and explain all the elements of a marketing plan, the actual written plan should abstract and condense only what is truly pertinent. There are two key elements to a successful marketing plan: (1) that it is workable, and (2) that it is realistic. Too many plans fail in one or both of these respects.

Marketing Management vs. Strategic Planning

We need also to differentiate between marketing management and strategic marketing. In fact, this entire book deals with both marketing management and strategic marketing. This helps explain our title *Marketing Leadership,* because leadership encompasses both.

There are numerous textbooks available entitled either *Marketing Management* or *Marketing Strategy.* Either one will cover the same subject areas covered in this text. The difference is in the approach. Some authors place strategy largely at the corporate or strategic business unit level (SBU) and management at the local level; we believe that both belong at both levels when good marketing leadership is practiced.

In the strategic marketing approach, market segments are identified as those that the company can best serve with competitive advantage. In marketing management, they are defined according to marketing mix variables. Strategic marketing takes an overall view, allocating resources and setting objectives after defining the market; marketing management develops the marketing mix to serve designated markets in accordance with those objectives and resources. This is, as Jain points out, why strategy must precede management. Management, with a short-term orientation, stresses a "winning marketing mix rather than an accurate definition of the market."[1] We have provided numerous examples of this throughout the book, such as inappropriately designing a hotel's restaurant without first correctly designating the market it is to serve.

Strategic marketing deals with the long-term view of the market and the business to be in; marketing management stresses running that business and seeks to optimize within the constraints established by the strategy. Other differences between the two approaches are delineated in Table 21-1.

We emphasize this distinction for a specific reason. Far too many marketing plans fail because they are based on the wrong strategy, or fail to flow from the right strategy. An excellent example of this, which has been mentioned before, is the strategy of a hotel to target an upscale market when that market does not exist, it is already overcrowded, or the product is not adequate to serve it. A marketing plan is then developed to implement the strategy, and fails.

In many cases, this type of situation is forced. For example, we have also previously discussed the influence of owners and management companies on hospitality enterprises. Many owners are not primarily in the hospitality industry, and sometimes have unrealistic expectations of their investments. The converse is true as well: Management companies are so anxious to obtain these management contracts that they submit

---

[1] Subhash C. Jain, *Marketing Planning and Strategy,* Cincinnati: South-Western Publishing, 1985, p. 54.

TABLE 21-1   Major Differences Between Strategic Marketing and Marketing Management

Point of Difference	Strategic Marketing	Marketing Management
Timeframe	Long-range; i.e., decisions have long-term implications	Day-to-day; i.e., decisions have relevance in a given financial year
Orientation	Inductive and intuitive	Deductive and analytical
Decision process	Primarily bottom-up	Mainly top-down
Relationship with environment	Environment considered everchanging and dynamic	Environment considered constant with occasional disturbances
Opportunity sensitivity	Ongoing to seek new opportunities	Ad hoc search for a new opportunity
Organizational behavior	Achieve synergy between different components of the organization, both horizontally and vertically	Pursue interests of the decentralized unit
Nature of job	Requires high degree of creativity and originality	Requires maturity, experience, and control orientation
Leadership style	Requires proactive perspective	Requires reactive perspective
Mission	Deals with what business to emphasize	Deals with running a delineated business

Source: Jain, *Marketing Planning and Strategy,* Cincinnati: South-Western Publishing, 1985, p. 55.

very aggressive pro formas to potential investors. These factors pressure the local marketing team to develop unrealistic and unworkable marketing plans.

Management should resist this pressure. The local marketing team's responsibility to owners and management companies for whom they work lies not in painting rosy forecasts that are bound to fail, but in constructing a marketing plan that is realistic and workable. If that is not consistent with the strategy, then the strategy needs to be reevaluated. This may appear contradictory after we have emphasized that the marketing plan flows from the strategy; now we seem to be saying the reverse. What we are talking about, however, is the test of the strategy as explained in the previous chapter.

If the strategy cannot be implemented, it is the wrong strategy. Marketing plan conclusions cannot be drawn until all the information has been assembled, and marketing management should not begin until the strategy and all the facts are in place. Too often a marketing plan is developed with the final conclusion drawn before the work begins, and the data collected are summarily "fitted" to the conclusion. The result is a marketing plan that is both unrealistic and unworkable.

Requirements for a Marketing Plan

As the number of hotels and restaurants built continues to increase, there is far more pressure to compete for the same hospitality dollar. The marketing team that develops a realistic marketing plan can take the appropriate actions to maintain the desired, realistic market share. The team that writes an unrealistic and unworkable plan will be doing all of the wrong things and is guaranteed to lose market share.

The marketing plan has to remain simple and easy to execute. Many marketing plans are developed at the designated time of the year and remain untouched until it is "that time of year again." The trap planners fall into is developing a plan with a list of one hundred action steps; while very impressive, it is also unproductively exhaustive. The local team gets so wrapped up in completing an endless assortment of laundry lists that it begins to lose sight of the basics. The result is poorer performance and frustration. The marketing plan that is the simplest, with a few key items to be completed, will be the most focused and successful.

The marketing plan must also be flexible. A professor of management and technology at Harvard University, Robert H. Hayes, said it well: "A road map is useful if one is lost in a highway system, but not in a swamp whose topography is constantly changing. A simple compass that indicates the general direction and allows you to use your own ingenuity in overcoming difficulties is far more valuable."[2]

Never before has the topography of the hospitality industry been in such a state of flux as it is today. Marketing plans, even less than strategic plans, should never be cast in cement and should always be adaptable to changes in the topography. Thus, marketing plans must constantly be reviewed and reevaluated. This is not to say that they should be changed at the sign of the slightest aberration; a good marketing plan has a certain stability to it. It simply means you mustn't be locked into a position when the situation changes and there is evidence that this position no longer is the most effective one to be in.

The marketing plan must be appropriate for the business in terms of capacity, image, scope, and risk, as well as being feasible in terms of time and resources. This would seem to be a fairly obvious statement, but we have seen it violated so often by hospitality firms that it has to be mentioned here. Owners' demands, corporate's demands, management's demands, ROI demands, and others lead to too many marketing plans that simply have little or no chance of success. Although a marketing plan will have objectives, it should be based solely and entirely on the characteristics of the market and the resources to implement the plan. Wild-eyed dreams and wishful thinking will not overcome these realities.

The marketing plan should assign specific responsibility, with times and dates for accomplishment. Continuous follow-up assures that these responsibilities will be met. This provision requires that the plan be thoroughly understood by everyone in the organization. A good plan indicates how marketing activities are integrated with all other activities of the operation, and it receives a commitment from all personnel.

What this last statement means is that the marketing plan doesn't stop at the door of

---

[2] Robert H. Hayes, "Why Strategic Planning Goes Awry," *New York Times*, April 20, 1986.

the marketing office. Although the details of the plan will not go to every person in the work force, the essence of the plan should do exactly that.

Consider, for example, as one overseas hotel did, a plan to attract the market segment of German families with children on vacation at a package rate. The promotion was a success and the families came, but no one had made adequate plans, as promised in the promotion, for children's activities, baby-sitters, or even extra beds to be placed in the rooms. Consider, again, attempting to attract an American market segment but having no fresh-squeezed orange juice until 10:00 A.M.

Any plan that succeeds in attracting the market but fails to fulfill its promises, explicit or implicit, to that market will in the long term be self-defeating. Personnel cannot deliver what marketing promises if they don't know what those promises are or don't have the tools to deliver on them.

A good marketing plan provides direction for an operation. It states where you are going and what you are going to have to do to get there. It builds employee and management confidence through shared effort and teamwork toward common goals. It recognizes weaknesses, emphasizes strengths, and deals with reality. It seeks and exploits opportunities. And last but certainly not least, a good marketing plan gets everyone into the act.

If you have previously thought of a marketing plan as a description of the facility, a list of possible competitors and their facilities, an advertising and sales plan, and a forecast and budget (as so many marketing programs are), think again. These are necessary but not sufficient elements of a marketing plan that succeeds. Like everything else we have said in this book, the test of the marketing plan is embodied in the question "How will the customer be served?"

Development of a Marketing Plan

Situation Analysis

As in strategic planning, the marketing plan begins with a situation analysis. Here, however, we are dealing with greater specifics. Our goal is to develop a marketing mix that will attract and serve designated markets.

It is well to begin, then, with a restatement of the firm's philosophy, the master strategy, and the mission statement of the property. This will establish the context within which the marketing plan will be developed. The next step is to complete the first major portion of the plan, data collection.

Data Collection—The External Environment Data collection can be divided into two parts, external and internal. External data deals with the environment, including everything from international and domestic trends such as currency exchange rates (more Europeans will be going to the United States this year), travel habits (more Americans are utilizing recreational vehicles), specials events (millions will be going to the World's Fair in Finland), to economic trends (the Singapore economy is weak, resulting in less business travel), political trends (Aquino's regime is threatened by political unrest in the Philippines), social trends (the senior citizen market is increasing in size and traveling more), and technological trends (expansion of the TGV fast-speed train routes in France means people can get to French destination areas faster and stay longer).

There are also numerous industry trends to be considered, such as growth or decline of various market segments, building trends affecting future supply, room occupancy and eating-out trends, new concept trends such as all-suite hotels and "grazing" restaurants, new taste trends such as Mexican food and Cajun cooking in America, less drinking of wine in France and of all alcoholic beverages in the United States, more eating of hamburgers (thanks to McDonald's) in Singapore, five weeks' vacation for all working people in Finland, and the "opening" of the market to tourism in Russia and China with new "American-style" hotels.

There are also legislative impacts (the U.S. 1986 tax law), and energy impacts and their ripple effects (the cost of oil). Still other trends include, for example, budget motel growth, *luxury* budget motel growth, convention centers, growth in incentive travel, increase in weekend package users, two-income households with high discretionary income, "short-tripping" at low cost (a New York City couple can now spend the weekend in Rio de Janeiro for little more than going to Cape Cod), and other demographic, psychographic, and population shifts.

Then there are external impacts such as state, regional, or national tourism promotions, major new tourist attractions, new industries in the area, new office buildings being built, new airline routes added, plant closings, companies merged and moved, new sources of visitor origin, and new convention centers being built.

This may seem like a long list but is actually only a small part of the environmental factors that can affect an operation. Every factor does not affect every operation; the key is to recognize those that may affect yours. The marketing plan has to deal with these factors, prepare for them, and, whenever possible, capitalize on them or counteract them.

For example, we know of one restaurateur who had operated a very successful restaurant for a number of years until business began declining quite drastically in the late 1970s. Because this operation was in the country and off a main highway, the operator concluded that people were simply not traveling as often or as far, because of the cost of gasoline. Closer analysis, however, revealed that his competition was doing better than ever. In fact, the tastes of the market had changed and new markets had emerged. Instead of adapting to the market (e.g., he refused to change his menu because his remaining old customers "loved it as it is"), he watched his business gradually disappear.

Data Collection—The Competition   The second area of external data collection is concerned with the competition. It is important that the local marketing team collect data on all feasible competitors within logical boundaries. Understand that "logical boundaries" may mean the hotel or restaurant across the street or it may mean the one 3000 miles away. The competition for the convention market for the Hotel del Coronado off the coast of California includes the Homestead Hotel in Virginia, the White Sulphur Springs Hotel in West Virginia, the Cloisters Hotel in Georgia, the Breakers Hotel in Florida, and the Hyatt Regency in Maui, not to mention many others.

The motel in North Overshoe, Maine, competes with the motel in South Skislope, Maine, even though they are 30 miles apart. The Club Med in Eleuthera in the Bahamas competes with the all-inclusive Couples in Jamaica. The restaurant in the city competes with the one in the suburbs. And McDonald's competes with the convenience store, but, by the same token, neither one competes with the French restaurant located between them. Competition, as defined in the marketing plan, is anyone competing for the same customer with the same or a similar product, or a reasonable alternative, that the customer has a reasonable opportunity to purchase at the same time and in the same context.

As in everything, of course, there may be exceptions. We may want to expand even from this perspective of competition in a highly competitive environment or a period of economic disruption. At these times it may be necessary to reach down-market from the current level of product in order to maintain acceptable profit margins.

These different views of who the competition is were discussed in Chapter 5 on competitive analysis and will not be repeated here. Let it suffice to say that the marketing plan should include data on any competitor that, in the forthcoming year, we can reasonably expect to take customers from, or to which we could conceivably lose customers.

The marketing team must take an objective stance when it comes to evaluating the competition. While we all like to believe we have the best product to sell in our product class, this may lull us into a false sense of security, and the competition can move by us very quickly. The marketing plan must be truly objective and realistic about the products evaluated for the best results. After making a list of all competitors for your product, the following information will be needed:

Description: A brief description of the physical attributes of the competing hotel or restaurant or lounge (or nation, country, state, or city, etc.). Emphasize good points as well as bad. Determine such things as when the product was last renovated, plans for upgrading in the near future, physical facilities, and all features that compete with yours—that is, the product/service mix. The description includes quality and level of both tangible and intangible features, personnel, procedures, management, reservations systems, distribution networks, marketing efforts and successes and failures, promotions, market share, image, positioning, chain advantages/ disadvantages, and so forth. All of these items will be important in the final analysis. A physical description—number of rooms, meeting space, F&B outlets and so on—is simply not enough. All strengths and weaknesses need to be defined.

Customer Base: Who are their customers? Why do these customers go there? Are they potentially your customers? Part of the marketing plan will focus on creating demand for your product. Most of the plan will focus on taking customers directly from your competitors. It will be difficult to take customers from your competition if you do not know who these customers are. In a restaurant situation, for example, do your competitors have a high volume of senior citizens eating at traditionally quiet times, a group that you desire? Does their lounge have a successful happy hour (still very legal and in practice in many states and countries) that you could augment for your lounge, and if so, what type of people go there? Does your competitive hotel have a higher percentage of transient guests than your own? What particular market segments does the competition attract?

Price Structure: Where is your competition in relation to price? While food and beverage prices are relatively easy to obtain, the product delivered for the price is also important. Is their $6.95 chef's salad as large as yours for $7.95? When analyzing prices it is important to compare "apples with apples."

Published guest room prices are relatively easy to find, but negotiated prices with volume producers take a little more effort. Be very careful how you obtain this information. Antitrust laws in the United States are very clear on this matter; you cannot share this kind of information with your competitors. The reason is that your discussions could be interpreted as price-fixing—that is, not offering the buyer the opportunity to purchase the product in a free market. However, this information can be obtained from purchasers. For example, if the travel planner for XYZ Company shared with you the negotiated rates of a competitor, your having that information is perfectly legal.

Future Supply: It is important to determine if there are any new projects that will affect your competitive environment in the future. This information can normally be obtained from the Chamber of Commerce or other local sources. The fact that a new 300-room hotel is scheduled to break ground soon is very important in the development of the marketing plan. Likewise, if the building that houses a major food and beverage competitor is scheduled for demolition to make way for a new office park, this could also influence your decision-making process for the following year.

Once again, keep in mind that competition is all relative. Traditional boundaries of location may no longer apply. For a restaurant in New York City the competition may encompass a three-block radius that is less than one-quarter square mile. For a five-star resort hotel the competition might be located thousands of miles away. When determining who your comeptition is, the question must be asked; "Where else do/might my customers/potential customers go?"

In the development of the marketing plan, it is also critical to keep in mind the fact that you want new customers and that you are looking for opportunities to get them. This means that sometimes you have to break the "rules" of competition. For example, a Hilton property might normally be positioned against Sheraton, Hyatt, and Westin as competition. In good times this might be correct. However, when occupancies are low the Hilton hotel might consider customers that it could capture at a profit from other competition. If rooms are going vacant, a "normal" Holiday Inn customer might be a target of the marketing plan of the hypothetical Hilton. A Holiday Inn customer paying $50 for a room that costs $25 to produce is a good customer to have when the room might otherwise be vacant. In addition, there might be a synergistic effect in being able to retain this person as a regular customer. On the other hand, the Red Roof Inn customer who can only afford a room at $29 would not be considered as an alternative target.

It can be helpful to look at the overall market as a product class triangle based on the width of the customer base for each product class. Figure 21-1 is a hypothetical example not intended in any way to reflect the actual situation of the marketplace. What this does is to provide a visual market positioning of the size of the various product classes and the alternative opportunities when seeking additional occupancy.

The same technique can be used for restaurants. For example, in Springfield, Massachusetts, a heavily ethnic Italian city and Italian restaurant supply, a steak house would not expect to compete directly against the Italian choices in the same context and time. The product class base, however, illustrates the demand potential. Seeking additional opportunity, the steak house might develop a plan to tap into this market in addition to its regular market.

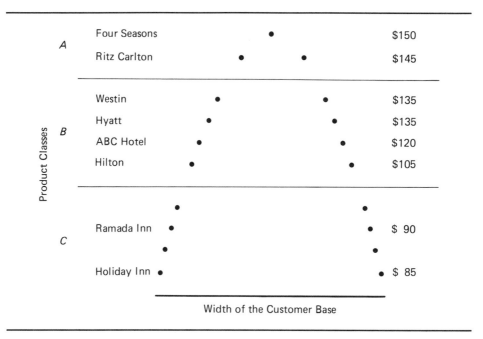

FIGURE 21-1   Product class perception of the market base

During the year of the marketing plan, it will be clear to the marketing team just where they are realistically competing, as well as what the alternative marketing opportunities are. The pyramid should be updated quarterly to keep abreast of the actions in the marketplace.

Data Collection—Internal   The third area of data collection is internal. One hopes that accurate and adequate records have been kept, and much of this information will be readily at hand. Once you have prepared your first marketing plan you will have said, at least a dozen times, "I wish I knew that." Thus, you will have set up procedures so that next year you will know "that."

Hotels and/or restaurants should have current data at all times on occupied rooms, occupancy ratio, revenues, average rate (totally and by market segment), market segments served, restaurant covers, seat turnovers, menu abstracts, average check, food to beverage check ratios (totally and for each outlet), and ratios as a percentage of gross revenue. These figures should be broken down by month, seasonally, and by days of the week.

These are the "hard" data and the easiest to obtain, but not the place to stop. List now what you know about the markets. Who are they, what do they like, what are their needs and wants? Why do they come here? Where would they go if they didn't come here? What are their complaints? Describe their characteristics, attitudes, opinions, and preferences. What is the market's perception and awareness? If you don't know the answers to these questions it is time to start doing some research. At the minimum, start talking to your customers. Have personnel in every single department keep logs on all customer comments—good, bad, and otherwise.

Failure to know these things can lead to making the same mistakes over and over.

How many times, do you suppose, did a waitress at the Holiday Inn in Kuala Lumpur have to tell customers that they can't get fresh orange juice until 10:00 A.M.?

The restaurant, essentially a coffee shop, at the Hilton Inn at Logan Airport in Boston had a captive audience, or at least management thought it did. There was virtually no place to eat at the airport other than snack bars. Passengers and friends with waiting time were advised by airport personnel to go to the Hilton, which they could do easily by shuttle, or by walking in nice weather. The menu prices started at about $15.00 per entree, à la carte. Scrod was $16.95—perhaps the highest price in Boston, where scrod is almost a staple.

These are not exactly the prices people hope to pay when "grabbing a bite" while waiting for a flight. Once there, however, they were stuck except for one alternative. At the bottom of the menu there was listed a hamburger sandwich for $5.95. "About how many of your customers order the hamburger?" we asked the waitress. "About 90 percent," was the response. Some people, such as international travelers who connect in Boston, had little choice: They ate hamburger. Those of us who drive to Logan, however, learned to stop and eat before we got there. Here was a property losing business and missing a tremendous opportunity because they didn't keep records, and/or refused to listen to their customers and/or employees.

Formal research is even better. The basic tenet of all marketing is to know your market. It is surprising how few hospitality establishments do. This is why so many marketing plans, the vast majority in our experience, rather than discuss what they will do for the customer, deal with bricks and mortar, physical facilities, inaccurate definition of competition (who is the competition for the Logan Hilton's restaurant?), broad market segments (e.g., the business traveler), vague budgets and forecasts, and undirected advertising.

The second category of internal data collection is the objective listing of resource strengths and weaknesses. This includes bricks and mortar. What is the condition of the property? Where is it weak and where is it strong? How can/should it be improved? What does it offer in terms of facilities? How effective is the location?

Then, the hardest part—how strong is management? The marketing staff? Personnel training, experience, and attitude? How are guests being treated? What do complaints look like? How successful have marketing efforts been in the past? What is the consumer image of the property? What is the position in the marketplace? This is the time for realistic objectivity, not glossing over or wishful thinking. Finally, make a list of what you do not know—that is, what research is needed.

To give an idea of how all this comes together, we list some abstractions from the data collection portion of the actual marketing plan of a hotel in Belgium.

Economy: Despite the economic recession and the bad position of the Belgian franc (which favors our incoming business), business is showing a slightly increasing trend. The percentage of international tourists is increasing. On the other hand, Belgian companies have substantially reduced or canceled budgets for meetings, seminars, and travel.

External Impacts: There are severe occupancy problems in winter. Bad weather conditions and lack of activities in the city center have strong negative impact on travel patterns. Competition is coming down hard on prices.

There are a large number of good à la carte restaurants downtown offering attractive weekend menus at good prices.

Our location away from the center of town is a disadvantage.

Internal Impacts: Customers are more and more cost-conscious, especially on F&B expenses.

We are receiving many complaints on lack of color TV sets and on the lack of soundproofing on the first, second, and third floors.

Quality of food is not up to standard, especially for groups.

Budgets were not finished until the end of last year and were not ready or effective at the beginning of this year.

Communication between departments is poor.

The entire staff is not sufficiently motivated.

Future of Our Markets: There is an increase of short holiday and weekenders from Netherlands and Germany.

There is an increase of the European tour series.

There is an increase of package bookings, especially during the summer.

There is a decrease of company individual bookings.

A new 230-room hotel will open next spring near the city center.

Data Analysis

Thus far, we have been engaged only in the collection of data. It is wise to complete this stage first without attempting to analyze the data, because you want to obtain the complete picture and the synergistic effect. Analyzing different factors in isolation can be misleading.

Analysis follows the same flow as the data collection process. Essentially, we want to draw some conclusions about market position, market segments, customer behavior, environmental impacts, growth potential, strengths and weaknesses, threats and opportunities, performance trends, customer satisfaction, resource needs and limitations, and other factors that will be germane to the marketing plan.

Environmental Analysis Let us look first at environmental trends. Are they positive or negative? How will/can they affect us? How can we take advantage of, or compensate for them? What are our alternatives? How long will they last? What courses of action are possible and feasible? How do these fit together? What would be the synergistic effect?

Competitive and Demand Analysis Next, the competitive and demand analysis needs to be completed. What are the potentials and opportunities in the marketplace? This requires a close analysis of all the demand factors, various market segments and target markets—for instance, what are the strongest market segments; what is their potential for further growth; are they steady, growing, or in decline; what is their contribution in room nights, covers, revenue; what can be done to accelerate a growing trend, begin growth in a steady trend, or reverse the direction of a declining trend? What other segments are there, perhaps untouched, that could be developed?

How do these segments affect our market mix? Are they compatible? Can they be expanded to fill gaps such as seasonal or day-of-the-week fluctuations? What types of business would complement these segments? What types of action could be taken to attract more business during low-occupancy periods? How does the competitive situation affect all these factors?

As you can see, the list can go on and on. We can't answers all these questions here, or even tell you how to find the answers, without a preponderance of information that alone could fill this book. Instead, let's take a hypothetical example based on the product class perception of the market base depicted in Figure 21-1 and look at how we might analyze the problem to head us in the right direction as to what we have to do.

Property Needs Analysis   This stage is what is called a property needs analysis; this means analyzing major profit areas to see what gaps have to be filled. These gaps could be in occupancy, market share, market segments, food sales, beverage sales, seasonal needs, and many other areas. In other words, instead of looking at where we can cut costs, we want to look at where we can obtain business. When we have done that we can match property needs with market needs to determine target markets and how to reach and serve them.

Needs analysis also means identifying other marketing problems. For example, this might be marketing strategies that aren't working, image changes that are needed, positioning problems, ineffective advertising or promotion, distribution channel problems, pricing problems, losing business to a particular competitor (perhaps because of a new facility, new product or service, or even just better marketing), or changing needs of a market segment that we can't meet.

In short, needs analysis is an identification of problems to be overcome. It makes the case clearer if we can apply some quantitative measurements to our analysis, which is no more than a best estimate based upon all of the data assembled. To demonstrate this we will use a simplified case to determine what the overall increase or decrease for the product will be for the forthcoming year. Ideally, this would be done by market segment.

In this example, we will say that we are anticipating an increase of 2 percent in demand for both group and transient hotel rooms in the midprice category. From the data collected, a competitive universe can be compiled as shown in Table 21-2, based on the same hotels as those in Figure 21-1.

Assume, also, for the purpose of this discussion, that a Holiday Inn Crowne Plaza of 200 rooms is opening in the following year with a projected occupancy of 55 percent. Its forecasted market mix is 50 percent group and 50 percent transient.

Now, for the purpose of developing the marketing plan, we have some quantitative data with which to work. One thing is immediately obvious: ABC Hotel not only has a low occupancy but is also not getting fair market share. After all the data collected in the situation analysis have been analyzed, two main areas of concentration are ready to be addressed: creating new business and capturing competitors' business.

Creation of New Business   Given the current situation, what plans can be developed to create a new demand for the product? McDonald's created a new demand for its product by opening for breakfast. Package weekends have created new demands for hotel products in the past. Creating a new demand in the hospitality industry, however, may be the toughest part of marketing. The important point to remember is that we are creating demand that until now did not exist for a product. This usually means creating a new use.

TABLE 21-2   Hypothetical Competitive Universe of ABC Hotel

Hotel Name	Rooms Available	Fair Market Share	Yearly Occupancy	Rooms Sold	Actual Market Share	Group Rooms	Transient Rooms
Four Seasons	400	16.3%	65%	95,000	16.4%	38,000	57,000
Ritz Carlton	200	8.2%	60%	44,000	7.6%	12,000	32,000
Westin	400	16.3%	65%	95,000	16.4%	57,000	38,000
Hyatt	500	20.4%	70%	128,000	22.1%	90,000	38,000
ABC Hotel	300	12.2%	60%	66,000	11.4%	33,000	33,000
Hilton	300	12.2%	70%	77,000	13.3%	45,000	32,000
Ramada Inn	200	8.2%	60%	44,000	7.6%	22,000	22,000
Holiday Inn	150	6.1%	55%	30,000	5.2%	15,000	15,000
Totals	2450	100.0%	65%	579,000	100.0%	312,000	267,000

Numbers rounded

The "Murder Mystery" weekend, previously discussed, is an example. In this case, the target market is couples with a sense of adventure who may be bored with alternatives. They might have stayed home for the weekend except for this exciting opportunity, or they have been enticed from a competitor offering the standard weekend package. The objective of the hotel, of course, is to build weekend business.

This is different than, for example, selling a corporate meeting package where meeting planners have already decided what they want to do, the only question being where. That constitutes direct marketing against the competition, rather than creating a new use for the product.

The rest of the marketing plan will carry out and specify the implementation of the murder weekend concept in terms of the specific target market, as discussed later.

Capturing Competitors' Business   Most efforts of the marketing plan will concentrate in this area. Specifically, let's return to the competitive universe depicted in Table 21-2. Let's assume that ABC Hotel's main competitors are Westin, Hyatt, and Hilton; Four Seasons and Ritz Carlton are in a different price and product category. Assume, however, that from a product and price point of view, Ramada is competitive and Holiday Inn is not.

A demand analysis for these five hotels, three of which are capturing more than fair market share while ABC and Ramada are not, might appear as follows:

Rooms Sold	Total	Group Segment	Transient Segment
Previous year	410,000	247,000	163,000
Next year projection with 2% increase in demand	418,200	251,940	166,260
New supply (Crowne Plaza)	40,000	20,000	20,000

A red flag should be raised with this scenario: Although the forecast is an increase in demand for the hotel product, the increase in supply will eclipse the increase in demand.

Each hotel will now be fighting for a smaller piece of the pie. If ABC Hotel does everything the same as the year before, they will be drawing on a smaller pool of rooms and occupancy will drop lower. In fact, ABC and its four competitors are now competing for 378,000 rooms vs. 410,000 of the previous year, after the new Holiday Inn takes its share.

ABC's marketing team can now see the task that lies before it. In order just to maintain the occupancies of the year before, it will have to create new demand for the product, aggressively attack competitors for new business, and maintain its own customer base, which the competition will be trying to lure away with their own marketing plans.

With this information, a projected market share can be derived:

	Total	Group Segment	Transient Segment
Projected room sales	418,200	251,940	166,260
ABC Hotel:			
FMS (6 hotels including new Crowne Plaza)	15.8%	15.8%	15.8%
	66,000	33,000	33,000
AMS	15.8%	13.1%	19.8%

The percent of rooms available is derived from the total rooms available (2450) minus the Four Seasons, Ritz Carlton, and Holiday Inn plus the 200 in the new Crowne Plaza (1900). The number of rooms available at the ABC Hotel is then divided by the 1900 total rooms to give a 15.8 percent fair market share (FMS).

ABC Hotel has 15.8 percent of the total competitive inventory available for sale. To maintain the same 66,000 occupied rooms as the previous year, ABC will have to maintain FMS, something they have not done in the past. The figures also show, however, that it is losing market share in the group segment while gaining it in the transient segment.

Two approaches are possible in this broad view of the market. Which one is chosen, or what combination of the two, will depend on full analysis of the remaining data, which obviously makes the situation far more complicated than it has been here. For example, ABC's strength may be as a transient hotel while this may be a weakness of the other properties. In this case, ABC might choose to direct its major marketing effort at that market.

Another possibility is that ABC has neglected the group market and needs to direct greater effort in that direction. Then, of course, it may have to make major efforts in both directions. Let us assume, for the sake of argument and because it is easier to demonstrate, that there is high price sensitivity in the market in either one or both of these segments. Looking back at the customer base pyramid in Figure 21-1, it can be seen that the broadest customer base is in the low end of the market. ABC might direct its marketing plan at the Ramada customer. Perhaps Ramada's low market share is indicative of other problems. Possibly pricing down, but still pricing just above Ramada could capture its customers.

The reverse situation applies to the Westin/Hyatt market. Perhaps ABC could pull the more price-sensitive customers from these competitors and should aim marketing efforts in that direction. In either case, specific marketing plans must be made to attack the competitive hotels in order to capture rooms from them. The plans might, perhaps, be directed at only specific days of the week or times of the year when ABC's occupancy suffers the most.

Although there is some hesitancy in the industry as to the positioning of a property offering lower prices during certain periods, there need not be if this is done properly. The airline industry has conditioned the traveling public to expect lower rates during certain periods and higher rates during others. In fact, the practice is common in many phases of the hospitality industry.

The ABC example is clearly an oversimplified one. There are innumerable other factors affecting any similar situation, and numerous alternative approaches. In fact, we haven't even mentioned the consumer in this discussion, and that data base would be the first one to consider! The point we want to make is that there is an absolute need for complete and adequate data and information followed by thorough analysis of all possible considerations. It is only through such methods that workable, realistic, and effective marketing plans can be developed.

Internal Analysis   We now turn to the internal analysis (not that we would have done the preceding without doing the internal analysis first!). Using the realistic and objective data we have gathered, we start by asking about the ability to serve certain markets. Let's start with an extreme example, perhaps, but a not uncommon one. Meridien Hotels (a subsidiary of Air France) and Nikko Hotels (a subsidiary of Japan Air Lines) both entered the New York City market anxious to position at the upper end of the scale. Both ran into problems and had to revise their marketing plans. The problems these companies had boil down to two main factors: They misjudged the market and they overrated their resources and capabilities.

Among other things, Nikko didn't understand Marriott customer loyalty (Nikko had taken over the Essex House on Central Park South from Marriott) and could only watch as their presumed customer base walked out the door. Although Nikko totally renovated the property, there was little market for their new upscale French restaurant or their $239 single rack rate. The general manager was German but most department heads were Japanese. Former Marriott employees, who stayed by contractual agreement, received crash courses in how to work with Japanese management and mentality, but turnover was still high. Occupancy dropped drastically as the upscale market failed to materialize. Similar problems occurred when New Otani, another Japanese firm, entered the Los Angeles market.

The Parker Meridien on 57th Street in New York City had an owner with "five-star fever." He wanted to target the same market as the Helmsley Palace, a deluxe five-star hotel, but didn't have the same quality product. Although Meridien attempted to go upscale in all respects, including prices, they didn't compete as well in that market. To compound the problem, even when special prices were advertised in *The New York Times*, reservationists were instructed to quote only rack rates over the phone!

Meridien tried to overcome the disadvantage with a restaurant. "Maurice," while one of the better restaurants in New York City, and one that helped to position the hotel, was not enough to overcome other deficiencies sufficiently to compete for the same target market as the Helmsley Palace. Today, the Parker Meridien does very well, better than the Helmsley Palace, with its appropriate positioning at the four-star level.

When doing an internal analysis, one should ask questions such as these:

What is the gap between what your customers want and need, what you promise them, and the product/service that is provided?

How well do you meet or exceed customer expectations?

How does the market's estimation of your product/service agree with yours? What makes you think so?

What items, product improvements, or services are needed to improve customer satisfaction?

Are you actually delivering what you think you are?

What patterns are appearing in guest comments? What types of problems seem to recur? What areas seem to need improvement?

Do you have the proper organization to accomplish what you are trying to—for instance, although the manager is a strong operations person, does he or someone else understand the customer?

Do you reward your staff strictly on bottom line results? If so, does it show up in matters affecting the customers?

Do you know, identify, and deal with your real strengths and weaknesses?

Once again, the list could go on indefinitely. Once again, we have to state that workable, effective, and realistic marketing plans can be developed only through the gathering of complete and adequate information and its thorough and objective analysis.

Market Analysis   Our final step in analysis is the market itself, the customer. Because this entire book is about the hospitality customer, it would be redundant to repeat here all that we have said about this strange individual who is the reason for the existence of any hospitality enterprise. For purposes of developing the marketing plan, this step means determining where the gaps are, where needs are unfulfilled, where problems are not being solved, and where the niches are that the competition is not filling.

This analysis must be matched with the environmental trends, the competitive and demand analysis, the property needs analysis, and the internal analysis. We would, of course, combine all these analyses by segment and target market. We are then ready to develop a mission statement for the property, determine opportunities, establish objectives, and begin the actual marketing plan, which will include a plan and course of action for each segment or target market.

The Mission Statement

In the previous chapter we discussed developing a mission statement for strategic planning. The mission statement of the marketing plan flows from the strategic mission statement and differs only in that it applies at the unit level (this could be an individual hotel or restaurant, or even an F&B outlet within a hotel, or a particular lounge or catering endeavor within a restaurant). It is the strategic planning mission statement that will guide initial efforts in developing the marketing plan—that is, the data collection and analysis.

Some people recommend that all marketing plan efforts begin with a mission statement. We do not necessarily recommend this, if the general guideline of the strategic mission statement serves the purpose. In an individual property, of course, the two are

TABLE 21-3   Marketing Plan Mission Statement

Mission Statement
Ala Moana Americana, Honolulu

The Ala Moana Americana is a first-class hotel located between Honolulu's business section and the Waikiki tourist area. There is no first-class hotel closer to the business section and Honolulu's special event areas. The hotel is adjacent to Hawaii's largest shopping center with 155 stores.

To be successful, the hotel must be No. 1 to Honolulu's business traveler, airline crews, Japanese special campaigns, Kamaaina individuals, and Kamaaina groups. These markets should be supplemented by Japanese package series business, government employees, special events, and one-shot group business.

The Ala Moana must have authentic Hawaiian atmosphere, entrance, decor, and uniformity. It should be known for its Hawaiian style service (language, dress, fruit, flowers, and special touches).

When Japanese and U.S. F.I.T. demand slackens in the Waikiki area, the hotel is vulnerable to competition and loses significant business to the first-class Waikiki hotels. During these periods, it must depend on its major market segments and get one-shot group business. The hotel's rooms product must be designed and maintained to meet the needs of its four major market segments. There is a potential F.I.T. market of frequent Hawaii visitors and stopover business.

Because of the hotel's difficult competitive position for tourist room business and its high vulnerability to tourist fall-off, the food and beverage outlets offer the only major opportunity for revenue growth. These outlets must appeal to its local community; however, they must be flexible enough to meet its room guest requirements as well.

The Ala Moana must be known by its employees as the "best hotel in Honolulu to work in." Its employees should have the Aloha Spirit and should communicate that spirit to each other and to the guest.

---

probably one and the same. In multiunit organizations, however, there can be great variety. For example, Goodyear Tire and Rubber Company can establish a corporate strategy for selling tires. Marketing plans can follow that strategy. Markets will be different, and the plans will so indicate, but the product and the usage will be the same.

The same does not hold true in the hospitality industry, for the most part. For Four Seasons Hotels, it may, but many chains have diversified products selling in diversified markets for diversified uses. Corporate strategies established in corporate headquarters in Memphis, Phoenix, New York, Hampton (NH), Paris, or Tokyo do not necessarily fit the situation in India, Germany, Kuwait, New York City, Minneapolis, or Los Angeles.

The local strategic mission statement will flow from the corporate one with some adjustment to the local scene. It is the situation analysis of the marketing plan, however, as previously stated, that provides the test of the strategy and may necessitate rewriting the local mission statement. Thus, only after the situation analysis has been completed do we recommend writing the marketing plan mission statement and, if necessary, adjusting the

TABLE 21-3   (continued)

Financial Goals

	Occupancy	Avgerage Rate	Room Revenue	Food Revenue	Beverage Revenue
'79	86.4%	$30.16	$11,357,300	$5,757,000	$2,194,000
'80	87.0%	32.14	12,186,000	6,670,000	2,632,800
'81	87.0%	35.00	13,270,400	7,670,000	3,036,000

Assumptions:
1. Major Market Segments—The sales and marketing efforts of the hotel are geared toward the following market segments:
    a. Airline Crews
    b. Japanese Special Campaigns
    c. Yes We Can
    d. Government
    e. Kamaaina
2. Rooms Rehab Program will continue as planned.
3. Food & Beverage Department—A master plan to reconceptualize total Food and Beverage outlets is being prepared in order to update and gear the operation toward the markets identified. This effort, in connection with increased sales and marketing efforts, will increase the growth in the Food & Beverage Department over the next several years.
4. Room Supply—Additional hotel rooms in the area are planned as follows:
    1978
    440 Rooms   Cinerama Reef Hotel-Waikiki Tower
    1979
    650 Rooms   Hawaiian Regent
    360 Rooms   Ala Wai Sunset Seaside Towers
    630 Rooms   Hawaiian Princess
    495 Rooms   Pacific Beach Hotel

Source: Michael A. Leven, "How to Develop Marketing Strategies," *Lodging,* March 1980, p. 14.

strategic mission statement. Recall, moreover, that the latter is your long-term mission; the marketing plan mission is designed for one year at a time.

We make this distinction emphatically because we have seen it done the other way so many times (for example, with Nikko and Parker Meridien above), following which the marketing plan is less than optimal. Recall, from the beginning of this chapter, that strategy decisions work from the bottom up; management decisions work from the top down. Too often it is done the other way. Probably the most flagrant abuse of this principle, at least in the hotel industry, is in pricing strategies, as we have shown in a number of examples.

Therefore, once you have done the situation analysis, it is now time to write the marketing plan mission statement if it should differ from the strategic mission statement. There is no need to discuss these further. Instead, Table 21-3 is presented as an individual unit mission statement that will drive the marketing plan for that hotel.

This mission statement is an excellent case in point. Americana Hotels had a very diversified set of properties. Each one required its own particular mission statement for its own particular product and market.

Opportunity Analysis

If a thorough job of data collection and analysis has been done, we should now be able to determine the opportunities available. The section heading is self-explanatory and can only be discussed by example. Therefore, we abstract from the marketing plan of the Belgian hotel previously mentioned, as shown below.

OPPORTUNITIES

A. Market segments relating to existing customer mix:
    1. Company groups
    2. Company residential seminars
    3. Company individual bookings
    4. Leisure tours
    5. Leisure clubs and societies
    6. Weekend packages
    7. Travel agents
    8. Walk-ins
B. New markets
    1. Winter packages for individual travelers
    2. Netherlands bank travel agencies
    3. Incentive market
    4. Magazine holiday or minitrip packages
    5. Incoming travel agencies
C. Image
    1. More professional and colorful F&B promotions
    2. Improved reputation of service and cuisine
    3. Provide better background information about city
    4. Renovations to improve image of bar, sauna, and swimming pool terrace
    5. Professional advertising to improve hotel image

The above opportunities, although perhaps too general, have been derived after analysis of the market, market segments, the competition, trends, the needs of the property, and so forth. Its brief form belies the groundwork that goes into identifying opportunities. Sometimes this groundwork is not done—that is, someone says something like, "How about the incentive market? We don't have any of that business. That's an opportunity! Let's put it down." Of course, a thorough study of the incentive market, its needs and wants, and the organization's ability to serve them is necessary first. Opportunities, in the true sense, are not just something that's "out there"; they are, instead, a match between consumer needs and an organization's competencies, and, one hopes, a lapse in the competition.

Consider, for example, the marketing plan for a hotel in Brazil. This hotel was being buffeted on all sides by a declining economy, rampant inflation, movement of industry out of the area, new hotel construction, vicious price cutting, and declining markets—in other words, the hotel was in a serious situation, to say the least. Following are excerpts from the marketing plan to counter this, with some of our questions in brackets.

- Service will differentiate us from existing or new hotels [Are you sure? Does the customer agree?]
- We will provide progressive discounts for a total of six visits over four months, with the second stay offering 10 percent off rack rate, and each subsequent stay (up to six) offering an additional 5 percent off. These rates will not be commissionable. [When no one is paying rack rate to begin with, will this really work? What will be the problems keeping track of it? Will it negate travel agent business?]
- Because 37 percent of package business is booked within the city, and 24 percent of these guests originate here, we could develop a new package and have it displayed in the city's largest supermarket, and other shopping centers. [Are these the places to reach weekend package buyers? Will they even notice?]

In short, this marketing plan was essentially "grasping at straws" rather than being a detailed situation and opportunity analysis.

One way to find opportunities through lapses in the competition is with positioning analysis, as discussed in Chapter 10. For example, consider the incentive travel market. We could take the major needs and wants of this market and place them on a ten-point scale of importance. We could then plot each need against the ability to fulfill them, on another ten-point scale, for both our organization and our major competitors for the same market. We can do the same for other specific target markets. When these scales are plotted on perceptual maps, it is relatively easy to visualize where needs and competencies match, or do not, and the same for the competition.

Objectives

The next step in the marketing plan is to establish the objectives and how they are to be accomplished. Again, this is better explained by doing, so we continue to abstract from the marketing plan of the Belgian hotel.

OBJECTIVES AND METHODS

A. To increase yearly occupancy
   1. Review annual forecast on a monthly and weekly basis to ensure an overall and continuous view of occupancies and early actions in case of problem periods or days
   2. Orient the room rate structure to the market
   3. Conduct permanent hard and aggressive sales actions to increase
      a. company and commercial rate business
      b. seminars and conferences, especially in summer and winter
      c. winter and summer weekend business with families

        d. incentive travel year-round

        e. tour business and stopovers, especially in off-season

B. To keep up with the competition

    1. Provide color and cable television

    2. Hospitality service and well-trained staff

    3. Continuous sales follow-up on existing clients

    4. Continuous sales calls to potential new customers

    5. Improve restaurant image

    6. Offer clients "just a little more" in rooms and restaurant, which will make their stay with us different from the others

    7. Refurbish bar (if possible enlarge)

    8. Develop more creativity in sales and F&B

C. To level out occupancy throughout the year

    1. Develop attractive (but not bargain) offers during weak periods for seminars and conferences

    2. Develop winter packages for individuals

    3. Provide seasonal rates for bus tours

    4. Develop new initiatives, such as room here and lunch in Bruges

    5. Develop incentive tour arrangements

    6. Promote Sunday night business to tour operators and wholesalers

D. To level out occupancy over the week

    1. Lower rate for winter seminars during the week

    2. Develop packages for individuals to be distributed to German and Netherlands travel agents with special commission rates

    3. Create special activities for tour operators to sell in United Kingdom, Germany, and the Netherlands

E. To increase average rate

    1. Increase company rates

    2. Increase bus tour rates

    3. Increase rates in the commercial business market

    4. Appeal more to walk-in guests with roadside advertising

    5. Build higher rate in luxury rooms through luxury room amenities

    6. Try to reduce low-rate contracts during high season

    7. Charge supplement on group rates on special event weekends

F. To increase F&B sales by

    1. Appealing more to in-house guests through

        a. promotional material in rooms, lobby, reception, and other guest service areas

        b. vouchers for first drink in bar at reduced rate

        c. food promotion frames inside and in front of elevators

        d. sales-trained people in bar, restaurant, and coffee shop

        e. dinner dance twice a week during winter

        f. more eye-catchers in restaurant and coffee shop

        g. training desk clerks to ask at check-in if guests want to reserve table in restaurant

2. Developing the local market through promotions
   a. candlelight dinner dance promotions
   b. Sunday family brunch
   c. wedding promotions
   d. charity dinners
   e. promotions for staff parties
   f. funeral banquet promotions through funeral agents
   g. attract companies in the neighborhood, e.g., with a sandwich bar
   h. more organized activities

The objectives listed above are specific and fairly typical of hotel marketing plans. Action plans are designed to carry out each one. There could be many other kinds of objectives, particularly those that derive from the identification of market needs, such as these:

- changes in marketing direction
- defensive or offensive marketing moves
- new opportunities
- other specific product line objectives
- market share objectives—overall and by market segment, such as geographic, demographic, psychographic, group, FIT, package, etc.
- pricing objectives
- sales and promotion objectives
- advertising objectives
- channel, distribution, and intermediary objectives, such as travel agents
- research objectives
- awareness, perception, image, and positioning objectives
- double occupancy objectives
- customer loyalty and repeat business objectives
- customer satisfaction objectives

We caution again not to try to do too many things at once. Make objectives reasonable, so they can be accomplished and can be done well.

A marketing plan needs to be employed for existing customers as well. These customers may, in fact, be the best opportunity and the target of the most important objectives. This part of the plan addresses current patrons, and should be designed to make them "competition proof." Because the main emphasis of the marketing plan will be on capturing competitors' business, so too will be the emphasis of competitors' marketing plans. If the focus is entirely on bringing in new customers and the present customers are forgotten, then the marketing plan is simply going to be one of robbing Peter to pay Paul. Replacing current customers with new customers is never cost-efficient.

Marriott and Holiday Corporation have developed plans to solve problems of their guests with in-house hot-line systems by which guests can get immediate attention to problems. Holiday also offers rebates on the spot if the customer is dissatisfied and management does not fix the problem. Action plans will vary with the local establishment, be it a restaurant, lounge, or hotel.

A documented plan to keep guests coming back and to reduce exposure to competitors' attempts to steal customers should be an integral part of any marketing plan. Once again, however, this does not necessarily mean giveaway programs. The basic task of marketing is to fulfill its promises, not give away the product. A customer should not have to join a "club" or even be a frequent guest to have guaranteed reservations or quick check-in or check-out.[3]

Action Plans

Action plans dictate how the marketing plan will be carried out. They assign specific responsibility to individuals and dates for accomplishment. An action plan is a detailed list of the action steps necessary for carrying out the strategies and tactics for reaching each objective. One format for an action plan is shown in Table 21-4, but there are numerous variations on the theme.

Action plans deal with the various parts of the marketing mix, which, of course, is the implementation of the marketing plan. For example, the action plan for the communications mix would incorporate advertising, direct mail, personal sales efforts, promotions, merchandising, and public relations campaigns. Each of these is coordinated for maximum impact of the strategies that are derived from the conclusions drawn from the creation of business and competitive strategies section of the plan.

The action plan should be developed for a full year, with all products and actions for new business, keeping current business, and strategies for taking business from competitors outlined in time frames that reflect achievable goals.

In the previous example of the murder mystery weekend, advertising support may be necessary in designated months to create awareness and requests for more information. An ad in a meeting magazine might be in support of a special meeting package, designed to counter a competitor's offering during the traditionally slower months in the fall. An advertisement in a travel agency index might be intended to offer an alternative to competition, at present more frequently utilized by travel agencies.

Yearly schedules for other support mechanisms of the communications mix are needed to coordinate the entire plan. A direct mail campaign might be used in conjunction with the advertising for the murder mystery weekend to generate the highest volume. Without action plans, too many things are forgotten too often, or are done too late to be effective.

There are other concerns as well. The communications mix is expensive to execute. The aggressive marketing executive will constantly be looking for ways to maximize communications mix dollars. Co-advertising is possible with related travel industries. Airlines are increasingly willing to work with hotels to generate business through col-

---

[3] Our mention throughout of guaranteed reservations being a given for every single customer has ignored the problem of no-shows and the resulting need to "overbook" rather than lose revenue. This is a serious problem and we do not treat it lightly. On the other hand, there are many ways to deal with the problem (beyond the scope of this book) and hotels have become quite adept at doing so. For one, American Express reservations are guaranteed at no loss to the hotel, thus minimizing risk. Regardless, the damage done by "walking" customers can be far greater than a night's revenue.

TABLE 21-4 Marketing Plan Action Plan

OBJECTIVE/GOAL

_____
_____
_____

STRATEGIES

A. _____
_____
_____
_____

B. _____
_____
_____
_____

C. _____
_____
_____
_____

ACTION STEPS	Person Responsible	Beginning Date	Targeted Completion Date	Actual Completion Date	Estimated Cost

Amount of Risk/Return   Other Departments Involved in Action Program
Estimated Cost $_____   _____
                                  _____
Estimated Return $_____   _____
                                  _____

lective advertising and direct mail. Credit card companies are doing dual promotions with restaurants and lounges on a consistent basis to differentiate their products and combine resources. All these efforts require considerable advance planning and specific actions being done on time.

Except for forecasts and budgeting, the marketing plan is now complete. Remember, this should be a "fluid" document, ready to be changed with shifts of the marketplace. This is not to suggest that the entire marketing plan be rewritten every time there is a shift in the market; if the situation analysis was done properly, the conclusions drawn should not change readily or dramatically.

Some opportunities, however, that present themselves during the year should be incorporated into an effective marketing plan. If an opportunity arose to do a combined direct mail piece to selected guests of a reputable credit card company, it should not be passed up just because it's not in the marketing plan. The plan should be analyzed and resources reallocated if necessary.

The Marketing Forecast

Making accurate marketing forecasts is one of the most difficult stages of the marketing plan. Regardless, the best attempt possible is essential. Forecasts are a venture into the unknown that are subject to any number of alterations in the marketplace. The answer to accuracy lies in the best information available, thorough analysis, and the best judgment of the forecaster.

Many hotel marketing plan formats require the projection of room nights for every day of the forthcoming year. We believe this is a "make-work" type of project, which bears no real fruit. The only real information that one has is confirmed group bookings and history. We prefer to make forecasts by important time periods instead, plus the overall forecast for the year.

These time periods may be seasonal, monthly, days of the week, or some combination thereof. They should definitely be by market segment, grouped together by room rate or average check. Traditional percentages can be used to forecast beverage sales and certain food sales except where special marketing efforts are planned to increase those sales.

It is not uncommon for forecasters to use some figure, say 5 percent, as the projected increase in sales over the previous year. Such a method is purely arbitrary and of little advantage. It is better to start with a zero base each year and build according to the marketing plan. In this way, room nights, covers, and other sources of revenue are based on the marketing objectives that have been realistically established. Monetary amounts such as average room rate per segment, average breakfast, lunch, and dinner check, and so on are used as the multipliers to forecast revenue.

Table 21-5 on pages 600–601 illustrates a forecast form used by one hotel company. Again, there are many variations on the theme according to the particular situation or needs of the operation.

The Marketing Budget

Industry-wide averages in 1985 for the marketing budgets of U.S. hotels were 5.7 percent of total sales. (There are no reported averages for restaurants except a general figure of 2 to 3 percent of sales spent on advertising for an individual sit-down mid-to-upper scale operation.) As a rule of thumb, the payroll expenses are normally about 4 percent of the total payroll, and 1 percent of the total revenue. Traditionally, resorts have slightly higher marketing expenses. The overall trend in the industry has been toward increasing the marketing budget as a total percentage of sales.[4]

An actual brief description of a marketing budget follows for an 1100-room convention chain hotel in a major U.S. city.

Sales revenues	$50 million
Marketing budget	$2.5 million
Includes: wages, supplies, advertising, direct mail, public relations, entertainment, national sales offices support, travel	
Sales staff: 1 director of marketing, 2 directors of sales, 8 sales managers	
Local advertising	$180,000
Support of chain's frequent traveler program	$400,000

Internationally, the expenses for marketing average slightly lower, at 4.1 percent of total sales for 1985. Latin America and Caribbean hotels spend over 5 percent of sales for their marketing budget, while hotels in Europe and the Middle East spend under 4 percent of their total sales.[5]

Unfortunately, these industry averages mean very little in the increasingly competitive environment that has been created in the hospitality industry. The traditional 5 percent of hotel sales allocated to marketing was sufficient for a property to maintain its market share and occupancies consistently in the days when the increase in demand for hotel rooms was exceeding the number of rooms being built.

While demand continues to be strong for the lodging product, supply of the product in many markets has eclipsed the growth curve. Some markets are facing a 20-plus percent increase in supply of hotel rooms, with a 5 percent increase in demand. More important, for marketing planning, what is taking place is a shift in the market into different product classes. To attack a problem of this kind with a traditional marketing budget of 5 percent of total sales would be like David fighting Goliath. (Recall, however, that David won, with a better strategy.)

The marketing budget should be a natural extension of the marketing plan—no more and no less. Once a strategy has been developed to create, steal, or keep customers, the funds need to be allocated to ensure success. The actual budget consists of two areas—payroll and expenses.

The budget will normally include the following categories in some degree, regardless of the size or type of the operation. This even includes a case in which, for example,

---

[4] *Trends in the Hotel Industry USA Edition 1986,* published by Pannell Kerr Forster Worldwide, New York, N.Y.
[5] *Trends in the Hotel Industry International Edition 1986,* published by Pannell Kerr Forster, New York, N.Y.

TABLE 21-5 Hotel Occupancy Forecasting Form, by Month

	LAST YEAR ACTUAL Rooms Occupied	LAST YEAR ACTUAL Average Rate	LAST YEAR ACTUAL Revenues	BUDGET Revenues	BUDGET Average Rate	BUDGET Rooms Rented	J	F	M
Pure/Transient									
Meeting Conv.									
Tour & Travel									
Individual									
Wholesaler									
Group									
Total Tour & Travel									
Contract									
Charter									
Other									
Total Contract									

Commercial										
Preferred Co.										
Pref. Guest										
Other										
Total Commercial										
Special Programs										
W/E Package										
Other										
Other										
Other										
Other										
TOTALS										
Rooms Avail.										
% of Occ.										

601

the manager of a restaurant (chain, individual, or within a hotel) performs all the marketing and sales duties. Parts of that person's salary and expenses should be allocated to the marketing budget.

Payroll will include all marketing and sales time plus any secretarial or related work.
Communication includes all advertising, promotion, direct mail, public relations, collateral, and related items.
Travel includes all related travel.
Office expenses include telephone and related office supplies.
Research includes all research expenses.
Entertainment includes entertainment of clients or prospective clients both in-house and out.

The above are broad and fairly obvious categories. Further breakdown depends on the needs of the operation. What is important is that marketing expenses be clearly and appropriately assigned. As with any other budget items, they are a cost of operating a particular department. Table 21-6 shows one hotel's monthly spread sheet for allocating particular expenses to a given month.

The budget should be carefully prepared, not done haphazardly or by guesswork. If you are not your own boss, you will probably have to have it approved by someone. In that case, you may have to justify each cost item as one that will produce tangible results.

The marketing budget should also be a fluid tool, reacting to the changes in the marketing plan. It is critical to protect the integrity of the budget and plan throughout the planning year. The plan and budget should be changed if results are falling short of forecasts. For instance, the murder mystery weekend might be considered cost-effective if it produced 50 rooms for a given Friday and Saturday night. If after three or four attempts, the demand never exceeds 35 rooms nights, the responsive marketing team will reevaluate the feasibility of the project.

The decision might be to try the promotion again at a later date, or to scrap it altogether and allocate the funds elsewhere. The difficult decisions when cutting the marketing budget occur when managers think only in short-term objectives (i.e., improving short-term financial performance by cutting costs) rather than execute longer-term strategies to increase and retain customers.

This type of situation occurs frequently in the careers of sales and marketing professionals. Although there is no clear-cut answer to the dilemma, the need to create and keep customers should be the paramount consideration for any successful organization. Short-term rewards are gained too many times at the expense of future business.

Marketing Controls

There is a final step and an important one—monitoring the marketing plan throughout the year and evaluating it at the end of the year.

The first step, of course, is to continuously match performance against the desired results and to detect when and where deviations occur. The extent of each deviation should be measured and the worst ones addressed. The cause of the deviation should be determined and dealt with either by bringing it into line, or by adjusting the plan.

TABLE 21-6   Monthly Spread Sheet for Allocating Expenses

	Dates	Market Segment	Costs
Sales Trips/Trade Shows			
Washington (WSAE)	5/82	Group	$1000.00
Atlanta/Delta & Agents	5/82	T&T/Whlslrs	500.00
Incentive House Trip	5/82	T&T	1400.00
Advertising			
Hotel Trvl Index 1 pg 4 c	Quarterly	T&T	1805.83
Fla Resident Ad 2 col 5″	1 week	Special	1350.00
Southern Living 4″ ad	Monthly	Trans.	518.35
Airport Display	Monthly	Trans.	1305.60
Travel Agent Mktplc	Bi-monthly	T&T	777.75
Trvl Weekly 20″ 4c	6×	T&T	2391.80
F&B Advertising			
Fla Tour. News	6×	F&B	271.19
Orlando Mag ½ pg BW	Monthly	F&B	420.75
Dining Out 1 pg BW	Monthly	F&B	152.00
Orlando Sentinel	5×	F&B	1520.00
Local News	1×	F&B	125.00
Special Promotions			
Mother's Day Coll. & Menu	Annual	F&B	300.00
Samantha's Calendar	Monthly	F&B	125.00
Direct Mail			
Bus. Reply	Ongoing	Group	1000.00
Samantha's Mailing	Monthly	F&B	50.00
Mother's Day Mailing	Annual	F&B	50.00
Collateral Proration			
5000 Rack Brochures	Ongoing	Group	500.00
5000 IT Brochures	Ongoing	T&T	500.00
7000 F&B Brochures	Ongoing	F&B	500.00

Yardsticks are set up in advance. These could include any of the following as well as others: market share, occupancy figures, covers served, seat turnovers, check averages, F&B ratios, revenue per guest room, average room rate by segment, product mix, business mix by segments, advance bookings, advertising results, return per marketing dollar, customer satisfaction, complaints/compliments, repeat business, revenue, and profit.

A feedback system should be established to synchronize with the yardsticks. You should be able to answer questions such as the following:

- Is the product meeting needs of the segment(s)?
- Is the segment growing, static, or declining?
- Is the segment profitable?
- Is customer perception as intended?
- Is your positioning correct?
- How are you doing vis-à-vis the competition?
- Are you solving consumers' problems?
- Are weaknesses showing?
- Are strengths being exploited?
- Is there price resistance?
- Are you having selling problems?
- What are the reasons for the variances?

You may have to make changes where necessary and/or move in contingency plans. You may have to reanalyze your strategy or your plan, or perform a new situation analysis. Marketing plans are not static, but dynamic; they operate under dynamic conditions and must be monitored in the same way.

Summary

The marketing plan and the marketing budget are fluid tools designed to create, capture, and retain customers. The process begins early in the year and continues until fall. It is based on a sound and realistic situation analysis, which requires good data collection, research where necessary, and acute analysis. Instead of relying on traditional methods to deal with unique situations, the marketing team needs to develop innovative strategies based on solid information. The funding of these strategies must then be realistic, to get the job done. The following is final checklist for developing a good marketing plan.

1. Keep good records. A situation analysis requires knowing what is happening and what has happened. The future is not necessarily built on the past, but neither should one repeat the same mistakes or reinvent the wheel. Good records identify strengths and weaknesses as well as opportunities and threats.
2. Allow sufficient time. Detailed analysis and planning are required, with ample time for the thought process to work. This is not done overnight.
3. Obtain cooperation from other departments to provide information in a useful form. Other departments are part of the information system that must be utilized.
4. Critically analyze the data, both qualitative and quantitative. Be realistic and totally objective. What do the figures really mean? Be certain to feed in information from customers and from marketing research.
5. Leave time to develop the plan and strategies, and then to analyze them. This should not be a crash job to meet a deadline.
6. Develop a plan that will ensure participation of the entire management team and, in turn, the entire work force. Marketing plans are not just for marketing departments;

they're for everyone. The greatest failure of good marketing plans usually lies in the failure of execution.

7. Make sure there is a control feedback loop in the plan so you will know immediately when it breaks down.

A final word: The marketing-driven organization must not be susceptible to a short-term mentality that will eventually lose customers. The marketing budget and plan should be adjusted according to the customers, not the accountants. To do otherwise is not unlike deferring maintenance to improve short-term bottom line figures, and then having to buy new equipment at some time in the future. Even so, accountants must have their say. Thus, plans and budgets must ultimately stand the test of concrete cost-effective results and proven revenues.

DISCUSSION QUESTIONS

1. Discuss the key differences between strategic marketing and marketing management in the development of the marketing plan.
2. Formulate a situation analysis for a restaurant or hotel where you have worked or with which you are familiar. Analyze the internal and external factors.
3. Construct a detailed property needs analysis for the same restaurant or hotel that will form the basis of a marketing plan.
4. Develop an internal marketing plan for a real or hypothetical hotel or restaurant.
5. Why is the realistic and objective analysis of the data collection critical to a successful marketing plan? Discuss. What happens when this is lacking?
6. Write a mission statement for the restaurant or hotel analyzed in question 2.

CHAPTER 22

International Marketing

Throughout this text we have provided examples of marketing situations in international arenas. We have done this not so much because these examples become different in an international context, but because they are similar. In fact, the basic principles of marketing are no different wherever you go; they always involve the needs and wants and problems of consumers. Likewise, the concepts of positioning, segmentation, and marketing planning or strategy are no different. What changes, of course, are the consumers. In essence, then, international marketing does not involve any changes in marketing concepts; instead, it involves understanding the changes in consumers.

We do not minimize other factors that vary from country to country. Distribution systems, political influences, and even the way of doing business will affect the marketing of hospitality from one country to another. These factors, however, impose constraints upon marketing (or, in some cases, remove them), rather than alter basic marketing principles. To substantiate this point we analyzed many hospitality marketing situations in a number of different countries. We dissected each one to see whether it was unique to the particular national situation—that is, to see whether it was different from what it would have been in the United States. It was difficult to find any cases that, transposed into a U.S. situation, were not similar to situations faced in the United States.

The greatest differences reflect not differences in basic marketing, but differences in culture, on the one hand, and the need for marketers to recognize differences, on the other hand. For instance, here are two examples of (1) not specifying and understanding the target market, and (2) influencing the target market.

> In France, as in the United States, the best time to eat asparagus is in the spring when it is fresh. For asparagus lovers this is a much-awaited time of the year. Asparagus is a vegetable that does not freeze well and aficionados relish it when it is fresh. The only

difference between France and the United States is that in France the asparagus is white; in the United States it is green.

It didn't seem unnatural, then, that a French hotel company would proclaim "Asparagus Week" as a promotion. What did seem far-fetched was that all hotels in the chain were prompted to join in this celebration. Hotels worldwide were urged to hang a banner in the lobby announcing the occasion. Menus featured everything from asparagus soufflés to asparagus desserts.

In Dubai, Abu Dhabi, Jeddah, and Kuwait, however, where this hotel chain had properties, native people hardly knew what asparagus was, let alone relishing it. Expatriates in these areas may have known asparagus and perhaps would have been the target market of the promotion. Instead, the result was much wasted effort, a confused clientele, and a promotion that failed.

On the other hand, such promotions can work if they are implemented locally by a marketing team that understands the market and does the appropriate public relations work. In Singapore, the Sheraton Century Park runs a Belgian Gastronomique Festival in August in one of its restaurants. There aren't many Belgians in Singapore, but the promotion is successful enough to warrant bringing in chef Pierrot of Brussels's Chez Pierrot au Surcouf, his sous chef, and over a ton of fresh basil, rosemary, sea bass, turbot—and asparagus. The promotion was implemented locally.

Whatever is hard to come by, is seasonal, and is available only in limited quantities makes excellent promotional material—but only if one understands how to promote it to the target market.

The same hotel company that failed with asparagus in Saudi Arabia designed a Christmas card picturing a Christmas tree surrounded by snow to be used by all its hotels, worldwide, to send to their customers. Fortunately, an alert sales manager of Lebanese descent caught it and informed corporate of its tactical error. Production was halted before the card was printed and sent out to the large Moslem clientele of this chain, who don't celebrate Christmas, and traditionally and historically oppose Christianity.

These are not differences in marketing. Rather, they point out the necessity of knowing your market. Obviously, anyone would know this. Why then did the largest company in the world, General Motors, promote the Chevrolet Nova in Spain and Puerto Rico? *No va* in Spanish means "it doesn't go."

The main thrust of this chapter, then, is not to tell you that international marketing is different, but to reemphasize that you have to know your market.

Having said that, we immediately revert to a defensive position. No company should be so naive as to not find out what "nova" means in Spanish, or that asparagus is unknown in Saudi Arabia, or that Moslems don't celebrate Christmas. But what do you do when your customer mix originates in the following countries, as does that of an American hotel chain's property in Brazil: United States, Canada, Mexico, Belgium, England, France, Germany, Holland, Italy, Portugal, Spain, Sweden, Switzerland, Latin America, the Caribbean, Australia, China, Japan, and Africa, not to mention "others," or Brazilians? Obviously, this makes for an entirely different picture, and yet some say that hospitality marketing is no different from goods marketing!

In recent years many American hospitality companies have gone international: Hilton, Hyatt, Marriott, Sheraton, Ramada (now owned by an Asian company), Holiday Inns, Quality, Days Inn and McDonald's, Burger King, Kentucky Fried Chicken, and Pizza

Hut. Many foreign hospitality companies have come to America: Accor (France), Meridien (France), Trusthouse Forte (England), Penta (England), and Nikko (Japan). Oberoi (India) is in the Middle East, as is Meridien; Mandarin (Hong Kong) is in Singapore and Bangkok; Trusthouse Forte is all over the world, and is expanding. In short, the hospitality industry, especially the hotel branch, has gone international. This means not only understanding the national market in which one locates, but also understanding the international traveler, who comes from many diverse geographical locations and cultures. This chapter will deal with some of those diversities.

Marketing decisions relevant to marketing principles remain the same in whatever country one does business. It is the environment in which these decisions are made that remains unique, determines the outcome, and makes international marketing different from marketing in one's home country. To illustrate this we will discuss various environmental issues, providing examples along the way.

The Economic Environment

Of all environmental concerns, the economic environment may be the most universally critical to the company doing business in foreign lands. It is the economic environment that opens doors to opportunities, and also closes them. This is because countries differ greatly in areas of growth rate, consumer consumption, and discretionary income.

Interestingly, American hotel companies that have gone abroad have almost always aimed at the top end of the market. Even Ramada and Holiday Corp., in general, did not aim at the same market level abroad as they did in the United States. Best Western is a notable exception to this rule, as is, more recently, Quality International.

There is good reason for this. These companies, traditionally, have targeted the international traveler abroad. In many cases, at least initially, this was largely the American expense account business traveler. Inter-Continental began as a subsidiary of Pan American Airways, and the first hotels were located at major destination points of the airline. When Hilton International became a subsidiary of Trans World Airlines the same practice was followed.

These companies were able to stay more or less "above" the economic vicissitudes of the countries in which they operated. Labor and operating costs were usually much lower than in America, while rates charged were based on American levels. Foreign business travelers also accepted these rates, because those who traveled either were on expense accounts or had ample means. The American tourist abroad paid the price to "feel at home away from home."

Changes in the Economy and the Market

As the economies of many countries grew stronger, particularly those of developing nations that had not previously developed their own upscale hotel chains, the situation began to change. Essentially, two things happened. The first was that foreign developers joined the game. Many at first brought in American companies to manage their properties. Eventually, they developed their own chains, also initially in the upscale market.

The second thing that happened was that the traveler changed. Persons of lower income or not on expense accounts began to travel. These people resisted the high prices of the upscale hotels and searched for alternatives. Americans especially no longer felt that they had to stay at an "American" hotel. The result has been that many of these hotels have had to learn to adjust to the local economy. An example is the Hilton International in Paris. This hotel priced and geared to the American market; when the American market fell apart in 1986, management realized that it had shut out much of the European market.

Hilton International was affected by other economic forces in Sao Paulo, Brazil. In this case, the local currency devalued at an incredibly high inflation rate. The economy weakened and international travelers no longer came to Sao Paulo in the same numbers. Hilton was forced to turn to the Brazilian market but this also had suffered. Companies in Rio de Janeiro persuaded airlines to add more morning and evening flights to Sao Paulo, a one-hour flight, so that business travelers could return in the same day. At the same time, new hotels opened with wealthy, prestige-seeking owners who were willing to cut prices to the bone in order to obtain business.

The collapse of the oil market in the mid-1980s had the same effect in the Middle East. International hotel companies, not just American ones, found themselves with few customers more than the airline crews they could capture. Although international hotel companies have always had to grapple with the intricacies of monetary exchange rates, they have only recently had to confront them at the local level. The environment has forced these companies to seek more national customers of the countries in which they operate, and such customers are less able to pay. Thus, the Maurya Sheraton in New Delhi, a five-star hotel that thrived on the diplomatic market due to its proximity to major embassies, decided to go after the "second level" of business traveler with a flexible rate policy.

Consider the case of another hotel in New Delhi. Over the five-year period from 1982 to 1986, the following changes occurred in its customer mix. American business declined from 17,155 to 11,873 room nights, and American occupancy declined from 19.1 percent to 17 percent. Italian business increased from 3.1 percent to 5.5 percent occupancy, while Japanese business increased from 8.3 percent to 14.5 percent. At the same time Indian business increased from 12 percent to 18.7 percent.

Hotel companies of countries other than the United States have also tended to enter foreign markets at the upper end of the scale. In fact, it is difficult to think of major companies that have done otherwise. An exception is Accor of France. This company took its two- and three-star concepts into neighboring European countries as well as to the United States, under the names of Ibis and Novotel. This may well be the forerunner of the future, as economic conditions continue to change.

There are many countries without sufficient satisfactory middle-tier hotel accommodations to serve the market, countries as diverse as Finland and India. Residents of these countries, as well as international travelers who visit them in increasing numbers, must often choose between top-rate hotels or less-than-desirable facilities. Quality International, Days Inn, and Accor of France are three companies moving to take advantage of these opportunities.

In Spain, Sol Hotels bought a chain of thirty-three hotels that had been taken over and run by the government, in order to move into the lower three-star and four-star categories. Although customer mix is 80 percent Spanish, Sol has had a problem with its position in foreign markets because of this move.

The Macroeconomy

Economically speaking, what happens is this. When the macroeconomic environment of a country is in high gear, companies from other nations see opportunities to enter new markets. For a goods company (e.g., Procter & Gamble) major marketing decisions (assuming a market exists) center on the name and communication and distribution strategies. For a hotel company the situation is more complex. First comes finding a developer. Contract negotiations and site location can easily take a year or more. Construction to opening can easily take three years or more. Hyatt, for example, has "built" a hotel in Jerusalem for thirteen years, as its developer periodically ran out of funds.

In the meanwhile, the macroeconomic environment is probably changing, slowly if not drastically. If the economy has declined, the market picture has changed as well and the marketing plan has to be altered accordingly. High-priced goods and services tend to suffer more in a declining economy. Conversely, McDonald's and Burger King have done well in international markets in spite of weak economies. It is the long-term perspective that must be kept in mind.

Hotel companies turned to the Taiwanese tourist market in the Philippines when that country's economy soured. This is a low-price market but it supported some hotels when they needed it most. With the economy on the rise, the marketer must now decide whether to continue to serve this market in the event it is needed again in the future.

Many countries have governments that threaten the hotel industry with their protectionist legislation. The Singapore industry, for example, was devastated when exit taxes (taxes that natives have to pay to leave the country) were implemented by three of its ASEAN neighbors in 1982 and 1983. Indonesia introduced a 25,000 rupiah exit tax in March 1982 and increased it in November. Visitation to Singapore was reduced by 35 percent of the previous 455,000 visitors a year. In 1986, the exit tax was increased to 250,000 rupiah, virtually wiping out the Indonesian market. The Philippines and Thailand had similar damaging exit taxes.

In France, a currency regulation was introduced in 1983, purportedly as an economic measure to promote domestic tourism and contain the export of French francs. This was reported to have reduced the number of French people traveling abroad by over a million.

Currency fluctuations also greatly affect the traveling market. We have recently seen travel "reverses" as the dollar strengthens and more Americans go to Europe; when it reverses and weakens, more Europeans come to the United States. It is the relative strength of one currency against another that is the critical factor.

Devaluation of the Hong Kong dollar, the French franc, the Australian dollar, the New Zealand dollar, and the Filipino peso in 1985 placed Singapore out of reach for many tourists from other countries. The country's attraction as a shopping destination was greatly reduced for Australians and Europeans. Package wholesalers were forced to look for cheaper stopover cities because Singapore accommodation costs had gone up proportionately.

Another related element for countries such as Singapore is the number of airline seats that arrive every day. The market is only as big as the number of airline seats, regardless of the number of hotel rooms. In that part of the world, the number of flights are a consequence of political and economic actions as much as they are of business practice.

The Microeconomy

On the other side of the coin exists the microeconomic environment. This environment is concerned with use of the product, awareness levels, and the competitive situation. A good example, again, is Singapore. In the early 1980s the Singapore economy was booming. Both tourism and international business travel were on the increase. Inter-Continental, another Sheraton, and Westin entered the market with over 2000 rooms. Mandarin, New Otani from Japan, Peninsula from Hong Kong, and others also opened new hotels. By the time most of these hotels were built (and others were still building or had construction halted), the macroeconomy had softened.

More critical, however, the microeconomy presented a totally different picture. Rate-cutting practices became intense and consumers could almost name their own price. Another important aspect of the microeconomic environment is that one may be competing against cost advantages that home-based competitors enjoy.

A country's economic policies affect international companies. In India, for example, the government mandated that a foreign company can only hold less than 50 percent equity in an Indian business. It is because of this that McDonald's, Coca-Cola, and IBM all withdrew from India. In some cases there is also government competition. The Ashok hotel chain in India is owned by the government (although also tied in with Trusthouse Forte). Such relationships can strongly affect the market and the way a company competes.

In the final analysis, any company seeking to penetrate the international market must carefully weigh all the economic considerations. Each country requires specific strategic approaches and marketing plans that must fit, although they will not necessarily mesh with, the company's resources and capabilities. The long-term economic environment is the primary consideration. Although many developing countries offer inducements such as tax incentives and low-cost employment, they may still be very unstable for market entry. Risk/reward analysis is critical.

Foodservice companies entering international markets must deal with the local consumer. Although there are obvious exceptions—for example, there are restaurants in Paris and other cities geared to Americans or Britains—these generally are not the purpose of entry by a foreign firm. This means understanding population size, wage levels, disposable income, standards of living, and other economic factors is important. Conventional wisdom of the home base country usually does not apply.

For hotel companies seeking to expand abroad there are two considerations. One, as for foodservice companies, concerns the local economic climate. This is a particularly strategic decision in terms of the geographical customer mix and that portion of room nights sought from the domestic market.

The other consideration is the international travel market: will it be sought, where will it come from and what economic factors will affect it? Regardless of its decision, the international hotel company will still have to confront the local market for its food and beverage outlets as well as a portion of its meetings business. Although hotel dining and drinking is not necessarily fashionable in the United States or countries like France and England, in some countries, such as India, hotels are where almost all "better" dining takes place. Hotel companies need to understand this market as well, and its economic impacts.

Cultural and Social Environment

Although the economic environment will probably have the greatest impact upon major international marketing decisions, it is certainly the cultural environment that will most deeply affect marketing behavior. Hospitality marketers need to be keenly aware of cultural traits of both the countries in which they operate and the countries or nationalities of their customers. It is sensible practice, of course, to have management personnel from the native country who understand at least that country's culture. Often, however, this practice is ignored, is not fulfilling, or is simply not possible.

In the Far East, southeast Asia, and the Middle East, general managers of hotels operated by American and European companies tend to be European. In America, hotels operated by international companies tend to have managers from the countries where the companies originate. It is not until you reach the middle management level that local people are found in key positions, including sales and marketing. Of course, what these international companies want in top positions are people who understand the *corporate* culture and system. There is good reason for this paradoxical situation, as well as a shortage of local national executive talent. Nevertheless, it has its negative consequences.

Some of these consequences result from corporate mandates issued far away from the scene of the action. In 1986 Ramada ran an advertising campaign in the United States headed, "What makes Madden mad" or "What makes Madden glad" (see Figure 15-9). John Madden is an American football figure, supposedly well known to all Americans, with a reputation for fierceness. Madden was featured in close-up describing what he liked and didn't like when staying at hotels. These things, of course, were properly taken care of by Ramada.

It would be interesting to know how many traveling Americans actually know who Madden is and are inspired to choose Ramada because of him (although he makes the point quite well without identification). However, when Madden showed up on the cover of Ramada's worldwide directory and in numerous lobby and front desk posters in European and Middle East hotels, you can be sure that even fewer people knew who he was. In fact, the following conversation was overheard at a Ramada front desk in Europe: "Who's that?" "John Madden." "Who's John Madden?" "A football coach." "What's football?" Whatever impact Madden may have in the United States, he apparently had little abroad.

This is not to suggest that Ramada lost any customers because of John Madden, but it may not have gained any either. "Football" in Europe means soccer. American football is unique to America and few other nationalities know it, much less follow it. If Ramada had wanted to use a sports figure, even an American one, they might have tried John McEnroe (who's he?). At least he plays in probably the only sport that has an international following (although that doesn't necessarily make him a drawing card for hotels).

Other faux pas can be more serious. When Meridien entered the American market, their hotel in Boston naturally had to have the best, most exclusive, and most expensive restaurant in the city. But it didn't fill hotel rooms, even though the hotel eventually did well in the marketplace. Meridien had the same experience in Saudi Arabia. A smaller French company opened a hotel and spa in California with, you guessed it, a classic French restaurant. The entire concept failed for undoubtedly other, but related, reasons as well.

Knowing the Local Market

Establishing a hotel in a foreign land requires giving up some preconceived notions, especially when it comes to the restaurants. The astute company will first go into the marketplace and determine the cultures, social customs, dining-out habits, and other environmental elements of the populace, not to mention do a competitive analysis, which we have covered in a previous chapter.

This is especially true of those companies that have finally decided that restaurants in hotels don't have to present no-win situations. To prosper, they must be supported by the local populace. Sofitel, a four-star hotel chain owned by the French firm Groupe Accor, initiated research in the local markets they planned to enter in the United States to determine local restaurant needs and wants. Hyatt International has begun steering away from the "grande salon" dining room concept. Instead it is installing smaller Italian, steak, and seafood concepts in its hotels. These outlets are operated as individual profit centers with their own chef and manager, by contrast with the traditional F&B manager and executive chef organization.

Of course, all this is no different from knowing your market, wherever you are—it just takes a little more effort. If you want to learn from guest complaints, for example, as suggested in an earlier chapter, you will have a tough time in Asia. Asian cultures emphasize always smiling and being pleasant, and never disagreeing.

Consider some problems of doing business in Islamic societies. When an Inter-Continental hotel was built in the holy city of Mecca, Christians were not allowed inside the holy city. Construction was supervised from a distance via television cameras. Consider, then, the implications of managing a property where only Moslems are allowed and where the entire work force must be Moslem, catering, of course, to an entirely Moslem clientele.

One does not have to go to an Islamic holy city to find such strong cultural differences. Five times a day, Moslems pray while facing Mecca. Hotels catering to the Moslem market—and there are many in that part of the world—must provide each room with a directional indicator oriented toward Mecca.

In Moslem countries such as Kuwait, alcoholic beverages are totally banned. This is no idle gesture. Even incoming airplanes were boarded to be certain that their liquor stock is locked and secured. Imagine developing weekend packages for a hotel in Kuwait, when Cairo with all its bars is just a short flight away. On the other hand, you couldn't even deplane in Kuwait if you had been to Israel and it was so stamped on your passport.

Values that are important to one culture may mean little to another. These conflicts become more intense in an industry that sells very personal services to a very diversified clientele. Different cultures reflect different beliefs, attitudes, motivations, moralities, perceptions, and rituals. Although preconceived notions of what the hotel guest wants may be discrepant with the guest's own notions in any country, they can result in disaster when marketing to different cultures. It thus goes without saying that cultural differences have a tremendous impact upon marketing mix decisions in international operations. Ignoring this impact has often resulted in expensive consequences for hotels operating in arenas outside their corporate homeland.

In Strasbourg, France, an historic city occupied alternately in history by the Germans and the French, was a Hilton International hotel that rarely achieved a satisfactory occupancy. This is a city so steeped in cultural tradition that one almost feels sacrilegious spending the night in American modernity; in other words, Strasbourg is not a traditional Hilton market. Hilton International had the same problem in Stratford-upon-Avon in England, a locale from which it soon withdrew.

Cultural and social traditions are not always so complex. In fact, they often descend to the totally mundane. How many Americans (aside from the authors) would go to a McDonald's and not expect to find a catsup bottle on the counter? In France, England, and other countries, catsup is sold separately at McDonald's and Burger King for those who "dare" to use it, and of course is nonexistent in better restaurants. McDonald's and Burger King have adapted to cultural differences.

To go a bit further, imagine, if you possibly can, an American wife who flies economy class while her husband flies first class, as the Moslems often do. Americans are often shocked, as well, to see male "chambermaids" in hotels in Moslem countries, where females are forbidden to work outside the home. In Kuwait, no one does "menial" labor and Filipinos are imported for these jobs.

What American would expect a fine French restaurant to feature pig's ears and tails on its menu (it sounds delicious in French) and not be shocked when this dish, so delectably described (in French), showed up on the dinner plate? Imagine an American without the traditional "cocktail sauce" that accompanies oysters—yet the French, who like to taste the oyster, use only lemon and "slurp" the liquid from the shell. Now consider fish. In America we order it deep-fried and cover it with tartar sauce. Who knows whether it is fresh or frozen, and for how long? Yet the average American abjures frozen fish. The same American abjures sushi, Japanese raw fish, which is so fresh that any not used by the day after it is caught is thrown away.

Of course, the situation works in reverse as well. In Paris, better restaurants don't open until 8:00 P.M., if then. At 9:00 P.M. you're the only party in the place. At 10:00 P.M., the place is packed. (In Madrid it isn't packed until 11:00 P.M.) So a French hotel company opens a hotel in America and thinks, "Who are these crazy people who want to eat at six o'clock?"

In India, liquor stores close on the first and seventh of every month, because these are pay days. In New Delhi, liquor stores cannot give away free gifts, such as calendars. In Bombay, the state government permits the opposite.

In 1983, the Indian parliament banned the use on menus of words such as beef and veal and their French equivalents. The Oberoi Hotel, as one example, resorted to the use of German names on French menus, so that escalope de veau Rossini became kalb Rossini, which confused just about everyone.

It is not easy to understand the cultures and social mores of other countries. It has been said that the French don't understand the French. But you don't have to be a Francophone or a Francophile to know that the 21 Club restaurant in New York City—famous, very expensive, and successful for many years—wouldn't last two weeks in Paris with what restaurant critic Mimi Sheraton has called its "dependably dreary pricy food."

And what would happen to the French Brasserie in New York City? Omni Hotels found out when it put one, albeit an ersatz one, in the Omni Park Central Hotel on Seventh Avenue, where the product was a poor fit with the market. A little market analysis instead of "conceptitis" would have provided the answer and saved tens of thousands of dollars.

There is an interesting social change taking place in many countries today. This is an increasing level of domestic travel by natives. This phenomenon has been occurring for some time in the United States but is really only beginning in some European countries. For example, in Scandinavia, people who traveled traditionally headed for southern Europe and warmer temperatures. Now, with high discretionary income and time, many other Scandinavians are traveling more, staying in hotels more, and eating out more in their own countries. In 1986, international arrivals in Norway were down but local travel increased 15 percent over the previous year—yet hotel occupancy decreased 3 percent. This is the kind of social change that creates marketing opportunities. In this case, the hospitality industry has an opportunity to create new markets for its product, and to develop product to fit new markets.

Other Environments

It is clear that political, competitive, and regulatory environments of countries other than one's own will differ from each other, and often radically. Obviously, too, these elements are intertwined with the economic and cultural elements. In some countries, in order to get anything of consequence done, it is largely who you know and who you pay "extra to" that will determine when, or if, it will be done. In other words, it takes economic influence to get the political influence to get around the regulatory barriers unless, of course, the competition knows someone higher than you do. That's the culture!

In Abu Dhabi, the same company (Abu Dhabi National Hotel Company) owns all the five-star competing hotels, each managed by different companies. The owning company tells the hotels which will charge what, where the hotel will be positioned, and what markets, or groups, each will serve. The fact that the owners of the parent company are also invested in Sheraton is not irrelevant to Sheraton's 75 percent occupancy vs. 40–50 percent for the other hotels.

In Al Khobar, Saudi Arabia, you can't get alcoholic beverages at all. The city, like the country, is totally dry; also, women are not allowed outside the home. During the day the shops are full because of their tax-free status. At night the hotels are relatively empty because it is a short ride across the bridge to Bahrain where liquor flows freely and women are allowed to work. Le Meridien, the most beautiful hotel in Al Khobar, is fortunate to have a 55 percent occupancy when facing this kind of competitive situation.

In Britain, the drinking laws vary depending upon the local legislature and, until very recently, you couldn't get drinks between 2:30 and 5:30 P.M. unless you were also eating, and so you were largely reliant on the eccentric opening hours of the famous British pub. In one case it's the cultural environment; in the other it's the regulatory environment.

Tax control, price control, and labor restrictions are other influences that can become gigantic headaches when doing business in foreign countries, quite apart from expropriation. Problems of political and regulatory environments are not limited only to Third World and developing countries; they occur in almost all countries, particularly those with less than stable governments. These include Spain, Italy, and even France. All of these problems impact upon marketing strategies and tactics. It does not serve our purpose to discuss these impacts in more detail here. We can only caution that today's great marketing opportunity (e.g., Iran in the early 1970s) can be tomorrow's high-risk situation (Iran in 1979), not to mention the myriad of small details that a business must cope with in an international environment.

In spite of all or any of these difficulties, companies from all countries with expanding economies will increasingly go abroad. Domestic markets get overbuilt, currency exchange rates fluctuate, and the need to continually expand the customer base and revenues leads in one direction—overseas.

Segmentation

Segmentation takes on a different perspective for the hotel company in the international arena. The potential market is so obviously diverse that special care must be taken in regard to customer mix. For the individual restaurant, on the other hand, segmentation strategies would be developed in much the same way as in the home country. The hotel restaurant will likewise segment both by its in-house market and by the local market it wishes to attract.

Home-based hotels in countries other than the United States, at least those in major cities, have long had to deal with wide geographic segmentation. These hotels may segment on the home national market, as many do throughout Europe outside the major cities. Groupe Accor's Formule1, Ibis division, and much of the Novotel division segment on the lower and middle portions of the French market. Its upper-end Sofitel division, however, and many other hotels in that category, as well as some in lower categories, segment primarily on the international market. In other countries, such as Singapore, the upscale hotels are almost totally dependent on the international market. In the United States, on the other hand, relatively very few hotels segment on the international market, except perhaps their own nationality if they are foreign-based.

When a hotel company strays to foreign lands, the picture changes. The company must first seek geographic definition of its markets. The Nikko hotel in New York City and the New Otani in Los Angeles initially sought to capture the Japanese market. More specifically, they segmented on both the Japanese business market and the Japanese pleasure travel market. Other companies, however, like those from France, do not necessarily seek the same nationality as their origin. Instead, this segment will be just one of a number of segments they hope to attract. When either these companies or American companies locate in other parts of the world, they seek a diverse international clientele. This is where the segmentation "fun" begins.

International hotel marketers must first make conscious decisions about the geographic segments they wish to attract. Many of these segments are not mutually compatible. For example, Arabs cook in their rooms in order to follow their religious codes; this may have unpleasant consequences for other guests. The Japanese market, the Taiwanese market, the Australian market, the ASEAN market, the German market, the European market, and the American market, all have special significance for hotels in ASEAN countries (Philippines, Singapore, Malaysia, Thailand, Indonesia, and Brunei). This is true whether the hotels are operated by companies of the native country, America, Hong Kong, Japan, or any other country. This situation is even more apparent in Hong Kong where, like Singapore, very few guests will be national residents.

It is also possible, of course, for some of these hotels to have guests from over twenty different countries at one time or another, as we have previously shown. Resources would be spread too thin, however, if a hotel made concentrated efforts to appeal to all of them. Thus, decisions should be made, though admittedly, they are made by default in many cases. On the other hand, many hotels try to avoid the stigma of being a one-origin hotel—a Japanese hotel, an Arab hotel, an American hotel.

A case in point is the Oberoi hotel in Bombay, which tried to shed the image of catering primarily to the international traveler while its rival, the Taj hotel, skimmed off the cream of the Indian market. Another case is a former Holiday Inn in Antwerp, Belgium, that wanted to dispel the image of being an "American" hotel, especially when the American market weakened. No one geographic market is large enough to maintain necessary occupancy in spite of the potential of obtaining a major share of that market.

Fine-Tuning Segments

It can be a mistake to segment on very broad geographical areas. All Europeans are clearly not the same, nor are all Moslems, and clearly not all Americans. Thus, some international hotel companies are beginning to fine-tune their segmentation strategies with a global perspective. This could mean, for example, a certain level of business executive regardless of geographic origin. This segment is more difficult and expensive to reach, but increasingly global communication media are easing the task. It also means more difficulty in servicing the diverse cultures included.

A good example of this is the Century Park Sheraton in Singapore. The prime market for this hotel is the business traveler. Main sources of this market are Japan, the United States, the United Kingdom, and Europe. All this hotel's business travelers have essentially the same needs—to wit, a business center, a location near the business area, dining and entertainment facilities, and a good communication infrastructure. Each ethnic group may have different priorities but the needs remain the same. The Century Park segments as follows:

Sheraton—business generated by the Sheraton reservation system
Corporate—business generated from companies located in Singapore
Diplomatic—business generated by local diplomatic missions

Crew—airline crew rooms booked by contract, travel agency and airline personnel, and
business generated by airline reservations systems

By carefully targeting these markets, the hotel has been able to maintain its image
even in bad times by refusing groups such as Australian tours. This hotel is a good
example of avoiding the trap that some other Singapore hotels have fallen into of not
utilizing careful segmentation strategies. The Westin Hotel in the same city, with over
2000 rooms and built for a convention market yet to appear, had to grab about anything it
could get.

Fine-tuning follows the pattern of good segmentation strategy—that is, complementary target markets. The Meridien at Porte Maillot in Paris, a 1000-room hotel, had
considerable segmentation difficulties with the mixture of executives and tour groups. The
company took over another hotel at Montparnasse in a commercially less desirable (for the
businessperson) location in Paris, where it booked most of its tour groups. This move
considerably enhanced the position of the Porte Maillot property.

One way to fine-tune is to look at the business market as something other than one
vast market. Kristian Moller and his colleagues researched over 700 business travelers in
Scandinavia on "regular" hotel usage—that is, congresses, conventions, and seminars
were excluded. Using a benefit clustering approach, they were able to show that business
travelers do not evaluate hotels homogeneously. The research defined six meaningful and
homogeneous segments based on four underlying dimensions. The four dimensions and
the six subjectively labeled segments that were identified are shown in Table 22-1.

It is informative to note some of the conclusions of Moller and his colleagues.

> [A] striking feature is the number of segments regarding business services clearly
> unimportant—covering 47% of respondents.
>   . . . both business service oriented segments differ from the other segments by
> including a larger share of top and middle mangement personnel, who also travel more
> than the average business customers. Moreover, they do more work during their stay at
> the hotel. The High Business Services & Restaurant & Image segment has some
> additional, fairly unique, features. Its members are keen on hotel advice . . . using the
> "right" hotels, and it has a high share of U.S. and UK visitors. . . . it has more loyal
> patronizing behavior than other segments, and its members are more favorable towards
> international "luxury" chains. . . . they also exhibit a more active recreation pattern.[1]

It is also worth noting that SAS Hotels in Scandinavia have been particularly
successful in using psychographic segmentation, concentrating on the efficiency-minded
segment. In Stavanger, Norway, SAS successfully operates an "efficient" businessper-
sons' hotel without the usual flourish of varied restaurants and lounges usually associated
with upscale hotels.

The pitfalls of poor segmentation are more acute in international markets than in the
American market. Some geographical markets collapse overnight, as occurred with the
fall of the American market in Europe due to terrorism activities in 1986. Market
segments in America don't collapse so quickly. Ignoring the possibility for internation-

---

[1] K. E. K. Moller, J. R. Lehtinen, G. Rosenqvist, and K. Storbacka, "Segmenting Hotel Business Customers: A
Benefit Clustering Approach," in T. Bloch, et al. (eds.), *Services Marketing in a Changing Environment*, Published by
(Chicago: American Marketing Association, 1985), pp. 72–76.

TABLE 22-1   Hotel Dimensions and Benefit Segments of Business Travelers in Scandinavia

---

Dimensions on Which Hotels are Evaluated

Efficient core service: The efficiency and friendliness of service, quiet rooms and good reception, and other intangible benefits

Business services: Variety of business services offered as well as working possibilities in rooms, and office options

Restaurants and image: Restaurants and nightclub image, business customer clientele, and interior decor

Accessibility: Location of the hotel

Benefit Segments of Business Customers

Indifferents: Regard core service and business services as unimportant, indifferent by contrast with other dimensions

High business service and access: Business services and location critical, restaurant and image insignificant

Core service: Basic services important; location, restaurant and image unimportant

High access and core service: Location and core services important; business services, restaurant, and image of no importance

High business services and restaurants: Business services and restaurants important, other dimensions unimportant

High restaurant and core services: Don't value business services

---

Source: K. E. K. Moller, J. R. Lehtinen, G. Rosenqvist, and K. Storbacka, "Segmenting Hotel Business Customers: A Benefit Clustering Approach," in T. Bloch et al. (eds.), *Services Marketing in a Changing Environment* (Chicago: American Marketing Association, 1985), pp. 74–75, Published by the American Marketing Association.

al markets can bring sudden shock to American companies abroad that are not fully cognizant of the frailty of market structures.

Globalization of Markets

Somewhat contrary to segmentation practice, Levitt considers that the era of multinational marketing must move to one of "globalization of markets." Levitt argues:

> . . . Though companies always customize for specific segments, success in a world whose wants become more homogenized requires of such companies strategic and operating modes that search for opportunities to sell to similar segments throughout the globe to achieve the scale economies that keep their costs competitive.
>
> Seldom these days is a segment in one country unique to that country alone. It is found everywhere, [and is] thus available to sellers from everywhere. Small local segments in this fashion become globally standardized, large, and therefore subject to global competition, especially price competition. . . . the successful global corporation does not abjure customization or differentiation for the requirements of markets that differ in product preferences, spending patterns, shopping preferences. . . . But the

global corporation accepts and adjusts to these differences only reluctantly, only after relentlessly testing their immutability—after trying in various ways to circumvent and reshape them.[2]

Does Levitt argue against segmentation? If a country or even a segment within that country is not homogeneous, can the world be one homogeneous marketplace? Does this apply to the hospitality industry? Is a hotel room, or a restaurant meal, basically the same worldwide with minor modifications? Should the marketer adjust only after testing the waters? We leave this discussion to the reader because the final chapter has yet to be written and Levitt's comments have been controversial. We include them here because they clearly come under the category of environmental scanning in the international arena.

Positioning

Closely related to segmentation issues, of course, is the issue of positioning. Relative to most of what we have already stated, most hotel companies that go abroad seek to position in the high upper end of the market. Perhaps this was a given when these companies were among the first to enter markets such as Singapore and Hong Kong. Today, Singapore is saturated with these hotels. Hong Kong, which has enjoyed high occupancy ratios for some time, may soon be in the same situation as heavy building plans continue.

Because it is easy to look at Singapore with hindsight, let's look at Hong Kong with foresight, since the situation will no doubt be different by the time the British crown colony reverts to Chinese sovereignty in 1997. Hong Kong has long been a top hotel market. Not only does the city achieve high occupancy (consistently 80 percent across all ranges of accommodation in 1987) but it contains some of the best world-class hotels. Every aspect of service is primed to perfection by intense competition.

In fact, it might be said that Hong Kong hotelkeeping has been recognized as the modern state of the art. This is the city where guests of the Mandarin and Peninsula Hotels are met at the airport by Rolls Royces, and a Holiday Inn has eight specialty cuisine restaurants. Every hotel is aware that the customer has many similar choices. As a result, hotels maintain continuous staff training, quality of food and beverage, and refurbishing. In spite of this situation, the hotel community has, relatively speaking, maintained reasonable rack rates.

When Singapore was in the same situation, rack rates increased drastically, building proliferated, and occupancy fell. In 1987, Singapore occupancy averaged below 50 percent during a number of months and discount rates made the city a bargain for the tourist.

In mid-1987, Hong Kong had 21,000 hotel rooms. Eighteen new projects were under development and hotel capacity was expected to increase to 29,000 rooms by 1990. Most of the present rooms and almost all of the new ones are in the top end of the market. Completed in 1988 was the massive Hong Kong Convention and Exhibition Centre, containing a 600-room Grand Hyatt.

Just about all major international hotel chains are in the Hong Kong market. These include two Holiday Inns, Hilton International, Inter-Continental, two Hyatts, Meridien,

---

[2] Theodore A. Levitt, "The Globalization of Markets," *Harvard Business Review*, May/June 1983, pp. 92–102. Copyright © 1983 by the President and Fellows of Harvard College; all rights reserved.

Sheraton, Nikko, and Regent, as well as top Hong Kong companies. Will Hong Kong suffer the same fate as Singapore? Will the new entries force rates up and occupancies down? This remains to be seen.

When international companies applied the same "top end of the market" positioning strategy in markets such as London and Paris the situation was different. These cities had individual (some are now chain or consortium members), classic hotels that held sway in the deluxe market category with a product that couldn't be duplicated, such as the Connaught and Dorchester in London and the Bristol and Ritz in Paris. Many of the new hotels were forced into down-market positions when they found they couldn't compete for the same customer. Interestingly, the first newly built hotel in central London in ten years, which opened in 1987, was Groupe Accor's 300-room Ibis Euston. This hotel offered no-frills accommodations at $65 per night, single. The lowest price five-star room in London in 1988 (Royal Garden Hotel) was $260. In Amsterdam, the Holiday Inn Crowne Plaza opened in 1987 positioned at the five-star level, a market it has yet to obtain.

Positioning at the upper end of the market is no longer a given in foreign market-places. As inevitably happens, the competition has moved in and there are too few non-price-sensitive customers to go around. As previously mentioned, even the Concorde Lafayette in Paris has moved to position at a lower level. Positioning opportunities should be the first stage of market analysis for any hospitality company seeking to penetrate foreign marketplaces. Amsterdam's Crowne Plaza suffers for forgetting this.

Another consideration for positioning in international markets is the use of a brand name. There are essentially three different common practices: single name, multinames, and individual names.

Perhaps the most common practice is to use a single name, as do Hilton, Sheraton, Hyatt, and Meridien. The purpose in this case is to create immediate identity. As Sheraton proclaimed in one ad:

> Knowing where you're going is knowing where to stay. In Sana'a, and around the world, that can only mean Sheraton Hotels. Where the art of hospitality finds new expressions of excellence. And sensitivity to the needs of the business and leisure traveler results in a superior guest experience. So when you come to Sana'a come to Sheraton to stay.

The multiname practice is followed by Groupe Accor to differentiate its product line. The corporate name is never used. To many people in the fifty-two foreign countries in which Groupe Accor operates, perhaps even in France, Sofitel, Novotel, and Ibis may be perceived as three separate and distinct chains.

A company that maintains individual names throughout the world is Trusthouse Forte of England. This company operates over 200 hotels in the United Kingdom and over 600 outside of it. Customers could stay at the Compleat Angler (Marlow, England) for a country inn; the Wynnstay (Machynlleth, Wales) for a small-town hotel; the Old England (Bowness-on-Windermere, England) for a lakeside resort; the Post House (Edinburgh, Scotland) for an outside-the-city hotel; the Strand Palace (London) for a touristy group hotel; or the George V (Paris), the Dom (Cologne), the Plaza Athenee (New York), the Ritz (Madrid), or the Sandy Lane (Barbados) for top-of-the-line luxury hotels—all without knowing they were in a Trusthouse Forte property, unless they recognized the small but ubiquitous "thf" initials.

Products and Services

If segmentation needs are different in the international arena, then it should stand to reason that products and services will also be different, yet Levitt appears to argue to the contrary. "High-touch products [hotels and restaurants] are as globalized as high-tech," according to Levitt, "and the globally-oriented company should seek global standardization. It digresses from this mode only at its peril."[3]

> The lower the price the greater the likelihood that the world will accept standardized modernity in all its major sectors and segments rather than insist on higher-priced customization in inherited preferences and ancient practices.[4]

However, the multinational hotel industry seems to be going in the other direction (with some exceptions, as we have previously discussed), while it might be said that the mutinational foodservice industry is following Levitt's advice. In fact, Levitt uses the example of McDonald's to make this point.

In the case of hotels, until the late 1980s each new hotel built in an international context seemed grander and more customized than the last—and higher priced. This is not to say that these were "inherited preferences," or "ancient practices" as Levitt suggests; to the contrary, they were efforts at new product development to minimize travelers' problems. The latest in meeting technology, health clubs, saunas, Turkish baths, jacuzzis, massages, squash courts, tennis courts, swimming pools, in-room amenities, and other customizations continue to appear in the international domain, although down market properties are becoming more common.

An excellent example of this, which is not as common in the United States, is the business service center. These centers provide telex services (a common form of communication in most of the world except the United States), computer facilities, facsimile services, stenographic services, translation services, business introductory services, courier service, round-the-clock currency exchange, and other services designed to make the foreign business traveler's life easier in a strange country (Figure 22-1). There is also a larger variety of food services, minibars, safes, personalized stationery, more elegant decor, and other customizations that are more common than in the United States.

Many product/service decisions are ones that must be made when the hotel is being designed. When Hilton International and Inter-Continental, the forerunners of international hotel companies, first started building hotels abroad, they essentially exported the American hotel. This practice is no longer adequate. Today, says Jain,

> the product decision must be made on the basis of careful analysis and review. The nature, depth, and breadth of the product line; the possibilities of new product development and product innovation; the importance attached to product design (the adaptation and customization of products to suit local conditions vis-à-vis standardization); the decision on foreign R&D; and a planned screening and elimination of unsuccessful products bear heavily on success in foreign markets.[5]

---

[3] Ibid., p. 93.
[4] Ibid., p. 98.
[5] Subhash C. Jain, *International Marketing Management*, Boston: Kent Publishing, 1984, p. 345.

FIGURE 22-1   Marketing to the international business traveler

It is clear that marketers should carefully consider Levitt's thesis of standardization vs. customization to local markets and preferences when developing product/service strategies in foreign markets. We have already given numerous examples of product differences in different countries, and have cited cases of the product not being adapted to the local market. The question of standardization vs. customization is a complex one. As with all product decisions, however, the answer should lie in the needs and wants of the marketplace and the degree of difference among the markets being served.

There are pitfalls in either case. Hilton International's standardization of product helped it to establish a common image worldwide so that first Americans, and then other international travelers, became accustomed to it and bought Hilton when available. As we have shown, however, this standardized product did not match the conditions in every market. Holiday Inns, on the other hand, has been more successful in foreign markets where it has adapted the product than in those where it has not.

Each international expansion requires designing the product line for the location and the markets to be served. With products as personal as hotels and restaurants, even aesthetic appeals (as well as the rest of the presentation mix) may need to be adapted to different countries and cultures. The product objectives for each country and market must be clearly delineated and related to the local situation as well as to the overall corporate objectives.

Pricing

Pricing is an exceedingly complex variable of the marketing mix in the international marketplace. There are two main reasons for this beyond the usual complexities of pricing. The first reason, previously mentioned, is the monetary exchange rates that, in most countries, fluctuate somewhat on a daily basis, and fluctuate radically during either national or international economic cycles. The second reason is the pricing tactics practiced by competitors, especially locally owned ones.

The president of one international hotel company with worldwide properties once said to one of of the authors, "We're not in the hotel business; we're in the monetary exchange business." While this statement was not to be taken literally, it demonstrates the concerns of a company operating internationally. Probably the greatest problem in this respect is pricing both for the natives of a host country and for the international traveler.

Good illustrations, though perhaps extreme cases, are the situations in Mexico and Brazil in recent years. Both these countries have experienced exceedingly high inflation rates. As the value of the peso and the cruzeiro dropped precipitously, the price of a hotel room for a Mexican or Brazilian increased precipitously in the other direction.

Consider Mexico: Not that long ago there were 50 pesos to the dollar. A hotel room at $80 to an American was 4,000 pesos to a Mexican. When, almost overnight, the peso devalued to 150 to the dollar, the American price was still $80, but the Mexican price was now 12,000 pesos. In spring 1988, there were about 2,400 pesos to the dollar but, during the same periods, the Mexican's or the Mexican company's earnings did not triple or increase 48-fold. Thus, Mexicans were shut out of their own market as well as the American market, where it took many more pesos to buy a hotel room. Americans, of course, flocked across the border to take advantage of the devalued peso. Balancing exchange rates is a full-time occupation for any company that operates internationally.

On a more gradual basis, exchange rates rise and fall. So too does international tourism. In 1984, with the French franc at 8 to the dollar, the American tourist could buy a 400 franc hotel room for $50. In 1986, at 10 francs to the dollar (if prices hadn't been increased proportionately, and they weren't), the same room cost an American $40. In 1987, the franc fell to 6 to the dollar and the same room cost $66.67—except, by now the French had "caught on" and the same room was over $100. All of these fluctuations have affected the incidence of American tourism in France.

Outside of four-star hotels in Paris that practice discounting when business is slow, as do American hotels, French hotels quote "straight" rates; in other words, for the ordinary traveler the rack rate (or rate posted with the government by law) is the rate you pay.[6] Thus France, or any other country, becomes either a bargain or costly, depending on the exchange rate between that country and the one you are coming from.

This is tricky business. Consider the following scenario: In the past, an American could book a room in an American company-operated hotel in Acapulco through an American travel agency for $80 per night, or could go to Mexico, exchange dollars for pesos, go to the hotel, and obtain the same room for $40. What may seem frustrating or even devious to the American consumer is a major headache for the operator who is trying to make a profit while serving markets with totally different monetary values.

The same scenario is repeated worldwide, one way or another, in various international markets. It is no wonder that the tourist is bewildered, but it is no less wonder that the hotel company has a difficult problem on its hands. Now consider the same scenario when the market mix of the hotel is from a dozen or more different countries, each with its own rate of exchange against the currency of the host country. The rate of exchange is affected by the inflation rate. Table 22-2 shows some inflation rates of countries from which a hotel in, say, Hong Kong might draw business.

Second, consider the pricing tactics of "unscrupulous" competitors. International hotel companies are primarily profit-driven, not to mention high-rate-oriented. When business is good, everyone gets top price. When business is bad, many local owners operating in their own countries, as well as some foreign chains, will do anything to get business—which here means to cut room rates to the bone. With "deep pockets" for survival, these hotels discount to a level at which their international counterparts, who need to show a profit, cannot compete.

The problem of pricing hotel rooms in foreign countries is compounded when the parent country reserves for itself the international pricing decisions. In the chapter on pricing, we described how one American chain simply ordered its international properties to increase prices. Obviously, each property operates under a different set of price constraints that the parent company chooses to ignore.

---

[6] This is also true in most of Europe. Many European countries also use an official or unofficial rating system based on the "number of stars system." There is minimum overlap in the rates between hotels with different star ratings. The ratings also indicate the physical facilities available. Thus, customers know pretty well what the property offers, and at what rate range, when they choose a one-, two-, three-, four-, or five-star hotel, which thus have different meanings than in the U.S.

In France the customer pays an additional penalty for going upscale. Four-star and four-star luxe (the highest rating) hotels add approximately 18 percent tax on the total bill, including food and beverage. Lower-rated hotels only add about 6 percent. Just about all hotels and restaurants in Europe add a 10 to 15 percent service charge.

TABLE 22-2   Inflation Rates of Selected Countries—June 1987

Country	Inflation Rate	Country	Inflation Rate
Hong Kong	2.5%	United States	1.5%
France	2.1%	Australia	8.9%
Greece	21.9%	India	8.7%
Italy	7.5%	Japan	0.5%
Norway	8.8%	Korea	1.3%
United Kingdom	3.0%	New Zealand	11.0%
West Germany	−1.2%	Philippines	−0.5%
		Singapore	−1.4%
Egypt	29.6%		
Israel	16.6%	Argentina	74.2%
Kuwait	1.3%	Brazil	94.4%
Saudi Arabia	−2.9%	Mexico	96.0%

Source: *Executive Travel*, June 1987, p. 90.

An analysis of pricing in various competitive international environments has been developed by Henley and is shown in Table 22-3. Each one of these environments can be found in various countries where international hotel companies operate. Clearly, it would be foolhardy to dictate prices from a remote country without considering these and many other factors.

It is not difficult to see that pricing a hotel room in the international market can be extremely risky, yet pricing is a marketing tool that can not be forsaken. Once again, a clear definition of target markets is essential. Pricing in anticipation of the economic environment becomes an even more critical part of the marketing mix. Vicious discounting when there simply isn't enough demand for the supply, as in Singapore, ends up being self-defeating for all. Generically speaking, of course, Singapore competes with Hong Kong. Its discount pricing has helped to stabilize Hong Kong prices.

In the food and beverage areas, a somewhat different situation exists. In most of Europe and in parts of Asia, "eating out" approximates a national pastime (at least for the middle and upper classes), far more so than in the United States. This causes a high demand and the prices reflect it. Even so-called moderate restaurants can be quite expensive, and some of the better ones are simply exorbitant. The natives seem to accept it. For Americans, to whom eating out is often something to do "before, during, or after" and in more of a hurry, it can come as quite a shock. The local nationals, on the other hand, see the meal more as an experience in itself, in all price ranges.

Communications

Communications in international markets are obviously affected by cultural differences and, like any communications efforts, the designated target markets. Other than these

TABLE 22-3 Competitive Environments in International Arenas

Points of Differentiation	Competitive Environment			
	Privileged Position	Leadership	Chaotic	Stabilized Competition
Definition	Lack of significant direct competition	Leader has ability to set price level Leader affects degree of variation from basic level	Price level and variation are unpredictable and frequently changing	Firms have pricing latitude Price levels and variations adjust smoothly to each firm's strategy
Characteristics	High degree of technical/service differentiation High cost of entry Good customer, competitor intelligence Considerable latitude in pricing	Few competitors, high cost of entry Leader has high market share Leader has recognized technical and marketing leadership, and generally is low-cost producer Leader has reputation for good pricing decisions Leader is able to communicate his policies Leader's actions are predictable	Price is the major competitive tool "Commodity" products —everybody viewed the same Customers are price sensitive, or made to be price sensitive Tendency to excess capacity No recognized leader and no restraint	No recognized industry price leader No firm has dominant market share Firms employ product differentiation and market segmentation Competition based on technology, service, delivery; not based on price Infrequent price changes
Implications	High margins and profits Responsibility for market development	Good margins and profits for leader Acceptable margins and profits for followers Customers are satisfied	Nobody making even acceptable profits Customer probably dissatisfied	Good or acceptable margins for all Customers are satisfied

Source: Donald S. Henley, "Evaluating International Product Line Performance: A Conceptual Approach," in *Multinational Product Management* (Cambridge, Mass.: Marketing Science Institute, 1976), pp. II–13 to II–16.

concerns, the coordination of communications efforts with other elements of the marketing mix in foreign markets is more difficult. The quality and availability of the means and the media vary from country to country and affect the usefulness and success of various techniques.

Global advertising (i.e., advertising using the same copy in different countries) is practiced by only very few companies of all industries. Cultural barriers make implementing a global campaign difficult. In a survey of 100 American advertisers, these barriers were defined as follows:

- 19 percent said their biggest mistake abroad was failure to allow for cultural differences.
- 79 percent develop distinctly different media plans in each country to reflect cultural and linguistic differences.
- 57 percent redesign the product or the packaging for each individual overseas market.
- 40 percent believe that universal advertising rises above cultural differences only on rare occasions.

Results from a separate study of marketers in the European Economic Community confirmed similar atttudes and concerns.[7]

Because of this and because of the need to communicate with numerous and dissimilar markets, there tends to be more emphasis on personal selling at the unit level, and less selling at the national level. Corporate hotel salespeople seem to spend their lives on airplanes and in foreign cities.

American hotel companies, however, tend to practice global advertising. We have shown that in Ramada's case, the international use of an American figurehead led to confusion abroad. In much Hyatt and Sheraton corporate advertising, one need only change the location references to use the same ad anywhere in the world.

This is not surprising, however. In most advertising by Asian hotel companies, even at the individual level, one could almost change the name of the hotel to Hyatt or Sheraton and use the same ad. The sameness of hotel advertising persists the world around. Figure 22-2, however, illustrates a differentiation. We suspect that if the Holiday Inn name were removed from the ad, very few would guess that it was a Holiday Inn. This ad avoids the sameness of most Holiday Inn advertising. There is good reason for this: Holiday Inns tend to have a very different image and position abroad than they have in the United States.

With the exception of Europe, most international hotel properties are new and modern, offer the same basic services, and make the same claims and promises. It is truly difficult, as it is in the United States, to differentiate one from the other in advertising copy. Thus many companies, like airlines, stress the destination and put the emphasis on the brand name, as mentioned above in the case of Sheraton. The strategy in these cases is largely one of awareness and reminder.

In Europe there are some differences. These are not the newer Hyatts, Hiltons, or Sheratons, but the older hotels that have charm, warmth, or historic atmosphere. These attributes are rarely if ever captured in modern hostelries or in their ads. In some cases

---

[7] Reported in "Differences, Confusion Slow Global Marketing Bandwagon," *Marketing News*, January 16, 1987, p. 1.

FIGURE 22-2 Creating a different image in a foreign country

FIGURE 22-3 Marketing historic charm in Portugal

Singapore's most elegant deluxe hotel featuring 462 rooms, cabanas and suites, non-smoking floor, 2 bars, 3 restaurants, a lounge, discotheque, health club, swimming pool and a businessman's centre.

Century Park Sheraton
Singapore

16 Nassim Hill, Singapore 1025,
Telephone: 7321222

FIGURE 22-4   Failing to capitalize on unique differences

these attributes are used to advantage in advertising. One example is the ad for a Pousada in Portugal illustrated in Figure 22-3. Pousadas are small inns housed in historic buildings, castles, palaces, and monasteries that reflect the history and cultural traditions of the region in which they are located.

On the other hand, true differences are often wasted, or not used to advantage. The Century Park Sheraton in Singapore is unlike many of its competitors. Its lobby is wood-paneled and is not atrium-like in scope, as are the lobbies of many of its competitors. In this and other ways it has a charm that differentiates it from, say, the nearby Hyatt, Inter-Continental, Ming Court, Mandarin, and Dynasty. Its market likes this difference, which helps the hotel to maintain a higher than fair market share. This hotel's postcard, however, shown in Figure 22-4, fails to capitalize on this difference and equates it with any other Sheraton (including another in the same city), and its claims on the card equate it with any other hotel in the same product class in Singapore.

Consider also the photograph from an Oberoi brochure, shown in Figure 22-5, of the Windsor Hotel in Melbourne, Australia, a beautifully restored 100-year-old, old-world hotel. One can see this beauty in the elegance of the dining room, but, at least as it appears to us, it is greatly damaged by the artificiality of the staged setting. Notice in Figure 22-6, on the other hand, how Meridien brings France to North American meetings.

The decision of whether to standardize advertising worldwide or to adapt it to each country and/or each market is a difficult one. The very diversity of the countries and the markets calls on the one hand for diversity in advertising; on the other hand, total diversity

FIGURE 22-5   Failing to maximize unique differences

would be prohibitively expensive and thus calls for standardization. Nevertheless, each hotel has its own specific collateral and, in many cases, does its own advertising to specific markets. In these cases, every attempt at differentiation should be made. There is little difference in cost between effective and ineffective advertising. In all cases, advertising by whatever medium should be consistent with the corporate image, should position the extablishment in its desired marketplace, and should be a cost-effective method for communicating with the market.

THE MERIDIEN INVITATION:
We find brilliant solutions without obligation.

Let us show you our genius for meetings even before you book anything. Just call the number below for the Meridien that interests you and speak to our representative. You'll hear your meeting logistics needs disappear right before your ears. Without making as much as one reservation. And if you're not sure about

location yet, call the Regional Sales Office nearest you, or fill out the business reply card attached to get more information on any hotel and how to make your meeting an enviable success. So pick up the phone and call on our brilliance. Le Meridien. A genius for meetings.

Le Meridien Montreal
4 Complexe Desjardins
Montreal, Quebec
(514) 285-1450

Le Parker Meridien New York
118 West 57th St.
New York, N.Y.
(212) 245-5000

Le Meridien Boston
250 Franklin St.
Boston, Mass.
(617) 451-1900

Le Meridien San Francisco
50 Third St.
San Francisco, Calif.
(415) 974-6400

Le Meridien New Orleans
614 Canal St.
New Orleans, La.
(504) 525-6500

Le Meridien Newport Beach
4500 MacArthur Blvd.
Newport Beach, Calif.
(714) 476-2001

Le Meridien Vancouver
845 Burrard Street
Vancouver, B.C.
(604) 682-5511

Le Meridien San Diego
at Coronado (Spring '88)
2000 Second St.
Coronado, Calif.
(619) 435-3000

Regional Sales Offices:
New York (212) 245-2920 Washington D.C. (202) 331-8856 Chicago (312) 951-6629 Los Angeles (213) 854-0841 Toronto (416) 598-3838

Le
MERIDIEN
Travel Companion of Air France Over 50 hotels worldwide.

FIGURE 22-6 Bringing France to North American meetings

Distribution

By and large, external distribution channels are more heavily relied upon by international hotel companies in foreign lands than in their own home country. The reasons for this extend from the previous discussion. Markets are drawn from many geographical areas with many cultural differences as well as different needs and wants. Reaching these markets fully and efficiently by advertising and/or direct selling is cost-prohibitive.

Hotel companies need someone in local markets who knows the market, knows its needs and wants, knows how to reach it, knows how to communicate with it, and knows how to sell it. Only the United States and the United Kingdom enjoy full toll-free telephone dialing; thus, companies in other countries turn in large number to consortiums, referral agencies, travel agencies, wholesalers, and brokers. As one example, Sol Hotels in Spain rely on wholesalers for 95 percent of their rooms sales in their resort properties.

Consider southeast Asia: Huge numbers of tourists come to this part of the world as part of tours or on individual travel packages from Europe, North America, Australia, and Japan. Consider Europe, where the largest outside markets are North America and Japan. Consider South America, which draws its bulk business from North America and Europe.

While these distribution channels are essential to international markets, they also cause problems. First of all they want bargain rates for their clients and have the clout to get them. Second, they want commissions. Third, they often make promises that are difficult to fulfill and for which the hotels will subsequently be blamed. Fourth, they can be manipulative. For example, some wholesalers will boycott a hotel if that hotel does business with another wholesaler. When the wholesaler cannot deliver all the business that the hotel needs, the hotel is caught between a rock and a hard place.

Nevertheless, heavy use of distribution channels is a necessary evil and a fact of life in international markets. Channel members are brought to the destination to see it and be sold on it. These are expenses that have to be absorbed. Even when channel members come on their pleasure trips, large discounts are granted as a matter of routine.

International franchising is also used by multinational companies to increase their distribution network. McDonald's, Burger King, Dairy Queen, and Denny's all have international franchisees. Although these franchisees essentially maintain the product line of the franchisor, they may make local adaptations. For example, Denny's serves ginger pork and curried rice in Japan; McDonald's serves wine in France and beet-root in Austria (and actually sells catsup); and Dairy Queen offers a type of bread called *roti*, and a fried vegetable and meat dish in the Middle East. Well-known hotel companies that franchise internationally are Days Inn, Ramada, Quality Inns, and Sheraton.

Marketing Research

Marketing research is no less important internationally than it is domestically. In fact, it may be even more important. The problems of doing it, however, are increased many-fold.

Consumers in other parts of the world are not as accustomed to answering research questions as are Americans. In some countries there may be outright refusal. Sampling methods can be grossly distorted for lack of adequate representative sampling frames. Telephone listings, street directories, census tract and block data, and social and economic characteristics of the population are frequently inaccurate, if available at all.

Mailing is expensive and may not reach the intended destination. Telephoning is expensive because of the lack of WATS lines or their equivalent. Both personal interviewing and written questionnaires have serious language problems even when conducted or written by natives of the area. In an area such as research, where scrupulous wording is essential to accuracy, the translation from one language to another can be less than precise. When questions are needed in multiple languages the problem is compounded.

In spite of all these problems, marketing research is needed but seldom done in the hospitality industry outside the United States. One international research firm specializes in hospitality research; it is called International Travel Research Institute (Intramar) and is based in Manila, with offices around the world. Intramar conducts ongoing tracking studies of hotel guests for international companies.

Reliance on guest comment cards is surely inadequate, if not grossly misleading, under the existing circumstances. Although it is difficult and expensive to research broad markets, it is not impossible to research one's own customers. The Century Park Sheraton in Singapore redesigned its rooms based on feedback from customer research. Focus groups with customers are certainly feasible and should be conducted more frequently. Feedback from employees on a regular basis can also be revealing.

Customs and regulations may even enhance the process in some ways. Hotel guests in many countries are required to provide information when registering, at which Americans in America would probably balk. Additional information can be obtained at this time. Government agencies and tourism boards also collect substantial information. Governments have the power—and sometimes use it, as in the case of Bermuda—to randomly sample departing visitors on cruise ships or airlines.

In today's increasingly competitive international marketplace, it is short-sighted for any international hospitality firm not to be doing some legitimate research.

Summary

International hospitality marketing is fraught with both conceptual and practical complexities. Many firms jump into the international arena without a full awareness of this. This can result in misjudged or lost opportunities and many costly mistakes. Too often, a multinational company does not know why it is in certain markets; it just "wants to be there." In turn, it may not understand the market and ends up simply taking the business that comes along. Communication efforts may be misdirected or misallocated.

Environmental influences may be largely ignored until they "hit." Because environmental forces are never truly known until they happen, there is a greater tendency in unfamiliar territory to react rather than plan ahead. In the hotel industry, overpricing is the most common tactical error when entering a new market. When the market collapses or competition becomes too intense, price-cutting is probably the most common tactical error.

All of this calls for even greater insight in strategic and marketing planning than when operating domestically. Many errors made by hospitality firms in foreign waters could be avoided with better analysis and planning. This goes far beyond the usual cursory feasibility study on which many firms rely. It has been shown conclusively, over and over again, that location and the "ultimate in facilities and physical plant" are insufficient for lasting success in the international marketplace.

DISCUSSION QUESTIONS

1. At the library, get a copy of *The Wall Street Journal* from three years ago and locate the foreign exchange rates at that time. Compare these rates with those from a current copy of the same paper. Assuming that hotel room rates have otherwise stayed constant in their native currency, calculate the impact on different markets traveling to different countries.
2. A hotel in a southeast Asian capital city was confronted with a unique marketing problem. This hotel refused to follow the practice of its competitors in freely allowing prostitutes in the hotel. As a result, it suffered a drastic loss in market share. How would you deal with this problem?
3. Why is segmentation so difficult in properties that target international markets? Discuss ways that markets could be segmented to overcome these difficulties.
4. Discuss Levitt's concept of globalization. Do you agree or disagree? How does it apply to the hospitality industry?
5. Discuss the future of Hong Kong under the conditions mentioned in the chapter. If it is subject to the fate of Singapore, what should hoteliers there do to combat it, now and later?
6. For a hotel in Hong Kong, develop a research design that would attempt to deal with the problems of doing research in a diverse international market.

FOR FURTHER STUDY

International Tourism Marketing

by **Linda L. Lowry**
Travel and Tourism Faculty
Department of Hotel, Restaurant, and Travel Administration
The University of Massachusetts-Amherst

In the global sense, tourism is not just one specific product but a conglomeration of many products and services. In many cases, the product exists only in the minds of consumers. In other words, the tourism business thrives on meeting the dreams, expectations, and perceptions of travel consumers. As a service industry, the tourism industry is a traffic system of consumer departure and arrival services, transportation services, and complementary support services.

Consumer departure services include motivation enterprises such as travel information centers, travel writers, tourist offices, travel photographers, and marketing and advertising firms specializing in tourism. Consumer departure services also include tour wholesalers and operators, travel agents, and travel planners who specialize in group, incentive, meeting, and convention planning. Transportation services such as airlines, automobiles, cruise lines, motorcoaches, and railroads provide the link between the consumer departure and arrival travel services.

Arrival travel services include businesses such as receptive ground operators, tourist information centers, local transportation, food and lodging, attractions and activities, and retail shops. To complement and support the business directly involved with serving the traveling consumer, regulatory organizations, training facilities, and the industrial sector must also become involved in satisfying the traveling consumer. Figure 22-7 illustrates the basic structure of the travel consumer service system.

As an industry of importation and exportation of dreams, international tourism depends largely on social, economic, and political situations. In that light, destinations can be viewed in much the same way as a wardrobe susceptible to the whim of fashion. Who is going where and what is going on there can have serious impact on any destination. These factors and others affect the rise and fall of a tourism destination's popularity.

Tourism Types   There are said to be five primary psychographic types of tourists: psychocentrics, near-psychocentrics, midcentrics, near-allocentrics, and allocentrics. These five types appear to be distributed along the normal population curve, as shown in Figure 22-8.[8] In simpler language, these types range from the timid and unadventurous to the bold and adventurous.

According to Plog, travelers choose their travel destinations based on their desire for and perception of novelty. In so doing, they shape the image of a destination by their presence or absence. For example, the extremely adventurous allocentrics pioneer new or seldom-visited destinations. In time, and as the novelty wears off, others follow.

Plog's scheme of destination popularity, based on traveler and destination types, places destinations in an unusual marketing position. Attracting too few tourists does little to justify the building of infrastructures and superstructure. Attracting too many tourists creates a social environment that tourists will no longer desire to visit. If this happens, the costly infrastructure and superstructure become underutilized or empty.

The quandary for international tourism marketers lies in a unique triadic relationship. How can one destination be all things to all people—that is, the travel consumers, the service systems that are in business to make a profit from travel consumers, and the host community that must share its scarce resources with the travel consumers? The answer is obvious yet often overlooked—it cannot. In thinking that this can be done, many destination marketers lose their way, and their baggage as well.

Elements of a Tourism Destination   Just as a market analyst of a single property must think about the product in relation to consumers' (the market's) needs, wants, and desires, so too must a market analyst of a destination. Before developing a marketing strategy for a particular destination, a tourism market analyst must first consider a number of factors.

---

[8] Stanley C. Plog, "Why Destination Areas Rise and Fall," *Cornell Hotel and Restaurant Administration Quarterly*, February 1974, pp. 55–58.

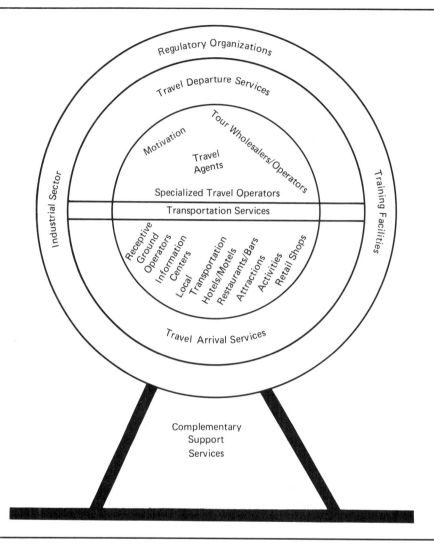

FIGURE 22-7   The travel consumer service system

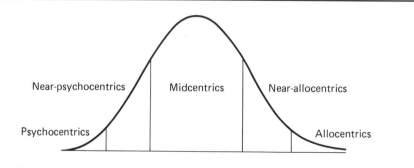

FIGURE 22-8   Psychographic model of tourist distribution

1. What are the natural resources of the destination area?

    Natural resources include such elements as climate, terrain, vegetation, animal life, bodies of water, beaches, drinking water supply, energy resources, and general natural beauty.

2. What is the existing infrastructure?

    Infrastructure includes the water supply and sewage disposal systems; gas, electric, and communication systems; roads; airports; bus and train stations; parking lots; public transportation; and so on.

3. What is the current development phase of the superstructure?

    Superstructure consists of such facilities as hotels/motels, restaurants/bars, retail shops, activity/entertainment centers, and business sectors involved in providing goods and services to the other parts of the consumer service system.

4. What forms of transportation are currently available to potential travel consumers who may choose to visit the destination?

    Primary forms of transportation include car, air, rail, bus, and ship.

5. Does the destination area have the necessary people (the host community) who are wiling and able to service the travel consumer?

    This factor sets a destination product apart from a product such as a hotel property. The hotel property exists to make a profit for its owners by serving the needs, wants, and desires of the travel consumer. It is not a living human being with needs, wants, and desires of its own.

    A critical factor in evaluating a destination for market potential lies in the residents of the destination area itself. For example, do the people (i.e., the natives/the host community) have the skills, motivation, and socioculture to fit with the notion of hosting others of different sociocultural systems? Do they want to share their place of residence with others who are fundamentally different from them?

6. What cultural/historical resources does a particular destination have that sets it apart from other destinations?

    In other words, is it unusual enough to have no specific product alternative, or must it compete with other destinations for the same potential travel consumer?

7. What types of travel consumers currently visit the destination? Why do they choose to visit that destination instead of the many other possible destinations?

    Determining what type of travel consumer is currently visiting the destination gives valuable insight into its life cycle as a travel consumer product. Referring again to the Plog model, are only the extremely adventurous allocentrics daring to explore the area, or is it being visited largely by travel consumers who fit into the midcentric category?

8. What is the government attitude toward, and treatment of, tourism?

    Does the government support tourism, both in action and resources as well as words? Does it provide funding to do the necessary marketing, or just lip service? Does it try to encourage government employees who deal with tourists, such as immigration officials, to make the tourist experience more trouble-free, both by regulation and by attitude? In some countries (e.g., the Scandinavian countries, Hong Kong, Singapore, Portugal, and Britain) there is generally a feeling when getting off the plane that this country wants and welcomes tourists. In other countries, particularly the United States, it seems that there is the opposite attitude toward foreigners.

FIGURE 22-9 Distribution of a developing tourism destination

This attitude is substantiated in the meager budget that the U.S. federal government allocates for tourism marketing—a pittance compared to what most other developed countries allocate, and some undeveloped ones.

Task of the Market Analyst   The market analyst's first job is to determine the answers to the above eight questions. The analyst then can begin to formulate an idea of how to maximize a destination's consumer market potential. At the same time, minimizing the overuse of the destination's natural resources and the negative impacts of stress and acculturation of the host community is also critical. Unfortunately, in many cases, the optimal number of travel consumers (in terms of economic return on investment to superstructure owners) often exceeds the social carrying capacity of the host community.

Perhaps the best answer to this difficult balancing act for those people involved in the marketing and development of a tourism area (i.e., the aforementioned travel consumers, the service systems that are in business to make a profit from travel consumers, and the host community that must share its scarce resources with the travel consumers) is the tried and true notion of research and careful planning. By ascertaining what the product (the destination) is, has, needs, and wants, and comparing that information with the needs, wants, and desires of current and potential travel consumers (the market), a profitable and socially satisfying market environment may be created.

If a sufficient fit is believed to be attainable (i.e., the marketing and development of an area as a travel consumer destination is feasible), the market analyst can then concentrate on how to coordinate the many separate entities involved in the travel consumer service system as shown in Figure 22-7. Once again, research and careful planning must be utilized to determine which service members within the travel consumer service system will best complement each other; the needs, wants, and desires of the travel consumers; and the destination itself. Another significant decision involves the choice or choices of how the information and sale of the product (the destination and the various superstructures designed to meet the needs, wants, and desires of consumers) are distributed. See, for example, the distribution of Barbados through travel agents in Figure 22-9.

Summary

A better understanding of international tourism marketing by a host country can be obtained only through research. Without sufficient knowledge about the complex and often conflicting objectives involved in the marketing and development of an area as a travel consumer destination, irreparable damage can be done to the physical and sociocultural environment of the destination area itself. Once a destination exceeds its social carrying capacity it becomes undesirable and can no longer attract tourism. When this happens, the service structure entities (superstructure) that exploited the land and the people of the destination area suffer losses due to the decline of the destination's popularity, and are themselves the victims of the whim of fashion. A workable and prudent solution to this cycle can be found in careful planning. The solution is not easy, but the challenge is an exciting one.

PART VII

Epilogue

EPILOGUE

Marketing Leadership in Hospitality

As we said at the beginning, and in the title, this entire book is about marketing leadership in hospitality. Why marketing *leadership?*

The answer is simple. It is too easy to accept marketing as a methodology—a set of tools to be used for wooing and winning the customer. Most of those tools have been discussed in this book, and many examples of their use and misuse have been given. But all those tools are of minimum value without marketing leadership.

In Chapter 1, we briefly discussed leadership in terms of leadership qualities and in terms of the customer. That was easy. It set us up for the following twenty-one chapters on marketing and its necessary ingredient: customer orientation. That's what marketing *is*. We can now boil it all down to the other necessary ingredient: leadership. That's what makes marketing *work*. Without marketing leadership, it really doesn't matter what your orientation is.

We, the authors, have often seen and heard marketing talked, preached, and managed, but we do not always find the leadership that really makes it work. Howard Johnson's and Victoria Stations dropped from major forces in the industry to dissolution and bankruptcy for lack of marketing leadership. These were large and well-known companies. There are many smaller and lesser-known ones that have done likewise.

We are not alone in our findings. Lawrence Miller states:

During recent decades there has arisen a cadre of executives at the top of our corporations who have served more to destroy purpose than to create it. These antileaders have put together some of the largest conglomerates in the nation. They have done so not by building a business but by the organization of finances. . . . They know numbers. They do not know products, services, or customers. Success to them is found solely in the numbers . . . while understanding nothing of the businesses within them or of the motivations and fears of their employees.

. . . managers . . . are judged only on financial criteria. . . . energies are directed more on the resulting numbers, . . . [and] the business deteriorates.[1]

There are many existing companies, both large and small, that are slipping at the time of this writing and will soon follow suit. Many others will survive and grow stronger. Given good operations management and quality of product in the product class, the difference will be made by marketing leadership.

The days of good operations and/or quality being the only keys to success, as Howard Johnson, Jr. and the founders of Victoria Stations proclaimed before they bailed out, are over. While these elements are essential, they are not sufficient. Even more recently, only token marketing, or only marketing management are also insufficient. They are simply not adequate. We began this book by describing how Jan Carlzon practiced marketing leadership to turn around SAS. In the following pages we discussed the foundations and practices of this type of leadership. We now provide two current examples of what happens when there is a lack of marketing leadership.

The Hotel Business

There is a hotel company that has been around for a number of years and has expanded steadily during that time. The company certainly must be considered successful by any form of measurement. In recent years, however, this company faced a huge increase in competition. Not only did occupancies begin to fall, but market share slipped in many locations. This, of course, affected profits—the bottom line. While gross revenue increased due to expansion, unit profits did not kept pace.

A concerned management at the top level reacted by putting more emphasis in the same place it had always placed its major emphasis—the bottom line. Unit management had long received annual bonuses based on profits. This emphasis was increased and unit management reacted accordingly. Payroll was cut wherever possible, food and liquor costs were lowered, and other cost-cutting methods were instituted to improve the bottom line.

A number of other things occurred. Staff and line employees became disenchanted. They were not able to serve their customers as they had been told they should. Many quit and went elsewhere when they could not get raises in spite of longer hours and more experience. They watched as huge company expenditures were made on capital improvements and company junkets when the company couldn't afford to give them a $2,000 raise. The company did little to halt the departure of these experienced employees. Unit management could save $5,000 to $10,000 a year by hiring new employees.

Customers waited longer at the front desk because of fewer, less skilled, and less motivated employees. Many turned to competitive hotels as their choice of accommodations. They also began to desert this company's food and beverage outlets as the price/value relationship eroded.

This company, which had long been product- and operations-oriented, tried to become marketing-oriented. It tried to change its corporate culture. It held meetings of

---

[1] Lawrence M. Miller, *American Spirit: Visions of a New Corporate Culture*, New York: William Morrow, 1984, p. 41.

both its marketing people and its management people. At these meetings and in various company memos, it described the new company as a marketing-driven, service-oriented company dedicated to two major objectives—the finest service and profitability. The company emphasized short parables of little things that had been done for customers. Rules for serving the customer were to be learned by all employees (for instance: smile at the customers and anticipate their needs—months of research had told the company that these things were important). Unfortunately, the company only mandated a customer orientation instead of motivating it.

Almost every commentary made by this company's executives contained two mandates—service and profit—along with new procedures to fulfill the mandates. But there was no question as to which of these mandates had top priority, with statements such as these: "This is a bottom-line profit-driven company," "What drives profit is service," "Profit is our end goal, service is the means to that end."

Not surprisingly, not much changed. By contrast with SAS, top management practiced management, not leadership. Unit middle management left the company meetings with such comments as "I've heard that before; when are they going to act as if they mean it?" For example, they saw guaranteed reservations for paying customers not honored, to accommodate company executives. Another comment was "How can they spend all this money on a meeting to say the same old thing, when they can't give us a raise?" And always the bottom line: "Service leads to higher profits" was the byword to remember, according to top management.

Everything was right. All the basic rules of marketing were there, laid out as they never had been before. Personal service was the new slogan. Then the final word came from the chairman of the company: The company, he proclaimed, would never compromise quality. But never forget: the company expects a minimum return and a strong cash flow, and all management was expected to keep it that way. With that masterful stroke, things went back to "normal."

A former top student, who had six job offers when she graduated, worked for this company for four years until she left, just recently. Discussion with her about her experiences indicated that she had adopted the bottom line orientation of this company and had "forgotten" all she had learned about customer orientation, even though she decried the company practices.

We had seen this happen to other former students in this and other companies, so we asked, "Why? You agreed with us then, you agree with us now, why do you do what you do?" Her answer was, "You assimilate the mentality of the company or you quit. You can't work in a situation where you have to fight your job every day that you go in."

In another company, we saw the management of one hotel stop replacing burned-out light bulbs in guest rooms, among other things, in order to try to achieve the yearly gross operating profit mandated for sizable management bonuses.

In still another company, we saw $15,000 allocated for a year's bonuses for nine sales personnel, to be rewarded on the basis of 50¢ per room sold above an established quota. When one salesperson brought in an account worth a $10,000 bonus on this basis, he was told the allocation didn't provide for that amount. He was given $3,000 and an extra week's vacation instead, as a reward for some $3 to $4 million worth of business. (He now works somewhere else.)

Unfortunately, we could fill another hundred pages with similar stories.

The Restaurant Business

Our story on leadership in the restaurant business comes from a nationally syndicated columnist, because we think he says it better than we could. It also addresses those who will be the largest users of this text—college hospitality students.

> The moment we sat down for lunch, I knew it was a mistake. About ten minutes later, I snared a waitress and asked, "Is there any chance we can see a menu?" She flung down a couple of menus and rushed off. About five minutes later she was back for the orders and apologizing because they were shorthanded.
>
> When she finally brought the food it was not what I had ordered. I decided to eat it anyway, but asked her about the beer I ordered. The beer arrived as I was finishing my last bite. When she brought the check, it was also wrong. "Who runs this place," I asked. "The manager," she said, "he's in the end booth having lunch."
>
> I stopped at the manager's booth on the way out. He and a clone were leisurely sipping their coffee and looking at a computer printout. He told me the restaurant was owned by one of those big corporations that operates in far-flung office buildings and health clubs. He also proudly told me that he had recently left college with a degree in restaurant and hotel mangement.
>
> That explained it all. His waitresses were shorthanded, his cook was goofing up the orders, the customers were grumbling, and what was he doing? He was having lunch. Or, as he'd probably say, he was *doing* lunch.
>
> When this nation collapses, this manager and his ilk will be the cause. First, we had the MBA. With his bottom-line approach, he did such a brilliant job that the Japanese might soon buy the whole country and evict us.
>
> The problem is that the service industry is being taken over by people like the restaurant manager and his corporation. They go to college and study service. Then they install computers programmed for service. And they have meetings and look at service charts and graphs and talk about service. But what they don't do is provide service.[2]

What does all this—bonuses, employee turnover, company meetings, raises, personnel, food and liquor costs, light bulbs, having lunch, hospitality education—have to do with leadership? If you have to ask, we have done a lousy job in writing this book. Write to the publisher and ask for your money back; whatever you do, do not plan a career in marketing.

Leadership and Management

Some managers act like leaders and some leaders act like managers. What is the difference? That question has been analyzed in minute detail by many researchers and writers in both the business field and the behavioral sciences. While no one has come up with the undisputed answer, there is much evidence that is worth discussion.

Managers are certainly expected to lead. They are also expected to plan, control, implement, and organize. Good managers are presumed to have abilities and skills that are

---

[2] Paraphrased from Mike Royko, "This Fern-Bedecked Restaurant Lacks Secret Ingredient for Success," syndicated column, 1986.

performed regardless of a particular situation. Yet, as well as managers may manage, it is generally agreed that leadership is what removes management from a mechanistic approach to planning, controlling, implementing, and organizing and extends it to an influential approach beyond the power of authority.

Managers have powers of reward and punishment; leaders have powers that go beyond these and that influence others to follow willingly, freely, and gladly. In marketing this is an especially crucial difference. This is because marketing leaders do not so much manage physical actions as they manage attitudes and behaviors. Leadership fills the gap between the theoretical and practical approaches to marketing. In marketing hospitality, management can sustain a firm for a limited period if the product and market conditions are right. Only marketing leadership, however, will sustain the growth and longevity of the firm over the long term. It is exactly this gap that is evident in many hospitality firms today.

Marketing management aims at executing prescribed objectives. Marketing leadership involves increasing marketing's effectiveness. Leaders are responsible for adaptation and change. "Staying close to the customer" is one characteristic of marketing leadership described by Peters and Waterman and by Peters and Austin in their *Excellence* books.

The customer changes, and marketing leadership changes with the customer; marketing management without leadership will only execute, and often much too late, as we have repeatedly shown throughout this book. As Austin says, "The common wisdom is that managers motivate. We think employees bring their own motivation to the job. What a leader does is less to motivate than to liberate, involve, make people accountable and cause them to reach for their potential."[3] Leaders create energy by instilling purpose; managers control and direct energy.

Leaders are responsible for the vision of ends, not just means. They initiate change and adaptation, and alter behavior to cope with new situations. The leader has the ability to see beyond what appears to be, to what really is. Leaders have the responsibility to sense the environment and to inspire others to larger visions of their duties. Leaders accept the responsibility of serving as models for management.

In hospitality marketing, this means "getting into the trenches," as demonstrated by Jan Carlzon, Pat Paterson, Mike Leven, Robert Hazard, Jim Nassikas, Bill Marriott, Kathy Ray, Richard Melman, and "the McDonald's"—all names we have mentioned before in this text. These are all people, and there are many others, who in one way or another never lose touch with their end-customers, uncover their problems, and provide solutions. They are also people who have by and large motivated those who work for them to follow suit and "think customer."

When "Pat" Paterson, then president of United Air Lines, told his people, "The customer doesn't give a damn about your problems, fix them," he was practicing marketing leadership that was clearly recognized. When United Air Lines had an unwritten policy that no executive, including Paterson himself, could ever "bump" a paying passenger off a flight, no one had to inquire into the meaning of the message.

Marketing leaders, whatever their title or whatever the level of management, lead by example. They create unity within the organization and between the organization and its members. They assume responsibility for performance and don't put the blame on

---

[3] Nancy Austin quoted in "How to Instill 'A Passion for Excellence,' " *Lodging*, July–August 1987, p. 21.

subordinates. They don't eat lunch while the place is "going to hell in a handbag." They don't pontificate at company meetings about the importance of the service and then provide reward and punishment based solely or primarily on the bottom line. They don't provide edicts of customer orientation; they provide examples. In essence they lead, not simply manage.

This has been a problem of marketing in the hospitality industry. We have seen hotel openings when the corporate staff on hand went out and partied all night, leaving the line employees to "make everything go right." We have seen restaurant owners demand the best table and service in the house while paying customers waited. We have seen managers of both hotels and restaurants stand by while the phone rang because answering the phone is what they hire someone else to do. We have seen front office managers read a newspaper while customers lined up fifty deep at the front desk, waiting to check in.

Marketing leadership is also marketing management; marketing management is not necessarily marketing leadership. In short, converting marketing orientation or marketing management into marketing leadership means only one thing: Practice what you preach. It doesn't matter whether you are the company president or the recent college graduate manager of a restaurant; it doesn't matter whether you have taken seven marketing courses or none: Marketing leadership means recognizing that absolutely everything in the hospitality industry involves marketing and that you shouldn't make a single decision without that in mind.

Corporate Culture

In every company and every unit of every company, there is a "corporate culture." Corporate culture shapes the behavior of an organization and its employees.[4] The right corporate culture eases the transition from marketing strategy to marketing action. In fact, it has been shown that a major obstacle to success is an inappropriate corporate culture.[5]

Corporate culture requires as much care and planning as do financial, product, and marketing strategies. These strategies cannot succeed unless human resources and performance are consistent with them. Too often, the culture that senior executives believe to exist is unlike that perceived by middle managers and front line employees. Many companies have been handicapped by failure to lead the culture of the firm, as was demonstrated in the earlier example in this chapter.

Corporate culture is an asset when it eases communication and generates high levels of cooperation and commitment. While this is efficient, it is not necessarily effective if the shared beliefs and values are not consistent with the mission of the organization. Leaders convey the culture by credibly communicating beliefs and values by words and deeds. Only when the organization's members internalize these beliefs and values can leadership actually shape the culture. Corporate culture is a liability when those beliefs are wrongly prioritized because the culture members know what priorities should prevail in the event of conflict. Webster states,

---

[4] H. Scwartz and S. M. Davis, "Matching Corporate Culture and Business Strategy," *Organizational Dynamics,* Summer 1981, pp. 30–48.

[5] B. Uttal, "The Corporate Culture Vultures," *Fortune,* October 1983, pp. 66–72.

Customer-oriented values and beliefs are uniquely the responsibility of top management. Only CEOs can take the responsibility for defining customer- and market-orientation as the driving force because, if they don't put the customer first they have, by definition, put something *else* first. Organization actors will know what that is and behave accordingly. CEOs must give clear signals and establish clear values and beliefs about serving the customer.[6]

Leadership decisions are made with consideration of the mission of the organization, not on the basis of expediency. Profit is the test of the validity of those decisions. Too many hospitality firms tend to be service-oriented as an expedience, when they need to be customer-oriented. They are more concerned with the functioning, production, and development of their product/services than they are with the customers use, or in response to customer requests or behavior.

Let's bring all this down to the real world. At the beginning of this chapter we described a hotel company that was trying to change its culture, and why it wasn't succeeding. Let's look at a company that did.

We have mentioned Bill Marriott as a marketing leader. Why? There are many customers who have had, and who will have, less than satisfactory experiences at Marriott hotels and restaurants. We have certainly criticized some Marriott practices in this book. Let's analyze this situation.

Marriott Corporate has become a massive but not monolithic organization. This has inevitably led to a process-centered culture with a high level of bureaucracy. The leadership at Marriott is dedicated to 20 percent annual growth but also—and it is an important also—Marriott is dedicated to the goal of being "employer of choice" in the hospitality industry.

To achieve these goals, Marriott must provide the right leadership. It goes without saying that success will result not only in obtaining quality employees, but also in a customer experience that will, in turn, provide the fuel for the 20 percent annual growth goal. How did Marriott get where it is today?

In the 1970s Marriott was a successful but relatively undistinguished company. Its product was standard. As with most hotel companies, it duplicated the same hotel over and over, and the guest experience was seldom more or less than the average. Success at that time required little more than this, plus some decent management, control of expenses, and a constant eye on the bottom line.

By the turn of the decade the environment was changing rapidly. Competition was becoming more and more intense, and many cities and some market segments were becoming saturated. Howard Johnson's was disappearing; Ramada and Holiday Corp. were struggling and enduring management shakeups. The barriers to industry entry were down, and new players were coming into the game.

It is said that Marriott is run by the book written by the people on Marriott Drive in Bethesda, Maryland. Marriott, like most of its competitors, concentrated on operations. It was around the turn of the decade that Marriott realized it had to make the shift from a purely operations-driven company to a marketing-oriented company. This meant changing the culture.

---

[6] Frederick E. Webster, Jr., "Rediscovering the Marketing Concept," working paper, Cambridge, Mass.: Marketing Science Institute, 1988, pp. 14–15.

Changing the culture at Marriott started in two places—with the employees and with the customers. Promotion paths and compensation programs were altered. No longer was it just how you ran the operation; now it was how you satisfied customers and met their expectations. To find out how to do that, Marriott began extensive consumer research, and also adopted what it learned.

Marriott is still run by the book, but that book has some loose pages. Says Bill Marriott, "We have to allow our people to break the rules when it is in the customer's interest." He also says that "marketing is really about managing change." And it was a culture change that Bill Marriott managed and led, by deed and example.

> At Marriott, we address change by committing ourselves to offering quality products at every price level, treating our employees fairly, providing consistently good service, and to really listening and responding to our customers. These commitments drive our marketing efforts, and I firmly believe that those companies that succeed in the times ahead will be those who understand marketing in its broadest definition and application.[7]

Bill Marriott practices what he preaches.

A far smaller company is Stouffer Hotels and Resorts, a fast-emerging leader in the hotel industry. Unbound by the size and magnitude of a Marriott, and aiming at only one major segment of the market, Stouffer is propelled by the leadership of Bill Hulett. *Participation* is Hulett's word to describe the culture at Stouffer's. Not participative management, a textbook term that has had its ups and downs, but participation in the action—the art of involving employees in what is going on. Hulett wants his managers to understand that employees want the freedom to decide how to do their own work, and that they work best when they have this freedom. Says Hulett,

> We listen to our employees. We understand that they want challenge and responsibility; we give it to them and then we reward them for doing a good job.
>
> . . . I'm talking about a total commitment to the guest, one that says we are always eager to find better ways of creating the most satisfying experience for that person from efficient check-ins to competitive room rates and the ultimate in service and amenities.

Many companies say this, but at Stouffer it shows. In Stouffer properties the employee attitude from top to bottom is one of genuine customer care and concern, with none of the obsequiousness and platitudinous behavior that so often derives from "smile training" alone. Top executives at Stouffer's answer their own phones. Such "culture rituals" send clear messages to those who work in the hotels and come face to face with the customer.

It would be easy to dismiss as ridiculous the notion of high-priced executives answering the phone. On the other hand, if you consider that the real job of these people concerns leadership and the customer experience, this is probably more cost-effective than all the smile training in the world.

Bill Hulett practices what he preaches.

Marketing leadership is a corporate culture. Marketing leadership companies are those that recognize the importance of nurturing customer contact. As well as placing a

---

[7] *Marketing News,* February 29, 1988, p. 2. Published by the American Marketing Association.

high value on consumer closeness, marketing leadership also emphasizes the importance of the individual employee. Both the customer and the employee are placed in high esteem. Not only is the consumer regarded as the essential ingredient, but employees are also treated with vital concern. Managerial concerns for customers and employees are synonomous. Customer and personnel orientation are related; customers and employees are both valued and looked to for guidance.

According to Darryl Hartley-Leonard, president of Hyatt Hotels:

> All hotels concentrate on good food, service, and special features. The only thing that makes us different is our employees and how they handle the guests. If you treat your employees well, the attitude will spill over to your guests. . . . Human resources are so important to our existence. If we don't treat them properly, all the work we put into technology, marketing, and operations will mean nothing.[8]

Things are no different in the restaurant business. One writer reports:

> Your management recognition and financial rewards programs have a dramatic impact on customer counts. Too often, the effect is negative. . . . I have seen too many good managers make a questionable decision because of a quarterly bonus. . . . A manager will cut cost to make a bonus even if that action hurts sales in the long run. . . . I have seen managers and area managers put off replacing chipped china just so they could make a quarterly profit bonus. Even company presidents [set the example by refusing] to allocate funds for these replacements simply to boost earnings. *It is easier to cut cost than build customer counts* [emphasis added].
>
> A manager will cut the soap concentrate level on the dishwasher to cut costs; . . . chipped tile, torn carpets, broken light fixtures, peeling formica, wobbling tables, parking lot potholes . . . get put off just to make the boss happy and paycheck fatter.
>
> Not replacing a stained tablecloth or chipped wine glass is common. Substituting a lower quality ingredient so the customer won't notice can start your sales on a downward spiral. . . . Since [labor] is one of the two largest cost areas in a restaurant and is highly controllable, managers pounce on it with a passion.
>
> . . . Change the way you reward the manager and you will change the manager's behavior.[9]

We've all heard of Bill Marriott. Have you heard of Denise Fugo? She owns and operates an independent restaurant in Cleveland called Sammy's. Here's what Denise says:

> Marketing starts with the customer; it starts with credibility; it starts with developing relationships; it starts with people. Not budgets, not dollars. . . . We respond to opportunities to do more for the customer, inform the customer, get customer feedback. My [advertising] dollars are spent more on sales with people—talking to my customers. I don't advertise. . . . In the early years I spent a lot of money trying to test this advertiser, this one, that one, and when I asked customers why they came, it was because someone told them to come.
>
> . . . Probably the number one thing that we work on with our staff—both management and our regular staff—is learning more about our customers.

---

[8] Quoted in Cherylann Coutts, "Hyatt Hotels: Growth in Leisure Travel Spurs 'Fantasy Resort' Concept," *The Travel Agent*, July 27, 1987, pp. 50–51.

[9] Don Shapiro, "Bonuses That Backfire," *Restaurant Business*, October 10, 1986, p. 182. Reprinted with permission of *Restaurant Business Magazine*.

We go as far as throwing pop quizzes at cue times to see how many more customers our front line people have actually learned about. . . . Our management staff answersphones. I think people who answer phones should be people who can help solve a problem. . . . That's very important for us.[10]

Denise Fugo practices what she preaches.

Marketing leadership is perceived management committment to the customer and the culture. No marketing orientation will work if management doesn't lead. Wanting excellent guest service is management; providing it is leadership.

[Marketing leadership] also requires programs for recognizing and rewarding superior marketing performance, not just by marketing managers but by all managers, bringing their contributions to the attention of other managers, developing strong role models, and reinforcing the basic commitment to customer-oriented beliefs and values.

- Marketing management must be held to its fundamental mission of being expert on the customer.
- The effort will suffer and come to naught if, in the final analysis, managers are evaluated solely in terms of sales volume and short-term profitability and rate of return measures.
- Managers will do those things for which they are evaluated and rewarded.
- Marketing is the whole business seen from the customer's viewpoint—Marketing is too important to be left to the marketing people![11]

The Winning Performance

Donald Clifford, Jr., and Richard Cavanagh were part of the McKinsey & Company team that in 1983 completed a two-year study of successful midsize companies. They found that the "wisdom of the seventies" had evolved into new traditions for success. We reiterate some of their findings here as they apply to our discussion.[12]

- Very few winners regard cost, scale, or price as their chief basis of competition. They keep a close eye on economy and efficiency, but the new tradition holds that the value the customer receives is much more important than the mere cost of the product or service.
- Business success is the art of leading people, nurturing them, and challenging their creativity so they will figure out what customers really need and want. When an organization adopts a single-minded focus on "cutting corners," creativity and new ideas only tend to get in the way of the process.
- It may well be that the biggest threat to a company is not the competition or the high labor costs. Rather, it may come from its own myopic perception—stifling innovation, substituting rules for common sense, stultifying decision-making, and straitjacketing initiative.

---

[10] Excerpted from "Marketing Roundtable," *Restaurant Management,* March 1988, pp. 32, 34.

[11] Webster, "Rediscovering the Marketing Concept," pp. 15–17.

[12] Donald K. Clifford, Jr., and Richard E. Cavanagh, *The Winning Performance,* New York: Bantam, 1985. This section draws from various parts of this book. It includes added comments by the authors.

- A company's culture is not only what it stands for, it is what it does. It is the articulation of values that give meaning to everyday performance. A culture is not what is said, it is how it is performed. It is not just word, it is deed promulgated by top management. When powerful and widely comprehended guiding principles are in place, rules, regulations, policies, procedures, instructions, and the like are only secondary to the way people perform. These latter are only the how; it is the culture that defines the why.

- A fanatic has been defined as one who, having lost sight of his objective, redoubles his effort. A leader never loses sight of his objective: to instill and institutionalize leadership throughout the organization into pervasive values and culture.

The Success Syndrome[13]

The success syndrome is the point at which a successful business begins to rest on its laurels. Its attributes are overconfidence and overcomplacency. Its symptoms are sliding standards, indifference to customers, and the belief that you can do no wrong. It can affect any business and goes something like this.

- You open for business and you do cartwheels in your effort to please. No request is impossible, no detail too small.

- Business is steady; you're a success. Time is money; you have a business to run. Suddenly there's not much time for little details anymore, and even less for customers.

- Employees start to slack off because they know you don't have time to notice, or to listen to them either. Service and standards slip but you're the last to notice—but facts don't cease to exist just because they're ignored, as T. H. Huxley once said. Your employees know it but have lost their motivation. They don't think you care. Customers know it; they aren't coming back. So you launch a few special promotions and develop some new advertising proclaiming how good you are. The trade press has noticed as you report lower earnings. They run special articles on you and how you're "turning things around" by going back to basics.

- In the meantime, you're making the bottom line look better by laying off a few employees, cutting the hours of others, and scrimping on services. You think the customers won't notice. The promotions bring in some new ones and some old ones come back. They find it as bad as ever, maybe worse. You are on the way down.

- There is a cure. The first step is recognizing the problem. The place to look is inside, not outside. All successful companies face intense competition and economic vagaries every day. These factors only increase the need for good leadership. The only way to know how customers see your business is to look at it through their eyes.

- Sit in the customer's chair. Sleep in the customer's bed. Call for a reservation. Find out how long it takes room service to arrive. Check the burned-out light bulbs and the dirt under the table. Evaluate employees' attitudes. Listen to your employees, who are the point of contact with the customers. Listen to your customers, who are the point of contact with the employees.

---

[13] This section draws from a column by Daniel R. Scoggin, then President and Chief Executive Officer of TGI Friday's Inc. restaurant chain ("Manager's Journal," *Wall Street Journal*, August 11, 1986). It includes added comments by the authors.

- Be honest. You can't conceal the fact that you have problems. The customers and the employees know better. The success syndrome doesn't attack from outside—it is a threat from within.

Leadership doesn't wait until the disease becomes malignant and terminal. Let us return, once again, to the wisdom of Peter Drucker.

The first thing to say about [leadership] is that it is work. . . . The foundation of effective leadership is thinking through the organization's mission, defining it and establishing it, clearly and visibly. The leader sets the goals, sets the priorities, and sets and maintains the standards. . . . The leader's first task is to be the trumpet that sounds a clear sound.

What distinguishes the leader from the misleader are his goals. Whether the compromise he makes with the constraints of reality . . . are compatible with his mission and goals or lead away from them determines whether he is an effective leader. And whether he holds fast to a few basic standards (exemplifying them in his own conduct) or whether "standards" for him are what he can get away with, determines whether the leader has followers or only hypocritical time-servers.

The second requirement is that the leader see leadership as responsibility rather than as rank and privilege. . . . precisely because an effective leader knows that he, and no one else, is ultimately responsible, he is not afraid of strength in associates and subordinates.

. . . The final requirement of effective leadership is to earn trust. Otherwise there won't be any followers—and the only definition of a leader is someone who has followers. To trust a leader, it is not necessary to like him. Nor is it necessary to agree with him. Trust is the conviction that the leader means what he says. It is a belief in something very old-fashioned, called "integrity." A leader's actions and a leader's professed beliefs must be congruent, or at least compatible.[14]

The Future of Hospitality Marketing

The hospitality industry is reaching the mature stage of its development. This is the stage, as we pointed out in Chapter 12, when marketing is most crucial. Hospitality marketing, on the other hand, is still coming of age. The near future will see it continue to grow, with maturity coming fast but still a few years away.

Twenty years ago, except in isolated cases, hospitality marketing was restricted to sales, advertising, and promotion. The 1970s saw a new recognition of the need for marketing. Titles were changed and new jargon was introduced, but the transition progressed slowly. Old habits die hard, and many marketing vice-presidents were still sales- and advertising-oriented. This attitude permeated the lower ranks and continues there in many places.

Today, however, there is a new wave cresting. New blood has come into the industry, with a new recognition of the customer. Those who are marketing-minded and work for those who are sales-minded are leaving to join companies (not always hospitality companies) that understand marketing. Eventually, these companies will be the survivors among the fittest, and hospitality marketing will reach its full maturity.

---

[14] Peter F. Drucker, "Leadership: More Doing than Dash," *The Wall Street Journal*, January 6, 1988, p. 14.

What does marketing maturity mean? Obviously, it means all those things we have discussed throughout this book. As a final conclusion, let's go beyond that and talk about hospitality marketing and its future in a more general sense.

There have been drastic changes in the hospitality industry in the past ten years. The supply/demand relationship has changed and will continue to change. Underlying this change, in the hotel industry at least, is that hotel companies no longer control the industry because they are not in ownership positions. Instead, "hotel companies have become suppliers of services to the industry and therefore are more interested in the growth of the industry than in the soundness and health of the industry."[15] These factors will lead to continued expansion of supply at a rate faster than that of demand. The same thing is occurring in the restaurant industry, as chain operations demand growth.

New concepts are always conceived of as those that will be more successful than the old ones. As a result, hotels and restaurants are no longer built to satisfy growing demand, but to take business away from others. Canas states, "The industry, from the point of view of the customer, will resemble more and more, supermarket shelves full of detergent. Customers will be faced with endless choices of essentially the same substance packaged differently and remarketed as 'new' and 'improved' variations on the same thing." This is exactly the trap into which the airlines have fallen. With the addition of severe service problems, they have incurred further government mandates to "get their act together."

On the consumer side, another critical trend that will affect hospitality services is the level of consumer expectation. People are increasingly wary of not receiving the services they are paying for. Large companies will find it increasingly difficult to differentiate themselves by the quality and consistency of their products and services. Thus, there exist two opposing trends: "Bigness" works against the needs of the customer.

At the same time, the industry is increasingly aware that customer needs must be understood and that products and services promised must be delivered. We believe the result will be as follows:

1. Increasing specialization as marketers seek to differentiate their products in the marketplace.
2. Increasing true segmentation as opposed to "conceptitis." Target marketing will become more refined, and products and services will be developed based on the needs and wants of those markets.
3. Increasing attention paid to employees, their incentives, and their motivations. Companies that give only lip service to these needs will fare poorly.
4. Customer fulfillment, customer perception, and favorable word-of-mouth will become the primary goals of marketing leaders. At its best, achievement of these goals will relegate selling and advertising to purely secondary roles.
5. There will be less emphasis on promotional gimmicks and a new emergence, recognition, and understanding of real services marketing as opposed to goods marketing. The future will bring, finally, a recognition that marketing services is not the same as marketing soap.
6. Management and marketing will be perceived as one and the same. Leadership will be the catalyst that makes it work.

---

[15] Jon Canas, Chief Executive Officer, Omni Hotels, in a talk given at International Hospitality Congress, Paris, May 18, 1987.

7. Successful marketers will be marketing subversives: "Individuals who challenge old practices and, when necessary, violate company rules and policies. . . . Predictable marketing practices and stable structures make eminent good sense when markets and strategies are unchanging. . . . today's marketing manager confronts rapidly changing conditions. A lasting competitive advantage comes not from products or policies alone, but from the people who do the job. That's why companies should refocus their attention on the kind of people who are doing their critical marketing tasks and make sure these people have the necessary incentives [and resources] to do the job."[16]

8. Successful marketing will be based on seizing opportunities, and innovation. In the past, the response to a problem has been to try to fix it. In the future, problems will be used as opportunities to find a new way to do something.

9. Successful leaders will lead through shared visions, values, and objectives. The "work hard, play hard" macho image of industry leaders, with few exceptions, has become an anachronism. As John Sculley, CEO of Apple states, "New-age leaders will lead not with toughness but with powerful ideas. . . . Yet, the new-age leader almost has to show his fallibility. Making mistakes is a very real and important part of succeeding. . . . At Apple, making mistakes is the only way to learn. If you fail to convey the idea at the top you can make mistakes, you can send the wrong message, isolate yourself from the people.[17]

10. Finally, in the words of Darryl Hartley-Leonard, the industry will stop just talking to each other and start to really listen to the customer.

These are our predictions for the future of hospitality marketing. As we said in the Preface, "In marketing we really don't know the right decision from the wrong one until after it has happened." Based on the foundations of marketing in this text, and as marketing leaders, we trust you will make the right decisions.

If so, the customer is yours!

---

[16] Thomas V. Bonoma, "Marketing Subversives," *Harvard Business Review*, November–December 1986, pp. 113–118.

[17] John Sculley, *Odyssey*, New York: Harper & Row, 1987, p. 333.

APPENDIX
World Maps

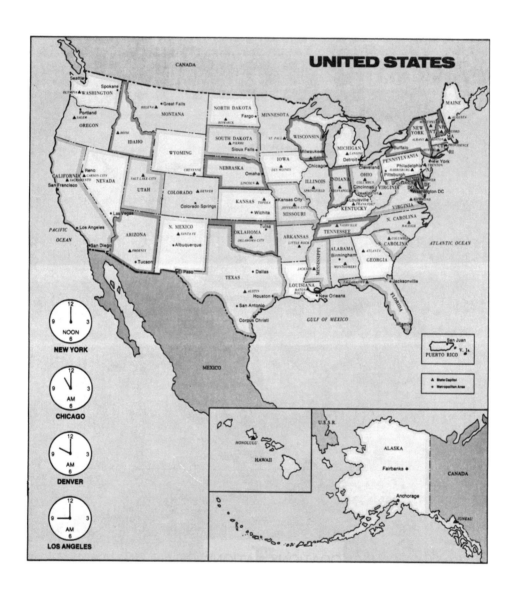

FIGURE A-1

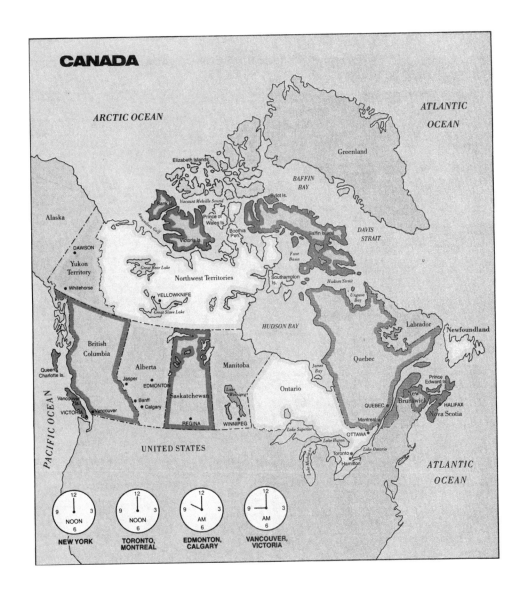

FIGURE A-2

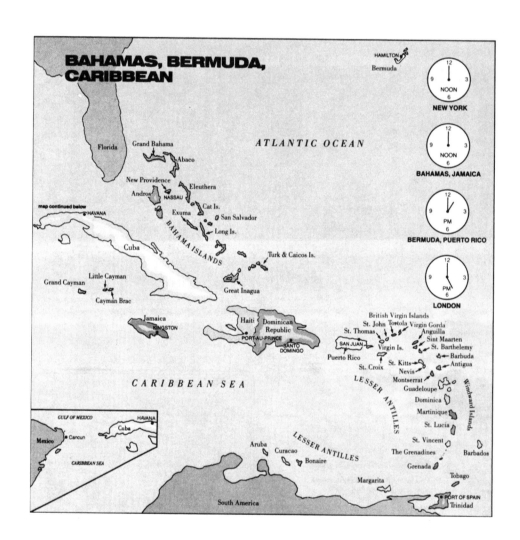

FIGURE A-3

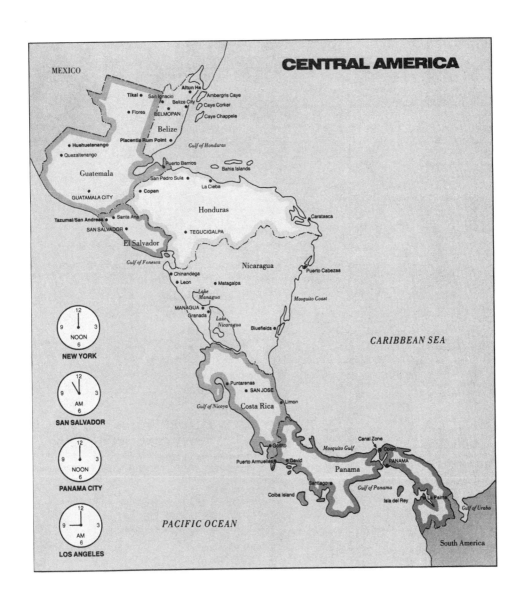

FIGURE A-4

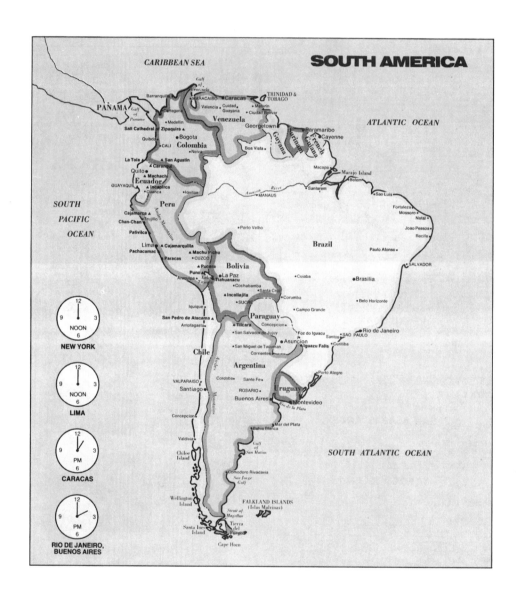

FIGURE A-5

FIGURE A-6

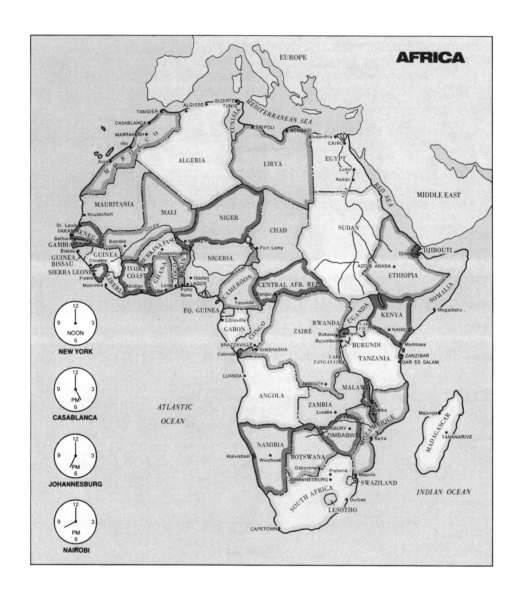

FIGURE A-7

666

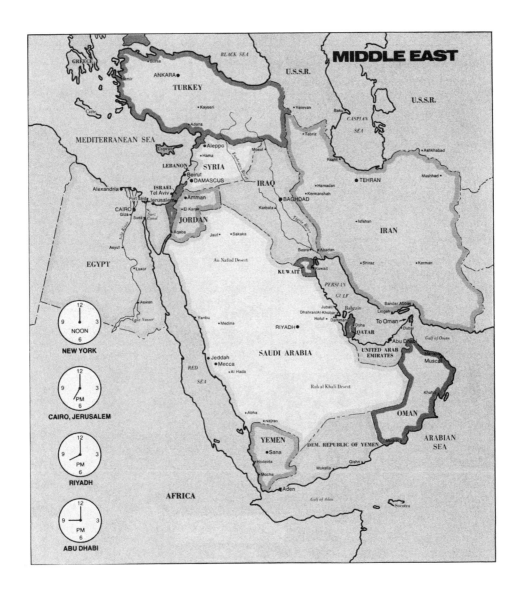

FIGURE A-8

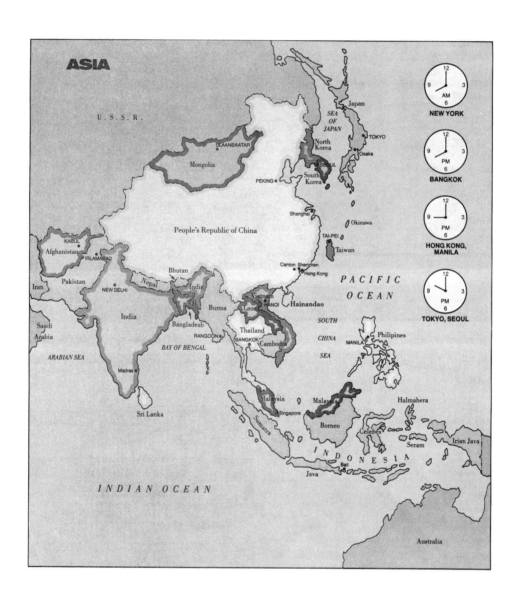

FIGURE A-9

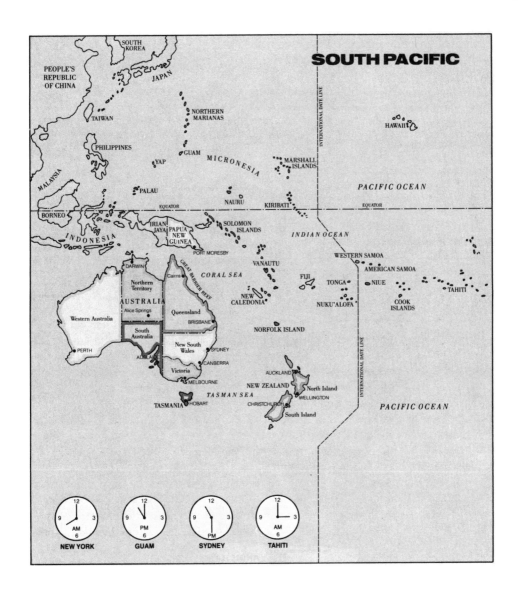

FIGURE A-10

Glossary

Ad hoc group: A segment of customers that has a specific destination in mind, travels by motorcoach, and usually stays at a hotel overnight.

Airline market: Housing of airline employees and crew members by a hotel on a contractual basis, normally over a period of at least one year. Also known as "base business."

Area of Dominant Influence (ADI): Specific geographic population bases determined by television audience but also used by newspaper and magazine media for distribution coverage.

Atmospherics: The conscious designing of a concept to create certain effects in buyers. The effort to design buying environments to produce specific emotional effects in the buyer that will enhance purchase probability.

Attitudes: Affective component of the belief-attitude-behavior trilogy. Emotional responses toward beliefs.

Augmented product: The totality of all benefits received or experienced by the customer when purchasing the product.

Average check: The method to track the spending habits of food customers, derived by dividing the total money collected within a meal period by the number of customers served. Some establishments include liquor purchased in the calculation.

Average room rate: The method to track the spending habits of rooms customers, derived by dividing the total money collected for room rent on a given day by the number of rooms sold. Establishments may or may not include complimentary rooms, out of order rooms, and day use rooms in the calculation.

Behavioral differences: The ways in which one segment (customer) behaves differently from another. Can lead to conflict among segments.

Belief: Something we think is fact (something we believe) about an object, for whatever reason or derivation; a belief is cognitive.

670

Benefits: Serve the needs and wants of the consumer. What a feature can do for the customer. The reason that a customer needs or uses the feature or product.

Bimodal or strongly skewed life cycle: Two possible configurations of the product life cycle when it does not always follow a bell-shaped curve.

Break-even pricing: Pricing to cover at least fixed costs beyond variable cost per unit.

Bus tour: Travelers arriving at a hospitality establishment by motorcoach, as part of a total tour package.

Business purpose: To create and keep a customer.

Business traveler: Customer who utilizes a hospitality product because of a need to conduct business in the particular destination. This person usually travels alone or with a limited number of individuals.

Cannibalized market: An offering by the same company of a similar product to the same customer in the same market. Giving the consumer an alternative to the existing hotel or restaurant, under the same ownership, when a customer gained is also a customer lost.

Cash flow pricing: A strategy to maximize short-run revenues to generate cash.

Catering salesperson: Handles meetings, banquets, and social events (such as weddings) that require few sleeping rooms.

Channels of distribution: Set of independent organizations involved in the process of delivering a product or service between producer and consumer.

Chapter 11 bankruptcy: The court protection of an existing business entity from its creditors. When a business is no longer viable and/or solvent the courts will assist in the reorganization and/or the orderly distribution of assets to creditors. Chapter 11 is voluntary on the part of the organization to gain protection before it is forced into involuntary bankruptcy, usually so it can continue to operate.

Close: Gaining a verbal or written commitment from the customer.

Closed probe: A communications method used during a sales call to direct customers who may not be aware of their needs, or cannot express those needs well.

Closing: The customer makes a commitment to buy.

Cognitive dissonance: A theory that recognizes a customer's potential uncertainty after the purchase decision has been made. A customer may believe that his or her choice of product was wrong, incorrect, or a mistake.

Collateral: A term used in advertising to include brochures, fliers, cocktail napkins, match books, and other promotional materials.

Communications mix: The variety of methods to tell the consumer about a product, including advertising, merchandising, promotions, public relations, and direct selling.

Communication strategy: The purpose, or desired effect, of the communication to the marketplace before it has been decided how to say it.

Comparative group: A target market that a customer may try to emulate. For example, teenagers may consider a rock band as a comparative group and make their product choices accordingly.

Compensatory models: The purchase decision model that assumes the willingness to trade one feature for another in order to make the buy decision.

Competitive intelligence: Includes information-gathering beyond industry statistics and trade gossip and involves close observation of competitors to learn what they do and why.

Competitive strategy: The firm chooses its competition and when and where it will compete. The firm then targets all its marketing forces towards the identified competitor(s).

Conceptitis: A word we have coined to describe those people who are afflicted with total immersion in design concepts with little or no regard as to how the customer will use the product.

Conjunctive model: Consumers might establish a minimum acceptable level for each important product attribute and make a choice only if each attribute equals or exceeds the minimum level.

Consortium: A loosely knit group of independently owned and managed hotels (or other companies such as travel agencies) with a joint marketing distribution process.

Construct validity: Measuring what you think you are measuring—for example, ensuring the behavior pattern being measured is actually significant to the customer's buy decision.

Consumer demand: Consists of existing, latent, and incipient demand.

Contribution margin pricing: A version of markup pricing that can be used to price a product. A margin is assigned to an offering above the variable cost to establish the price. The contribution is to fixed cost after the variable cost has been covered, even when there is no absolute profit.

Control: The feedback loop of the marketing system, which includes research and marketing intelligence that tells if the system is working right.

Core product: What the customer is really buying. Often abstract and intangible attributes.

Cost percentage or markup pricing: Favored by the restaurant industry, this method features either a dollar markup on the variable ingredient cost of the item, a percentage markup based on the desired ingredient cost percentage, or a combination of both.

Cost plus pricing: Establish the total cost of a product, including overhead, plus a predetermined gross profit margin.

Cottage industries: Subordinate companies that feed off and supply a major product offering, and/or sell directly to the consumer.

Cover: Generic term applied to a meal served—for instance, twenty customers in a restaurant are twenty covers.

Customized product: The design of a product to fit the specific needs of a particular target market.

Data collection, external: The assembling of information from environmental sources such as currency rates, international terrorism, population growth, demographics, and so on, that may indicate trends that affect the purchase decisions of customers.

Data collection, internal: The assembling of information within the context of the hospitality establishment, such as average room rate, menu preferences, and so on, that may indicate trends that affect the purchase decisions of customers.

Data collection, primary: The assembling of information directly from the consumer, as in consumer research.

Demand analysis: An analysis of a market to determine whether it is ready, willing, and able to buy.

Demographic segmentation: Customer definition based on location, income, race, age, nationality, and so on.

Descriptive data: Information that tells us who and what, but not why.

Descriptive quantitative research: Research that tells us how many, how often, and what percentage, such as how old people are, their sex, or their income.

Designated Market Area (DMA): Developed by the A. C. Nielsen research company, these are geographic areas serviced by television stations. Data include demograhic characteristics that can be used for reaching specific audiences.

Determinant attributes: Attributes that determine choice.

DEWKS: Acronym for couples of dual employment, with kids. Forty eight percent of U.S. married couples, June 1987.

Differentiation: The ability to convey a tangible or intangible advantage of one product over another to a customer.

DINKS: Acronym for couples with a double income, no kids. Fourteen percent of U.S. married couples, June 1987.

Director of Marketing (as commonly applied): Within the hierarchy of a hospitality entity's organizational chart, the department head responsible for producing revenues, usually through the utilization of the communications mix. This position is normally found in larger hotels and restaurant chains. The director of marketing reports to the general manager and oversees the position of Director of Sales, if applicable.

Director of Sales: In smaller hospitality entities, the same job description as Director of Marketing applies. In larger organizations, this position reports to the Director of Marketing and heads the direct sales effort.

Disjunctive model: The consumer establishes a minimum level of expectation based on only one or a few attributes.

Edifice/Oedipus complex: An emphasis on the edifice or building as the primary selling point in the product and/or communications mix. When used pejoratively, the hotel structure fails to differentiate itself from other hotels in both a physical and positioning sense, thus losing any possible differentiation in the customer's mind. In Greek mythology, Oedipus was banished from the kingdom as a child. As an adult he returned and, ignorant of his heritage, murdered his father and wed his mother. In psychology, the term Oedipus complex is used to define a male who has a fixation for his mother. In the sense described above, the term "edifice complex" is used colloquially as a play on words to mean not recognizing the real reason people buy hotel rooms because of a fixation on the physical property.

Elasticity: The economic model that establishes the relationship between pricing of a product and demand for the product.

Environmental scanning: The analysis of trends that may affect both the production and the purchase of a product by the customer.

Expatriate: Person that lives and works in a country not of his or her own origin or nationality.

Expectancy-value model: Assumes that people have a measurement of belief about the existence of an attribute and that each attribute has an importance weight relative to the other attributes.

Expectation pricing: Pricing according to what it is believed people expect to pay, regardless of intrinsic value.

External information: Data gathered from distribution members such as suppliers, vendors, and local, state, and national agencies and associations.

Facilitating goods: Tangible goods that accompany an intangible product or service to facilitate its purchase—for instance, airport limo service or an 800 reservation phone number.

Family life cycle: Spans the basic stages of life (e.g., single, married, married with children, married with grown children, widowed), and how these stages affect the purchasing decision.

Feasibility study: The thorough evaluation and determination of a business venture and its ability to perform in a marketplace. Market feasibility indicates market demand; financial feasibility indicates financial performance.

Feature: A tangible or intangible component of a product that is offered to solve the customer's problem.

Fern bars: A trendy concept of the 1970s that features an atmosphere filled with plants, brass, and glass.

Focus group: An assemblage of typical customers used to discuss and critique products. (Typicality is determined by the use of screening techniques.) A moderator normally leads the discussion of five to ten people.

Food and Beverage (F&B): The term applied to the department within a hotel that services the food and beverage products.

(FIT) Foreign or Free Independent Traveler: A visitor from another country, or simply any individual without a preset itinerary such as a package or tour; variously used in the industry.

Franchisee: An organization or person that purchases a brand name to distribute the product or service.

Franchising: A method for a hospitality entity to increase its distribution network, both to create more revenue and to obtain increased geographic presence. Management of the hospitality entity that is franchised is not retained by the parent company.

Franchisor: The parent company of a franchising distribution network.

Freestanding: A slang term for a customer who needs function or meeting space without accompanying guest rooms. This term can also be applied to food and beverage outlets not associated, or positioned not to be associated, with a host hotel.

Frequent flyer programs: Programs that reward the airline passenger for repeated patronage with free mileage credit toward future flights and other awards such as rental cars and hotel rooms.

Frequent traveler: By industry definition, a traveler who spends at least ten nights per year in a hotel room for any number of reasons.

Frequent traveler programs: Emulation of frequent flyer programs that offer free hotel rooms, upgrades, and other benefits and prizes for repeat patronage.

Functional strategies: The "what" of the strategic system—that is, "what" we are going to do specifically within the marketing mix to reach the customer.

General Manager (GM): This position is normally the head of the individual hospitality entity, such as a restaurant or hotel.

Goods: Tangible, physical factors over which management has direct control, or, in other industries, manufactured goods.

Grazing restaurants: A concept of restaurants where the customers are offered a variety of foods throughout the day and night. The customer is allowed to walk up to many food stations in the restaurant, sampling more than just one entrée—hence the term *grazing*. The customer may also "nibble" at any time rather than at set meal periods.

Group product line: For customers who purchase a number of rooms, catering, and related services.

Group market segment: Five or more single attendees at a meeting whose purpose is business and/or pleasure, usually within the facilities of the hotel.

Group salesperson: The member of the hotel sales force who handles the needs of customers booking ten or more hotel rooms at a time, and generally accompanying meeting space.

Hassle-Free: A common industry term that describes a customer's experience as being without any problems or hang-ups.

Heterogeneity: Variation and lack of uniformity in a service being performed. Also, variation of consumers in the marketplace.

Hospitality marketing mix: Contains four major submixes: product/service mix, presentation mix, communications mix, and distribution mix.

Hospitality product: The goods and services offered by the hospitality entity. The goods and services include guest rooms, food, beverages, health clubs, pools, and so on, and all services whether included in the price or priced separately.

Importance attributes: Items that are important to the consumer in making a choice of product, or in consuming the product, but are not necessarily determinant.

Inbound operator: A channel of distribution that handles international travel to the host country from all locations outside the country.

Incentive houses: Companies that specialize in handling the needs of organizations that reward their employees with travel.

Incipient demand: Demand for which even the customer does not yet recognize there is a need, (i.e., the demand is in its embryonic stage.)

Incongruities: Discrepancies between what is and what ought to be.

Inferential quantitative research: This method allows the extrapolation of findings from a survey sample to a larger population base. For this sample, each person in the population being studied has an equal chance of being selected in the sample.

Innovators: A consumer term identifying those who are the first to try a new product.

Intangible: Unable to be perceived by the sense of touch. Used in marketing as unable to be perceived by the five senses.

Intention: The conative stage of the buying process—what people intend to do.

Internal information: Data collected from sources within the organization such as occupancy, average room rate, average check, number of covers, frequently ordered menu items, and so on.

Internal marketing: Applying the philosophies and practices of marketing to people who serve the external customers so that (1) the best possible people can be employed and retained, and (2) they will do the best possible work. Management emphasis is equally on the employee, the customer, and the job as the product.

Internal marketing concept: Organization's internal market of employees can be influenced effectively and motivated to customer-consciousness, market-orientation, and sales-mindedness by a marketing-like internal approach and by using marketing-like activities internally.

Internal rate of return (IRR): The method of determining the percentage of profit needed for projects funded with existing cash.

Internal validity: Reported research findings that are free from bias and are valid in their conclusions.

Judgmental sample: A nonprobability sample using a specified variation. Subjects are "screened" to ensure they meet criteria specified.

Latent demand: A consumer need for which no suitable product is available to satisfy the need (e.g., fast-food before McDonald's).

Leader: Someone who has followers.

Loss leaders: Items that are offered to customers at low (loss) prices to create traffic, and the potential purchase of a more desirably priced item. For example, a soup special may be priced at 50¢ in the hope that the customer will also order a sandwich.

Macro competition: Anything that is competing for the same consumer's dollar that you are, regardless of the product similarity—for instance, a new car might compete with an extended vacation.

Market demand: The measurement of the amount of demand in the marketplace. See *demand analysis*.

Market positioning: Creating an image of a product in the marketplace in the consumer's mind.

Market segmentation: Assumes a heterogeneity in the marketplace and a divergent demand. Segmentation divides the market into various segments, with homogeneity along one or more common dimensions.

Market share: The determination of a hospitality entity's actual success rate in attracting customers. Once a determination of total supply for the product is made, each business competing has a "fair" market share—that is, its proportion of the total supply. Its proportion of actual sales is its "actual" market share. The market share establishes who has sold more or less than their fair share of the available supply.

Marketing: Communicating to and giving the customers what they want, when they want it, where they want it, and at a price they are willing to pay.

Marketing concept: The theory that the customer has a choice and does not have to buy a product, or your product—hence the need to market or attract the customer to the product.

Marketing leader: A marketer who practices what he or she preaches.

Marketing mix: The product/service, presentation, communication, and distribution that directly affects the consumer.

Marketing opportunity: Exists when the needs (problems) of the customer are not being satisfied, or could be enhanced.

Marketing orientation: The philosophy, foundations, and practices of marketing as evidenced in the philosophy of the firm.

Marketing-oriented management: The philosophy that customer needs are primary to all processes—for example, when designing a product before the sale, when delivering a product after the sale, and while the customer consumes the product.

Marketing plan: Working document that the hospitality enterprise develops for action during the forthcoming year. A situation analysis and all phases of the communications mix should be addressed as needed.

Marketing system: Makes marketing orientation and marketing concept work. Comprises leadership, opportunity, planning, and control.

Maslow's hierarchy: A hierarchy of needs in which higher-level needs do not become primary until lower-level needs have been fulfilled.

Master strategy: Shapes objectives after developing and weighing alternatives. Specifies where the firm is going and is the framework of the marketing effort. Normally a long-term planning process.

Micro competition: Any business that is competing for the same customers in the same product class—that is, is a direct competitor with a similar product in a similar context.

Mission statement: The statement that delineates the total perspectives or purpose of a business. It states why the business exists, the competitors, the marketplace, and how the business serves its constituents.

Multiple brand strategy: A firm that crosses over a variety of levels of consumer needs for the same product. For example, Marriott Hotels offers six brands of hotels, from deluxe all-suites for the non-price-sensitive guest to the Courtyard concept for the traveler, to Fairfield Inns for the budget traveler.

New markets: The attempt to increase the customer base of a business by developing new markets through the solicitation of current nonusers, or fulfilling unfulfilled, latent, or incipient demand.

No-equity deals: The management of a hospitality entity without significant capital investment on the part of the managing company.

Noncompensatory models: When the customer perceives no trade-off of attributes (e.g., conjunctive or disjunctive models). For example, some customers would not accept a double-bed guest room in lieu of a promised king-bed guest room, even if the price is much lower.

Nonprobability sample: Everyone in the population does not have an equal chance of being selected. Includes judgmental, quota, or convenience samples.

Nontargeted prospecting: Using list of potential clients to make "cold" calls (i.e., calls with no advance contact).

Normative beliefs: The thought process that certain individuals or groups should conform to a particular behavior.

Objective positioning: The process of creating an image about a product that reflects its physical characteristics and functional features.

Odd numbered pricing: A pricing methodology employed to create a perception of a lower price by charging, for example, $6.99 rather than $7.00.

Open probe: A question phrased to encourage a customer to speak freely.

Opening specials: A pricing methodology used as inducement to try the product in the initial phases of the product life cycle. Also called introductory pricing.

Operations orientation: A work ethic within a hospitality entity that focuses on the internal mechanism of the organization rather than the customer. Sometimes, similarly, called the F&B mentality because of that department's historical emphasis on controlling cost and running a smooth operation regardless of customers' needs or wants.

Opportunity analysis: Matching product strengths to opportunity while avoiding threats caused by product weaknesses.

Outbound operator: A channel of distribution that handles international travel from the host country to all points of destination outside the country.

Package market: Offering of a combination of room and amenities for an inclusive price to consumers.

Penetration pricing: Practiced more typically by restaurants than hotels. The company will drastically reduce prices to initially create awareness and trial of product, eventually stealing customers and building volume.

Perception: What is real to the consumer; that is, what the consumer perceives or believes.

Perceptual mapping: Process that helps to determine the positioning strategy relative to the competition by "mapping" competitive positions or product attributes.

Perishability: A characteristic of a product that indicates the length of time available for sale to a customer. A rock has a perishability of 100+ years; a hotel guest room, one day.

Perpetuability: A word we have coined to describe the characteristic and ability to perpetuate repeated sales of the same product, e.g., a hotel room or an airline seat.

Personal constructs: Devices that individuals use to interpret or make sense out of what they confront. Personal constructs are bipolar—for instance, good-bad.

Physical plant: The term for the actual building and its components that house the hospitality entity.

Physical supports: Materials necessary for the production of a service. From this support, both the contact personnel and the customer will draw services.

Planning: Defining what has to be done and allocating the resources to do it.

Porte cochére: A covered carriage entrance at the front of a building.

Positioning: The consumer's mental perception of a product, which may or may not differ from the actual physical characteristics of a product or brand.

Positioning strategy: The planning by the hospitality entity to maintain, enhance, or change the consumer's mental perception of the product.

Presentation mix: All elements used by the firm to increase the perception of the product/service mix in the mind of the consumer.

Presentation strategy: The idea that the presentation mix must be consistent with the product/service and the overall master strategy.

Press release: A document prepared for the press providing the salient points of a story that the hospitality entity would like published.

Price: A statement of value, usually in monetary terms, that can be used to express the cost of a good or service.

Price lining: This technique clumps prices together so that a perception of substantially increased quality is created.

Price skimming: The pricing of a product at the high end of the scale to create a perceived value, and then eventually reducing the price to include a larger number of potential consumers.

Pricing objective: The desired results of a pricing strategy, which should be consistent with the hospitality entity's other marketing objectives.

Primary reference groups: Small, usually intimate groups whose behavior patterns may directly influence individuals within the group.

Proact: Opposed to react; act before the event rather than afterward (commonly used in strategy vernacular).

Probing: Method to determine the needs of the customer through a series of inquiries.

Product: An offering of a business entity as it is perceived by both present and potential customers. It is a bundle of benefits designed to satisfy the needs and wants, and solve the problems of specified target markets. A product is composed of both tangible and intangible elements; it may be as concrete as a chair or a dinner plate, or as abstract as a feeling. The utility of a product derives from what it does for the customer.

Product awareness: Whether consumers are familiar with a product.

Product differentiation: Perceived difference in a product when compared with others.

Product life cycle: The description of the various stages that a product experiences during its tenure in the market. These phases include an introduction or embryonic stage, growth stage, mature stage, and stage of decline.

Product orientation: An organizational approach to marketing that focuses on the product itself and assumes that the product will sell itself—for instance, emphasis on atrium lobbies as the product the customer is buying; related to *edifice complex*.

Product parity: The competition is selling the same thing, or the consumer perceives no difference between offerings.

Product strategy: Deals with the benefits the product provides, the problems it solves, and how it differentiates from the competition.

Production line orientation: An organizational approach based on how fast, how many, and how cheaply to produce a product to get it to the market in bulk at the lowest possible price.

Product/service: The totality of what hospitality companies offer their customers, including goods, services, and environment.

Product/service mix: Combination of products and services, whether free or for sale, aimed at satisfying the needs of the target market.

Profit center concept: The idea of breaking a larger organization into smaller, more manageable pieces by assigning profit contribution goals to individual departments.

Profit Impact of Marketing Strategy (PIMS): Program that is a computerized cross-sectional study based on about 200 pieces of data supplied by more than 450 companies in more than 3000 businesses. This program has shown that the profitability of a business is affected by 37 basic factors that explain more than 80 percent of the profitability variation among the businesses.

Proprietary research: When research is conducted for a particular organization for the specific use of that organization as opposed to general use.

Prospecting: The methodology used in finding new customers. An example would be making sales calls on customers who are not currently using the product.

Psychographers: People who correlate factors into relatively homogeneous categories using classification terms for consumers' life-styles, such as homebodies, traditionalists, swingers, and so on.

Psychographic segmentation: Life-style patterns combine the virtues of demographics with the way people live, think, and behave in their everyday lives to divide them into market segments, i.e., by their attitudes, interests, and opinions (AIO).

Psychological pricing: Pricing strategy utilized to elicit consumer reactions such as perceived quality or value.

Public relations: The organized attempt by a business to get favorable stories concerning their product or services carried by the media.

Publicity: The format used in public relations to "create" a story. Stories are created through organized promotions.

Pull strategy: Inducements are offered to make the consumer want to purchase a product, or "pull" the product down the channel of distribution.

Push strategy: Inducements are offered to the channel member to sell, or "push" the product down the channel of distribution.

Probability sample: One in which every member of the population has an equal chance of being selected.

Qualitative research: The process of obtaining information on consumer attitudes and behavior on a subjective basis. This research is largely exploratory in nature and the findings cannot be generalized to a larger population. An example is the use of focus groups.

Quantitative research: The process of obtaining information on consumer attitudes and behavior on an objective basis. This research is factual in nature and the findings sometimes can be generalized to a larger population.

Raise the numbers: Hotel industry parlance to raise occupancy and average rate.

Reference groups/Referents: Groups that form small pockets of influence that affect consumers.

Relationship marketing: The emphasis on retaining existing customers through building good relationships.

Reliability: In research, findings can be projected to a larger population if it is the intent of the researcher to do so; also, if the study is repeated, similar findings will emerge.

Repositioning: Changing the position or image of a product to consumers in the marketplace.

Representative firm: Channel of distribution that brings a hotel to a marketplace. They market a hotel to a customer base for a fee.

Research design: The process of establishing the total objectives and method of research to be conducted.

Research problem: The designation of the problem of the research—that is, stating what the research is going to answer; not necessarily the same as the management problem.

Research purpose: What you intend to do with the findings; what kind of business decisions you plan to make after you have the results.

Reservation networks: Central reservations systems that serve multiple companies or properties.

Retail market: Middlemen such as travel agents who sell directly to the consumer. A member of the distribution mix.

Return on Assets (ROA): The ratio of profits to assets that is generated by a business.

Return on Investment (ROI): The ratio of profits to investment that is generated by a business.

Run-of-the-house room: The generic term for the random assignment of guest rooms to customers. Customers are not promised a certain type of room before their arrival at the hotel.

Salient attributes: Those attributes that readily come to mind when you think of a product or product class.

Sample: A group derived from the population at large. From it we hope to learn the characteristics of many based on a few.

Segmentation: The dividing of a large customer base into smaller homogeneous categories, based on a variety of applicable factors.

Selective acceptance: The theory that customers accept only what they choose to accept, that they select from a variety of information only what is applicable.

Selective attention: The theory that customers attend to only what is of particular interest to them.

Selective comprehension: The theory that customers will try to comprehend, digest, and evaluate something only if they are still interested in it after attending to and accepting it.

Selective retention: The theory that customers retain in memory for future reference only what suits their particular interest after attention, acceptance, and comprehension.

Selling orientation: To practice "hard sell" techniques; the emphasis is on persuading the customer to buy rather than on the needs of the customer.

Service: Nonphysical, intangible attributes that management controls (or should), including friendliness, efficiency, attitude, professionalism, responsiveness, and so on.

Service augmentation: The marketing strategy to add to a generic product by enhancing services—for instance, the perception of a hotel room may be enhanced by the availability of a shoe-shine service.

Share of mind: Marketing jargon associated with positioning. It means that the positioning has been established in the consumer's mind.

Simultaneous production and consumption: Unique service characteristic whereby consumption depends on participation of the seller and the seller requires the participation of the buyer.

Soft opening: Product introduction begins a few days to a few weeks before the official opening.

Standard metropolitan statistical area (SMSA): Area that the government defines as a large economic area in terms of supposed economic boundaries. Government pro duces data on these areas such as population, ethnic mix, income, and so on.

Standard product: The attempt to provide a similar experience to the customer despite different locations or managers. For example, McDonald's offers a standard hamburger throughout the United States.

Strategic business unit (SBU): Units of a business that have a common market base. Each SBU serves a clearly defined product-market base with its own strategy.

Strategic marketing: Long-term view of the market and the business to be in; marketing management stresses running that business and seeks to optimize objectives within the constraints established by the strategy.

Strategic planning: Developing a plan for how to get from here (situation analysis) to there (objectives). It is concerned with setting business objectives, the match between products and markets, the choices of competition, the allocation of resources, and planning ahead to reach the objectives.

Subjective norm: People's perception of the social pressures put on them to perform or not perform in a particular way.

Subjective positioning: The perceived image that does not necessarily belong to the product or brand, but is the property of the consumer's mental perceptions.

Suitcase party: Customers come to a hotel with their suitcases packed, and during the evening, an exotic weekend away is awarded randomly, and the couple is whisked away to their destination.

Supporting goods: Tangible goods that support a service or, without which, it would not be possible to provide the service, e.g., a bed or desk is a supporting good for hotel services.

Tactics: The step-by-step procedure of executing a strategic plan.

Tangibilize the intangible: Service marketing jargon to describe use of a tangible product to reflect the perception of an intangible construct, e.g., a tangible atrium lobby reflects intangible constructs such as awe, aesthetic pleasure, or excitement.

Target marketing: The marketing strategy to aim a product or service at one portion of a specific market segment.

Target markets: Homogeneous markets that allow for more detailed analysis and evaluation of potential customers of a segment.

Technology orientation: Belief that success in the marketplace is a result of the finest technological development. This thought process is similar to the business philosophy exemplified by Polaroid for many years. Also akin to atrium lobbies with lakes and waterfalls.

Tour series: Prearranged link of stopovers for customers traveling by bus, usually carrying a theme.

Transient salespeople: The salesperson who is designated to sell to organizations that have a need to book guest rooms on an individual basis.

Trial: This stage of product introduction attempts to get the consumer to try a product.

Two-fer: Restaurant promotion that offers two meals or drinks for the price of one.

Vertical integration: Company becomes its own supplier of products—for instance, Holiday has a subsidiary that sells hotel furnishings; or its own distributor—for instance, Radisson Hotels and Carlson Travel Agency belong to the same company.

Walked customers: Result of overbooking hotel rooms. Customers' reservations are not honored and they are sent to a different hotel.

Wholesale market: Middlemen, such as wholesale tour operators, who create hospitality packages and in turn market their product to retailers, such as travel agents. A member of the distribution mix.

Wholesale tour operator: Middlemen who create hospitality packages, such as group tours, and sell to the customer through retail agents. A member of the distribution mix.

Word-of-mouth advertising: The marketing strategy that satisfied customers are the best form of communication. Satisfied customers will tell potential customers of their experience, thus increasing the customer base.

Yield management: The concept of maximizing the revenue yield by raising or lowering prices depending upon the demand.

Index